BUSINESS FORECASTING

THE IRWIN/MCGRAW-HILL SERIES

STATISTICS

Aczel,
Complete Business Statistics,
Third Edition

Bowerman and O•Connell,
Applied Statistics: Improving Business Processes,
First Edition

Bryant and Smith,
Practical Data Analysis: Case Studies in Business Statistics, Volumes I and II,
First Edition

Cooper and Schindler,
Business Research Methods,
Sixth Edition

Delurgio,
Forecasting Principles and Applications,
First Edition

Doane, Mathieson, and Tracy,
Visual Statistics,
First Edition

Duncan,
Quality Control & Industrial Statistics,
Fifth Edition

Gitlow, Oppenheim, and Oppenheim,
Quality Management: Tools and Methods for Improvements,
Second Edition

Hall,
Computerized Business Statistics,
Fourth Edition

Hanke and Reitsch,
Understanding Business Statistics,
Second Edition

Lind and Mason,
Basic Statistics for Business and Economics,
Second Edition

Mason and Lind,
Statistical Techniques in Business and Economics,
Ninth Edition

Neter, Kutner, Nachtsheim, and Wasserman,
Applied Linear Statistical Models,
Fourth Edition

Neter, Kutner, Nachtsheim, and Wasserman,
Applied Linear Regression Models,
Third Edition

Shin,
The Irwin Statistical Software Series: Minitab, SAS, SPSS Guides,
Second Editions;
Statgraphics,
First Edition

Siegel,
Practical Business Statistics,
Third Edition

Webster,
Applied Statistics for Business and Economics,
Second Edition

Wilson and Keating,
Business Forecasting,
Third Edition

QUANTITATIVE METHODS AND MANAGEMENT SCIENCE

Bodily, Carraway, Frey, Pfeifer,
Quantitative Business Analysis: Casebook,
First Edition

Bodily, Carraway, Frey, Pfeifer,
Quantitative Business Analysis: Text and Cases,
First Edition

Bonini, Hausman, and Bierman,
Quantitative Analysis for Business Decisions,
Ninth Edition

Hesse,
Managerial Spreadsheet Modeling and Analysis,
First Edition

Lofti and Pegels,
Decision Support Systems for Operations and Management Science,
Third Edition

Stevenson,
Introduction to Management Science,
Second Edition

Turban and Meredith,
Fundamentals of Management Science,
Sixth Edition

T H I R D   E D I T I O N

BUSINESS FORECASTING

J. Holton Wilson
Central Michigan University

Barry Keating
University of Notre Dame

Irwin
McGraw-Hill

Boston   Burr Ridge, IL   Dubuque, IA   Madison, WI   New York   San Francisco
St. Louis   Bangkok   Bogotá   Caracas   Lisbon   London   Madrid
Mexico City   Milan   New Delhi   Seoul   Singapore   Sydney   Taipei   Toronto

Irwin/McGraw-Hill

A Division of The **McGraw·Hill** *Companies*

1 2 3 4 5 6 7 8 9 0 DOC/COC 1 0 9 8

ISBN: 0-07-290718-5
CD ISBN: 0-07-290617-0
Package ISBN: 0-256-23956-8

Vice president and editorial director: *Michael W. Junior*
Publisher: *Jeffrey J. Shelstad*
Senior sponsoring editor: *Scott Isenberg*
Editorial assistant: *Nicolle Kendall*
Senior marketing manager: *Nelson W. Black*
Project manager: *Alisa Watson*
Production supervisor: *Heather D. Burbridge*
Compositor: *Publication Services, Inc.*
Typeface: *10/12 Times Roman*
Printer: *R. R. Donnelley & Sons Company*

Library of Congress Cataloging-in-Publication Data

Wilson, J. Holton, 1942–
    Business forecasting / J. Holton Wilson, Barry Keating. — 3rd ed.
      p.   cm.
    Includes bibliographical references and index.
    ISBN 0-256-23956-8
    1. Business forecasting.   I. Keating, Barry, 1945–   .
  II. Title.
  HD30.27.W56   1998
  658.4′0355—dc21   97-32388

http://www.mhhe.com

To Eva, Ronnie,
and Clara
and
To Robert Vincent Keating

The third edition of *Business Forecasting* builds on the success of the first two editions. While a number of significant changes have been made in this third edition, it remains a book about forecasting methods for managers, for forecasting practitioners, and for students who will one day be business professionals who have a need to understand practical issues related to forecasting. Our emphasis is on authentic learning of the forecasting methods that practicing forecasters have actually found useful. *Business Forecasting* is written for students and others who want to know how it's really done.

Our emphasis is on authentic learning of the forecasting methods that practicing forecasters have actually found useful.

The third edition of the text includes the following new features, which we are confident will enhance the process of learning how to forecast:

- A new user-friendly and more powerful **Windows version of the SORITEC econometric/forecasting software.** Every method discussed in the text can be implemented with this software.
- **A continuing case** involving forecasting sales of The Gap has been added at the end of chapters to provide a linkage from chapter to chapter.
- A **CD** accompanies the text. This CD contains all the data sets from the text as well as the ECONDATA database (with 100 long-run time series), the SORITEC software with an easy-to-use Install routine, a demonstration of the SORITEC program, the complete manual for the SORITEC software, and directed student exercises. Also included on the instructor's CD are answers to text problems, the **COMPUTEST test software,** banks of test questions for each chapter, and Power Point templates for each figure and table in the text, which can be used to master overheads or in an electronic presentation using a run-time version of Power Point (also included on the CD).
- **Data** for text problems, figures, and tables are provided in ASCII (generic text) files for use in any software package, as well as in the SORITEC format. Thus, it is easy for users of this text to work some, or all, problems in SPSS, EXCEL, MINITAB, or other software (although not all methods demonstrated in this text can be fully implemented by these packages, they can all be fully implemented in SORITEC).
- **Comments from the field** by forecasting practitioners provide quick insights into issues and problems faced on a daily basis by individuals who are actively engaged in the forecasting process. These provide a very practical perspective from the "real world" to help students appreciate the relevance of the concepts presented in the text.
- **A database (ECONDATA)** containing 100 variables is available in a form similar to the way data are obtained by business professionals. This database is useful for student projects and for additional problems instructors may

wish to develop. The variables included are listed in the Appendix to Chapter 2 and can be accessed directly using the SORITEC software packaged with the text.

- The emerging technique known as **bootstrapping** can now be implemented with the software provided with the text.
- The **discussion of forecast accuracy** in Chapter 1 has been expanded to include a greater selection of accuracy measures.
- The **"User's Guide to BEA Information"** is the updated text appendix. The Bureau of Economic Analysis (BEA) publishes a wide variety of data that are useful to business forecasters. This appendix will help readers learn to access these data.

Today, most business planning routinely begins with a sales forecast. Whether you are an accountant, a marketer, or a financial analyst, you will have to forecast something sooner or later. This book is designed to lead you through the most helpful techniques to use in any forecasting effort. The examples we offer are, for the most part, based on actual historical data much like the data you may encounter in your own forecasts. The techniques themselves are explained as procedures that you may replicate with your own data.

The examples we offer are, for the most part, based on actual historical data

Because most forecasting today is done in a PC environment, we provide the new Windows version of SORITEC for use with the text. We are able to do this because of a cooperative working arrangement with Full Information Software and their commitment to higher education and the training of forecast professionals. For many years SORITEC has been used by firms and government agencies in the United States and abroad to prepare forecasts for clients and for internal use. It has also been widely used in academic settings. Among financial institutions using SORITEC are the World Bank, Chase Manhattan Bank, and Citibank. In government, the Central Intelligence Agency, the Federal Aviation Administration, the National Bureau of Economic Research, and the Joint Economic Committee all use SORITEC. Private firms using SORITEC include E. I. du Pont, General Motors, Hallmark Cards, and Intelsat. In addition, many universities use SORITEC. A table containing a more complete list of SORITEC users follows this preface.

Windows users will find this version of SORITEC very easy to learn.

Those who use *Business Forecasting* receive a free copy of a special student version of SORITEC packaged with the text. This student version of SORITEC differs from the commercial version only in terms of the size of the work space permitted. You will see, from the real-world examples used in the text, that this student version is fully functional and will handle relatively large problems. Windows users will find this version of SORITEC very easy to learn and powerful in its use.

The text includes instructions at the end of chapters on how to use the software for topics covered in that chapter. An extensive Help file is also provided within the software, and a comprehensive user's manual is provided on the CD that accompanies the text.

The authors would like to thank the students at the University of Notre Dame and Central Michigan University for their help in working with materials included in this book during development. Their comments were invaluable in preparing clear expositions and meaningful examples for this third edition. The final product owes a great debt to the inspiration and comments of our colleagues, especially Professor

Edward Trubac of the University of Notre Dame and Professor Thomas Bundt of Oregon Graduate Institute, Portland.

Adopters of the first two editions who have criticized, challenged, encouraged, and complimented our efforts deserve our thanks. The authors are particularly grateful to the following faculty who used the first two editions of the text and have provided comments that have helped to further improve this third edition.

Paul Altieri, Central Connecticut State University

Margaret M. Capen, East Carolina University

Ali Dogramaci, Rutgers, the State University of New Jersey

Robert Fetter, Yale University

Benito Flores, Texas A & M University

Kenneth Gaver, Montana State University

Rakesh Gupta, Adelphi University

Joseph Kelley, California State University, Sacramento

Thomas Kelly, BMW of Canada

Krishna Kool, University of Rio Grande

John Mathews, University of Wisconsin, Madison

Elam McElroy, Marquette University

Thomas Needham, US Bancorp

Gerald Platt, San Francisco State University

Melissa Ramenofsky, University of Southern Alabama

Helmut Schneider, Louisiana State University

Stanley Schultz, Cleveland State University

Nancy Serafino, United Telephone

John Sneed and Robert Sneed, The SORITES Group

Donald N. Stengel, California State University, Fresno

Kwei Tang, Louisiana State University

Dick Withycomb, University of Montana

In addition, the following reviewers have provided insights that have helped to make this edition better than it would have been without their thoughtful comments: Katy Azouri (San Francisco State University), Gerald Evans (University of Montana), D. S. Gill (California State Polytechnic University), Rakesh Gupta (Adelphi University), and Soo N. Jang (Plymouth State College). We are especially grateful to have worked with publishing professionals at Irwin/McGraw-Hill, including our editor, Scott Isenberg, and Jeff Collins, John Agnew, Alisa Watson, and Nicolle Kendall.

We hope that all of the above will be pleased with this new edition.

J. Holton Wilson
Holt.Wilson@cmich.edu
Barry Keating
Barry.P.Keating.1@nd.edu

SORITEC: *Econometric Language*

Representative Client List

Financial Institutions

Aetna Life
Bank of Montreal
Central National Bank of Cleveland
Chase Manhattan Bank
CIT Financial
Citibank, N.A.
First Pennsylvania Bank
Fleet National Bank

Guyerzeller Zurmont Bank (Switz.)
Morgan Guaranty Trust
National Provident Institution (U.K.)
North Carolina National Bank
Royal Bank of Canada
Toronto Dominion Bank
Union Mutual Life
United Banks of Colorado

Government Agencies

Australia Department of Labor
Canadian Transport Commission
Central Bank of Barbados
Central Bureau of Statistics (Neth.)
Central Intelligence Agency
Colorado Legislative Council
Congressional Budget office
Directorate of Food Crops (Indonesia)
D.C. Public Service Commission
Executive Office of the President
Federal Aviation Administration
Federal Emergency Management Agency
Federal Home Loan Bank Board
Federal Land Bank of St. Paul
Federal Reserve Bank of Atlanta
Federal Reserve Bank of San Francisco
Federal Reserve Board of Governors
Haiti Ministry of Finance
Inter-American Development Bank
International Monetary Fund
Joint Economic Committee
Kansas Corporation Commission
Monetary Authority of Singapore
National Atmospheric and Oceanographic
   Administration
North Carolina Employment and Security
   Commission
Norwegian Telecommunications Authority
Ontario Ministry of Energy
Puget Sound Council of Governments
Reserve Bank of Malawi
Saudi Arabian Embassy, London
Secretario Regional do Comercio e Industria
   (Azores)

State of Alaska
State of Florida
State of Illinois
State of Massachusetts
State of Minnesota
State of Montana
State of New York
State of North Carolina
State of Oregon
Supply Information Systems Group (Canada)
Transport Canada
U.K. Business Statistics Office
U.K. Civil Aviation Authority
U.K. Civil Service College
U.K. Department of Environment
U.K. Department of Health and Social Security
U.K. Department of Trade and Industry
U.K. Ministry of Agriculture, Fisheries, and Food
U.K. Ministry of Defense
U.K. Treasury/Central Statistics Ofc.
United National ESCAP (Thailand)
U.S. Bureau of the Census
U.S. Department of Agriculture
U.S. Department of Commerce
U.S. Department of Interior
U.S. Department of State
U.S. Department of Transportation
U.S. Environmental Protection Agency
U.S. General Accounting Office
U.S. Internal Revenue Service
U.S. Postal Service
U.S. Senate Computing Center
U.S. Veterans Administration
World Bank

Public Utilities

Bay State Gas
Bell Atlantic
Bell South Corporation
Bell Telephone Co. of Pennsylvania
Central Maine Power
Central Research Institute of the Electric Power
  Industry (Japan)
Cincinnati Gas and Electric
Comision Ejecutiva Hidroelectrica del Rio Lempa
  (El Salvador)
Detroit Edison

Gulf States Utilities
Houston Light and Power
Middle South Services
New York Telephone
Northern States Power
Orange and Rockland Utilities
Pacific Bell
Southern Union Gas
Southwestern Bell
Toronto Hydro

Industrial and Commodities

A. T. Cross and Co., Inc.
Atchison, Topeka, and Santa Fe Railroad
Babcock and Wilcox
Broken Hill (Pty.) Iron and Steel (Australia)
Cable and Wireless (U.K.)
Cehave NV Veghel
Celanese Corporation
Centerwood Securities (Neth.)
Certainteed Corporation
Clayton Brokerage of St. Louis
Columbia Broadcasting System
Con-Agra, Inc.
Cooper Industries
E. I. du Pont
General Motors
Hallmark Cards
Hill, Samuel (U.K.)
IC Industries
Intelsat

IZI (Italy)
Maritz, Inc.
McCann-Erickson
Mead Data Central
Merrill Lynch Futures Corporation
National Farmers' Union (U.K.)
National Gypsum
Nova and Alberta Corp. (Canada)
O'Connor & Associates
Paine Webber
Reynolds Metals
Sentinel Communications Company
Simon and Coates (U.K.)
Transway International
United Parcel Service
Vitro Envases (Mexico)
Warren Springs Labs (U.K.)
Yellow Freight
Zapata

Associations and Consulting Firms

Abba Consultants (U.K.)
American Paper Institute
Battelle Northwest Labs
BDM Corporation
Centro de Estudios Monetarios Latinamericanos
  (Mexico)
Chemonics International
Commodities Research Unit
Coopers & Lybrand
Engineering and Economic Research
Fiscal Associates
Food Studies Group (U.K.)
Gas Research Institute
Goldman, Sachs

M.G. Lewis and Company
McKinsey and Company
Midwest Research Institute
National Association of Furniture Manufacturers
National Bureau of Economic Research
Netherlands Economic Institute
Price Waterhouse
The Rand Corporation
TASC
Thailand Development Research Institute
TRW
R.S. Weinberg and Associates
The Wyatt Company

Academic Institutions

Aston University (U.K.)
Babson College
Boston University
Brandeis University
California State University
Cambridge University (U.K.)
Catholic University
Central Michigan University
Columbia University
Erasmus University (Neth.)
Florida International University
Florida State University
Fordham University
Free University of Amsterdam (Neth.)
George Mason University
George Washington University
Goldsmith's College (U.K.)
Howard University
Imperial College (U.K.)
Iowa State University
James Madison University
Kansas State University
Kyoto University (Japan)
Laval University (Canada)
London Business College (U.K.)
London School of Economics (U.K.)
Nagasaki University (Japan)
New School for Social Research
North Carolina A&T State University
Oberlin College
Plymouth Polytechnic (U.K.)
Polytechnic of North London (U.K.)
Preston Polytechnic (U.K.)
Queen Mary College (U.K.)
Rutgers University
State University of New York
Technische Universitat Berlin (Germany)

Temple University
Thames Polytechnic (U.K.)
Tulane University
Union College
Universite Libre de Bruxelles (Belgium)
University of Arkansas
University of Baltimore
University of Bristol (U.K.)
University of California
University of Essex (U.K.)
University of Hawaii
University of Illinois
University of Indonesia
University of Linz (Austria)
University of Maine
University of Maryland
University of Minnesota
University of Missouri
University of New Orleans
University of North Dakota
University of Notre Dame
University of Paris (France)
University of Reading (U.K.)
University of South Dakota
University of Uppsala (Sweden)
University of Virginia
*University of Wales Institute of Science and
    Technology*
University of West Indies
U.S. Air Force Academy
Villanova University
Virginia Wesleyan College
Washington State University
Western Australia Institute of Technology
Western Illinois University
Williams College

CONTENTS

9   Forecast Implementation   409

10   Computationally Intensive Statistics: The Bootstrap   427

Appendix   User's Guide to BEA Information   452

Index   486

1 INTRODUCTION TO BUSINESS FORECASTING

Introduction

Forecasting involves making the best possible judgment about some future event. In today's rapidly changing business world such judgments can mean the difference between success and failure. It is no longer reasonable to rely solely on intuition, or one's "feel for the situation," in projecting future sales, inventory needs, personnel requirements, and other important economic or business variables. Quantitative methods have been shown to be helpful in making better predictions about the future course of events,[1] and a number of sophisticated computer software packages have been developed to make these methods accessible to nearly everyone. There is a danger, however, in using canned forecasting software unless you are familiar with the concepts upon which the programs are based.

Do not become so enamored with quantitative methods and computer results that you fail to think *carefully about the series you wish to forecast.*

This text and its accompanying computer software have been carefully designed to provide you with an understanding of the conceptual basis for many modern quantitative forecasting models, along with programs that have been written specifically for the purpose of allowing you to put these methods to use. You will find both the text and the software to be extremely user-friendly. After studying the text and using the software to replicate the examples we present, you will be able to forecast economic and business variables with greater accuracy than you might now expect. But a word of warning is appropriate. Do not become so enamored with quantitative methods and computer results that you fail to *think* carefully about the series you wish to forecast. Personal judgments based on practical experience and/or thorough research should always play an important role in the preparation of any forecast.

---

[1] J. Holton Wilson and Deborah Allison-Koerber, "Combining Subjective and Objective Forecasts Improves Results," *Journal of Business Forecasting* 11, no. 3 (Fall 1992), pp. 12–16.

Forecasting in Business Today

Business decisions almost always depend on some forecast about the course of events. Virtually every functional area of business makes use of some type of forecast. For example:

1. Accountants rely on forecasts of costs and revenues in tax planning.
2. The personnel department depends on forecasts as it plans recruitment of new employees and other changes in the workforce.
3. Financial experts must forecast interest rates to be able to manage cash flow.
4. Production managers rely on forecasts to determine raw-material needs and the desired inventory of finished products.
5. Marketing managers use a sales forecast to establish promotional budgets.

The sales forecast is often the root forecast from which others, such as employment requirements, are derived. As early as the mid-1980s a study of large American-operated firms showed that roughly 94 percent made use of a sales forecast.[2] The ways in which forecasts are prepared and the manner in which results are used vary considerably among firms.

As a way of illustrating the application of forecasting in the corporate world we will summarize aspects of the forecasting function in nine companies. In these examples you may see some terms with which you are not fully familiar at this time. However, you probably have a general understanding of them, and when you have completed the text you will understand them all quite well.

Bell Atlantic

At Bell Atlantic the forecasting process begins with the collection of historical data on a monthly basis.[3] These data are saved both for service classifications and geographic regions. The Demand Forecasting Group at Bell Atlantic developed a data repository so that the data can be shared and integrated across the entire corporation. In preparing forecasts, subjective forecasting methods are used along with time-series methods, and regression modeling based on economic, demographic, and other exogenous variables. The forecasts are continually monitored and compared with actual results monthly and annually to ensure that Bell Atlantic meets customer needs.

Rubbermaid: Home Products Division

Richard B. Barrett and David J. Kitska—manager of marketing information and forecast analyst, respectively, for the Home Products Division of Rubbermaid—have

---

[2]Guisseppi A. Forgionne, "Economic Tools Used by Management in Large American-Operated Corporations," *Business Economics* 19, no. 3 (April 1984), p. 6.

[3]Sharon Harris, "Forecasting with Demand Forecast Group Database at Bell Atlantic," *Journal of Business Forecasting,* Winter 1995–96, p. 23.

noted that at Rubbermaid, "The forecasts are not just 'show' numbers; they are incorporated into the short-term and long-term business plans to which people willingly react."[4] They also note that input to the forecasts comes from all functional areas and that modern statistical methods—such as exponential smoothing and Box-Jenkins—are combined with practical business knowledge and experience in developing forecasts. A one-year forecast and 30-, 60-, and 90-day forecasts are prepared for roughly 600 item packs. One week of every month is designated as "forecast week," during which product managers, group product managers, the vice president for sales, the vice president for marketing, and others devote considerable time to reviewing and revising forecasts initially prepared by those personnel who work daily on the forecasting process. In addition, every Friday morning a new report on forecasts and the demand history is distributed to product managers and group product managers.

Segix Italia

Segix Italia is a pharmaceutical company in Italy that produces products that are sold domestically and are exported to countries in Europe, such as Belgium, Holland, Germany, and England, as well as to African, South American, Asian, and Middle Eastern countries.[5] The forecasting function at Segix is housed within the marketing group, and forecasts are reviewed by the marketing director and the sales director, both of whom may make subjective adjustments to the forecasts based on market forces not reflected in the original forecasts. The forecasts are prepared monthly for seven main prescription drug products. The monthly forecasts are then aggregated to arrive at annual forecasts. These forecasts are used to develop targets for sales representatives.

Peter Paul Cadbury, Inc.

Douglas Newell—manager of sales information and development at Peter Paul Cadbury, Inc.—has reported that his division makes 4,680 original short-term forecasts per year (concerning 120 items for each of 3 shipping centers for 13 periods per year).[6] They use time-series analysis, smoothing, regression, and judgmental methods in developing forecasts of sales. Forecasts of total gross sales for a year were reported to be accurate to within 1 percent. Narrow, short-term forecasts have a higher degree of error, perhaps 25 percent or more when forecasting a single item for one of the three shipping centers for a particular four-week period. Mr. Newell advised that forecasters should not "get carried away with sophisticated models unless they prove themselves in real situations,"[7] and that users of forecasts must realize that no forecast is going to be exactly correct at all times.

---

[4]Richard B. Barrett and David J. Kitska, "Forecasting System at Rubbermaid," *Journal of Business Forecasting* 6, no. 1 (Spring 1987), pp. 7–9.

[5]Anna Maria Rosati, "Forecasting at Segix Italia: A Pharmaceutical Company," *Journal of Business Forecasting,* Fall 1996, pp. 7–9.

[6]Douglas Newell, "Simple Methods Work for Candyman at Peter Paul Cadbury," *Journal of Business Forecasting* 1, no. 3 (Spring 1982), pp. 24–27.

[7]Ibid., p. 27.

Fiat Auto

Top management at Fiat considers the forecasting function as an essential aspect of their decision-making process.[8] Midway through the 1990s Fiat was selling over 2 million vehicles annually and employed some 81,000 people in Italy and about another 38,000 overseas. All functional areas in the company make use of the forecasts that are prepared primarily in the Planning, Finance and Control Department and in the Product Strategy Department. Macroeconomic data such as gross domestic product, the interest rate, the rate of inflation, and raw-material prices are important inputs in Fiat's forecasting process. At Fiat forecasts are first prepared for total sales of vehicles, engines, and gears and then broken down to specific SKUs. Sales are measured by orders rather than shipments because their system is customer driven.

Douglas Aircraft

In discussing how forecasts are prepared at Douglas Aircraft, Adrian LeRoy and Adam Pilarski relate how two alternative forecasts are reconciled within the company.[9] Since the number of passenger-miles flown is an important determinant of airplane sales, they prepare two passenger-miles forecasts: a top-down forecast and a bottom-up forecast. The former starts with an econometric forecast of the entire market for each of 32 regions of the world. These regional forecasts are then broken down for individual airlines that serve each market. Another forecast begins with a separate econometric model for each of the top 50 airlines in the world (which includes about 85 percent of the market) for each market. Less sophisticated forecasts for another 110 airlines are added to arrive at a bottom-up forecast for each market. The total of 160 airlines accounts for about 98 percent of the market. The econometric models are augmented with commonsense judgments about the industry in arriving at final forecasts for the two approaches, which are then reconciled.

Trans World Airlines

Paul Biederman, director of economic analysis and forecasting at TWA, has the responsibility for revenue forecasting for the entire company.[10] TWA's financial plan for each year is driven by his revenue forecasts, which are done twice each year. A first forecast for the following year is prepared in the November of the previous year. This forecast is then recalibrated in May of the forecast year. Thus, for the 1998 year a forecast is prepared in November of 1997 and that forecast is updated in May of 1998. Ultimately the revenue forecasts are combined with expense

---

[8]Anna Maria Rosati, "Forecasting at Fiat Auto," *Journal of Business Forecasting,* Spring 1996, pp. 28–29.

[9]Adrian D. LeRoy and Adam M. Pilarski, "The Way to Improve Accuracy—Douglas Aircraft's Experience," *Journal of Business Forecasting* 4, no. 2 (Summer 1985), pp. 10–12.

[10]Paul S. Biederman, "The Role of Forecasting at Trans World Airlines," *Journal of Business Forecasting,* Fall 1993, pp. 3–4.

estimates that come from the office of the controller. In addition to these short-term forecasts, TWA prepares long-term forecasts for equipment planning.

Rather than forecasting each market separately and adding them together to get the total company forecast, TWA uses a top-down and industry-share approach. They start by forecasting total industry passenger traffic and then they estimate TWA's share of the total. The reason for the top-down approach is related to data availability issues. Total industry data are available for each month within a week after the end of the month. On the other hand, it takes about nine months to get market-by-market data from the Department of Transportation. TWA uses a combination regression and trend models in developing annual forecasts, which are then converted to a monthly basis according to seasonal relationships.

Howmedica Division of Pfizer Hospital Products Group

Mr. Terry Anderson, manager of forecasting and analysis for Howmedica, a division of the Pfizer Hospital Products Group, has indicated that his division has responsibility for forecasting sales of reconstructive products for total joint replacement, trauma products to aid in healing bone fractures, and both system-specific and generic instrumentation.[11] These categories include over 6,000 items, and so the division needs to be as efficient as possible in developing forecasts. Forecasts by individual items are necessary because it is Howmedica's policy to ship orders directly from stock. Howmedica's manufacturing department uses the forecasted sales in units (demand forecasts) for inventory and human resource planning as well as to determine requirements for plant and equipment. Demand forecasts are also valuable as an input to sales and departmental budgets. Sales forecasts, in dollars, are provided to the finance department as an input to the financial budgeting process. Each month all product forecasts are evaluated for reasonability and revised if necessary. Even when forecasts are tracking well they are revised at least every three months.

Brake Parts, Inc.

Brake Parts, Inc. (BPI) is a manufacturer of replacement brake parts for both foreign and domestic cars and light trucks.[12] They have nine manufacturing plants and seven distribution centers in the United States and Canada. Overall BPI has roughly 250,000 stock-keeping units at various distribution locations (SKULs) to forecast. *The development and implementation of a multiple forecasting system (MFS) has saved BPI over $6 million per month, resulting from sales not being lost due to stockouts.* The MFS used at BPI uses up to 19 time-series forecasting techniques, such as a variety of exponential smoothing methods, and causal regression models

---

[11]Terry Anderson, "Demand Forecasting at Howmedica," *Journal of Business Forecasting* 10, no. 2 (Summer 1991), pp. 2–4.

[12]John T. Mentzer and Jon Schroeter, "Multiple Forecasting System at Brake Parts, Inc.," *Journal of Business Forecasting,* Fall 1993, pp. 5–9.

in tandem. Forecasts are first developed with a time-series method and then the errors, or residuals, are forecast using regression. The two forecasts are then added together and provided to management in a form that allows management to make subjective adjustments to the forecasts.

Forecasts are evaluated using three measures: percent error (PE), mean absolute percent error (MAPE), and year-to-date mean absolute percent error (YTD MAPE). The first two of these are common error measures but the third is someone unique. The YTD MAPE is used to give management a feeling for how each forecast is performing in the most current time frame. The PE and MAPE contain errors that have occurred at any time in the historical period and thus may not reflect how well the method is working currently.

These examples illustrate the role forecasting plays in nine representative firms. Similar scenarios exist in thousands of other businesses throughout the world and, as you will see in the following section, in various nonbusiness activities as well.

Forecasting in the Public and Not-for-Profit Sectors

The need to make decisions based on judgments about the future course of events extends beyond the profit-oriented sector of the economy. Hospitals, libraries, blood banks, police and fire departments, urban transit authorities, credit unions, and a myriad of federal, state, and local governmental units rely on forecasts of one kind or another. Social service agencies such as the Red Cross and the Easter Seal Society must also base their yearly plans on forecasts of needed services and expected revenues.

Brooke Saladin, working with the research and planning division of the police department in a city of about 650,000 people, has been effective in forecasting the demand for police patrol services.[13] This demand is measured by using a call-for-service work-load level in units of hours per 24-hour period. After a thorough statistical analysis, five factors were identified as influential determinants of the call-for-service work load (W):

POP   a population factor
ARR   an arrest factor
AFF   an affluence factor
VAC   a vacancy factor
DEN   a density factor

The following multiple-regression model was developed on the basis of a sample of 40 cruiser districts in the city:

$$W = 5.66 + 1.84POP + 1.70ARR - 0.93AFF + 0.61VAC + 0.13DEN$$

Using the remaining 23 cruiser districts to test this model, Saladin found that "the absolute error in forecasting workload ranged from 0.07827 to 1.49764, with an

---

[13]Brooke A. Saladin, "A Police Story with Business Implications and Applications," *Journal of Business Forecasting* 1, no. 6 (Winter 1982–83), pp. 3–5.

average of 0.74618."[14] This type of model is useful in planning the needs for both personnel and equipment.

In Texas, the Legislative Budget Board (LBB) is required to forecast the growth rate for Texas personal income, which then governs the limit for state appropriations. The state comptroller's office also needs forecasts of such variables as the annual growth rates of electricity sales, total nonagricultural employment, and total tax revenues. Richard Ashley and John Guerard have used techniques like those to be discussed in this text to forecast these variables and have found that the application of time-series analysis yields better one-year-ahead forecasts than naive constant-growth-rate models.[15]

Dr. Jon David Vasche, senior economist for the California Legislative Analysis Office (LAO), is involved with economic and financial forecasting for the state. He has noted that these forecasts are essential, since the state's budget must be prepared long before actual economic conditions are known.[16] The key features of the LAO's forecasting approach are:

1. *Forecasts of national economic variables.* The Wharton econometric model is used with the adaptations that reflect the LAO's own assumptions about such policy variables as monetary growth and national fiscal policies.
2. *California economic submodel.* This model forecasts variables such as trends in state population, personal income, employment, and housing activity.
3. *State revenue submodels.* These models are used to forecast the variables that affect the state's revenue. These include such items as taxable personal income, taxable sales, corporate profits, vehicle registrations, and cash available for investment.
4. *Cash-flow models.* These models are used to forecast the flow of revenues over time.

In developing and using forecasting models, "the LAO has attempted to strike a balance between comprehensiveness and sophistication on the one hand, and flexibility and usability on the other."[17] LAO's success is determined by how accurately it forecasts the state's revenues. In the three most recent years reported, the "average absolute value of the actual error was only about 1.6 percent."[18] Errors of 5 percent or more have occurred when unanticipated movements in national economic activity have affected the state's economy.

A multiple-regression forecasting model has been developed to help forecast a hospital's nursing staff requirements.[19] This model forecasts the number of patients

---

[14]Ibid., p. 5.

[15]Richard Ashley and John Guerard, "Applications of Time-Series Analysis to Texas Financial Forecasting," *Interfaces* 13, no. 4 (August 1983), pp. 46–55.

[16]Jon David Vasche, "Forecasting Process As Used by California Legislative Analyst's Office," *Journal of Business Forecasting* 6, no. 2 (Summer 1987), pp. 9–13.

[17]Ibid., pp. 9, 12.

[18]Ibid., p. 12.

[19]F. Theodore Helmer, Edward B. Opperman, and James D. Suver, "Forecasting Nursing Staffing Requirements by Intensity-of-Care Level," *Interfaces* (June 1980), pp. 50–55.

that need to be served and the nature of care required (e.g., pediatric or orthopedic) for each month, day of the week, and time of day. Such models have become very valuable for directors of nursing personnel in determining work schedules.

In a study of a hospital that holds over 300 beds, we have found that the forecasting methods discussed in this text are effective in forecasting monthly billable procedures (BILLPROC) for the hospital's laboratories.[20] The primary purpose of producing monthly forecasts is to help laboratory managers make more accurate staffing decisions in the laboratory. Also, an accurate forecast can help in controlling inventory costs and in providing timely customer service. This can streamline operations and lead to more satisfied customers.

For preparing short-term forecasts of billable procedures, two models are used: a linear-regression model and Winters' exponential-smoothing model. The linear-regression model is based on inpatient admissions, a time index, and 11 monthly dummy variables to account for seasonality. The second model is a Winters' exponential smoothing that incorporates a multiplicative seasonal adjustment and a trend component.

The root-mean-squared error (RMSE) is used to evaluate the accuracy of forecast models at the hospital. The first annual forecast, by month, of billable procedures for the laboratory prepared with these quantitative methods provided good results. The linear-regression model provided the most accurate forecast, with an RMSE of 1654.44. This was about 3.9 percent of the mean number of procedures per month during that year. The Winters' model had a higher RMSE of 2416.91 (about 5.7 percent of the mean number of procedures per month). For the entire fiscal year in total, the forecast of the annual number of laboratory procedures resulted in an error of only 0.7 percent.

Computer Use and Quantitative Forecasting

In today's business environment computers are readily available to nearly everyone. There was a time when only very large business enterprises had the resources to spend on computer systems, and within those businesses access to the computer's power was limited. Today things are quite different. The cost of large-scale computer systems has dropped significantly, and the advent of mini-and microcomputers has made computer technology available to virtually any business professional interested in utilizing it. As early as 1966 a study reported that 68 percent of the companies surveyed used computers in preparing forecasts.[21] In 1986 a survey of economists found that over 93 percent used a mainframe computer, a microcomputer, or both in developing forecasts.[22] Of that number, less than 6 percent relied

---

[20]J. Holton Wilson and Steven J. Schuiling, "Forecasting Hospital Laboratory Procedures," *Journal of Medical Systems,* December 1992, pp. 269–79.

[21]Spyros Makridakis, Steven C. Wheelwright, and Victor E. McGee, *Forecasting: Methods and Applications,* 2nd ed. (New York: John Wiley & Sons, 1983), p. 782.

[22]Barry Keating and J. Holton Wilson, "Forecasting: Practices and Teachings," *Journal of Business Forecasting* 6, no. 3 (Winter 1987–88), p. 12.

solely on a mainframe. A similar study of marketing professionals found that about 87 percent were using computers in forecasting and that only about 2 percent of those relied solely on a mainframe computer. Just over 30 percent of the marketing professionals surveyed who use a computer in developing forecasts relied solely on a microcomputer.[23] Thus, it is clear that microcomputers are now widely used in the preparation of forecasts.

The widespread availability of computers has contributed to the use of quantitative forecasting techniques, many of which would not be practical to carry out by hand. Most of the methods described in this text fall into the realm of quantitative forecasting techniques that are reasonable to use only when appropriate computer software is available. A number of software packages, at costs that range from about $100 to several thousands of dollars, are currently marketed for use in developing forecasts. You will find that the SORITEC software that accompanies this text will enable you to apply the most commonly used quantitative forecasting techniques to data of your choosing.

The use of microcomputers or PCs (personal computers) in forecasting has been made possible by rapid technological changes that have made these desktop (or laptop) computers very fast and capable of storing and processing large amounts of data. User-friendly software makes it easy for people to become proficient in using forecasting programs in a short period of time. Dr. Vasche has said in this regard that "reliance on such PC systems has given state economists added flexibility in their forecasting work. By minimizing use of mainframe computers, it has also reduced the state's costs of preparing forecasts."[24] The same is true in most business situations as well. The dominance of PC forecasting software is clear at the annual meetings of the International Association of Business Forecasting and of the International Institute of Forecasters. At these meetings various vendors of PC-based forecasting software packages display and demonstrate their products.

The importance of quantitative methods in forecasting has been stressed by Charles W. Chase, Jr., who was director of forecasting at Johnson & Johnson Consumer Products, Inc., and now works in a similar capacity for Coca-Cola. He says, "Forecasting is a blend of science and art. Like most things in business, the rule of 80/20 applies to forecasting. By and large, forecasts are driven 80 percent mathematically and 20 percent judgmentally."[25]

Subjective Forecasting Methods

Quantitative techniques using the power of the computer have come to dominate the forecasting landscape. However, there is a rich history of forecasting based on

---

[23]J. Holton Wilson and Hugh G. Daubek, "Marketing Managers Evaluate Forecasting Methods," *Journal of Business Forecasting* 8, no. 1 (Spring 1989), p. 20.

[24]Vasche, "Forecasting Process," p. 12.

[25]Charles W. Chase, Jr., "Forecasting Consumer Products," *Journal of Business Forecasting* 10, no. 1 (Spring 1991), p. 2.

subjective and judgmental methods, some of which remain useful even today. These methods are probably most appropriately used when the forecaster is faced with a severe shortage of historical data and/or when quantitative expertise is not available. In some situations a judgmental method may even be preferred to a quantitative one. Very long-range forecasting is an example of such a situation. The computer-based models that are the focal point of this text have less applicability to such things as forecasting the type of home entertainment that will be available 40 years from now than do those methods based on expert judgments. In this section several subjective or judgmental forecasting methods are reviewed.

Sales-Force Composites

The sales force can be a rich source of information about future trends and changes in buyer behavior. These people have daily contact with buyers and are the closest contact most firms have with their customers. If the information available from the sales force is organized and collected in an objective manner, considerable insight into future sales volumes can be obtained.

Members of the sales force are asked to estimate sales for each product they handle. These estimates are usually based on each individual's subjective "feel" for the level of sales that would be reasonable in the forecast period. Often a range of forecasts will be requested, including a most optimistic, a most pessimistic, and a most likely forecast. Typically these individual projections are aggregated by the sales manager for a given product line and/or geographic area. Ultimately the person responsible for the firm's total sales forecast combines the product-line and/or geographic forecasts to arrive at projections that become the basis for a given planning horizon.

While this process takes advantage of information from sources very close to actual buyers, a major problem with the resulting forecast may arise if members of the sales force tend to underestimate sales for their product lines and/or territories.[26] This behavior is particularly likely when the salespeople are assigned quotas on the basis of their forecasts and when bonuses are based on performance relative to those quotas. Such a downward bias can be very harmful to the firm. Scheduled production runs are shorter than they should be, raw-material inventories are too small, labor requirements are underestimated, and in the end customer ill will is generated by product shortages. The sales manager with ultimate forecasting responsibility can offset this downward bias, but only by making judgments that could, in turn, incorporate other bias into the forecast. Robin Peterson has developed a way of improving sales-force composite forecasts by using a prescribed set of learned routines as a guide for salespeople as they develop their forecasts.[27]

---

[26]Robin T. Peterson, "Sales Force Composite Forecasting—An Exploratory Analysis," *Journal of Business Forecasting* 8, no. 1 (Spring 1989), pp. 23–27.

[27]Robin T. Peterson, "Improving Sales Force Composite: Forecasting by Using Scripts," *Journal of Business Forecasting,* Fall 1993, pp. 10–14.

These sets of learned routines are referred to as *scripts,* which can serve as a guide in developing an essentially subjective forecast. An example of a hypothetical script adapted from Peterson's work follows.

Review data on gross domestic product
Review forecasts of gross domestic product
Review industry sales data for the preceding year
Review company sales data for the preceding year
Review company sales forecasts for the previous years
Survey key accounts concerning their purchasing plans
Review last year's sales data in the salesperson's territory
Review the employment situation in the salesperson's territory
Do a simple trend projection of sales in the salesperson's territory
Examine competitors' actions in the salesperson's territory
Gather internal data about the company's promotional plans
Gather internal data about the company's product introduction plans
Gather internal data about the company's customer service plans
Gather internal data about the company's credit-granting plans
Check to see if there are planned changes in the company's pricing structure
Evaluate the pricing practices of competitors
Track the company's sales promotions
Track the competitors' sales promotions

A script such as this can be developed, based on interviews with successful salespeople concerning procedures they have used in preparing their forecasts.

Surveys of Customers and the General Population

In some situations it may be practical to survey customers for advanced information about their buying intentions. This practice presumes that buyers plan their purchases and follow through with their plans. Such an assumption is probably more realistic for industrial sales than for sales to households and individuals. It is also more realistic for big-ticket items such as cars or personal computers than for convenience goods like toothpaste or tennis balls.

Survey data concerning how people feel about the economy are sometimes used by forecasters to help predict certain buying behaviors. One of the commonly used measures of how people feel about the economy comes from a monthly survey conducted by the University of Michigan Survey Research Center (SRC). The SRC produces an Index of Consumer Sentiment (ICS) based on a survey of 500 individuals, 40 percent of whom are respondents who participated in the survey six months earlier and the remaining 60 percent are new respondents selected on a random basis. This index has its base period in 1966, when the index was 100. High values of the ICS indicate more positive feelings about the economy than do lower values.

Thus, if the ICS goes up, one might expect that people are more likely to make certain types of purchases.

Jury of Executive Opinion

The judgments of experts in any area are a valuable resource. Based on years of experience, such judgments can be useful in the forecasting process. Using the method known as the *jury of executive opinion,* a forecast is developed by combining the subjective opinions of the managers and executives who are most likely to have the best insights about the firm's business. To provide a breadth of opinions, it is useful to select these people from different functional areas. For example, personnel from finance, marketing, and production might be included.

The person responsible for making the forecast may collect opinions in individual interviews or in a meeting where the participants have an opportunity to discuss various points of view. The latter has some obvious advantages such as stimulating deeper insights, but it has some important disadvantages as well. For example, if one or more strong personalities dominate the group, their opinions will become disproportionately important in the final consensus that is reached.

The Delphi Method

The Delphi method is similar to the jury of executive opinion in taking advantage of the wisdom and insight of people who have considerable expertise about the area to be forecast. It has the additional advantage, however, of anonymity among the participants. The experts, perhaps five to seven in number, never meet to discuss their views; none of them even knows who else is on the panel.

The Delphi method can be summarized by the following six steps:

1. Participating panel members are selected.
2. Questionnaires asking for opinions about the variables to be forecast are distributed to panel members.
3. Results from panel members are collected, tabulated, and summarized.
4. Summary results are distributed to the panel members for their review and consideration.
5. Panel members revise their individual estimates, taking account of the information received from the other, unknown panel members.
6. Steps 3 through 5 are repeated until no significant changes result.

Through this process there is usually movement toward centrality, but there is no pressure on panel members to alter their original projections. Members who have strong reason to believe that their original response is correct, no matter how widely it differs from others, may freely stay with it. Thus, in the end there may not be a consensus.

The Delphi method may be superior to the jury of executive opinion, since strong personalities or peer pressures have no influence on the outcome. The processes of sending out questionnaires, getting them back, tabulating, and summarizing can be speeded up by using advanced computer capabilities, including networking and electronic mail.[28]

Some Advantages and Disadvantages of Subjective Methods

Subjective (i.e., qualitative or judgmental) forecasting methods are sometimes considered desirable because they do not require any particular mathematical background of the individuals involved. As future business professionals, like yourself, become better trained in quantitative forms of analysis, this advantage will become less important. Historically, another advantage of subjective methods has been their wide acceptance by users. However, our experience suggests that users are increasingly concerned with how the forecast was developed, and with most subjective methods it is difficult to be specific in this regard. The underlying models are, by definition, subjective. This subjectivity is nonetheless the most important advantage of this class of methods. There are often forces at work that cannot be captured by quantitative methods. They can, however, be sensed by experienced business professionals and can make an important contribution to improved forecasts. Wilson and Allison-Koerber have shown this dramatically in the context of forecasting sales for a large piece of food-service equipment produced by the Delfield Company.[29] Quantitative methods reduced errors to about 60 percent of those that resulted from the subjective method that had been in use. When the less accurate subjective method was combined with the quantitative methods, errors were further reduced to about 40 percent of the level when the subjective method was used alone. It is clear from this result, and others, that there is often important information content in subjective methods.

The disadvantages of subjective methods were nicely summarized by Charles W. Chase, Jr., when he was with Johnson & Johnson Consumer Products, Inc. He stated that "the disadvantages of qualitative methods are: (1) they are almost always biased; (2) they are not consistently accurate over time; (3) it takes years of experience for someone to learn how to convert intuitive judgment into good forecasts."[30]

New-Product Forecasting

Quantitative forecasting methods, which are the primary focus of this text, are not usually well suited for predicting sales of new products, because they rely on a historical data series to establish model parameters. Often judgmental methods are better suited to forecasting new-product sales because there are many uncertainties and few known relationships. One way to deal with the lack of known information

---

[28] See, for example, Bernard S. Husbands, "Electronic Mail System Enhances Delphi Method," *Journal of Business Forecasting* 1, no. 4 (Summer 1982), pp. 24–27.

[29] Wilson and Allison-Koerber, "Combining Subjective and Objective Forecasts," p. 15.

[30] Charles W. Chase, Jr., "Forecasting Consumer Products," p. 4.

in the forecasting of new products is to incorporate a modified version of the Delphi method. This was done by Ken Goldfisher while he worked in the Information Services Division of the Nabisco Foods Group. Goldfisher has also found some relatively simple quantitative methods, such as moving averages, to be helpful in developing new-product forecasts at Nabisco.[31]

Various market research activities can be helpful in new-product forecasting. Surveys of potential customers can provide useful preliminary information about the propensity of buyers to adopt a new product. Test-market results and results from the distribution of free samples can also provide estimates of initial sales. On the basis of predictions about the number of initial innovators who will buy a product, an S-shaped market-penetration curve can be used to forecast diffusion of the new product throughout the market.

Terry Anderson has described a process for new-product forecasting at Howmedica that is based on various judgmental factors.[32] It begins with an estimate of the total number of customers, based on a consensus within the marketing and sales groups. A customer usage rate is derived based on experience with past new introductions. Inventory requirements are also included in making projections.

Whitlark, Geurts, and Swenson have used customer purchase intention surveys as a tool to help prepare forecasts of new products.[33] They describe a three-step process that starts with the identification of a demographic profile of the target market, then the probability of purchase is estimated from survey data, and finally a forecast is developed by combining this probability with information on the size of the target market. A sample of consumers from the target market are asked to respond to an intent-to-purchase scale such as: definitely will buy; probably will buy; might or might not buy; probably will not buy; and definitely will not buy. Probabilities are then assigned to each of the intention-to-buy categories, using empirical evidence from a longitudinal study of members of the target market covering a length of time comparable to the length of time for the proposed forecast horizon. An example of these probabilities for a three- and a six-month time horizon is shown in Table 1–1. Note that the probabilities of purchase increase as the time horizon increases.

Applying this method to two products produced good results. For the first product the three-month forecast purchase rate was 2.9 percent compared with an actual purchase rate of 2.4 percent. In the six-month time horizon the forecast and actual rates were 15.6 percent and 11.1 percent, respectively. Similar results were found for a second product. In the three-month horizon the forecast and actual percents were 2.5 percent versus 1.9 percent, while in the six-month forecast horizon the forecast was 16.7 percent and the actual was 16.3 percent.

---

[31] Ken Goldfisher, "Modified Delphi: A Concept for New Product Forecasting," *Journal of Business Forecasting* 11, no. 4 (Winter 1992–93), pp. 10–11; and Ken Goldfisher and Colleen Chan, "New Product Reactive Forecasting," *Journal of Business Forecasting* 13, no. 4 (Winter 1994–95), pp. 7–9.

[32] Anderson, "Demand Forecasting at Howmedica," pp. 2–3.

[33] David B. Whitlark, Michael D. Geurts, and Michael J. Swenson, "New Product Forecasting with a Purchase Intention Survey," *Journal of Business Forecasting* 10, no. 3 (Fall 1993), pp. 18–21.

TABLE 1–1   Probabilities Assigned to Purchase-Intention Categories

Intention-to-Purchase Category	Three-Month Time Horizon	Six-Month Time Horizon
Definitely will buy	64%	75%
Probably will buy	23%	53%
Might or might not buy	5%	21%
Probably will not buy	2%	9%
Definitely will not buy	1%	4%

Adapted from Whitlark et al., p. 20.

Two Simple Naive Models

The simplest of all forecasting methods is to assume that the next period will be identical to the present. You may have used this method today in deciding what clothes to wear. If you had not heard a professional weather forecast, your decision about today's weather might be based on the weather you observed yesterday. If yesterday was clear and the temperature was 70°F, you might assume today to be the same. If yesterday was snowy and cold, you might expect a similar wintry day today. In fact, without evidence to suggest otherwise, such a weather forecast is quite reasonable. Forecasts based solely on the most recent observation of the variable of interest are often referred to as "naive forecasts."

In this section we will use such a method, and a variation on it, to forecast the yearly U.S. average annual unemployment rate using data for an arbitrary 10-year period. These data are given in Table 1–2 and are shown graphically in Figure 1–1. In both forms of presentation you can see that the unemployment rate (UR) varied considerably throughout this period, from a low of 5.3 percent in year 9 to a high of 9.7 percent in year 2. The fluctuations in most economic and business series (variables) are usually best seen after converting the data into graphic form, as in Figure 1–1. You should develop the habit of observing data in graphic form when forecasting.

(c1t2)

TABLE 1–2   U.S. Average Annual Unemployment Rate

Year	UR	Year	UR
1	7.6%	6	7.0%
2	9.7%	7	6.2%
3	9.6%	8	5.5%
4	7.5%	9	5.3%
5	7.2%	10	5.5%

Figure 1–1

*U.S. Average
Annual
Unemployment
Rate*
(same as c1t2)

U.S. Unemployment Rate (UR)

*The U.S. average annual unemployment rate (UR) from year 1 through year
10 shows a low of 5.3 percent in year 9 and a high of 9.7 percent in year 2.
A plot such as this provides a helpful way of viewing data.*

The simplest naive forecasting model, in which the forecast value is equal to the previous observed value, can be described in algebraic form as follows:

$$F_t = A_{t-1}$$

where F_t represents the forecast value for time period t and A_{t-1} represents the observed value one period earlier ($t - 1$). In terms of the unemployment-rate data we wish to forecast, the model may be written as:

$$\text{URF1}_t = \text{UR}_{t-1}$$

where URF1_t is the unemployment-rate naive forecast number 1 at time period t and UR_{t-1} is the observed unemployment rate one period earlier ($t - 1$). We call this *naive forecast one* because we will very shortly look at another naive forecast.

This first naive forecast was actually done using SORITEC, but were we to do it by hand it would produce the following tabulation:

Year	Actual Value UR	Forecast Value URF1
1	7.6%	Missing
2	9.7%	7.6%
3	9.6%	9.7%
4	7.5%	9.6%
5	7.2%	7.5%
6	7.0%	7.2%
7	6.2%	7.0%
8	5.5%	6.2%
9	5.3%	5.5%
10	5.5%	5.3%
11	Missing	5.5%

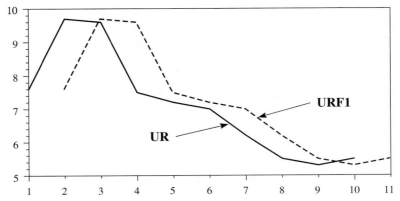

FIGURE 1–2

Unemployment Rate and First Naive Forecast (c1f2)

This figure shows the actual unemployment rate (solid line = UR), and the forecast value (dashed line = URF1) for year 2 through year 11. The forecast values were generated by the naive model: $URF1_t = UR_{t-1}$.

Note that each forecast value simply replicates the actual value for the preceding year. Since we are assuming that the stream of known data ended in year 10, we have "Missing" for the observed unemployment rate in year 11. These results are presented in graphic form in Figure 1–2, which clearly shows the one-year shift between the two series. The forecast for every year is exactly the same as the actual value for the year before.

One might argue that in addition to considering just the most recent observation, it would make sense to consider the direction from which we arrived at the latest observation. If the series dropped to the latest point, perhaps it is reasonable to assume some further drop. Alternatively, if we have just observed an increase, it may make sense to factor into our forecast some further increase. Such adjustments can be made in a second naive forecasting model, which includes some proportion of the most recently observed rate of change in the series. In general algebraic terms the model becomes

$$F_t = A_{t-1} + P(A_{t-1} - A_{t-2})$$

where F_t is the forecast for period t, A_{t-1} is the actual observation at period $t - 1$, A_{t-2} is the observed value at period $t - 2$, and P is the proportion of the change between periods $t - 2$ and $t - 1$ that we choose to include in the forecast.

Applying this second naive model to the unemployment-rate data, we have

$$URF2_t = UR_{t-1} + P(UR_{t-1} - UR_{t-2})$$

where $URF2_t$ represents the unemployment-rate naive forecast number 2 for time period t; UR_{t-1} and UR_{t-2} are the observed unemployment rates one and two periods earlier, respectively; and P is the fraction of the most recent change in the unemployment rate that we decide to include in our forecast. This is illustrated with $P = 0.5$ as follows:

Year	Actual UR	Forecast (URF2)	Year	Actual UR	Forecast (URF2)
1	7.6%	Missing	7	6.2%	6.9%
2	9.7%	Missing	8	5.5%	5.8%
3	9.6%	(10.8%)	9	5.3%	5.2%
4	7.5%	9.6%	10	5.5%	5.2%
5	7.2%	6.4%	11	Missing	5.6%
6	7.0%	7.0%			

Let us look closely at the circled value in the table above to help you see the exact calculations that are involved in developing this forecast. To get the forecast for year 3, we take the observed value for year 2 and adjust it by including some information from the most recent trend. (For illustrative purposes we have used one-half of that recent change, but one could try other values to see whether improved forecasts are possible.) Thus, the circled value (i.e., the forecast for year 3, $URF2_3$) is:

$$
\begin{aligned}
URF2_3 &= UR_2 + 0.5(UR_2 - UR_1) \\
&= 9.7 + 0.5(9.7 - 7.6) \\
&= 9.7 + 0.5(2.1) \\
&= 9.7 + 1.05 \\
&= 10.75, \text{ or } 10.8
\end{aligned}
$$

All forecast values have been rounded to one decimal place. The values for this second naive forecast of the unemployment rate are shown in graphic form in Figure 1–3, along with the actual unemployment rate for each year.

FIGURE 1–3

Unemployment Rate and Second Naive Forecast

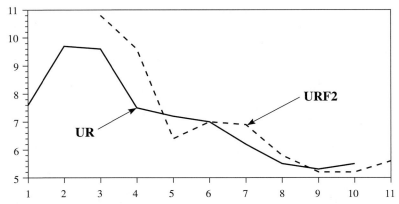

This figure shows the actual unemployment rate (solid line = UR) and the second naive model's forecast value (dashed line = URF2). The forecast values were calculated by the following naive model: $URF2_t = UR_{t-1} + 0.5(UR_{t-1} - UR_{t-2})$.

Evaluating Forecasts

You have now looked at two alternative forecasts of the yearly unemployment rate in the United States. Which forecast is best depends on the particular year or years you look at. For example, the first model (URF1) did a better job of forecasting the unemployment rate for year 3, whereas the second model (URF2) did a better job for year 6. Results for these two years are summarized as follows (the better forecast in each year is in boldface):

		Forecasts	
Year	*UR*	*URF1*	*URF2*
3	9.6%	**9.7%**	10.8%
6	7.0%	7.2%	**7.0%**

It is rare to find one model that is always best for any given set of business or economic data.

In retrospect it is easy to say which forecast was better for any one year. However, it is rare to find one model that is always best for any given set of business or economic data. But we need some way to evaluate the accuracy of forecasting models over a number of years so that we can identify the model that generally works the best. Among a number of possible criteria that could be used, eight common ones are the mean error (ME), the mean absolute error (MAE), the mean percentage error (MPE), the mean absolute percentage error (MAPE), the adjusted mean absolute percentage error (AdjMAPE), the mean-squared error (MSE), the root-mean-squared error (RMSE), and Theil's U.

To illustrate how each of these is calculated, let

A_t = Actual value in period t
F_t = Forecast value in period t
n = Number of periods used in the calculation

1. The mean error is calculated as:

$$ME = \frac{\sum (A_t - F_t)}{n}$$

2. The mean absolute error is then calculated as:

$$MAE = \frac{\sum |A_t - F_t|}{n}$$

3. The mean percentage error is calculated as:

$$MPE = \frac{\sum [(A_t - F_t)/A_t]}{n}$$

4. The mean absolute percentage error is calculated as:

$$\text{MAPE} = \frac{\sum |(A_t - F_t)/A_t|}{n}$$

5. The adjusted mean absolute percentage error is calculated as:

$$\text{AdjMAPE} = \sum \frac{|(A_t - F_t) \div (A_t + F_t)/2|}{n}$$

6. The mean-squared error is calculated as:

$$\text{MSE} = \frac{\sum (A_t - F_t)^2}{n}$$

7. The root-mean-squared error is:

$$\text{RMSE} = \sqrt{\frac{\sum (A_t - F_t)^2}{n}}$$

8. Theil's U can be calculated in several ways, two of which are shown here.

$$U = \sqrt{\sum (A_t - F_t)^2} \div \sqrt{\sum (A_t - A_{t-1})^2}$$

$$U = \text{RMSE (model)} \div \text{RMSE (no-change model)}$$

The no-change model here is the model called naive forecast number 1 above, in which $F_t = A_{t-1}$.

For criteria one through seven, lower values are preferred to higher ones. For Theil's U a value of zero means that the model forecast perfectly (no error in the numerator). If $U < 1$, the model forecasts better than the consecutive-period no-change naive model; if $U = 1$, the model does only as well as the consecutive-period no-change naive model; and if $U > 1$, the model does not forecast as well as the consecutive-period no-change naive model.

The values for these measures, for both forecasts of the unemployment rate (URF1 and URF2), are shown in Table 1–3. From these results we see that five of the eight measures (MAE, MSE, AdjMAPE, RMSE, and Theil's U) indicate that the URF1 is the more accurate forecast. Using ME or MPE, one would pick URF2 as the better model. MAPE results are so close that neither model would be evaluated as clearly superior.

Mean error (ME) and mean percentage error (MPE) are not often used as measures of forecast accuracy because large positive errors ($A_t > F_t$) can be offset by large negative errors ($A_t < F_t$). In fact, a very bad model could have an ME or MPE of zero. ME and MPE are, however, very useful as measures of forecast bias. A negative ME or MPE suggests that, overall, the forecasting model overstates the forecast, while a positive ME or MPE indicates forecasts that are generally too low.

The other measures (MAE, MAPE, AdjMAPE, MSE, RMSE, and Theil's U) are best used to compare alternative forecasting models for a given series. Because of different units used for various series, only MAPE, AdjMAPE, and Theil's U should

TABLE 1–3   Eight Measures of Forecast Accuracy for Two Alternative Unemployment Rate Forecasts

Error Measure	Forecast 1 URF1	Forecast 2 URF2
ME	−0.53	−0.39*
MAE	0.58*	0.69
MPE	−0.08	−0.05*
MAPE	0.09	0.09
AdjMAPE	0.08*	0.09
MSE	0.72*	0.90
RMSE	0.85*	0.95
Theil's U	1.00*	1.12
Number of times best	5	2

The best forecast as indicated by each measure is marked with a *. Only years for which both forecasts are available are included in the calculations so that these criteria for measuring error are applied consistently.

be interpreted across series. For example, a sales series may be in thousands of units, while the prime interest rate is a percentage. Thus, MAE, MSE, and RMSE would be lower for models used to forecast the prime rate than for those used to forecast sales.[34]

Throughout this text we will focus on root-mean-squared error (RMSE) to evaluate the relative accuracy of various forecasting methods. The RMSE is easy for most people to interpret because of its similarity to the basic statistical concept of a standard deviation, and it is one of the most commonly used measures of forecast accuracy.

All quantitative forecasting models are developed on the basis of historical data. When measures of accuracy, such as RMSE, are applied to the historical period, they are often considered measures of how well various models fit the data (i.e., how well they work "in sample"). To determine how accurate the models are in actual forecasts ("out of sample"), a holdout period is often used for evaluation. It may be that the best model "in sample" may not hold up as the best "out of sample."[35] Terry Anderson, of Howmedica, has said, "We often test models for their accuracy by preparing expost forecasts (forecasts for which actuals are known). This helps us in selecting an appropriate model."[36]

---

[34]Brian P. Mathews and Adamantios Diamantopoulos, "Towards a Taxonomy of Forecast Error Measures," *Journal of Forecasting,* August 1994, pp. 409–16.

[35]Pamela A. Texter and Peg Young, "How Accurate Is a Model That Fits Best the Historical Data?" *Journal of Business Forecasting* 8, no. 4 (Winter 1989–90), pp. 13–16; and Spyros Makridakis, "Accuracy Measures: Theoretical and Practical Concerns," *International Journal of Forecasting,* December 1993, pp. 527–29.

[36]Anderson, "Demand Forecasting at Howmedica," p. 4.

Using Multiple Forecasts

When forecasting sales or some other business or economic variable, it is usually a good idea to consider more than one model. We know it is unlikely that one model will always provide the most accurate forecast for any series. Thus, it makes sense to "hedge one's bets," in a sense, by using two or more forecasts. This may involve making a "most optimistic," a "most pessimistic," and a "most likely" forecast. In our example of forecasting the unemployment rate, using the two naive models described in previous sections, we could take the lowest forecast value in each year as the most optimistic and the highest as the most pessimistic. This provides a range of values into which we feel the actual value will probably fall. These are shown in Table 1–4, along with a value called *most likely*. The latter was calculated as the mean of the two other forecast values in each year. That is:

In making a final forecast, we again stress the importance of using well-reasoned judgments based on expertise regarding the series under consideration.

$$\text{Most likely forecast} = \frac{URF1 + URF2}{2}$$

This is probably the simplest way to combine forecasts.

The purpose of a number of studies has been to identify the best way to combine forecasts to improve overall accuracy.[37] After we have covered a wider array of

TABLE 1–4   Most Optimistic, Most Pessimistic, and Most Likely Forecasts of the U.S. Civilian Unemployment Rate

	Forecast			
Year	*Most Optimistic*	*Most Pessimistic*	*Most Likely**	*Actual UR*
1	Missing	Missing	Missing	7.6%
2	Missing	Missing	Missing	9.7%
3	9.7%	10.8%	10.25%	9.6%
4	9.6%	9.6%	9.60%	7.5%
5	6.4%	7.5%	6.95%	7.2%
6	7.0%	7.2%	7.10%	7.0%
7	6.9%	7.0%	6.95%	6.2%
8	5.8%	6.2%	6.00%	5.5%
9	5.2%	5.5%	5.35%	5.3%
10	5.2%	5.3%	5.25%	5.5%
11	5.5%	5.6%	5.55%	Missing

*The most likely forecast in this example is the mean of the most optimistic and the most pessimistic. The RMSE for the most likely forecast for year 3 through year 10 is 0.85. Comparing this with values shown in Table 1–3, we see that for this example, and this method of combining forecasts, the combined forecast has the same accuracy, as measured by RMSE, as does URF1.

---

[37]For example, see Wilson and Allison-Koerber, "Combining Subjective and Objective Forecasts."

forecasting models, we will come back to this issue of combining different forecasts (see Chapter 8). For now, we just want to call attention to the desirability of using more than one method in developing any forecast. In making a final forecast, we again stress the importance of using well-reasoned judgments based on expertise regarding the series under consideration.

Sources of Data[38]

The quantity and type of data needed in developing forecasts can vary a great deal from one situation to another. Some forecasting techniques require only the data series that is to be forecast. These methods include the naive methods discussed in previous sections as well as more sophisticated time-series techniques such as time-series decomposition, exponential smoothing, and ARIMA models, which will be discussed in subsequent chapters of this text. On the other hand, multiple-regression methods require a data series for each variable included in the forecasting model. This may mean that a large number of data series must be maintained to support the forecasting process.

The most obvious sources of data are the internal records of the organization itself. Such data include unit product sales histories, employment and production records, total revenue, shipments, orders received, inventory records, and so forth. However, it is surprising how often an organization fails to keep historical data in a form that facilitates the development of forecasting models. Often, monthly and/or quarterly data are discarded after three or four years. Thus, models that depend on such data may be difficult to develop. Another problem with using internal data is getting the cooperation necessary to make them available both in a form that is useful and in a timely manner. As better information systems are developed and made available through computer technology, internal data will become even more important and useful in the preparation of forecasts.

For many types of forecasts the necessary data come from outside the firm. Various trade associations are a valuable source of such data, which are usually available to members at a nominal cost and sometimes to nonmembers for a fee. But the richest sources of external data are various governmental and syndicated services.

You will also find a wealth of data available on the Internet. Using various search engines you can uncover sources for most macroeconomic series that are of interest to forecasters. The specific URLs (Web addresses) may change over time, but when you find that one of your favorites has disappeared it is likely that a new search will find it in another location on the Web.

Forecasting Domestic Car Sales

In each chapter of the text where new forecasting techniques are developed, we will apply at least one of the new methods to preparing a forecast of domestic car sales

---

[38] A set of data is available in the ECONDATA.SDB file, on the disk that accompanies this text. There are 100 series in this file in either monthly or quarterly form. Access to the data in this file is described in the "Using SORITEC" section of Chapter 2.

(DCS). As you will see, there is a fair amount of variability in how well different methods work for this very important economic series. The data we will be using are shown graphically and in tabular form in Figure 1–4. As you see, we have quarterly domestic car sales figures from the first quarter of 1980 through the fourth quarter of 1995. The data represent domestic car sales in thousands of units and have not been seasonally adjusted. After this chapter we will discuss only each new forecast of DCS and will not repeat the original data. We will, however, keep a running summary of the root-mean-squared errors for the various models used.

In this chapter we apply a modified naive model to forecast domestic car sales for the four quarters of 1995. The model is:

$$DCSF_t = DCS_{t-4}$$

where $DCSF_t$ is the forecast of domestic car sales for time t and DCS_{t-4} is the actual domestic car sales four quarters earlier. As seen in Figure 1–4, the level of domestic

FIGURE 1–4

Domestic Car Sales in Thousands of Units (c1f4)

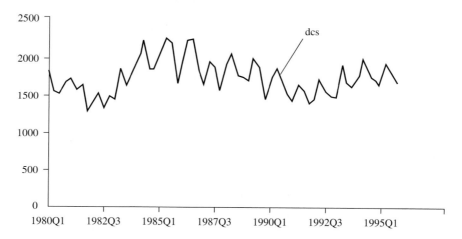

Year	Quarter 1	Quarter 2	Quarter 3	Quarter 4
1980	1849.9	1550.8	1515.3	1665.4
1981	1733.0	1576.0	1618.5	1281.3
1982	1401.4	1535.3	1327.9	1493.6
1983	1456.9	1875.8	1646.2	1814.1
1984	1994.6	2251.8	1854.3	1851.0
1985	2042.2	2272.6	2217.7	1672.2
1986	1898.7	2242.2	2246.9	1827.2
1987	1669.3	1972.8	1878.2	1560.6
1988	1914.0	2076.0	1787.1	1762.3
1989	1707.4	2018.6	1898.5	1453.6
1990	1706.2	1878.2	1752.1	1560.4
1991	1445.1	1683.9	1586.6	1421.3
1992	1455.4	1746.1	1571.7	1503.4
1993	1483.5	1917.9	1690.3	1642.3
1994	1762.3	2001.5	1766.6	1724.8
1995	1658.2	1938.4	1845.3	1686.9

(c1t5)

TABLE 1–5 Domestic Car Sales (DCS) and a Modified Naive Forecast of Domestic Car Sales (DCSF) in Thousands of Units

Period	DCS	DCSF
1980Q1	1849.90	MISSING
1980Q2	1550.80	MISSING
1980Q3	1515.30	MISSING
1980Q4	1665.40	MISSING
1981Q1	1733.00	1849.90
1981Q2	1576.00	1550.80
1981Q3	1618.50	1515.30
1981Q4	1281.30	1665.40
1982Q1	1401.40	1733.00
1982Q2	1535.30	1576.00
1982Q3	1327.90	1618.50
1982Q4	1493.60	1281.30
⋮	⋮	⋮
1993Q1	1483.50	1455.40
1993Q2	1917.90	1746.10
1993Q3	1690.30	1571.70
1993Q4	1642.30	1503.40
1994Q1	1762.30	1483.50
1994Q2	2001.50	1917.90
1994Q3	1766.60	1690.30
1994Q4	1724.80	1642.30
1995Q1	*1658.20**	1762.30
1995Q2	*1938.40**	2001.50
1995Q3	*1845.30**	1766.60
1995Q4	*1686.90**	1724.80

*These values were held out in developing the forecast and were used only to calculate the RMSE for the four quarters of 1995.

Using 1995Q1–1995Q4:   Root-Mean-Squared Error = 74.9

Using 1981Q1–1994Q4:   Root-Mean-Squared Error = 207.3

car sales for the fourth quarter of 1994 (DCS_{94Q4}) was 1724.8. Thus our forecast for the fourth quarter of 1995 (DCS_{95Q4}) is 1724.8.

Table 1–5 and Figure 1–5 show how this naive model has fared over the historical period. The root-mean-squared error for this modified naive model for the period from 1981Q1 through 1994Q4 is 207.3. For the four quarters of 1995 the RMSE is 74.9.

Overview of the Text

Business Forecasting has been organized in such a way that by working consecutively through the text you will gradually develop a rather sophisticated forecasting capability. In this first chapter you have been given an introduction to business forecasting that has included three naive models that can be implemented using the

FIGURE 1–5

Domestic Car Sales (DCS) and a Modified Naive Forecast of Domestic Car Sales (DCSF) in Thousands of Units
(c1f5)

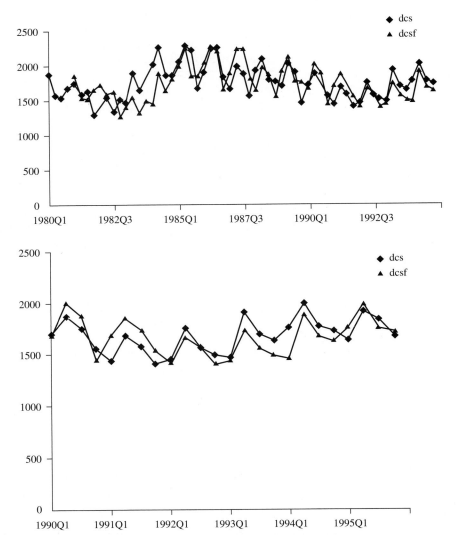

The upper panel shows the entire 1980Q1 through 1995Q4 time frame. The lower panel focuses on the most recent years. The actual values (DCS) are represented by diamonds and the forecast values (DCSF) are shown as triangles.

SORITEC software. The second chapter provides a discussion of data exploration through visualization, an overview of model-selection criteria, and a review of some statistical concepts that will be helpful as you learn about additional forecasting methods.

Chapter 3 presents moving-average and exponential smoothing techniques. These methods are widely used, quite simple from a computational standpoint, and often very accurate. Chapter 4 provides an explanation of simple linear-regression analysis and its applications to business forecasting. Both simple trend models and simple two-variable causal models are presented. In Chapter 5 the simple regression model is expanded to include more than one independent variable. Multiple-regression models are applied to specific forecasting problems, and a method for accounting for seasonality is presented.

Classical time-series decomposition, discussed in Chapter 6, provides accurate forecasts for many series. In addition, it can be used to develop seasonal indexes that help identify the degree of seasonality in the data. These indexes can also be used to deseasonalize the data series. ARIMA forecasting models are presented in Chapter 7.

Chapter 8 contains a discussion of alternative methods for combining individual forecasts to take advantage of information contained in different methods to improve forecast accuracy. Chapter 9 focuses on how to select appropriate forecasting methods for a particular situation and on how to establish an effective forecasting process. The role of judgments based on experience with the series to be forecast is stressed once more. The use of bootstrapping in forecasting is discussed in Chapter 10.

At the end of each chapter you will find suggested readings that will provide additional insight into the topics covered. In addition, a set of exercises in each chapter will help you to validate your understanding of the material. Many of these exercises will also help you to become proficient in the use of the SORITEC software.

Comments from the Field

N. Carroll Mohn

Manager of field services, European Community Group, in the Corporate Marketing Research Department of The Coca-Cola Company.[*]

Why Try to Forecast?

Forecasts are critical inputs to a wide range of business decision-making processes. From letters, teaching forecasting, managing the function, and consulting work, I know that many people are striving to get a practitioner's grasp of the subject—some feeling for the applied state of the art and its science.

As forecasters, at one time or another, we have to ask ourselves why we should try to forecast in the first place. First, the power of forces such as economics, competition, markets, social concerns, and the ecological environment to affect the individual firm is severe and continues growing. Secondly, forecast assessment is a major input in management's evaluation of different strategies at business decision-making levels. Thirdly, the inference of *no* forecasting is that the future either contains "no significant change" or there is ample time to react "after the fact."

Forecasting is far too important to the organization not to have appropriate management and resource backing. Each firm must develop its own *explicit* forecast system so that alternative courses of action can be identified.

We can see the future coming if we know what to look for because many things often progress in an astonishingly orderly manner over time. This consistent progress provides a basis for forecasting. At the same time, many things respond to needs, opportunities, and support resources. If these driving forces can be identified, we believe future progress can be forecast.

---

[*]Adapted from an address given at the Fourth Annual Conference of the International Association of Business Forecasters, Philadelphia, September 1989.

INTEGRATIVE CASE
Forecasting Sales of The Gap

Part 1: Background of The Gap and Its Sales

Throughout the text we will be using Gap sales in an integrative case at the end of the chapter. In these cases concepts from the chapter will be applied to this sales series. In this chapter we will apply concepts as well as provide an overview of the company.

The Gap: An Introduction

Few retailers have accomplished what The Gap has. The Gap has managed to successfully market its retail stores and the apparel they carry. In 1992, The Gap was the number 2 clothing brand in America, and in 1994 they placed in the top 25 of the 50 most recognizable brands in the United States. There are only two private-brand retailers that achieved this coveted brand image for their stores' products: Victoria's Secret and The Gap. While many other retailers, such as The Limited, lost strong brand images, The Gap continued to redefine its strategy and managed to maintain market dominance. By the end of 1995, The Gap operated over 1,500 stores in its four domestic divisions, which include The Gap, GapKids, Banana Republic, and the Old Navy Clothing Co. The Gap's fifth division, its International Division, operated 164 stores by the end of 1995 in countries such as Canada, the United Kingdom, France, Germany, and Japan.

The first Gap store was opened in 1969 by founder Donald Fisher, who decided to open a store after he had a problem exchanging a pair of Levi's jeans that were an inch too short. He felt that there was a need for a store that would sell jeans in a full array of sizes. He opened his first store in San Francisco, which advertised that it had "four tons" of Levi's. The store was an instant success and Gap stores were on their way to national prominence. Levi's were the mainstay of The Gap's business, and due to Levi Strauss & Co.'s fixed pricing, Fisher maintained a 50 percent margin on the sales of these jeans. This changed in 1976, however, when the Federal Trade Commission prohibited manufacturers from dictating the price that retailers could charge for their products. There was suddenly massive discounting on Levi's products, which drastically cut The Gap's margins. Fisher recognized the need to expand his product offerings to include higher-margin items, and therefore began to offer private-label apparel.

In 1983, Fisher recruited Millard Drexler as president, with his objective being to revamp The Gap. Drexler did this by liquidating their existing inventories and focusing on simpler, more classic styles that offered the consumer "good style, good quality, good value." The Gap started to design its own clothes to fit into this vision. The Gap already had formed strong relationships with manufacturers from their earlier entry into the private-label business. This enabled them to monitor manufacturing closely, which kept costs low and quality high. The Gap's strategy didn't end with high-quality products. Drexler paid equally close attention to visual presence of the stores. He replaced the old pipe racks and cement floors with hardwood floors and attractive tables and shelves with merchandise neatly folded, which made it easier for the customers to shop. As new merchandise came in, store managers were given detailed plannograms, which told them precisely where the items would go. With this control, Drexler ensured that each Gap store would have the same look, and would therefore present the same image to the customer.

The Gap capitalized on these same concepts as they entered the kids' clothing market. The idea originated after Drexler was disappointed with the lack of selection he found while shopping for his own child. Drexler organized a meeting with his employees who had children to discuss their thoughts about the children's clothing market. Their mutual frustration with the selection of children's clothing triggered the idea for GapKids. Drexler and his team believed that they could use the same merchandising principles that made The Gap a success and apply them to the children's clothing market. GapKids was launched in 1986, and was a success in its first year of operation with sales of $2 million.

Drexler's retailing prowess also became evident when he turned around the poor performance of the Banana Republic division. In 1983, The Gap bought Banana Republic, which featured the then-popular safari-style clothing. This trend toward khakis had been brought on by the popularity of movies such as *Raiders of the Lost Ark* and *Romancing the Stone.* By 1987, Banana Republic's sales had reached $191 million. Then the safari craze ended, and this once popular division lost roughly $10 million in the two years that followed. Banana Republic was repositioned as a more upscale Gap, with fancier decor as well as more updated fashions that offered a balance between sophistication and comfort. By 1992, the chain was once again profitable, with about $300 million in sales.

Although these other Gap divisions had grown and prospered, the traditional Gap stores began to falter in the early 1990s. Coupled with the effects of a retailing recession, their strong emphasis on basic styles had made them a target of competition. The market became flooded with "Gap-like" basics. Other retailers were also mimicking their presentation strategy, and started folding large-volume commodity items such as jeans, T-shirts, and fleece, some selling them at substantially lower prices. Drexler and his team recognized that several major changes were taking place in the retailing environment, and they needed to identify ways to respond to this competition if they were to continue to grow.

One way The Gap responded to increasing competition was to revise its merchandise mix. Customers were shifting away from the basics toward more fashion items, in gender-specific styles. To respond to this trend, The Gap took advantage of aggressive changes already underway in their inventory management programs, which gave them faster replenishment times. This enabled The Gap to reduce its inventories in basics by as much as 40 percent, giving them more room for hot-selling, high-profit items. In addition to shifting to more fashion, The Gap also fine-tuned its product mix so that merchandise would be more consistent between stores.

Another way that The Gap has responded to increased competition and changing retailing trends was by entering into strip malls. This move has been facilitated in part by the reduction of available spaces in large malls. As fewer spaces became available, retailers wishing to expand have had to explore other possible options. Many strip centers have been upgraded in response to this trend, and retailers found that they could offer their customers easier access to stores and more convenient parking than they could in their traditional mall locations. With carefully placed geographic locations, retailers also discovered that they could often do the same volume that they could in the large malls. Additionally, strip-center rents are substantially lower than those of their mall counterparts. Their common charges are sometimes a mere 25 percent of what they would be in a typical large mall.

As other retailers and discounters found success by knocking off The Gap's classic styles and their presentation standards, The Gap responded by entering the "discount" market itself in 1993, with the transformation of 48 of its lowest-performance stores into "Gap Warehouse" stores. By doing so, The Gap capitalized on the new surge of price-conscious consumers. Gap Warehouse stores offer Gap-type styles at prices about 30 percent lower than Gap apparel.

Their success with this discount concept led to the launch of the Old Navy Clothing Co. in April of 1994, which targeted consumers in households with incomes between $20,000 and $50,000, who make about one-half of the nation's $150 billion apparel purchases each year. Old Navy stores carry a different assortment of apparel than traditional Gap stores. They differentiate themselves from The Gap stores by offering alternative versions of basic items, with different fabric blends that enable them to charge lower retail prices. In fact, 80 percent of their assortment retailed $22 or less. There are other ways in which The Gap differentiates its Old Navy stores from their traditional Gap stores, however. To help keep costs down, they also scaled down the decor of these stores, with serviceable concrete floors and shopping carts instead of the hardwood floors found in The Gap. They are venturing away from The Gap's traditional means of advertising for these new stores and are offering more short-term promotions. Old Navy stores are further positioning themselves as one-stop-shopping stores by offering clothing for the whole family in one location.

With its current mix of stores, The Gap has successfully carved out a position for itself in every retail clothing category: Banana Republic at the high end of the market, Gap (and GapKids) stores in the middle, and Old Navy at the low end. Although there have been some hurdles along the way, The Gap has proven that it has the ability to respond to changes in the retail environment and has, therefore, managed to stay in the race. This is evidenced by the increased quarterly sales shown in the table and graphic below.

Quarter	GAP Sales in Thousands of Dollars	Quarter	GAP Sales in Thousands of Dollars
1985Q1	105,715	1990Q3	501,690
1985Q2	120,136	1990Q4	624,726
1985Q3	181,669	1991Q1	490,300
1985Q4	239,813	1991Q2	523,056
1986Q1	159,980	1991Q3	702,052
1986Q2	164,760	1991Q4	803,485
1986Q3	224,800	1992Q1	588,864
1986Q4	298,469	1992Q2	614,114
1987Q1	211,060	1992Q3	827,222
1987Q2	217,753	1992Q4	930,209
1987Q3	273,616	1993Q1	643,580
1987Q4	359,592	1993Q2	693,192
1988Q1	241,348	1993Q3	898,677
1988Q2	264,328	1993Q4	1,060,230
1988Q3	322,752	1994Q1	751,670
1988Q4	423,669	1994Q2	773,131
1989Q1	309,925	1994Q3	988,346
1989Q2	325,939	1994Q4	1,209,790
1989Q3	405,601	1995Q1	848,688
1989Q4	545,131	1995Q2	868,514
1990Q1	402,368	1995Q3	1,155,930
1990Q2	404,996	1995Q4	1,522,120

(c1gap)

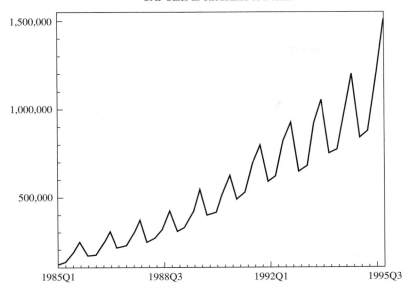

GAP Sales in Thousands of Dollars

Case Questions

1. Based on the tabular and the graphic presentations of the GAP sales data, what do you think explains the seasonal pattern in their sales data?

2. Using a modified naive forecasting method, such as the one used for domestic car sales in this chapter, make a forecast of GAP sales for the four quarters of 1996. Based on inspection of the graph of GAP sales, what is your expectation in terms of forecast accuracy?

3. Calculate the RMSE for your forecast of the four quarters of 1996, given that the actual sales were: Quarter 1—1,113,154; Quarter 2—1,120,335; Quarter 3—1,382,996; Quarter 4—1,667,896.

Solutions to Case Questions

1. The seasonal pattern is one in which sales typically have a small increase from the first to the second quarter, followed by a considerable increase in the third quarter and yet another large increase in the fourth quarter. The third quarter increase is related to back-to-school buying, while the increase in the fourth quarter is caused by the Christmas shopping season.

2. The model would be: GAPF = GAPSALES(−4). GAPF represents the forecast values, while GAPSALES(−4) is the actual value four periods earlier. An inspection of the GAP sales series would lead one to expect that a naive forecasting model with a lag of four periods would pick up the seasonality fairly well but would not account for the upward trend in GAP sales. This can be seen in the graph of actual and predicted values. The actual values are consistently above the forecast values.

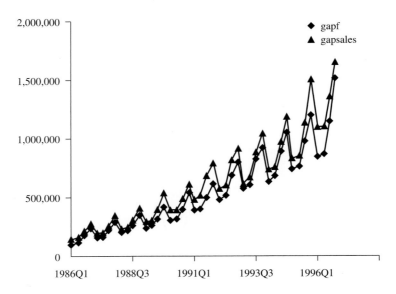

3. The actual and predicted values for 1996Q1 through 1996Q4 are shown below. The RMSE for these four quarters is: RMSE = 227,029. This is about a 17 percent error, based on the average quarterly sales for the year (1,321,095.25).

The RMSE for the 1986Q1 through 1995Q4 historic period was 107,150. The reason the RMSE was so much lower in the historic period is that the level of sales over that period was also much lower, averaging 589,392 per quarter.

	GAPSALES	*GAPF*
1996Q1	1,113,154	848,688
1996Q2	1,120,335	868,514
1996Q3	1,383,996	1,155,930
1996Q4	1,667,896	1,522,120

Case References

Arlen, Jeffrey. "Gap Knocks Off Gap." *Discount Store News* (Sept. 6, 1993), p. A8.

———. "It's a Trend." *Discount Store News* (Sept. 6, 1993), p. A5.

Cuneo, Alice. "Gap Floats Lower-Price Old Navy Stores." *Advertising Age* (July 25, 1994), p. 36.

Edelson, Sharon. "Strip Centers: The Chain Reaction." *WWD* (Aug. 9, 1995), p. 9.

Mitchell, Russell. "A Bit of a Rut at The Gap." *Business Week* (Nov. 30, 1992), p. 100.

———. "The Gap: Can the Nation's Hottest Retailer Stay on Top?" *Business Week* (March 9, 1992), p. 58.

———. "The Gap Dolls Itself Up." *Business Week* (March 21, 1994), p. 46.

———. "A Humbler Neighborhood for The Gap." *Business Week* (Aug. 16, 1993), p. 29.

Popiel, Leslie A. "Old Navy Store Is Gap's Answer to the Penny-Pinching Shopper." *Christian Science Monitor* (Oct. 28, 1994), p. 8.

Street, Pamela. "Old Navy Fills Off-Price Gap for The Gap." *Daily News Record* (March 31, 1994), p. 3.

Wilson, Marianne. "The Magic of Brand Identity." *Chain Store Age Executive* (Feb. 1994), p. 66.

The Gap, Inc. 1995 Annual Report.

ABOUT THE SORITEC SOFTWARE

The SORITEC software that accompanies this text provides you with a professional software package that will do the computations for all of the methods covered in the text (and more). The list that follows will give you an idea about the breadth of use of this software in the "real world" of forecasting. It is also used at many universities in the United States and other countries around the world.

Representative List of Nonacademic Users of the SORITEC Econometric Software

FINANCIAL INSTITUTIONS
Aetna Life
Bank of Montreal
Chase Manhattan Bank
Guyerzeller Zurmont Bank (Switz.)
Morgan Guaranty Trust
North Carolina National Bank
Royal Bank of Canada

GOVERNMENT AGENCIES
Australia Department of Labor
Canadian Transport Commission
Colorado Legislative Council
Congressional Budget Office
DC Public Service Commission
Federal Home Loan Bank Board
Federal Reserve Board of Governors
International Monetary Fund
Monetary Authority of Singapore
Norwegian Telecommunications Authority
State of Illinois
State of Massachusetts
State of New York
State of Oregon
UK Department of Environment
U.S. Bureau of the Census
U.S. Department of Agriculture
U.S. Department of Commerce
World Bank

INDUSTRIAL AND OTHERS
A.T. Cross and Co., Inc.
American Paper Institute
Atchison, Topeka, and Santa Fe R.R.
Battelle Northwest Labs
Celanese Corporation
Certainteed Corporation
Columbia Broadcasting System
Con-Agra, Inc.
Coopers and Lybrand
E. I. du Pont
General Motors
Gas Research Institute
Goldman, Sachs
Hallmark Cards
Intelsat
IZI (Italy)
McCann-Erickson
Mead Data Central
Merrill Lynch Futures Corporation
The Rand Corporation
TRW

PUBLIC UTILITIES
Bell Atlantic
BellSouth Corporation
Cincinnati Gas and Electric
Detroit Edison

You will learn more about how to use SORITEC in each chapter of the text as you learn various forecasting methods. At this point we will provide you with an overview of the software and show you how to read a data file and how to prepare a time-series plot.

An Overview of SORITEC

SORITEC requires an IBM-compatible computer running Windows 3.1 or later, with an 80386 or later processor, a math coprocessor, a hard disk with at least 5 megabytes of free space, and 8 megabytes of RAM. On machines with less RAM, performance may be degraded.

To start the program, double-click on the SORITEC icon 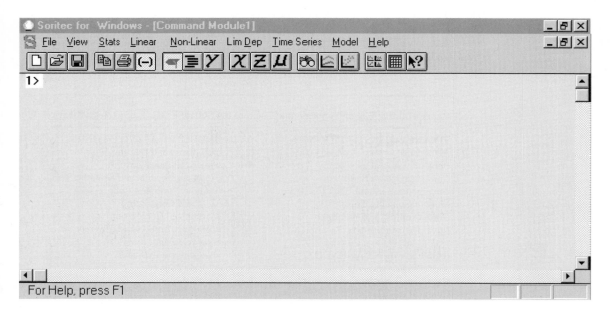. The SORITEC window will then appear, as shown below.

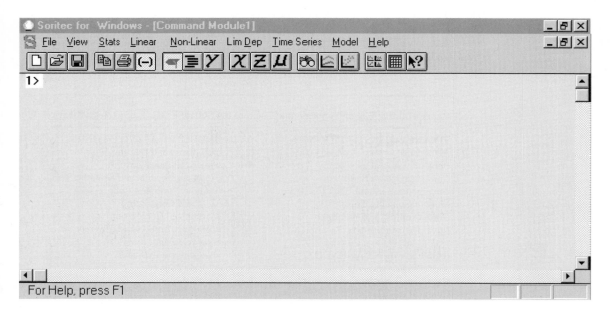

SORITEC is controlled either through the graphical user interface (GUI)—which consists of menus, toolbars, and associated dialog boxes—or the command line, indicated by the 1> prompt. To initiate actions through the GUI, use the mouse to make selections from the menus or toolbar buttons, and respond to the dialog boxes that appear to prompt you for any additional information. To use the command line interface, enter commands from the keyboard using the SORITEC command set. As you work through the text you will become familiar with much of the SORITEC command language. Users with good knowledge of the command line language will find that it is often faster to work from the keyboard than to use the GUI, though the GUI makes it possible to be productive almost immediately without much knowledge of the command language.

You can terminate a SORITEC session in either of two ways:

1. Open the **System** menu (the small box in the upper left corner of the window frame) and select **Close,** or double-click on the menu box with the left mouse button.

2. From the menu bar, select **File | Exit.**

The SORITEC graphical interface conforms to the general layout and functionality of most Windows programs, so Windows users should find its operation to be an intuitive and straightforward process. By default, commands generated by the graphical interface are echoed on the command line for easy review of the command history, to facilitate editing and reissuing commands, and as a mechanism to help new users learn the command line syntax. The command line facilitates programming, provides backward compatibility to existing users, and allows commands to be edited visually and reinitiated with minimum effort.

Menu and toolbar controls combine with dialog boxes to lead users through most operations. Generally, modeling activities and methods are initiated from the pull-down menus. Menu selections trigger displays of dialog boxes that query for selections or additional information needed to complete the selected operation. The menu and dialog box labels and nomenclature follow common usage in econometric and business forecasting literature. The menu system is organized by topic.

The table on the following page outlines the general function and content of each top-level menu entry.

As you would guess from the above, the SORITEC software is very sophisticated and contains many high-level procedures that are not covered in this text. As you further develop your statistical background you will find SORITEC to be helpful, especially for time-series data and econometric analyses.

The Command Line

The command line interface resembles simple scrolling text editors. However, it is designed strictly to accept inputs into an interactive session with a math program, so it has some particular rules.

1. Only the current line can be edited [e.g., using (**Backspace**), (**Delete**), and the other editing keys]; all other lines are part of the record of the actual command sequence transmitted and the program's response, and therefore cannot be edited in place.
2. The mouse or the arrow keys can be used to place the text caret anywhere on the screen.
3. When the text caret is located on a previous command line, pressing the (**Enter**) key will copy the entire line where the caret is located to the current (last) command line, where it can be reissued (after editing if desired). If there are existing entries in the current command line, SORITEC will splice the previous command immediately onto the end of the new command line (SORITEC will not copy its own output onto the current command line).
4. Pressing the (**Enter**) key from anywhere on the current command line will transmit the entire line, as currently written, to the parser for execution.

New users may find it helpful to operate the system from the GUI, and let the echo commands facility help them learn the command set and syntax.

Screen Display of Information Stored in SORITEC's Memory

The **PRINT** command is the primary means of showing information on the screen. It has a syntax of

```
print item1 [item2 ...]
```

where *item1 [item2 ...]* is the list of items to be displayed. The **PRINT** command must have at least one item to be displayed. As a shortcut, you can use just the letter **P** rather than **PRINT.**

Variable Names

SORITEC variable names can be made up of letters A to Z, the digits 0 to 9, and the symbols @, %, $\wedge$, and _. The name must begin with a letter and must be no more than 32 characters long. Mathematical operators may not be used in variable names.

An Example Using The Gap Sales Data

What follows is a set of extended examples to illustrate how to use SORITEC to get data from a data file and prepare a time-series plot. You may find it helpful to follow this example, using the program and the accompanying data, as a quick way to get started.

Menu	Entries	Function
File	File controls	Access .sdb (databank), .sal (ASCII) data files, and .sac command script files; execute .sac files; save data files; control the log file
	Copying to the clipboard	Copy highlighted selection in the command window to the Windows clipboard
	Forecasting	Forecast using a single-equation method
	Print controls	Print the record of the current session, or the current graph if the graphics window is active
View	Display options	Display of the tool and status bars
	Graphic controls	Selection of line, bar, pie, and scatter graphs
	Data tool	Selection of the spreadsheet data entry tool
Stats	Univariate statistics	Analysis of a single variable
	Multivariate statistics	Analysis of two or more variables
	Economic statistics	Common economic calculations
Linear	Basic least-squares regression options	OLS and GLS
	Serial correlation and hetero-skedasticity options	Corrections for first- and second-order serial correlation and for unconditional heteroskedasticity
	Two stage / IVT options	Instrumental variables and two-stage least-squares with and without corrections for serial correlation
	Restricted estimation	Restricted least-squares and mixed estimation; mixed estimation can be corrected for serial correlation
	Distributed lags	Almon and Shiner distributed lag models, with and without correction for serial correlation
	Ridge regression	Ordinary ridge regression
	Variable parameters	Variable parameter models using classifying indicator variables
	Principal components	Principal component analysis
Nonlinear	Nonlinear least squares	
	Two-stage	Nonlinear two-stage least-squares
	FIML	Uses robust solution algorithms to fit nonlinear models, including, e.g., models specified to correct for serial correlation
Lim Dep	Logit, probit models and discriminant analysis	Methods for dealing with discrete dependent variables
Time Series	Trend	Linear, exponential growth, and S-curve models
	Smoothing	A variety of exponential smoothing methods
	Autocorrelations examination	Correlograms
	ARIMA	Integrated autoregressive moving-average models
	Transfer functions	ARIMA models combined with transfer functions
	Seasonal adjustment	Data deseasonalization
Model	Setting parameters and equations	Controls for viewing and specifying system equations and parameters
	Data selection	Controls to select variables for specific purposes (explanatory, dependent, instrumental, etc.)
	Multiequation model estimation	Controls for model specification, choice of estimating method (FIML, three-stage least-squares, or seemingly unrelated regressions), and multiequation simulation
	Multiequation model simulation	Controls for establishing, estimating, and simulating multiequation models.
Help	Help indexes	

Reading Data

To read data from *gapdata.sal,* a SORITEC alternate load (SAL) file that was included with your software:

1. Select the Open option from the File menu.

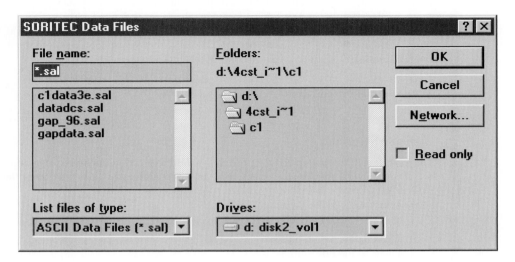

2. When the SORITEC **Data Files** dialog box appears, select the *.sal* extension from the **List files of type** box.
3. Then select the drive from which you will be reading the data file from the **Drives** box.
4. Then select the desired folder from the **Folders** box.
5. Select *gapdata.sal* from the list of files in the **File name** box.
6. Click on the **OK** button.

SORITEC will open the file and read the data in it. To confirm that the data have been read into the workspace, select **Symbols** from the **View** menu. The following will appear on the screen:

```
2> symbols (full)

SORITEC symbol table:
User variables

SYM NO NAME        ADDRESS TYPE      LENGTH

    141 Q4         32390 SERIES      48 1985Q1-1996Q4
    155 Q3         32292 SERIES      48 1985Q1-1996Q4
    169 Q2         32194 SERIES      48 1985Q1-1996Q4
    183 Q1         32096 SERIES      48 1985Q1-1996Q4
    197 GAPSALES   31998 SERIES      48 1985Q1-1996Q4

3>
```

First, note that a command line entry, symbols (full), has appeared, even though you didn't type anything (there was also an entry for the file read). Unless you suppress the output by clicking on the toggle entry at **View | Echo Commands** (or the 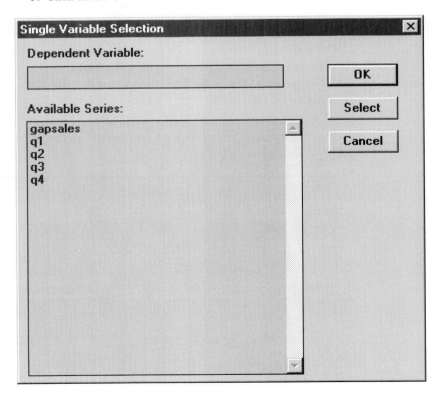 toolbar button), SORITEC will show the command line equivalent for most actions initiated through the menu system (the exception is the graphical displays). Second, note that the response to your selection was to show all the items currently in the workspace, their length, and (for data series) the dates (case numbers for undated variables) for which the series is defined.

Reading the SAL file will also have established a USE period (the dates and times/ observation numbers of the active example), because that information is part of the information entered in a SAL file format. To confirm that, enter

```
3> use
```

SORITEC will respond with

```
USING 1985Q1-1996Q4
```

Variable Selection

Click on the toolbar button **Y**. The **Single Variable Selection** dialog box that appears has a list box showing the series (variables) in the system, and an edit box showing the series (variables) currently available, as shown in the screen shot below.

To select the variable *gapsales,*

1. Click the left mouse button on *gapsales* to select it.
2. Click on the **Select** button.
3. Click on the **OK** button.

A shortcut to select the variable is to double-click on its entry in the **Available Series** list box.

Graphing Gap Sales

To get a time-series plot of Gap sales, click on the 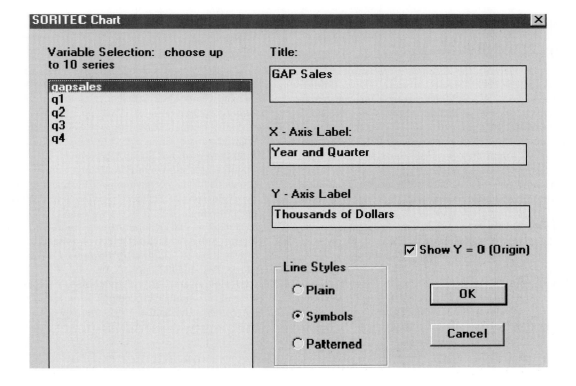 icon in the main SORITEC tool-bar. A new window will open. Click on the icon once more. A box will appear in which you can select the variable (series) to be plotted along with some attributes for the plot. For this example we have clicked on *gapsales* (the other variables listed there will be explained and used in later chapters). You can have the line plotted with or without a symbol being shown at each observation. Here we have marked the circle to have a symbol shown. If more than one series is plotted, the lines will have different colors and the symbols will have different shapes for each series. We have also checked the box **Show Y=0 (Origin)** and typed in a title and labels for both the X and Y axes.

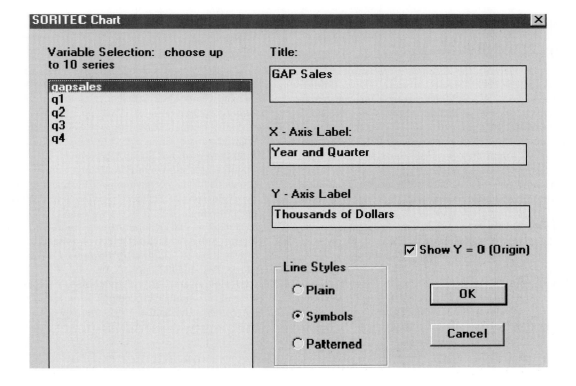

The graph resulting from these selections is shown on the next page.

Suggested Readings

Adams, F. Gerard. *The Business Forecasting Revolution.* New York: Oxford University Press, 1986.

Chase, Charles W., Jr. "Forecasting Consumer Products." *Journal of Business Forecasting* 10, no. 1 (Spring 1991), pp. 2–6.

Jain, C. L. "Forecasting at Colgate-Palmolive Company." *Journal of Business Forecasting* 11, no. 1 (Spring 1992), pp. 16–20.

Makridakis, Spyros. "Accuracy Measures: Theoretical and Practical Concerns." *International Journal of Forecasting,* December 1993, pp. 527–29.

Mathews, Brian P.; and Adamantios Diamantopulos. "Towards a Taxonomy of Forecast Error Measures." *Journal of Forecasting* (August 1994), pp. 409–16.

Mentzer, John T.; and Jon Schroeter. "Multiple Forecasting System at Brake Parts, Inc." *The Journal of Business Forecasting* 14, no. 3 (Fall 1993), pp. 5–9.

Moriarty, Mark M.; and Arthur J. Adams. "Management Judgment Forecasts, Composite Forecasting Models, and Conditional Efficiency." *Journal of Marketing Research* (August 1984), pp. 239–50.

Rosati, Anna Maria. "Forecasting at Segix, Italia: A Pharmaceutical Company." *Journal of Business Forecasting* 17, no. 3 (Fall 1996), pp. 7–9.

Van Vught, F. A. "Pitfalls of Forecasting: Fundamental Problems for the Methodology of Forecasting from the Philosophy of Science." *Futures* (April 1987), pp. 184–96.

Wilson, J. Holton; and Deborah Allison-Koerber. "Combining Subjective and Objective Forecasts Improves Results." *Journal of Business Forecasting* 11, no. 3 (Fall 1992), pp. 12–16.

Wilson, J. Holton; and Steven J. Schuiling. "Forecasting Hospital Laboratory Procedures." *Journal of Medical Systems* (December 1992), pp. 269–79.

Exercises

1. Write a paragraph in which you compare what you think are the advantages and disadvantages of subjective forecasting methods. How do you think the use of quantitative methods relates to these advantages and disadvantages?

2. Suppose that you work for a U.S. senator who is contemplating writing a bill that would put a national sales tax in place. Because the tax would be levied on the sales revenue of retail stores, the senator has asked you to prepare a forecast of retail store sales for year 8, based on data from year 1 through year 7. The data are:

(c1p2)

Year	Retail Store Sales
1	1,225
2	1,285
3	1,359
4	1,392
5	1,443
6	1,474
7	1,467

   a. Use the first naive forecasting model presented in this chapter to prepare a forecast of retail store sales for each year from 2 through 8.
   b. Prepare a time-series graph of the actual and forecast values of retail store sales for the entire period. (You will not have a forecast for year 1 or an actual value for year 8.)
   c. Calculate the root-mean-squared error for your forecast series using the values for year 2 through year 7.

3. Use the second naive forecasting model presented in the chapter to answer parts (*a*) through (*c*) of Exercise 2. Use $P = 0.2$ in preparing the forecast. Which model do you think works the best? Explain why. (c1p3)

4. Suppose that you work for a major U.S. retail department store that has outlets nationwide. The store offers credit to customers in various forms, including store credit cards, and over the years has seen a substantial increase in credit purchases. The manager of credit sales is concerned about the degree to which consumers are using credit and has started to track the ratio of consumer installment credit to personal income. She calls this ratio the credit percent, or CP, and has asked that you forecast that series for year 8. The available data are:

(c1p4)

Year	CP
1	12.96
2	14.31
3	15.34
4	15.49
5	15.70
6	16.00
7	15.62

   a. Use the first naive model presented in this chapter to prepare forecasts of CP for years 2 through 8.
   b. Plot the actual and forecast values of the series for the years 1 through 8. (You will not have an actual value for year 8 or a forecast value for year 1.)
   c. Calculate the root-mean-squared error for your forecasts for years 2 through 7.

5. Go to the library and look up annual data for personal savings as a percentage of disposable personal income in the United States from 1981 through the most recent year available. One good source for such data is the *Economic Report of the President,* published each year by the U.S. Government Printing Office. This series is also on your software disk in the ECONDATA.SDB file, on a quarterly basis under the name GPSAV. You can access it by issuing the following commands after opening the ECONDATA database from the FILE menu:

```
USE 1981 1996
CONVERT (AVERAGE) GPSAV = GPSAV
PRINT GPSAV
```

Plot the actual data along with the forecast you would get by using the first naive model discussed in this chapter. (c1p5)

6. Pick a corporation you are interested in and go to the library to find annual reports for that company. Look at five consecutive annual reports and find the firm's total revenue for each of those years. Plot the firm's actual revenue along with the forecast of revenue you would get by using the first naive model discussed in this chapter.

7. Go to the library and find the most recent edition of *U.S. Industrial Outlook,* published annually by the U.S. Department of Commerce. Write a paragraph in which you summarize the information given there for passenger cars.

8. CoastCo Insurance, Inc., is interested in developing a forecast of larceny thefts in the United States. It has found the following data:

Year	Larceny Thefts*	Year	Larceny Thefts*
1	4,151	10	7,194
2	4,348	11	7,143
3	5,263	12	6,713
4	5,978	13	6,592
5	6,271	14	6,926
6	5,906	15	7,257
7	5,983	16	7,500
8	6,578	17	7,706
9	7,137	18	7,872

*Data are in thousands.

(c1p8)

Plot this series in a time-series plot and make a naive forecast for years 2 through 19. Calculate the RMSE and MAD for years 2 through 18. On the basis of

these measures and what you see in the plot, what do you think of your forecast? Explain.

9. As the world's economy becomes increasingly interdependent, various exchange rates between currencies have become important in making business decisions. For many U.S. businesses, the Japanese exchange rate (in yen per U.S. dollar) is an important decision variable. This exchange rate (EXRJ) is shown in the following table by month for a two-year period:

(c1p9)

Period	EXRJ	Period	EXRJ
Year 1		Year 2	
M1	127.36	M1	144.98
M2	127.74	M2	145.69
M3	130.55	M3	153.31
M4	132.04	M4	158.46
M5	137.86	M5	154.04
M6	143.98	M6	153.70
M7	140.42	M7	149.04
M8	141.49	M8	147.46
M9	145.07	M9	138.44
M10	142.21	M10	129.59
M11	143.53	M11	129.22
M12	143.69	M12	133.89

Prepare a time-series plot of this series, and use the naive forecasting model to forecast EXRJ for each month from year 1 M2 (February) through year 3 M1 (January). Calculate the RMSE for the period from year 1 M2 through year 2 M12.

2 THE FORECAST PROCESS, DATA CONSIDERATIONS, AND MODEL SELECTION

Introduction

In this chapter we will outline a nine-step forecasting process that is a useful guide to the establishment of a successful forecasting system. The number of steps in such a process is arbitrary, but it is important that forecasting be viewed as a process that contains certain key components. This process includes the selection of one or more forecasting techniques applicable to the data that need to be forecast. This, in turn, depends on the type of data that are available. Therefore, in selecting a forecasting model, one should first evaluate the data for trend, seasonal, and cyclical components.

In evaluating a data series for its trend, seasonal, and cyclical components, it is useful to look at the data in graphic form. In this chapter we evaluate data for GDP, for U.S. billings of the Leo Burnett advertising agency, and private housing starts to see which time-series components exist in each. This chapter also includes a review of statistics and an introduction to the use of autocorrelation coefficients, which can provide useful information about the underlying components in a time series.

The Forecast Process

The forecast process begins with recognizing the need to make decisions that depend on the future—and unknown—value(s) of some variable(s). It is important for managers who use forecasts in making decisions to have some familiarity with the methods used in developing the forecast. It is also important for the individuals involved in developing forecasts to have an understanding of the needs of those who make decisions based on the forecasts. Thus, good communication among all involved with forecasting is paramount.

There are a variety of ways in which one could outline the overall forecasting process. We have found the nine-step sequence shown below to be a useful paradigm.

1. Specify objectives
2. Determine what to forecast
3. Establish time dimensions
4. Data considerations
5. Model selection
6. Model evaluation
7. Forecast preparation
8. Forecast presentation
9. Tracking results

This flow of relationships in the forecasting process will be discussed in more detail in Chapter 9, after a solid base of understanding of quantitative forecasting methods has been established.

It may seem obvious that the forecasting process should begin with a clear statement of objectives that includes how the forecast will be used in a decision context. Objectives and applications of the forecast should be discussed between the individual(s) involved in preparing the forecast and those who will utilize the results. Good communication at this phase will help to ensure that the effort that goes into developing the forecast results in improved decision outcomes.

The second step of the process involves specifying explicitly what to forecast. For a traditional sales forecast, one must decide whether to forecast unit sales or dollar sales. Should the forecast be for total sales, or sales by product line, or sales by region? Should it include domestic sales, export sales, or both? A hospital may want to forecast patient load, which could be defined as admissions, discharges, patient-days, or acuity-days. In every forecasting situation, care must be taken to carefully determine exactly what variable(s) should be forecast.

Next, two different issues that relate to the time dimensions of the forecast need to be considered. One of these dimensions involves the length and periodicity of the forecast. Is the forecast needed on an annual, a quarterly, a monthly, a weekly, or a daily basis? In some situations an even shorter time period may be necessary, such as in forecasting electricity demand for a generating facility. The second time dimension to be considered is related to the urgency of the forecast. If there is little time available before the forecast is needed, the choice of methods that can be used will be limited. When forecasting is established as an ongoing process, there should be ample time to plan for the use of any forecasting technique.

The fourth element of the forecasting process involves a consideration of the quantity and the type of data that are available. Some data may be available internally, while other data may have to be obtained from external sources. Internal data are often the easiest to obtain, but not always. Sometimes data are not retained in a form that makes them useful for a particular forecast. It is surprising how frequently we find that data are kept only on an annual basis rather than for shorter periods such as quarterly or monthly. Similarly, we often run into situations where only dollar values are available rather than units. External data are available from a wide variety of sources, some of which were discussed in Chapter 1. Most external sources provide data in both printed and electronic form.[1]

Model selection, the fifth phase of our forecasting process, depends on a number of criteria, including:

1. The pattern exhibited by the data
2. The quantity of historic data available
3. The length of the forecast horizon
4. The quantitative background of forecast users and preparers

Table 2–1 summarizes how these criteria relate to the quantitative forecasting methods that are included in this text. While all of these criteria are important, the first is the most important. We will discuss the evaluation of patterns in data and model selection in greater detail after completing our review of the forecasting process.

The sixth phase of the forecasting process involves testing the models on the specific series that we want to forecast. This is often done by evaluating how each model works in a retrospective sense. That is, we see how well the results fit the historic data that were used in developing the models. Measures such as the root-mean-squared error (RMSE) are typically used for this evaluation. We often make a

TABLE 2–1   A Guide to Selecting an Appropriate Forecasting Method

Forecasting Method	Data Pattern	Quantity of Historical Data (Number of Observations)	Forecast Horizon	Quantitative Background
Naive	Stationary	1 or 2	Very short	None
Moving averages	Stationary	Number equal to the periods in the moving average	Very short	Very little
Exponential smoothing				
Simple	Stationary	5 to 10	Short	Little
Adaptive response	Stationary	10 to 15	Short	Moderate
Holt's	Linear trend	10 to 15	Short to medium	Little
Winters'	Trend and seasonality	At least 4 or 5 per season	Short to medium	Moderate
Regression-based				
Trend	Linear and nonlinear trend with or without seasonality	Minimum of 10 with 4 or 5 per season if seasonality is included	Short to medium	Little
Causal	Can handle nearly all data patterns	Minimum of 10 per independent variable	Short, medium, and long	Moderate
Time-series decomposition	Can handle trend, seasonal, and cyclical patterns	Enough to see two peaks and troughs in the cycle	Short, medium, and long	Little
ARIMA	Stationary or transformed to stationary	Minimum of 50	Short, medium, and long	High

---

[1]The data that are provided in the ECONDATA.SDB file on the disk accompanying this text are an example of how such data may be made available. The ECONDATA file contains 100 economic series that can be accessed using the software provided with this text.

Fit refers to how well the model works retrospectively. *Accuracy* relates to how well the model works in the forecast horizon.

distinction between *fit* and *accuracy* in evaluating a forecast model. *Fit* refers to how well the model works retrospectively. *Accuracy* relates to how well the model works in the forecast horizon (i.e., outside the period used to develop the model). When we have sufficient data, we often use a "holdout" period to evaluate forecast accuracy. For example, suppose that you have 10 years of historic quarterly sales data and want to make a 2-year forecast. In developing and evaluating potential models, you might use just the first 8 years of data to forecast the last 2 years of the historical series. RMSEs could then be calculated for the 2 holdout years to determine which model or models provide the most accurate forecasts. These models would then be respecified using all 10 years of historic data, and a forecast would be developed for the true forecast horizon. If the models selected in phase 6 did not yield an acceptable level of accuracy, you would return to step 5 and select an alternative model.

Phase 7, forecast preparation, is the natural result of having found models that you believe will produce acceptably accurate results. We recommend that more than one technique be used whenever possible. When two, or more, methods that have different information bases are used, their combination will frequently provide better forecasts than would either method alone. The process of combining forecasts is sufficiently important that Chapter 8 is devoted to this topic.

The eighth phase of the forecasting process involves the presentation of forecast results to those who rely on them to make decisions. Here, clear communication is critical. Sometimes technicians who develop forecasts become so enamored with the sophistication of their models that they focus on technical issues rather than on the substance of the forecast. In both written and oral presentations, the use of objective visual representations of the results is very important.[2]

Finally, the forecasting process should include continuous tracking of how well forecasts compare with the actual values observed during the forecast horizon. Over time, even the best of models are likely to deteriorate in terms of accuracy and need to be respecified, or replaced with an alternative method. Forecasters can learn from their mistakes. A careful review of forecast errors may be helpful in leading to a better understanding of what causes deviations between the actual and forecast series.

Trend, Seasonal, and Cyclical Data Patterns

The data that are used most often in forecasting are time series. For example, you might have sales data by month from January 1972 through December 1997, or you might have the number of visitors to a national park every year for a 30-year period, or you might have stock prices on a daily basis for several years. These would all be examples of time-series data.

Such time series can display a wide variety of patterns when plotted over time. Displaying data in a time-series plot is an important first step in identifying various component parts of the times series. A time series is likely to contain some, or all,

---

[2]An excellent discussion of how to present information in graphic form can be found in Edward R. Tufte, *The Visual Display of Quantitative Information* (Cheshire, Conn.: Graphics Press, 1983).

of the following components:

Trend

Seasonal

Cyclical

Irregular

Let us first define and discuss each of these in general terms, and then we will look at several specific data series to see which components we can visualize through graphic analyses.

The *trend* in a time series is the long-term change in the level of the data. If, over an extended period of time, the series moves upward, we say that the data show a positive trend. If the level of the data diminishes over time, there is a negative trend. Data are considered *stationary* when there is neither a positive nor a negative trend (i.e., the series is essentially flat in the long term).

A *seasonal* pattern occurs in a time series when there is a regular variation in the level of the data that repeats itself at the same time each year. For example, ski lodges in Killington, Vermont, have very regular high occupancy rates during December, January, and February (as well as regular low occupancy rates in the spring of the year). Housing starts are always stronger in the spring and summer than during the fall and winter. Retail sales for many products tend to peak in November and December because of Christmas sales. Most university enrollments are higher in the fall than in the winter or spring and are typically the lowest in the summer. All of these patterns recur with reasonable regularity year after year. No doubt you can think of many other examples of time-series data for which you would expect similar seasonal patterns.

A *cyclical* pattern is represented by wavelike upward and downward movements of the data around the long-term trend. Cyclical fluctuations are of longer duration and are less regular than are seasonal fluctuations. The causes of cyclical fluctuations are less readily apparent as well. They are usually attributed to the ups and downs in the general level of business activity that are frequently referred to as *business cycles.*

The *irregular* component of a time series contains the fluctuations that are not part of the other three components. These are often called *random* fluctuations. As such, they are the most difficult to capture in a forecasting model.

To illustrate these components, let us analyze three specific sets of data. One of these is a quarterly macroeconomic series, gross domestic product (GDP, in 1992 dollars), which many forecasters refer to as a *prime mover* because of its important influence on many other variables in the economy. The second series we will analyze is quarterly industry-level data on private housing starts (PHS). The last data set is at the firm level: annual U.S. billings of the Leo Burnett advertising agency (LBB). The integrative case at the end of this chapter also involves a similar evaluation of the sales of Gap stores.

Figure 2–1 shows a times-series plot of real GDP on a quarterly basis starting with the first quarter of 1970 (1970Q1) and ending with the fourth quarter of 1995 (1995Q4). From a visual inspection of this graph, it is fairly easy to see that there has been a positive trend to GDP over the 21-year period shown. The long-term trend

---

Data are considered *stationary* when there is neither a positive nor a negative trend.

A *seasonal* pattern occurs in a time series when there is a regular variation in the level of the data that repeats itself at the same time each year.

FIGURE 2–1

Quarterly Values of Gross Domestic Product in Constant 1992 Dollars, Along with the Long-Term Trend (c2f1)

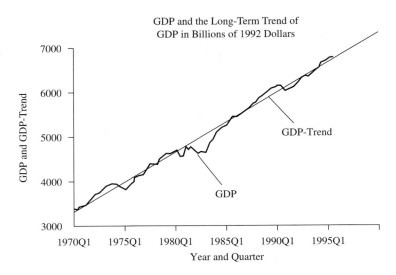

is shown by the straight line in Figure 2–1. (In later chapters, you will learn how to determine an equation for this long-term trend line.) In this graphic representation of the raw data along with the trend line, the wavelike cyclical movement of GDP above and below the long-term trend can also be discerned. Thus, GDP is nonstationary and has a cyclical component. Because GDP is nonstationary, some models would not be appropriate in forecasting GDP (see Table 2–1). Later in this chapter we will show one method that could be used to transform GDP to a stationary series.

Private housing starts (PHS) are plotted in Figure 2–2 for the period from 1980Q1 through 1995Q4. Probably the most striking feature of this visualization of the private housing starts data is the regular and sharp upward and downward movements that repeat year after year. This indicates a seasonal pattern, with housing starts reaching a peak in the spring of each year (quarter 2—April, May, and June). Overall, there also appears to be some upward trend to the data and some cyclical movement as well.

The straight line in Figure 2–2 shows the long-term trend in the PHS series. The third line, which moves above and below the long-term trend but is smoother than the plot of PHS, is what the PHS series looks like after the seasonality has been removed. Such a series is said to be "deseasonalized," or "seasonally adjusted," and is represented by PHSSA (the "SA" at the end of the name is meant to indicate that the data have been seasonally adjusted). By comparing PHSSA with the trend, the cyclical nature of private housing starts becomes clearer. You will learn how to deseasonalize data in Chapter 6.

Now let us turn to a visual analysis of firm-specific data. Figure 2–3 shows U.S. billings of the Leo Burnett advertising agency (LBB), one of the largest firms in this industry. Data are shown on an annual basis from 1950 through 1995. Clearly, there is an upward trend in the data, and it is a trend that appears to be accelerating (i.e., becoming increasingly steep). You will learn to forecast such nonlinear trends later

FIGURE 2–2

*Quarterly Values
of Private
Housing Starts
(PHS) in Thousands
of Units
(c2f2)*

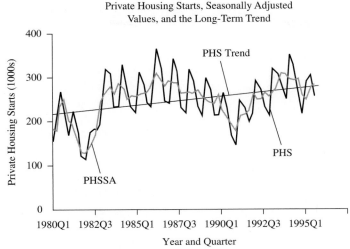

Private Housing Starts, Seasonally Adjusted
Values, and the Long-Term Trend

in this text. There does not appear to be a cyclical component to the series, and since these are annual data, there is no need to consider seasonality.

Data Patterns and Model Selection

As discussed earlier in this chapter, the pattern that exists in the data is an important consideration in determining which forecasting techniques are appropriate. On the basis only of the pattern of data, let us apply the information in Table 2–1 to determine which methods might be good candidates for forecasting each of the three specific series just discussed and plotted in Figures 2–1 through 2–3.

For GDP, which has a trend and a cycle but no seasonality, the following might be appropriate:

The pattern that
exists in the data
is an important
consideration
in determining
which forecasting
techniques are
appropriate.

Holt's exponential smoothing

Linear regression trend

Causal regression

Time-series decomposition

Because of the cycle component, the last two may be better than the first two.

Private housing starts (PHS) have a trend, seasonality, and a cycle. Therefore, the likely candidate models for forecasting PHS would include:

Winters' exponential smoothing

Linear regression trend with seasonal adjustment

Causal regression

Time-series decomposition

Again, the existence of a cycle component would suggest that the latter two may be the best candidates.

FIGURE 2–3

U.S. Billings of the Leo Burnett Advertising Agency on an Annual Basis for 1950 through 1995 (c2f3)

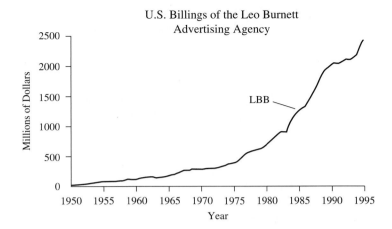

For U.S. billings of Leo Burnett advertising (LBB), there is a nonlinear trend, with no seasonality and no cycle. Thus, the models most likely to be successful are:

Nonlinear regression trend
Causal regression

In subsequent chapters of the text, we will return to these three series from time to time as examples. By the time you finish with the text you will be able to develop good forecasts for these series and others that exhibit a wide variety of data patterns. After a review of some statistical concepts, we will return to an evaluation of data patterns that goes beyond the simple, yet powerful, visualization of data and that will be of additional help in selecting appropriate forecasting techniques.

A Statistical Review[3]

The approach that we will take in this discussion is more intuitive than theoretical. Our intent is to help you recall a small part of what is normally covered in an introductory statistics course. We begin by discussing descriptive statistics, with an emphasis on measures of central tendency and measures of dispersion. Next we review two important statistical distributions. These topics lead to statistical inference, which involves making statements about a population based on sample statistics. We then present an overview of hypothesis testing and finish with a discussion of correlation.

Descriptive Statistics

We often want to use numbers to describe one phenomenon or another. For example, we might want to communicate information concerning the sales of fast-food restaurants in a community. Or we might want to describe the typical consumption

---

[3]Students with a good statistical background may be able to skip this section.

(c2t2)

TABLE 2–2   Twenty-Five Consecutive Months of Total Sales

Month	Sales	Month	Sales
1	3	14	4
2	4	15	7
3	5	16	3
4	1	17	4
5	5	18	2
6	3	19	5
7	6	20	7
8	2	21	4
9	7	22	5
10	8	23	2
11	1	24	6
12	13	25	4
13	4		

of soft drinks in U.S. households. Or we might want to convey to someone the rate at which sales have been increasing over time. All of these call for the use of descriptive statistics.

When we want to describe the general magnitude of some variable, we can use one or more of several *measures of central tendency*. The three most common measures of central tendency are the mean, median, and mode. To grasp each of these measures, let us consider the data in Table 2–2. These data represent 25 consecutive months of computer sales for a small office-products retailer. The *mode* is the response that occurs most frequently. If you count the number of times each value for sales is found in Table 2–2, you obtain the following results:

Sales	Number of Occurrences
1	2
2	3
3	3
4	6
5	4
6	2
7	3
8	1
13	1
Total	25

Since the largest number of occurrences is 6 (for sales of four computers), the mode is 4.

The *median* is the value that splits the responses into two equal parts when they are arrayed from smallest to largest. In this set of data, the median is 4. This is shown in the following diagram:

Responses Arrayed from Low to High

$$\underbrace{1\ 1\ 2\ 2\ 2\ 3\ 3\ 3\ 4\ 4\ 4\ 4}_{\text{12 Values}}\quad\textcircled{4}\quad\underbrace{4\ 5\ 5\ 5\ 5\ 6\ 6\ 7\ 7\ 7\ 8\ 13}_{\text{12 Values}}$$

Median

There are 12 numbers to the left of the circled 4, and 12 numbers to the right. When there are an even number of observations, the median is the midpoint of the two center values. For example, in the series 1, 4, 6, 10, the median is 5. Note that the median may be a number that is not actually in the data array.

The *mean* is the arithmetic average of all the numbers in the data set. To find the mean, add up all the values and divide by the number of observations. If the set of numbers is a population, rather than a sample, the mean is designated by the Greek mu (μ). It is calculated as:

$$\mu = \sum_{i=1}^{N} X_i/N$$

where the subscript i is used to identify each X value and

$$\sum_{i=1}^{N} X_i$$

means the sum of all the values of X_i, in which i ranges from 1 to N. X is simply a shorthand way of representing a variable. For the data in Table 2–2, $X_3 = 5$ and $X_{15} = 7$. N represents the total number of elements, or observations, in the population. In this case $N = 25$. Adding up all 25 values, we get:

$$\sum X = 115$$

Note that we have dropped the subscript here. This will often be done to simplify the notation. The population mean is then:

$$\mu = \sum X/N = 115/25 = 4.6$$

If the data represent a sample (i.e., a portion of the entire population), the mean is designated $\overline{X}$ and the number of elements in the sample is designated n. Thus, a sample mean is:

$$\overline{X} = \sum_{i=1}^{n} X_i/n$$

If the data in Table 2–2 represented a sample of months, the mean would be calculated as:

$$\overline{X} = \sum X/n = 115/25 = 4.6$$

All three of these measures of central tendency provide some feel for what we might think of as a "typical case." For example, knowing that the median and mode for sales are both 4 and the mean is 4.6 gives you an idea about what is a typical month's sales.

These sales data are plotted over time in Figure 2–4, along with the trend line. You see in this plot that sales fluctuate around a nearly flat trend. Thus, this sales series is stationary.

We have seen that for the data in Table 2–2, the mean is 4.6, and both the mode and the median are 4.0. Note that the mean is above both of the other measures of central tendency. This can result when there is one relatively large value (in this example, the 13). That large value pulls up the mean but has little or no effect on the median or mode. Without that observation the median and mode for this example would still be 4, but the mean would be 4.25 (4.25 = 102/24).

Let us now consider dispersion in data. A measure of dispersion tells us something about how spread out (or dispersed) the data are. Such information helps us to gain a clearer picture of the phenomenon being investigated than we get by looking just at a measure of central tendency. Look, for example, at the following two data sets marked *A* and *B:*

A:	18	19	20	21	22
B:	0	10	20	30	40

In both cases the mean and median are 20. (Since no value occurs more frequently than the others, there is no mode.) However, the two data sets are really very different. Measures of dispersion can be helpful in conveying such a difference.

The simplest measure of dispersion is the *range,* which is the difference between the smallest value and the greatest value. In Table 2–2 the smallest value is 1

FIGURE 2–4

Sales and Sales Trend
(c2f4)

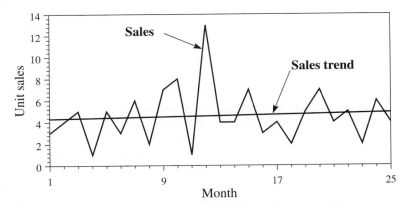

For this sales series, the trend is almost perfectly flat, so that the data are stationary. Note that the level of the trend line is fairly close to the sample mean of 4.6.

(observations 4 and 11); the greatest is 13 (observation 12). Thus,

$$\text{Range} = \text{Greatest value} - \text{Smallest value}$$
$$= 13 - 1$$
$$= 12$$

For the two data sets *A* and *B* just given, the range for *A* is 4 and the range for *B* is 40.

Think for a moment about the different perception you get from the following two statements:

> "The data set *A* has a mean of 20 and a range of values equal to 4, from 18 to 22."

> "The data set *B* has a mean of 20 and a range of values equal to 40, from 0 to 40."

You can see how much your perception is affected by knowing this measure of dispersion in addition to the mean.

Two other measures of dispersion, the variance and the standard deviation, are probably the ones that are most used. The standard deviation is a measure of the "average" spread of the data around the mean. Thus, it is based on the mean and tells us how spread out the data are from the mean. The variance is the square of the standard deviation.

The calculation of sample and population standard deviations and variances can be shown in the shorthand of mathematical expressions as follows (let X_i represent the *i*th observation):

	For a Sample	*For a Population*
Standard deviation	$S = \sqrt{\dfrac{\sum(X_i - \overline{X})^2}{n - 1}}$	$\sigma = \sqrt{\dfrac{\sum(X_i - \mu)^2}{N}}$
Variance	$S^2 = \dfrac{\sum(X_i - \overline{X})^2}{n - 1}$	$\sigma^2 = \dfrac{\sum(X_i - \mu)^2}{N}$

For the computer sales data in Table 2–2, the calculations of the standard deviation and variance are illustrated in Table 2–3. Note that the sum of the unsquared differences between each observation and the mean is equal to zero. This is always true. Squaring the differences gets around the problem of offsetting positive and negative differences. The standard deviation for the sales data is (assuming the data represent a sample) 2.582 units around a mean of 4.6. That is, the "average" spread around the mean is 2.582. The corresponding variance is 6.667 "units squared." You can see that the interpretation of the variance is a bit awkward. What is a "squared computer"? Because of this squaring of the units of measurement, the variance is less useful in communicating dispersion than is the standard deviation. In statistical

(c2t3) **TABLE 2–3** **Calculation of the Standard Deviation and Variance for the Computer Sales Data (Assuming a Sample)**

Observation Number	Computer Sales (X_i)	$(X_i - \overline{X})$	$(X_i - \overline{X})^2$
1	3	−1.6	2.56
2	4	−0.6	0.36
3	5	0.4	0.16
4	1	−3.6	12.96
5	5	0.4	0.16
6	3	−1.6	2.56
7	6	1.4	1.96
8	2	−2.6	6.76
9	7	2.4	5.76
10	8	3.4	11.56
11	1	−3.6	12.96
12	13	8.4	70.56
13	4	−0.6	0.36
14	4	−0.6	0.36
15	7	2.4	5.76
16	3	−1.6	2.56
17	4	−0.6	0.36
18	2	−2.6	6.76
19	5	0.4	0.16
20	7	2.4	5.76
21	4	−0.6	0.36
22	5	0.4	0.16
23	2	−2.6	6.76
24	6	−1.4	1.96
25	4	−0.6	0.36
Total	115	0.0	160.00

$$\text{Mean} = \overline{X} = \frac{\sum X_i}{n} = \frac{115}{25} = 4.6$$

$$\text{Variance} = S^2 = \frac{\sum(X_i - \overline{X})^2}{n - 1} = \frac{160}{25 - 1} = 6.667$$

$$\text{Standard deviation} = S = \sqrt{\frac{\sum(X_i - \overline{X})^2}{n - 1}} = \sqrt{\frac{160}{24}} = \sqrt{6.667} = 2.582$$

analysis, however, the variance is frequently far more important and useful than the standard deviation. Thus, both are important to know and understand.

Look back at the two small data sets *A* and *B* referred to earlier. For both sets the mean was 20. Assuming that these are both samples, the standard deviations are:

$$\text{For } A: \quad S = 1.58$$
$$\text{For } B: \quad S = 15.8$$

You see that knowing both the mean and the standard deviation gives you a much better understanding of the data than you would have if you knew only the mean.

The Normal Distribution

Many statistical distributions are important for various applications. Two of them—the normal distribution and Student's *t*-distribution—are particularly useful for the applications in forecasting to be discussed in this text. In this section we will describe the normal distribution. We will consider the *t*-distribution in a later section.

The normal distribution for a continuous random variable is fully defined by just two characteristics: the mean and the variance (or standard deviation) of the variable. A graph of the normal distribution has a bell shape such as the three distributions shown in Figure 2–5.[4] All such normal distributions are symmetrical around the mean. Thus, 50 percent of the distribution is above the mean and 50 percent is below the mean. It follows that the median must equal the mean when the distribution is normal.

In Figure 2–5 the top graph represents the normal curve for a variable with a population mean of 4 and a standard deviation of 2. The middle graph is for a variable with the same mean but a standard deviation of 3. The lower graph is for a normal

FIGURE 2–5

Three Normal Distributions

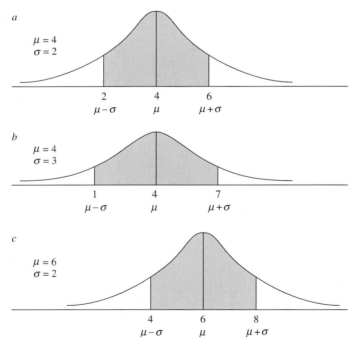

The top and middle distributions have the same mean but different standard deviations. The top and bottom distributions have the same standard deviation but different means.

_____

[4]Technically, these are probability density functions, for which the area under the curve between any two points on the horizontal axis represents the probability of observing an occurrence between those two points. For a continuous random variable, the probability of any particular value occurring is considered zero, because there are an infinite number of possible values in any interval. Thus, we discuss only probabilities that values of the variable will lie between specified pairs of points.

distribution with a mean of 6 and a standard deviation of 2. While each is unique, the three graphs have similar shapes, and they have an important common feature: for each of these graphs the shaded area represents roughly 68 percent of the area under the curve.

This brings us to an important property of all normal curves. The area between one standard deviation above the mean and one standard deviation below the mean includes approximately 68 percent of the area under the curve. Thus, if we were to draw an element at random from a population with a normal distribution, there is a 68 percent chance that it would be in the interval $\mu \pm 1\sigma$. This 68 percent is represented by the shaded areas of the graphs in Figure 2–5.

If you remember that the normal distribution is symmetrical, you will realize that 34 percent must be in the shaded area to the left of the mean and 34 percent in the shaded area to the right of the mean. Since the total area to the right (or left) of the mean is 50 percent, the area in either tail of the distribution must be the remaining 16 percent (these are the unshaded regions in the graphs in Figure 2–5).

If one extends the range to plus or minus two standard deviations from the mean, roughly 95 percent of the area would be in that interval. And if you go out three standard deviations in both directions from the mean, about 99 percent of the area would be included. These concepts can be summarized as follows:

$\mu \pm 1\sigma$ includes about 68% of the area
$\mu \pm 2\sigma$ includes about 95% of the area
$\mu \pm 3\sigma$ includes about 99% of the area

These three rules of thumb are helpful to remember.

In Figure 2–5 you saw three similar yet different normal distributions. How many such distributions are there? There may be billions of them. Every variable or measurement you might consider could have a different normal distribution. And yet any statistics text you look in will have just one normal distribution. The reason for this is that every other normal distribution can be transformed easily into a *standard* normal distribution called the Z-distribution. The transformation is simple:

$$Z = \frac{X - \mu}{\sigma}$$

In this way any observed value (X) can be standardized to a corresponding Z-value. The Z-value measures the number of standard deviations by which X differs from the mean. If the calculated Z-value is positive, then X lies to the right of the mean (X is larger than μ). If the calculated Z-value is negative, then X lies to the left of the mean (X is smaller than μ).

The standard normal distribution is shown in the lower part of Figure 2–6. Note that it is centered on zero. A normal distribution for product sales (X) with a mean of 50 and a standard deviation of 10 is shown immediately above the standard normal distribution. For every value of X there is a corresponding value for Z, which can be found by using the transformation shown in the preceding equation. Let us calculate the Z-values that correspond to X = 40 and to X = 65:

$$Z = \frac{X - \mu}{\sigma}$$

FIGURE 2–6

*Transformation
to the Standard
Normal Distribution*

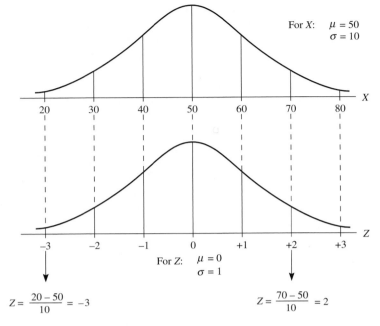

For X: $\mu = 50$
           $\sigma = 10$

For Z: $\mu = 0$
           $\sigma = 1$

$$Z = \frac{20 - 50}{10} = -3$$

$$Z = \frac{70 - 50}{10} = 2$$

The normal distribution for the sales variable, represented by X, is shown above the standard normal distribution. Any level of sales can be transformed to the standard normal variable, Z, as follows:

$$Z = \frac{X - \mu}{\sigma}$$

Two representative calculations are shown.

For $X = 40$, $Z = \dfrac{40 - 50}{10} = -1$

For $X = 65$, $Z = \dfrac{65 - 50}{10} = 1.5$

Through this process every normal variable can be transformed to the standard normal variable Z.

Although this standardization is a simple process, it is very powerful and opens the door to answers for many questions. For example, suppose we want to know what percent of sales would be between the mean of 50 and 65. Since the sales variable can so easily be transformed into the standard normal variable, Z, we can answer such a question with the help of the standard normal table shown as Table 2–4. The Z-value that corresponds to sales of 65 ($X = 65$) is:

$$Z = \frac{65 - 50}{10} = 1.5$$

Looking for $Z = 1.5$ in Table 2–4, we find that the area under the normal curve between the midpoint (the mean for sales, or $Z = 0$) and $Z = 1.5$ is 0.4332. Thus, 43.32 percent of sales would be in the interval between 50 and 65.

TABLE 2–4   **The Standard Normal Distribution***

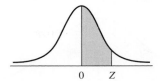

Z	.00	.01	.02	.03	.04	.05	.06	.07	.08	.09
0.0	.0000	.0040	.0080	.0120	.0160	.0199	.0239	.0279	.0319	.0359
0.1	.0398	.0438	.0478	.0517	.0557	.0596	.0636	.0675	.0714	.0753
0.2	.0793	.0832	.0871	.0910	.0948	.0987	.1026	.1064	.1103	.1141
0.3	.1179	.1217	.1255	.1293	.1331	.1368	.1406	.1443	.1480	.1517
0.4	.1554	.1591	.1628	.1664	.1700	.1736	.1772	.1808	.1844	.1879
0.5	.1915	.1950	.1985	.2109	.2054	.2088	.2123	.2157	.2190	.2224
0.6	.2257	.2291	.2324	.2357	.2389	.2422	.2454	.2486	.2518	.2549
0.7	.2580	.2612	.2642	.2673	.2704	.2734	.2764	.2794	.2823	.2852
0.8	.2881	.2910	.2939	.2967	.2995	.3023	.2051	.3078	.3106	.3133
0.9	.3159	.3186	.3212	.3238	.3264	.3289	.3315	.3340	.3365	.3389
1.0	.3413	.3438	.3461	.3485	.3508	.3531	.3554	.3577	.3599	.3621
1.1	.3643	.3665	.3686	.3708	.3729	.3749	.3770	.3790	.3810	.3830
1.2	.3849	.3869	.3888	.3907	.3925	.3944	.3962	.3980	.3997	.4015
1.3	.4032	.4049	.4066	.4082	.4099	.4115	.4131	.4147	.4162	.4177
1.4	.4192	.4207	.4222	.4236	.4251	.4265	.4279	.4292	.4306	.4319
1.5	.4332	.4345	.4357	.4370	.4382	.4394	.4406	.4418	.4429	.4441
1.6	.4452	.4463	.4474	.4484	.4495	.4505	.4515	.4525	.4535	.4545
1.7	.4554	.4564	.4573	.4582	.4591	.4599	.4608	.4616	.4625	.4633
1.8	.4641	.4649	.4656	.4664	.4671	.4678	.4686	.4693	.4699	.4706
1.9	.4713	.4719	.4726	.4732	.4738	.4744	.4750	.4756	.4761	.4767
2.0	.4772	.4778	.4783	.4788	.4793	.4798	.4803	.4808	.4812	.4817
2.1	.4821	.4826	.4830	.4834	.4838	.4842	.4846	.4850	.4854	.4857
2.2	.4861	.4864	.4868	.4871	.4875	.4878	.4881	.4884	.4887	.4890
2.3	.4893	.4896	.4898	.4901	.4904	.4906	.4909	.4911	.4913	.4916
2.4	.4918	.4920	.4922	.4925	.4927	.4929	.4931	.4932	.4934	.4936
2.5	.4938	.4940	.4941	.4943	.4945	.4946	.4948	.4949	.4951	.4952
2.6	.4953	.4955	.4956	.4957	.4959	.4960	.4961	.4962	.4963	.4964
2.7	.4965	.4966	.4967	.4968	.4969	.4970	.4971	.4972	.4973	.4974
2.8	.4974	.4975	.4976	.4977	.4977	.4978	.4979	.4979	.4980	.4981
2.9	.4981	.4982	.4982	.4983	.4984	.4984	.4985	.4985	.4986	.4986
3.0	.49865	.4987	.4987	.4988	.4988	.4989	.4989	.4989	.4990	.4990
4.0	.49997									

*Z is the standard normal variable. Other variables can be transformed to Z as follows:

$$Z = \frac{X - \mu}{\sigma}$$

For $Z = 1.96$, the shaded area in the distribution is 0.4750 (found at the intersection of the 1.9 row and the .06 column).

SOURCE: Adapted from Owen P. Hall, Jr., and Harvey M. Adelman, *Computerized Business Statistics* (Homewood, Ill.: Richard D. Irwin, 1987), p. 91.

Let us look at one more example. What percent of sales would be greater than 30? The shaded area of the following normal curve is the area of interest:

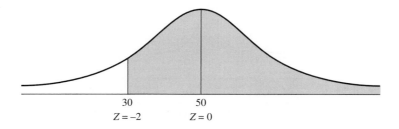

30	50
$Z = -2$	$Z = 0$

Since the Z-distribution is symmetrical, negative values would be superfluous in Table 2–4. The area between $Z = 0$ and $Z = -2$ is identical to the area between $Z = 0$ and $Z = +2$. From Table 2–4, we see that this is 0.4772 (or 47.72 percent). Thus, 47.72 percent would lie between 30 and 50. Since 50 percent is always above the mean (i.e., $Z = 0$), the total that would be above $X = 30$ is 97.72 percent ($= 47.74$ percent $+ 50$ percent).

The Sampling Distribution of the Mean

Statistical theory tells us some very interesting and useful things about the *distribution of sample statistics.* For example, when the population is normally distributed or when the sample size is large, sample means are distributed normally. That means that a graph of the distribution of sample means ($\overline{X}$'s) would look like the bell-shaped curves in Figure 2–5. Second, the distribution of sample means is centered on the population mean μ. That is, the mean of the sample means is equal to the population mean. Third, the standard deviation of the sample means is equal to the standard deviation of the population divided by the square root of the sample size. The standard deviation of sample means is denoted $\sigma_{\overline{X}}$ and is usually called the *standard error of the mean.* It is:

$$\sigma_{\overline{X}} = \frac{\sigma}{\sqrt{n}}$$

We will use other types of standard errors as we work with regression models in Chapters 4 and 5.

When we select a sample, we get just one sample from a great many that could have been selected. Knowing that the distribution of sample means is normal with a mean equal to the population mean and a standard error equal to $\sigma/\sqrt{n}$ gives us a great deal of power in working with a sample. Suppose, for example, that a sample of $n = 100$ is selected and that it has a mean of 300. For now we will assume that the population standard deviation is known and is equal to 60. We can now answer a question such as, What is the probability that a sample of 100 elements with a mean of 300 or more would be selected if the true population mean were 288? To answer such a question, we have to transform this information from the distribution of sample means to the standard normal distribution (Z). This is done as follows:

$$Z = \frac{\overline{X} - \mu}{\sigma_{\overline{X}}}$$

where $\sigma_{\overline{X}} = \sigma/\sqrt{n}$. Notice that this is the same as the Z-transformation used earlier except that now the variable of interest is $\overline{X}$ (rather than X), and that we use the standard deviation of the mean ($\sigma_{\overline{X}}$ rather than σ).

$$Z = \frac{\overline{X} - \mu}{\sigma/\sqrt{n}}$$

$$Z = \frac{300 - 288}{60/\sqrt{100}} = \frac{12}{6} = 2$$

From Table 2–4 we see that the area between $Z = 0$ and $Z = 2$ is 0.4772. Since 0.5000 is the total area above $Z = 0$, the area beyond $Z = 2$ must be 0.5000 − 0.4772 = 0.0228. Thus, there is a 2.28 percent chance of selecting a sample with a mean greater than 300 when the true population mean is 288 and the population standard deviation is 60.

The Student's t-Distribution

When the population standard deviation is not known, or when the sample size is small, the Student's t-distribution should be used rather than the normal distribution. The Student's t-distribution resembles the normal distribution but is somewhat more spread out for small sample sizes. As the sample size becomes very large, the two distributions become the same. The formula for standardizing the distribution of sample means to the t-distribution is similar to the Z-transformation except that the sample standard deviation (s) is used instead of the population standard deviation (σ). The formula is:

$$t = \frac{\overline{X} - \mu}{s/\sqrt{n}}$$

Like the normal distribution, the t-distribution is centered at zero (i.e., has a mean of zero) and is symmetrical.

Since the t-distribution depends on the number of degrees of freedom (df), there are many t-distributions. The number of degrees of freedom appropriate for a given application depends on the specific characteristics of the analysis. Throughout this text, we will specify the value for df in each application. In our present application there are $n - 1$ degrees of freedom. Table 2–5 has a t-distribution for 29 different degrees of freedom plus infinity. The body of this table contains t-values such that the shaded area in the graph is equal to the subscript on t at the top of the column, for each number of degrees of freedom (df).

To learn how to read the t-table, let us consider three examples. First, what value of t would correspond to 5 percent of the area in the shaded region if there are 15 degrees of freedom? To answer this, go to the row for 15 degrees of freedom, then to the column that has .050 for the subscript on t. The t-value at the intersection of that row and column is 1.753. Second, if there are 26 degrees of freedom and

TABLE 2–5   Student's *t*-Distribution*

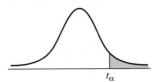

t_α

df	$t_{.100}$	$t_{.050}$	$t_{.025}$	$t_{.010}$	$t_{.005}$
1	3.078	6.314	12.706	31.821	63.657
2	1.886	2.920	4.303	6.965	9.925
3	1.638	2.353	3.182	4.541	5.841
4	1.533	2.132	2.776	3.747	4.604
5	1.476	2.015	2.571	3.365	4.032
6	1.440	1.943	2.447	3.143	3.707
7	1.415	1.895	2.365	2.998	3.499
8	1.397	1.860	2.306	2.896	3.355
9	1.383	1.833	2.262	2.821	3.250
10	1.372	1.812	2.228	2.764	3.169
11	1.363	1.796	2.201	2.718	3.106
12	1.356	1.782	2.179	2.681	3.055
13	1.350	1.771	2.160	2.650	3.012
14	1.345	1.761	2.145	2.624	2.977
15	1.341	1.753	2.131	2.602	2.947
16	1.337	1.746	2.120	2.583	2.921
17	1.333	1.740	2.110	2.567	2.898
18	1.330	1.734	2.101	2.552	2.878
19	1.328	1.729	2.093	2.539	2.861
20	1.325	1.725	2.086	2.528	2.845
21	1.323	1.721	2.080	2.518	2.831
22	1.321	1.717	2.074	2.508	2.819
23	1.319	1.714	2.069	2.500	2.807
24	1.318	1.711	2.064	2.492	2.797
25	1.316	1.708	2.060	2.485	2.787
26	1.315	1.706	2.056	2.479	2.779
27	1.314	1.703	2.052	2.473	2.771
28	1.313	1.701	2.048	2.467	2.763
29	1.311	1.699	2.045	2.462	2.756
Inf.	1.282	1.645	1.960	2.326	2.576

*The *t*-distribution is used for standardizing when the population standard deviation is unknown and the sample standard deviation is used in its place.

$$t = \frac{\overline{X} - \mu}{s/\sqrt{n}}$$

SOURCE: Adapted from Owen P. Hall, Jr., and Harvey M. Adelman, *Computerized Business Statistics* (Homewood, Ill.: Richard D. Irwin, 1987), p. 93.

the *t*-value is 2.479, how much area would be in the shaded region? Looking across the row for 26 degrees of freedom we see that 2.479 is in the column for which *t* is subscripted with .010. Thus, 1 percent of the area would be in that tail.

For our third example, consider the following question: If there are 85 degrees of freedom, what value of *t* would be associated with finding 97.5 percent of the area in the unshaded portion of the curve? For any number of degrees of freedom greater than 29, we would use the infinity (Inf.) row of the table. If we want 97.5 percent in the clear area, then 2.5 percent must be in the shaded region. Thus, we need the column for which *t* is subscripted with .025. The *t*-value at the intersection of this row and column is found to be 1.960. (Note that this is the same as the Z-value for which 2.5 percent would be in the tail, or 0.4750 is in the shaded section of the normal distribution shown in Table 2–4.)

While *t*-tables are usually limited to four or five areas in the tail of the distribution and perhaps 30 levels for degrees of freedom, most statistical software incorporates the equation for the *t*-distribution and will give exact areas, given any *t*-value and the appropriate number of degrees of freedom. We will rely on the *t*-distribution extensively in Chapters 4 and 5 as part of the evaluation of statistical significance in regression models.

From Sample to Population: Statistical Inference

We are usually much less interested in a sample than in the population from which the sample is drawn. The reason for looking at a sample is almost always to provide a basis for making some inference about the whole population. For example, suppose we are interested in marketing a new service in Oregon and want to know something about the income per person in the state. Roughly 3 million people live in Oregon. Clearly, trying to contact all of them to determine the mean income per person would be impractical and very costly. Instead we might select a sample and make an inference about the population based on the responses of the people in that sample of Oregon residents.

A sample statistic is our best point estimate of the corresponding population parameter. While it is best, it is also likely to be wrong. Thus, in making an inference about a population it is usually desirable to make an interval estimate.

For example, an interval estimate of the population mean is one that is centered on the sample mean and extends above and below that value by an amount that is determined by how confident we want to be, by how large a sample we have, and by the variability in the data. These elements are captured in the following equation for a confidence interval:

$$\mu = \overline{X} \pm t(s/\sqrt{n})$$

Recall that $s/\sqrt{n}$ is the standard error of the sample mean. The *t*-value is determined from Table 2–5 after choosing the number of degrees of freedom ($n - 1$ in this case), and the level of confidence we desire as reflected by the area in the shaded tail of the distribution.

If we want a 95 percent confidence interval that is symmetrical around the mean, we would want a total of 5 percent in the two extreme tails of the distribution. Thus,

2.5 percent would be in each tail. The following diagram will help you see this:

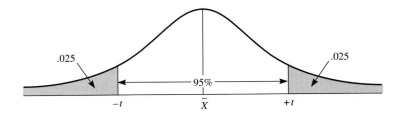

The *t*-value that would correspond to 2.5 percent in each tail can be determined from Table 2–5, given the appropriate number of degrees of freedom. Several examples follow:

Number of Degrees of Freedom	t-Value for 95% Confidence Interval
5	2.571
10	2.228
20	2.086
50	1.960
100	1.960

Suppose that a sample of 100 responses gives a mean of $15,000 and a standard deviation of $5,000. Our best point estimate for the population mean would be $15,000, and a 95 percent confidence interval would be:

$$\mu = 15,000 \pm 1.96\left(5,000/\sqrt{100}\right)$$
$$= 15,000 \pm 980$$

that is,

$$14,020 \le \mu \le 15,980$$

See if you can correctly find the endpoints for a 90 percent confidence interval given this same set of sample results.[5]

Hypothesis Testing

Frequently we have a theory or hypothesis that we would like to evaluate statistically. For example, we might hypothesize that the mean expenditure on entertainment in some city is equal to the national average for all age groups. Or we may theorize that

---

[5]The lower bound is $14,177.5; the upper bound is $15,822.5. Notice that at this lower confidence level the value of *t* is smaller (other things equal) and thus the confidence interval is narrower.

consumption of soft drinks by retired people is less than the national level. Or we may want to evaluate the assumption that women professionals work more than the standard 40-hour work week. All of these can be evaluated by using an appropriate hypothesis testing procedure.

The process begins by setting up two hypotheses, the null hypothesis (designated H_0:) and the alternative hypothesis (designated H_1:). These two hypotheses should be structured so that they are mutually exclusive and exhaustive. For example, if we hypothesize that the mean expenditure on entertainment by people in some city is different from the national average, the null and alternative hypotheses would be (let μ_0 = the national average and μ be this city's population mean):

$$\text{Case I} \begin{cases} H_0: & \mu = \mu_0 \\ \text{i.e., } H_0: & \text{The city mean equals the national mean.} \\ H_1: & \mu \neq \mu_0 \\ \text{i.e., } H_1: & \text{The city mean is not equal to the national mean.} \end{cases}$$

If we theorize that the consumption of soft drinks by retired people is *less* than the national average, the null and alternative hypotheses would be (let μ_0 = national average and μ be the mean for retired people):

$$\text{Case II} \begin{cases} H_0: & \mu \geq \mu_0 \\ \text{i.e., } H_0: & \text{The mean for retired people is greater than or} \\ & \text{equal to the national average.} \\ H_1: & \mu < \mu_0 \\ \text{i.e., } H_1: & \text{The mean for retired people is less than} \\ & \text{the national average.} \end{cases}$$

If we want to evaluate the assumption that women professionals work *more* than the standard 40-hour work week, the null and alternative hypotheses would be (let μ_0 = the standard work week and μ = the mean for professional women):

$$\text{Case III} \begin{cases} H_0: & \mu \leq \mu_0 \\ \text{i.e., } H_0: & \text{The mean for professional women is less than or} \\ & \text{equal to the standard.} \\ H_1: & \mu > \mu_0 \\ \text{i.e., } H_1: & \text{The mean for professional women is greater} \\ & \text{than the standard.} \end{cases}$$

In each of these cases the null and alternative hypotheses are mutually exclusive and exhaustive.

In statistical hypothesis testing, the approach is to see whether you find sufficient evidence to reject the null hypothesis. If so, the alternative is found to have support. For questions of the type we are considering, this is done by using a *t*-test. To perform a *t*-test, we must first determine how confident we want to be in our decision regarding whether or not to reject the null hypothesis. In most business applications a 95 percent confidence level is used. A measure that is closely related to the confidence level is the significance level for the test. The significance level, often denoted α (alpha), is equal to 1 minus the confidence level. Thus, a 95 percent

---

TABLE 2–6   Type I and Type II Errors

Statistical Decision	The Truth	
	H_0: *Is True*	H_0: *Is Not True*
Reject H_0:	Type I error	No error
Fail to Reject H_0:	No error	Type II error

---

confidence level is the same as a 5 percent significance level. The significance level is the probability of rejecting the null hypothesis when in fact it is true.

In testing hypotheses, there are four possible outcomes, two of which are good and two of which are bad. These are summarized in Table 2–6. If we reject H_0: when in fact it is true, we have what is termed a *type I error.* The other possible error results when we fail to reject a null hypothesis that is in fact incorrect. This is a *type II error.* These two errors are related in that by reducing the chance of a type I error we increase the chance of a type II error and vice versa. Most of the time, greater attention is given to type I errors. The probability of making a type I error is determined by the significance level (α) we select for the hypothesis test. If the cost of a type I error is large, we would use a low α, perhaps 1 percent or less.

Hypothesis tests may be one- or two-tailed tests. When the sign in the alternative hypothesis is an unequal sign ($\neq$), the test is a two-tailed test. Otherwise, a one-tailed test is appropriate. For a two-tailed test the significance level (α) is split equally into the two tails of the distribution. For a one-tailed test the entire significance level (α) goes in the one tail of the distribution that is indicated by the direction of the inequality sign in the alternative hypothesis. Consider the three situations described a few paragraphs back. These are summarized in the following diagrams, which show where the significance level would be (a 5 percent significance level is used in all three cases).

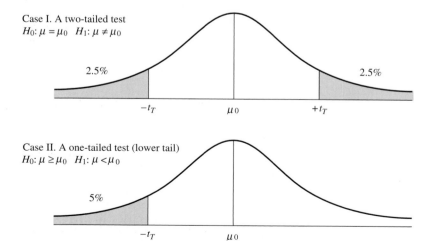

Case I. A two-tailed test
$H_0: \mu = \mu_0$ $H_1: \mu \neq \mu_0$

2.5%   2.5%

$-t_T$ μ_0 $+t_T$

Case II. A one-tailed test (lower tail)
$H_0: \mu \geq \mu_0$ $H_1: \mu < \mu_0$

5%

$-t_T$ μ_0

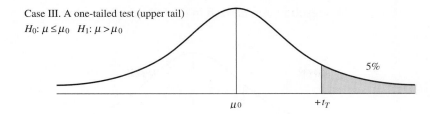

Case III. A one-tailed test (upper tail)

$H_0: \mu \leq \mu_0 \quad H_1: \mu > \mu_0$

5%

μ_0 $+t_T$

The t_T values are determined from a t-distribution, such as that in Table 2–5, at the appropriate number of degrees of freedom ($n - 1$, in the examples used here) and for the tail areas indicated in these diagrams ($\alpha/2$ for two-tailed tests and α for one-tailed tests).

For each hypothesis test, a t-value is calculated (t_{calc}) and compared with the critical value from the t-distribution (t_T). If the calculated value is further into the tail of the distribution than the table value, we have an observation that is extreme, given the assumption inherent in H_0, and so H_0 is rejected. That is, we have sufficient evidence to reject the null hypothesis (H_0) when the *absolute value* of t_{calc} is greater than t_T. Otherwise we fail to reject the premise in H_0.

The calculated t-statistic is found as follows:

$$t_{calc} = \frac{\overline{X} - \mu_0}{s/\sqrt{n}}$$

where $\overline{X}$ is our sample mean and our best point estimate of μ. The value we are testing against is μ_0. The sample standard deviation is s and the sample size is n.

Let us now apply these concepts to our three situations. Starting with case I, let us assume that a sample of 49 people resulted in a mean of \$200 per month with a standard deviation of \$84. The national average is \$220 per month. The hypotheses are:

$$H_0: \mu = 220$$
$$H_1: \mu \neq 220$$

The calculated value is:

$$t_{calc} = \frac{200 - 220}{84/\sqrt{49}} = \frac{-20}{12} = -1.67$$

If we want a 95 percent confidence level ($\alpha = 0.05$), the critical or table value of t is ± 1.96. Notice that the $t_{.025}$ column of Table 2–5 was used. This is because we have a two-tailed test, and the α of 0.05 is split equally between the two tails. Since our calculated t-value (t_{calc}) has an absolute value that is less than the critical value from the t-table (t_T), we fail to reject the null hypothesis. Thus, we conclude that the evidence from this sample is not sufficient to say that entertainment expenditures by people in this city are any different from the national average.

This result is summarized in the following diagram:

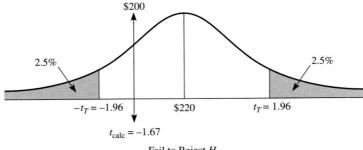

We see here that the observed mean of $200 or its corresponding *t*-value (-1.67) is not extreme. That is, it does not fall into either of the shaded areas. These shaded areas taken together are often called the *rejection region,* because t_{calc} values in the shaded areas would call for rejection of H_0.

Let us now look at case II. Assume that for a sample of 25 retired people the mean was 1.2 six-packs per week with a standard deviation of 0.6. The national average (μ_0) is 1.5. The hypotheses are:

$$H_0: \mu \geq 1.5$$
$$H_1: \mu < 1.5$$

The calculated *t*-value is:

$$t_{calc} = \frac{1.2 - 1.5}{0.6/\sqrt{25}} = \frac{-0.3}{0.12} = -2.50$$

The critical value from the *t*-distribution in Table 2–5, assuming a 95 percent confidence level ($\alpha = 0.05$), is $t_T = -1.711$. Note that there are 24 degrees of freedom. Since the absolute value of t_{calc} is greater than the table value of *t*, we reject H_0. Thus, we conclude that there is sufficient evidence to support the notion that retired people consume fewer soft drinks than the national average.

This result is shown in graphic form as follows:

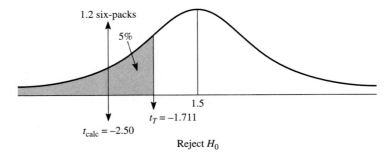

Here we see that the sample mean of 1.2 is extreme, given $\alpha = 0.05$ and $df = 24$, and so we reject H_0. The calculated value of *t* falls in the rejection region.

Finally, let us consider case III. We will assume that we have a sample of 144 professional women and that the mean number of hours per week worked for that sample is 45 with a sample standard deviation of 29. The national norm is the 40-hour work week. The hypotheses are:

$$H_0: \mu \leq 40$$
$$H_1: \mu > 40$$

Our calculated *t*-value is:

$$t_{calc} = \frac{45 - 40}{29/\sqrt{144}} = \frac{5}{2.42} = 2.07$$

The relevant table value is 1.645 ($\alpha = 0.05$ and $df = 143$). Since $T_{calc} > t_T$, we reject the null hypothesis and conclude that the mean for professional women is greater than 40 hours per week.

This result is shown graphically as follows:

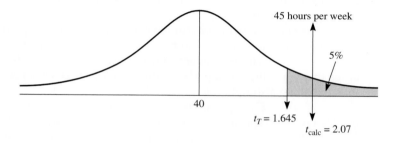

The calculated *t*-value lies in the shaded (or rejection) region, and so H_0 is rejected.

The *t*-tests illustrated in this section involved making judgments about a population mean based on information from a sample. In each *t*-test, the calculated value of *t* was determined by dividing some difference ($\overline{X} - \mu_0$) by a standard error ($s/\sqrt{n}$). All *t*-statistics are calculated in this general way:

$$t = \frac{\text{The difference being evaluated}}{\text{The corresponding standard error}}$$

We will use this general form later in this chapter as well as in subsequent chapters of the text when *t*-tests are appropriate.

There are other statistical tests and other distributions that are applicable to forecasting. These include *F*-tests, Durbin-Watson tests, and chi-square tests, which will be discussed later in the text as they are applied. If you have a basic understanding of the use of *t*-tests, these other statistical tests will not be difficult to use.

Correlation

It is often useful to have a measure of the degree of association between two variables. For example, if you believe that sales may be affected by expenditures on advertising, you might want to measure the degree of association between sales and advertising. One measure of association that is often used is the Pearson product-moment correlation coefficient, which is designated ρ (rho) for a population and r for a sample. There are other measures of correlation, but Pearson's is the most common and the most useful for the type of data encountered in forecasting situations. Thus, when we refer to correlation or a correlation coefficient, we mean the Pearson product-moment correlation.

There are several alternative ways to write the algebraic expression for the correlation coefficient. For our purposes the following is the most instructive:

$$r = \frac{\sum(X - \overline{X})(Y - \overline{Y})}{\sqrt{[\sum(X - \overline{X})^2][\sum(Y - \overline{Y})^2]}}$$

where X and Y represent the two variables of interest (e.g., advertising and sales). This is the sample correlation coefficient. The calculation of the population correlation coefficient (ρ) is strictly analogous except that the population means for X and Y would be used rather than the sample means. It is important to note that the correlation coefficient defined here measures the degree of *linear* association between X and Y.

The correlation coefficient can have any value in the range from -1 to $+1$. A perfect positive correlation would be $r = +1$, while a perfect negative correlation would be $r = -1$. These cases are shown in scatterplots A and B of Figure 2–7. You can see that when there is a perfect correlation (positive or negative) all of the data points fall along a straight line.

In scatterplot C it appears that in general when X increases, Y_C increases as well. That is, there appears to be a positive (or direct) association between X and Y_C. However, all five points do not fall along a single straight line, and so there is not a perfect linear association. In this case the correlation coefficient is $+0.80$. Scatterplot D shows a negative (or inverse) association between X and Y_D, but one that is not perfectly linear. For scatterplot D, $r = -0.85$.

The remaining two scatterplots in Figure 2–7 illustrate cases for which the correlation coefficient is zero. In both cases there is no linear association between the variables. However, note that in panel F there is a clear nonlinear association between X and Y_F.

We could perform a hypothesis test to determine whether the value of a sample correlation coefficient (r) gives us reason to believe that the true population correlation coefficient (ρ) is significantly different from zero. If it is not, then there would be no linear association between the two measures. The hypothesis test would be:

$$H_0: \rho = 0$$

$$H_1: \rho \neq 0$$

and t would be calculated as:

$$t = \frac{r - 0}{\sqrt{(1 - r^2)/(n - 2)}}$$

where $\sqrt{(1 - r^2)/(n - 2)}$ is the standard error of r.

FIGURE 2–7

Representative Scatterplots with the Corresponding Correlation Coefficients

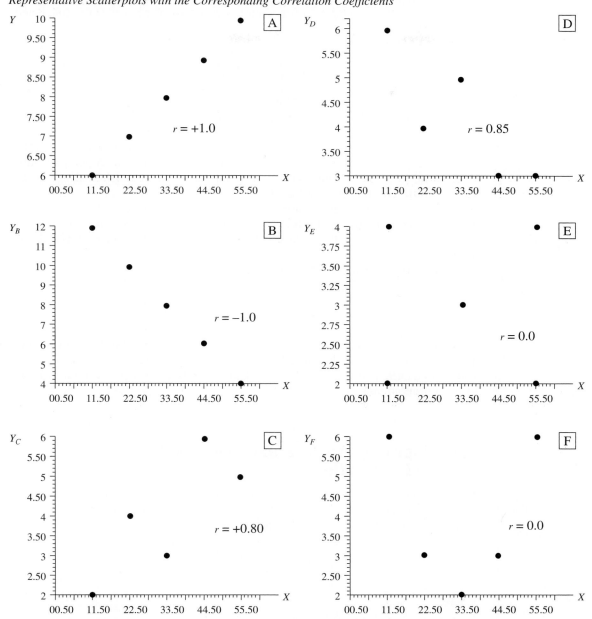

These scatterplots show correlation coefficients that range from a perfect positive correlation (A) and a perfect negative correlation (B) to zero correlations (E and F).

Let us apply this to the data in scatterplots D and F of Figure 2–7. In both of these cases, for a two-tailed test, with $\alpha = 0.05$ and $n = 5$, the table value of t_T is 3.182 (there are $n - 2$, or 3 degrees of freedom for this test). For panel D the calculated value of t is:

$$t_{calc} = \frac{0.85 - 0}{\sqrt{[1 - (-0.85)^2]/(5 - 2)}}$$

$$= \frac{-0.85}{\sqrt{0.2775/3}} = \frac{-0.85}{\sqrt{0.0925}} = -2.795$$

Since t_{calc} is in the interval between $\pm t_T$ (i.e., ± 3.182), we would fail to reject the null hypothesis on the basis of a sample of five observations at a 95 percent confidence level ($\alpha = 0.05$). Thus, we conclude that there is not enough evidence to say that ρ is different from zero. While the $r = -0.85$ is a fairly strong correlation, we are not able to say it is significantly different from zero in this case, largely because we have such a small sample. If $n = 50$ and $r = -0.85$, the calculated value for t would be -11.18, and the table value would be 1.96, so that the null hypothesis would be rejected.

For the data in panel F, the calculated value of t is:

$$t_{calc} = \frac{0 - 0}{\sqrt{(1 - 0^2)/(5 - 2)}} = 0$$

Since this t_{calc} is again in the interval between $\pm t_T$, we would fail to reject H_0 and would conclude that we do not have enough evidence to suggest that ρ is different from zero (at a 95 percent confidence level, or $\alpha = 0.05$, and on the basis of a sample of five observations).

Correlograms: An Alternative Method of Data Exploration

In evaluating a time series of data, it is useful to look at the correlation between successive observations over time. This measure of correlation is called an autocorrelation.

In evaluating a time series of data, it is useful to look at the correlation between successive observations over time. This measure of correlation is called an *autocorrelation* and may be calculated as follows:

$$r_k = \frac{\sum_{t=1}^{n-k}(Y_{t-k} - \overline{Y})(Y_t - \overline{Y})}{\sum_{t-1}^{n}(Y_t - \overline{Y})^2}$$

where:

r_k = Autocorrelation for a k-period lag
Y_t = Value of the time series at period t
Y_{t-k} = Value of the time series k periods before period t
$\overline{Y}$ = Mean of the time series

If the time series is stationary, the value of r_k should diminish rapidly toward zero as k increases. If, on the other hand, there is a trend, r_k will decline toward zero slowly. If a seasonal pattern exists, the value of r_k will be significantly different from zero at $k = 4$ for quarterly data, or $k = 12$ for monthly data. (For quarterly data, r_k for $k = 8$, $k = 12$, $k = 16,\ldots$ may also be large. For monthly data, a large r_k may also be found for $k = 24$, $k = 36$, etc.)

A k-period plot of autocorrelations is called an *autocorrelation function (acf)*, or a *correlogram*. We will look at a number of such graphics as we further analyze GDP, Leo Burnett U.S. billings, and private housing starts.

To determine whether the autocorrelation at lag k is significantly different from zero, the following hypothesis test and rule of thumb may be used:

$$H_0: \rho_k = 0$$
$$H_1: \rho_k \neq 0$$

For any k, reject H_0 if $|r_k| > 2/\sqrt{n}$, where n is the number of observations. This rule of thumb is for a 95 percent confidence level.[6]

The use of autocorrelations and correlograms can be illustrated by looking at some of the data used earlier in this chapter. Let us begin with the gross domestic product data that were graphed in Figure 2–1. From that plot it was clear that GDP has a fairly strong positive trend, so that we might expect high autocorrelation coefficients. The autocorrelation structure of GDP is shown in Figure 2–8.

In this case 104 observations were used, from 1970Q1 through 1995Q4. Thus, $2/\sqrt{n} = 2/\sqrt{104} = 0.196$. Since all of the autocorrelation coefficients in Figure 2–8 are greater than 0.196, we can conclude, by our rule of thumb, that they are all significantly different from zero. Therefore, we have additional evidence of a trend in the GDP data.[7] The actual 95 percent confidence interval is shown by the two

---

[6]The complete t-test would be to reject H_0 if $|t_{calc}| > t_T$, where:

$$t_{calc} = \frac{(r_k - 0)}{(1/\sqrt{n - k})}$$

and t_T is from the t-table for $\alpha/2$ and $n - k$ degrees of freedom (n = number of observations, k = period of the lag).

[7]The more formal hypothesis test is:

$$H_0: \rho_k = 0$$
$$H_1: \rho_k \neq 0$$

and the calculated t-ratio is:

$$t_{calc} = \frac{r_k - 0}{1/\sqrt{n - k}}$$

For example, for $k = 15$ where $r_k = 0.426$,

$$t_{calc} = \frac{0.426 - 0}{1/\sqrt{84 - 15}} = 3.539$$

which is greater than the table value of 1.96 at $\alpha/2 = 0.025$ (a 95 percent confidence level).

FIGURE 2–8

Autocorrelation Structure of GDP (c2f8)

```
                              Autocorrelations
                  Lag        . . . . . . . . . . . . . . . . .
                   0            1.000000
                   1             .971454
                   2             .941462
                   3             .911642
                   4             .880327
                   5             .849431
                   6             .818744
                   7             .788488
                   8             .758847
                   9             .730455
                  10             .703703
                  11             .677253
                  12             .651347
                  13             .626529
                  14             .602495
                  15             .578524
                  16             .555346
                  17             .532015
                  18             .508423
```

```
                  Plot of Autocorrelations (+) for GDP

       Lag   -1.0                          0.0                          1.0
             +----------------------------+----------------------------+
         1 |                              |    :    |                    +|
         2 |                              |    :    |                  +  |
         3 |                              |    :    |               +     |
         4 |                              |    :    |             +       |
         5 |                              |    :    |           +         |
         6 |                              |    :    |          +          |
         7 |                              |    :    |         +           |
         8 |                            |    :    |        +             |
         9 |                            |    :    |      +               |
        10 |                            |    :    |      +               |
        11 |                            |    :    |    +                 |
        12 |                            |    :    |   +                  |
        13 |                            |    :    |  +                   |
        14 |                            |    :    | +                    |
        15 |                            |    :    | +                    |
        16 |                            |    :    |+                     |
        17 |                            |    :    +                      |
        18 |                            |    :   +                       |
             +----------------------------+----------------------------+
```

vertical lines on either side of 0.0. Note that it becomes wider as the length of the lag increases because $n - k$ is used in the calculation of the standard error to account for the loss in degrees of freedom as k increases.

If we want to try a forecasting method for GDP that requires stationary data, we must first transform the GDP data to a stationary series. Often this can be done by using first differences. For GDP, the first differences can be calculated as:

$$\mathrm{DGDP}_t = \mathrm{GDP}_t - \mathrm{GDP}_{t-1}$$

FIGURE 2–9

Time-Series Plots of GDP and the First Difference in GDP
(c2f9)

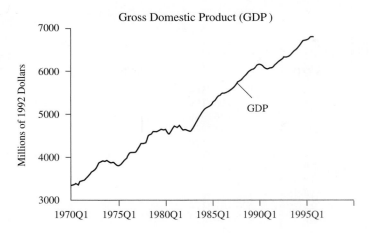

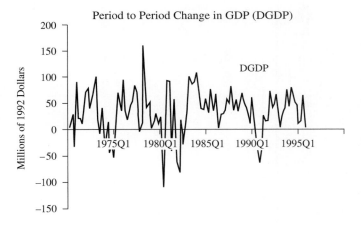

where $DGDP_t$ is the first difference (or change) in GDP. Figure 2–9 shows a plot of GDP in the left panel and DGDP in the right panel. The series in the right panel appears more stationary.

We can check for stationarity in DGDP by examining the autocorrelation structure for DGDP shown in Figure 2–10.

For 103 observations (one was lost in calculating DGDP), $2/\sqrt{n} = 2/\sqrt{103} = 0.197$. At the second-period lag, r_k has dropped below this ($0.165 < 0.197$), so we can conclude that for DGDP the autocorrelation coefficients do drop quickly toward zero. Note that after r_1, nearly all the autocorrelations are within the 95 percent confidence bounds. Thus, DGDP can be considered stationary, and forecasting methods requiring stationarity could be used to forecast DGDP. Once DGDP is forecast, the transformation can be reversed to forecast GDP.

Let us now look at the U.S. billings of Leo Burnett advertising. As illustrated in Figure 2–3, there is a strong positive trend to the LBB series. The first difference in LBB (defined as $DLBB_t = LBB_t - LBB_{t-1}$) also shows a positive trend. These

FIGURE 2–10

*Autocorrelation
Structure of
DGDP*
(c2f10)

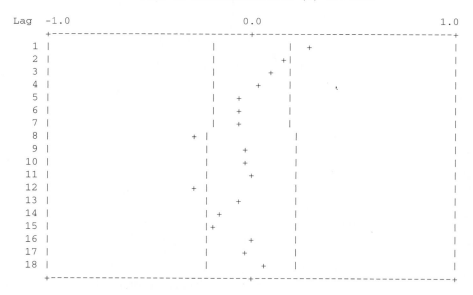

```
                              Autocorrelations for DGDP
              Lag      ................................
               0            1.000000
               1             .286229
               2             .164737
               3             .075561
               4             .034864
               5            -.066106
               6            -.080040
               7            -.082992
               8            -.271884
               9            -.033761
              10            -.020000
              11             .011887
              12            -.254416
              13            -.078372
              14            -.169182
              15            -.182729
              16            -.011845
              17            -.036684
              18             .058894
```

```
                   Plot of Autocorrelations (+) for DGDP

      Lag   -1.0                            0.0                          1.0
            +----------------------------------+----------------------------------+
         1  |                                  |             |  +                 |
         2  |                                  |          +  |                    |
         3  |                                  |        +    |                    |
         4  |                                  |       +     |                    |
         5  |                                  |   +         |                    |
         6  |                                  |   +         |                    |
         7  |                                  |   +         |                    |
         8  |                           +  |               |                    |
         9  |                                  |     +       |                    |
        10  |                                  |     +       |                    |
        11  |                                  |       +     |                    |
        12  |                           +  |               |                    |
        13  |                                  |    +        |                    |
        14  |                              |  +            |                    |
        15  |                              | +             |                    |
        16  |                                  |      +      |                    |
        17  |                                  |    +        |                    |
        18  |                                  |        +    |                    |
            +----------------------------------+----------------------------------+
```

trends can be confirmed by looking at the corresponding autocorrelation structures in Figure 2–11. For LBB, an $r_k > 0.295$ is significant ($n = 46$), while for DLBB, an $r_k > 0.298$ is significant ($n = 45$).

For LBB the autocorrelations are significant through r_9, and for DLBB five of the first eight r_s are significant. Thus, neither series is stationary.

In a case like this, we may do a further transformation to the second difference, that is, the difference in the first difference. In this case the second difference,

FIGURE 2–11

The Autocorrelation Structure of LBB, DLBB, and DDLBB

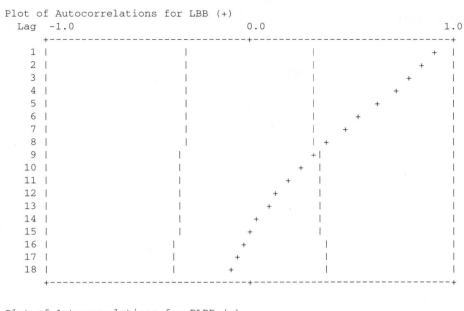

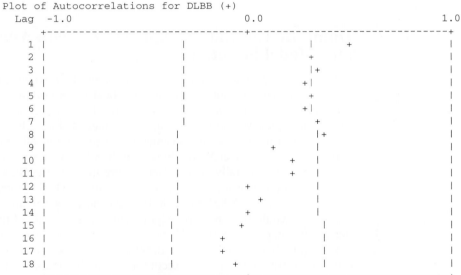

DDLBB, is:

$$DDLBB = DLBB_t - DLBB_{t-1}$$

The autocorrelation structure of DDLBB is shown in the lower panel of Figure 2–11. For DDLBB, an $r_k > 0.302$ ($n = 44$) is significant. In this case even $|r_1|$ is less than 0.302. Thus, we can conclude that DDLBB is stationary and could be forecast using methods that require stationarity.

FIGURE 2–11
(continued)

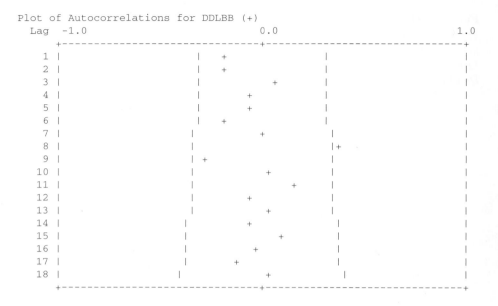

```
Plot of Autocorrelations for DDLBB (+)
 Lag  -1.0                              0.0                             1.0
      +---------------------------------+-----------------------------------+
   1  |                                 |   +               |               |
   2  |                                 |   +               |               |
   3  |                                 |        +          |               |
   4  |                                 |      +            |               |
   5  |                                 |      +            |               |
   6  |                                 |   +               |               |
   7  |                                 |          +        |               |
   8  |                                 |                   |+              |
   9  |                             |   +                   |               |
  10  |                                 |          +        |               |
  11  |                                 |             +     |               |
  12  |                                 |      +            |               |
  13  |                                 |          +        |               |
  14  |                                 |      +        |                   |
  15  |                                 |             +   |                 |
  16  |                                 |      +        |                   |
  17  |                                 |    +          |                   |
  18  |                             |        +          |                   |
      +---------------------------------+-----------------------------------+
```

Domestic Car Sales: Exploratory Data Analysis and Model Selection

Let us apply exploratory data analysis techniques to the domestic car sales data that were introduced in Chapter 1 and that will be used as a running example throughout the text. Figure 2–12 shows the raw data for domestic car sales (DCS) and a trend line. In this plot we see several things of interest. First, there appear to be fairly regular sharp up-and-down movements that may be a reflection of seasonality in domestic car sales. Second, the long-term trend of domestic car sales appears only slightly positive. Finally, it looks as if there may be a cyclical pattern around the long-term trend. The autocorrelation of structure of DCS is shown in Figure 2–13.

For $n = 64$ (1980Q1 through 1995Q4) an autocorrelation coefficient greater than 0.250 would be considered significant, using the rule of thumb described earlier in this chapter ($0.250 = 2/\sqrt{64}$). We see that the autocorrelations for DCS do not fall quickly to zero. For lags 1 through 5, the autocorrelation coefficients are significantly different from zero, except for r_2, which is 0.245. Thus, we have evidence of a significant, albeit modest, trend in DCS.

The DCS data can be de-trended by finding the first differences (i.e., the period-to-period changes in DCS). These differences are defined as $DDCS_t = DCS_t - DCS_{t-1}$. The autocorrelation structure of the differenced data, DDCS, is shown in Figure 2–13. Here the autocorrelation coefficient for the first lag is less than 0.252, indicating that it is not significantly different from zero ($0.252 = 2/\sqrt{63}$), and so we can conclude that there is no trend in DDCS. Notice that the autocorrelations for lags of 4 and 8 quarters are both significantly different from zero. This is indicative of a seasonal pattern to the data.

FIGURE 2–12

Domestic Car Sales and the Long-Term Trend in Thousands of Units (c2f12)

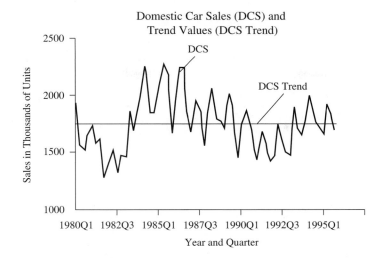

From this exploratory analysis of the domestic car sales data, we can conclude that there is trend, seasonality, and some cycle. From Table 2–1 we can, therefore, suggest the following as potential forecasting methods for retail car sales:

Winters' exponential smoothing
Regression trend with seasonality
Causal regression
Time-series decomposition
ARIMA

Business Forecasting: A Process Not an Application

Charles W. Chase, Jr.

Current literature and experience dictate that the best forecasting system provides easy access, review and modification of forecast results across all corporate disciplines; provides alternative modeling capabilities (multi-dimensional); includes the ability to create a knowledge base by which future forecasts can be refined; provides timely and accurate automated link/feed interfaces with other systems such as I.R.I (Information Resources Inc.)/Nielsen syndicated databases and the mainframe shipment database. The present industry trend has been redirected away from mainframe systems toward PC based software applications due to the lack of flexibility associated with mainframe access and reporting. Mainframes are being utilized primarily as storage bins for PC based systems to extract and store information.

Source: *Journal of Business Forecasting* 11, no. 3 (Fall 1992), pp. 12–13. Reprinted by permission.

FIGURE 2–13

Autocorrelation Structures for Domestic Car Sales (DCS) and the First Difference in Domestic Car Sales (DDCS)

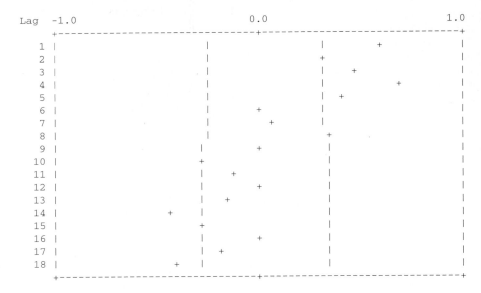

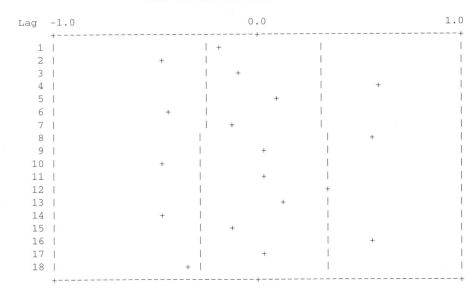

Note that ARIMA is included, since the data can be transformed to a stationary state, as was demonstrated. If the cycle component of this time series proves to be important, the regression trend with seasonality would probably be less accurate than some of the other methods listed.

INTEGRATIVE CASE
The Gap

Part 2: Data Analysis of The Gap Sales Data

The sales of Gap stores for the 44 quarters covering 1985 quarter 1 through 1995 quarter 4 are shown below.

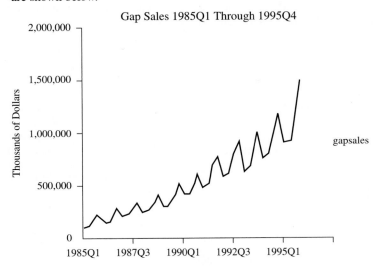

From this graph it is clear that Gap sales are seasonal and increasing over time (a positive trend). There does not appear to be a cycle.

Case Questions

1. In 1995 Gap sales by quarter were as given below:

Quarter	Gap Sales in Thousands of Dollars
1995Q1	848,688
1995Q2	868,514
1995Q3	1,155,930
1995Q4	1,522,120

Based on these data, calculate a 95 percent confidence interval for quarterly sales of The Gap.

2. Gap sales on an annual basis are shown below.

Year	Gap Sales (000)
1985	647,333
1986	848,009
1987	1,062,020
1988	1,252,100
1989	1,586,600
1990	1,933,780
1991	2,518,890
1992	2,960,410
1993	3,295,680
1994	3,722,940
1995	4,395,250

Plot these data in a time-series plot. Based on this graph, what pattern do you see in annual Gap sales?

3. Using data for 1985Q1 through 1995Q4, calculate the autocorrelation coefficients for quarterly Gap sales (the quarterly data were given in the Integrative Case for Chapter 1 and are in the *gapdata.sal* data file) using six lags, and construct the corresponding correlogram (plot of the autocorrelations) for lags of 1 through 6. What do the autocorrelation coefficients and the correlogram tell you about the series?

4. Calculate the first differences in quarterly Gap sales (call them DGAP), using data for 1985Q1 through 1995Q4, then calculate the autocorrelation coefficients for DGAP using six lags and construct the corresponding correlogram. What do the autocorrelation coefficients and the correlogram tell you about the DGAP series?

5. Based on the plot of Gap sales, on what you learned from questions 3 and 4, as well as the information in Table 2–1, what forecasting methods might you suggest if you were to forecast The Gap's quarterly sales?

Solutions to Case Questions

1. The 95 percent confidence interval is calculated as:

Mean of Gap Sales

$\pm$ *t*(Standard Deviation of Gap Sales $\div \sqrt{n}$)

In this case $n = 4$ and $df = n - 1$, so $df = 3$.

$$1,098,813 \pm 3.182(315,199 \div \sqrt{4})$$

$$1,098,813 \pm 501,481.6$$

$$597,331.4 \text{ to } 1,600,294.6$$

2. The plot of annual Gap sales shown below indicates that there is a positive trend to their sales over time.

3. The critical value of r_6 for an *n* of 44 (11 years of quarterly data) is 0.302. As you see from the autocorrelations and correlogram on the following page, the first six values for r_6 are all greater than the critical value at a 95 percent confidence level. Thus, we have further evidence of a trend in the Gap data.

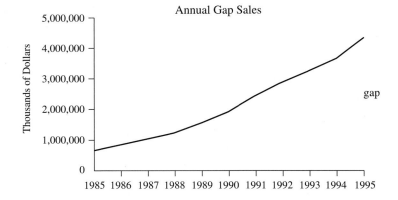

```
                    Lag    Autocorrelation
                    ----------------------
                     0     1.00000
                     1      .775806
                     2      .625026
                     3      .656997
                     4      .731502
                     5      .559541
                     6      .429422
```

```
Lag   -1.0                             0.0                             1.0
      +--------------------------------+--------------------------------+
   1 |                                |                        +       |
   2 |                                |                   +            |
   3 |                                |                 +              |
   4 |                                |                    +           |
   5 |                                |              +                 |
   6 |                                |        +                       |
      +--------------------------------+--------------------------------+
```

4. The critical value of r_6 for an n of 43 (one period was lost in calculating the first differences) is 0.305. As you see from the autocorrelations and correlogram below, the first six values for r_6—except for lags 2, 4, and 6—are all less than the critical value at a 95 percent confidence level. Thus we have evidence that there is no trend in the DGAP data.

```
                    Lag    Autocorrelation
                    ----------------------
                     0         1.0000
                     1         -.026091
                     2         -.618153
                     3         -.189381
                     4          .786694
                     5         -.016580
                     6         -.517047
```

```
Lag   -1.0                             0.0                             1.0
      +--------------------------------+--------------------------------+
   1 |                                |     +                          |
   2 |              +                 |                                |
   3 |                                |   +                            |
   4 |                                |                        +       |
   5 |                                |     +                          |
   6 |            +                   |                                |
      +--------------------------------+--------------------------------+
```

The high absolute values for the autocorrelations at lags of 2, 4, and 6 are indicative of the seasonal pattern in which sales are negatively correlated with sales two (or six) periods earlier but are positively correlated with sales four periods earlier.

5. Based on the plot of The Gap's quarterly sales, as well as the data analysis from questions 3 and 4, the following forecasting methods might be suggested from the information in Table 2–1:

> Winters' exponential smoothing
> Regression trend with seasonality
> Causal regression
> Time-series decomposition
> ARIMA (if the series is transformed to stationarity and deseasonalized)

USING SORITEC FOR EXPLORATORY DATA ANALYSIS AND BASIC STATISTICS

In this section we will show you how you can use SORITEC to analyze data using the techniques covered in this chapter. In addition we will discuss data entry within SORITEC and the use of data that may be in some other type of file (such as a spreadsheet or word processing file).

Integrating SORITEC with a Word Processor

Before we begin, however, let us address an issue related to making statistical software user-friendly in terms of incorporating the results into some type of report. It is a good idea to have your word processor running at the same time as the statistical software so that you can move easily between the programs. Suppose that you have SORITEC and your word processor both running. One way (there are others) to move between them is to hold down the (**Alt**) key while you press the (**Tab**) key. With each press of the (**Tab**) key you cycle to another open program that is indicated by a box in the middle of your screen. When the name of the program you want appears in the box, let up on both keys and you'll jump right into that program. When you want to leave that program to go back to the other, just repeat the process. This will work in both Windows 3.x and Windows 95/NT.

Suppose you have a time-series plot on-screen in SORITEC that you would like to have in your word processing document. Just click on the **Copy** button 📋, then using the (**Alt/Tab**) keys, move to the word processing document and paste the graphic where you want it. Use (**Alt/Tab**) again to go back to SORITEC. The text of statistical output can be highlighted in SORITEC, copied, and then pasted into a word processing document in a similar manner.

However, SORITEC makes another useful option available to you. You can create a log of all of your work in a session that is saved as a text (ASCII) file, which can then be read by any word processor. The process is simple. Pull down the drop-down menu from **FILE** on the main toolbar in SORITEC and click on the word **LOG.** A check mark will go next to **LOG** and from then on all the statistical results you generate will be kept in a file named *soritec.log* until you click on **LOG** again to remove the check. The *soritec.log* file will be found in the directory in which SORITEC is found. When you quit the SORITEC session this file will be closed and can then be inserted into, or opened by, a word processor. The following screen shot illustrates how this log file is initiated.

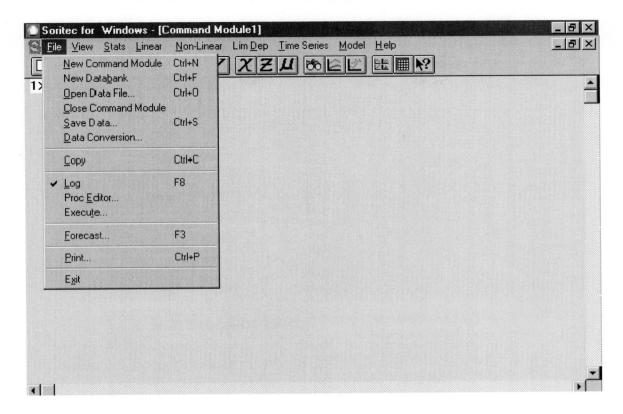

Entering Data into SORITEC

SORITEC provides a spreadsheet-type data tool to facilitate keyboard entry of data series. It facilitates data entry and display of as many as 59 series (variables) with up to 499 elements (observations). Access the spreadsheet data entry tool either by selecting **Data Tool** from the **View** menu, or by clicking on the ▦ button on the toolbar. To enter data:

1. Enter the date and time of the first observation in the first column, second row (the column labeled Date), in one of the SORITEC date formats (see the **USE** command below).
2. If you desire, SORITEC will fill in a complete date series in the Date column:
   a. With the mouse, select the date you entered in column 1, row 2;
   b. Hold down the left mouse button, and drag down to highlight the cells to hold the dates;
   c. Click on the **Fill** button and SORITEC will fill the selected cells with sequential dates/times.
3. Enter the names of the variables in the first row, starting with the second column (labeled Series 1) and continuing for as many data series as you want to enter.
4. In the column below each variable name, enter the data for that variable.
5. When the data are entered and the data entry tool looks something like the one that follows, click on **Update** to enter the data into the workspace.

Data Entry and Editing				
	Date	Series1	Series2	Series3
1			xvar1	xvar2
2	1985q1		23.4001	31.7563
3	1985q2		23.9382	32.4865
4	1985q3		24.4888	33.2338
5	1985q4		25.0520	33.9981
6	1986q1		25.6282	34.7800
7	1986q2		26.2176	35.5799
8	1986q3		26.8206	36.3982
9	1986q4		27.4375	37.2354
10	1987q1		28.0686	38.0919
11	1987q2		28.7142	38.9680
12	1987q3		29.3746	39.8643
13	1987q4		30.0502	40.7811
14	1988q1		30.7414	41.7192
15	1988q2		31.4485	42.6788
16	1988q3		32.1718	43.6603
17	1988q4		32.9118	44.6646
18	1989q1		33.6688	45.6919
19	1989q2		34.4432	46.7429
20	1989q3		35.2354	47.8180
21				
22				

[Update] [Cancel] [Display...] [Calc] [Fill]

Note 1: When you enter data or use the date fill facility in the spreadsheet tool, the **use** period will be updated, and the line counter in the prompt will skip one or two numbers; this is normal.

Note 2: SORITEC will determine the number of observations in the data entry by the number of consecutive nonblank entries for the first data series or consecutive date entries, whichever is greater.

Any nonnumerical entry (including a blank) will be treated as a missing value.

The USE Command.   SORITEC has a time-series data management focus, and sample selection is controlled by establishing the date and time reference for active observations through the **USE** command. Cross-sectional or undated data are controlled simply by assigning sequential numbers to the data entries.

The **USE** command determines which observations are active in analytic, transformation, data entry, and file management operations. It must be set prior to most SORITEC operations that involve data series.

The basic syntax is

```
use datetime1 datetime2
```

where *datetimei* refers to a time and date construct. The time and date syntax for SORITEC is given in the table below. Except for some forecasting activities that are automated, the **use** period must be set from the command line.

Use Period Designators

Example	Periodicity
Any positive integer	Undated (cross-sectional) data or data whose periodicity is not explicitly covered
1996	Annual data
1996s1	Semiannual data
1996q1	Quarterly data
1996m1	Monthly data
1996t1	Ten-day data
1996w1	Weekly data
1996d001, or 1996d0101	Daily data. In the first form, Julian dates can be entered; the leading zeros are optional; the second form is month, then day
1996b001, or 1996b0101	Business daily data. In the first form, Julian dates can be entered; the leading zeros are optional; the second form is month, then day
19960101h00	Hourly data; the sequence is year, month, day, the "h" designator, and the hour, on a 24-hour basis starting with midnight (00)

The **use** period can be set with gaps. For example, the command

```
use 1980 1983 1985 1996
```

selects 1980 to 1983 and 1985 to 1996, but omits 1984. Some commands dealing with dynamic calculations will not work with gaps in the **use** period.

Examining Data with the Data Tool.   To examine data using the tool:

1. Set the **use** period to cover the data to be reviewed.
2. Click on the toolbar or menu to invoke the data tool.
3. Click on the **Display** button to select series for display according to the current **use** period.
4. Select the desired series from the **Variables Selection** dialog box, and then click on **OK.**

SORITEC will display the selected data series, provided the periodicity of the selected series matches the periodicity of the **use** period.

   If you have only a small amount of data in the workspace, you can direct SORITEC to load it automatically when the data tool is invoked. Type the command **AUTOLOAD** from the command line to enable this feature. To turn it off, type the command **NOAUTO.**

Copying Data from a Spreadsheet into SORITEC.   You can use the Windows clipboard to copy data from a spreadsheet program to SORITEC:

1. Array the data in the spreadsheet in "flat file" form (variables in consecutive columns, observations in consecutive rows).
   a. If you include variable labels, make sure they are the first entry in each data column.
   b. If you include SORITEC-style date and time labels, make sure they are in the first column.
2. Highlight the data you want to transfer to SORITEC, and copy them to the clipboard.

3. Activate the SORITEC spreadsheet tool.
4. Select the upper left cell of the area in the SORITEC data tool where you want to paste the data.
    a. If the copied information includes only numerical data, select the cell at the intersection of the second row and second column.
    b. If variable labels are included, select the first row.
    c. If dates are included, select the first column.
5. Paste the data into SORITEC.
    a. Click the right mouse button in the spreadsheet tool.
    b. Select **Paste** from the floating menu (or press <**Control+v**> on the keyboard).
6. If the data do not include variable labels, enter the name of each variable above its column.
7. If the data do not include dates, enter the dates for the data in column 1.
    a. Put the date of the first observation in row 2 (the first observation on the data).
    b. Drag the mouse to highlight the desired date entries.
    c. Click on **Fill**.
8. Click on **Update** to bring the data into the workspace.

Reading ASCII Files.   SORITEC data files are called *SAL files;* they have a *.sal* extension and are ASCII files. These can contain data only or can contain both data and two associated commands. When SORITEC reads an ASCII file, it loads the data into named data series in the workspace. Therefore, it needs to have two pieces of information:

The name of the data series

The period and periodicity (**use** period) of the data series

The data file itself can contain **use** statements that set the period and periodicity of the data and **read** statements that identify the variable names. For example, a SAL file may be set up like this (upper- or lowercase or a mix may be used):

```
Use 1989m1 1990m3
read x
7.4 7.4 7.4 7.5 7.4 7.3 7.3 7.4 7.5
7.6 7.6 7.7 7.8 7.9 8.0;
use 850101h12 850102H01
READ y
4 3 6 6 7 8 8 10 11 9 9 8 7 7;
end
```

The **use** statements establish the period and periodicity of the data. The first indicates 15 monthly observations starting in January 1989 for the variable named x, and the second indicates 14 hourly observations for y starting at 1200 (12:00 p.m.) on January 1, 1985.[8]
    The **read** statements give the names by which the data that follow are to be known in the workspace (x and y in our example). If the number of items in the data stream does not match exactly the number implied by the **use** statement, SORITEC aborts the process.
    When a data file is in the SAL format, it can be read into the workspace with a **READ** command that only identifies the file. The command line syntax is

```
read ('<path><name.ext>')
```

---

[8]SORITEC syntax is based on a 24-hour clock.

where *<path>* is the path needed to locate the file if it is not in the same directory as the SORITEC for Windows program, and *<name.ext>* is the complete file name, including the extension. SAL files can also be input with the **File | Open Data File** menu option from the main toolbar.

Reading "Flat Files."   Data often come in the "flat-file" format, where each row contains an observation on the variables in the file, and each column contains the data on a given variable. There are often no entries in the file other than the data. Flat files can be produced, for example, by saving data from a spreadsheet or word processor in text (ASCII) format. The following illustrates a "flat-file" format:

1	2	3	4	5
6	7	8	9	10
11	12	13	14	15
16	17	18	19	20
21	22	23	24	193

To read data in flat-file format, you must set the **use** period and include the variable list in the **read** statement. The syntax of the **read** statement for a flat file is

```
read ('<path><name.ext>') var1 var2 ...
```

where *<path>* identifies the complete path to the directory where the file is located, *<name.ext>* is the complete file name (including extension), and *var1, var2,* etc., is the list of variable names to associate with the data. Note that the list of variables in the **read** statement must be in the same sequence as the variables (columns) that appear in the flat file. For example,

```
use 1995q1 1996q1
read ('data.sal') v1 v2 v3 v4 v5
```

will read the file illustrated above, provided it is named *data.sal* and located in the default directory. Five variables will be created, named *v1* through *v5*. Extensions other than *.sal* may be used, such as *.txt,* but the file must be an ASCII (text) file.

Flat files can also include a **USE** command to tell SORITEC how many observations are coming and what periods to assign them to, and a **read** statement giving the variable list.

Reading SAL Files Using the File Menu.   Reading ASCII files in the SAL format is a four-step process.

1. Open the **File** menu and click on **Open** (or click on the 📂 icon on the toolbar).
2. If the file has a *.sal* extension, select **.sal* as the file type; otherwise, select **.**.
3. Select the directory (if necessary).
4. Select the file you want to read from the list of available files.

This is the equivalent of issuing the **READ** command from the command line. To use the menu, however, the file must be in the SAL format, which means it must as a minimum contain a **read** statement complete with the list of variables (the **USE** command can be issued from the command line, so long as the first line on the file contains the **read** statement listing the variable names).

Saving ASCII Data in SAL-File Format

To write a self-documenting file that can be imported directly into most spreadsheets or back into SORITEC:

1. Make sure the data you want to save to the file are in the workspace.
2. Set the **Use** period to cover the period of the data you want to save.
3. Open the **File** menu and select **Save Data.**
4. When the **Variable Save List** dialog box appears,
   a. Select the variable you want written to file,
   b. Check the **Include USE** box if you want the **Use** command written to an ASCII file (SORITEC will automatically put the **Read** statement at the head of an ASCII file, as a record of the variables in the file),
   c. Enter the desired file name.
5. Click on **OK.**
6. When the SORITEC **Data File** dialog box appears, select a name and path for the file, and click on **OK** to complete the process and save the file.

Calculating Statistics

You can calculate a wide variety of statistics on your data using SORITEC. The following screen shot shows the basic path to obtaining the statistics you desire.

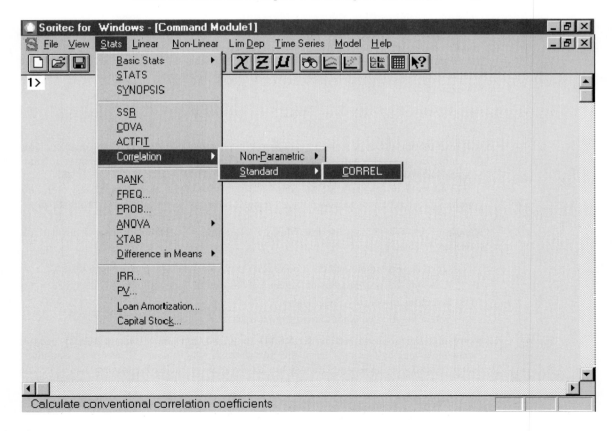

The STATS Selection (Stats Menu). The **stats** selection calculates and displays the mean(s) and standard deviation(s) of one or more data series.

Once you have data in the workspace,

1. Open the **Variables Selection** dialog box by clicking on the χ toolbar button.
2. Select the variable(s) for which you want the means and standard deviations computed.
3. Open the **Stats** menu, and select **STATS.**

SORITEC will respond with a table of the means and standard deviations of the selected variable(s).

The same result can be obtained from the command line by typing:

```
stats series1 series2 ...
```

where *series1* and *series2* are the variables being analyzed.

The Synopsis Selection (Stats Menu). Synopsis produces a detailed summary of a data series, including mean, standard deviation, median, mode, quartiles, deciles, variance, skewness, kurtosis, coefficient of variation, number of observations, number of missing values, minimum, maximum, range, mode, and the frequency of the mode.

Assuming that you have data in the workspace, you use Synopsis as follows:

1. Open the **Variables Selection** dialog box by clicking on the χ toolbar button.
2. Select the variable(s) for which you want the detailed summary computed.
3. Open the **Stats** menu, and select **SYNOPSIS.**

SORITEC will respond by presenting a table of the statistical results.

This can also be done from the command line by typing:

```
synopsis series1 series2 ...
```

where *series1* and *series2* are variables being analyzed.

The CORREL Selection (Stats menu | Correlation | Standard | Correl). This calculates the Pearson correlation matrix for two or more data series.

1. Open the **Variables Selection** dialog box by clicking on the χ toolbar button.
2. Select the variable(s) for which you want the correlation matrix computed.
3. Select the **Stats | Correlation | Standard | CORREL.**

SORITEC will display a correlation matrix for the selected variables. Alternatively, from the command line type:

```
correl series1 series2 ...
```

where *series1 series2 ...* are the variables for which the correlation matrix is being calculated.

Scatter Plots

The following describes the process used to produce a scatter Plot.

1. Initiate the process by clicking on **View** then the **Graphics** Window and then on 🖼 toolbar button.
2. When the SORITEC **Scatter Plot** dialog box (see below) appears,
   a. Select the variable to scale the X-axis (in effect, the variable against which all other variables are plotted) in the **Abscissa (X Axis) Variable** drop-down selection box;

    b. Select the variables to plot from the list of active variables (limit: 10 variables) from the **Ordinate (Y Axis)** list box;

    c. Enter the main title for the graph in the **Title** edit box (optional);

    d. Enter the text label for the horizontal axis in the **X-Axis Label** edit box (optional) (SORITEC automatically places numerical labels on the tic marks of the horizontal axis);

    e. Enter the text label for the vertical axis in the **Y-Axis Label** edit box (optional) (SORITEC will automatically put numerical labels on the vertical axis tic marks);

    f. If you want to leave the Y=0 origin out of the graph, do not check the **Show Y = 0 Origin** box;

    g. If you want to leave the X=0 origin out of the graph, do not check the **Show X = 0 Origin** box.

3. Click on **OK** to draw the graph.

The default is for SORITEC not to force the graph to show the 0,0 origin in the plot. If you override the default by checking one or both of the controlling check boxes, you may see less detail in the plot but will include the origin.

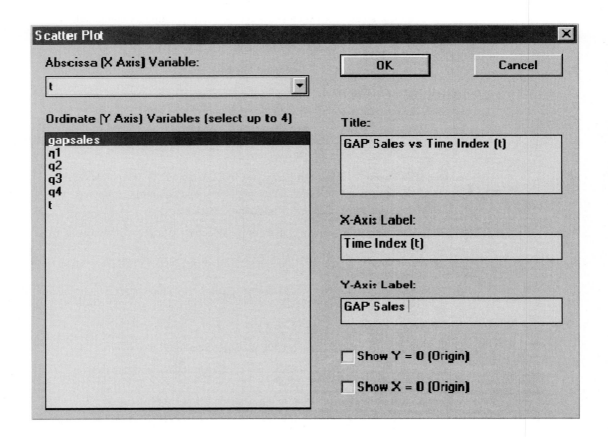

Creating a Time Index (t)

To create a time index named t that starts at 1 for the first time period in the current **Use** period and increments by one for each successive period, type the following on the command line:

```
TIME t
```

then press (**Enter**).

Developing Correlograms

Begin by turning on the plot flag by typing ON PLOT on the command line.

The calculation of autocorrelation coefficients and the plotting of the corresponding correlogram is most easily done by selecting **Time Series** from the main toolbar, then **Examine Autocorrelations.**

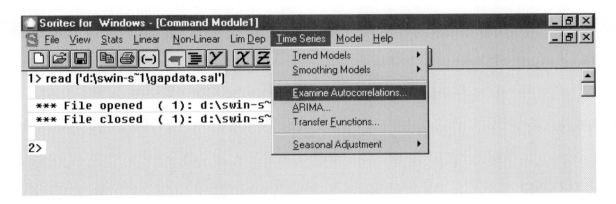

If a variable for analysis has not been selected, you will be prompted to make a selection. Select the number of lags you want to use (the autocorrelation order) and click on **OK.**

Doing Calculations in SORITEC

On any command line you can type in an algebraic statement to do virtually any data transformations. You can add (or subtract) variables, you can multiply (or divide) variables, you can convert variables to their logarithmic form, and so on. The following examples illustrate how to perform such operations. In each case the variable to the left of the equal sign is a new variable determined by the calculation, while the variables to the right of the equal sign are existing variables in the workspace.

1> Y1 = X1 + X2 − X3	Addition and Subtraction
2> Y2 = X1 ∗ X2	Multiplication
3> Y3 = X1/X2	Division
4> Y4 = X1∗∗2	Raising to a Power
5> Y5 = sqrt(X1)	Square Root
6> Y6 = LOG(X1)	Natural Log (Use LOG10 for Common Log)
7> Y7 = EXP(X1)	Exponentiation
8> Y8 = X2(−1)	Makes Y8 equal to the value of X2 one period earlier.

These examples are not exhaustive but cover all of the needed calculations for this course.

Suggested Readings

Aghazadeh, Seyed-Mahmoud; and Jane B. Romal. "A Directory of 66 Packages for Forecasting and Statistical Analyses." *Journal of Business Forecasting* 11, no. 2 (Summer 1992), pp. 14–20.

Bowerman, Bruce L.; and Richard T. O'Connell. *Applied Statistics: Improving Business Processes.* Chicago: Richard D. Irwin, 1997. (Especially chapters 5 and 7.)

Drumm, William J. "Living with Forecast Error." *Journal of Business Forecasting* 11, no. 2 (Summer 1992), p. 23.

Ermer, Charles M. "Cost of Error Affects the Forecasting Model Selection." *Journal of Business Forecasting* 10, no. 1 (Spring 1991), pp. 10–11.

Huff, Darrell. *How to Lie with Statistics.* New York: W. W. Norton, 1954.

Makridakis, Spyros. "Forecasting: Its Role and Value for Planning and Strategy." *International Journal of Forecasting* 12, no. 4 (December 1996), pp. 513–37.

Mentzer, John T.; and Kenneth B. Kahn. "Forecasting Technique Familiarity, Satisfaction, Usage, and Application." *Journal of Forecasting* 14, no. 5 (September 1995), pp. 465–76.

———. "State of Sales Forecasting Systems in Corporate America." *Journal of Business Forecasting* 16, no. 1 (Spring 1997), pp. 6–13.

O'Clock, George; and Priscilla M. O'Clock. "Political Realities of Forecasting." *Journal of Business Forecasting* 8, no. 1 (Spring 1989), pp. 2–6.

Tufte, Edward R. *Invisioning Information.* Cheshire, Conn.: Graphics Press, 1990.

———. *The Visual Display of Quantitative Information.* Cheshire, Conn.: Graphics Press, 1983.

Winklhofer, Heidi; Adamantios Diamantopoulos; and Stephen F. Witt. "Forecasting Practice: A Review of the Empirical Literature and an Agenda for Future Research." *International Journal of Forecasting* 12, no. 2 (June 1996), pp. 193–221.

Exercises

1. The mean volume of sales for a sample of 100 sales representatives is $25,350 per month. The sample standard deviation is $7,490. The vice president for sales would like to know whether this result is significantly different from $24,000 at a 95 percent confidence level. Set up the appropriate null and alternative hypotheses and perform the appropriate statistical test.

2. Larry Bomser has been asked to evaluate sizes of tire inventories for retail outlets of a major tire manufacturer. From a sample of 120 stores he has found a mean of 310 tires. The industry average is 325. If the standard deviation for the sample was 72, would you say that the inventory level maintained by this manufacturer is significantly different from the industry norm? Explain why. (Use a 95 percent confidence level.)

3. Twenty graduate students in business were asked how many credit hours they were taking in the current quarter. Their responses are shown as follows:

Student Number	Credit Hours	Student Number	Credit Hours	Student Number	Credit Hours
1	2	8	8	15	10
2	7	9	12	16	6
3	9	10	11	17	9
4	9	11	6	18	6
5	8	12	5	19	9
6	11	13	9	20	10
7	6	14	13		

(c2p3)

a. Determine the mean, median, and mode for this sample of data. Write a sentence explaining what each means.

b. It has been suggested that graduate students in business take fewer credits per quarter than the typical graduate student at this university. The mean for all graduate students is 9.1 credit hours per quarter, and the data are normally distributed.

Set up the appropriate null and alternative hypotheses and determine whether the null hypothesis can be rejected at a 95 percent confidence level.

4. Arbon Computer Corporation (ACC) produces a popular PC clone. The sales manager for ACC has recently read a report that indicated that sales per sales representative for other producers are normally distributed with a mean of $255,000. She is interested in knowing whether her sales staff is comparable. She picked a random sample of 16 salespeople and obtained the following results:

(c2p4)

Person	Sales	Person	Sales
1	$177,406	9	$110,027
2	339,753	10	182,577
3	310,170	11	177,707
4	175,520	12	154,096
5	293,332	13	236,083
6	323,175	14	301,051
7	144,031	15	158,792
8	279,670	16	140,891

At a 5 percent significance level, can you reject the null hypothesis that ACC's mean sales per salesperson was $255,000? Draw a diagram that illustrates your answer.

5. Assume that the weights of college football players are normally distributed with a mean of 205 pounds and a standard deviation of 30.
   a. What percent of players would have weights greater than 205 pounds?
   b. What percent of players would weigh less than 250 pounds?
   c. Ninety percent of players would weigh more than what number of pounds?
   d. What percent of players would weigh between 180 and 230 pounds?

6. Mutual Savings Bank of Appleton has done a market research survey in which people were asked to rate their image of the bank on a scale of 1 to 10, with 10 being the most favorable. The mean response for the sample of 400 people was 7.25, with a standard deviation of 2.51. On this same question a state association of mutual savings banks has found a mean of 7.01.

a. Clara Wharton, marketing director for the bank, would like to test to see whether the rating for her bank is significantly greater than the norm of 7.01. Perform the appropriate hypothesis test for a 95 percent confidence level.
b. Draw a diagram to illustrate your result.
c. How would your result be affected if the sample size had been 100 rather than 400, with everything else being the same?

7. In a sample of 25 classes, the following numbers of students were observed:

(c2p7)

40	50	42	20	29
39	49	46	52	45
51	64	43	37	35
44	10	40	36	20
20	29	58	51	54

a. Calculate the mean, median, standard deviation, variance, and range for this sample.
b. What is the standard error of the mean based on this information?
c. What would be the best point estimate for the population class size?
d. What is the 95 percent confidence interval for class size? What is the 90 percent confidence interval? Does the difference between these two make sense?

8. CoastCo Insurance, Inc., is interested in forecasting annual larceny thefts in the United States using the following data:

(c2p8)

Year	Larceny Thefts*	Year	Larceny Thefts*	Year	Larceny Thefts*
1972	4,151	1980	7,137	1988	7,706
1973	4,348	1981	7,194	1989	7,872
1974	5,263	1982	7,143	1990	7,946
1975	5,978	1983	6,713	1991	8,142
1976	6,271	1984	6,592	1992	7,915
1977	5,906	1985	6,926	1993	7,821
1978	5,983	1986	7,257	1994	7,876
1979	6,578	1987	7,500		

*Data are in thousands.
SOURCE: U.S. Bureau of the Census, at www.census.gov.

a. Prepare a time-series plot of these data. On the basis of this graph, do you think there is a trend in the data? Explain.

b. Look at the autocorrelation structure of larceny thefts for lags of 1, 2, 3, 4, and 5. Do the autocorrelation coefficients fall quickly toward zero? Demonstrate that the critical value for r_k is 0.471. Explain what these results tell you about a trend in the data.

c. On the basis of what is found in parts *a* and *b*, suggest a forecasting method from Table 2–1 that you think might be appropriate for this series.

9. Use exploratory data analysis to determine whether there is a trend and/or seasonality in mobile home shipments (MHS). The data by quarter are shown in the following table (note: these data can also be obtained from the ECONDATA database):

(c2p9)

		Quarter		
Year	Q1	Q2	Q3	Q4
1981	54.9	70.1	65.8	50.2
1982	53.3	67.9	63.1	55.3
1983	63.3	81.5	81.7	69.2
1984	67.8	82.7	79.0	66.2
1985	62.3	79.3	76.5	65.5
1986	58.1	66.8	63.4	56.1
1987	51.9	62.8	64.7	53.5
1988	47.0	60.5	59.2	51.6
1989	48.1	55.1	50.3	44.5
1990	43.3	51.7	50.5	42.6
1991	35.4	47.4	47.2	40.9
1992	43.0	52.8	57.0	57.6
1993	56.4	64.3	67.1	66.4
1994	69.1	78.7	78.7	77.5
1995	79.2	86.8	87.6	86.4

Data are in thousands.

On the basis of your analysis, do you think there is a significant trend in MHS? Is there seasonality? What forecasting methods might be appropriate for MHS according to the guidelines in Table 2–1?

10. Housing starts are often considered an important determinant of the future health of the economy. Thus, there is widespread interest in being able to forecast private housing starts (PHS). Data for PHS are available in the ECONDATA database on a monthly basis; you can access them and convert them to quarterly data using SORITEC. The converted quarterly data are shown in the following table in thousands of units:

(c2p10)

		Quarter		
Year	Q1	Q2	Q3	Q4
1981	166.5	229.9	184.8	124.1
1982	113.6	178.2	186.7	184.1
1983	202.9	322.3	307.5	234.8
1984	236.5	332.6	280.3	234.7
1985	215.3	317.9	295.0	244.1
1986	234.1	369.4	325.4	250.6
1987	241.4	346.5	321.3	237.1
1988	219.7	323.7	293.4	244.6
1989	212.7	302.1	272.1	216.5
1990	217.0	271.3	233.0	173.6
1991	146.7	254.1	239.8	199.8
1992	218.5	296.4	276.4	238.8
1993	213.2	323.7	309.3	279.4
1994	252.6	354.2	325.7	265.9
1995	214.2	296.7	308.2	257.2

Data are in thousands.

a. Prepare a time-series plot of PHS. Describe what you see in this plot in terms of trend and seasonality.

b. Calculate and plot the first eight autocorrelation coefficients for PHS. What does this autocorrelation structure suggest about trend and seasonality?

c. De-trend the data by calculating first differences:

$$DPHS_t = PHS_t - PHS_{t-1}$$

Calculate and plot the first eight autocorrelation coefficients for DPHS. Is there a trend in DPHS? Do the values of r_4 and r_8 suggest seasonality? Explain.

11. Problem 9 of Chapter 1 includes data on the Japanese exchange rate (EXRJ) by month. On the basis of a time-series plot of these data and the autocorrelation structure of EXRJ, would you say the data are stationary? Explain your answer. (c2p11)

APPENDIX 2.1
DATA AVAILABLE IN ECONDATA.SDB

	ECONDATA Name	Periodicity*	Units	Description[†]
1	FM1	M	$Billions	Money supply: M1 (SA)
2	FZM1	M	$Billions	Money supply: M1
3	FM1	M	$Billions	Money supply: M2 (SA)
4	FZMS1	M	$Billions	Money supply: M2
5	FYFF	M	%	Federal funds rate
6	FYPR	M	%	Prime rate
7	FYCM	M	%	Conventional mortgage rate—fixed
8	FY20M	M	%	20 municipal bonds—average rate
9	FWAFIT	M	%	Weighted average foreign interest rate (SA)
10	EXRJAN	M	Yen/US$	Exchange rate—Japan
11	EXRGER	M	Mark/US$	Exchange rate—Germany
12	FYMCLE	M	%	Conventional mortgage rate—loans closed
13	CCIOT	M	$Millions	Consumer installment credit (SA)
14	CCIPY	M	Ratio	Ratio consumer installment credit to personal income (SA)
15	FSNCOM	M	12/31/65 = 50	N.Y. Stock Exchange composite
16	FSPCOM	M	1941–1943 = 10	S&P's 500 composite
17	FSDJ	M	Average price	Dow Jones 30 industrials
18	FB	M	$Billions	Federal surplus or deficit (−)
19	FBD	M	$Billions	Gross federal debt outstanding
20	HHSNTR	M	Feb. 1966 = 100	University of Michigan Index of Consumer Sentiment
21	HS6P1	M	1000	Private housing starts—single units
22	HZNS	M	1000	New houses sold—single-family
23	HNMP	M	$1000	Median sales price—new homes—single-family
24	HEMP	M	$1000	Median sales price—existing homes—single-family
25	HMOB6	M	1000	Mobile home shipments
26	RTRR	M	$Millions	Retail sales—current dollars (SA)
27	RTR82	M	$Millions	Retail sales—1982 dollars (SA)
28	RT525R	M	$Millions	Hardware store sales (SA)
29	RT566R	M	$Millions	Shoe store sales (SA)
30	RCAR6T	M	1000	Total car sales
31	RCAR6D	M	1000	Domestic car sales
32	RCAR6F	M	1000	Foreign car sales
33	IOVRAT	M	$/car	Average expenditure/car—total
34	IOVRAD	M	$/car	Average expenditure/car—domestic
35	IOVRAF	M	$/car	Average expenditure/car—foreign
36	RZTRU	M	Units	Retail truck sales
37	PZUNEW	N	82–84 = 100	CPI—all items—urban consumers
38	PZU812	M	82–84 = 100	CPI—food at home—urban consumers
39	PZU19	M	82–84 = 100	CPI—food not at home—urban consumers
40	PZU211	M	82–84 = 100	CPI—residential rent—urban consumers

*Most data in ECONDATA are current through the end of 1996. Historic data varies according to when each series began to be recorded. Most series go back at least to 1970 and many go back into the 1950s.

[†]Not seasonally adjusted unless indicated. SA indicates data that have been seasonally adjusted. SAAR indicates data that are reported at a seasonally adjusted annual rate.

	ECONDATA *Name*	*Periodicity**	*Units*	*Description*[†]
41	PZUHSC	M	12/82 = 100	CPI—homeowners' cost—urban consumers
42	PZU45	M	82–84 = 100	CPI—new cars—urban consumers
43	PZU46	M	82–84 = 100	CPI—used cars—urban consumers
44	PZU471	M	82–84 = 100	CPI—gasoline—urban consumers
45	PZU53	M	82–84 = 100	CPI—public transportation—urban consumers
46	PZU63	M	82–84 = 100	CPI—tobacco products—urban consumers
47	PZU671	M	82–84 = 100	CPI—college tuition—urban consumers
48	PZUP82	M	82–84 = 100	CPI—Purchasing power of the dollar
49	PCGOLD	M	$/oz.	Gold price (London noon fix): average of daily rate
50	POP	M	1000	Population—including armed forces overseas
51	PM20	M	1000	Civilian noninstitutional population—male 20+
52	PF20	M	1000	Civilian noninstitutional population—female 20+
53	LHUR	M	%	Unemployment rate (SA)
54	LHEMPA	M	Ratio	Ratio civilian employment to total working-age population (SA)
55	LEW	M	$	Gross average weekly earnings: current $ (SA)
56	LUINC	M	1000	Initial unemployment claims (SA)
57	GMPY	M	$Billions	Personal income—current dollars (SAAR)
58	GMPYQ	M	$Billions	Personal income—1992 dollars (SAAR)
59	GMYDPC	M	$	Disposable personal income/capita—current dollars
60	GMYDPQ	M	$	Disposable personal income/capita—1992 dollars
61	DLEAD	M	1987 = 100	Index of 11 leading indicators (SA)
62	DCOINC	M	1987 = 100	Index of 4 coincident indicators (SA)
63	EEGP	M	¢/gal.	Gas price: U.S. city average—all types of gas
64	EEPSG	M	1000 barrels/day	Finished motor gasoline produced
65	RT554R	M	$Millions	Retail trade: gas and service stations (SA)
66	GMCNG	M	$Billions	Personal consumption expenditure: gas and oil—current $—(SAAR)
67	GMCNGQ	M	$Billions	Personal consumption expenditure: gas and oil—1992 $—(SAAR)
68	IP	M	87 = 100	Index of industrial production—U.S.
69	IPOECD	M	87 = 100	Index of industrial production—OECD (SA)
70	IPJP	M	87 = 100	Index of industrial production—Japan (SA)
71	IPWG	M	87 = 100	Index of industrial production—West Germany (SA)
72	IPFR	M	87 = 100	Index of industrial production—France (SA)
73	IPUK	M	87 = 100	Index of industrial production—U.K. (SA)
74	IPCAN	M	87 = 100	Index of industrial production—Canada (SA)
75	PC6JP	M	82–84 = 100	Index of consumer prices—Japan
76	PC6WG	M	82–84 = 100	Index of consumer prices—West Germany
77	PC6FR	M	82–84 = 100	Index of consumer prices—France
78	PC6UK	M	82–84 = 100	Index of consumer prices—U.K.
79	PC6CA	M	82–84 = 100	Index of consumer prices—Canada
80	FMD14	Q	$Millions	Outstanding mortgage debt: 1–4 family
81	IXIQ	Q	$Billions	Expenditures on new plant (&) equipment: 87$—(SAAR)
82	GDP	Q	$Billions	Gross domestic product: current $—(SAAR)
83	GDPQ	Q	$Billions	Gross domestic product: 1992 $—(SAAR)
84	GC	Q	$Billions	Personal consumption expenditure: current $—(SAAR)
85	GCQ	Q	$Billions	Personal consumption expenditure: 1992 $—(SAAR)
86	GPI	Q	$Billions	Gross private domestic investment: current $—(SAAR)
87	GPIQ	Q	$Billions	Gross private domestic investment: 1992 $—(SAAR)
88	GNET	Q	$Billions	Net exports: current $—(SAAR)
89	GNETQ	Q	$Billions	Net exports: 1992 $—(SAAR)

	ECONDATA *Name*	*Periodicity**	*Units*	*Description*[†]
90	GGE	Q	$Billions	Government spending: current $—(SAAR)
91	GGEQ	Q	$Billions	Government spending: 1992 $—(SAAR)
92	GNP	Q	$Billions	Gross national product: current $—(SAAR)
93	GNPQ	Q	$Billions	Gross national product: 1992 $—(SAAR)
94	GPY	Q	$Billions	Personal income: current $—(SAAR)
95	GYD	Q	$Billions	Disposable personal income: current $—(SAAR)
96	GYDQ	Q	$Billions	Disposable personal income: 1992 $—(SAAR)
97	GYDPCQ	Q	$	Disposable personal income/capita: 1992 $—(SAAR)
98	GPSAV	Q	$Billions	Personal saving: current $—(SAAR)
99	GCNG	Q	$Billions	Personal consumer expenditure: fuel and coal—(SAAR)
100	GCNGQ	Q	$Billions	Personal consumer expenditure: gas & oil—(SAAR)

3   Moving Averages and Exponential Smoothing

Consider the situation facing a manager who must periodically forecast the inventories for hundreds of products. Each day, or week, or month, updated forecasts for the many inventories are required within a short time period. While it might well be possible to develop sophisticated forecasting models for each of the items, in many cases some very simple short-term forecasting tools are adequate for the job.

A manager facing such a task is likely to use some form of time-series *smoothing*. All the time-series smoothing methods use a form of weighted average of past observations to smooth up-and-down movements, that is, some statistical method of suppressing short-term fluctuations. The assumption underlying these methods is that the fluctuations in past values represent random departures from some smooth curve that, once identified, can plausibly be extrapolated into the future to produce a forecast or series of forecasts.

We will examine five basic smoothing techniques in this chapter. All five of these have the common characteristic that only a past history of the time series to be forecast is necessary to produce the forecast. Further, all are based on the concept that there is some underlying pattern to the data; that is, all time-series data to be forecast are assumed to have some cycles or fluctuations that tend to recur. The five methods, to be examined in turn, are:

1. Moving averages
2. Simple exponential smoothing
3. Holt's exponential smoothing
4. Winters' exponential smoothing
5. Adaptive–response-rate single exponential smoothing

Moving Averages

The simple statistical method of moving averages may mimic some data better than a complicated mathematical function. Figure 3–1 shows the exchange rate between the Japanese yen and the United States dollar from 1980 quarter 1 through 1995 quarter 4. Figure 3–1 does not exhibit a simple linear, exponential, or quadratic trend similar to those we will examine in Chapters 4 and 5. Instead, the series appears to show substantial randomness, which we may be able to eliminate with a technique that averages the most recent values.

The simple statistical method of moving averages may mimic some data better than a complicated mathematical function.

To illustrate how a moving average is used, consider Table 3–1, which displays the exchange rate between the Japanese yen and the United States dollar shown in Figure 3–1. To calculate the three-quarter moving average first requires that we sum the first three observations (243.529, 232.129, and 219.844). This three-quarter total is then divided by 3 to obtain 231.834, which is the first number in the "Three-Quarter Moving Average" column. This "smoothed" number, 231.834, becomes the forecast for period 1980Q4, that is, quarter 4 of 1980.

The final value in the "Three-Quarter Moving Average" column (93.3957) is the forecast for quarter 1 of 1996; it was arrived at by summing the final three values in the "Actual" column and then dividing by 3 (280.1872/3 = 93.3957).

The five-quarter moving averages displayed in the same table are calculated in like manner: the first moving average of 222.342 is calculated by summing the first five actual values and dividing by 5:

$$\frac{243.529 + 232.129 + 219.844 + 210.585 + 205.624}{5} = \frac{1,111.7110}{5} = 222.3422$$

Thus, 222.3422 becomes the forecast for the next period, 1981Q2 (quarter 2 of 1981). The five entries from 1994Q4 through 1995Q4 in the "Actual" column are averaged

FIGURE 3–1

Exchange Rate with Japan in Yen per U.S. Dollar (c3f1)

(c3t1) Table **3–1**   **Exchange Rate with Japan and Two Moving-Average Forecasts**

Period	Actual	Three-Quarter Moving Average	Three-Quarter Moving-Average Forecast	Five-Quarter Moving Average	Five-Quarter Moving-Average Forecast
1980Q1	243.529	MISSING	MISSING	MISSING	MISSING
1980Q2	232.129	MISSING	MISSING	MISSING	MISSING
1980Q3	219.844	231.834	MISSING	MISSING	MISSING
1980Q4	210.585	220.853	231.834	MISSING	MISSING
1981Q1	205.624	212.017	220.853	222.342	MISSING
1981Q2	219.938	212.049	212.017	217.624	222.342
1981Q3	231.738	219.100	212.049	217.545	217.624
1981Q4	224.549	225.408	219.100	218.486	217.545
1982Q1	233.729	230.005	225.408	223.115	218.486
1982Q2	244.012	234.096	230.005	230.793	223.115
1982Q3	259.075	245.605	234.096	238.620	230.793
1982Q4	259.160	254.082	245.605	244.105	238.620
⋮	⋮	⋮	⋮	⋮	⋮
1993Q1	120.929	122.959	126.112	125.592	127.302
1993Q2	110.056	118.002	122.959	121.864	125.592
1993Q3	105.678	112.221	118.002	116.922	121.864
1993Q4	108.274	108.003	112.221	113.592	116.922
1994Q1	107.657	107.203	108.003	110.519	113.592
1994Q2	103.259	106.397	107.203	106.985	110.519
1994Q3	99.0564	103.324	106.397	104.785	106.985
1994Q4	98.8655	100.394	103.324	103.422	104.785
1995Q1	96.1079	98.0099	100.394	100.989	103.422
1995Q2	84.4869	93.1535	98.0099	96.3551	100.989
1995Q3	94.1613	91.5854	93.1535	94.5356	96.3551
1995Q4	101.539	93.3957	91.5854	95.0321	94.5356
1996Q1	*105.827**	MISSING	93.3957	MISSING	95.0321

*Value assumed not to be known in developing moving-average forecasts.

	RMSE for 1980Q1–1995Q4
Three-Quarter Moving-Average Model	14.4643
Five-Quarter Moving-Average Model	18.2970

	Percent Error for 1996Q1
Three-Quarter Moving-Average Model	11.7%
Five-Quarter Moving-Average Model	10.2%

to give the final five-quarter moving average:

$$\frac{98.8655 + 96.1079 + 84.4869 + 94.1616 + 101.539}{5} = \frac{475.1606}{5} = 95.0321$$

This final moving average serves as the forecast for quarter 1 of 1996.

Obviously, three- and five-quarter moving averages are not the only kinds of moving averages. We could calculate seven- or nine-quarter moving averages if we wished, or eight- or ten-quarter averages, and so on. The choice of the interval for

The choice of the interval for the moving average depends on the length of the underlying cycle or pattern in the original data.

the moving average depends on the length of the underlying cycle or pattern in the original data. If we believe the actual data to be exhibiting a cycle that recurs every four periods, we would choose a four-period moving average in order to best dampen the short-run fluctuation. The simplest naive model of Chapter 1 used each period's actual value as the forecast for the next period; you could correctly think of this model as a one-period moving average, that is, a special case of the model we are examining here.

In order to compute whether the three-quarter or five-quarter moving average is the better forecasting model, it is useful to compute the root-mean-squared error (RMSE) as we calculated it in Chapter 1. Table 3–1 shows the squared errors for each forecast model and shows the RMSE for both forecasts at the bottom of the table. The RMSE of 14.4643 for the three-quarter moving average is less than the 18.2970 calculated for the five-quarter case, and so we might conclude that the better forecast in this particular case is generated by the three-quarter model.

In preparing the forecasts for 1996Q1 it was assumed that the actual value for that quarter was unknown. However, the actual value for that quarter is known in this situation and is shown in Table 3–1. Thus, we can see which of the two moving-average forecasts developed above was really the best for 1996Q1. The error for the three-quarter moving average forecast was 11.7 percent, while for the five-quarter moving average forecast the error was 10.2 percent.

The three- and five-quarter moving averages are shown graphically in Figures 3–2 and 3–3, respectively. Notice in Figures 3–2 and 3–3 that the peaks and troughs of the actual series are different from those for either moving average. This failure of the moving averages to predict peaks and troughs is one of the shortcomings of moving-average models.

One final and important observation: The moving average forecasting method has fooled more than one forecaster by appearing to identify a cycle when, in fact,

FIGURE 3–2

Three-Quarter Moving Average Forecast of the United States Exchange Rate with Japan (c3f2)

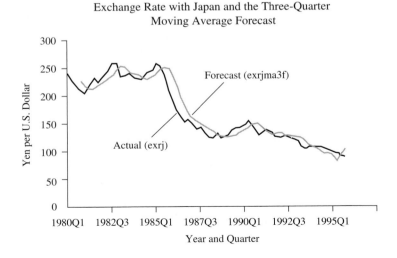

Exchange Rate with Japan and the Three-Quarter Moving Average Forecast

FIGURE 3–3

Five-Quarter Moving Average Forecast of the United States Exchange Rate with Japan (c3f3)

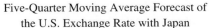

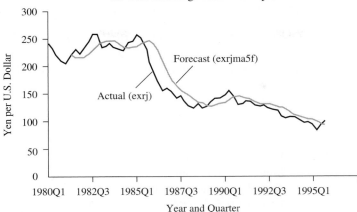

The moving-average forecasting method has fooled more than one forecaster by appearing to identify a cycle.

no cycle was present in the actual data. Such an occurrence can be understood if you think of an actual data series as being simply a series of random numbers. Since any moving average is serially correlated, because a number of contiguous periods have been averaged, *any* sequence of random numbers could appear to exhibit cyclical fluctuation.[1]

Simple Exponential Smoothing

With exponential smoothing, the forecast value at any time is a weighted average of all the available previous values.

Simple exponential smoothing, like moving averages, uses only past values of a time series to forecast future values of the same series and is properly employed when there is no trend or seasonality present in the data. With exponential smoothing, the forecast value at any time is a weighted average of all the available previous values; the weights decline geometrically as you go back in time. Moving-average forecasting gives equal weights to the past values included in each average; exponential smoothing gives more weight to the recent observations and less to the older observations. The weights are made to decline geometrically with the age of the observation to conform to the argument that the most recent observations contain the most relevant information, so that they should be accorded proportionately more influence than older observations.

---

[1]This incorrect conclusion is sometimes called the *Slutsky-Yule effect,* named after Eugen Slutsky and G. Udny Yule, who first pointed out the possibility of making a mistake in this manner. See Eugen E. Slutsky, "The Summation of Random Causes as the Source of Cyclic Processes," *Econometrica* 5 (1937), pp. 105–46; and G. Udny Yule, "On a Method of Investigating Periodicities in Disturbed Series, with Special Reference to Wolfer's Sunspot Numbers," Royal Society of London, *Philosophical Transactions* (1927), pp. 267–98.

Exponential smoothing proceeds as do moving averages by smoothing past values of the series; the calculations for producing exponentially smoothed forecasts can be expressed as an equation. The weight of the most recent observation is assigned by multiplying the observed value by α, the next most recent observation by $(1 - \alpha)\alpha$, the next observation by $(1 - \alpha)^2\alpha$, and so on. The number we choose for α is called the *smoothing constant*.

The number we choose for α is called the *smoothing constant*.

The simple exponential smoothing model can be written in the following manner:

$$F_{t+1} = \alpha X_t + (1 - \alpha)F_t \qquad (3.1)$$

where[2]

$$
\begin{aligned}
F_{t+1} &= \text{Forecast value for period } t + 1 \\
\alpha &= \text{Smoothing constant } (0 < \alpha < 1) \\
X_t &= \text{Actual value now (in period } t) \\
F_t &= \text{Forecast (i.e., smoothed) value for period } t
\end{aligned}
$$

In using this equation the forecaster does not need to deal with every actual past value at every step; only the exponentially smoothed value for the last period and the actual value for this period are necessary. An alternative way of writing Equation 3.1 results from rearranging the terms as follows:

$$
\begin{aligned}
F_{t+1} &= \alpha X_t + (1 - \alpha)F_t \qquad (3.2)\\
&= \alpha X_t + F_t - \alpha F_t \\
&= F_t + \alpha(X_t - F_t)
\end{aligned}
$$

From this form we can see that the exponential smoothing model "learns" from past errors. The forecast value at period $t + 1$ is increased if the actual value for period t is greater than it was forecast to be, and it is decreased if X_t is less than F_t. Forecasting the value for the next period (F_{t+1}) requires us to know only the actual value for this period (X_t) and the forecast value for this period (F_t). However, all historical observations are included, as follows:

$$F_{t+1} = \alpha X_t + (1 - \alpha)F_t \qquad (3.3)$$

and, $\qquad F_t = \alpha X_{t-1} + (1 - \alpha)F_{t-1}$

therefore, $\quad F_{t+1} = \alpha X_t + (1 - \alpha)\alpha X_{t-1} + (1 - \alpha)^2 F_{t-1}$

and, $\qquad F_{t-1} = \alpha X_{t-2} + (1 - \alpha)F_{t-2}$

thus, $\qquad F_{t+1} = \alpha X_t + (1 - \alpha)\alpha X_{t-1} + (1 - \alpha)^2\alpha X_{t-2} + (1 - \alpha)^3 F_{t-2}$

---

[2]Our notation throughout the chapter for exponential smoothing follows approximately the notation found in Everette S. Gardner, "Exponential Smoothing: The State of the Art," *Journal of Forecasting* 4, no. 1 (1985), pp. 1–28. This article contains a very complete description of different forms of smoothing that are in common use and explains (with advanced mathematics) that there may be theoretical advantages for employing smoothing in situations where it can be shown that certain assumptions concerning the probability distribution of the series are met.

We could continue this expansion to include X terms as far back as we have data, but this is probably far enough to help you see how the weights for previous time periods become smaller and smaller at a rate that depends on the value of α, as will be shown in the following tables for two alternative values of α.

The value of the smoothing constant α must be between 0 and 1. The value of the smoothing constant cannot be *equal* to 0 or 1; if it is, the entire idea of exponential smoothing is negated. If a value close to 1 is chosen, recent values of the time series are weighted heavily relative to those of the distant past when the smoothed values are calculated. Likewise, if the value of α is chosen close to 0, then the values of the time series in the distant past are given weights comparable to those given the recent values. The rate at which the weights decrease can be seen from their values for an α of 0.1:

Time	$\alpha = 0.1$ Calculation	Weight
t		0.1
$t - 1$	0.9×0.1	0.090
$t - 2$	$0.9 \times 0.9 \times 0.1$	0.081
$t - 3$	$0.9 \times 0.9 \times 0.9 \times 0.1$	0.073
$\vdots$		
Total		1.000

Regardless of the smoothing constant chosen, the weights will eventually sum to 1. Whether the sum of the weights converges on 1 quickly or slowly depends on the smoothing constant chosen. If, for example, we choose a smoothing constant of 0.9, the sum of the weights will approach 1 much more rapidly than when the smoothing constant is 0.1:

Time	$\alpha = 0.9$ Calculation	Weight
t		0.9
$t - 1$	0.1×0.9	0.09
$t - 2$	$0.1 \times 0.1 \times 0.9$	0.009
$t - 3$	$0.1 \times 0.1 \times 0.1 \times 0.9$	0.0009
$\vdots$		
Total		1.000

As a guide in choosing α, select values close to 0 if the series has a great deal of random variation; select values close to 1 if you wish the forecast values to depend strongly on recent changes in the actual values. The root-mean-squared error

In practice
relatively small
values of alpha
(α) generally
work best when
simple exponential
smoothing is the
most appropriate
model.

(RMSE) is often used as the criterion for assigning an appropriate smoothing constant; the smoothing constant giving the smallest RMSE would be selected as the model likely to produce the smallest error in generating additional forecasts. In practice relatively small values of alpha (α) generally work best when simple exponential smoothing is the most appropriate model.

The following example will demonstrate the technique. Suppose we wish to forecast the University of Michigan Index of Consumer Sentiment for January of 1996 (1996M1) based on data from 1994M1 through 1995M12. These values are shown in the "Actual" column of Table 3–2 for January 1994 through December 1995. Since no previous forecast is available for the first period (January 1994), we have arbitrarily chosen to use the first actual value in its place; thus 94.3 becomes the first entry in the "Forecast" column. This process of choosing an initial value for the

(c3t2)

TABLE 3–2　Simple Exponential Smoothing
Forecast of the University of Michigan Index
of Consumer Sentiment

Period	Actual	Forecast	Error	Pct Error
1994M1	94.3000	94.3000		
1994M2	93.2000	94.3000	−1.1000	1.1803%
1994M3	91.5000	93.8586	−2.3586	2.5777%
1994M4	92.6000	92.9121	−0.3121	0.3371%
1994M5	92.8000	92.7869	0.0131	0.0141%
1994M6	91.2000	92.7921	−1.5921	1.7458%
1994M7	89.0000	92.1533	−3.1533	3.5430%
1994M8	91.7000	90.8879	0.8121	0.8856%
1994M9	91.5000	91.2138	0.2862	0.3128%
1994M10	92.7000	91.3286	1.3714	1.4794%
1994M11	91.6000	91.8789	−0.2789	0.3045%
1994M12	95.1000	91.7670	3.3330	3.5047%
1995M1	97.6000	93.1045	4.4955	4.6061%
1995M2	95.1000	94.9084	0.1916	0.2014%
1995M3	90.3000	94.9853	−4.6853	5.1886%
1995M4	92.5000	93.1052	−0.6052	0.6543%
1995M5	89.8000	92.8623	−3.0623	3.4102%
1995M6	92.7000	91.6335	1.0665	1.1505%
1995M7	94.4000	92.0615	2.3385	2.4773%
1995M8	96.2000	92.9999	3.2001	3.3265%
1995M9	88.9000	94.2840	−5.3840	6.0563%
1995M10	90.2000	92.1235	−1.9235	2.1325%
1995M11	88.2000	91.3517	−3.1517	3.5733%
1995M12	91.0000	90.0870	0.9130	1.0033%
1996M1		90.4533		

Alpha = .401
Root-mean-squared error (RMSE) = 2.5143
Historical data for 1994M1 (January of 1994) through 1995M12
(December of 1995) were used to forecast January 1996.

smoothed series is called *initializing* the model, or *warming up* the model.[3] All the other values in the "Forecast" column were calculated by using Equation 3.1 with a smoothing constant (α) of 0.401, which was selected by SORITEC to minimize the RMSE. The actual and forecast values are shown in Figure 3–4.

Let us illustrate the calculation of the forecast value for March of 1994 (1994M3) by using Equation 3.1 as follows:

$$F_{t+1} = \alpha X_t + (1 - \alpha)F_t$$

$$F_{2+1} = \alpha X_2 + (1 - \alpha)F_2$$

$$F_3 = 0.401(93.2) + (1 - 0.401)94.3 = 93.8586$$

This smoothed value of 93.8586 is the forecast for March ($t = 3$). Once actual data for March become available, the model is used to forecast April, and so on.

Taking this one step further, assume now that the actual sales figure for March 1994 has become available. In Table 3–2 we see that this figure is 91.5. We now wish to forecast the sales figure for $t = 4$ (April 1994). The technique applied before is repeated:

$$F_{t+1} = \alpha X_t + (1 - \alpha)F_t$$

$$F_{3+1} = \alpha X_3 + (1 - \alpha)F_3$$

$$F_4 = 0.401(91.5) + (1 - 0.401)93.8586 = 92.9121$$

FIGURE 3–4

A Simple Exponential Smoothing Forecast of the University of Michigan Index of Consumer Sentiment (c3f4)

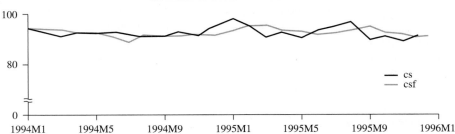

Simple Exponential Smoothing Forecast of the Index of Consumer Sentiment

In this forecast an alpha of .401 was selected by SORITEC to minimize the root-mean-squared error (RMSE).

---

[3]The choice of a starting value in exponential smoothing models has been a matter of some discussion, with little empirical evidence favoring any particular approach. R. G. Brown first suggested using the mean of the data for the starting value, and this suggestion has been quite popular in actual practice. A linear regression (like that described in Chapter 4) is sometimes used when selecting starting values for seasonal factors, and time-series decomposition (as discussed in Chapter 6) has also been used. If the data include trend, backcasting is sometimes used to select a starting value, but if the trend is erratic, this sometimes leads to negative starting values, which make little sense. A discussion of the various alternatives (including using the first value in the series or using the mean of the series, which are both popular in practice) appears in the Gardner article (footnote 2).

The error for the March 1994 forecast is calculated as:

$$e_3 = X_3 - F_3 = 91.5 - 93.8586 = -2.3586$$

The error for the April 1994 forecast is calculated as:

$$e_4 = X_4 - F_4 = 92.6 - 92.9121 = -0.3121$$

The predominant reason for using simple smoothing is that it requires a limited quantity of data and it is simpler than most other forecasting methods. Its limitations, however, are that its forecasts lag behind the actual data and it has no ability to adjust for any trend or seasonality in the data.

Holt's Exponential Smoothing

Two further extensions of the smoothing model can be used in order to bring the forecast values closer to the values observed if the data series exhibits a trend and/or seasonality (the first extension is discussed in this section, and the second in the following section). In real-world situations one or both of these techniques are often used because real-world data are not very often so simple in their patterns that simple exponential smoothing provides an accurate forecast.

The first extension is to adjust the smoothing model for any trend in the data; with a trend in the data the simple smoothing model will have large errors that usually tend from positive to negative or vice versa. When a trend exists, the forecast may then be improved by adjusting for this trend by using a form of smoothing named after its originator, C. C. Holt. Holt's two-parameter exponential smoothing method is an extension of simple exponential smoothing; it adds a growth factor (or trend factor) to the smoothing equation as a way of adjusting for the trend. Three equations and two smoothing constants are used in the model.

Holt's two-parameter exponential smoothing method is an extension of simple exponential smoothing; it adds a growth factor (or trend factor) to the smoothing equation as a way of adjusting for the trend.

$$F_{t+1} = \alpha X_t + (1 - \alpha)(F_t + T_t) \tag{3.4}$$

$$T_{t+1} = \beta(F_{t+1} - F_t) + (1 - \beta)T_t \tag{3.5}$$

$$H_{t+m} = F_{t+1} + mT_{t+1} \tag{3.6}$$

where:

$$
\begin{aligned}
F_{t+1} &= \text{Smoothed value for period } t + 1 \\
\alpha &= \text{Smoothing constant for the data } (0 < \alpha < 1) \\
X_t &= \text{Actual value now (in period } t) \\
F_t &= \text{Forecast (i.e., smoothed) value for time period } t \\
T_{t+1} &= \text{Trend estimate} \\
\beta &= \text{Smoothing constant for the trend estimate } (0 < \beta < 1) \\
m &= \text{Number of periods ahead to be forecast} \\
H_{t+m} &= \text{Holt's forecast value for period } t + m
\end{aligned}
$$

Equation 3.4 adjusts F_{t+1} for the growth of the previous period, T_t, by adding T_t to the smoothed value of the previous period, F_t. The trend estimate is calculated in Equation 3.5, where the difference of the last two smoothed values is calculated.

Because these two values have already been smoothed, the difference between them is assumed to be an estimate of trend in the data. The second smoothing constant, β in Equation 3.5, is arrived at by using the same principle employed in simple exponential smoothing. The most recent trend $(F_{t+1} - F_t)$, is weighted by β and the last previous smoothed trend, T_t, is weighted by $(1 - \beta)$. The sum of the weighted values is the new smoothed trend value T_{t+1}.

Equation 3.6 is used to forecast m periods into the future by adding the product of the trend component, T_{t+1}, and the number of periods to forecast, m, to the current value of the smoothed data F_{t+1}.

This method accurately accounts for any linear trend in the data.[4] Table 3–3 illustrates the application of Holt's model to disposable personal income per capita. The two smoothing constants are $\alpha = 0.720$ and $\beta = 0.200$. Two starting values are needed: one for the first smoothed value and another for the first trend value. The initial smoothed value is often a recent actual value available; the initial trend value is often 0.00 if no past data are available (see footnote 3).

For the disposable personal income per capita data, Equations 3.4 through 3.6 can be used to calculate the Holt's forecast for 1985Q2. To do so we will arbitrarily select the first actual value as our initial smoothed value $(F_1 = 16,481)$ and 100 as our initial trend $(T_1 = 100)$. The smoothed value for period 2 (1985Q2) is calculated by:

$$F_{t+1} = \alpha X_t + (1 - \alpha)(F_t + T_t)$$

$$F_2 = 0.72(X_1) + (1 - 0.72)(F_1 + T_1)$$
$$= 0.72(16,481) + 0.28(16,481 + 100) = 16,509$$

The trend estimate for period 2 is calculated as:

$$T_{t+1} = \beta(F_{t+1} - F_t) + (1 - \beta)T_t$$

$$T_3 = 0.2(F_2 - F_1) + (1 - 0.2)T_1$$
$$= 0.2(16,509 - 16,481) + 0.8(100) = 85.6$$

The forecast for period 2 is calculated as:

$$H_{t+m} = F_{t+1} + mT_{t+1}$$

$$H_2 = F_2 + 1T_2$$
$$= 16,509 + 1(85.6) = 16,594.6$$

Our calculated forecast for 1985Q2 differs from what you see in Table 3–3 by 89.4. This is because our arbitrary selection of seed values differs from those selected

---

[4]All trends, of course, do not have to be linear, and there are smoothing models that can account for multiplicative trend. In this chapter we are examining only a subset of the number of possible smoothing models. For a listing of smoothing models, see Carl C. Pegels, "Exponential Forecasting: Some New Variations," *Management Science* 15, no. 12 (1969), pp. 311–15, or the Gardner article (1985). Both of these articles cover many smoothing models, including some that are very rarely used in actual practice.

(c3t3)   TABLE **3–3**   **Holt's Exponential Smoothing
Forecast of Disposable Personal Income per Capita**

Period	Actual	Forecast	Error	Pct Error
1985Q1	16481.0000			
1985Q2	16750.0000	16674.0000	76.0000	0.4537%
1985Q3	16632.0000	16932.6242	−300.6242	1.8075%
1985Q4	16749.0000	16876.9629	−127.9629	0.7640%
1986Q1	16952.0000	16927.1932	24.8068	0.1463%
1986Q2	17065.0000	17090.9492	−25.9492	0.1521%
1986Q3	17107.0000	17214.4432	−107.4432	0.6281%
1986Q4	17032.0000	17263.8403	−231.8403	1.3612%
1987Q1	17162.0000	17190.3847	−28.3847	0.1654%
1987Q2	16957.0000	17259.2946	−302.2946	1.7827%
1987Q3	17160.0000	17087.6111	72.3889	0.4218%
1987Q4	17379.0000	17196.0205	182.9795	1.0529%
⋮	⋮	⋮	⋮	⋮
1994Q1	18082.0000	18308.6701	−226.6701	1.2536%
1994Q2	18367.0000	18155.4610	211.5390	1.1517%
1994Q3	18436.0000	18348.0643	87.9357	0.4770%
1994Q4	18564.0000	18464.3356	99.6644	0.5369%
1995Q1	18698.0000	18603.3700	94.6300	0.5061%
1995Q2	18668.0000	18752.3784	−84.3784	0.4520%
1995Q3	18819.0000	18760.4148	58.5852	0.3113%
1995Q4	18971.0000	18879.7724	91.2276	0.4809%
1996Q1		19035.7342		
1996Q2		19126.0318		
1996Q3		19216.3294		
1996Q4		19306.6270		

$\alpha = 0.720$ $\beta = 0.200$
Root-mean-squared error (RMSE) = 149.43
Mean pct error (MPE) = −0.1037%
Mean absolute pct error (MAPE) = 0.6738%

by SORITEC. Over the course of 44 quarters the effect of differing seed values would diminish to almost nothing, and if we continued the hand calculations our final forecasts would be virtually identical to those in Table 3–3.

Figure 3–5 shows a plot of both the actual values and the forecast values generated by this model. Some commercially available forecasting packages allow the forecaster to minimize the value of RMSE (or some similar summary statistic) by automatically adjusting the smoothing constants (SORITEC automatically adjusts). This, of course, is preferable to making numerous adjustments by hand. We picked the smoothing constants here using SORITEC.

Holt's form of exponential smoothing is then best used when the data show some linear trend but little or no seasonality. A descriptive name for Holt's smoothing might be *linear-trend smoothing*.

FIGURE 3–5

Holt's Exponential Smoothing Forecast of Disposable Personal Income per Capita ($\alpha = 0.720$; $\beta = 0.200$) (c3f5)

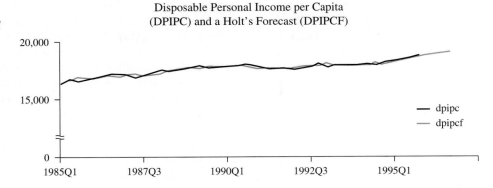

Disposable Personal Income per Capita (DPIPC) and a Holt's Forecast (DPIPCF)

Winters' Exponential Smoothing

Winters' exponential smoothing model is the second extension of the basic smoothing model; it is used for data that exhibit both trend and seasonality.

Winters' exponential smoothing model is the second extension of the basic smoothing model; it is used for data that exhibit both trend and seasonality. It is a three-parameter model that is an extension of Holt's model. An additional equation adjusts the model for the seasonal component. The four equations necessary for Winters' model are:

$$F_t = \alpha X_t/S_{t-p} + (1 - \alpha)(F_{t-1} + T_{t-1}) \tag{3.7}$$

$$S_t = \beta X_t/F_t + (1 - \beta)S_{t-p} \tag{3.8}$$

$$T_t = \gamma(F_t - F_{t-1}) + (1 - \gamma)T_{t-1} \tag{3.9}$$

$$W_{t+m} = (F_t + mT_t)S_{t+m-p} \tag{3.10}$$

where:

F_t = Smoothed value for period t
α = Smoothing constant for the data ($0 < \alpha < 1$)
X_t = Actual value now (in period t)
F_{t-1} = Average experience of series smoothed to period $t - 1$
T_{t+1} = Trend estimate
S_t = Seasonality estimate
β = Smoothing constant for seasonality estimate ($0 < \beta < 1$)
γ = Smoothing constant for trend estimate ($0 < \gamma < 1$)
m = Number of periods in the forecast lead period
p = Number of periods in the seasonal cycle
W_{t+m} = Winters' forecast for m periods into the future

Equation 3.7 updates the smoothed series for both trend and seasonality; note that the equation is only slightly different from Equation 3.4 in Holt's model. In Equation 3.7, X_t is divided by S_{t-p} to adjust for seasonality; this operation deseasonalizes the data or removes any seasonal effects left in the data. It is easy to see how this deseasonalizes the data if you consider what happens when S_{t-p} is greater than 1, as it would be when the value in period $t - p$ is greater than average in its seasonality. Dividing X_t by S_{t-p} reduces the original value by a percentage equal to the percentage that the seasonality of the period was above the average. An opposite adjustment would take place if the period were below average in terms of seasonality.

The seasonality estimate itself is smoothed in Equation 3.8, and the trend estimate is smoothed in Equation 3.9; each of these processes is exactly the same as in simple exponential smoothing. The final equation, 3.10, is used to compute the forecast for m periods into the future; the procedure is almost identical to that in Holt's model (Equation 3.6).

To illustrate Winters' exponential smoothing we will use data for the sales of trucks in the United States by quarter. Truck sales are quite seasonal, with quarter 2 typically being the strongest sales quarter (this includes the months of April, May, and June). As you can see in Figure 3–6, there has been an overall upward trend in the data since our 1980Q1 starting point. You have seen above how to apply the equations to do a few of the calculations for simple and Holt's exponential smoothing. We will not repeat that process for the Winters' model.

Having SORITEC determine the parameters that would minimize the RMSE results in an alpha of 0.586, a beta of 0.980, and a gamma of 0.082.

As with simple and Holt's exponential smoothing, initial values must be selected to *initialize* or *warm up* the model. Over a long time period, such as in this example, the particular values selected have little effect on the forecast of truck sales for 1996. These initial values are also determined within the software.

The results of the Winters' exponential smoothing forecast of truck sales are shown in Table 3–4 and in Figure 3–6. You can see, especially in the graph, that the model works quite well. The root-mean-squared error (RMSE) of 58,511.1 for

FIGURE 3–6

Quarterly Truck Sales in Units (TS) and a Winters' Exponential Smoothing Forecast of Truck Sales (TSF). Alpha = 0.586, Beta = 0.980, and Gamma = 0.082. (c3f6)

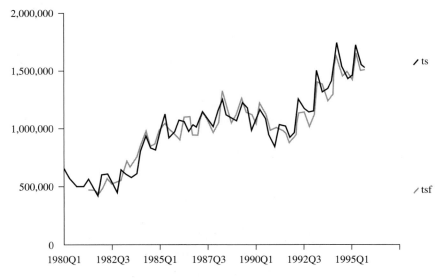

Historic Period: Root-Mean-Squared Error = 78,335.0
Forecast Period: Root-Mean-Squared Error = 58,511.1

(c3t4)   TABLE **3–4**   **Winters' Three-Parameter Linear and Seasonal Exponential Smoothing for Truck Sales**

Period	Actual	Forecast	Error	Pct Error
1980Q1	634427.0000			
1980Q2	568758.0000			
1980Q3	532143.0000			
1980Q4	496188.0000			
1981Q1	499968.0000			
1981Q2	559593.0000	469811.0659	89781.9341	16.0441%
1981Q3	495349.0000	472664.9879	22684.0121	4.5794%
1981Q4	417391.0000	439124.7752	−21733.7752	5.2071%
1982Q1	597296.0000	480742.7274	116553.2726	19.5135%
1982Q2	605965.0000	563497.0849	42467.9151	7.0083%
1982Q3	516173.0000	514948.8656	1224.1344	0.2372%
1982Q4	528238.0000	453758.3672	74479.6328	14.0996%
⋮	⋮	⋮	⋮	⋮
1994Q1	1430080.0000	1293835.6914	136244.3086	9.5270%
1994Q2	1636760.0000	1745909.3093	−109149.3093	6.6686%
1994Q3	1456740.0000	1531125.3119	−74385.3119	5.1063%
1994Q4	1502440.0000	1435521.2009	66918.7991	4.4540%
1995Q1	1438960.0000	1471047.1951	−32087.1951	2.2299%
1995Q2	1661130.0000	1719962.0478	−58832.0478	3.5417%
1995Q3	1490620.0000	1538764.7730	−48144.7730	3.2298%
1995Q4	1500120.0000	1511446.1392	−11326.1392	0.7550%
1996Q1	1551470*	1454011.7396		
1996Q2	1750260*	1706816.2717		
1996Q3	1591650*	1556772.8032		
1996Q4	1605000*	1571921.7224		

Alpha = 0.586   Beta = 0.980   Gamma = 0.082
Historic root-mean-squared error (RMSE) = 78,335.0
Mean percentage error (MPE) or bias = 1.6651%
Mean absolute percentage error (MAPE) = 6.9554%

*These values were not used in developing the model but have been added so that the RMSE for 1996Q1 through 1996Q4 could be calculated.

the forecast period is only about 3.6 percent of the average quarterly sales for 1996 (the average quarterly sales for 1996 were 1,624,595 per quarter).

Adaptive–Response-Rate Single Exponential Smoothing

An interesting variant on simple smoothing called *adaptive–response-rate single exponential smoothing (ADRES)* has an important advantage over normal smoothing models because of the manner in which the smoothing constant is chosen. In ADRES smoothing there is no requirement to actually choose an α value! This is an attractive feature if what you need is a very low-cost method of forecasting requiring no sophisticated knowledge of the technique. Real-world situations requiring the frequent forecasting of many items (perhaps thousands) would be ideal candidates for ADRES smoothing forecasts.

Adaptive-response smoothing does not use one single α value like the simple exponential smoothing model.

Adaptive-response smoothing does not use one single α value like the simple exponential smoothing model. The word *adaptive* in its name gives a clue to how the model works. The α value in the ADRES model is not just a single number, but rather *adapts* to the data. When there is a change in the basic pattern of the data, the α value adapts.

For instance, suppose that some data to be forecast fluctuate around a mean value of m. The best estimate of the next observation of the data might then be that mean value (m). But suppose further that after some time an outside force changes the mean value of m and the new value is now m'. The data then fluctuate around the new mean value of m'. If we had a way of adapting to the new mean of m', we could then use that adapted estimate as the forecast for future values of the data. In fact, we would like to be able to adapt each time the mean value of the data changed; sometimes we would adapt very often, if the mean changed frequently, and at other times we would adapt very rarely, if the data changed only infrequently.

Because of the simplicity of the ADRES smoothing model and its ability to adapt to changing circumstances, it is quite often used in actual practice. Keep in mind, however, that it is a variant of the simple smoothing model and so assumes that the data to be forecast have little trend or seasonality (or that the trend or seasonality in the data has been removed).

The ADRES model looks very much like the simple smoothing model presented earlier:

$$F_{t+1} = \alpha_t X_t + (1 - \alpha_t)F_t \qquad \text{(ADRES equation)} \qquad (3.11)$$

where:

$$\alpha_t = \left| \frac{S_t}{A_t} \right| \qquad (3.12)$$

$$S_t = \beta e_t + (1 - \beta)S_{t-1} \qquad \text{(Smoothed error)} \qquad (3.13)$$

$$A_t = \beta|e_t| + (1 - \beta)A_{t-1} \qquad \text{(Absolute smoothed error)} \qquad (3.14)$$

$$e_t = X_t - F_t \qquad \text{(Error)} \qquad (3.15)$$

Note carefully the subscripts on the α term! There may now be a different α value for each period.

The ADRES equation is the same as the one for simple exponential smoothing with the exception of the manner in which the α value is chosen. In the simple exponential smoothing model we chose the α value by selecting the value that minimized the root-mean-squared error associated with the model. But in simple smoothing we were allowed to choose only a single value for α. In the ADRES smoothing model we may allow the α value to adapt as the data change.

The smoothing value (α) is now given as the absolute value of the smoothed error divided by the absolute smoothed error. The smoothed error is itself a smoothed value, with a smoothing factor of β. The absolute smoothed error is also a smoothed value, again using the smoothing constant β. In most cases, β is assigned a value of either 0.1 or 0.2. Thus, the first term of both the smoothed error and absolute smoothed error equations has a lighter weight than the second term.

To explain ADRES smoothing, consider Table 3–5, which lists 12 values of an observed data series. We would like to model the series using an adaptive–response-rate smoothing model. Note that the first six values of the series average about 100; the last six values in the series average about 125. This is a situation similar to that described in the preceding paragraphs and one conducive to the use of this technique. An adaptive–response-rate model should do quite well in modeling these data.

For period 5 the computations are as follows (with some rounding difference in the third decimal place):

$$
\begin{aligned}
F_5 &= \alpha_4 X_4 + (1 - \alpha_4)F_4 \\
&= (0.143)(98) + (1 - 0.143)(102.042) \\
&= 14.014 + 87.450 \\
&= 101.464
\end{aligned}
$$

TABLE 3–5   Adaptive-Response Example

Period	Observed	Forecast	Error	Smoothed Error	Absolute Smoothed Error	α
1	100					
2	96	100.000	−4.00	−0.800	0.800	1.000
3	107	96.000	11.00	1.560	2.840	0.549
4	98	102.042	−4.04	0.440	3.080	0.143
5	103	101.464	1.53	0.659	2.771	0.238
6	99	101.830	−2.83	−0.039	2.783	0.014
7	126	101.790	24.21	4.811	7.068	0.681
8	128	118.267	9.73	5.795	7.601	0.762
9	122	125.687	−3.69	3.899	6.818	0.572
10	130	123.579	6.42	4.403	6.739	0.653
11	125	127.774	−2.77	2.968	5.946	0.499
12	124	126.390	−2.39	1.896	5.235	0.362

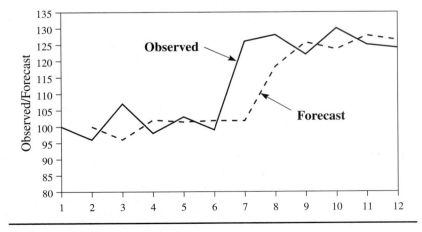

Once the observed value of 103 becomes available for period 5, it is possible to make the following computations (assuming Beta = .2):

$$e_5 = 103 - 101.464 = 1.536$$
$$S_5 = (0.2)(1.536) + (1 - 0.2)(0.440) = 0.659$$
$$A_5 = (0.2)(|1.536|) + (1 - 0.2)(3.080) = 2.771$$

and finally

$$\alpha_5 = \left| \frac{0.659}{2.771} \right| = 0.238$$

The process continues iteratively for all the remaining values in the example. In SORITEC you will get somewhat different results due to their use of a somewhat different algorithm.

Perhaps the most important consideration in adaptive–response-rate single exponential smoothing is the selection of the appropriate β factor. The β factor is usually set near 0.1 or 0.2 because these values reduce the effects of previous errors (i.e., they allow adaptation) but the values are small enough that the adaptation takes place gradually.

The ADRES model has no explicit way to handle seasonality. There are ways of using the ADRES model, however, with seasonal data. In fact, simple smoothing, Holt's smoothing, and the ADRES smoothing model may all be used with seasonal data. An example follows in the next section.

Using Single, Holt's, or ADRES Smoothing to Forecast a Seasonal Data Series

When data have a seasonal pattern, the Winters' model provides an easy way to incorporate the seasonality *explicitly* into the model. An alternative method, however, is widely practiced. This alternative consists of first "deseasonalizing" the data. Deseasonalizing is a process that removes the effects of seasonality from the raw data before the forecasting model is employed.[5] The forecasting model is then applied to the deseasonalized data, and finally, the results are "reseasonalized" to provide accurate forecasts. In sum, the process consists of these steps:

1. Calculate seasonal indices for the series. This can be done in different ways, one of which is to use the ADJUST routine in SORITEC.
2. Deseasonalize the original data by dividing each value by its corresponding seasonal index.
3. Apply a forecasting method (such as simple, Holt's, or adaptive-response exponential smoothing) to the deseasonalized series to produce an intermediate forecast of the deseasonalized data.
4. Reseasonalize the series by multiplying each deseasonalized forecast by its corresponding seasonal index.

---

[5] A complete description of deseasonalizing and reseasonalizing data appears in Chapter 6. The results that follow here are computed with SORITEC using the ADJUST command (with arithmetic normalization), which uses the moving-average method described in that chapter.

Many forecasters have found this method more accurate than using Winters' smoothing to incorporate seasonality. This method is more flexible than the Winters' method alone because it allows for the use of simple smoothing in situations without any trend whatsoever while allowing Holt's smoothing to be used if a trend is present. (Recall that Winters' model assumes that a trend is present.) Further, the ADRES model could be used in situations where some adaptation of the α factor is desirable.

To illustrate this approach to forecasting a seasonal series, let us return to the truck sales data used in our example of the application of Winters' exponential smoothing. Table 3–6 shows the first and last portions of the truck sales series (TS), the deseasonalized truck sales data (TSSA), a Holt's exponential smoothing forecast of the deseasonalized truck sales (TSSAF), the seasonal indices (SI) that were obtained from the ADJUST routine in SORITEC, and the reseasonalized forecast of truck sales (TSF). In this table TSSA = TS ÷ SI, and TSF = TSSAF × SI. You

(c3t6) **TABLE 3–6   Truck Sales (TS), Seasonally Adjusted Truck Sales (TSSA), Holt's Exponential Smoothing Forecast of Seasonally Adjusted Truck Sales (TSSA_FCST), the Seasonal Indices (SI), and the Reseasonalized Forecast of Truck Sales (TSF)**

Period	ts	tssa	tssa_fcst	si	tsf
1980Q1	634,427	655,216	missing	0.96827	missing
1980Q2	568,758	515,432	584,253	1.10346	644,700
1980Q3	532,143	534,328	462,471	0.99591	460,581
1980Q4	496,188	532,187	427,170	0.93236	398,275
1981Q1	499,968	516,351	434,521	0.96827	420,734
1981Q2	559,593	507,126	451,299	1.10346	497,991
1981Q3	495,349	497,383	469,564	0.99591	467,644
1981Q4	417,391	447,673	481,260	0.93236	448,706
1982Q1	597,296	616,868	454,646	0.96827	440,220
1982Q2	605,965	549,150	564,130	1.10346	622,495
1982Q3	516,173	518,292	583,776	0.99591	581,389
1982Q4	528,238	566,562	562,341	0.93236	524,303
⋮	⋮	⋮	⋮	⋮	⋮
1994Q1	1,430,080	1,476,940	1,489,830	0.96827	1,442,560
1994Q2	1,636,760	1,483,300	1,542,200	1.10346	1,701,760
1994Q3	1,456,740	1,462,720	1,557,340	0.99591	1,550,970
1994Q4	1,502,440	1,611,440	1,531,210	0.93236	1,427,630
1995Q1	1,438,960	1,486,110	1,610,280	0.96827	1,559,180
1995Q2	1,661,130	1,505,380	1,558,690	1.10346	1,719,960
1995Q3	1,490,620	1,496,740	1,528,040	0.99591	1,521,800
1995Q4	1,500,120	1,608,950	1,500,160	0.93236	1,398,690
1996Q1	*1,551,470		1,567,820	0.96827	1,518,070
1996Q2	*1,750,260		1,582,650	1.10346	1,746,390
1996Q3	*1,591,650		1,597,470	0.99591	1,590,940
1996Q4	*1,605,000		1,612,300	0.93236	1,503,240

*These values were not used in developing the forecast but are shown for comparison.

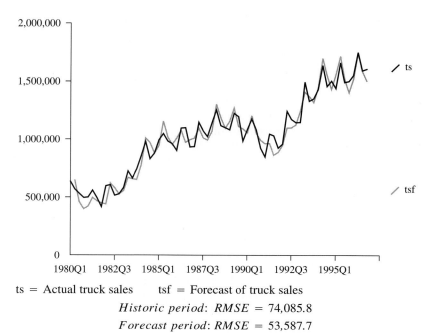

FIGURE 3–7

Truck Sales and Truck Sales Forecast Based on a Holt's Exponential Smoothing Forecast of Deseasonalized Truck Sales (c3f7)

ts = Actual truck sales   tsf = Forecast of truck sales

Historic period: *RMSE* = 74,085.8

Forecast period: *RMSE* = 53,587.7

Truck sales were first deseasonalized, then a Holt's forecast was done and the results were reseasonalized.

may want to check a couple of these calculations to verify the process for yourself (you may get slightly different answers due to rounding effects).

The results of this forecast of truck sales are shown in Figure 3–7. The RMSEs for both the historic period and the forecast period are lower than those from the Winters forecast (see Figure 3–6). For this approach the forecast period RMSE is about 3.3 percent of the average quarterly sales for 1996 compared to 3.6 percent for the Winters forecast.

Summary

If the time series you are forecasting is a stationary one, the moving-average method of forecasting may accurately predict future values. The moving-average method calculates the average of the past observations, and this average becomes the forecast for the next period.

When recent-past observations are thought to contain more information than distant-past observations, some form of exponential smoothing may be appropriate. Exponential smoothing provides self-correcting forecasts that adjust so as to regulate the forecast values by changing them in the opposite direction from recent errors. It is a characteristic of smoothing models in general, however, that their forecasts lag behind movements in the original time-series data. Exponential smoothing requires the specification of a smoothing constant, which determines the relative weights accorded to recent as opposed to more distant historical observations.

A suggested method for choosing an optimal smoothing constant is to minimize the root-mean-squared error (RMSE); the RMSE is found by dividing the sum of the squared errors by the number of observations and then taking the square root of the result.

When some trend is observed in the original time series, simple exponential smoothing becomes less able to perform accurate prediction; adding a procedure to adjust for the trend results in Holt's two-parameter exponential smoothing. Holt's smoothing adds a growth factor to the smoothing model to account for trend; in a sense, the growth or trend factor itself is smoothed in the same manner as the original data.

When seasonality is also present in the original data, Winters' three-parameter exponential smoothing adds a correction factor to Holt's smoothing model to correct for the seasonality. The correction factor is provided by an additional equation.

Adaptive–response-rate single exponential smoothing provides another technique that can be useful when the "level" of the forecasted variable changes infrequently. Adaptive-response models adjust the smoothing factor for changing conditions rather than choosing a constant smoothing factor.

In addition to trying Winters' exponential smoothing for seasonal data, one might also deseasonalize the data and then use another forecasting tool to forecast the deseasonalized series. The deseasonalized forecast can then be reseasonalized by multiplying the deseasonalized forecast by the corresponding seasonal indices.

Forecasting Domestic Car Sales with Exponential Smoothing

You will recall that in Chapter 1 we presented quarterly data on domestic car sales (in thousands of units); these data were presented in order to provide a single series that could be used to compare the various forecasting techniques presented in this text. In Chapter 1, Figure 1–5, you saw that the DCS series shows a great deal of seasonality, some cycle, and only a very slight positive trend.

In this chapter Winters' exponential smoothing was the only method that we used in which seasonality is explicitly taken into account. Thus, Winters would appear to be an excellent candidate as a forecasting technique for domestic car sales. You might want to go back to Table 2–1, which provided a guide to model selection, to see how this handy table would help you select Winters' for this series. The adaptive-response (ADRES) exponential smoothing model might also be a good candidate *if we first deseasonalize the DCS data.* You will note that we do not apply simple or Holt's exponential smoothing to the domestic car sales data because neither of those methods would be an appropriate model given the guidelines in Table 2–1.

Applying the Winters model, the software found the optimum values for the weights to be: alpha = 0.397; beta = 0.658; and gamma = 0.037. The historic RMSE for this Winters model was 177.1, while the RMSE for the 1995Q1 through 1995Q4 forecast horizon was 55.8. This RMSE corresponds to about 3 percent of the average quarterly sales for the 1995 year. In terms of total sales for the year, the actual was 7128.8, while the forecast was 7226.69—an error for the yearly total of 1.4 percent.

When the DCS series is deseasonalized, the seasonal factors turn out to be: 0.966, 1.102, 1.008, and 0.924 for quarters one through four, respectively. From these we see that on average quarter two is the strongest season for domestic car sales, while quarter four is the weakest. Applying an optimal adaptive-response model to the deseasonalized series, then making the forecast, and finally reseasonalizing the data, we obtain another forecast of DCS. The RMSE for the historic period was 169.5 and for the 1995 forecast horizon the RMSE was 67.7.

FIGURE 3–8

Two Forecasts of Domestic Car Sales (c3f8)

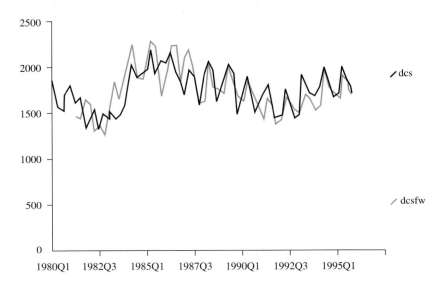

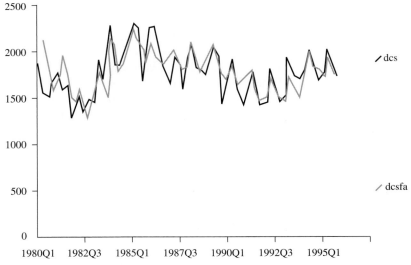

Actual values of DCS are shown along with the Winters' forecast (dcsfw) in the top graph, while the actual and the adaptive-response forecast (dcsfa) are shown in the bottom graph.

Figure 3–8 shows both of these forecasts of domestic car sales in comparison to the actual data. The top panel shows the results from the Winters model (dcsfw), while the lower panel is for the adaptive-response forecast (dcsfa).

Table 3–7 provides a summary of root-mean-squared errors for various methods used to forecast domestic car sales. A similar table will appear at the end of the corresponding section of each chapter in which a new forecast of DCS is developed.

TABLE 3–7   Summary Table of RMSEs for Domestic Car Sales

Chapter	Method	Period	RMSE
1	Naive—with 4-period lag	Historic before '95	207.3
		Holdout 95Q1–95Q4	74.9
2	Not applicable	Historic before '95	na
		Holdout 95Q1–95Q4	na
3	Winters' exponential smoothing	Historic before '95	177.1
		Holdout 95Q1–95Q4	55.8
	ADRES with	Historic before '95	169.5
	seasonal adjustment	Holdout 95Q1–95Q4	67.7

INTEGRATIVE CASE
The Gap

Part 3: Forecasting The Gap Sales Data with Exponential Smoothing

The sales of Gap stores for the 44 quarters covering 1985 quarter 1 through 1995 quarter 4 are once again shown below. From this graph it is clear that Gap sales are quite seasonal and are increasing over time. See page 30 for 85Q1–95Q4 data and page 31 for 1996 data.

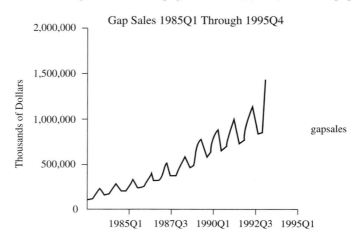

Gap Sales 1985Q1 Through 1995Q4

Case Questions

1. Using Gap data, which are not adjusted to remove the seasonality, what exponential smoothing model do you think would be the most appropriate if you want to develop a quarterly forecast for 1996 sales? Explain why. Make a forecast for Gap sales using the method you selected and use the RMSE to evaluate your historic fit and your forecast accuracy for the four quarters of 1996. For the entire year of 1996, what percent error is there in your forecast?

2. What are the seasonal indices for the Gap sales and what do they tell you about this company's sales pattern?

3. If the Gap data are deseasonalized, what exponential smoothing model do you think would be the most likely to work well in preparing a forecast of sales for the four quarters of 1996? Apply that method and evaluate your results.

Solutions to Case Questions

1. Of the exponential smoothing models discussed in the text the one that is most appropriate for the nonseasonally-adjusted data is Winters' exponential smoothing. This model takes both trend and seasonality into account. Allowing SORITEC to determine the optimal smoothing weights we obtain: alpha = 0.278, beta = 0.999, and gamma = 0.249. The RMSE using the historic period is 37,935.5, while for the four quarters of 1996 the RMSE is 84,460.7 (remember that our data are in thousands of dollars). If we compare the RMSE for these last four quarters to the mean level of sales for those quarters (1,321,095.25), we find that the RMSE is about 6.4 percent of the mean actual quarterly sales. For the entire year of 1996 our forecast was for yearly sales of 5,097,915. This compares favorably with

actual sales of 5,284,381 (an error for the year of about 3.5 percent).

The actual (GAPSALES) and the Winters forecast (GAPFW) of Gap sales (in thousands of dollars) are shown below for the four quarters of 1996.

	GAPSALES	GAPFW
1996Q1	1,113,154	993,966
1996Q2	1,120,335	1,021,065
1996Q3	1,382,996	1,354,804
1996Q4	1,667,896	1,728,080

The graph below shows actual Gap sales (gapsales) and the Winters' forecast of Gap sales (gapfw) for both the historic and forecast periods.

2. The seasonal factors for Gap sales in quarters one through four are: 0.854, 0.846, 1.046, and 1.254. This indicates strong sales during the fall back-to-school buying season (for Gap the third quarter includes the months of August, September, and October) followed by even stronger sales in their fourth quarter due to the Christmas season (the fourth quarter includes November, December, and January).

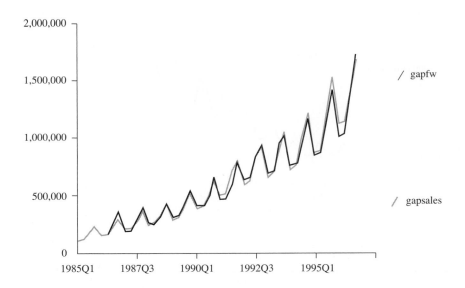

3. When Gap sales are deseasonalized, about all that remains is the positive trend and some noise around that trend. Using Holt's exponential smoothing (alpha = 0.999 and beta = 0.082) to forecast the deseasonalized series for Gap sales, then multiplying this forecast by the seasonal factors provides another forecast of Gap sales. The RMSE for this forecast in the historic period was 31,272.5, while in the 1996Q1–1996Q4 forecast period the resulting RMSE was 33,341.3. If we compare the RMSE for these last four quarters to the mean level of sales for those quarters (1,321,095.25) we find that the RMSE is about 2.5 percent of the mean actual quarterly sales. For the entire year of 1996 our Holt's forecast was for yearly sales of 5,235,840. This compares even more favorably with actual sales of 5,284,381 (an error for the year of about 0.9 percent) than did the Winters model.

The actual (GAPSALES) and Holt's forecast (GAPFH) of Gap sales (after reintroducing the seasonality) are shown below for the four quarters of 1996.

	GAPSALES	GAPFH
1996Q1	1,113,154	1,066,140
1996Q2	1,120,335	1,086,950
1996Q3	1,382,996	1,381,400
1996Q4	1,667,896	1,701,350

A time-series plot of this forecast, along with the actual data, is shown below. The following table provides a summary of root-mean-squared errors for various methods used to forecast Gap sales. A similar table will appear along with the Integrative Case for each chapter in which a new forecast of Gap sales is developed.

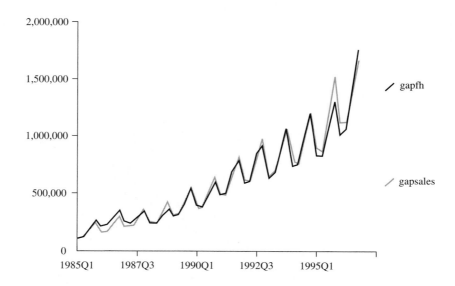

Chapter	Method	Period	RMSE
1	Naive—with 4-period lag	Historic before '96	107,150
		Holdout 96Q1–96Q4	227,029
2	Not applicable	Historic before '96	na
		Holdout 96Q1–96Q4	na
3	Winters' exponential smoothing	Historic before '96	37,935.5
		Holdout 96Q1–96Q4	84,460.7
	Holt's exponential smoothing with seasonal readjustment	Historic before '96	31,272.5
		Holdout 96Q1–96Q4	33,341.3

USING SORITEC FOR MOVING-AVERAGE AND EXPONENTIAL SMOOTHING FORECASTS

In this section we begin by explaining how you can deseasonalize data and derive seasonal indices using SORITEC. We then show you how to develop forecasts using a moving average or any of the four exponential smoothing methods discussed in this chapter.

Deseasonalizing Data and Calculating Seasonal Indices

To deseasonalize a data series and calculate the seasonal indices, begin by going to **Time Series** on the main tool bar, then to **Seasonal Adjustment,** and then to **ADJUST,** as shown below.

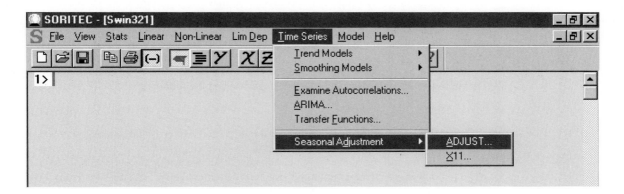

Clicking on **ADJUST** will lead to the following dialog box:

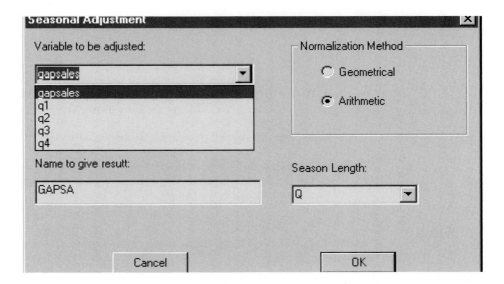

(If you had no data loaded, you would get a message to that effect.) From the drop-down menu for the **Variable to be adjusted** select the variable you want to adjust. For this example we selected *gapsales*. Then in the open space below type the name you want to give to the result (that is, the seasonally adjusted series). We used the name GAPSA. It is common to use **SA** to represent "Seasonally Adjusted."

For **Normalization Method** select **Arithmetic,** which will normalize the seasonal indices so that they average 1. From the drop-down menu for **Season Length** select **Q** if you have quarterly data (such as our Gap sales data) and **M** if you have monthly data.

Finally click on the **OK** button and you will see the following:

```
2> adjust (q a) gapsa gapsales
   Seasonal Factors
        .854023 .846179 1.04595 1.25385
```

where the first line is the echo of the command initiated by the completion of the seasonal adjustment dialog box (under **View** on the main toolbar you must have "echo" checked to see the command line).

The seasonal factors (indices) are stored by SORITEC under the name ^FACTOR, which may be used just as any other variable in subsequent operations. This is helpful when we want to reseasonalize data. We recommend that you use the name SI for seasonal indices. Therefore, on the next command line we suggest typing the following:

```
SI = ^FACTOR.
```

In making a forecast we want the seasonal indices in the forecast horizon that would usually extend beyond the period for which the seasonal indices have been calculated. Suppose, for example, we did the above seasonal adjustment for the **use** period of 1985Q1 through 1995Q4 but want to forecast out through the fourth quarter of 1997. Our SI would only exist through 1995Q4. To extend it, enter the following five commands:

```
ON DYNAMIC
USE 96Q1 97Q4
REVISE SI = SI(-4)
USEALL SI
PRINT SI
```

Note the use of REVISE. We are revising an existing variable, so REVISE is the appropriate command. The ON DYNAMIC flag just tells SORITEC to do the revision for the quarters of 1997 after doing so for 1996. Otherwise there would be missing values for 1997. The USEALL command simply changes the current **use** period to all periods for which the named variable exists. PRINT SI will cause the list of values for SI to be printed in your output screen. You will see that they repeat themselves every fourth quarter, as you would expect.

Suppose we have a Holt's exponential smoothing forecast of the deseasonalized trend for Gap sales (assume we have named it GAPFHSA). We can now convert the deseasonalized forecast to its seasonal counterpart (we'll call it GAPF) as follows:

```
GAPF = SI * GAPFHSA
```

We now have a forecast of the actual expected values for Gap sales in the quarters of the forecast period.

Moving Average Forecasts

The calculation of moving averages is done from the command line in SORITEC and is quite easy. Suppose that we want to prepare a moving-average forecast of the Gap sales series. In general form the moving-average command (ma) is:

```
ma output input length
```

where "output" is the name you want to assign to the calculated moving averages, "input" is the name of the existing series for which you want to calculate the moving average, and "length" is the number of periods you want included in each moving average.

For our example, the moving-average command is:

```
ma gapma4 gapsales 4
```

where we have chosen a 4-period moving average of gapsales and named the output series (the moving averages) gapma4.

Now to develop the forecast we would first extend the **use** period one period forward (in this example we started with data for 1985Q1–1995Q4). We then calculate the forecast as the moving average one period earlier. This is illustrated as follows:

```
use 85q1 96q1
gapfma4 = gapma4(-1)
```

where "gapfma4" is the name we are using for the forecast. An abbreviated table of the results follows:

Period	GAPSALES	GAPMA4	GAPFMA4
1985Q1	105715.	MISSING	MISSING
1985Q2	120136.	MISSING	MISSING
1985Q3	181669.	MISSING	MISSING
1985Q4	239813.	161833.	MISSING
1986Q1	159980.	175400.	161833.
1986Q2	164760.	186556.	175400.
1986Q3	224800.	197338.	186556.
1986Q4	298469.	212002.	197338.

Simple Exponential Smoothing Forecasts

While the exponential smoothing forecasts can also be done by entering commands on the command line, we will illustrate their use from the SORITEC menus. We begin with simple exponential smoothing.

You begin with **Time Series** on the main toolbar then select **Smoothing Models** and then **Simple Exponential,** as shown below.

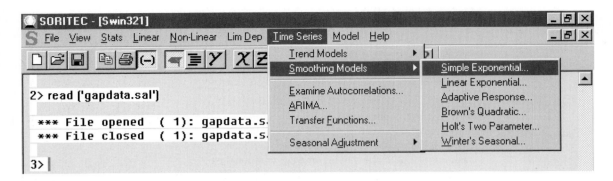

After you click on **Simple Exponential** you will see the following dialog box:

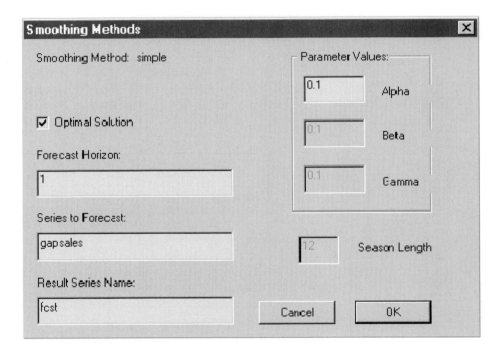

We recommend checking the box next to **Optimal Solution,** which allows SORITEC to determine the best value of alpha (the smoothing constant). For simple exponential smoothing it is most likely that your forecast horizon would be just one period; however, you can select a longer forecast horizon. In the box for **Series to Forecast,** type the name of the series you want to forecast (such as "gapsales"). In the **Result Series Name** box you can type in a name for the forecast series (such as "gapf") or leave the default name "fcst."

It is possible that the program will fail to converge to an optimal solution and you will get a message to this effect. If that ever happens, you can usually get an optimal solution by changing the value of alpha in the dialog box. Indeed, with the Gap data and alpha = 0.1 the model does fail to converge to an optimal solution but by typing in .3 for alpha it works well. The value of alpha provides a starting place for the search process when you have checked the **Optimal Solution** box, and changing the starting point usually leads to convergence.[6]

Holt's Exponential Smoothing

From what you have seen for simple exponential smoothing, you already have a pretty good idea about how to use SORITEC for Holt's. From the main toolbar go to **Time Series,** then to **Smoothing Models,** then to **Holt's Two Parameter.** After clicking on **Holt's Two Parameter** the following dialog box appears.

You see that this is almost identical to the dialog box for simple smoothing. The main difference is that there are now two parameters we can specify, alpha and beta. However, we again suggest allowing SORITEC to determine the optimal solution. If the model fails to converge to an optimal solution in Holt's, you may change either alpha or beta or both until an optimal solution is found.

---

[6]Simple exponential smoothing would not be a good choice for the Gap sales data because of the trend and seasonality. We use it here only to explain how the dialog boxes are used. We will use the same series for the rest of this section as well.

Winters' Exponential Smoothing

From what you have seen for simple and Holt's exponential smoothing you can probably reason out how to use SORITEC for Winters' method. From the main toolbar go to **Time Series,** then to **Smoothing Models,** then to **Winters' Seasonal.** After clicking on **Winters' Seasonal** the following dialog box appears:

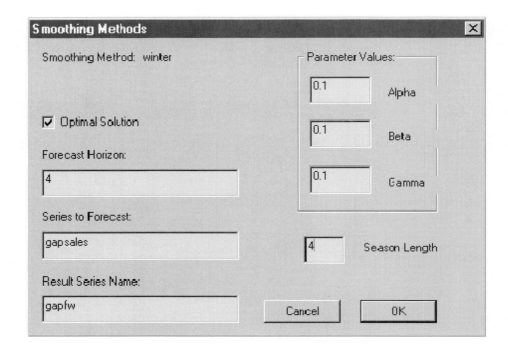

This is again similar to what you have seen before, except that now you can select values for alpha, beta, and gamma. In addition, since Winters' deals with seasonality you must type in the correct season length. This will be 4 if you have quarterly data and 12 if you have monthly data.

Notice that in this case we have opted to forecast four periods ahead and have named the forecast series "gapfw." Once again we recommend having SORITEC select the optimal values for the three parameters. If convergence fails, change the values of one or more of the parameters to establish a different starting point for the search process.

Adaptive–Response-Rate Exponential Smoothing

To invoke the adaptive–response-rate exponential smoothing model from the main toolbar go to **Time Series,** then to **Smoothing Models,** then to **Adaptive Response.** After clicking on

Adaptive Response the following dialog box appears:

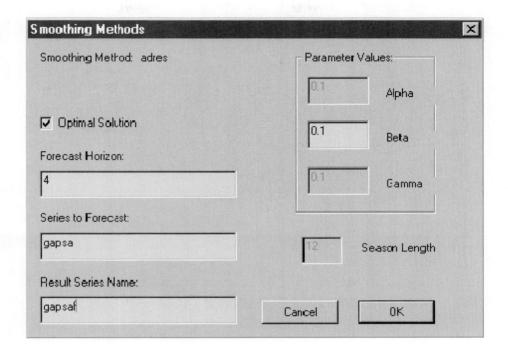

Here we have deseasonalized Gap sales into a series named "gapsa," which we have typed into the **Series to Forecast** box. We have typed in "gapsaf" as the name for the forecast values and have set the forecast horizon for 4 periods. Once more we are having SORITEC determine the optimal value for the parameter beta (remember that alpha varies in this method and so is not given a specific value). If the model fails to converge, try a different value for beta.

Calculating the Root-Mean-Squared Error

We often want to determine the root-mean-squared error (RMSE) for a forecast model. This can be done using the ACTFIT command from the command line as follows:

```
ACTFIT actual forecast
```

where **actual** and **forecast** are the actual and forecast values of the series you are working with. Alternatively this can be done from the menus.

From the main toolbar pull down the **Stats** menu and click on **ACTFIT:**

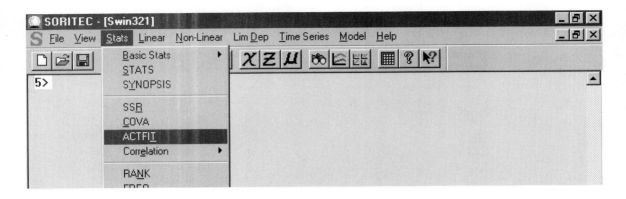

A box appears telling you to select the two variables. Click on **OK** and the following dialog box appears:

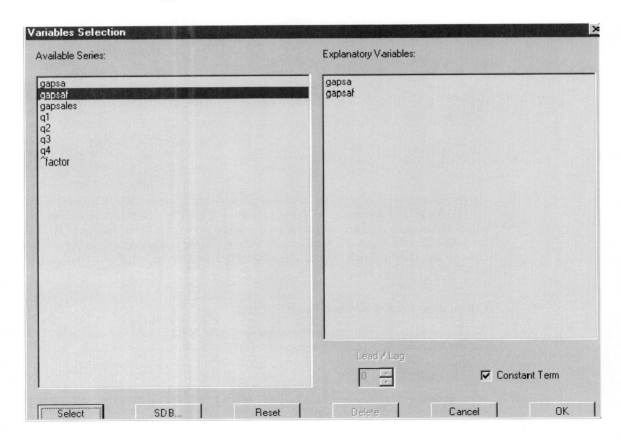

In this box click on one of the series you want, then click on **Select,** and then repeat the process for the other variable. In our example we selected *gapsa* (Gap sales seasonally adjusted) and *gapsaf* (the adaptive response forecast of the seasonally adjusted Gap sales). Then click on **OK.**

A full set of evaluative statistics will result, comparing the actual series (*gapsa* in our example) with the forecast series (*gapsaf*). The RMSE is among the statistics reported as are many of the other measures of forecast accuracy discussed in Chapter 2.

Data Conversion

Frequently we have data that are in one periodicity but we would like to work with those data in a different periodicity. For example, in the ECONDATA database file that is provided with this book, foreign car sales are in a monthly series named RCAR6F and we may want to work with a quarterly series for this variable. Thus, we need to convert the series from monthly to quarterly. SORITEC has a built-in procedure to do this.

Using the graphical interface, the conversion process can be summarized as follows:

1. Set the **use** period to span the appropriate time period, in terms of the *original* periodicity, and make sure the original data series is in the workspace. If it is not in the workspace open the data file with that variable or open a database (.sdb) file that has that variable and **COPY** the variable to the workspace; for example **COPY RCAR6F.**
2. Select **Data Conversion** from the **File** menu, as shown below.

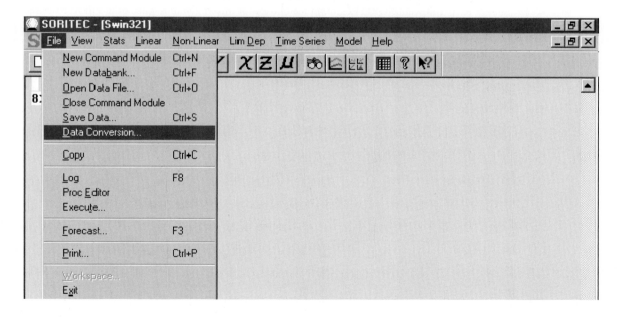

3. When the **Calendar Conversion Options** dialog box appears,
   a. Select the data series to be converted.
   b. Select the new periodicity in the **New Series Periodicity** list box.
   c. Type in the conversion method that is appropriate to what you want to achieve in the **Conversion Method** box (see example below).

The choices for aggregation (for example monthly to quarterly, or quarterly to annual) are:

sum	sum of observations (default)
msum	sum of nonmissing observations
average	average of observations
maverage	average of nonmissing observations
min	minimum of the observations
max	maximum of the observations
first	first observation in the period
middle	middle observation/average of two middle observations
last	last observation

The choices for disaggregation (for example, quarterly to monthly) are:

fill	use value for all observations
share	divide value equally among all observations (default)

d. Type in a new name in the **New Series/Tag** box.
e. If you want SORITEC to impute entries for missing values, check the **Fill in Missing Values** box.

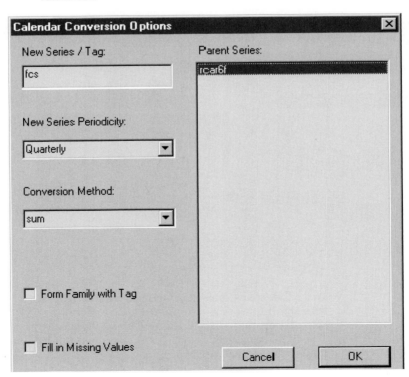

4. Click on **OK** to complete the conversion.

Conversion may also be done from the command line using the **CONVERT** command. The **CONVERT** command converts data into the **use** period currently in effect. The primary form of the **CONVERT** command is:

```
CONVERT [rule] new_variable_name = old_variable_name
```

The conversion rules are the same as described above. For aggregation within a target periodicity, the options for rule are

sum	sum of observations (default)
msum	sum of nonmissing observations
average	average of observations
maverage	average of nonmissing observations
min	minimum of the observations
max	maximum of the observations
first	first observation in the period
middle	middle observation/average of two middle observations
last	last observation

For disaggregation to a target periodicity, the options for rule are

fill	use value for all observations
share	divide value equally among all observations (default)

The following short example shows how a conversion of the monthly foreign car sales series (rcar6d) from ECONDATA is converted to a quarterly series named "fcs."

```
1> access 'econdata'
*** File opened (1): econdata.sdb
2> use 90m1 96m12
3> copy rcar6f
4> use 90q1 96q4
5> convert (sum) fcs=rcar6f
```

Suggested Readings

Gardner, Everette S. "Exponential Smoothing: The State of the Art." *Journal of Forecasting* 4, no. 1 (1985), pp. 1–28.

Holt, C. C. "Forecasting Seasonal and Trends by Exponentially Weighted Moving Averages." Office of Naval Research, Memorandum No. 52, 1957.

Makridakis, Spyros; and Steven C. Wheelwright. *Forecasting Methods for Management.* 5th ed. New York: John Wiley & Sons, 1989.

Makridakis, Spyros, et al. "The M2-Competition: A Real-Time Judgementally Based Forecasting Study." *International Journal of Forecasting* 9 (1), April 1993, pp. 5–22.

Makridakis, Spyros; Steven C. Wheelwright; and Victor E. McGee. *Forecasting: Methods and Applications.* 2nd ed. New York: John Wiley & Sons, 1983.

Pegels, Carl C. "Exponential Forecasting: Some New Variations." *Management Science* 15, no. 12 (January 1969), pp. 311–15.

West, Douglas C. "Number of Sales Forecast Methods and Marketing Management." *Journal of Forecasting* 13 (4), August 1994, pp. 395–407.

Winters, P. R. "Forecasting Sales by Exponentially Weighted Moving Averages." *Management Science* 6 (1960), pp. 324–42.

Exercises

1. Assume you were to use α values of 0.1, 0.5, and 0.9 in a simple exponential smoothing model. How would these different α values weight past observations of the variable to be forecast? How would you know which of these α values provided the best forecasting model? If the $\alpha = 0.9$ value provided the best forecast for your data, would this imply that you should do anything else? Does exponential smoothing place more or less weight on the most recent data when compared with the moving-average method? What weight is applied to each observation in a moving-average model? Why is smoothing (simple, Holt's, and Winters') also called *exponential* smoothing?

2. Under what conditions would you choose to use simple exponential smoothing, Holt's exponential smoothing, and Winters' exponential smoothing? Are these the only smoothing models possible to construct? If there are other possible models, suggest one that might be useful.

3. Exponential smoothing is meant to be used with time-series data when the data are made up of some or all of the basic components of average, trend, seasonality, and error. If the data series only fluctuates about an average with no trend and no seasonality, which form of smoothing would you employ? If the data include all of these components, which form of smoothing would you employ? How should the correct smoothing factors be chosen?

4. The smoothing factor chosen in simple exponential smoothing determines the weight to be placed on different terms of time-series data. If the smoothing factor is high rather than low, is more or less weight placed on recent observations? If α is .3, what weight is applied to the observation four periods ago?

5. Consider the following rates offered on certificates of deposit at a large metropolitan bank during a recent year:

(c3p5)

Month	Rate	Month	Rate
January	7.025%	July	7.575%
February	9.047%	August	8.612%
March	8.280%	September	8.985%
April	8.650%	October	9.298%
May	9.714%	November	7.454%
June	8.963%	December	8.461%

Use a three-month average to forecast the rate for the following January.

6. The following inventory pattern has been observed in the Zahm Corporation over 12 months:

Month	Inventory	Month	Inventory
January	1,544	July	1,208
February	1,913	August	2,467
March	2,028	September	2,101
April	1,178	October	1,662
May	1,554	November	2,432
June	1,910	December	2,443

(c3p6)

Use both three-month and five-month moving-average models to forecast the inventory for the next January. Use root-mean-squared error (RMSE) to evaluate these two forecasts.

7. Consider the following data on mobile-home shipments taken from the ECONDATA database provided with your text. Calculate both the three-month

and five-month moving averages for these data and compare the forecasts by calculating the root-mean-squared errors. The data are in thousands of units.

(c3p7) **Mobile Homes: Manufacturers' Shipments (Thousands of Units), Not Seasonally Adjusted**

Month	Shipments	Month	Shipments
1986Q1	58.1	1991Q1	35.4
1986Q2	66.8	1991Q2	47.4
1986Q3	63.4	1991Q3	47.2
1986Q4	56.1	1991Q4	40.9
1987Q1	51.9	1992Q1	43.0
1987Q2	62.8	1992Q2	52.8
1987Q3	64.7	1992Q3	57.0
1987Q4	53.5	1992Q4	57.6
1988Q1	47.0	1993Q1	56.4
1988Q2	60.5	1993Q2	64.3
1988Q3	59.2	1993Q3	67.1
1988Q4	51.6	1993Q4	66.4
1989Q1	48.1	1994Q1	69.1
1989Q2	55.1	1994Q2	78.7
1989Q3	50.3	1994Q3	78.7
1989Q4	44.5	1994Q4	77.5
1990Q1	43.3	1995Q1	79.2
1990Q2	51.7	1995Q2	86.8
1990Q3	50.5	1995Q3	87.6
1990Q4	42.6	1995Q4	86.4

8. Forecasters at Siegfried Corporation are using simple exponential smoothing to forecast the sales of its major product. They are trying to decide what smoothing constant will give the best results. They have tried a number of smoothing constants with the following results:

Smoothing Constant	RMSE
0.1	125
0.15	97
0.2	136
0.25	141

Which smoothing constant appears best from these results? Why? Could you perhaps get even better

results given these outcomes? How would you go about improving the RMSE?

9. The number of tons of brake assemblies received at an auto parts distribution center last month was 670. The forecast tonnage was 720. The company uses a simple exponential smoothing model with a smoothing constant of 0.6 to develop its forecasts. What will be the company's forecast for the next month?

10. The number of service calls received at LaFortune Electric during four months is shown in the following table:

(c3p10)

Month	Number of Service Calls
April	19
May	31
June	27
July	29

Forecast the number of service calls in August by using a simple exponential smoothing model with a smoothing constant of 0.1. (Assume the forecast for April was 21.)

11. *a.* Plot the data presented in Exercise 7 to examine the possible existence of trend and seasonality in the data.

b. Prepare four separate smoothing models to examine the mobile-home shipment data using those 10 years of quarterly data. (c3p11)
   1. A simple smoothing model
   2. Holt's model
   3. Winters' model
   4. Adaptive–response-rate model (Deseasonalize the data first then reseasonalize to get your forecasts.)

c. Examine the accuracy of each model by calculating the root-mean-squared error for each during the 10-year historic period. Explain carefully what characteristics of the original data led one of these models to minimize the root-mean-squared error.

d. Calculate the RMSE for each of the four models based on the four quarters of 1996 and explain your interpretation of the results. The actual values for 1996 were: Q1 = 84.4, Q2 = 97.2, Q3 = 94.9, Q4 = 86.9.

12. The data in the table below represent single-family houses sold (HS) in the United States on a quarterly basis in thousands of units from 1986Q1 through 1995Q4. These data are converted to quarterly from the monthly series (HZNS) in the ECONDATA database that accompanies this text.

(c3p12)

Period	HS	Period	HS
1986Q1	203	1991Q1	121
1986Q2	225	1991Q2	144
1986Q3	169	1991Q3	126
1986Q4	151	1991Q4	116
1987Q1	185	1992Q1	159
1987Q2	192	1992Q2	158
1987Q3	163	1992Q3	159
1987Q4	132	1992Q4	134
1988Q1	166	1993Q1	154
1988Q2	197	1993Q2	183
1988Q3	170	1993Q3	169
1988Q4	143	1993Q4	160
1989Q1	161	1994Q1	178
1989Q2	179	1994Q2	185
1989Q3	172	1994Q3	165
1989Q4	138	1994Q4	142
1990Q1	153	1995Q1	154
1990Q2	152	1995Q2	185
1990Q3	130	1995Q3	181
1990Q4	100	1995Q4	145

a. Prepare a time-series plot of the data and visually inspect that plot to determine the characteristics you see in this series.

b. Use a smoothing model to develop a forecast of HS for the four quarters of 1996 and explain why you selected that model. Plot the actual and forecast values. Determine the RMSE for your model during the historic period (prior to 1996).

c. The actual values for 1996 are: Q1 = 192, Q2 = 204, Q3 = 201, Q4 = 161. Based on these values determine the RMSE for the four quarters of 1996. Explain why you think your forecast was (or was not) a good forecast.

13. The data in the table below are for the college tuition consumers' price index (CTCPI) by quarter (converted from the corresponding monthly series [PZU671] in the ECONDATA database that came with your text).

(c3p13)

Period	CTCPI	Period	CTCPI
1986Q1	126.500	1991Q1	185.297
1986Q2	126.633	1991Q2	186.098
1986Q3	129.540	1991Q3	194.525
1986Q4	135.800	1991Q4	205.100
1987Q1	136.200	1992Q1	206.004
1987Q2	136.666	1992Q2	207.764
1987Q3	139.687	1992Q3	215.115
1987Q4	144.935	1992Q4	225.103
1988Q1	146.127	1993Q1	227.500
1988Q2	146.499	1993Q2	227.965
1988Q3	150.811	1993Q3	234.953
1988Q4	156.500	1993Q4	243.466
1989Q1	157.862	1994Q1	244.066
1989Q2	157.968	1994Q2	244.631
1989Q3	162.605	1994Q3	251.489
1989Q4	169.099	1994Q4	258.900
1990Q1	169.997	1995Q1	259.524
1990Q2	170.199	1995Q2	259.466
1990Q3	176.607	1995Q3	266.496
1990Q4	183.000	1995Q4	273.700

a. Plot these data and examine the plot. Does this view of the data suggest a particular smoothing model? Do the data appear to be seasonal? Explain.

b. Use a smoothing method to forecast the four quarters of 1996. Plot the actual and forecast values.

c. Calculate the RMSE for the historic period (prior to 1996) and again for just the four quarters of 1996, given the following actual values for 1996:

1996Q1	274.464
1996Q2	274.833
1996Q3	281.533
1996Q4	288.300

4 INTRODUCTION TO FORECASTING WITH REGRESSION METHODS

In this chapter the fundamentals of bivariate regression analysis are presented in the context of forecasting applications. Regression models are developed for retail sales (RS), private housing starts (PHS), and disposable personal income (DPI), all based on 10 years of quarterly data starting with the first quarter of 1986 (1986Q1) and ending with the fourth quarter of 1995 (1995Q4). These regression models are then used to make forecasts of each series for the four quarters of 1996. At the end of the chapter, we return to our continuing example of forecasting domestic car sales and to the continuing Gap case study.

The Bivariate Regression Model

Bivariate regression analysis (also called *simple regression*) is a statistical tool that gives us the ability to estimate the mathematical relationship between a dependent variable (usually called Y) and a single independent variable (usually called X).[1] The dependent variable is the variable for which we want to develop a forecast. While various nonlinear forms may be used, simple linear regression models are the most common. Nonlinear models will be discussed in Chapter 5.

In using regression analyses we begin by supposing that Y is a function of X. That is:

$$Y = f(X)$$

---

[1] For a more detailed discussion of the regression model, including underlying assumptions, see Robert S. Pindyck and Daniel L. Rubinfeld, *Econometric Models and Economic Forecasts,* 3rd ed. (New York: McGraw-Hill, 1991).

141

Since we most often begin by using linear functions, we may write the population regression model as:

$$Y = \beta_0 + \beta_1 X + \varepsilon$$

where β_0 represents the intercept of the regression line on the vertical (or Y) axis and β_1 is the slope of the regression line. Thus, β_1 tells us the rate of change in Y per unit change in X. The intercept (β_0) is the value that the dependent variable would have if $X = 0$. While this is a correct interpretation from an algebraic perspective, such an interpretation is often not valid in applications, since a value of $X = 0$ is frequently not in the relevant range of observations on X. The ε in this model represents an error term. That is, every Y is not likely to be predicted exactly from the values of β_0 and $\beta_1 X$. The resulting error is ε.

We would like to estimate values of β_0 and β_1 such that the resulting equation best fits the data. To do so we need to decide on a criterion against which the fit of the estimated model can be evaluated. The most common such rule is called the *ordinary least-squares* (OLS) criterion. This rule says that the best model is the one that minimizes the sum of the squared error terms.

The unobserved model that describes the whole population of data is expressed as

$$Y = \beta_0 + \beta_1 X + \varepsilon$$

These values of the intercept (β_0) and slope (β_1) are population parameters that are typically estimated using sample data. The corresponding sample statistics are b_0 and b_1. The estimated regression model is expressed as

$$\hat{Y} = b_0 + b_1 X$$

Deviations of predicted values ($\hat{Y}$) from the actual values of Y are called *residuals* and are denoted by e, where

$$e = Y - \hat{Y}$$

or,

$$e = Y - b_0 - b_1 X$$

The ordinary least-squares method seeks to find estimates of the slope and intercept parameters that minimize the sum of squared residuals:

$$Minimize \sum e^2 = \sum (Y - b_0 - b_1 X)^2$$

By taking partial derivatives of the sum of squared residuals with respect to b_0 and b_1, setting the partial derivatives equal to zero, and solving the two equations simultaneously, we obtain estimating formulas:

$$b_1 = \left(\sum XY - n\overline{X}\,\overline{Y} \right) \Big/ \left(\sum X - n\overline{X}^2 \right)$$

$$b_0 = \overline{Y} - \beta_1 \overline{X}$$

These formulas could be used to calculate b_0 and b_1 by hand. However, even for simple regression, a computer program is normally used for such calculations.

Visualization of Data:
An Important Step in Regression Analysis

There was a time when regression lines were estimated in a rather ad hoc manner, based solely on an analyst's visual interpretation of the data. The analyst would plot the data by hand and would "eyeball" the resulting scatter of points to determine the position of a straight line that was believed to "best" represent the general relationship between Y and X. Such a straight line was then drawn through the scatterplot, and by selecting two points from the line, its algebraic equation was calculated (i.e., values for b_0 and b_1 were estimated). One obvious problem with such a procedure is that different analysts would almost surely come up with differing estimates of b_0 and b_1.

Today it is doubtful that anyone would take this approach to estimating a regression equation. Modern computer technology makes it very easy to obtain the OLS equation without ever looking at the data. This equation is best, according to the ordinary least-squares criterion, and numerous evaluative statistics can be simultaneously determined. Every analyst obtains precisely the same results, and those results are easily replicated. Thus it may appear that computer-based regression analysis is a clearly superior method. However, something is lost. Analysts may just enter data, issue appropriate commands, get the corresponding statistical results, and run off to apply the model in some decision-based context such as forecasting. In the process, they would never have *looked* at the data. Such blind attention to statistical estimates can be dangerous.

To illustrate this point, consider the four data sets in Table 4–1. For all four of the data sets in Table 4–1, the regression results show an OLS equation of:

$$\hat{Y} = 3 + 0.5X$$

(c4t1)   **TABLE 4–1   Four Dissimilar Data Sets with Similar Regression Results**

Set A		Set B		Set C		Set D	
X	Y	X	Y	X	Y	X	Y
10	8.04	10	9.14	10	7.46	8	6.58
8	6.95	8	8.14	8	6.77	8	5.76
13	7.58	13	8.74	13	12.74	8	7.71
9	8.81	9	8.77	9	7.11	8	8.84
11	8.33	11	9.26	11	7.81	8	8.47
14	9.96	14	8.10	14	8.84	8	7.04
6	7.24	6	6.13	6	6.08	8	5.25
4	4.26	4	3.10	4	5.39	19	12.50
12	10.84	12	9.13	12	8.15	8	5.56
7	4.82	7	7.26	7	6.42	8	7.91
5	5.68	5	4.74	5	5.73	8	6.89

SOURCE: F. J. Anscombe, "Graphs in Statistical Analysis," *American Statistician* 27 (February 1973), pp. 17–21; as reported in Edward R. Tufte, *The Visual Display of Quantitative Information* (Cheshire, Conn.: Graphics Press, 1983), p. 13.

It might also be noted that the mean of the X's is 9.0 and the mean of the Y's is 7.5 in all four cases. The standard deviation is 3.32 for all of the X variables and 2.03 for all of the Y variables. Similarly, the correlation for each pair of X and Y variables is 0.82.[2]

From these results, an analyst who looks only at these summary statistics would be likely to conclude that the four data sets are identical or, at the very least, quite similar. But oh, how wrong this conclusion would be. If one were to take the time to prepare a scattergram of each of the four data sets, dramatic differences would become apparent. In Figure 4–1 we have plotted each XY pair in a separate plot, along with the corresponding OLS regression lines (all four of the regression lines have the same equation: $\hat{Y} = 3 + 0.5X$).

Visualization of these data allows us to see stark differences that would not be apparent from the descriptive statistics we have reviewed. The regression line is most clearly inappropriate for the data in the lower right plot. The lower left plot has, with the exception of one outlier, a perfectly linear relationship between Y and X, which

FIGURE 4–1

Scatterplots of Four XY Data Sets That Have Very Similar Statistical Properties but Are Visually Quite Different
(c4f1)

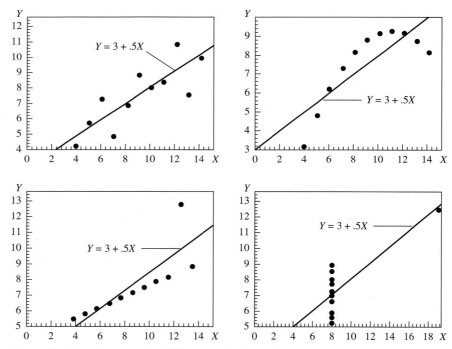

For each of the data sets, the OLS regression equation is

$$Y = 3 + 0.5X$$

---

[2]Many statistical diagnostics on the regression equations, which we will cover later in this chapter, are also equal. These include standard errors of the regression, t-ratios for the coefficients, R^2, and the regression sum of squares. Statistics related to the evaluation of residuals, such as the Durbin-Watson statistic, show some differences.

is not so clear without visual inspection of the data. The upper right-hand plot of data suggests that a nonlinear model would fit the data better than a linear function. Only the plot on the upper left suggests a data set that is a good candidate for a linear regression model. Visually, these data sets are quite dissimilar even though they have some very similar statistical properties.

Forecasters can benefit from this example. It is important to *look* at the data before plunging into data analysis and the selection of an appropriate set of forecasting techniques.

A Process for Regression Forecasting

It is usually useful to have a plan at hand when approaching any task. And so it is with developing a regression-based forecast. In this section we suggest one such plan, or process, that helps to organize the task of preparing a regression forecast. What we say here is not separate from the forecast process discussed in Chapter 2. Rather, it complements that process, especially data considerations, model selection, model evaluation, and forecast preparation.

We begin with data considerations, which become somewhat more complex for regression models. Not only do we need to pay attention to the dependent variable, the series to be forecasted, but we must also consider the independent variable(s) that will drive the regression forecast. One should utilize graphic techniques to inspect the data, looking especially for trend, seasonal, and cyclical components, as well as for outliers. This will help in determining what type of regression model may be most appropriate (e.g., linear versus nonlinear, or trend versus causal).

> One should utilize graphic techniques to inspect the data, looking especially for trend, seasonal, and cyclical components, as well as for outliers.

Next one must make a forecast of the independent variable(s). This becomes a separate, yet related, forecasting effort. Each potential independent variable should be forecast using a method that is appropriate to that particular series, taking into account the model-selection guidelines discussed in Chapter 2 and summarized in Table 2–1.

Once the data have been thoroughly reviewed and the type of regression model has been selected, it is time to specify the model. By model specification, we mean the statistical process of estimating the regression coefficients (b_0 and b_1, in simple bivariate regression models). In doing so we recommend using a holdout period for evaluation. Thus, if you have 10 years of quarterly data ($n = 40$), you might use 9 years of data ($n = 36$) to estimate the regression coefficients. Initial evaluation of regression models (based on diagnostic statistics we will discuss shortly) can be done on this subsample of the historic data. However, the real test of a forecasting model is in the actual forecast. Thus, if you have set aside a holdout period of data, you can then test the model in this period to get a truer feel for how well the model meets your needs.

This relates to our discussion of fit versus accuracy in Chapter 2. When the model is evaluated in comparison with the data used in specifying the model, we are determining how well the model "fits" the data. This is a retrospective approach, often called an *in-sample* evaluation. By using a holdout period, we have an opportunity to evaluate the model "out of sample." That is, we can determine how "accurate" the model is for an actual forecast horizon. After an evaluation of fit and accuracy, a forecaster may respecify the best of the models using the entire span of data that are available. The newly specified model is then used to forecast beyond the frontier of what is known at the time of the forecast.

Forecasting with a Simple Linear Trend

It is sometimes possible to make reasonably good forecasts on the basis of a simple linear time trend. To do so we set up a time index (T) to use as the independent or X variable in the basic regression model, where T is usually set equal to 1 for the first observation and increased by 1 for each subsequent observation. The regression model is then:

$$\hat{Y} = b_0 + b_1(T)$$

where Y is the series we wish to forecast.

To illustrate this process, consider the data in the top part of Table 4–2. DPI is disposable personal income per capita in 1992 dollars and is given for the 40 quarters from the first quarter of 1986 (1986Q1) through the fourth quarter of 1995 (1995Q4). This is an important economic series, since income is an important determinant for many kinds of sales. The linear time-trend model for DPI is:

$$\widehat{DPI} = b_0 + b_1(T)$$

You see in Table 4–2 that T (time) equals 1 for 1986Q1 and 40 for 1995Q4.

It is usually a good idea to look at data such as those given in Table 4–1 in graphic form before beginning to do any regression analysis. A visual inspection of the data can be helpful in deciding whether a linear or nonlinear model would be most appropriate. A scattergram of DPI versus T is shown in Figure 4–2. From this scattergram one can get a good feel for how this important measure of income has increased over the 40 quarters presented. All 40 points do not fall on a single straight line. However, it does appear that a linear trend line may fit the data reasonably well. The positive trend to DPI is more easily seen in the graphic form of Figure 4–2 than in the tabular form shown at the top of Table 4–2.

Suppose that you are asked to forecast DPI for the four quarters of 1996, using a simple linear trend. The first thing you would do is to use the linear regression part of your regression software to provide the estimates of b_0 and b_1 for the following model:

$$DPI = b_0 + b_1(T)$$

The regression results are shown at the bottom of Table 4–2. From those results we see that the intercept (b_0) is 17,052.1 and that the coefficient on T (b_1, or the slope) is 41.0672. Thus, the regression forecast model may be written as:

$$\widehat{DPI} = 17,052.1 + 41.0672(T)$$

The slope term in this model tells us that, on average, disposable personal income per capita in 1992 dollars increased by 41.0672 per quarter. The other statistical results

(c4t2) **TABLE 4–2** **Disposable Personal Income Per Capita, 1986Q1–1995Q4.** The table at the top contains the raw data used to generate the bivariate regression results summarized at the bottom.

Period	DPI*	Time Index (T)	Period	DPI*	Time Index (T)
1986Q1	16951.7	1	1991Q1	17748.0	21
1986Q2	17064.7	2	1991Q2	17861.3	22
1986Q3	17107.3	3	1991Q3	17815.3	23
1986Q4	17032.3	4	1991Q4	17811.0	24
1987Q1	17162.0	5	1992Q1	18000.3	25
1987Q2	16956.0	6	1992Q2	18085.7	26
1987Q3	17159.7	7	1992Q3	18035.3	27
1987Q4	17378.7	8	1992Q4	18330.0	28
1988Q1	17622.7	9	1993Q1	17962.3	29
1988Q2	17623.3	10	1993Q2	18132.3	30
1988Q3	17704.3	11	1993Q3	18143.0	31
1988Q4	17760.3	12	1993Q4	18305.7	32
1989Q1	17919.7	13	1994Q1	18081.7	33
1989Q2	17804.0	14	1994Q2	18366.3	34
1989Q3	17833.7	15	1994Q3	18436.0	35
1989Q4	17858.7	16	1994Q4	18564.3	36
1990Q1	18034.7	17	1995Q1	18697.7	37
1990Q2	18062.7	18	1995Q2	18668.3	38
1990Q3	18031.3	19	1995Q3	18818.7	39
1990Q4	17855.7	20	1995Q4	18971.3	40

*DPI is disposable personal income per capita in constant 1992 dollars.

```
REGRESS : dependent variable is DPI
Using   1986Q1-1995Q4

    Variable        Coefficient        Std Err        T-stat        Signf

  ^CONST              17052.1          59.6121       286.051         .000
  T                   41.0672          2.53382       16.2076         .000


                          Equation Summary
     No. of Observations =      40      R2=   .8736    (adj)=    .8703
     Sum of Sq. Resid. =  .130035E+07  Std. Error of Reg.=  184.986
                                       Durbin-Watson     =   .62196
                                       F ( 1,   38)      =  262.687
                                       Significance      =  .000000
```

The regression equation is DPI $= 17,052.1 + 41.0672(T)$.

shown at the bottom of Table 4–2 are helpful in evaluating the usefulness of the model. Most of these will be discussed in detail in the section "Statistical Evaluation of Regression Models," later in this chapter. Our discussion of others will be held in abeyance until Chapter 5. For now we will just comment that statistical evaluation suggests that this linear equation provides a reasonably good fit to the data.

FIGURE 4–2

Scatterplot of Disposable Personal Income Per Capita in 1992 Dollars (DPI) Versus a Time Index (T) for 1986Q1 through 1995Q4 (40 Quarters) (c4f2)

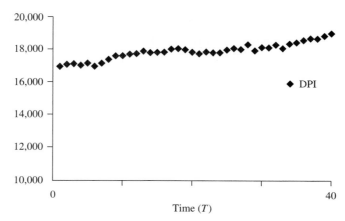

While these points do not fall on a perfectly straight line, they do show a positive trend that is close to linear.

To use this equation to make a forecast for the four quarters of 1996, we need only substitute the appropriate values for time (*T*). These are 41, 42, 43, and 44 for 1996Q1, 1996Q2, 1996Q3, and 1996Q4, respectively. The trend estimates of DPI for 1996 are as follows:

$$1996Q1: \text{DPIT} = 17,052.1 + 41.0672(41) = 18,735.8$$

$$1996Q2: \text{DPIT} = 17,052.1 + 41.0672(42) = 18,776.9$$

$$1996Q3: \text{DPIT} = 17,052.1 + 41.0672(43) = 18,818.0$$

$$1996Q4: \text{DPIT} = 17,052.1 + 41.0672(44) = 18,859.0$$

You can see in Figure 4–3 that the simple linear trend line does fit the actual data reasonably well through the period from 1986 through 1996.

The actual values of DPI for 1996 are shown in the following table, along with the trend values (DPIT) in order to determine the root-mean-squared error (RMSE) for the forecast period:

Period	Actual DPI	Trend Forecast of DPI	Actual Minus Forecast	Square of Actual Minus Forecast
1996Q1	19,028.0	18,735.8	292.173	85,365.1
1996Q2	19,053.0	18,776.9	276.106	76,234.5
1996Q3	19,233.0	18,818.0	415.039	172,257
1996Q4	19,314.7	18,859.0	455.672	207,637

Sum of squared errors = 541,493.6

Mean-squared error (MSE) = 541,493.6 ÷ 4 = 135,373.4

Root-mean-squared error (RMSE) = Square root of MSE = 367.931

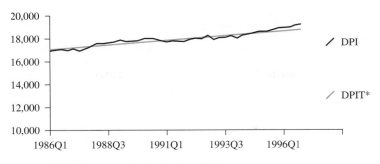

FIGURE 4–3

DPI with a Linear Trend Line (c4f3)

*DPIT represents the trend value of DPI.

The linear trend (DPIT) follows the general upward movement in DPI quite well. The trend equation is DPI = 17,052.1 + 41.0672(T).

This RMSE is about 1.9 percent of the mean for DPI during the forecast period, another indication that the simple trend forecasting model works reasonably well for this series. The RMSE for this method could be compared with that of other techniques to determine the most appropriate method to use.[3]

Obviously, in this example we knew the 1996 values of DPI, and so we used the four quarters of 1996 as a holdout period. If we wanted to then forecast DPI for the four quarters of 1997, we could have respecified the model using the latest available data. A comparison of the models specified for 1986Q1 through 1995Q4 and 1986Q1 through 1996Q4 follows:

Data Period	Constant	Slope for T	Historic RMSE
1986Q1–1995Q4	17,052.1	41.0672	180.302
1986Q1–1996Q4	16,992.5	45.1679	195.138

You can see that using the four quarters of 1996 shifts the intercept down slightly and increases the slope of the trend line. This is an expected result, since we have seen that the original model underestimated DPI for 1996.

Trend models such as this can sometimes be very helpful in forecasting, and, as you see, they are easy to develop and to implement. In such models we simply track the past time trend and project it forward for the forecast horizon of interest. Note that we do not imply any sense of causality in such a model. Time does not cause income to rise. Income has increased over time at a reasonably steady rate for reasons not explained in our model.

---

[3] For example, based on 1986 through 1995 data the optimal Holt's exponential smoothing model for DPI (alpha = 0.734; beta = 0.036) produces a forecast for the four quarters of 1996 that has an RMSE for that period of 128.9 (i.e., the smoothing model would be a better model because of the lower RMSE).

Using a Causal Regression Model to Forecast

Trend models, such as the one we looked at in the previous section for real disposable personal income, use the power of regression analysis to determine the best linear trend line. However, such uses do not exploit the full potential of this powerful statistical tool. Regression analysis is especially useful for developing causal models.

In a causal model, expressed as $Y = f(X)$, a change in the independent variable (X) is assumed to cause a change in the dependent variable (Y). The selection of an appropriate causal variable (X) should be based on some insight that suggests that a causal relationship is reasonable. One does not arbitrarily select an X variable, but rather looks to past experience and understanding to identify potential causal factors. For example, suppose that you were attempting to develop a bivariate regression model that might be helpful in explaining and predicting the level of retail sales in the United States. What factors do you think might have an impact on retail sales? Some potential causal variables that might come to mind could include income, some measure of the level of interest rates, and the unemployment rate, among others.

Discussions with knowledgeable people in the retailing industry would help you determine other variables and would be helpful in prioritizing those that are identified. Library research in areas related to retail sales and to consumer behavior may turn up yet other potential X variables. One thing you would learn quickly is that there is a substantial seasonal aspect to retail sales.

It is important that the independent variable be selected on the basis of a logical construct that relates it to the dependent variable. Otherwise one might find a variable through an arbitrary search process that works well enough in a given historic

FIGURE 4–4

Retail Sales in Millions of Dollars (c4f4)

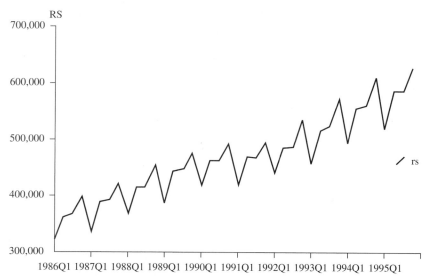

This graph of retail sales shows a clear positive trend and a reasonably consistent seasonal pattern. Source: The Bureau of the Census (http://www.census.gov/).

(c4t3)

TABLE 4–3   Retail Sales (RS) in Millions of Dollars

Period	RS	Period	RS
1986Q1	320,566	1991Q1	417,357
1986Q2	360,948	1991Q2	470,851
1986Q3	369,596	1991Q3	469,494
1986Q4	398,526	1991Q4	498,235
1987Q1	335,520	1992Q1	437,388
1987Q2	390,337	1992Q2	486,553
1987Q3	393,813	1992Q3	489,541
1987Q4	421,629	1992Q4	538,107
1988Q1	369,185	1993Q1	456,050
1988Q2	415,351	1993Q2	519,830
1988Q3	415,531	1993Q3	523,405
1988Q4	456,135	1993Q4	573,503
1989Q1	389,123	1994Q1	493,778
1989Q2	444,746	1994Q2	556,848
1989Q3	448,724	1994Q3	562,860
1989Q4	476,378	1994Q4	613,839
1990Q1	418,436	1995Q1	519,991
1990Q2	464,944	1995Q2	587,346
1990Q3	464,490	1995Q3	587,208
1990Q4	496,741	1995Q4	629,493

SOURCE: The Bureau of the Census (http://www.census.gov/).

period, more or less by accident, but then breaks down severely out of sample. Consider, for example, William Stanley Jevons' sunspot theory of business cycles. For a certain historic period a reasonably strong correlation appeared to support such a notion. Outside that period, however, the relationship was quite weak. In this case it is difficult to develop a strong conceptual theory tying business cycles to sunspot activity.

To illustrate the use of a causal model, we will consider how well retail sales (RS) can be forecast on the basis of two different causal variables: (1) disposable personal income per capita in 1992 dollars as a measure of overall purchasing power; and (2) the mortgage rate as one possible measure of the general level of interest rates, since many "big ticket" items such as cars and home appliances may be financed.

Before we start to develop a forecast of retail sales, we should take a look at a time-series plot of the series. In this example we will assume that we have quarterly data for retail sales from 1986Q1 through 1995Q4 and that we want to forecast RS for each of the four quarters of 1996. A time-series plot of RS is found in Figure 4–4 and the raw data are in Table 4–3.

A Retail Sales Forecast Based on Disposable Personal Income Per Capita

If we hypothesize that disposable personal income per capita (DPI) is influential in determining RS, we might initially want to look at a scattergram of these two variables. This is shown in Figure 4–5, where RS is plotted on the vertical axis and DPI is on the horizontal axis. You see that higher values of RS appear to be associated with higher incomes. All 40 observations (for 1986Q1 through 1995Q4) do not fall on a single straight line, but a straight line through those points appears to provide a reasonably good fit to the data. You also see that all of these 40 observations are well away from the origin. The importance of this observation will be apparent as we discuss the regression results below.

The bivariate regression model for RS as a function of DPI may be written as:

$$RS = b_0 + b_1(DPI)$$

The RS data used to estimate values for b_0 and b_1 are given in Table 4–3 and the data for DPI are in Table 4–2. The basic regression results are shown in Figure 4–6, along with a graph of the actual and predicted values based on this model. On the basis of these results the forecast model (equation) for retail sales as a function of disposable personal income per capita is:

$$RS = -1,931,730 + 134.056(DPI)$$

Note the "large" negative value for the vertical (RS) intercept, as we expected based on the plot in Figure 4–5. The positive slope (134.056) indicates that on average, RS (in millions) increases by 134.056 for each additional 1-dollar increase in disposable personal income per capita. A major problem with this model is apparent in Figure 4–6. It is clear from the graph of actual and predicted retail sales that this model fails to deal with the seasonality in RS.

FIGURE 4–5

Scatterplot of Retail Sales Versus Disposable Personal Income Per Capita (c4f5)

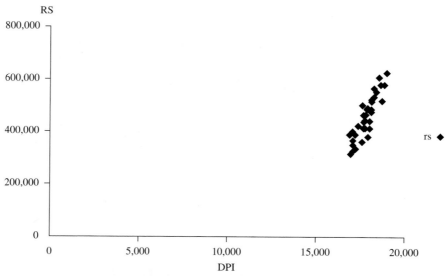

In this graph you see a fairly tight clustering of the 40 data points for RS and DPI. Note that all the data are quite far from the origin. If you picture a straight line drawn through these points and extended clear to the vertical axis, you can see that the vertical intercept would be negative.

FIGURE 4–6

Actual Retail Sales (RS) and Values Predicted (^yfit) by the Regression Model: RS = f(DPI), Without Accounting for Seasonality (c4f6)

Basic Regression Results : RS as a function of DPI

```
Using    1986Q1-1995Q4
Variable          Coefficient      Std Err          T-stat           Signf

^CONST             -.193173E+07     188112.          -10.2691         .000
 DPI                134.056         10.5084           12.7571         .000
```

The regression equation is: RS = −1,931,730 + 134.056(DPI). Notice that the predicted values in the graph, based on this model, do not replicate the seasonal pattern in retail sales very well.

The failure of this model to deal well with the seasonal nature of retail sales suggests that either we should use a model that can account for seasonality directly or we should deseasonalize the data before developing the regression forecasting model. In Chapter 3 you learned how to forecast a seasonal series with Winters' exponential smoothing. In the next chapter you will see how regression methods can also incorporate seasonality, and in Chapter 6 you will see how a seasonal pattern can be modeled using time-series decomposition. For the remainder of this chapter we will develop models based on deseasonalized retail sales data (RSSA), then reintroduce the seasonality as we develop forecasts.

When retail sales are seasonally adjusted, the following seasonal indices are found (arithmetically normalized to average 1): Q1 = 0.908107; Q2 = 1.01351; Q3 = 1.00575; and Q4 = 1.07264. From these we see that retail sales are the highest in the fourth quarter (the Christmas season) and lowest in the first quarter.

When we regress the seasonally adjusted values of retail sales (RSSA) as a function of disposable personal income, we get the results shown at the top of Figure 4–7 and summarized by the following equation:

$$RSSA = -1,813,520 + 127.429(DPI)$$

FIGURE 4–7

*Retail Sales
and Forecasts
Derived from a
Regression Model
of Seasonally
Adjusted Retail
Sales Based
on Disposable
Personal Income
Per Capita
(c4f7)*

Regression Results : RSSA as a function of DPI, taking seasonality into account

```
REGRESS : dependent variable is RSSA (Retail Sales Seasonally Adjusted)
Using    1986Q1-1995Q4
```

Variable	Coefficient	Std Err	T-stat	Signf
^CONST	-.181352E+07	116433.	-15.5757	.000
DPI	127.429	6.50421	19.5918	.000

```
                              Equation Summary
        No. of Observations =      40      R2=   .9099   (adj)=   .9075
        Sum of Sq. Resid. =   .165411E+11  Std. Error of Reg.= 20863.7
        Log(likelihood)   =  -453.562      Durbin-Watson     =  .74951
        Schwarz Criterion = -457.251       F ( 1,    38)     = 383.840
        Akaike Criterion  = -455.562       Significance      =  .000000
```

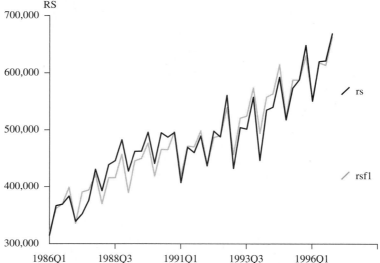

*The regression equation is: RSSA = −1,813,520 + 127.429(DPI). Values
for DPI are substituted into this equation, and the results are multiplied
by the seasonal indices to arrive at the predicted values for retail sales
shown in the graph. That is: RSF1 = (Regression prediction of RSSA) ×
(SI) = [−1,813,520 + 127.429(DPI)] × (SI)*

We can substitute values of DPI into this equation to get predictions for seasonally
adjusted retail sales (RSSA). Then, multiplying RSSA by the seasonal index for each
quarter, we obtain a prediction of the unadjusted retail sales for each quarter.

To forecast RS as a function of DPI, one must first forecast DPI. Forecasts for
primary macroeconomic series such as DPI are often purchased from one of the
econometric firms that provide such services. These causal variables may also be
forecast "in-house" by using an appropriate method. If we want to use the above
regression model to forecast RS for the four quarters of 1996, we must first develop

forecast values for DPI for those same quarters. As indicated in footnote 3, Holt's exponential smoothing model provides a good forecast for DPI. That model generates the following forecast values of DPI for 1996: Q1 = 18,981.0; Q2 = 19,027.1; Q3 = 19,073.3; and Q4 = 19,119.4. Recall that the seasonal indices (SI) are: Q1 = 0.908107; Q2 = 1.01351; Q3 = 1.00575; and Q4 = 1.07264. Our retail sales forecasts (RSF) for 1996 can now be calculated as follows:[4]

$$RSF = (\text{Regression Prediction of RSSA}) \times (SI)$$

$$RSF = [-1,813,520 + 127.429(DPI)] \times (SI)$$

1996Q1: RSF = $[-1,813,520 + 127.429(18,981.0)] \times (0.908107) = 549,595.300$

1996Q2 : RSF = $[-1,813,520 + 127.429(19,027.1)] \times (1.01351) = 619,340.075$

1996Q3 : RSF = $[-1,813,520 + 127.429(19,073.3)] \times (1.00575) = 620,519.132$

1996Q4 : RSF = $[-1,813,520 + 127.429(19,119.4)] \times (1.07264) = 668,089.558$

These values, as well as the values the model predicts for the historical period, are plotted in Figure 4–6, along with the actual data for 1986Q1 through 1996Q4. During the historic period, actual values of DPI were used to calculate RSF, while in the forecast period (1996Q1 to 1996Q4) forecast values of DPI were used as described.

Actual and predicted values of retail sales for 1996 are shown in the following table, along with the calculation of the root-mean-squared error (RMSE) for the forecast period:

Period	Actual RS	Forecast RSF	$(RS - RSF)^2$
1996Q1	552,928	549,595.300	11,106,889.29
1996Q2	617,069	619,340.075	5,157,781.66
1996Q3	612,813	620,519.132	59,384,470.40
1996Q4	662,486	668,089.558	31,399,862.26

Sum of squared errors = 107,049,003.61

Mean-squared error: MSE = $107,049,003.61 \div 4 = 26,762,250.90$

Root-mean-squared error: RMSE = $\sqrt{26,762,250.90} = 5,173.22$

This RMSE is about 0.8 percent of the mean for RS during these four quarters.

A Retail Sales Forecast Based on the Mortgage Rate

As mentioned above, a portion of retail sales involves "big ticket" items that are financed by many consumers, and thus we might expect that interest rates would influence purchasing decisions. Examples of products that may be bought on credit

---

[4]If you do these same calculations on a computer, you will get slightly different results due to the rounding and truncating done in the manual calculations shown here.

would include dishwashers, washing machines, dryers, refrigerators, home computers, home entertainment centers, and, of course, cars. To measure the influence of interest rates on retail sales, what we would really like is a weighted average of all different interest rates used for consumer purchases.

In reality we often find that the measure we most want is not available and so we use a "proxy" variable. That is, we use another variable that is available and that is closely related to the variable we want. We will show an example of this in the forecasting of retail sales. Because all interest rates tend to be closely related, we will use the mortgage rate as a proxy measure of the effect that interest rates may have on retail sales. We are not suggesting that people take out a mortgage to buy a car or a new washer and dryer, but rather that this rate may be indicative of the actual rate used for such purchases. It might be noted in passing that some people do get a new, or additional, mortgage on their home to borrow money that is then used to purchase a car or other consumer good.

Figure 4–8 shows a scatterplot of the relationship between retail sales and the mortgage rate. In general it appears in that graph that these two variables have an inverse relationship. Higher levels of retail sales appear to be related to lower mortgage rates, and vice versa.

Of the two causal variables we are considering, a measure of income per person and an interest rate, which do you think would be of the most help in forecasting retail sales? Most people would probably pick the income measure, since it takes money for all consumer purchases but only some retail sales are purchased using credit. Let's see how our models compare.

To develop the forecast model, seasonally adjusted retail sales were first regressed on the mortgage rate using data from 1986Q1 through 1995Q4. This resulted in the following model:

$$RSSA = 883,226 - 45,053.6(MR)$$

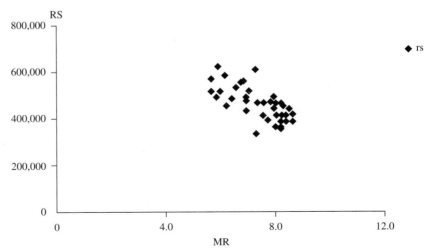

FIGURE 4–8

Scatterplot of Retail Sales Versus the Mortgage Rate (c4f8)

In this graph you see an inverse relationship between retail sales and the mortgage rate.

The negative coefficient for the mortgage rate is consistent with the idea that higher interest rates make credit purchases more expensive and should therefore reduce sales. The full regression model of seasonally adjusted retail sales as a function of the mortgage rate is given in Figure 4–9.

To get a forecast of RSSA for the four quarters of 1996, we needed to have a forecast of the mortgage rate for 1996Q1 through 1996Q4. This forecast was done using a linear-regression trend model. The predictions of RSSA from the model are

FIGURE 4–9

Retail Sales and Forecasts Derived from a Regression Model of Seasonally Adjusted Retail Sales Based on the Mortgage Rate (c4f9)

Regression Results: RSSA as a function of MR, taking seasonality into account

```
REGRESS : dependent variable is RSSA (Retail Sales Seasonally Adjusted)
Using    1986Q1-1995Q4

Variable          Coefficient      Std Err        T-stat        Signf

^CONST             883226.         55826.5        15.8209        .000
  MR              -45053.6          5991.24       -7.51991        .000


                               Equation Summary
       No. of Observations =         40      R2=  .5981   (adj)=    .5875
       Sum of Sq. Resid. =   .737999E+11    Std. Error of Reg.=   44069.3
       Log(likelihood)   =    -483.472      Durbin-Watson     =   .27464
       Schwarz Criterion =    -487.161      F ( 1,  38)       =   56.5491
       Akaike Criterion  =    -485.472      Significance      =   .000000
```

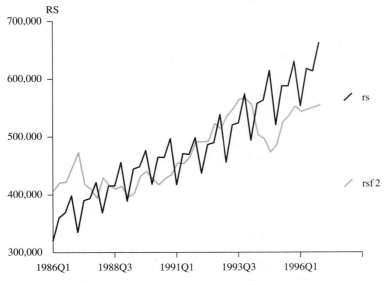

The regression equation is: RSSA = 883,226 − 45,053.6(MR). Values for MR are substituted into this equation and the results are multiplied by the seasonal indices to arrive at the predicted values for retail sales shown in the graph. That is: RSF2 = (Regression prediction of RSSA) × (SI) = [883,226 − 45,053.6(MR)] × (SI)

multiplied by the seasonal indices to arrive at the forecasts of retail sales.[5] These forecast values, along with actual retail sales, are plotted in the time-series graph of Figure 4–9. A visual inspection of this time-series plot in comparison with the results shown in Figure 4–7 supports the notion that DPI is a more important determinant of retail sales than is MR.

Actual and predicted values of retail sales for 1996, based on the mortgage rate model, are shown below, along with the root-mean-squared error (RMSE) for the forecast period:

Period	*Actual RS*	*Predicted RS*
1996Q1	552,928	542,988
1996Q2	617,069	546,710
1996Q3	612,813	550,431
1996Q4	662,486	554,153

Root-mean-squared error = 62,624.8

Note that this RMSE is greater than the RMSE for the DPI model (5,173.22). This supports our conclusion that the DPI is the better predictor of retail sales.

In the next chapter we will investigate the possibility of using the influence of both disposable personal income per capita and the mortgage rate in the same model. This will take us into the realm of multiple regression.

Statistical Evaluation of Regression Models

Now that you have a basic understanding of how simple bivariate regression models can be applied to forecasting, let us look more closely at some things that should be considered in evaluating regression models. Three of the regression models developed above will be used as the basis for our initial discussion. These are reproduced in Table 4–4. After evaluating these models in more detail we will turn our attention to the use of bivariate regression models to forecast domestic car sales and the sales of The Gap.

Basic Diagnostic Checks for Evaluating Regression Results

There are several things you should consider when you look at regression results. First, ask yourself whether the sign on the slope term makes sense. There is almost always an economic or business logic that indicates whether the relationship between the dependent variable (Y) and the independent variable (X) should be positive or negative.

---

[5]The seasonal indices are: Q1 = 0.908107; Q2 = 1.01351; Q3 = 1.00575; and Q4 = 1.07264. These are the same indices used for our model involving DPI.

TABLE 4–4 Statistical Results for Three Bivariate Regression Models*

Regression Results : DPI as a function of Time (T)

```
REGRESS : dependent variable is DPIO

Using   1986Q1-1995Q4

    Variable        Coefficient      Std Err      T-stat        Signf
    ^CONST            17052.1        59.6121      286.051        .000
    T                 41.0672        2.53382       16.2076       .000

                           Equation Summary
        No. of Observations =       40      R2=  .8736 (adj)=     .8703
        Sum of Sq. Resid. =   .130035E+07   Std. Error of Reg.= 184.986
        Log(likelihood)   =  -264.543       Durbin-Watson    =   .62196
        Schwarz Criterion =  -268.232       F ( 1,   38)     =  262.687
        Akaike Criterion  =  -266.543       Significance     =  .000000
```

Regression Results : RSSA as a function of DPI

```
REGRESS : dependent variable is RSSA (Retail Sales Seasonally Adjusted)
Using   1986Q1-1995Q4

    Variable        Coefficient      Std Err      T-stat        Signf
    ^CONST          -.181352E+07     116433.     -15.5757        .000
    DPI               127.429        6.50421       19.5918       .000

                           Equation Summary
        No. of Observations =       40      R2=  .9099  (adj)=    .9075
        Sum of Sq. Resid. =   .165411E+11   Std. Error of Reg.= 20863.7
        Log(likelihood)   =  -453.562       Durbin-Watson    =   .74951
        Schwarz Criterion =  -457.251       F ( 1,   38)     =  383.840
        Akaike Criterion  =  -455.562       Significance     =  .000000
```

Regression Results : RSSA as a function of MR

```
REGRESS : dependent variable is RSSA (Retail Sales Seasonally Adjusted)
Using   1986Q1-1995Q4

    Variable        Coefficient      Std Err      T-stat        Signf
    ^CONST            883226.        55826.5      15.8209        .000
    MR               -45053.6        5991.24      -7.51991       .000

                           Equation Summary
        No. of Observations =       40      R2=  .5981  (adj)=    .5875
        Sum of Sq. Resid. =   .737999E+11   Std. Error of Reg.= 44069.3
        Log(likelihood)   =  -483.472       Durbin-Watson    =   .27464
        Schwarz Criterion =  -487.161       F ( 1,   38)     =   56.5491
        Akaike Criterion  =  -485.472       Significance     =  .000000
```

*Some of the more advanced statistics shown here will not be discussed until Chapter 5.

In two of the examples considered so far in this chapter, a positive sign makes sense. In the first model we know that real disposable personal income per capita in the United States has generally increased over time. There have been some short periods of decline but such periods have been exceptions. Thus, we would expect the positive sign on the coefficient of T, the time index, in the trend model for DPI. In the second example, where retail sales (RS) is modeled as a function of real disposable personal income per capita (DPI), a positive sign is also logical. For most goods and services, sales can be expected to increase as income increases. In the third model, for which retail sales is a function of the mortgage rate, the negative coefficient for MR is also to be expected. The mortgage rate is used as a proxy for the rate of interest on consumer installment loans, and as that rate increases we would expect consumers to borrow less. Thus, retail sales should decrease as interest rates rise.

What if the signs do not make sense? This is a clear indication that something is wrong with the regression model. It may be that the model is incomplete and that more than one independent variable is needed. In such a case the model is said to be *underspecified.* If so, a multiple-regression model may be appropriate. (Such models will be discussed in Chapter 5.) It would not be wise to use regression models that have coefficients with signs that are not logical.

The second thing that should be considered in an initial evaluation of a regression model is whether or not the slope term is significantly positive or negative. If not, then there is probably no statistical relationship between the dependent and independent variables. If the slope is zero, the regression line is perfectly horizontal, indicating that the value of Y is independent of the value of X (i.e., there is probably no relationship between X and Y).

But how far from zero need the slope term be? In the first example in Table 4–4 the slope is 41.0672, in the second it is 127.429, and in the third model the coefficient is $-45,053.6$. These are the relatively large numbers in terms of how much above or below zero they are, but we must be cautious about evaluating just the size of the slope term. To determine if the slope is significantly greater or less than zero, we must test a hypothesis concerning the true slope. Remember that our basic regression model is:

$$Y = \beta_0 + \beta_1 X + \varepsilon$$

If $\beta_1 = 0$, then $Y = \beta_0$ regardless of the value of X.

When we have a predisposition about whether the coefficient should be positive or negative based on our knowledge of the relationship, a one-tailed hypothesis test is appropriate. If our belief suggests a positive coefficient, the hypothesis would be set up as follows:

$$H_0: \beta \leq 0$$

$$H_1: \beta > 0$$

This form would be correct for the first two cases in Table 4–4, since in both cases a direct (positive) relationship is expected.

It would not be wise to use regression models that have coefficients with signs that are not logical.

When our belief suggests a negative coefficient, the hypothesis would be set up as follows:

$$H_0: \beta \geq 0$$

$$H_1: \beta < 0$$

This form would be correct for the third case in Table 4–4 because an inverse (negative) relationship is expected.

In some situations we may not have a specific expectation about the direction of causality, in which case a two-tailed hypothesis test is used. The hypothesis would be set up as follows:

$$H_0: \beta = 0$$

$$H_1: \beta \neq 0$$

The appropriate statistical test is a *t*-test, where the calculated value of *t* (t_{calc}) is equal to the slope term.[6] That is:

$$t_{calc} = (b_1 - 0)/(\text{s.e. of } b_1)$$

It is typical to use a 95 percent confidence level (an α, or significance level, of 5 percent) in testing this type of hypothesis. The appropriate number of degrees of freedom in bivariate regression is always $n-2$, where *n* is the number of observations used in estimating the model. As described above, when we have a greater-than or less-than sign in the alternative hypothesis, a one-tailed test is appropriate.

For our present examples there are 38 degrees of freedom (40 − 2). From the *t*-table in Chapter 2 we find the critical value of *t* (such that 0.05 is in one tail) to be 1.645 (using the infinity row). The calculated values of *t* are:

For the DPI Trend Model	For the RS = f(DPI) Causal Model	For the RS = f(MR) Causal Model
$t_{calc} = (41.0672 - 0)/2.53382$	$t_{calc} = (127.429 - 0)/6.50421$	$t_{calc} = (-45,053.6 - 0)/5,991.24$
$= 16.2076$	$= 19.5918$	$= -7.5199$

For the first two cases the calculated values are larger than the critical, or table, value so we can reject H_0 in both cases and conclude that the regression coefficients are significantly greater than zero. In the third case the calculated *t* is more negative than the negative of the table value, and so once again we can reject H_0. In this case we conclude that the coefficient on MR is significantly negative. If this statistical evaluation of the coefficients in a regression analysis results in failure to reject the

---

[6]The standard error of the estimated regression coefficient measures the sampling variability of b_1 about its expected value β_1, the true population parameter.

null hypothesis, then it is probably not wise to use the model as a forecasting tool.[7] However, it is not uncommon to relax the criterion for evaluation of the hypothesis test to a 90 percent confidence level (a 10 percent significance level).

In determining whether or not to reject H_0, an alternative to comparing t-values is to consider the significance level given in most computer output. Let us assume that we desire a 95 percent confidence level. This is the equivalent of saying that we desire a 5 percent significance level.[8]

For a two-tailed hypothesis test ($H_1: \beta_1 \neq 0$), we can then reject H_0 if the reported two-tailed significance level[9] in our output is less than 0.05. For a one-tailed hypothesis test ($H_1: \beta_1 < 0$ or $H_1: \beta_1 > 0$), we can reject H_0 if one-half of the reported two-tailed significance level is less than 0.05.

In all three of the examples in Table 4–4 the two-tailed significance levels associated with the calculated t-ratios are 0.000. Clearly, one-half of 0.000 is less than 0.05, so it is appropriate to reject H_0 in all three cases. Note that we reach the same conclusion whether we evaluate the hypotheses by comparing the calculated and table t-ratios or by looking at the significance levels.

The third check of regression results is to evaluate what percent of the variation (i.e., up-and-down movement) in the dependent variable is explained by variation in the independent variable. This is evaluated by interpreting the R-squared value that is reported in regression output. R-squared is the coefficient of determination, which tells us the fraction of the variation in the dependent variable that is explained by variation in the independent variable. Thus, R-squared can range between zero and one. Zero would indicate no explanatory power, while one would indicate that all of the variation in Y is explained by the variation in X. (A related statistic, adjusted R-squared, will be discussed in Chapter 5.)

Our trend model for disposable personal income per capita (DPI) has an R-squared of .8736. Thus, 87.36 percent of the variation in real disposable personal income per capita is accounted for by this simple linear-trend model. The causal model for retail sales as a function of DPI has an R-squared of .9099, which suggests that 90.99 percent of the variation in retail sales is explained by variations in real disposable personal income per capita. The model for retail sales as a function of the mortgage rate has the lowest R-squared of the three models in Table 4–4; $R^2 = .5981$. Thus, variations in the mortgage rate explain only 59.81 percent of the variation in retail sales.

It is possible to perform a statistical test to determine whether the the coefficient of determination (R^2) is significantly different from zero. The hypothesis test may be stated as:

$$H_0: R^2 = 0$$
$$H_1: R^2 \neq 0$$

---

[7]A phenomenon known as *serial correlation* (which we will discuss shortly) may cause coefficients to appear significantly different from zero (as measured by the t-test) when in fact they are not.

[8]Remember that the confidence level and the significance level add to one. Thus, if we know one of these we can easily determine the other.

[9]In SORITEC, as well as most other statistical packages, two-tailed significance levels are reported.

The appropriate statistical test is an *F*-test, which will be presented in Chapter 5. With bivariate regression it turns out that the *t*-test for the slope term in the regression equation is equivalent to the *F*-test for R^2. Thus, we will wait until we explore multiple-regression models to discuss the application of the *F*-test.

Before considering other statistical diagnostics, let us summarize these three initial evaluative steps for bivariate regression models:

1. Ask whether the sign for the slope term makes sense.
2. Check to see whether the slope term is statistically positive or negative at the desired significance level by using a *t*-test.
3. Evaluate how much of the variation in the dependent variable is explained by the regression model using the *R*-squared (R^2) value.

These three items can be evaluated from the results presented in standard computer output, such as the SORITEC results given in Table 4–4.

Using the Standard Error of the Regression

The forecasts we made in the preceding paragraphs—using a simple linear-trend model and the two causal regression models—were point estimates. In each case we substituted a value for the independent variable into the regression equation to obtain a single number representing our best estimate (forecast) of the dependent variable. It is sometimes useful to provide an interval estimate rather than a point estimate.

The standard error of the regression can be used to generate *approximate* confidence intervals with relative ease. The confidence intervals we present here are approximate because the true confidence band is not parallel to the regression line but rather bows away from the regression line at values of *Y* and *X* far from the means. This is illustrated in Figure 4–10. The approximate 95 percent confidence interval can be calculated as follows.[10]

$$\text{Point estimate} \pm 2 \text{ (standard error of the regression)}$$

The value of 2 is used as an easy approximation for the correct *t*-value. Recall that if there is a large number of degrees of freedom, $t = 1.96$.

The calculation of approximate 95 percent confidence bands for the regression forecasts developed for DPI and RSSA are shown in Table 4–5. The standard errors of the regressions are taken from Table 4–4, while the point estimates for each model and each quarter are those that were found in the sections "Forecasting with a Simple Linear Trend" and "Using a Causal Regression Model to Forecast."

---

[10]The true 95 percent confidence band for predicting *Y* for a given value of *X* (X_0) can be found as follows:

$$\hat{Y} \pm t(\text{s.e.r.})\sqrt{1 + (1/n) + [(X_0 - \overline{X})^2 / \sum(X - \overline{X})^2]}$$

where *t* is the appropriate value from the *t*-distribution at $n - 2$ degrees of freedom and the desired significance level; s.e.r. is the standard error of the regression; and $\hat{Y}$ is the point estimate determined from the estimated regression equation.

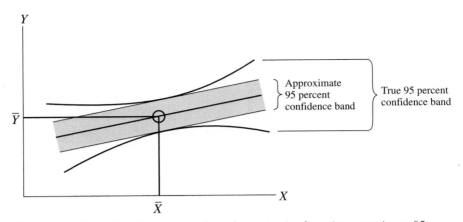

FIGURE 4–10

*Confidence
Bands around
a Regression Line*

*The true confidence band bows away from the regression line. An approximate 95
percent confidence band can be calculated by taking the point estimate for each X, plus
or minus 2 times the standard error of the regression.*

**TABLE 4–5   Calculation of Approximate 95 Percent Confidence Intervals:
Point Estimate $\pm 2 \times$ Standard Error of the Estimate (s.e.r.)***

**For DPI $= f(T) = 17{,}052.1 + 41.0672(T)$
$2 \times$ s.e.r. $= 2 \times 184.986 = 369.972$**

Period	95 Percent Confidence Interval	Actual DPI
1996Q1	$18{,}736 \pm 369.972 = 18{,}366.03$ to $19{,}105.97$	19,028.0
1996Q2	$18{,}777 \pm 369.972 = 18{,}407.03$ to $19{,}146.97$	19,053.0
1996Q3	$18{,}818 \pm 369.972 = 18{,}448.03$ to $19{,}187.97$	19,233.0
1996Q4	$18{,}859 \pm 369.972 = 18{,}489.03$ to $19{,}228.97$	19,314.7

**For RSSA $= f(\text{DPI}) = 1{,}813{,}520 + 127.429(\text{DPI})$
$\times$s.e.r. $= 2 \times 20{,}863.7 = 41{,}727.4$**

Period	95 Percent Confidence Interval	Actual RSSA**
1996Q1	$605{,}210 \pm 41{,}727.4 = 563{,}482.6$ to $646{,}937.4$	608,880
1996Q2	$611{,}084 \pm 41{,}727.4 = 569{,}356.6$ to $652{,}811.4$	608,845
1996Q3	$616{,}972 \pm 41{,}727.4 = 575{,}244.6$ to $658{,}699.4$	609,311
1996Q4	$622{,}846 \pm 41{,}727.4 = 581{,}118.6$ to $664{,}573.4$	617,624

**For RSSA $= f(\text{MR}) = 883{,}226 - 45{,}053.6(\text{MR})$
$\times$s.e.r. $= 2 \times 44{,}069.3 = 88{,}138.6$**

Period	95 Percent Confidence Interval	Actual RSSA**
1996Q1	$597{,}934 \pm 88{,}138.6 = 509{,}795.4$ to $686{,}072.6$	608,880
1996Q2	$539{,}422 \pm 88{,}138.6 = 451{,}283.4$ to $627{,}560.6$	608,845
1996Q3	$547{,}284 \pm 88{,}138.6 = 459{,}145.4$ to $635{,}422.6$	609,311
1996Q4	$516{,}625 \pm 88{,}138.6 = 428{,}486.4$ to $604{,}763.6$	617,624

*Point estimates have been rounded to integers.
**Note that these are for retail sales seasonally adjusted.

Serial Correlation

Business and economic data used in forecasting are most often time-series data. The retail sales data and the real disposable personal income data used in this chapter are typical of such time series. In using regression analysis with time-series data, the problem known as *serial correlation* can cause some difficulty.

One of the assumptions of the ordinary least-squares regression model is that the error terms are independent and normally distributed, with a mean of zero and a constant variance. If this is true for a particular case, we would not expect to find any regular pattern in the error terms. When a significant time pattern that violates the independence assumption is found in the error terms, serial correlation is indicated.

Figure 4–11 illustrates the two possible cases of serial correlation. In the left-hand graph, the case of negative serial correlation is apparent. Negative serial correlation exists when a negative error is followed by a positive error, then another negative error, and so on. The error terms alternate in sign. Positive serial correlation is shown in the right-hand graph in Figure 4–11. In positive serial correlation, positive errors tend to be followed by other positive errors, while negative errors are followed by other negative errors.

When serial correlation exists, problems can develop in using and interpreting the OLS regression function. The existence of serial correlation does not bias the coefficients that are estimated, but it does make the estimates of the standard errors smaller than the true standard errors. This means that the *t*-ratios calculated for each coefficient will be overstated, which in turn may lead to the rejection of null hypotheses that should not have been rejected. That is, regression coefficients may be deemed statistically significant when indeed they are not. In addition, the existence of serial correlation causes the R^2 and *F*-statistics to be unreliable in evaluating the overall significance of the regression function (the *F*-statistic will be discussed in Chapter 5).

FIGURE 4–11

Negative and Positive Serial Correlation

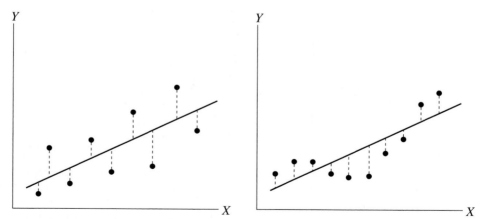

The left-hand graph shows an example of negative serial correlation; the right-hand graph illustrates positive serial correlation. The latter is common when dealing with business data.

There are a number of ways to test statistically for the existence of serial correlation. The method most frequently used is the evaluation of the Durbin-Watson statistic (DW). This statistic is calculated as follows:

$$\text{DW} = \frac{\sum (e_t - e_{t-1})^2}{\sum e_t^2}$$

where e_t is the residual for the time period t, and e_{t-1} is the residual for the preceding time period $(t - 1)$. Almost all computer printouts for regression analysis include the Durbin-Watson statistic, so you are not likely to have to calculate it directly.

The DW statistic will always be in the range of 0 to 4. As a rule of thumb, a value close to 2 (e.g., between 1.75 and 2.25) indicates that there is no serial correlation. As the degree of negative serial correlation increases, the value of the DW statistic approaches 4. If positive serial correlation exists, the value of DW approaches 0.

To be more precise in evaluating the significance and meaning of the calculated DW statistic, we must refer to a Durbin-Watson table, such as Table 4–6. Note that for each number of independent variables (k), two columns of values labeled d_l and d_u are given. The values in these columns for the appropriate number of observations (N) are used in evaluating the calculated value of DW according to the criteria shown in Figure 4–11.

To illustrate, let us consider the simple trend regression for real disposable personal income per capita (DPI). From Table 4–2 (see page 147) you see that the calculated Durbin-Watson statistic is approximately 0.622. Using Table 4–6, we find for $k = 1$ and $N = 40$ that:

$$d_l = 1.44$$

$$d_u = 1.54$$

Using these values and our calculated value, we can evaluate the criteria in Figure 4–12:

Region	Comparison	Result
A	$4 > 0.622 > (4 - 1.44)$	False
B	$(4 - 1.44) > 0.622 > (4 - 1.54)$	False
C	$(4 - 1.54) > 0.622 > 1.54$	False
D	$1.54 > 0.622 > 1.44$	False
E	$1.44 > 0.622 > 0$	True

Since our result is in region E, we can conclude that positive serial correlation exists in this case.[11] You can see evidence of this positive serial correlation if you look in

---

[11] Check for serial correlation in the regression of RSSA as a function of DPI. You should find that with a calculated Durbin-Watson statistic of 0.7495, with $k = 1$, and with $N = 40$, the criterion in region E is satisfied, indicating positive serial correlation.

Table 4–6   The Durbin-Watson Statistic

N	k = 1		k = 2		k = 3		k = 4		k = 5	
	d_l	d_u	d_l	d_u	d_l	d_u	d_l	d_u	d_l	d_u
15	1.08	1.36	0.95	1.54	0.82	1.75	0.69	1.97	0.56	2.21
16	1.10	1.37	0.98	1.54	0.86	1.73	0.74	1.93	0.62	2.15
17	1.13	1.38	1.02	1.54	0.90	1.71	0.78	1.90	0.67	2.10
18	1.16	1.39	1.05	1.53	0.93	1.69	0.82	1.87	0.71	2.06
19	1.18	1.40	1.08	1.53	0.97	1.68	0.86	1.85	0.75	2.02
20	1.20	1.41	1.10	1.54	1.00	1.68	0.90	1.83	0.79	1.99
21	1.22	1.42	1.13	1.54	1.03	1.67	0.93	1.81	0.83	1.96
22	1.24	1.43	1.15	1.54	1.05	1.66	0.96	1.80	0.86	1.94
23	1.26	1.44	1.17	1.54	1.08	1.66	0.99	1.79	0.90	1.92
24	1.27	1.45	1.19	1.55	1.10	1.66	1.01	1.78	0.93	1.90
25	1.29	1.45	1.21	1.55	1.12	1.66	1.04	1.77	0.95	1.89
26	1.30	1.46	1.22	1.55	1.14	1.65	1.06	1.76	0.98	1.88
27	1.32	1.47	1.24	1.56	1.16	1.65	1.08	1.76	1.01	1.86
28	1.33	1.48	1.26	1.56	1.18	1.65	1.10	1.75	1.03	1.85
29	1.34	1.48	1.27	1.56	1.20	1.65	1.12	1.74	1.05	1.84
30	1.35	1.49	1.28	1.57	1.21	1.65	1.14	1.74	1.07	1.83
31	1.36	1.50	1.30	1.57	1.23	1.65	1.16	1.74	1.09	1.83
32	1.37	1.50	1.31	1.57	1.24	1.65	1.18	1.73	1.11	1.82
33	1.38	1.51	1.32	1.58	1.26	1.65	1.19	1.73	1.13	1.81
34	1.39	1.51	1.33	1.58	1.27	1.65	1.21	1.73	1.15	1.81
35	1.40	1.52	1.34	1.53	1.28	1.65	1.22	1.73	1.16	1.80
36	1.41	1.52	1.35	1.59	1.29	1.65	1.24	1.73	1.18	1.80
37	1.42	1.53	1.36	1.59	1.31	1.66	1.25	1.72	1.19	1.80
38	1.43	1.54	1.37	1.59	1.32	1.66	1.26	1.72	1.21	1.79
39	1.43	1.54	1.38	1.60	1.33	1.66	1.27	1.72	1.22	1.79
40	1.44	1.54	1.39	1.60	1.34	1.66	1.29	1.72	1.23	1.79
45	1.48	1.57	1.43	1.62	1.38	1.67	1.34	1.72	1.29	1.78
50	1.50	1.59	1.46	1.63	1.42	1.67	1.38	1.72	1.34	1.77
55	1.53	1.60	1.49	1.64	1.45	1.68	1.41	1.72	1.38	1.77
60	1.55	1.62	1.51	1.65	1.48	1.69	1.44	1.73	1.41	1.77
65	1.57	1.63	1.54	1.66	1.50	1.70	1.47	1.73	1.44	1.77
70	1.58	1.64	1.55	1.67	1.52	1.70	1.49	1.74	1.46	1.77
75	1.60	1.65	1.57	1.68	1.54	1.71	1.51	1.74	1.49	1.77
80	1.61	1.66	1.59	1.69	1.56	1.72	1.53	1.74	1.51	1.77
85	1.62	1.67	1.60	1.70	1.57	1.72	1.55	1.75	1.52	1.77
90	1.63	1.68	1.61	1.70	1.59	1.73	1.57	1.75	1.54	1.78
95	1.64	1.69	1.62	1.71	1.60	1.73	1.58	1.75	1.56	1.78
100	1.65	1.69	1.63	1.72	1.61	1.74	1.59	1.76	1.57	1.78

k = the number of independent variables; N = the number of observations used in the regression.

SOURCE: J. Durbin and G. S. Watson, "Testing for Serial Correlation in Least Squares Regression," *Biometrika* 38 (June 1951), p. 173.

Figure 4–3 at how the regression line (fitted) is at first above, then below, then above, and then below the actual data in a recurring pattern.

You might well ask: What causes serial correlation and what can be done about it? A primary cause of serial correlation is the existence of long-term cycles and

FIGURE 4–12

*A Schematic
for Evaluating
Serial Correlation
Using the Durbin-
Watson Statistic*

Value of Calculated Durbin-Watson	Result	Region Designator
4		
	Negative serial correlation (reject H_0)	A
$4 - d_l$		
	Indeterminate	B
$4 - d_u$		
	No serial correlation (do not reject H_0)	C
2------		
d_u		
	Indeterminate	D
d_l		
	Positive serial correlation (reject H_0)	E
0		

d_u = Upper value of Durbin-Watson from Table 4–6

d_l = Lower value of Durbin-Watson from Table 4–6

H_0: $\rho = 0$ (i.e., no serial correlation)

H_1: $\rho \neq 0$ (i.e., serial correlation exists)

A primary
cause of serial
correlation is the
existence of long-
term cycles and
trends in economic
and business data.

trends in economic and business data. Such trends and cycles are particularly likely to produce positive serial correlation. Serial correlation can also be caused by a mis-specification of the model. Either leaving out one or more important variables or failing to include a nonlinear term when one is called for can be a cause.

We can try several relatively simple things to reduce serial correlation. One is to use first differences of the variables rather than the actual values when performing the regression analysis. That is, use the change in each variable from period to period in the regression. For example, we could try the following:

$$\Delta Y = b_0 + b_1(\Delta X)$$

where Δ means "change in" and is calculated as follows:

$$\Delta Y_t = Y_t - Y_{t-1}$$

$$\Delta X_t = X_t - X_{t-1}$$

This process of "first-differencing" will be seen again in Chapter 7, when we discuss ARIMA forecasting models.

Other approaches to solving the serial-correlation problem often involve moving into the realm of multiple regression, where there is more than one independent variable in the regression model. For example, it may be that other causal factors account for the differences between the actual and predicted values. For example, in the retail sales regression, we might add the interest rate and the unemployment rate as additional independent variables.

A third, and somewhat related, approach to dealing with serial correlation is to introduce the square of an existing causal variable as another independent variable.

Also, we might introduce a lag of the dependent variable as an independent variable. Such a model might look as follows:

$$Y_t = b_0 + b_1 X_t + b_2 Y_{t-1}$$

where t represents the current time period and $t - 1$ represents the previous time period.

There are other procedures, based on more sophisticated statistical models, that are helpful in dealing with the problems created by serial correlation. These are typically based on an extension of the use of first differences in that they involve the use of generalized differencing to alter the basic linear regression model into one for which the error terms are independent of one another (i.e., $\rho = 0$, where ρ (rho) is the correlation between successive error terms).

The basic regression model is:

$$Y_t = \beta_0 + \beta_1 X_t + \varepsilon_t$$

and since this is true for all time periods, it follows that:

$$Y_{t-1} = \beta_0 + \beta_1 X_{t-1} + \varepsilon_{t-1}$$

Multiplying the second of these equations by ρ and subtracting the result from the first yields the following generalized-differencing transformed equation:

$$Y_t^* = (1 - \rho)\beta_0 + \beta_1 X_t^* + v_t$$

where:

$$Y_t^* = Y_t - \rho Y_{t-1}$$

$$X_t^* = X_t - \rho X_{t-1}$$

$$v_t = \varepsilon_t - \rho \varepsilon_{t-1}$$

It can be shown that the resulting error term, v_t, is independently distributed with a mean of zero and a constant variance.[12] The problem with this generalized-differencing model is that we do not know the correct value for ρ. Two common methods for estimating ρ and the corresponding regression model are the Cochrane-Orcutt procedure and the Hildreth-Lu procedure.[13]

The Cochrane-Orcutt procedure uses an iterative approach to estimate the value for ρ, starting with the standard OLS regression model, from which the residuals (e_t) are used to estimate the equation $e_t = \rho e_{t-1} + v_t$. The estimated value of ρ is then used to perform the generalized-differencing transformation, and a new regression is run. New error terms result and are used to make another estimate of ρ. This process continues until the newest estimate of ρ differs from the previous one by a prescribed amount (such as 0.01).

---

[12]Most econometrics books describe the underlying statistical theory as well as the two correction procedures we include herein. For example, see Pindyck and Rubinfeld, *Econometric Models and Economic Forecasts,* pp. 137–47.

[13]Both of these advanced methods are available in the software accompanying this text.

Applying the Cochrane-Orcutt procedure to the RSSA $= f(\text{DPI})$ model yields the following results:

```
Dependent variable is RSSA.          Using 1986Q2-1995Q4

Variable             Coefficient      Std Err        T-stat       Signf
^CONST                  551125.       143406.        3.84312       .001
DPI                    10.8673        6.58502        1.62161       .113
^RHO                    .981313       .308118E-01   31.8486        .000

Durbin-Watson = 2.57            R2=.9925
```

Notice that in comparison with the OLS results shown in Figure 4–7, the *t*-statistic for DPI is lower, as would be expected if the OLS estimate of the standard error were too low (1.62 compared with the 19.59 shown in Figure 4–7). Using the Cochrane-Orcutt procedure, DW = 2.57 (versus 0.7495 in the OLS specification). This Durbin-Watson statistic (2.57) falls in region B of Figure 4–12, indicating that the result is indeterminate. In this example the Cochrane-Orcutt procedure took care of the positive serial correlation problem that results in many business or economic situations. However, the resulting model is quite close to the region in which there is negative serial correlation. (For this Durbin-Watson test, $N = 39$ and $k = 1$, so $d_l = 1.43$ and $d_u = 1.54$.)

Applying these results to make estimates for the dependent variable involves rewriting the generalized-difference model as:

$$Y_t = \beta_0 + \beta_1 X_t + \rho[Y_{t-1} - (\beta_0 + \beta_1 X_{t-1})] + v_t$$

$$\hat{Y}_t = b_0 + b_1 X_t + \hat{\rho}[Y_{t-1} - (b_0 + b_1 X_{t-1})]$$

Thus, for our model of retail sales (RSSA) as a function of disposable personal income (DPI), we would have:

$$\text{RSSA}_t = b_0 + b_1 \times \text{DPI}_t + \hat{\rho}[\text{RSSA}_{t-1} - (b_0 + b_1 \times \text{DPI}_{t-1})]$$

$$= 551,125 + 10.6783 \times \text{DPI}_t$$

$$+ 0.981313[\text{RSSA}_{t-1} - (551,125 + 10.6783 \times \text{DPI}_{t-1})]$$

Professional software packages (such as the SORITEC Sampler that comes with this text) make all the algebra involved in this method transparent to the user.

The Hildreth-Lu procedure is also based on the generalized-differencing transformed equation. In this method a grid of possible values is specified for ρ such as: 0, 0.1, 0.2, 0.3, and 0.4. The procedure uses the values in this grid to estimate the parameters for the model and selects the equation that has the lowest sum of squared residuals. A new grid with finer divisions can then be established around this first value of ρ, and a new value is determined. This process can be continued until the desired level of accuracy is obtained. (This method is also available in the software that accompanies this text.)

Heteroscedasticity

One of the assumptions of regression analysis is that the error terms in the population regression (ε_i) have a constant variance across all values of the independent variable (X). When this is true, the model is said to be homoscedastic, and if this assumption is violated the model is termed heteroscedastic. With heteroscedasticity, the standard errors of the regression coefficients may be underestimated, causing the calculated *t*-ratios to be larger than they should be, which may lead us to conclude incorrectly that a variable is statistically significant.

We can evaluate a regression model for heteroscedasticity by looking at a scatterplot of the residuals (on the vertical axis) versus the independent variable (on the horizontal axis). In an ideal model the plot of the residuals would fall within a horizontal band, as shown in the top graph of Figure 4–13. This graph illustrates a residual pattern representative of homoscedasticity. A typical heteroscedastic situation is shown by the funnel-shaped pattern of residuals in the lower graph of Figure 4–13.

One common way to reduce or eliminate a problem of heteroscedasticity is to use the logarithm of the dependent variable in the estimation of the regression model.

FIGURE 4–13

Residual Patterns Indicative of Homoscedasticity (Top Graph) and Heteroscedasticity (Bottom Graph)

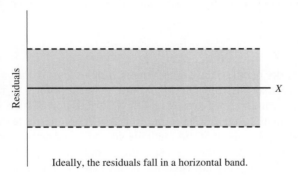

Ideally, the residuals fall in a horizontal band.

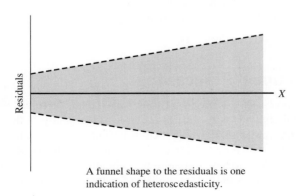

A funnel shape to the residuals is one indication of heteroscedasticity.

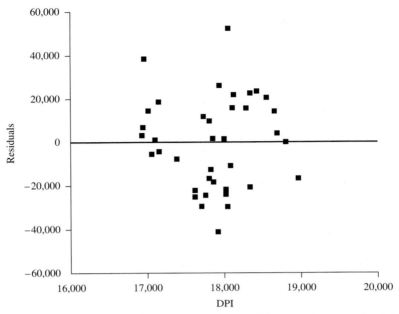

FIGURE 4–14

*Scatterplot of the
Residuals from
the Regression of
RSSA with DPI*
(c4f14)

This scatterplot does not show a pattern that would suggest heteroscedasticity.

This often works because the logarithms will have less overall variability than the raw data. A second possible solution would be to use a form of regression analysis other than the ordinary least-squares method. Discussion of such methods is beyond the scope of this text but can be found in many econometric texts. (The SORITEC software will handle many of the methods you will find suggested.)

To illustrate the evaluation of a specific model for heteroscedasticity, let us look at the model of seasonally adjusted retail sales (RSSA) as a function of disposable personal income per capita (DPI). Figure 4–14 shows a scattergram of the residuals from that model. There does not appear to be a systematic pattern to the residuals that would lead us to suspect heteroscedasticity in this case.

Cross-Sectional Forecasting

While most forecasting is based on time-series data, there are situations in which cross-sectional analysis is useful. In cross-sectional analysis the data all pertain to one time period rather than a sequence of periods. Suppose, for example, that you are the sales manager for a firm that sells small specialty sandwiches through convenience stores. You currently operate in eight cities and are considering expanding into another. You have the following data for the most recent year's sales and the

While most forecasting is based on time-series data, there are situations in which cross-sectional analysis is useful. In cross-sectional analysis the data all pertain to one time period rather than a sequence of periods.

population of each city:

City	Sales (000)	Population (000)
1	372	505
2	275	351
3	214	186
4	135	175
5	81	132
6	144	115
7	90	108
8	97	79

You may try to predict sales based on population by using a bivariate regression model. The model may be written as:

$$\text{Sales} = b_0 + b_1(\text{POP})$$

Regression results for this model, given the eight data points just shown, are presented in Table 4–7.

These results show the expected positive sign for the coefficient of population. The critical value of t from the t-table at six degrees of freedom ($n - 2 = 6$) and a 5 percent significance level (one-tailed test) is 1.943. Since the calculated value is greater ($8.004 > 1.943$), we conclude that there is a statistically significant positive relationship between sales and population. The coefficient of determination (R-squared) is 0.914, which tells us that 91.4 percent of the variation in sales is explained by the variation in population.

Now suppose that the city that you are considering expanding into has a population of 155,000. You can use the regression results to forecast sales as

TABLE 4–7   Regression Results for Sales as a Function of Population

```
Variable    | Coefficient |       Std Err |  t-stat   |  Signf
-----------------------------------------------------------------
 ^CONST     |    37.0219  |     20.8634  | 1.77449   |  0.126
  POP       |    .673425  | .841293E-01  | 8.00465   |  0.000
-----------------------------------------------------------------
                    Equation Summary
No. of Observations =        8      R2 = 0.9144 (adj)  =   0.9001
Sum of Sq. Resid.   =  6424.15      Std. Error of Reg. =  32.7214
                                    Durbin-Watson       =  2.64387
                                    F (1,6)             =  64.0744
                                    Significance        = 0.000302
```

follows:

$$\text{Sales} = 37.02 + 0.6734(\text{POP})$$
$$= 37.02 + 0.6734(155)$$
$$= 141.397$$

Remember that sales are in thousands, so this is a point estimate of 141,397 sandwiches. An approximate 95 percent confidence band could be constructed as follows:

$$\text{Point estimate} \pm 2(\text{standard error of regression}) = 141.397 \pm 2(32.721)$$
$$= 141.397 \pm 65.442$$
$$= 75.955 \text{ to } 206.839$$

That is, about 76,000 to 207,000 sandwiches.

Forecasting Domestic Car Sales with Bivariate Regression

You may recall that the domestic car sales series (DCS) that we forecast in Chapters 1 and 3 shows quite a bit of variability, including a substantial seasonal component. Therefore, you might expect that it would be difficult to forecast such a series based on a simple regression equation with one causal variable. One thing that would make the process more workable would be to deseasonalize DCS prior to attempting to build a regression model.

What are the causal factors that you think would influence the sales of domestic cars? You might come up with a fairly long list. Some of the variables that might be on such a list are:

Income
Unemployment rate
Interest rates
Consumer attitudes
Domestic car prices
Foreign car prices

In this section we will focus on consumer attitudes as measured by the University of Michigan's Index of Consumer Sentiment. This is an index that is released each month by the University of Michigan Survey Research Center. Each month 500 respondents in a national survey are interviewed about a variety of topics. There are five specific questions in the survey that go into the calculation of the Index of Consumer Sentiment, which has been adjusted to a base of 100 for 1966. Those five questions are:

1. We are interested in how people are getting along financially these days. Would you say that you (and your family living there) are better off or worse off financially than you were a year ago?

2. Now looking ahead—do you think that a year from now you (and your family living there) will be better off financially, or worse off, or about the same as now?

3. Now turning to business conditions in the country as a whole—do you think that during the next twelve months we'll have good times financially, or bad times, or what?

4. Looking ahead, which would you say is more likely—that in the country as a whole we'll have continuous good times during the next five years or so, or that we will have periods of widespread unemployment or depression, or what?

5. About the big things people buy for their homes—such as furniture, a refrigerator, stove, television, and things like that. Generally speaking, do you think now is a good or bad time for people to buy major household items?

The way in which the index is computed makes it higher when people's responses to these questions are more positive.

When seasonally adjusted quarterly data for domestic car sales (DCSSA) are regressed as a function of the University of Michigan Index of Consumer Sentiment (CS), the following results are obtained:

```
REGRESS : dependent variable is DCSSA
Using    1981Q1-1994Q4

Variable        Coefficient     Std Err        T-stat       Signf

^CONST            381.696        157.942        2.41668      .019
CS                15.9937        1.82957        8.74176      .000


                          Equation Summary
       No. of Observations =       56       R2=    .5859    (adj)=   .5783
       Sum of Sq. Resid. =    .102852E+07   Std. Error of Reg.=  138.009
       Log(likelihood)   =   -354.372       Durbin-Watson     =    1.53794
       Schwarz Criterion =   -358.398       F ( 1,   54)      =   76.4183
       Akaike Criterion  =   -356.372       Significance      =    .000000
```

The equation for seasonally adjusted domestic car sales is:

$$DCSSA = 381.696 + 15.9937(CS)$$

Given the makeup of the index of consumer sentiment, the positive coefficient (15.9937) for that variable is logical and from the *t*-ratio (8.74) we see that CS is quite statistically significant in this model (the significance level is .000—even at a two-tailed level). The *R*-squared (R^2) tells us that 58.59 percent of the variation in seasonally adjusted retail car sales is explained by this model. From Figure 4–12 we see that the Durbin-Watson test for serial correlation is indeterminate.

To make a forecast of DCSSA for the four quarters of 1996 with this model we first need a forecast of CS for those quarters. A simple exponential smoothing

TABLE 4–8   **Summary Table of RMSEs for DCS**

Chapter	Method	Period	RMSE
1	Naive—with 4-period lag	Historic before '95	207.3
		Holdout 95Q1–95Q4	74.9
2	Not applicable	Historic before '95	na
		Holdout 95Q1–95Q4	na
3	Winters' exponential smoothing	Historic before '95	177.1
		Holdout 95Q1–95Q4	55.8
	ADRES with seasonal adjustment	Historic before '95	169.5
		Holdout 95Q1–95Q4	67.7
4	Simple regression model using seasonally adjusted DCS as a function of the University of Michigan Index of Consumer Sentiment	Historic before '95	134.570
		Holdout 95Q1–95Q4	102.242

FIGURE 4–15

Domestic Car Sales (DCS) and a Simple Regression Forecast (DCSRF) (c4dcs)

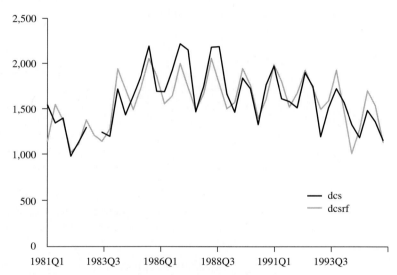

To develop this forecast, DCS were first deseasonalized, then those values were regressed as a function of the University of Michigan's Index of Consumer Sentiment. The resulting model was used to predict deseasonalized values for DCS, which were multiplied by the seasonal indices to arrive at the forecast (DCSRF) shown in the graph.

forecast was used in this instance. The forecast values of CS were substituted into the above model to obtain a forecast of DCSSA for the four quarters of 1996. These forecasts were then multiplied by the seasonal indices to obtain the following forecasts for domestic car sales (DCSRF):

Period	Actual DCS	Forecast DCSRF
1995Q1	1658.20	1794.13
1995Q2	1938.40	2079.12
1995Q3	1845.30	1897.65
1995Q4	1686.90	1715.09

The root-mean-squared errors for this model in the historic period and in the 1996 forecast horizon are shown in Table 4–8. A graphic comparison of actual (DCS) and predicted (DCSRF) domestic car sales is shown in Figure 4–15.

Comments from the Field

While working for Dow Plastics, a business group of the Dow Chemical Company, Jan Neuenfeldt received on-the-job training while assisting others in developing forecasts. This led her to enroll in an MBA forecasting class in which she obtained formal training in quantitative forecasting methods.

The methodology that Jan uses most is regression analysis. On occasion she also uses exponential smoothing models, such as Winters'. However, the marketing and product managers who use the forecasts usually are interested in *why* as well as in the forecast values. Most of the forecasts Jan prepares are on a quarterly basis. It is fairly typical for annual forecasts one year out to be within a 5 percent margin of error. For large-volume items in mature market segments the annual margin for error is frequently only about 2 percent.

Each quarter, Jan reports forecast results to management, using a newsletter format. She begins with an exposition of the results, followed by the supporting statistical information and a graphic presentation of the forecast. She finds that graphics are extremely useful as she prepares forecasts as well as communicates results to end users.

This comment is based on an interview with Jan Neuenfeldt.

INTEGRATIVE CASE
The Gap

Part 4: Forecasting The Gap Sales Data with a Simple Regression Model

The sales of Gap stores for the 44 quarters covering 1985 quarter 1 through 1995 quarter 4 are shown in the graph below. From this graph it is clear that Gap sales are quite seasonal and are increasing over time.

(c4gap)

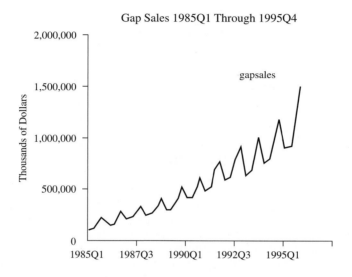

Gap Sales 1985Q1 Through 1995Q4

Case Questions

1. Do you think that the general growth path of Gap sales has followed a linear path over the period shown? As part of your answer show a graph of the deseasonalized Gap sales along with a linear-trend line. What does this graph suggest to you about the results you might expect from using a linear trend as the basis of a forecast of Gap sales for 1996?

2. Use a bivariate regression of deseasonalized Gap sales as the basis for a forecast of Gap sales for 1996.

Be sure to reseasonalize your forecast, then graph the actual Gap sales along with your forecast. What do you think would happen to the accuracy of your forecast if you extended it out through 1997? Why?

3. Calculate the root-mean-squared errors for both the historic period and for the 1996Q1 through 1996Q4 forecast horizon.

Solutions to Case Questions

1. When the Gap sales data are deseasonalized and a linear trend is plotted through the deseasonalized series, it becomes clear that the trend in sales was increas-

ing at an increasing rate during the 1985Q1 through 1995Q4 period. This can be seen in the graph below, in which actual sales (seasonally adjusted) are at first above the trend line, then fall below the linear trend, and finally are again greater than the trend. It might be expected based on this graph that a forecast based on a linear trend would underestimate sales for the coming quarters. This graph also suggests that a regression-trend model would have positive serial correlation.

2. The Gap sales data were deseasonalized using the following seasonal indices: Q1 = 0.854, Q2 = 0.846, Q3 = 1.046, and Q4 = 1.254. The deseasonalized sales data (Gap_SA) for 1985Q1 through 1995Q4 were then regressed against a time index, where $T = 1$ for 1985Q1 through $T = 44$ for 1995Q4. The regression results follow.

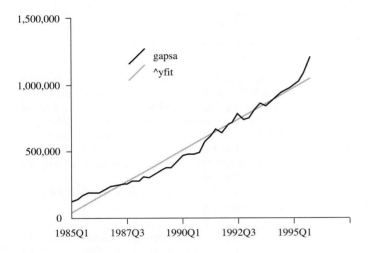

```
REGRESS : dependent variable is GAP_SA
Using    1985Q1-1995Q4

 Variable          Coefficient      Std Err       T-stat       Signf

 ^CONST             21049.8         16145.2       1.30378      .199
 T                  23340.5         624.910       37.3501      .000


                            Equation Summary
    No. of Observations = 44    R2=    .9708   (adj)=   .9701
    Durbin-Watson  = .29249     F ( 1,   42)    =    1395.03
                                Significance    =    .000000
```

The trend equation is: GAP_SA = 21,049.8 + 23,340.5(T). All of the diagnostic statistics for this model look good (t-ratio = 37.3501 and R^2 = .9708) except for the Durbin-Watson statistic (DW = .29249). From the tests in Figure 4–12 it is determined that this model does exhibit positive serial correlation. In this situation the positive serial correlation looks to be caused by the nonlinearity in the data. (In Chapter 5 you will learn how to account for such a nonlinearity using more advanced regression methods.)

The predicted values of GAP_SA were multiplied by the seasonal indices to get the forecast values graphed below.

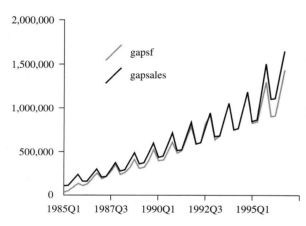

The actual (GAPSALES) and forecast (GAPSF) of Gap sales (in thousands of dollars) are shown below for the four quarters of 1996.

	GAPSALES	*GAPSF*
1996Q1	1,113,154	914,975
1996Q2	1,120,335	926,321
1996Q3	1,383,996	1,169,420
1996Q4	1,667,896	1,431,140

Notice that in the forecast horizon (1996) the forecast is below the actual in all four quarters. This is because the linear trend that underlies this forecast fails to take into account the fact that Gap sales have been increasing at an increasing rate. If this model was used to forecast through 1997, it is likely that this tendency for low forecasts would continue and probably become worse.

3. The RMSEs for the historic period and the 1996 forecast horizon are:

1985Q1–1995Q4	Root-mean-squared error = 56,110.6
1996Q1–1996Q4	Root-mean-squared error = 211,550.0

If we compare the RMSE for these last four quarters to the mean level of sales for those quarters (1,321,095.25), we find that the RMSE is about 16 percent of the mean actual quarterly sales.

TABLE 4–9   Summary Table of RMSEs for Gap Sales

Chapter	Method	Period	RMSE
1	Naive—with 4-period lag	Historic before '96	107,150.0
		Holdout 96Q1–96Q4	227,029.0
2	Not applicable	Historic before '96	na
		Holdout 96Q1–96Q4	na
3	Winters' exponential smoothing	Historic before '96	37,935.5
		Holdout 96Q1–96Q4	84,460.7
	Holt's exponential smoothing with seasonal readjustment	Historic before '96	31,272.5
		Holdout 96Q1–96Q4	33,341.3
4	Linear trend of deseasonalized data with forecast reseasonalized	Historic before '96	56,110.6
		Holdout 96Q1–96Q4	211,550.0

USING SORITEC FOR SIMPLE REGRESSION FORECASTS

Getting the Data

The first thing that we need to do is get some data to work with in estimating a regression model. To do so, go to **FILE** on the main menu and select **OPEN DATA FILE,** then select a data file (typically a .SAL file) or a database file (a .SDB file), such as the ECONDATA file that came with your text.

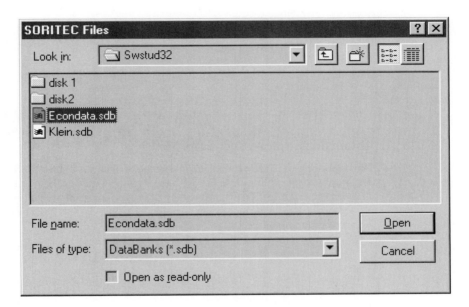

For this example we will assume that you have opened the ECONDATA file and want to develop a forecast of shoe store sales (named RT566R in ECONDATA) as a function of the total U.S. population (named POP in ECONDATA). Both these variables are in ECONDATA on a monthly basis with shoe store sales already seasonally adjusted in millions of dollars, and population in thousands of people. We will call shoe store sales SSS and use POP for population. Let us use data from January 1994 through December 1995 (24 observations) to forecast shoe store sales for the first six months of 1996. The following shows how to set up the time period, including the forecast horizon, so that we can check the accuracy of our forecast and set up the variables with the names we desire.

```
1> access 'econdata'    {echoed from our use of the menu above to open ECONDATA}

   *** File opened  ( 1): econdata.sdb

2> use 94m1 96m6    {sets up the time period for which we get the data}

3> sss = rt566r     {brings shoe store sales into the workspace with the name sss}

4> copy pop         {brings population into the workspace with the name pop}

5> use 94m1 95m12   {sets the period to 24 months to be used to estimate
                     the regression model}
```

Clicking on **VIEW** then on **SYMBOLS** will show what we have in the workspace, as follows:

```
6> symbols (full)

 SORITEC symbol table:

 User variables

 SYM NO NAME                    ADDRESS    TYPE       LENGTH

    155 RT566R                  3733582    SERIES       363  1967M1-1997M3

 RETAIL SALES: SHOE STORES (MIL$,SA)

    169 SSS                     3733510    SERIES        30  1994M1-1996M6

    183 POP                     3732284    SERIES       602  1947M1-1997M12

 POPULATION: TOTAL, INC. ARMED FORCES OVERSEAS (THOUS.,NSA)
```

Estimating a Simple Regression Model

The first thing we should do is look at a graph of shoe store sales (SSS) to see what characteristics the data exhibit. (Use the 🖿 button.) Such a time-series plot for the historic period (1994M1 through 1995M12) is shown to the right. We see that there is some upward trend, no seasonality (the shoe store sales series in ECONDATA has been deseasonalized), and an apparent drop in January 1995.

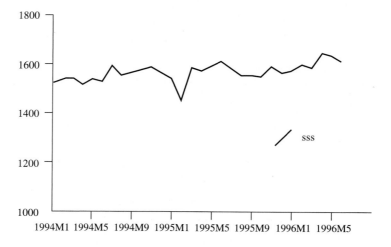

We hypothesize that shoe store sales may be related to population, so we want to regress SSS on POP. To do this we first click the **𝒴** icon on the main menu to define the dependent variable. The **Single Variable Selection** dialog box appears. We highlight **SSS,** click on **SELECT,** then click on **OK.** This is illustrated at the top of page 183.

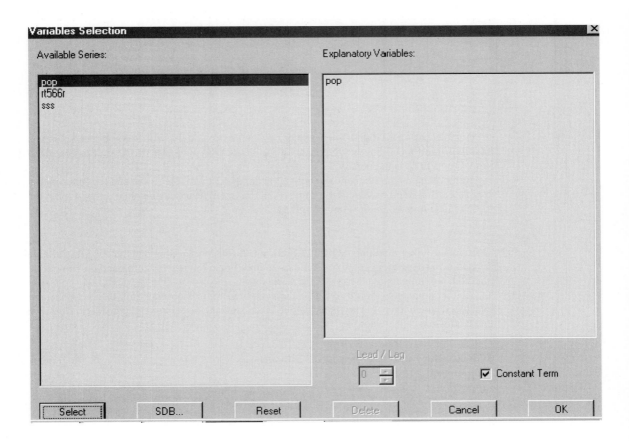

Next we need to select the independent variable. This is done by clicking the χ icon on the main menu. The **Variables Selection** dialog box appears, as shown below. To select POP you highlight **POP,** then click on **SELECT,** then click on **OK.**

To estimate the regression model for SSS = f(POP) first be sure the **use** period is 1994M1–1995M12 (on the command line type **USE 94M1 95M12** to be sure) then click on **LINEAR** on the main menu, then on **LEAST SQUARES,** then on **OLS** (for ordinary least-squares regression), as illustrated below.

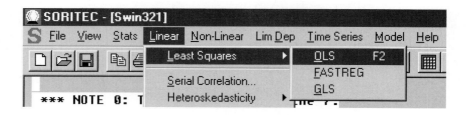

This will produce the following regression results:

```
REGRESS : dependent variable is SSS
Using    1994M1-1995M12

Variable        Coefficient      Std Err          T-stat         Signf
 ^CONST          -631.128         1180.95          -.534423        .598
 POP             .836633E-02      .450656E-02      1.85648         .077

                              Equation Summary
      No. of Observations =      24        R2=     .1354  (adj)=    .0961
      Sum of Sq. Resid. =    22638.0       Std. Error of Reg.=   32.0781
      Log(likelihood)    =  -116.247       Durbin-Watson      =   1.78490
      Schwarz Criterion  =  -119.425       F ( 1,    22)      =   3.44651
      Akaike Criterion   =  -118.247       Significance       =   .076828
```

A table with actual and fitted values, as well as residuals, will follow these statistical results if the **PLOT** flag is **ON.** You can turn it on by typing **ON PLOT** on the command line. OFF PLOT is the default.

Rather than using the menus to define the dependent variable (SSS) and the independent variable (POP), and to select OLS regression, this same result can be obtained by typing the following command on the command line:

```
regress sss pop.
```

Without any other modifiers SORITEC knows to do OLS regression and that the first variable named is the dependent variable. Some users find typing the regress command the preferable method, but both approaches yield the same result.

At this point you should evaluate the estimated regression equation, using the criteria discussed in Chapter 4. The model above is satisfactory on all counts, considering that we have only one causal variable.

Developing Forecasts Based on Simple Regression Models

There is a "forecast" button, 🔭, on the SORITEC toolbar that can be used to facilitate developing a regression forecast. (It can be used for other forecasting methods as well.) We will use this graphic interface to prepare a bivariate regression forecast of shoe store sales as a function of population size. In this section we assume that the variables SSS and POP are already in the workspace (see above discussion "Getting the Data") for the 1994M1 through 1996M6 period. We will consider 1994M1 to 1995M12 as the historic period on which to base the forecast and 1996M1 to 1996M6 as a holdout period to allow us to evaluate the accuracy of our forecast "out of sample."

Forecasting the Independent Variable.   To use population as a causal variable to forecast shoe store sales, we must first develop a forecast of POP for the forecast horizon (1996M1– 1996M6). A time-series plot of population shows it to be increasing in essentially a linear manner over time. Therefore we will forecast POP for 1996M1–1996M6 using a regression-based linear-trend model. Thus we need to define a time variable T ($T = 1$ for 1994M1 through $T = 36$ for 1996M6). This is done by setting the **use** period to 94M1–96M6 (type USE 94m1 96m6 on the command line) then on the next command line type: time t.

Now click on the 🐦 icon, and the **Forecast Options** dialog box shown below appears. From the pull-down box (**Select variable to forecast**) select **POP**. Click on **Regression Models** as the forecasting method, type in **94ml** as the **First Period in Estimation, 95m12** as the **Last Period in Estimation,** and **6** as the **Number of Periods to Forecast.**

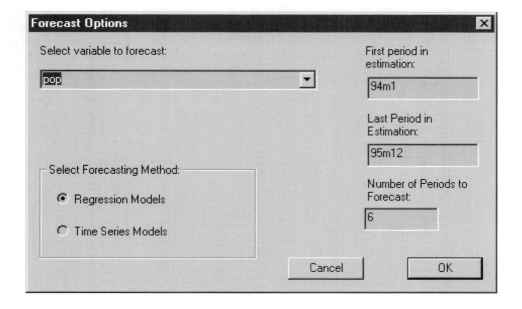

Then click on **OK** and the following dialog box appears.

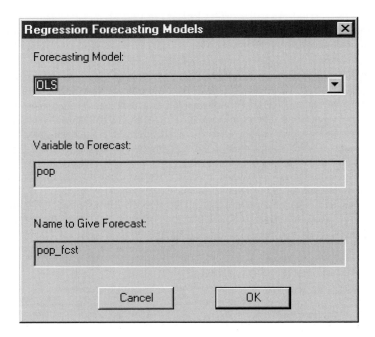

Select **OLS** as the forecasting model and assign a name that you want for the resulting forecast series (the default will be the name of the variable to be forecast followed by an underscore and the letters *fcst;* thus, we have pop_fcst in this example). Then click on **OK.** You will be prompted to select or confirm the independent variable for the regression model—click on **OK** and the following dialog box appears. Highlight **t,** then click on **SELECT** and **OK** in that order. (Delete any variables from the **Explanatory Variables** list that you do not want to use.)

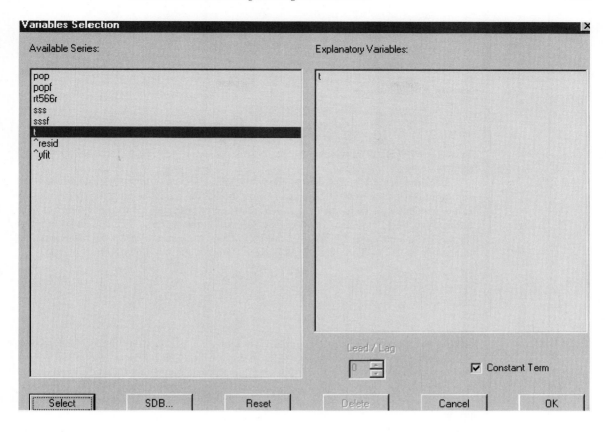

The regression model, some SORITEC commands, and the forecast values of POP_FCST for 96M1–96M6 appear on screen as follows:

```
37> use 94m1 95m12
38> regress pop t

REGRESS : dependent variable is POP
Using    1994M1-1995M12

     Variable      Coefficient      Std Err        T-stat        Signf
      ^CONST         259425.         17.2172        15067.8        .000
        T            209.825         1.20495        174.135        .000

                            Equation Summary
         No. of Observations =       24      R2=    .9993   (adj)=     .9992
         Sum of Sq. Resid. =     36733.3     Std. Error of Reg.=    40.8619
         Log(likelihood)   =    -122.055     Durbin-Watson     =     .38474
         Schwarz Criterion =    -125.233     F (  1,   22)     =    30323.1
         Akaike Criterion  =    -124.055     Significance      =    .000000
```

(A set of automatically invoked SORITEC commands will appear here.)

```
                              POP_FCST
1996M1                         264671.
1996M2                         264881.
1996M3                         265090.
1996M4                         265300.
1996M5                         265510.
1996M6                         265720.
```

The series POP_FCST now contains the forecast values of population for 1994M1 through 1996M6.

To construct a regression model of shoe store sales (SSS) as a function of population and use it to forecast shoe store sales, you want to estimate the model using actual population as the independent variable in the historic period; but you want to use the forecast values of population (POP_FCST) to make the forecast of SSS using the regression model. To accomplish this we create a new variable we will call POPM that is equal to POP in the historic period but equal to POP_FCST in the forecast horizon. This is done as follows:

```
USE 94M1 95M12      (The historic period)
POPM = POP
USE 96M1 96M6       (The forecast horizon)
REVISE POPM = POP_FCST
```

Making the Forecast of the Dependent Variable.   As you would expect, the process of forecasting the dependent variable (SSS in this example) with a regression model is very much like the above description of using a regression-trend model to forecast the independent variable.

Start by again clicking on the forecast icon 🐝, and the "**Forecast Options**" dialog box appears.

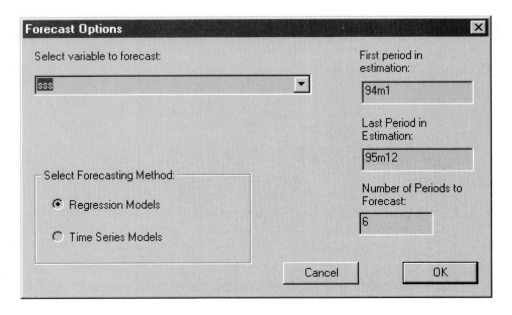

From the pull-down box (**Select variable to forecast**) select **SSS.** Click on **Regression Models** as the forecasting method, type in **94m1** as the **First Period in Estimation, 95m12** as the **Last Period in Estimation,** and **6** as the **Number of Periods to Forecast.** Then click on **OK** and the **Regression Forecasting Models** dialog box will appear. In this dialog box select **OLS** as the forecasting model and either take the default as the name to give the forecast (sss_fcst in this example) or type a name of your choice in that space.

You will be prompted to select or confirm the independent variable for the regression model—click on **OK** and a new dialog box (shown at the top of page 190) appears in which you select the independent variable. Highlight **POPM**, then click on **SELECT** and **OK** in that order. (Delete any variables from the **Explanatory Variables** list that you do not want to use.) This will give you the regression model, some SORITEC commands, and the forecast values for the first six months of 1996. The regression equation, the statistical results, and the forecasts for 96M1 through 96M6 are shown at the bottom of page 190 and at the top of page 191.

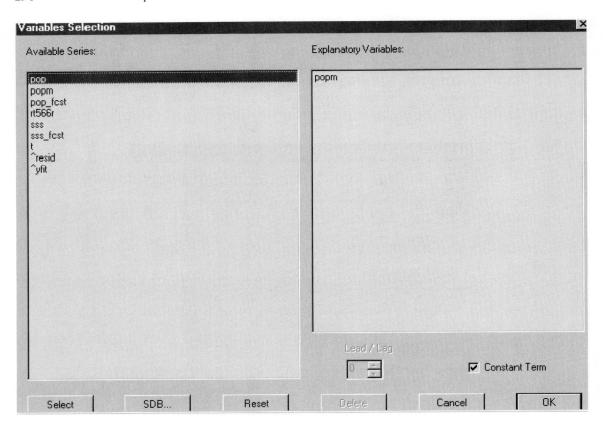

The equation is: **SSS = −631.128 + 0.00836633(POPM)**

```
REGRESS : dependent variable is SSS
Using    1994M1-1995M12

Variable          Coefficient       Std Err        T-stat      Signf
^CONST            -631.128          1180.95        -.534423     .598
POP               .836633E-02       .450656E-02    1.85648      .077

                          Equation Summary
      No. of Observations =      24      R2=    .1354   (adj)=     .0961
      Sum of Sq. Resid. =    22638.0     Std. Error of Reg.=    32.0781
      Log(likelihood)   =   -116.247     Durbin-Watson    =     1.78490
      Schwarz Criterion =   -119.425     F ( 1,   22)     =     3.44651
      Akaike Criterion  =   -118.247     Significance     =     .076828
```

(A set of automatically invoked SORITEC commands will appear here.)

The forecast values for 1996M1 through 1996M6 are:

	SSS_FCST
1996M1	1583.19
1996M2	1584.95
1996M3	1586.70
1996M4	1588.46
1996M5	1590.22
1996M6	1591.97

Checking the Fit and Accuracy of the Model Using RMSEs.   The series SSS_FCST contains the forecast values of shoe store sales for 1994M1 through 1996M6. Now you can determine the RMSEs in the historic period and the forecast (holdout) period as follows:

```
use 94m1 95m12
actfit  sss  sss_fcst
use  96m1  96m6
actfit  sss  sss_fcst
```

For this example the RMSEs are:

Using 1994M1–1995M12 Root-mean-squared error $= 30.7124$

Using 1996M1–1996M6   Root-mean-squared error $= 31.4159$

The mean for actual shoe store sales in 1996M1–1996M12 was 1609.5, so the forecast period RMSE was about 2 percent of the average actual value during that period.

Suggested Readings

Aykac, Ahmed; and Antonio Borges. "Econometric Methods for Managerial Applications." In *The Handbook of Forecasting: A Managers' Guide.* Eds. Spyros Makridakis and Steven C. Wheelwright. New York: John Wiley & Sons, 1982, pp. 185–203.

Bassin, William M. "How to Anticipate the Accuracy of a Regression Based Model." *The Journal of Business Forecasting* 6, no. 4 (Winter 1987–88), pp. 26–28.

Bowerman, Bruce L.; and Richard T. O'Connell. *Applied Statistics: Improving Business Processes,* Chicago: Irwin, 1997.

Dalrymple, Douglas J.; William M. Strahle; and Douglas B. Bock. "How Many Observations Should Be Used in Trend Regression Forecasts?" *Journal of Business Forecasting* 8, no. 1 (Spring 1989), pp. 7–9.

Harris, John L.; and Lon-Mu Liu. "GNP as a Predictor of Electricity Consumption." *Journal of Business Forecasting* (Winter 1990–91), pp. 24–27.

Johnson, Aaron C., Jr.; Marvin B. Johnson; and Reuben C. Buse. *Econometrics: Basic and Applied.* New York: Macmillan, 1987.

Meade, Nigel; and Towhidul Islam. "Forecasting with Growth Curves: An Empirical Comparison," *International Journal of Forecasting* 11, no. 2 (June 1995), pp. 199–215.

Monaco, Ralph M. "MEXVAL: A Simple Regression Diagnostic Tool." *Journal of Business Forecasting* (Winter 1989–90), pp. 23–27.

Morrison, Jeffrey S. "Target Marketing with Logit Regression," *Journal of Business Forecasting* 14, no. 4 (Winter 1995–96), pp. 10–12.

Pindyck, Robert S.; and Daniel L. Rubinfeld. *Econometric Models and Economic Forecasts,* 3rd ed. New York: McGraw-Hill, 1991.

Wang, George C. S.; and Charles K. Akabay. "Heteroscedasticity: How to Handle in Regression Modeling." *Journal of Business Forecasting* 13, no. 2 (Summer 1992), pp. 11–17.

Exercises

1. What are the steps that should be used in evaluating regression models? Write each step in the order it should be evaluated, and following each one write a sentence or two in your own words to explain its importance.

2. In this chapter a number of graphic displays have been presented. What advantage(s) do you see in showing data in graphic form rather than, or in addition to, tabular form?

3. In evaluating regression models we have tested a hypothesis to determine whether the slope term is significantly different from zero. Why do we test this hypothesis? Why do we not test the comparable hypothesis for the intercept?

4. The following regression results relate to a study of the salaries of public school teachers in a midwestern city:

Variable	Coefficient	Standard Error	t-ratio
Constant	20,720	6,820	3.04
EXP	805	258	

R-squared = 0.684; *n* = 105.
Standard error of the regression = 2,000.
EXP is the experience of teachers in years of full-time teaching.

a. What is the *t*-ratio for EXP? Does it indicate that experience is a statistically significant determinant of salary if a 95 percent confidence level is desired?

b. What percentage of the variation in salary is explained by this model?

c. Determine the point estimate of salary for a teacher with 20 years of experience.

d. What is the approximate 95 percent confidence interval for your point estimate from part (*c*)?

5. Nelson Industries manufactures a part for a type of aircraft engine that is becoming obsolete. The sales history for the last 10 years is as follows:

(c4p5)

Year	Sales	Year	Sales
1	945	6	420
2	875	7	305
3	760	8	285
4	690	9	250
5	545	10	210

a. Plot sales versus time.

b. Estimate the regression model for a linear time trend of sales.

c. What is the root-mean-squared error of the linear regression estimates for these 10 years?

d. Using this model, estimate sales for year 11.

6. Mid-Valley Travel Agency (MVTA) has offices in 12 cities. The company believes that its monthly airline bookings are related to the mean income in those cities and has collected the following data:

(c4p6)

Location	Bookings	Income
1	1,098	$43,299
2	1,131	45,021
3	1,120	40,290
4	1,142	41,893
5	971	30,620
6	1,403	48,105
7	855	27,482
8	1,054	33,025
9	1,081	34,687
10	982	28,725
11	1,098	37,892
12	1,387	46,198

a. Develop a linear regression model of monthly airline bookings as a function of income.

b. Use the process described in the chapter to evaluate your results.

c. Make a point and approximate 95 percent confidence interval estimate of monthly airline bookings for another city in which MVTA is considering opening a branch, given that income in that city is $39,020.

7. Barbara Lynch is the product manager for a line of skiwear produced by HeathCo Industries and privately branded for sale under several different names, including Northern Slopes and Jacque Monri. A new part of Ms. Lynch's job is to provide a quarterly forecast of sales for the northern United States, a region composed of 27 states stretching from Maine to Washington. A 10-year sales history is shown:

Sales ($000)

Year	1st Quarter	2nd Quarter	3rd Quarter	4th Quarter
1988	$ 72,962	$ 81,921	$ 97,729	$142,161
1989	145,592	117,129	114,159	151,402
1990	153,907	100,144	123,242	128,497
1991	176,076	180,440	162,665	220,818
1992	202,415	211,780	163,710	200,135
1993	174,200	182,556	198,990	243,700
1994	253,142	218,755	225,422	253,653
1995	257,156	202,568	224,482	229,879
1996	289,321	266,095	262,938	322,052
1997	313,769	315,011	264,939	301,479

(c4p7)

a. Because Ms. Lynch has so many other job responsibilities, she has hired you to help with the forecasting effort. First, she would like you to prepare a time-series plot of the data and to write her a memo indicating what the plot appears to show and whether it seems likely that a simple linear trend would be useful in preparing forecasts.

b. In addition to plotting the data over time, you should estimate the least-squares trend line in the form:

$$SALES = a + b(TIME)$$

Set TIME = 1 for 1988Q1 through TIME = 40 for 1997Q4. Write the trend equation:

SALES = _____ +/− _____ (TIME)

(Circle + or − as appropriate)

c. Do your regression results indicate to you that there is a significant trend to the data? Explain why or why not.

d. On the basis of your results, prepare a forecast for the four quarters of 1998.

Period	TIME	Sales Forecast (F1)
1998Q1	41	_____
1998Q2	42	_____
1998Q3	43	_____
1998Q4	44	_____

e. A year later, Barbara gives you a call and tells you that the actual sales for the four quarters of 1998 were: Q1 = 334,271; Q2 = 328,982; Q3 = 317,921; and Q4 = 350,118. How accurate was your model? What was the root-mean-squared error?

8. Dick Staples, another product manager with HeathCo (see Exercise 7), has mentioned to Barbara Lynch that he has found both the unemployment rate and the level of income to be useful predictors for some of the products under his responsibility.

a. Suppose that Ms. Lynch provides you with the following unemployment data for the northern region she is concerned with:

Unemployment Rate (%)

Year	1st Quarter	2nd Quarter	3rd Quarter	4th Quarter
1988	8.4%	8.2%	8.4%	8.4%
1989	8.1%	7.7%	7.5%	7.2%
1990	6.9%	6.5%	6.5%	6.4%
1991	6.3%	6.2%	6.3%	6.5%
1992	6.8%	7.9%	8.3%	8.0%
1993	8.0%	8.0%	8.0%	8.9%
1994	9.6%	10.2%	10.7%	11.5%
1995	11.2%	11.0%	10.1%	9.2%
1996	8.5%	8.0%	8.0%	7.9%
1997	7.9%	7.9%	7.8%	7.6%

(c4p8)

b. Plot a scattergram of SALES versus northern-region unemployment rate (NRUR). Does there appear to be a relationship? Explain.

c. Prepare a bivariate regression model of sales as a function of NRUR in the following form:

$$SALES = a + b(NRUR)$$

Write your answer in the following equation:

$$SALES = \underline{\hspace{1.5cm}} +/- \underline{\hspace{1.5cm}} (NRUR)$$

(Circle + or − as appropriate)

d. Write a memo to Ms. Lynch in which you evaluate these results and indicate how well you think this model would work in forecasting her sales series.

e. Use the model to make a forecast of sales for each quarter of 1998, given the forecast for unemployment (FNRUR) that HeathCo has purchased from a macroeconomic consulting firm (MacroCast):

Period	FNRUR	Sales Forecast (F2)
1998Q1	7.6%	_____
1998Q2	7.7%	_____
1998Q3	7.5%	_____
1998Q4	7.4%	_____

f. For the actual sales given in Exercise 7(e), calculate the root-mean-squared error for this model. How does it compare with what you found in Exercise 7(e)?

g. Barbara Lynch also has data on income (INC), in billions of dollars, for the region as follows:

	Income ($Billions)			
Year	1st Quarter	2nd Quarter	3rd Quarter	4th Quarter
1988	$ 218	$ 237	$ 263	$ 293
1989	318	359	404	436
1990	475	534	574	622
1991	667	702	753	796
1992	858	870	934	1,010
1993	1,066	1,096	1,162	1,187
1994	1,207	1,242	1,279	1,318
1995	1,346	1,395	1,443	1,528
1996	1,613	1,646	1,694	1,730
1997	1,755	1,842	1,832	1,882

Plot a scattergram of SALES with INCOME. Does there appear to be a relationship? Explain.

h. Prepare a bivariate regression model of SALES as a function of income (INC) and write your results in the equation:

$$SALES = a + b(INC)$$

$$SALES = \underline{\hspace{1.5cm}} +/- \underline{\hspace{1.5cm}} (INC)$$

(Circle + or − as appropriate)

i. Write a memo to Ms. Lynch in which you explain and evaluate this model, indicating how well you think it would work in forecasting sales.

j. HeathCo has also purchased a forecast of income from MacroCast. Use the following income forecast (INCF) to make your own forecast of SALES for 1998:

Period	INCF	Sales Forecast (F3)
1998Q1	$1,928	_____
1998Q2	1,972	_____
1998Q3	2,017	_____
1998Q4	2,062	_____

k. On the basis of the actual sales given in Exercise 7(e), calculate the root-mean-squared error for this model. How does it compare with the other two models you have used to forecast sales?

l. Prepare a time-series plot with actual sales for 1988Q1 through 1997Q4 along with the sales forecast you found in part (j) of this exercise. To accompany this plot, write a brief memo to Ms. Lynch in which you comment on the strengths and weaknesses of the forecasting model.

9. Carolina Wood Products, Inc., a major manufacturer of household furniture, is interested in predicting expenditures on furniture (FURN) for the entire United States. It has the following data by quarter for 1988 through 1997:

FURN (in Billions of Dollars)

Year	1st Quarter	2nd Quarter	3rd Quarter	4th Quarter
1988	$ 98.1	$ 96.8	$ 96.0	$ 95.0
1989	93.2	95.1	96.2	98.4
1990	100.7	104.4	108.1	111.1
1991	114.3	117.2	119.4	122.7
1992	125.9	129.3	132.2	136.6
1993	137.4	141.4	145.3	147.7
1994	148.8	150.2	153.4	154.2
1995	159.8	164.4	166.2	169.7
1996	173.7	175.5	175.0	175.7
1997	181.4	180.0	179.7	176.3

(c4p9)

a. Prepare a naive forecast for 1998Q1 based on the following model (see Chapter 1):

$$\text{NFURN}_t = \text{FURN}_{t-1}$$

Period	Naive Forecast
1998Q1	_____

b. Estimate the bivariate linear-trend model for the data where TIME = 1 for 1988Q1 through TIME = 40 for 1997Q4.

$$\text{FURN} = a + b(\text{TIME})$$

$$\text{FURN} = \underline{\hspace{1cm}} +/- \underline{\hspace{1cm}} (\text{TIME})$$

(Circle + or − as appropriate)

c. Write a paragraph in which you evaluate this model, with particular emphasis on its usefulness in forecasting.

d. Prepare a time-trend forecast of furniture and household equipment expenditures for 1998 based on the model in part (b).

Period	TIME	Trend Forecast
1998Q1	41	_____
1998Q2	42	_____
1998Q3	43	_____
1998Q4	44	_____

e. Suppose that the actual values of FURN for 1998 were as shown in the following table. Calculate the RMSE for both of your forecasts and interpret the results. (For the naive forecast, there will be only one observation, for 1998Q1.)

Period	Actual FURN ($Billions)
1998Q1	177.6
1998Q2	180.5
1998Q3	182.8
1998Q4	178.7

10. Fifteen Midwestern and Mountain states have united in an effort to promote and forecast tourism. One aspect of their work has been related to the dollar amount spent per year on domestic travel (DTE) in each state. They have the following estimates for disposable personal income per capita (IPC) and DTE:

(c4p10)

State	IPC	DTE ($Millions)
Minnesota	$17,907	$4,933
Iowa	15,782	1,766
Missouri	17,158	4,692
North Dakota	15,688	628
South Dakota	15,981	551
Nebraska	17,416	1,250
Kansas	17,635	1,729
Montana	15,128	725
Idaho	15,974	934
Wyoming	17,504	778
Colorado	18,628	4,628
New Mexico	14,587	1,724
Arizona	15,921	3,836
Utah	14,066	1,757
Nevada	19,781	6,455

a. From these data estimate a bivariate linear regression equation for domestic travel expenditures (DTE) as a function of income per capita

(IPC):

$$DTE = a + b(IPC)$$

$$DTE = \underline{\hspace{2cm}} +/- \underline{\hspace{2cm}}(IPC)$$

(Circle + or − as appropriate)

Evaluate the statistical significance of this model.

b. Illinois, a bordering state, has asked that this model be used to forecast DTE for Illinois under the assumption that IPC will be $19,648. Make the appropriate point and approximate 95 percent interval estimates.

c. Given that actual DTE turned out to be $7,754 (million), calculate the percentage error in your forecast.

11. Collect data on population for your state over the past 20 years and use a bivariate regression trend line to forecast population for the next 5 years. Prepare a time-series plot that shows both actual and forecast values. Do you think the model looks as though it will provide reasonably accurate forecasts for the five-year horizon? (c4p11)

12. AmerPlas, Inc., produces 20-ounce plastic drinking cups that are embossed with the names of prominent beers and soft drinks. It has been observed that sales of the cups match closely the seasonal pattern associated with beer production but that, unlike beer production, there has been a positive trend over time. The sales data, by month, for 1994 through 1997 are as follows:

Period	T	Sales	Period	T	Sales
1994M01	1	857	1995M04	16	1,497
1994M02	2	921	1995M05	17	1,560
1994M03	3	1,071	1995M06	18	1,586
1994M04	4	1,133	1995M07	19	1,597
1994M05	5	1,209	1995M08	20	1,615
1994M06	6	1,234	1995M09	21	1,535
1994M07	7	1,262	1995M10	22	1,543
1994M08	8	1,258	1995M11	23	1,493
1994M09	9	1,175	1995M12	24	1,510
1994M10	10	1,174	1996M01	25	1,604
1994M11	11	1,123	1996M02	26	1,643
1994M12	12	1,159	1996M03	27	1,795
1995M01	13	1,250	1996M04	28	1,868
1995M02	14	1,289	1996M05	29	1,920
1995M03	15	1,448	1996M06	30	1,953
					(continued)

Period	T	Sales	Obs.	T	Sales
1996M07	31	1,980	1997M04	40	2,202
1996M08	32	1,989	1997M05	41	2,288
1996M09	33	1,897	1997M06	42	2,314
1996M10	34	1,910	1997M07	43	2,343
1996M11	35	1,854	1997M08	44	2,339
1996M12	36	1,957	1997M09	45	2,239
1997M01	37	1,955	1997M10	46	2,267
1997M02	38	2,008	1997M11	47	2,206
1997M03	39	2,171	1997M12	48	2,226

(c4p12)

a. Use these data to estimate a linear time trend as follows:

$$SALES = a + b(T)$$

$$SALES = \underline{\hspace{2cm}} +/- \underline{\hspace{2cm}}(T)$$

(Circle + or − as appropriate)

Do your regression results support the notion that there has been a positive time trend in the SALES data? Explain.

b. Use your equation to forecast SALES for the 12 months of 1998:

Period	SALES Forecast	Period	SALES Forecast
1998M01	_____	1998M07	_____
M02	_____	M08	_____
M03	_____	M09	_____
M04	_____	M10	_____
M05	_____	M11	_____
M06	_____	M12	_____

c. Actual SALES for 1998 are:

Period	Actual SALES	Period	Actual SALES
1998M01	2,318	1998M07	2,697
M02	2,367	M08	2,702
M03	2,523	M09	2,613
M04	2,577	M10	2,626
M05	2,646	M11	2,570
M06	2,674	M12	2,590

On the basis of your results in part (*b*) in comparison with these actual sales, how well do you think your model works? What is the RMSE for 1998?

d. Prepare a time-series plot of the actual sales and the forecast of sales for 1994M01 through 1998M12. Do the same for just the last two years (1997M01 to 1998M12). Do your plots show any evidence of seasonality in the data? If so, how might you account for it in preparing a forecast?

13. Alexander Enterprises manufactures plastic parts for the automotive industry. Its sales (in thousands) for 1993Q1 through 1997Q4 are as follows:

Period	Sales	Period	Sales
1993Q1	3,816.5	1996Q1	4,406.4
Q2	3,816.7	Q2	4,394.6
Q3	3,978.8	Q3	4,422.3
Q4	4,046.6	Q4	4,430.8
1994Q1	4,119.1	1997Q1	4,463.9
Q2	4,169.4	Q2	4,517.8
Q3	4,193.0	Q3	4,563.6
Q4	4,216.4	Q4	4,633.0
1995Q1	4,238.1	1998Q1	NA
Q2	4,270.5	Q2	NA
Q3	4,321.8	Q3	NA
Q4	4,349.5	Q4	NA

(c4p13)

You are asked to forecast sales for 1998Q1 through 1998Q4.

a. Begin by preparing a time-series plot of sales. Does it appear from this plot that a linear-trend model might be appropriate? Explain.

b. Use a bivariate linear regression trend model to estimate the following trend equation:

$$\text{SALES} = a + b(\text{TIME})$$

Is the sign for *b* what you would expect? Is *b* significantly different from zero? What is the coefficient of determination for this model? Is there a potential problem with serial correlation? Explain.

c. Based on this model, make a trend forecast of sales (SALESFT) for the four quarters of 1998.

d. Given that actual sales (SALESA) for the four quarters of 1998 are:

1998Q1	4,667.1
1998Q2	4,710.3
1998Q3	4,738.7
1998Q4	4,789.0

calculate the root-mean-squared error for this forecast model in the historic period (1993Q1–1997Q4) as well as for the forecast horizon (1998Q1–1998Q4). Which of these measures accuracy and which measures fit?

14. If you did Exercise 13, you found that your trend model for Alexander Enterprises had positive serial correlation. (c4p14)

a. Use the Cochrane-Orcutt procedure to respecify the model. Does the use of this method improve the Durbin-Watson statistic? Is positive serial correlation still a problem? Use this model to prepare a forecast for the four quarters of 1998. What is the RMSE for these four quarters?

b. Now use the Hildreth-Lu procedure to estimate this sales trend. Does this method adequately adjust for the serial-correlation problem? Explain. Prepare a forecast for the four quarters of 1998 using this model. Calculate the RMSE for this forecast.

5   FORECASTING WITH MULTIPLE REGRESSION

In this chapter we will build on the introduction to the use of regression in forecasting developed in Chapter 4. The model used to forecast retail sales (RS) will be extended to include the interest rate as an explanatory variable, in addition to real disposable personal income. We will also forecast private housing starts (PHS). We will examine the mortgage rate as a causal factor. In addition we will add variables to account for seasonality in the data and also consider the effect that disposable personal income has on our ability to forecast PHS. We will also continue with our ongoing example of forecasting domestic car sales and the continuing Gap case study at the end of this chapter. These extensions of the bivariate regression model take us into the realm of multiple regression, so let us begin by looking at the general multiple-regression model.

The Multiple-Regression Model

Multiple regression is a statistical procedure in which a dependent variable (Y) is modeled as a function of more than one independent variable ($X_1, X_2, X_3, \ldots, X_n$).[1] The population multiple-regression model may be written as:

$$Y = f(X_1, X_2, X_3, \ldots, X_n)$$
$$= \beta_0 + \beta_1 X_1 + \beta_2 X_2 + \beta_3 X_3 + \cdots + \beta_k X_k + \varepsilon$$

where β_0 is the intercept and the other β_i's are the slope terms associated with the respective independent variables (i.e., the X_i's). In this model ε represents the

---

[1] For more-detailed discussions of the multiple-regression model, see the following: John Neter, William Wasserman, and Michael H. Kutner, *Applied Linear Statistical Models* (Homewood, Ill.: Richard D. Irwin, 1990); and George O. Wesolowsky, *Multiple Regression and Analysis of Variance: An Introduction for Computer Users in Management and Economics* (New York: John Wiley & Sons, 1976). The latter is particularly recommended for readers whose statistical background is limited.

199

population error term, which is the difference between the actual Y and that predicted by the regression model ($\hat{Y}$).

The ordinary least-squares (OLS) criterion for the best multiple-regression model is that the sum of the squares of all the error terms be minimized. That is, we want to minimize $\sum \varepsilon^2$, where

$$\sum \varepsilon^2 = \sum (Y - \hat{Y})^2$$

Thus, the ordinary least-squares criterion for multiple regression is to minimize:

$$\sum (Y - \beta_0 - \beta_1 X_1 - \beta_2 X_2 - \beta_3 X_3 - \cdots - \beta_k X_k)^2$$

The process of achieving this is more complicated than in the bivariate regression case and involves the use of matrix algebra.

Values of the true regression parameters (β_i) are typically estimated from sample data. The resulting sample regression model is:

$$\hat{Y} = b_0 + b_1 X_1 + b_2 X_2 + b_3 X_3 + \cdots + b_k X_k$$

where b_0, b_1, b_2, b_3, and so on, are sample statistics that are estimates of the corresponding population parameters β_0, β_1, β_2, β_3, and so on. Deviations between the predicted values based on the sample regression ($\hat{Y}$) and the actual values (Y) of the dependent variable for each observation are called *residuals* and are equal to ($Y - \hat{Y}$). The values of the sample statistics b_0, b_1, b_2, b_3, and so on, are almost always determined for us by a computer software package such as SORITEC. Standard errors, *t*-ratios, the coefficient of determination, the Durbin-Watson statistic, and other evaluative statistics, as well as a table of residuals, are also found in most regression output.

Selecting Independent Variables

As with bivariate regression, the process of building a multiple-regression model begins by identifying the dependent variable.

As with bivariate regression, the process of building a multiple-regression model begins by identifying the dependent variable. In our context that is the variable that we are most interested in forecasting. It may be some "prime mover" such as disposable personal income or another macroeconomic variable, or it may be total company sales, or sales of a particular product line, or the number of patient-days for a hospital, or state tax revenues.

Once the dependent variable is determined, we begin to think about what factors contribute to its changes. In our bivariate example of retail sales (RS) we first thought of real disposable personal income (DPI) as an explanatory variable. In this chapter, as we think of other potential independent variables that might improve that model, we want to think of other things that influence RS but that do not measure the same basic relationship that is being measured by DPI. Think, for example, of the possibility of adding GDP to the model. Both GDP and DPI are measures of aggregate income in the economy, so there would be a lot of overlap in the part of the variation in RS they explain. In fact, the correlation between real GDP and real disposable personal income is +0.99. A similar overlap would result if population and DPI were used in the same model. There is a high correlation between population size and real disposable personal income (approximately +0.95), and so they would have a lot of overlap in their ability to explain variations in RS. Such overlaps can cause a problem known as *multicollinearity,* which we will discuss in this chapter (see "Multicollinearity").[2]

Considering the set of independent variables to use, we should find ones that are not highly correlated with one another.

Thus, in considering the set of independent variables to use, we should find ones that are not highly correlated with one another. For example, suppose that we hypothesize that at least some portion of RS may be influenced by the mortgage interest rate, since many purchases are financed. It seems less likely that there would be a stronger correlation between real personal income and the mortgage interest rate than between real personal income and either real GDP or population size. The correlation between the mortgage interest rate and real disposable personal income turns out to be just −0.65, so there is less overlap between those two variables.

Sometimes it is difficult, or even impossible, to find a variable that measures exactly what we want to have in our model. For example, in the RS model we might like to have as a measure of the interest rate a national average of the rate charged on installment loans. However, a more readily available series, the mortgage rate (MR), may be a reasonable proxy for what we want to measure, since all interest rates tend to be closely related.

In our model of private housing starts (PHS), we will begin by looking at the relationship between PHS and the mortgage rate. However, in plotting the data we notice that there is a regular seasonal pattern in PHS that is not accounted for by the mortgage rate (see Figure 5–5). We would like to consider adding another variable (or set of variables) to account for the seasonality in PHS. But how do we measure spring, or fall, or summer, or winter? The seasons are qualitative attributes that have no direct quantitative counterpart. We will see (in the section "Accounting for Seasonality in a Multiple-Regression Model") that a special kind of variable, known as a *dummy variable,* can be used to measure such a qualitative attribute as spring.

Forecasting with a Multiple-Regression Model

Our first example of a multiple-regression model in forecasting will involve retail sales (RS).

The data for RS from 1986Q1 through 1995Q4 are shown in Figure 5–1. Our beginning bivariate regression forecasting model is:

$$RSF = b_0 + b_1(MR)$$
$$= 894,067 - 46,187.1(MR)$$

---

[2]Note that multicollinearity in regression analysis is really just strong correlation between two or more independent variables. Correlation here is measured just as we did in Chapter 2 with the Pearson product-moment correlation coefficient.

FIGURE 5–1

Retail Sales (RS) Unadjusted in Millions of Dollars (c5t1)

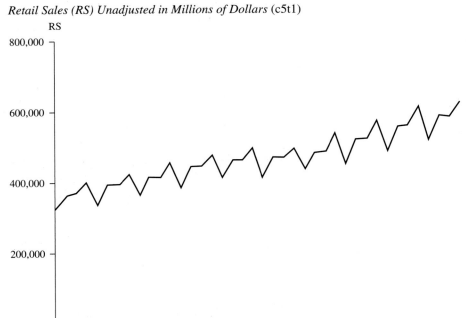

Source: The Bureau of the Census (http://www.census.gov/).

where RSF stands for the forecast of retail sales (RS) and (MR) is the mortgage interest rate.

Now we will expand this model to include disposable personal income per capita (DPI) as a second independent variable. We will let RSF2 represent the second forecasting model for RS.

$$\text{RSF2} = b_0 + b_1(\text{DPI}) + b_2(\text{MR})$$

Before running the regression, one should think about what signs should be expected for b_1 and b_2. Business and economic logic would suggest that b_1 should be positive ($b_1 > 0$) and that b_2 should be negative ($b_2 < 0$). As shown in Table 5–1, the regression results support this notion. The model estimate is:

$$\text{RSF2} = 1,423,270 - 14150.5(\text{MR}) + 112.952(\text{DPI})$$

The raw data for this model, along with the complete regression results, are shown in Table 5–1. Statistical evaluation of this model, based on the information

TABLE 5–1 **Data and Regression Results for Retail Sales (RS) as a Function of Disposable Income Per Capita (DPI) and the Mortgage Interest Rate (MR) (c5t1)**

	RS	DPI	MR		RS	DPI	MR
1986Q1	320,566	16,951.7	10.5600	1991Q1	417,357	17,748.0	9.50333
1986Q2	360,948	17,064.7	10.2600	1991Q2	470,851	17,861.3	9.53000
1986Q3	369,596	17,107.3	10.2400	1991Q3	469,494	17,815.3	9.27667
1986Q4	398,526	17,032.3	9.66667	1991Q4	498,235	17,811.0	8.69000
1987Q1	335,520	17,162.0	9.10667	1992Q1	437,388	18,000.3	8.71000
1987Q2	390,337	16,956.0	10.3233	1992Q2	486,553	18,085.7	8.67667
1987Q3	393,813	17,159.7	10.5000	1992Q3	489,541	18,035.3	8.01000
1987Q4	421,629	17,378.7	10.8500	1992Q4	538,107	18,330.0	8.20333
1988Q1	369,185	17,622.7	10.0667	1993Q1	456,050	17,962.3	7.72333
1988Q2	415,351	17,623.3	10.3733	1993Q2	519,830	18,132.3	7.45000
1988Q3	415,531	17,704.3	10.5033	1993Q3	523,405	18,143.0	7.07667
1988Q4	456,135	17,760.3	10.3933	1993Q4	573,503	18,305.7	7.05333
1989Q1	389,123	17,919.7	10.8033	1994Q1	493,778	18,081.7	7.30000
1989Q2	444,746	17,804.0	10.6733	1994Q2	556,848	18,366.3	8.44000
1989Q3	448,724	17,833.7	10.0000	1994Q3	562,860	18,436.0	8.58667
1989Q4	476,378	17,858.7	9.82000	1994Q4	613,839	18,564.3	9.10000
1990Q1	418,436	18,034.7	10.1233	1995Q1	519,991	18,697.7	8.81333
1990Q2	464,944	18,062.7	10.3367	1995Q2	587,346	18,668.3	7.95000
1990Q3	464,490	18,031.3	10.1067	1995Q3	587,208	18,818.7	7.70333
1990Q4	496,741	17,855.7	9.95000	1995Q4	629,493	18,971.3	7.35333

```
REGRESS: dependent variable is RS

Using 1986Q1-1995Q4

      Variable   Coefficient       Std Err      T-stat      Signf


^CONST        -.142327E+07       268992.     -5.29113      .000
MR             -14150.5          5654.04     -2.50273      .017
DPI            112.952           12.9653      8.71185      .000


                        Equation Summary
    No. of Observations =      40      R2 =  .8381   (adj)=  .8294
    Sum of Sq. Resid. =   .369254E+11  Std. Error of Reg.= 31590.9
    Log(likelihood)   = -469.623      Durbin-Watson    = 2.60588
    Schwarz Criterion = -475.157      F ( 2,   37)     = 95.7747
    Akaike Criterion  = -472.623      Significance     = .000000
```

provided in Table 5–1, will be considered in the next section. For now, we can see that at least the signs for the coefficients are consistent with our expectations.

To use this model to forecast retail sales for 1996, one must first forecast the independent variables: real disposable personal income (DPI) and the mortgage rate (MR). Forecasts for 1996Q1 through 1996Q4 for these two independent variables, based on Holt's exponential smoothing models, are:

Period	MR	DPI
1996Q1	7.2364	18981.0375
1996Q2	7.1192	19027.2120
1996Q3	7.0020	19073.3865
1996Q4	6.8848	19119.5610

Our second forecasts of retail sales (RSF2) can be found as follows:

$$RSF2 = -1,423,270 - 14,150.5(MR) + 112.952(DPI)$$

1996Q1: $RSF2 = -1,423,270 - 14,150.5(7.2364) + 112.952(18,981.0375)$
$\approx 618,273$

1996Q2: $RSF2 = -1,423,270 - 14,150.5(7.1192) + 112.952(19,027.2120)$
$\approx 625,147$

1996Q3: $RSF2 = -1,423,270 - 14,150.5(7.0020) + 112.952(19,073)$
$\approx 632,021$

1996Q4: $RSF2 = -1,423,270 - 14,150.5(6.8868) + 112.952(19,119.5610)$
$\approx 638,895$

These values are plotted in Figure 5–2 along with the values predicted by the equation for the historic period. The forecasts here were produced in SORITEC and the calculations involve more significant digits than shown here.

	RS	Forecasted RS		RS	Forecasted RS		RS	Forecasted RS
1986Q1	320566.	342026.	1990Q1	418436.	470532.	1994Q1	493778.	515792.
1986Q2	360948.	359034.	1990Q2	464944.	470675.	1994Q2	556848.	531806.
1986Q3	369596.	364129.	1990Q3	464490.	470383.	1994Q3	562860.	537603.
1986Q4	398526.	363771.	1990Q4	496741.	452766.	1994Q4	613839.	544831.
1987Q1	335520.	386345.	1991Q1	417357.	446921.	1995Q1	519991.	563956.
1987Q2	390337.	345861.	1991Q2	470851.	459341.	1995Q2	587346.	572851.
1987Q3	393813.	366368.	1991Q3	469494.	457730.	1995Q3	587208.	593330.
1987Q4	421629.	386152.	1991Q4	498235.	465546.	1995Q4	629493.	615519.
1988Q1	369185.	424797.	1992Q1	437388.	486645.	1996Q1	552928.	618273.
1988Q2	415351.	420526.	1992Q2	486553.	496763.	1996Q2	617069.	625147.
1988Q3	415531.	427835.	1992Q3	489541.	500504.	1996Q3	612813.	632021.
1988Q4	456135.	435717.	1992Q4	538107.	531055.	1996Q4	662486.	638895.
1989Q1	389123.	447920.	1993Q1	456050.	496315.			
1989Q2	444746.	436691.	1993Q2	519830.	519384.			
1989Q3	448724.	449573.	1993Q3	523405.	525876.			
1989Q4	476378.	454944.	1993Q4	573503.	544583.			

In Figure 5–2 one line shows actual values of retail sales (RS) for 1986Q1 through 1996Q4. The other line shows the values predicted by this model for

FIGURE 5–2

*Retail Sales (RS)
and Forecasted
Retail Sales
(RSF2) in Millions
of Dollars*

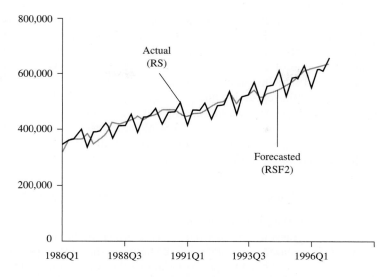

1986Q1 through 1996Q4 (RSF2). For the historic period, actual values for the independent variables were used in determining RSF2. In the forecast period, forecast values (from smoothing models) for DPI and MR, as shown in the preceding computations, were used to calculate RSF2.

Actual and forecast values of retail sales for the four quarters of 1996 are shown, along with the calculation of the root-mean-squared error (RMSE) for the forecast period:

Period	*Actual RS*	*Forecast RSF2*	$(RS - RSF2)^2$
1996Q1	552,928	618,273	4,269,969,025
1996Q2	617,069	625,147	65,254,084
1996Q3	612,813	632,021	368,947,264
1996Q4	662,486	638,895	556,535,281

Sum of squared errors = 5,260,705,654
Mean-squared error (5,269,926,662/4) = 1,315,176,414
Root-mean-squared error (RMSE) = $\sqrt{1,315,176,414}$ = 36,265

This RMSE is about 5 percent of the mean for RS during these four quarters. The total for RS in 1996 was 2,445,296, and the total of the four quarterly forecasts was 2,514,336, so the error for the year was 69,040, or about 2.8 percent.

The Regression Plane

In our three-variable case (with RS as the dependent variable and with DPI and MR as independent variables), three observations are made for each sample point (i.e., for each quarter). Table 5–1 shows these three observations for every quarter. In the period 1986Q1, for instance, the three values are 320,566 for RS, 16,951.7 for DPI, and 10.56 for MR. These observations can be depicted in a scatter diagram like those of Chapter 2, but the scatter diagram must be three-dimensional. Figure 5–3 shows the retail sales (RS) of any observation as measured vertically from the origin (labeled as RS in Figure 5–3). The value of MR is measured along the "MR" axis and the value of DPI is measured along the "DPI" axis. All 40 observations are represented as points in the diagram.

In multiple-regression analysis, our job is to suspend a three-dimensional plane (called the *regression plane*) among the observations in such a way that the plane best represents the observations. Multiple-regression analysis estimates an equation ($Y = a + b_1X + b_2Z$) in such a manner that all the estimates of Y made with the equation fall on the surface of the linear plane. The exact equation we estimated for retail sales,

$$RS = -1,423,270 - 14,150.5(MR) + 112.952(DPI)$$

is graphed as the plane shown in Figure 5–4. This regression plane, like the simple bivariate regression line of Chapter 4, is drawn in such a way as to minimize the sum of the squared vertical deviations between the sample points and the estimated plane. Some of the actual points lie above the regression plane, while other actual points lie below the regression plane.

Note that the b_1 estimate indicates how RS changes with respect to MR *while DPI is held constant.* If the sign of b_1 is negative, as it is in this example, then RS must decrease as MR increases. Looking at Figure 5–4 again, note that the plane "tilts down" as you move from 10 to 20 along the MR axis. Clearly, the regression plane is reacting to the negative relationship between MR and RS.

FIGURE 5–3

Retail Sales (RS) in Millions of Dollars Viewed in Three Dimensions (c5t1)

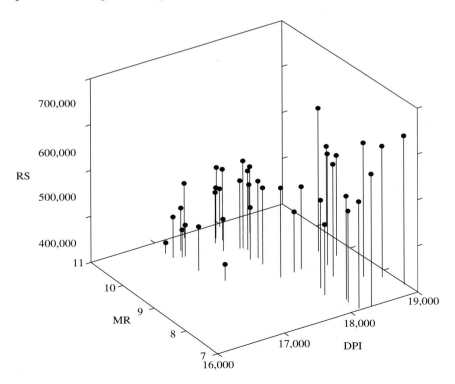

FIGURE 5–4

Retail Sales (RS) Viewed in Three Dimensions with Regression Plane Superimposed (c5t1)

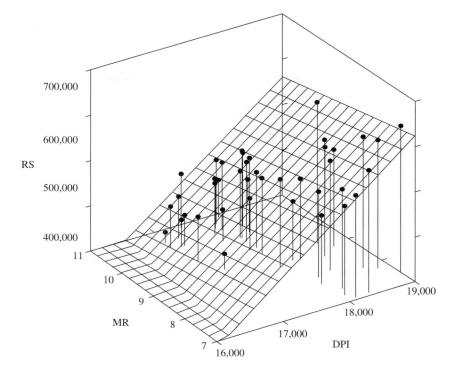

Regression plane has the equation: RS = −1,423,270 − 14,150.5(MR) + 112.952(DPI). See Table 5–2 for the estimation of this equation.

Similarly, the sign for b_2 in this regression represents the relationship between DPI and RS *while MR is held constant.* Since the estimated sign of b_2 is positive, we should expect that as DPI increases in value, all else being equal, RS will increase. This is also easily seen by examining the regression plane. Note that the plane is tilted in such a way that higher incomes (DPI) are associated with higher retail sales (RS) values.

Finally, if all the actual data points were to lie very close to the regression plane, the R^2 of the equation would be very high. If, on the other hand, most of the actual points were far above and below the regression plane, the R^2 would be lower than it otherwise would be. Normally, regression packages do not have a provision for the graphing of output in three-dimensional form. This is because relatively few of the problems faced in the real world involve exactly three variables. Sometimes you are working with only two variables, while at other times you will be working with more than three. Thus, while the three-dimensional diagram will be useful only in a few cases, it is instructive to see it once in order to understand that a regression package is simply estimating the equation of a plane in three-space when multiple regression is used. The plane is a normal plane when there are two independent variables, and it is called a *hyperplane* (more than three-dimensional) when there are more than two independent variables.

If all the actual data points were to lie very close to the regression plane, the R^2 of the equation would be very high.

Statistical Evaluation of Multiple-Regression Models

The statistical evaluation of multiple-regression models is similar to that discussed in Chapter 4 for simple bivariate regression models. However, some important differences will be brought out in this section. In addition to evaluating the multiple-regression model, we will be comparing these results with the corresponding bivariate model. Thus, in Table 5–2 you see the regression results for both models. The multiple-regression results appear at the bottom of the table.

The first thing one should do in reviewing regression results is to see whether the signs on the coefficients make sense.

Three Quick Checks in Evaluating Multiple-Regression Models

As suggested in Chapter 4, the first thing one should do in reviewing regression results is to see whether the signs on the coefficients make sense. For our current

(c5t1)

TABLE 5–2   Regression Results for Multiple- and Bivariate-Regression Models of Retail Sales (RS)

```
REGRESS: dependent variable is RS
Using 1986Q1-1995Q4
```

Variable	Coefficient	Std Err	T-stat	Signf
^CONST	894067.	68978.7	12.9615	.000
MR	-46187.1	7402.71	-6.23922	.000

Equation Summary

No. of Observations =	40	R2 = .5060 (adj)=	.4930
Sum of Sq. Resid. =	.112669E+12	Std. Error of Reg.=	54451.5
Log(likelihood) =	-491.934	Durbin-Watson =	1.09712
Schwarz Criterion =	-495.623	F (1, 38) =	38.9278
Akaike Criterion =	-493.934	Significance =	.000000

```
REGRESS : dependent variable is RS
Using   1986Q1-1995Q4
```

Variable	Coefficient	Std Err	T-stat	Signf
^CONST	-.142327E+07	268992.	-5.29113	.000
MR	-14150.5	5654.04	-2.50273	.017
DPI	112.952	12.9653	8.71185	.000

Equation Summary

No. of Observations =	40	R2 = .8381 (adj)=	.8294
Sum of Sq. Resid. =	.369254E+11	Std. Error of Reg.=	31590.9
Log (likelihood) =	-469.623	Durbin-Watson =	2.60588
Schwarz Criterion =	-475.157	F (2, 37) =	95.7747
Akaike Criterion =	-472.623	Significance =	.000000

MR = Mortgage interest rate.
DPI = Disposable income per capita.

model, that is,

$$RS = b_0 + b_1(MR) + b_2(DPI)$$

we have said that we expect a negative relationship between RS and the interest rate, and a positive relationship between real disposable personal income and RS. Our expectations are confirmed, since:

$$b_1 = -142{,}370 < 0$$
$$b_2 = +112.952 > 0$$

The second thing to consider is whether these results are statistically significant at our desired level of confidence.

The second thing to consider is whether these results are statistically significant at our desired level of confidence. We will follow the convention of using a 95 percent confidence level, and thus a 0.05 significance level. The hypotheses to be tested are summarized as follows:

For DPI	For MR
$H_0: \beta_1 \leq 0$	$H_0: \beta_2 \geq 0$
$H_1: \beta_1 > 0$	$H_1: \beta_2 < 0$

These hypotheses are evaluated using a t-test where, as with bivariate regression, the calculated t-ratio is found by dividing the estimated regression coefficient by its standard error (i.e., $t_{calc} = b_i/\text{s.e. of } b_i$). The table value of t (t_T) can be found from Table 2–5 at $n - (K + 1)$ degrees of freedom, where $n =$ the number of observations and $K =$ the number of independent variables. For our current problem $n = 40$ and $K = 2$, so df $= 40 - (2 + 1) = 37$. We will follow the rule that if df ≥ 30 the infinity row of the t-table will be used. Thus, the table value is 1.645. Note that we have used the 0.05 column, since we have one-tailed tests, and in such cases the entire significance level (0.05) goes in one tail.

Remember that since the t-distribution is symmetrical, we compare the absolute value of t_{calc} with the table value. For our hypothesis tests, the results can be summarized as follows:

For MR	For DPI
$t_{calc} = -2.50273$	$t_{calc} = 8.71185$
$|t_{calc}| > t_T$	$|t_{calc}| > t_T$
$+2.50273 > 1.645$	$8.71185 > 1.645$
$\therefore$ Reject H_0	$\therefore$ Reject H_0

In both cases the absolute value of t_{calc} is greater than the table value at $\alpha = .05$ and df $= 37$. Therefore, we reject the null hypotheses and conclude that the coefficients on MR and DPI are significantly positive and negative, respectively.

An alternative to comparing t-values to determine whether or not to reject H_0 is to consider the significance level given in most computer output (see the "Signf" column of Table 5–2). If we set a 95 percent confidence level as our criterion, we are at the same time saying that we are willing to accept a 5 percent chance of error, or, alternatively, we set a 5 percent desired significance level. For a two-tailed hypothesis test (H_1: $\beta_1 \neq 0$), we can reject H_0 if the reported two-tailed significance level in our output is less than 0.05 (i.e., our risk of error is less than 5 percent). For a one-tailed hypothesis test (H_1: $\beta_1 < 0$ or H_1: $\beta_1 > 0$) we can reject H_0 if one-half of the reported two-tailed significance level is less than 0.05. In the case of DPI the two-tailed significance level associated with the large calculated t-ratios is 0.000. Clearly, one-half of 0.000 is less than 0.05, so it is appropriate to reject H_0. For the MR variable the significance level is given as 0.017. Half of 0.017 is also less than 0.05, so it is appropriate to reject H_0. Note: In SORITEC, as well as most other statistical packages, two-tailed significance levels are reported.

The third part of our quick check of regression results involves an evaluation of the coefficient of determination, which, you may recall, measures the percentage of the variation in the dependent variable that is explained by the regression model. In Chapter 4 we designated the coefficient of determination as R^2. If you look at the second SORITEC output in Table 5–2, you will see that in addition to R-squared there is another measure called the *adjusted R*-squared. [See "(adj) = .8294" at the top right of the equation summary.] In evaluating multiple-regression equations, you should always consider the adjusted R-squared value. The reason for the adjustment is that adding another independent variable will always increase R-squared even if the variable has no meaningful relation to the dependent variable. Indeed, if we added enough independent variables, we could get very close to an R-squared of 1.00—a perfect fit for the historic period. However, the model would probably work very poorly for values of the independent variables other than those used in estimation. To get around this and to show only meaningful changes in R-squared, an adjustment is made to account for a decrease in the number of degrees of freedom.[3] The adjusted R-squared is often denoted $\overline{R}^2$ (called R-bar-squared).

For our multiple-regression model of retail sales (RS), we see, in Table 5–2, that the adjusted R-squared is .8294. Thus, this model explains 82.94 percent of the variation in retail sales. This compares with an adjusted R-squared of .4930 for the bivariate model.

In looking at regression output, you often see an F-statistic. This statistic can be used to test the following hypothesis:

$$H_0: \beta_1 = \beta_2 = \beta_3 = \cdots \beta_k = 0$$

(i.e., all slope terms are simultaneously equal to zero);

$$H_1: \text{All slope terms are not simultaneously equal to zero}$$

If the null hypothesis is true, it follows that none of the variation in the dependent variable would be explained by the regression model. It follows that if H_0 is true, the true coefficient of determination would be zero.

> The third part of our quick check of regression results involves an evaluation of the coefficient of determination.

---

[3] These concepts are expanded in J. Scott Armstrong, *Long-Range Forecasting* (New York: John Wiley & Sons, 1978), pp. 323–25, 466.

The *F*-statistic is calculated as follows:

$$F = \frac{\text{Explained variation}/K}{\text{Unexplained variation}/[n - (K + 1)]}$$

To test the hypothesis, this calculated *F*-statistic is compared with the *F*-value from Table 5–3 at *K* degrees of freedom for the numerator and $n - (K + 1)$ degrees of freedom for the denominator.[4] For our current regression, $K = 2$ and $[n-(K+1)] = 37$, so the table value of *F* is 3.23 (taking the closest value). In using an *F*-test, the criterion for rejection of the null hypothesis is that $F_{\text{calc}} > F_T$ (the calculated *F* must be greater than the table value). In this case the calculated value is 95.7747, so we would reject H_0 (i.e., our equation passes the *F*-test).

Multicollinearity

In multiple-regression analysis, one of the assumptions that is made is that the independent variables are not highly correlated with each other or with linear combinations of other independent variables. If this assumption is violated, a problem known as *multicollinearity* results.

In multiple-regression analysis, one of the assumptions that is made is that the independent variables are not highly correlated with each other or with linear combinations of other independent variables. If this assumption is violated, a problem known as *multicollinearity* results. If your regression results show that one or more independent variables appear not to be statistically significant when theory suggests that they should be, and/or if the signs on coefficients are not logical, multicollinearity may be indicated. Sometimes it is possible to spot the cause of the multicollinearity by looking at a correlation matrix for the independent variables.

To illustrate the multicollinearity problem, suppose that we model retail sales (RS) as a function of real disposable personal income (DPI), the mortgage rate (MR), and the municipal bond interest rate (BI). The model would be:

$$RS = b_0 + b_1(\text{MR}) + b_2(\text{DPI}) + b_3(\text{BI})$$

Business and economic logic would tell us to expect a negative sign for b_1, a positive sign for b_2, and a negative sign for b_3. The actual regression results are:

	Coefficient	*t-Ratio*	*Two-Tailed Significance*
b_0	$-.153924E+07$	-5.33605	.000
b_1	-32300.3	-1.84347	.074
b_2	117.053	8.69425	.000
b_3	30831.7	1.09406	.281

b_0 = Constant term
b_1 = Mortgage rate coefficient
b_2 = Disposable personal income coefficient
b_3 = Municipal bond interest rate coefficient

We see that the coefficient for BI is positive, which does not make sense. It would be difficult to argue persuasively that RS would rise as BI rises.

---

[4]This *F*-table corresponds to a 95 percent confidence level ($\alpha = 0.05$). One could use any α value and the corresponding *F*-distribution.

If we look at the correlations between these variables, we can see the source of the problem. The correlations are:

Variable Pair	Correlation Coefficient
MR, DPI	$-.650394$
DPI, BI	$-.682382$
MR, BI	$.969537$

Clearly there is a very strong linear association between MR and BI. In this case both of these variables are measuring essentially the same thing. There are no firm rules in deciding how strong a correlation is too great. Two rules of thumb, however, provide some guidance. First, we might avoid correlations between independent variables that are close to 1 in absolute value. Second, we might try to avoid situations in which the correlation between independent variables is greater than the correlation of those variables with the dependent variable. One thing to do when multicollinearity exists is to drop all but one of the highly correlated variables. The use of first differences can also help when there is a common trend in the two highly correlated independent variables.

Serial Correlation: A Second Look

Serial correlation results when there is a significant time pattern in the error terms of a regression analysis.

The problem known as *serial correlation* (or autocorrelation) was introduced in Chapter 4, where we indicated that serial correlation results when there is a significant time pattern in the error terms of a regression analysis that violates the assumption that the errors are independent over time. Positive serial correlation, as shown in the right-hand graph of Figure 4–11, is common in business and economic data.

A test involving six comparisons between table values of the Durbin-Watson statistic and the calculated Durbin-Watson statistic is used to detect serial correlation. These six comparisons are repeated here, where d_l and d_u represent the lower and upper bounds of the Durbin-Watson statistic from Table 4–6 and DW is the calculated value:

Test	Value of Calculated DW	Conclusion
1	$d_l < \text{DW} < d_u$	Result is indeterminate
2	$0 < \text{DW} < d_l$	Positive serial correlation exists
3	$2 < \text{DW} < (4 - d_u)$	No serial correlation exists
4	$d_u < \text{DW} < 2$	No serial correlation exists
5	$(4 - d_l) < \text{DW} < 4$	Negative serial correlation exists
6	$(4 - d_u) < \text{DW} < (4 - d_l)$	Result is indeterminate

TABLE 5–3　**Critical Values of the *F*-Distribution at a 95 Percent Confidence Level**
($\alpha = .05$)

	1*	2	3	4	5	6	7	8	9
1†	161.4	199.5	215.7	224.6	230.2	234.0	236.8	238.9	240.5
2	18.51	19.00	19.16	19.25	19.30	19.33	19.35	19.37	19.38
3	10.13	9.55	9.28	9.12	9.01	8.94	8.89	8.85	8.81
4	7.71	6.94	6.59	6.39	6.26	6.16	6.09	6.04	6.00
5	6.61	5.79	5.41	5.19	5.05	4.95	4.88	4.82	4.77
6	5.99	5.14	4.76	4.53	4.39	4.28	4.21	4.15	4.10
7	5.59	4.74	4.35	4.12	3.97	3.87	3.79	3.73	3.68
8	5.32	4.46	4.07	3.84	3.69	3.58	3.50	3.44	3.39
9	5.12	4.26	3.86	3.63	3.48	3.37	3.29	3.23	3.18
10	4.96	4.10	3.71	3.48	3.33	3.22	3.14	3.07	3.02
11	4.84	3.98	3.59	3.36	3.20	3.09	3.01	2.95	2.90
12	4.75	3.89	3.49	3.26	3.11	3.00	2.91	2.85	2.80
13	4.67	3.81	3.41	3.18	3.03	2.92	2.83	2.77	2.71
14	4.60	3.74	3.34	3.11	2.96	2.85	2.76	2.70	2.65
15	4.54	3.68	3.29	3.06	2.90	2.79	2.71	2.64	2.59
16	4.49	3.63	3.24	3.01	2.85	2.74	2.66	2.59	2.54
17	4.45	3.59	3.20	2.96	2.81	2.70	2.61	2.55	2.49
18	4.41	3.55	3.16	2.93	2.77	2.66	2.58	2.51	2.46
19	4.38	3.52	3.13	2.90	2.74	2.63	2.54	2.48	2.42
20	4.35	3.49	3.10	2.87	2.71	2.60	2.51	2.45	2.39
21	4.32	3.47	3.07	2.84	2.68	2.57	2.49	2.42	2.37
22	4.30	3.44	3.05	2.82	2.66	2.55	2.46	2.40	2.34
23	4.28	3.42	3.03	2.80	2.64	2.53	2.44	2.37	2.32
24	4.26	3.40	3.01	2.78	2.62	2.51	2.42	2.36	2.30
25	4.24	3.39	2.99	2.76	2.60	2.49	2.40	2.34	2.28
26	4.23	3.37	2.98	2.74	2.59	2.47	2.39	2.32	2.27
27	4.21	3.35	2.96	2.73	2.57	2.46	2.37	2.31	2.25
28	4.20	3.34	2.95	2.71	2.56	2.45	2.36	2.29	2.24
29	4.18	3.33	2.93	2.70	2.55	2.43	2.35	2.28	2.22
30	4.17	3.32	2.92	2.69	2.53	2.42	2.33	2.27	2.21
40	4.08	3.23	2.84	2.61	2.45	2.34	2.25	2.18	2.12
60	4.00	3.15	2.76	2.53	2.37	2.25	2.17	2.10	2.04
120	3.92	3.07	2.68	2.45	2.29	2.17	2.09	2.02	1.96
∞	3.84	3.00	2.60	2.37	2.21	2.10	2.01	1.94	1.88

*Degrees of freedom for the numerator $= K$
†Degrees of freedom for the denominator $= n - (K + 1)$

Earlier in this chapter we indicated that for the bivariate regression of RS with MR, the DW of 1.09712 indicated positive serial correlation.

For the multiple regression of RS with DPI and MR the calculated Durbin-Watson statistic is approximately 2.6. (See Table 5–2, which has DW for both the bivariate and the multiple regressions.) This satisfies test 6:

$$4 - d_u < DW < d_l$$
$$(4 - 1.6) < 2.6 < 4 - 1.39$$

where d_u was found from Table 4–6 for $k = 2$ and $N = 40$. Thus, we conclude that the result is indeterminate. This illustrates one possible solution to the serial-correlation problem. Our bivariate model was underspecified: an important independent variable was missing. In this case it was the mortgage rate (MR). While the addition of this variable did not solve the problem in this case, the DW statistic did move in the correct direction.

Another possible solution that was indicated in Chapter 4 was to add an independent variable that is the lagged value of the dependent variable. This can be illustrated by looking at the regression of real disposable personal income (DPI) as a function of time. Results of that regression were shown in Table 4–2; relevant parts are reproduced here:

$$DPI = 17,052.1 + 41.0672(TIME)$$
$$R^2 = 0.8736 \quad DW = 0.62$$
$$t\text{-ratio for TIME} = 16.2$$

As shown in Chapter 4, this Durbin-Watson statistic satisfied test 2, indicating positive serial correlation.

A multiple regression with DPI as a function of time and DPI lagged one quarter [DPI(-1)] was run, with the following result:

$$DPI = 5,224 + 12.7(TIME) + 0.69[DPI(-1)]$$
$$\text{adj } R^2 = 0.922 \quad DW = 2.27$$
$$t\text{-ratio for TIME} = 2.36$$
$$t\text{-ratio for DPI}(-1) = 5.54$$

This DW satisfies test 3, indicating that there is no serial correlation in the regression.

Serial Correlation and the Omitted-Variable Problem

Table 5–4 presents data for a firm's sales, the price the firm charges for its product, and the income of potential purchasers. The most common reason for serial correlation is that an important explanatory variable has been omitted. To address this situation it will be necessary at times to add an additional explanatory variable to the equation to correct for serial correlation.

In the first regression displayed in Table 5–4 price is used as the single independent variable to explain the firm's sales. The results are somewhat less than satisfactory on a number of accounts. First, the R^2 is quite low, explaining only about 39 percent of the variation in sales. More importantly, the sign on the price coefficient is positive, indicating that as price increases, sales also increase. This does not seem to follow economic theory. Finally, the Durbin-Watson statistic is only 0.34, indicating a serious case of serial correlation.

The problem may be that an important variable that could account for the correlation of the error terms has been omitted from the regression. The second regression in Table 5–4 adds income as a second explanatory variable. The results are dramatic. The adjusted R^2 shows that the model now accounts for about 95 percent of the

TABLE 5–4   **Regression Results for a Regression with an Omitted Variable**

	SALES	PRICE	INCOME		SALES	PRICE	INCOME
1993Q1	80.0000	5.00000	2620.00	1995Q1	111.000	5.55000	4016.00
1993Q2	86.0000	4.87000	2733.00	1995Q2	113.000	5.72000	4152.00
1993Q3	93.0000	4.86000	2898.00	1995Q3	110.000	5.74000	4336.00
1993Q4	99.0000	4.79000	3056.00	1995Q4	112.000	5.59000	4477.00
1994Q1	106.000	4.79000	3271.00	1996Q1	131.000	5.50000	4619.00
1994Q2	107.000	4.87000	3479.00	1996Q2	136.000	5.48000	4764.00
1994Q3	109.000	5.01000	3736.00	1996Q3	137.000	5.47000	4802.00
1994Q4	110.000	5.31000	3868.00	1996Q4	139.000	5.49000	4916.00

```
REGRESS : dependent variable is SALES

Using   1993Q1-1996Q4

    Variable        Coefficient      Std Err       T-stat       Signf

^CONST                -51.2362       54.3217      -.943200       .362
PRICE                  30.9231       10.3202       2.99638       .010




                        Equation Summary
     No. of Observations =      16     R2=   .3907   (adj)=   .3472
     Sum of Sq. Resid. =    2796.82    Std. Error of Reg.=  14.1341
     Log(likelihood)   =   -64.0122    Durbin-Watson     =   .34478
     Schwarz Criterion =   -66.7848    F ( 1,   14)      =  8.97829
     Akaike Criterion  =   -66.0122    Significance      =  .009620

REGRESS : dependent variable is SALES

Using   1993Q1-1996Q4


    Variable        Coefficient      Std Err       T-stat       Signf

^CONST                 123.472       19.3994       6.36473       .000
PRICE                 -24.8447       4.95184      -5.01726       .000
INCOME             .306334E-01    .226065E-02      13.5507       .000




                        Equation Summary
     No. of Observations =      16     R2=   .9597   (adj)=   .9535
     Sum of Sq. Resid. =    184.917    Std. Error of Reg.=  3.77152
     Log(likelihood)   =   -42.2815    Durbin-Watson     =  1.66946
     Schwarz Criterion =   -46.4404    F ( 2,   13)      =  154.858
     Akaike Criterion  =   -45.2815    Significance      =  .000000
```

variation in sales. The signs of both the explanatory variable coefficients are as expected. The price coefficient is negative, indicating that sales decrease as price increases, while the income coefficient is positive, indicating that sales of the good rise as incomes increase (which would be reasonable for a "normal" economic good).

The Durbin-Watson statistic has risen to 1.67 and is within the rule of thumb 1.5 to 2.5 range. There does not seem to be serial correlation (and so the R^2 and t-statistics are probably accurate). The formal test for serial correlation requires us to look for the upper and lower values in the Durbin-Watson table (Table 4–6). Note carefully that the appropriate values are 0.95 and 1.54 (i.e., $N = 15$ and column $k = 2$).

Using these values and our calculated value, we can evaluate each of the criteria presented in Figure 4–12:

Region	Comparison	Result
A	$4 > 1.67 > (4 - 0.95)$	False
B	$(4 - 0.95) > 1.67 > (4 - 1.54)$	False
C	$(4 - 1.54) > 1.67 > 1.54$	True
D	$1.54 > 1.67 > 0.95$	False
E	$0.95 > 1.67 > 0$	False

Since our result is in region C, we conclude that no serial correlation is present. Apparently, the addition of the second explanatory variable explained the pattern in the residuals that the Durbin-Watson statistic identified.

The Cochrane-Orcutt Solution to Serial Correlation

Another manner of handling the serial correlation problem that is used in multiple regression is the Cochrane-Orcutt procedure described in Chapter 4. Table 5–5 presents the results for a Cochrane-Orcutt multiple-regression model of the retail sales (RS) data. Note that the Durbin-Watson statistic is very close to the ideal 2 (the calculated value is 1.96695). This indicates that serial correlation is not a problem for this regression. It is best to remember that when autocorrelation is caused by omitted variables, a better solution is to respecify the model. Cochrane-Orcutt may make the errors appear well behaved, but it will do nothing about the likely bias introduced by omitting a variable.[5]

Alternative-Variable Selection Criteria

There is a strong tendency for forecasters to use a single criterion for deciding which of several variables ought to be used as independent variables in a regression. The

---

[5] Kmenta and Doran have pointed out that the Cochrane-Orcutt procedure occasionally results in multiple solutions (usually one "correct" solution and another "spurious" solution). Realizing this, the forecaster should probably use another forecasting technique to see if the Cochrane-Orcutt forecasts are reasonable.

(c5t1)   TABLE 5–5   **Regression Results for a Cochrane-Orcutt Multiple Regression**

```
REGRESS : dependent variable is RS

Using    1986Q1-1995Q4
```

Variable	Coefficient	Std Err	T-stat	Signf
^CONST	-.138343E+07	201873.	-6.85295	.000
MR	-15226.8	4213.99	-3.61339	.001
DPI	111.284	9.72906	11.4383	.000
^RHO	-.317325	.149942	-2.11632	.041

```
                     Equation Summary
     No. of Observations =      40      R2=   .8542   (adj)=   .8463
     Sum of Sq. Resid. =    .332587E+11 Std. Error of Reg.= 29981.4
     Log(likelihood)   = -467.532       Durbin-Watson     = 1.96695
     Schwarz Criterion = -473.065       F ( 2,   37)      = 108.373
     Akaike Criterion  = -470.532       Significance      = .000000

                 Autocorrelation Estimation Summary
     Initial Rho(1)      =   .00000     Final Rho(1)       = -.31733
     Std Error of Rho(1) =   .14994     t-value (sig) = -2.116 ( .041)
     Convergence at iteration 3
```

criterion most people use appears to be the coefficient of multiple determination, or R^2. Recall that R^2 is a measure of the proportion of total variance accounted for by the linear influence of the explanatory variables (only *linear* influence is accounted for, since we are using linear least-squares regression). The R^2 measure has at least one obvious fault when used in this manner: it can be increased by simply increasing the number of independent variables. Because of this, we proposed the corrected or adjusted R^2, which uses unbiased estimators of the respective variances. Most forecasters use the adjusted R^2 to lead them to the correct model by selecting the model that maximizes adjusted R^2. The adjusted R^2 measure is based on selecting the correct model by using a quadratic form of the residuals or squared errors in which the true model minimizes those squared errors. But the adjusted R^2 measure may not be the most powerful of the measures involving the squared errors.

> There are two other model-specification statistics reported by SORITEC and other statistical packages that can be of use in selecting the "correct" independent variables.

There are two other model-specification statistics reported by SORITEC and other statistical packages that can be of use in selecting the "correct" independent variables. These are the Akaike information criterion (AIC) and the Schwarz criterion (SC).

The Akaike information criterion selects the best model by considering the accuracy of the estimation and the "best" approximation to reality. The statistic (which is minimized by the best model) involves both the use of a measure of the accuracy of the estimate *and* a measure of the principle of parsimony (i.e., the concept that fewer independent variables are better than more, all other things being equal). The calculation of the AIC is detailed in Judge et al.[6] We can say that the statistic is constructed so that as the number of independent variables increases, the AIC has a tendency to increase as well; this means that there is a penalty for "extra" independent variables that must be sufficiently offset by an increase in estimation accuracy to keep the AIC from increasing. In actual practice, a decrease in the AIC as a variable is added indicates that accuracy has increased after adjustment for the rule of parsimony.

The Schwarz criterion is quite similar to the AIC. The SC uses Bayesian arguments about the prior probability of the true model to suggest the correct model. While the calculation routine for the SC is quite different from that for the AIC, the results are usually quite consistent.[7] The SC is also to be minimized, so that if the SC decreases after the addition of a new independent variable, the resulting model specification is seen as superior to the prior model specification.

In a study of the model-selection process, Judge and coauthors created five independent variables that were to be used to estimate a dependent variable. Two of the five independent variables were actually related to the dependent variable, while the remaining three were extraneous variables. Various combinations of the five independent variables were used to estimate the dependent variable, and three measures were used to select the "best" model. The three measures used were the adjusted R^2, the AIC, and the SC.

The correct model containing only the two variables actually related to the dependent variable was chosen 27 percent of the time in repeated experiments by the adjusted R^2 criterion. The AIC chose the correct model in 45 percent of the cases, and the SC chose the correct model in 46 percent of the cases. The results should make the forecaster wary of accepting only the statistical results of what constitutes the best model without some economic interpretation of why a variable is included. It should be clear, however, that the adjusted R^2 criterion is actually quite a poor judge to use in model selection; either the AIC or the SC is far superior. The same study also showed that in 9 percent of the repeated trials the adjusted R^2 criterion chose the model with all five variables (i.e., the two "correct" ones and the three extraneous ones). The AIC and the SC made the same incorrect choice in only 3 percent of the cases.

Examine the SORITEC output in Table 5–2, which includes the calculated Akaike and Schwarz criteria. In the upper half of Table 5–2, the retail sales (RS) regression includes only the mortgage rate (MR) as an independent variable. For this specification of the model, the AIC is −493.934, while the SC is −495.623. When the disposable personal income (DPI) variable is added to the regression, the AIC (in absolute terms) decreases to −472.623 and the SC decreases (again in absolute terms) to −475.157. These changes in the AIC and SC indicate that the addition of MR to the model was a correct choice.

In Table 5–4 we added a second variable to a regression. When both price and income were included, the AIC (again in absolute terms) decreased to −45 from

---

[6]For a complete description of the calculation routine, see George G. Judge, R. Carter Hill, William E. Griffiths, Helmut Lutkepohl, and Tsoung-Chao Lee, *Introduction to the Theory and Practice of Econometrics,* 2nd ed. (New York: John Wiley & Sons, 1988), Chapter 20.

[7]Again see Judge et al. for a complete description of the calculation routine.

−66 and the SC decreased (in absolute terms) to −46 from −66. Apparently, the inclusion of income as a variable was also a correct choice.

In Table 5–5 the Cochrane-Orcutt procedure is used to overcome serial correlation. Compare the AIC and the SC for this regression with that at the bottom of Table 5–2, which included only DPI and MR as independent variables. The AIC and the SC are better for the Cochrane-Orcutt regression, indicating that the inclusion of the ^RHO term was a correct choice.

Accounting for Seasonality in a Multiple-Regression Model

Many business and economic data series display pronounced seasonal patterns that recur with some regularity year after year. The pattern may be associated with weather conditions typical of four seasons of the year. For example, sales of ski equipment would be expected to be greater during the fall and winter (the fourth and first quarters of the calendar year, respectively) than during the spring and summer (quarters 2 and 3).

Other regular patterns that would be referred to as seasonal patterns may have nothing to do with weather conditions. For example, jewelry sales tend to be high in November and December because of Christmas shopping, and turkey sales are also highest in these months because of traditions surrounding Thanksgiving and Christmas dinners.

A special type of variable known as a *dummy variable* can be used effectively to account for seasonality or any other qualitative attribute.

Patterns such as these are not easily accounted for by the typical causal variables that we use in regression analysis. However, a special type of variable known as a *dummy variable* can be used effectively to account for seasonality or any other qualitative attribute. A dummy variable has a value of either 0 or 1. It is 0 if the condition does not exist for an observation, and it is 1 if the condition does exist.

Suppose that we were studying monthly data on turkey sales at grocery stores and that we would like to include the November and December seasonality in our model. We could define a dummy variable called M11, for the eleventh month, to be equal to 1 for November observations and 0 otherwise. Another dummy variable, M12, could be defined similarly for December. Thus, for every year these variables would be as follows:

Month	*M11*	*M12*	*Month*	*M11*	*M12*
January	0	0	July	0	0
February	0	0	August	0	0
March	0	0	September	0	0
April	0	0	October	0	0
May	0	0	November	1	0
June	0	0	December	0	1

In the regression results the coefficients for M11 and M12 would reveal the degree of difference in sales for November and December, respectively. In both of these cases we would expect the coefficients to be positive.

To illustrate very specifically the use of dummy variables to account for and measure seasonality, let us use private housing starts in the United States measured in thousands of units. These data are plotted for 1986Q1 through 1996Q4 in Figure 5–5. To help you see the seasonality, each first quarter is marked with the number 1. You see in this figure that through the 11 years, there are typically few housing starts during the first quarter of the year (January, February, March); there is usually a big increase in the second quarter (April, May, June), followed by some decline in the third quarter (July, August, September) and further decline in the fourth quarter (October, November, December). The first quarter is almost always the lowest quarter for the year. This pattern is reasonably consistent, although there is variability in the degree of seasonality and some deviation from the overall pattern.

To account for and measure this seasonality in a regression model, we will use three dummy variables: Q2 for the second quarter, Q3 for the third quarter, and Q4 for the fourth quarter. These will be coded as follows:

Q2 = 1 for all second quarters and zero otherwise
Q3 = 1 for all third quarters and zero otherwise
Q4 = 1 for all fourth quarters and zero otherwise

Data for private housing starts (PHS), the mortgage rate (MR), and these seasonal dummy variables are shown in Table 5–6. Look at the data carefully to verify your understanding of the coding for Q2, Q3, and Q4.

Since we have assigned dummy variables for the second, third, and fourth quarters, the first quarter is the base quarter for our regression model. Any quarter could be used as the base, with dummy variables to adjust for differences in other quarters.

FIGURE 5–5

Private Housing Starts (PHS) in Thousands of Units, 1986Q1– 1996Q4
(c5t6)

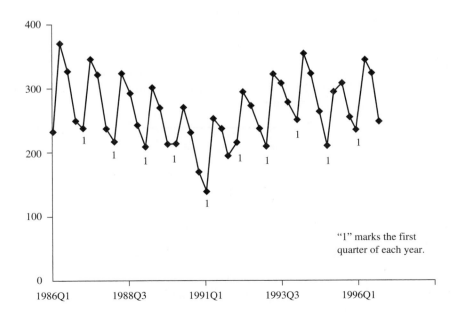

"1" marks the first quarter of each year.

(c5t6)   TABLE 5–6   **Data for Private Housing Starts (PHS), the Mortgage Rate (MR), and Seasonal Dummy Variables for the Second, Third, and Fourth Quarters (Q2, Q3, Q4)**

	PHS	MR	Q2	Q3	Q4
1986Q1	234.100	10.5600	0.00000	0.00	0.00000
1986Q2	369.400	10.2600	1.00000	0.00	0.00000
1986Q3	325.400	10.2400	0.00000	1.00	0.00000
1986Q4	250.600	9.66667	0.00000	0.00	1.00000
1987Q1	241.400	9.10667	0.00000	0.00	0.00000
1987Q2	346.500	10.3233	1.00000	0.00	0.00000
1987Q3	321.300	10.5000	0.00000	1.00	0.00000
1987Q4	237.100	10.8500	0.00000	0.00	1.00000
1988Q1	219.700	10.0667	0.00000	0.00	0.00000
1988Q2	323.700	10.3733	1.00000	0.00	0.00000
1988Q3	293.400	10.5033	0.00000	1.00	0.00000
1988Q4	244.600	10.3933	0.00000	0.00	1.00000
1989Q1	212.700	10.8033	0.00000	0.00	0.00000
1989Q2	302.100	10.6733	1.00000	0.00	0.00000
1989Q3	272.100	10.0000	0.00000	1.00	0.00000
1989Q4	216.500	9.82000	0.00000	0.00	1.00000
1990Q1	217.000	10.1233	0.00000	0.00	0.00000
1990Q2	271.300	10.3367	1.00000	0.00	0.00000
1990Q3	233.000	10.1067	0.00000	1.00	0.00000
1990Q4	173.600	9.95000	0.00000	0.00	1.00000
1991Q1	146.700	9.50333	0.00000	0.00	0.00000
1991Q2	254.100	9.53000	1.00000	0.00	0.00000
1991Q3	239.800	9.27667	0.00000	1.00	0.00000
1991Q4	199.800	8.69000	0.00000	0.00	1.00000
1992Q1	218.500	8.71000	0.00000	0.00	0.00000
1992Q2	296.400	8.67667	1.00000	0.00	0.00000
1992Q3	276.400	8.01000	0.00000	1.00	0.00000
1992Q4	238.800	8.20333	0.00000	0.00	1.00000
1993Q1	213.200	7.72333	0.00000	0.00	0.00000
1993Q2	323.700	7.45000	1.00000	0.00	0.00000
1993Q3	309.300	7.07667	0.00000	1.00	0.00000
1993Q4	279.400	7.05333	0.00000	0.00	1.00000
1994Q1	252.600	7.30000	0.00000	0.00	0.00000
1994Q2	354.200	8.44000	1.00000	0.00	0.00000
1994Q3	325.700	8.58667	0.00000	1.00	0.00000
1994Q4	265.900	9.10000	0.00000	0.00	1.00000
1995Q1	214.200	8.81333	0.00000	0.00	0.00000
1995Q2	296.700	7.95000	1.00000	0.00	0.00000
1995Q3	308.200	7.70333	0.00000	1.00	0.00000
1995Q4	257.200	7.35333	0.00000	0.00	1.00000

The number of seasonal dummy variables to use depends on the data. There is one important rule, however:

If we have P periods in our data series, we cannot use more than P − 1 seasonal dummy variables.

In our current example $P = 4$, since we have quarterly data, and so we would use only three seasonal dummy variables. We could use fewer than three if we found that all three were unnecessary by evaluating their statistical significance by t-tests.

Let us now add these variables to the regression model for private housing starts (PHS). Our regression model will include the mortgage rate (MR) and the three dummy variables for seasonality (Q2, Q3, and Q4) as independent variables. The model is:

$$\text{PHS} = b_0 + b_1(\text{MR}) + b_2(\text{Q2}) + b_3(\text{Q3}) + b_4(\text{Q4})$$

In this model we would expect b_1 to have a negative sign, and we would expect b_2, b_3, and b_4 all to have positive signs, since the first quarter of the year has been seen to be the lowest (see Figure 5–5).

Regression results for this model are shown in Table 5–7 along with the results for PHS $= f(\text{MR})$, where the mortgage rate is the only independent variable. The bivariate model was discussed in Chapter 4, but the results are shown here to facilitate comparison. Looking at the output at the top of Table 5–7, you see that the signs for the coefficients are all consistent with our expectations. Further, from the t-statistics you can see that all of the coefficients are statistically significant.

A comparison of the two sets of regression results shown in Table 5–7 shows that important improvements result from adding the seasonal dummy variables. Note that the model with the dummy variables explains about 58.5 percent of the variation in private housing starts (see the adjusted R-squared), which is a considerable improvement over the bivariate model. The AIC and SC both reflect the improvement from the addition of the seasonal dummy variables. Also, the standard error of the regression has fallen from 51.22 to 32.66. The Durbin-Watson statistic shows serial correlation for the multiple-regression model, while the test was indeterminate for the bivariate model. In the next section, we will work further with the PHS model and see some improvement in the serial-correlation problem.

Let us now use this model to make a forecast for each of the four quarters of 1996. The mortgage rate (MR) was forecast for 1996 earlier in this chapter as follows:

Period	MR Forecast
1996Q1	7.2364%
1996Q2	7.1192%
1996Q3	7.0020%
1996Q4	6.8848%

Our forecasts for private housing starts (PHS) are:

PHSF2 $= 265.965 - 5.28046(\text{MR}) + 97.4882(\text{Q2}) + 73.0769(\text{Q3}) + 18.4793(\text{Q4})$

1996Q1:

PHSF2 $= 265.965 - 5.28046(7.2364) + 97.4882(0) + 73.0769(0) + 18.4793(0)$
$= 227.75$

(c5t6)   TABLE 5–7   **Regression Results for Private Housing Starts (PHS) as a Function of the Mortgage Rate (MR) Both with and without Seasonal Dummy Variables**

```
REGRESS : dependent variable is PHS

Using    1986Q1-1995Q4

        Variable        Coefficient    Std Err      T-stat      Signf

^CONST                    265.965      42.6168      6.24085      .000
MR                       -5.28046      4.45972     -1.18403      .244
Q2                        97.4882      14.6196      6.66831      .000
Q3                        73.0769      14.6115      5.00134      .000
Q4                        18.4793      14.6261      1.26344      .215


                       Equation Summary
        No. of Observations =     40    R2=    .6279   (adj)=   .5854
        Sum of Sq. Resid. =   37344.2   Std. Error of Reg.=  32.6646
        Log(likelihood)   = -193.539    Durbin-Watson    =   .33492
        Schwarz Criterion = -202.761    F ( 4,   35)     =  14.7676
        Akaike Criterion  = -198.539    Significance     =  .000000


REGRESS : dependent variable is PHS

Using    1986Q1-1995Q4


        Variable        Coefficient    Std Err      T-stat      Signf

^CONST                    297.141      64.8850      4.57950      .000
MR                       -3.54063      6.96338      -.508464     .614


                       Equation Summary
        No. of Observations =     40    R2=    .0068   (adj)=  -.0194
        Sum of Sq. Resid. =   99692.7   Std. Error of Reg.=  51.2200
        Log(likelihood)   = -213.177    Durbin-Watson    =  1.46292
        Schwarz Criterion = -216.866    F ( 1,   38)     =   .258536
        Akaike Criterion  = -215.177    Significance     =  .614067
```

1996Q2:

$$PHSF2 = 265.965 - 5.28046(7.1192) + 97.4882(1) + 73.0769(0) + 18.4793(0)$$
$$= 325.86$$

1996Q3:

$$PHSF2 = 265.965 - 5.28046(7.0020) + 97.4882(0) + 73.0769(1) + 18.4793(0)$$
$$= 317.91$$

1996Q4:

$$PHSF2 = 265.965 - 5.28046(6.8848) + 97.4882(0) + 73.0769(0) + 18.4793(1)$$
$$= 248.09$$

These forecasts are plotted in Figure 5–6 along with the actual and predicted values and the simple bivariate forecast for the historical period. If you examine Figure 5–6, you will see how much better the multiple regression model appears to be in comparison with the model of private housing starts as a function of only the mortgage rate.

To see whether this model actually did provide better forecasts for the four quarters of 1996, let us look at the root-mean-squared error (RMSE):

Period	Actual PHS	Second Forecast (PHSF2)	$(PHS - PHSF2)^2$
1996Q1	240.000	227.75	150.0625
1996Q2	344.500	325.86	347.4496
1996Q3	324.000	317.91	37.0881
1996Q4	252.400	248.09	18.5761

$$\text{Sum of squared errors} = 991.1063$$
$$\text{Mean-squared error (MSE)} = 553.1763 = 138.294075$$
$$\text{Root-mean-squared error (RMSE)} = \sqrt{138.294075} = 11.76$$

This RMSE of 11.76 compares with an RMSE of 48.31 for the bivariate model using the mortgage rate as the only independent variable.

FIGURE 5–6

*Private Housing
Starts (PHS)
with a Simple-
Regression
Forecast (PHSF1)
and a Multiple-
Regression
Forecast (PHSF2)
in Thousands
of Units*
(c5t6)

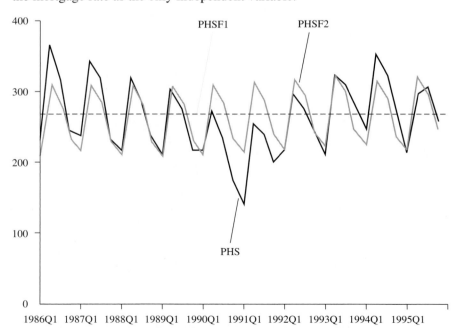

*PHSF1 uses only the mortgage interest rate as an explanatory variable while PHSF2
use the mortgage interest rate as well as three dummy variables accounting for seasonality*

Extensions of the Multiple-Regression Model

In some situations, nonlinear terms may be called for as independent variables in a regression analysis. Why? Business or economic logic may suggest that some non-linearity is expected. A graphic display of the data may be helpful in determining whether nonlinearity is present. One common economic cause for nonlinearity is diminishing returns. For example, the effect of advertising on sales may diminish as increased advertising is used. In this section we will add real income per person as an independent variable to the model for private housing starts and will investigate to see whether there are diminishing returns in the effect of per capita income on private housing starts.

Some common forms of nonlinear functions are the following:

$$Y = b_0 + b_1(X) + b_2(X^2)$$
$$Y = b_0 + b_1(X) + b_2(X^2) + b_3(X^3)$$
$$Y = b_0 + b_1(1/X)$$
$$Y = B_0 X^{b_1} \text{ where } B_0 = e^{b_0}$$
$$\text{based on the regression of } \ln Y = f(\ln X) = b_0 + b_1(\ln X)$$

The first of these will be illustrated later in this section. In these examples only one explanatory variable (X) is shown. Other explanatory variables could be used in each model as well.

To illustrate the use and interpretation of a nonlinear term, let us return to the problem of developing a forecasting model for private housing starts (PHS). So far we have estimated the following two models:

$$\text{PHS} = b_0 + b_1(\text{MR})$$
$$\text{PHS} = b_0 + b_1(\text{MR}) + b_2(\text{Q2}) + b_3(\text{Q3}) + b_4(\text{Q4})$$

where MR = mortgage rate and Q2, Q3, and Q4 are dummy variables for quarters 2, 3, and 4, respectively. Our results have been encouraging, but the best of these—in terms of adjusted R-squared and RMSE (the second model)—still explains only about 58 percent of the variation in PHS during the historical period and has been shown to have positive serial correlation.

Results for three additional regression models for PHS are summarized in Table 5–8 along with the results for the first two models that have been discussed previously. Models 1 and 2 are those we have already discussed. Model 3 adds real disposable personal income per capita (DPI) as an independent variable. Unexpectedly, the coefficient for DPI is negative and insignificant. In comparison with model 2 we see that the adjusted R-squared is virtually identical.

It is in model 4 that we introduce a nonlinear term into the regression. The square of disposable personal income per capita (DPI^2) is included in the regression model. The t-statistic for DPI^2 in this model is 3.31. Inclusion of DPI^2 increases the adjusted R-squared to .70, reduces the standard error of the regression to 27.79, and increases DW to 0.5497.

The values for private housing starts predicted by model 4 are plotted in Figure 5–7 along with the original data. The forecast values (PHSF4) are shown by

(c5t8)   **TABLE 5–8**   **Estimated Regression Coefficients and Other Statistics for Five Models of Private Housing Starts (PHS)**

Independent Variable*	Model				
	1	*2*	*3*	*4*	*5*
Intercept	297.14	265.97	756.99	15180.4	3957
MR	−3.54	−5.28	−12.06	−9.55	−7.87
DPI			−0.024	−1.65	−0.42
DPI^2				0.00005	0.00001
LPHS					0.76
Q2		97.49	99.44	97.19	111.85
Q3		73.08	74.77	73.38	14.48
Q4		18.48	21.43	17.25	−22.38
R^2 or $\bar{R}^2$	.0068	.58	.61	.70	.89
Std. Err. of Reg.	51.22	32.66	31.60	27.79	16.96
DW	1.46	0.334	0.4483	0.5497	2.0691
RMSE†	49.92	30.56	29.14	25.24	15.12‡

*MR = Mortgage rate
†RMSEs are for the period 1986Q1 through 1995Q4.
‡RMSE for model 5 is for the period 1986Q2 through 1995Q4.
DPI = Real disposable income per capita
DPI^2 = Square of real disposable personal income per capita
LPHS = Private housing starts lagged one quarter
Q2 = Dummy variable for quarter 2
Q3 = Dummy variable for quarter 3
Q4 = Dummy variable for quarter 4

FIGURE 5–7

Private Housing Starts (PHS) with Forecast Values (PHSF4) Using Model 4 from Table 5–8

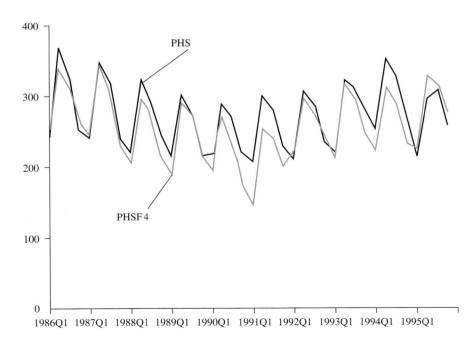

the dashed line, which follows the actual data quite well throughout the historical period. If you compare the dashed lines in Figures 5–6 and 5–7, you can see the improvement between model 2 and model 4 visually (the forecast series are PHSF2 and PHSF4, respectively). This graphic comparison should reinforce the statistical findings for the two models presented in Table 5–8.

Model 5, in Table 5–8, is the same as model 4 except that the dependent variable, lagged one quarter, is added as an independent variable. You may recall that such a procedure was suggested as a way to help reduce serial correlation. As shown in Table 5–8, the Durbin-Watson statistic does increase, although not enough to rule out positive serial correlation. The adjusted R-squared increases, and the standard error of the regression is further reduced. The root-mean-squared errors (RMSEs) are shown in Table 5–8 for models 1 through 5. You see that model 5 worked best for 1986Q1 to 1995Q4.

Data that were used in all of the regression models for private housing starts (PHS) are shown in Table 5–9.

Advice on Using Multiple Regression in Forecasting

Multiple-regression models are a very important part of the set of tools available to anyone interested in forecasting. Apart from their use in generating forecasts, they have considerable value in helping us to uncover structural relationships between the dependent variable and some set of independent variables. Knowing such relationships helps the forecaster understand the sensitivity of the variable to be forecast to other factors. This enhancement of our understanding of the business environment can only serve to improve our ability to make judgments about the future course of events. It is important not to downplay the role of judgments in forecasting. No one should ever rely solely on some quantitative procedure in developing a forecast. Expert judgments are crucial, and multiple-regression analyses can be helpful in improving one's level of expertise.

In developing forecasts with regression models, perhaps the best advice is to follow the "KIS" principle: keep it simple.[8] The more complex the model becomes, the more difficult it is to use. As more causal variables are used, the cost of maintaining the needed database increases in terms of both time and money. Further, complex models are more difficult to communicate to others who may be the actual users of the forecast. They are less likely to trust a model that they do not understand than a simpler model that they do understand.

In evaluating alternative multiple-regression models, is it better to compare adjusted R-squared values, or root-mean-squared errors? Remember that R-squared relates to the in-sample period, that is, to the past. A model may work well for the in-sample period but not work nearly so well in forecasting. Thus, it is usually best to focus on RMSE for actual forecasts (note that we say "focus on" and not "use exclusively"). You might track the RMSE for several alternative models for some period

---

[8]This is also called the *principle of parsimony* by Box and Jenkins. G. E. P. Box and G. M. Jenkins, *Time Series Analysis: Forecasting and Control,* 2nd ed. (San Francisco: Holden Day, 1976).

(c5t9)   TABLE 5–9   **Data for Regression Models of Private Housing Starts**

	PHS	MR	DPI	Q2	Q3	Q4
1986Q1	234.100	10.5600	16951.7	0.00	0.00000	0.00000
1986Q2	369.400	10.2600	17064.7	1.00	0.00000	0.00000
1986Q3	325.400	10.2400	17107.3	0.00	1.00000	0.00000
1986Q4	250.600	9.66667	17032.3	0.00	0.00000	1.00000
1987Q1	241.400	9.10667	17162.0	0.00	0.00000	0.00000
1987Q2	346.500	10.3233	16956.0	1.00	0.00000	0.00000
1987Q3	321.300	10.5000	17159.7	0.00	1.00000	0.00000
1987Q4	237.100	10.8500	17378.7	0.00	0.00000	1.00000
1988Q1	219.700	10.0667	17622.7	0.00	0.00000	0.00000
1988Q2	323.700	10.3733	17623.3	1.00	0.00000	0.00000
1988Q3	293.400	10.5033	17704.3	0.00	1.00000	0.00000
1988Q4	244.600	10.3933	17760.3	0.00	0.00000	1.00000
1989Q1	212.700	10.8033	17919.7	0.00	0.00000	0.00000
1989Q2	302.100	10.6733	17804.0	1.00	0.00000	0.00000
1989Q3	272.100	10.0000	17833.7	0.00	1.00000	0.00000
1989Q4	216.500	9.82000	17858.7	0.00	0.00000	1.00000
1990Q1	217.000	10.1233	18034.7	0.00	0.00000	0.00000
1990Q2	271.300	10.3367	18062.7	1.00	0.00000	0.00000
1990Q3	233.000	10.1067	18031.3	0.00	1.00000	0.00000
1990Q4	173.600	9.95000	17855.7	0.00	0.00000	1.00000
1991Q1	146.700	9.50333	17748.0	0.00	0.00000	0.00000
1991Q2	254.100	9.53000	17861.3	1.00	0.00000	0.00000
1991Q3	239.800	9.27667	17815.3	0.00	1.00000	0.00000
1991Q4	199.800	8.69000	17811.0	0.00	0.00000	1.00000
1992Q1	218.500	8.71000	18000.3	0.00	0.00000	0.00000
1992Q2	296.400	8.67667	18085.7	1.00	0.00000	0.00000
1992Q3	276.400	8.01000	18035.3	0.00	1.00000	0.00000
1992Q4	238.800	8.20333	18330.0	0.00	0.00000	1.00000
1993Q1	213.200	7.72333	17962.3	0.00	0.00000	0.00000
1993Q2	323.700	7.45000	18132.3	1.00	0.00000	0.00000
1993Q3	309.300	7.07667	18143.0	0.00	1.00000	0.00000
1993Q4	279.400	7.05333	18305.7	0.00	0.00000	1.00000
1994Q1	252.600	7.30000	18081.7	0.00	0.00000	0.00000
1994Q2	354.200	8.44000	18366.3	1.00	0.00000	0.00000
1994Q3	325.700	8.58667	18436.0	0.00	1.00000	0.00000
1994Q4	265.900	9.10000	18564.3	0.00	0.00000	1.00000
1995Q1	214.200	8.81333	18697.7	0.00	0.00000	0.00000
1995Q2	296.700	7.95000	18668.3	1.00	0.00000	0.00000
1995Q3	308.200	7.70333	18818.7	0.00	1.00000	0.00000
1995Q4	257.200	7.35333	18971.3	0.00	0.00000	1.00000
1996Q1	240.000	7.24333	19028.0	0.00	0.00000	0.00000
1996Q2	344.500	8.10667	19053.0	1.00	0.00000	0.00000
1996Q3	324.000	8.16000	19233.0	0.00	1.00000	0.00000
1996Q4	252.400	7.71333	19314.7	0.00	0.00000	1.00000

PHS = Private housing starts in thousands of units
MR = Mortgage rate (conventional fixed-rate) percent
DPI = Disposable personal income per year per capita
Note that the models estimated in Table 5–8 use a historical estimation period of 1986Q1 through 1995Q4.
This table, however, also includes the forecast period of 1996Q1 through 1996Q4.

to see whether any one model consistently outperforms others in the forecast horizon. Use the AIC and SC measures to help select appropriate independent variables. It is also desirable periodically to update the regression models to reflect possible changes in the parameter estimates.

Forecasting Domestic Car Sales with Multiple Regression

In this section we apply the concepts covered in this chapter to the problem of forecasting domestic car sales by using a multiple-regression model. The explanatory variables selected are based on business logic and are ones for which data are readily available, should you want to look up the most recent data to update the results shown here. The model used here builds on the model in Chapter 4, in which domestic car sales (DCS) was a function of the unemployment rate (UR). New explanatory variables added in the multiple regression are:

$$DPI = \text{Disposable personal income in constant 1987 dollars (expected sign of coefficient is positive)}$$
$$DPI^2 = \text{Square of DPI}$$
$$PR = \text{Prime interest rate (expected sign negative)}$$
$$Q2 = \text{Dummy variable equal to 1 for second quarters and zero otherwise (expected sign positive because of spring car buying)}$$
$$Q3 = \text{Dummy variable equal to 1 for third quarters and zero otherwise (expected sign negative because of anticipation of new models)}$$
$$Q4 = \text{Dummy variable equal to 1 for fourth quarters and zero otherwise (expected sign positive because of introduction of new models)}$$
$$INDEX = \text{Univ. of Michigan Index of Consumer Sentiment}$$
$$TIME = \text{Time index}$$
$$TIME^2 = \text{Square of time}$$

Two regressions for domestic car sales (DCS) are presented in Table 5–10. The data used to generate both regressions appear in Table 5–11.

At the top of Table 5–10 is the regression of DCS with only disposable personal income (DPI) and the prime rate (PR) used as independent variables. The overall regression has an adjusted R^2 of only 0.0412. The Durbin-Watson statistic is also quite low at 0.97247. The signs of the coefficients are, however, as expected. DCS rises as DPI increases, but DCS falls as PR increases. We show this regression because it is again possible to examine a figure showing the data points with the regression plane superimposed.

Figure 5–8 depicts the data points for the 60 observations and the estimated regression plane. It is easy to see in the figure that as the prime rate increases, domestic car sales decrease. This can clearly be seen by looking at the edge of the regression plane along which DPI equals 14,000; as PR increases from 0 to 30, the regression plane slopes downward. Remember that the "height" of the regression plane is the measure of domestic car sales, so that as the plane slopes downward, DCS is decreasing. Thus, as PR increases (while DPI is held constant at 2,500), DCS decreases.

(c5t11)   TABLE 5–10   **Regression Results for Domestic Car Sales**

REGRESS : dependent variable is DCS

Using   1980Q1–1994Q4

Variable	Coefficient	Std Err	T-stat	Signf
^CONST	1793.92	847.417	2.11693	.039
DPI	.463700E-02	.425425E-01	.108997	.914
PR	-12.1914	14.6443	-.832502	.409

Equation Summary

No. of Observations =	60	R2 = .0412	(adj)= .0075
Sum of Sq. Resid. =	.327047E+07	Std. Error of Reg.=	239.534
Log(likelihood) =	-412.319	Durbin-Watson =	.97247
Schwarz Criterion =	-418.461	F (2, 57) =	1.22405
Akaike Criterion =	-415.319	Significance =	.301648

6> regress dcs dpi dpi2 pr index time time2 q2 q3 q4

REGRESS : dependent variable is DCS

Using   1980Q1–1994Q4

Variable	Coefficient	Std Err	T-stat	Signf
^CONST	-31553.9	8398.76	-3.75697	.001
DPI	3.76585	1.02482	3.67464	.001
DPI2	-.104362E-03	.309574E-04	-3.37116	.002
PR	-16.8160	9.12450	-1.84294	.071
INDEX	10.2264	2.03623	5.02222	.000
TIME	-61.2355	10.5632	-5.79708	.000
TIME2	.608094	.119975	5.06852	.000
Q2	219.093	43.0816	5.08553	.000
Q3	62.4583	42.8792	1.45661	.151
Q4	-59.3869	42.8939	-1.38451	.172

Equation Summary

No. of Observations =	60	R2 = .7994	(adj)= .7633
Sum of Sq. Resid. =	684345.	Std. Error of Reg.=	116.991
Log(likelihood) =	-365.393	Durbin-Watson =	2.01760
Schwarz Criterion =	-385.864	F (9, 50) =	22.1346
Akaike Criterion =	-375.393	Significance =	.000000

TABLE 5–11 **Domestic Car Sales Data Used for Regressions in Table 5–10**

	DCS	DPI	DPI^2	PR	INDEX	TIME	$TIME^2$	Q2	Q3	Q4
1980Q1	1849.90	15006.4	.225192E+09	16.4	63.3912	1.00000	1.00000	0.00	0.00000	0.00000
1980Q2	1550.80	14680.3	.215511E+09	16.3	54.3374	2.00000	4.00000	1.00	0.00000	0.00000
1980Q3	1515.30	14772.0	.218212E+09	11.6	67.7022	3.00000	9.00000	0.00	1.00000	0.00000
1980Q4	1665.40	15009.5	.225285E+09	16.7	72.0163	4.00000	16.0000	0.00	0.00000	1.00000
1981Q1	1733.00	15041.8	.226256E+09	19.2	68.3122	5.00000	25.0000	0.00	0.00000	0.00000
1981Q2	1576.00	14927.4	.222827E+09	18.9	73.9593	6.00000	36.0000	1.00	0.00000	0.00000
1981Q3	1618.50	15183.3	.230533E+09	20.3	74.8185	7.00000	49.0000	0.00	1.00000	0.00000
1981Q4	1281.30	15104.8	.228155E+09	17.0	65.7348	8.00000	64.0000	0.00	0.00000	1.00000
1982Q1	1401.40	14972.4	.224173E+09	16.2	66.5000	9.00000	81.0000	0.00	0.00000	0.00000
1982Q2	1535.30	15123.2	.228711E+09	16.5	66.2473	10.0000	100.000	1.00	0.00000	0.00000
1982Q3	1327.90	15048.3	.226451E+09	14.7	66.6717	11.0000	121.000	0.00	1.00000	0.00000
1982Q4	1493.60	15069.9	.227102E+09	11.9	72.4707	12.0000	144.000	0.00	0.00000	1.00000
1983Q1	1456.90	15085.9	.227584E+09	10.8	75.2889	13.0000	169.000	0.00	0.00000	0.00000
1983Q2	1875.80	15196.8	.230943E+09	10.5	91.5527	14.0000	196.000	1.00	0.00000	0.00000
1983Q3	1646.20	15384.8	.236692E+09	10.7	91.5848	15.0000	225.000	0.00	1.00000	0.00000
1983Q4	1814.10	15659.1	.245207E+09	11.0	91.5380	16.0000	256.000	0.00	0.00000	1.00000
1984Q1	1994.60	15997.2	.255910E+09	11.0	99.5462	17.0000	289.000	0.00	0.00000	0.00000
1984Q2	2251.80	16260.0	.264388E+09	12.3	96.5835	18.0000	324.000	1.00	0.00000	0.00000
1984Q3	1854.30	16480.0	.271590E+09	12.9	98.8446	19.0000	361.000	0.00	1.00000	0.00000
1984Q4	1851.00	16494.8	.272078E+09	11.8	94.9587	20.0000	400.000	0.00	0.00000	1.00000
1985Q1	2042.20	16482.7	.271679E+09	10.5	94.4922	21.0000	441.000	0.00	0.00000	0.00000
1985Q2	2272.60	16753.5	.280680E+09	10.1	94.2725	22.0000	484.000	1.00	0.00000	0.00000
1985Q3	2217.70	16633.0	.276657E+09	9.50	92.8413	23.0000	529.000	0.00	1.00000	0.00000
1985Q4	1672.20	16749.9	.280559E+09	9.50	91.0685	24.0000	576.000	0.00	0.00000	1.00000
1986Q1	1898.70	16952.7	.287394E+09	9.36	95.5211	25.0000	625.000	0.00	0.00000	0.00000
1986Q2	2242.20	17064.7	.291204E+09	8.60	96.7451	26.0000	676.000	1.00	0.00000	0.00000
1986Q3	2246.90	17107.5	.292667E+09	7.85	94.8652	27.0000	729.000	0.00	1.00000	0.00000
1986Q4	1827.20	17032.4	.290103E+09	7.50	92.0402	28.0000	784.000	0.00	0.00000	1.00000
1987Q1	1669.30	17161.2	.294507E+09	7.50	90.4756	29.0000	841.000	0.00	0.00000	0.00000
1987Q2	1972.80	16958.5	.287591E+09	8.04	91.7923	30.0000	900.000	1.00	0.00000	0.00000
1987Q3	1878.20	17159.6	.294452E+09	8.39	93.9033	31.0000	961.000	0.00	1.00000	0.00000
1987Q4	1560.60	17379.0	.302030E+09	8.86	86.4359	32.0000	1024.00	0.00	0.00000	1.00000
1988Q1	1914.00	17621.7	.310524E+09	8.58	92.3495	33.0000	1089.00	0.00	0.00000	0.00000
1988Q2	2076.00	17623.4	.310584E+09	8.78	93.5802	34.0000	1156.00	1.00	0.00000	0.00000
1988Q3	1787.10	17704.5	.313449E+09	9.70	96.1096	35.0000	1225.00	0.00	1.00000	0.00000
1988Q4	1762.30	17760.7	.315442E+09	10.1	93.0000	36.0000	1296.00	0.00	0.00000	1.00000
1989Q1	1707.40	17919.2	.321098E+09	10.9	95.8822	37.0000	1369.00	0.00	0.00000	0.00000
1989Q2	2018.60	17803.8	.316975E+09	11.3	90.9308	38.0000	1444.00	1.00	0.00000	0.00000
1989Q3	1898.50	17834.1	.318055E+09	10.6	92.4304	39.0000	1521.00	0.00	1.00000	0.00000
1989Q4	1453.60	17858.4	.318922E+09	10.5	91.7761	40.0000	1600.00	0.00	0.00000	1.00000
1990Q1	1706.20	18034.1	.325229E+09	10.0	91.3256	41.0000	1681.00	0.00	0.00000	0.00000
1990Q2	1878.20	18062.3	.326247E+09	10.0	90.9297	42.0000	1764.00	1.00	0.00000	0.00000
1990Q3	1752.10	18031.8	.325146E+09	10.0	79.2022	43.0000	1849.00	0.00	1.00000	0.00000
1990Q4	1560.40	17855.9	.318833E+09	10.0	65.1239	44.0000	1936.00	0.00	0.00000	1.00000
1991Q1	1445.10	17748.7	.315106E+09	9.19	75.1189	45.0000	2025.00	0.00	0.00000	0.00000
1991Q2	1683.90	17861.1	.319019E+09	8.66	80.7066	46.0000	2116.00	1.00	0.00000	0.00000
1991Q3	1586.60	17815.3	.317385E+09	8.40	82.6293	47.0000	2209.00	0.00	1.00000	0.00000
1991Q4	1421.30	17811.4	.317246E+09	7.59	71.8967	48.0000	2304.00	0.00	0.00000	1.00000
1992Q1	1455.40	17999.8	.323993E+09	6.50	70.8099	49.0000	2401.00	0.00	0.00000	0.00000
1992Q2	1746.10	18085.7	.327093E+09	6.50	78.9363	50.0000	2500.00	1.00	0.00000	0.00000
1992Q3	1571.70	18035.1	.325265E+09	6.00	76.1054	51.0000	2601.00	0.00	1.00000	0.00000
1992Q4	1503.40	18331.9	.336059E+09	6.00	83.1772	52.0000	2704.00	0.00	0.00000	1.00000
1993Q1	1483.50	17962.2	.322641E+09	6.00	87.2889	53.0000	2809.00	0.00	0.00000	0.00000
1993Q2	1917.90	18132.7	.328795E+09	6.00	82.4429	54.0000	2916.00	1.00	0.00000	0.00000
1993Q3	1690.30	18143.1	.329172E+09	6.00	77.3946	55.0000	3025.00	0.00	1.00000	0.00000
1993Q4	1642.30	18307.5	.335165E+09	6.00	84.0641	56.0000	3136.00	0.00	0.00000	1.00000
1994Q1	1762.30	18079.5	.326868E+09	6.02	92.9933	57.0000	3249.00	0.00	0.00000	0.00000
1994Q2	2001.50	18367.4	.337361E+09	6.89	92.2066	58.0000	3364.00	1.00	0.00000	0.00000
1994Q3	1766.60	18435.8	.339879E+09	7.50	90.7250	59.0000	3481.00	0.00	1.00000	0.00000
1994Q4	1724.80	18564.6	.344644E+09	8.13	93.1500	60.0000	3600.00	0.00	0.00000	1.00000

(c5t11)

FIGURE 5–8

Regression Plane for DCS = f(DPI, PR) (c5t11)

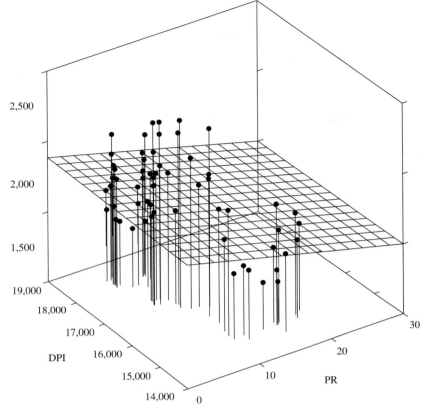

This figure shows the data points and the estimated regression plane for the two-independent variable model estimated in the upper half of Table 5–10. The regression plane has the equation:

$$DCS = 1,793.92 + 0.004637(DPI) - 12.1914(PR)$$

Likewise it is easy to see the effect of disposable personal income (DPI) on DCS. Look at the edge of the plane along which PR equals 0; as DPI increases from 14,000 to 19,000, the regression plane tilts upward. Thus, as DPI increases (while PR is held constant at 0), DCS also increases.

It is obvious why the adjusted R^2 for the regression is quite low: many of the data points are quite a distance above or below the estimated regression plane. Because the adjusted R^2 is quite low and also because the Durbin-Watson statistic suggests that we may have left out an important explanatory variable, the regression presented in the lower half of Table 5–10 was estimated.

This equation (in the lower half of Table 5–10) adds dummy variables for the last three quarters of each year, the Index of Consumer Sentiment, squared DPI, TIME, and squared TIME. Recall that the DCS time series is quite seasonal (which would suggest the use of seasonal dummies) with a mild trend (which might suggest the use of a trend variable). The forecasting equation is improved in a number of ways by the addition of these independent variables. Note that the adjusted R^2 has increased from 0.0075 to 0.7633. The standard error of the regression has fallen, both the Schwarz and Akaike criteria show improvement, the F-statistic has increased, and the Durbin-Watson statistic now indicates that no serial correlation is present. Note that it is impossible to graph the data points and the regression plane for this estimate (which has six independent variables) because it would require a drawing in seven dimensions. In fact, the regression plane would now be referred to as a *hyperplane.*

This last regression can be used to forecast for the next four quarters (1995Q1 to 1995Q4). In making our forecasts, we again used estimates of DPI and PR for the period 1995Q1 through 1995Q4 that were the results of a Holt smoothing model. The Index of Consumer Sentiment forecast uses a Winters model. This approximates a forecast that might have actually been done with only the information available at the end of 1994Q4.

The results of the forecasting efforts are presented in Table 5–12. In the second column the root-mean-squared error (RMSE) for each of our previous models is presented along with the results for this model for the in-sample period of 1981Q1 through 1994Q4. The RMSE for the most recent model of 106.798 is the best yet for the in-sample period. In the third column of the table, the RMSEs for the forecast, or out-of-sample, period are presented. The RMSE for the most recent model of 56.8954 is better than the RMSE for Winters' model in Chapter 3. In most cases, the better test of a model's forecasting accuracy is the RMSE for the forecast period (i.e., the numbers in the third column of Table 5–12).

Figure 5–9 presents the actual and predicted DCS using the nine–independent variable regression presented in the bottom half of Table 5–10. The forecast results for 1995Q1 through 1995Q4 were estimated using the DPI and PR estimates from a

TABLE 5–12 Summary Table of RMSEs for DCS

Chapter	Method	Period	RMSE
1	Naive—with 4-period lag	Historic before '95	207.3
		Holdout 95Q1–95Q4	74.9
2	Not applicable	Historic before '95	na
		Holdout 95Q1–95Q4	na
3	Winters' exponential smoothing	Historic before '95	177.1
		Holdout 95Q1–95Q4	55.8
	ADRES with	Historic before '95	169.5
	seasonal adjustment	Holdout 95Q1–95Q4	64.2
4	Simple regression model using seasonally adjusted DCS as a function of the University of Michigan Index of Consumer Sentiment	Historic before '95	134.570
		Holdout 95Q1–95Q4	102.242
5	Multiple regression	Historic 81Q1–94Q4	106.8
		Holdout 95Q1–95Q4	56.9

FIGURE 5–9

Domestic Car Sales (DCS) and Multivariate Regression Forecast (DCSF) in Thousands of Units (c5t11)

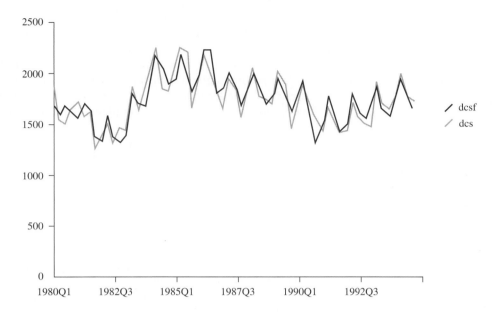

Holt smoothing model. The Index of Consumer Sentiment forecast was done with a Winters model. Comparing this figure with the bivariate regressions presented in Figure 4–8 shows graphically the improvement in model specification achieved with the use of additional variables.

Forecasting Consumer Products

Charles W. Chase, Jr.
Reckitt & Colman

The job of a practicing forecaster is very different from that of the academic one. He has to prepare forecasts for thousands of different items on a monthly, quarterly, or annual basis; versus one or two products, as is usually the case with an academic forecaster. Unlike an academic forecaster, he has deadlines to meet. If forecasts are not prepared at a set time, the entire planning process comes to a halt. His concern for bringing the error down to the last decimal point is not as great as that of an academic forecaster. He constantly weighs the costs and benefits of reducing the error further. In some cases, any further reduction in the error may not have any effect on the decision. Plus, each time a practicing forecaster prepares forecasts, his job is at stake. If the forecasts go awry, so does his future. The stake of an academic forecaster, on the other hand, is whether or not his article on forecasting is accepted for publication. The objective of this article is to explain how forecasts of consumer products are prepared in a business situation where thousands of items are involved, and deadlines are for real.

Procedure

Here is a step-by-step procedure for forecasting the sales demand for consumer products:

Step 1.   Establish an objective, which in this case is to forecast the sales of consumer products. For the purposes of simplicity we will refer to these products as Brand X. Aggregate forecasts are generally more accurate than individual forecasts. "Aggregate forecasts" in this case refers to the forecasts of all the products of Brand X. Individual forecasts, then, will be the forecasts of each item (product code) of this brand.

Step 2.   Decide on the method to be used for forecasting the sales of Brand X. There are several considerations that have to be made in the selection of a method. How much error is the company willing to tolerate? In this case, 10% error at the brand level was the chosen target. The industry average is much higher according to several recent studies. Next, consider the time horizon (how far ahead we want to forecast—one month, one quarter, or one year). This certainly has a bearing on the selection of a method, because some methods are good for short-term forecasting and others for long-term forecasting. In the consumer products industry the time horizon is generally three to twelve months out into the future. This is necessary to accommodate the long lead times of several of the components used in producing various consumer products. Components include such things as plastic bottles, labels, and cartons.

Forecasting is 80% mathematics and 20% judgment. Within mathematical methods, there are two categories: (1) time-series and (2) cause-and-effect. In time-series methods, forecasts are made simply by extrapolating the past data. They assume that the sales are related to time and nothing else. Time-series methods include simple moving averages, exponential smoothing, decomposition, and Box-Jenkins. Cause-and-effect methods use causal relationships. For example, sales are a function of advertising expenditures, price, trade and consumer promotions, and inventory levels. Sales, in this case, are a dependent variable, and advertising expenditures, price, etc., are independent variables. These methods assume that there exists a constant relationship between dependent and independent variables. Such methods are simple and multiple regressions, and econometrics.

The consumer products industry in recent years has encountered a shift in power from manufacturers to the trade. Today, the dominant players in the markets are not manufacturers but big chains such as Wal-Mart, K-mart, Kroger, CVS, and Walgreen. As a result, manufacturers have reduced their expenditures on national advertising and increased them on consumer and trade promotions. This shift has played havoc with forecasting, as it has made time-series methods obsolete. Constant changes in amount and period of promotions have disrupted the seasonality and trend of the historical data. Thus, forecasting with time-series methods is like driving down a highway in your car with the windshield blacked out. It's all well and good if you are driving in a desert with no bends in the road. However, if you are driving on a normal highway, sooner or later you will hit a turn. When you do, you won't see it until it's in your rearview mirror. At that point, it would be too late to react.

Taking this information into consideration, multiple regression was chosen as the forecasting method. There are several reasons for this. First, multiple regression has the ability to incorporate all the variables that impact the demand for a brand. Second, it produces extremely accurate forecasts for periods anywhere from three months to one year out into the future. Finally, multiple regression has the ability to measure the relationships of each independent variable with the demand for a brand. (The latter attribute has important implications for making managerial decisions. It helps management to determine how much to spend on national advertising, what should be the appropriate pricing strategy, and what are the most effective promotional programs.)

Step 3.   Choose proper independent variables and gather proper data. This is an important step in the forecasting process for two reasons: (1) judgmental influence comes into play; (2) it involves the users in the process. We found that the best way to make the users accept our forecasts is to use the variables they believe have strong impact on their products, and to use the source of data that they are most comfortable with. In the consumer products industry, the marketing department, in most cases, is the primary user of sales forecasts. In fact, those same forecasts ultimately become the marketing plan. Since they are the main users, we chose from their variables—the variables they believe had a strong impact on their products. We used Nielsen syndicated data (Scantrack and Audit), as well as the data furnished by the marketing department. The Nielsen syndicated data was used because the marketing people were most comfortable with it. When Step 3 is completed, the best possible match has been made between the situation and the method.

TABLE 1   Variables and Statistics of Consumption Model

$R^2 = .96$	$F\text{-stat} = 24.55$
Adj. $R^2 = .92$	DW $= 2.26$

Variable	t-stat
1. Time	$-.72$
2. Average retail price	-2.70
3. National advertising expenditures	2.52
4. Nielsen shipment data in units	6.48
5. FSI 1	4.38
6. FSI 2	2.31
7. Direct mail coupon	1.93
8. FSI 3	1.25
9. FSI 4	2.15
10. FSI 5	2.81

NOTES: (1) Dummy variables are used to capture the effects of variables that have no quantitative data.

(2) FSI stands for "Free Standing Insert."

TABLE 2   Forecasts versus Actuals: Consumption Model
Brand X

Month	Actuals	Forecasts	Absolute Error
January	2578	2563	1%
February	2788	2783	0%
March	2957	2957	0%
April	2670	2758	3%
May	2447	2466	1%
June	3016	3016	0%

NOTE: Mean absolute percentage error (MAPE) $= .81\%$

In the consumer products industry, trade shipments are forecasted—shipments to the brokers, food and drug chains, and mass merchandisers who sell the products to the consumer. The relationship between the trade and retail consumption plays a significant role in predicting trade shipments. Most users (brand managers) agree that retail consumption has some impact on trade shipments. For Brand X, ten variables were selected to predict retail consumption (see Table 1). Several dummy variables were used to capture the impact of consumer promotions along with average retail price, national advertising expenditures, and Nielsen shipment data of the category for Brand X. Dummy variables are used where the variable is defined in terms of yes (when a certain element exists) and no (when it doesn't exist). It is used in the form of "1" for yes and "0" for no. For example, for FSI (free standing insert) coupon 1, we used "1" in the equation when this coupon was used, and "0" when it was not.

Step 4. Compute the predictive regression equation for retail consumption of Brand X. The equation gives an excellent fit with an R^2 of .96. (See Table 1 for this and other statistics.) The ex post forecasts had a MAPE (mean absolute percentage error) of less than 1% (see Table 2). (Ex post forecasts are those for which actuals are known.)

Step 5. Forecast the retail consumption by plugging the values of independent variables into the predictive equation computed above. To do so, we need the values of the independent variables for the periods we want to forecast. For example, if we want to develop a forecast for Brand X for 2000 we need the values of average retail price, Nielsen shipment data of that category, national advertising expenditures, etc., for those periods. As for the dummy variables we have no problem because we control them. However, for Nielsen shipment data we have to forecast the value, which we do by extrapolating the historical data.

Step 6. Compute the predictive regression equation for trade shipments. The equation included retail consumption as the primary variable along with Nielsen inventory, trade price, and several dummy variables to capture trade promotions (see Table 3). Again, the fit was excellent with an R^2 of .96. The ex post forecasts had a MAPE of 3%, which is significantly lower than the original target of 10% (see Table 4). Those familiar with the rule of thumb for the t-statistic (variables are not significant if their value is less than 2) may feel that several of the variables should have been excluded from the model. I found through experience that if the forecasts are more accurate with the variables whose t-statistics are less than 2, then they should be left in the model. As you know, as a practitioner, our primary objective is to produce good forecasts.

Step 7. Forecast trade shipments by plugging the values of the independent variables (retail consumption, Nielsen inventory, etc.) into the predictive equation computed above. Here again, we need the values of independent variables for the period we want to forecast. The only independent variable over which we have no control is the Nielsen inventory, which we estimate by extrapolating its historical data.

Step 8. Prepare item-by-item forecasts for all the products of Brand X. This is achieved by using the past-six-month rolling average ratio of each item. If item 1 represents 5% of the total, then the forecast of item 1 will be 5% of the trade total of Brand X; if item 2 represents 10% of the total, then 10% of the total will be the forecast of item 2; and so on.

Clearly, the main challenge to a business forecaster is to improve the quality of forecasts and consequently the decisions. This can best be achieved by sharing our forecasting experience with others.

TABLE 3   Variables and Statistics of Trade Shipment Model

$$R^2 = .96 \qquad F\text{-stat} = 36.93$$
$$\text{Adj. } R^2 = .93 \qquad DW = 2.41$$

Variable	t-stat
1. Time	2.40
2. Retail consumption	3.59
3. Trade inventory	1.87
4. Trade price	−1.55
5. Trade promotion 1 early shipment	5.82
6. Trade promotion 1 sell in	16.01
7. Trade promotion 1 post shipment	4.19
8. Trade promotion 2 early shipment	9.57
9. Trade promotion 2 sell in	1.18
10. Trade promotion 3 early shipment	2.62
11. Trade promotion 3 sell in	7.29
12. Trade promotion 3 post shipment	13.55

NOTE: Dummy variables are used to capture the effects of variables that have no quantitative data.

TABLE 4   Forecasts versus Actuals: Trade Shipment Model

Brand X

Month	Actuals	Forecasts	Absolute Error
January	69,158	69,190	0%
February	45,927	47,216	3%
March	40,183	40,183	0%
April	56,427	54,841	3%
May	81,854	72,788	12%
June	50,505	52,726	4%
July	37,064	36,992	0%
August	58,212	57,347	2%
September	96,566	95,112	2%

NOTE: Mean absolute percentage error (MAPE) = 3.0%

Source: *Journal of Business Forecasting* 10, no. 1 (Spring 1991), pp. 2–6. Reprinted by permission.

INTEGRATIVE CASE
The Gap

Part 5: Forecasting the Gap Sales Data with a Multiple-Regression Model

The sales of Gap stores in thousands of dollars for the 44 quarters covering 1985 quarter 1 through 1995 quarter 4 are again shown in the graph below. Recall that the Gap sales data are quite seasonal and are increasing over time.

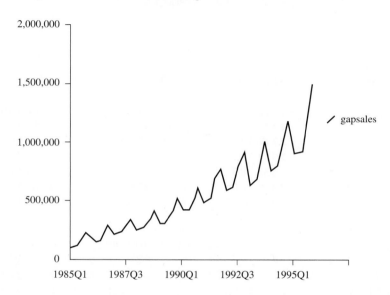

Case Questions

1. Have Gap sales generally followed a linear path over time? Does the graph suggest to you that some accommodation for seasonality should be used in any forecast? Does the graph suggest that some nonlinear term should be used in any forecast model?

2. Use a multiple regression of raw (i.e., non-seasonally-adjusted Gap sales) as the basis to forecast sales for 1996. What would happen to the accuracy of the model if your forecast is extended through 1997? Why?

3. Calculate the root-mean-squared errors both for the historic period and for the 1996Q1 through 1996Q4 forecast horizon.

Solutions to Case Questions

1. Gap sales appear to have followed a highly seasonal pattern over time; in addition, the sales pattern appears to show an increase in the rate of sales over time. In other words, the pattern over time appears to be nonlinear and may require some accommodation in a forecasting model.

2. The raw (or non-seasonally-adjusted) Gap sales were used as a dependent variable in a multiple regression

that includes the following explanatory (or independent) variables:

time = The index of time
time^2 = The index of time squared
    (to account for the nonlinearity)
Q2 = A seasonal dummy variable
    for quarter 2

Q3 = A seasonal dummy variable
    for quarter 3
Q4 = A seasonal dummy variable
    for quarter 4
SP500 = The Standard & Poor's 500 stock index

The regression results follow:

```
REGRESS : dependent variable is GAPSALES

Using    1985Q1-1995Q4
```

Variable	Coefficient	Std Err	T-stat	Signf
^CONST	-127204.	85551.0	-1.48688	.146
TIME	433.177	3812.44	.113622	.910
Q4	277833.	26221.0	8.68897	.000
Q3	103175.	26351.3	3.91539	.001
Q2	-7634.88	26198.1	-.291429	.772
TIME2	325.340	67.6760	4.80732	.000
SP500	1049.31	420.768	2.49381	.017

```
                          Equation Summary
    No. of Observations =       44     R2=    .9710    (adj)=    .9664
    Sum of Sq. Resid.  =   .138863E+12  Std. Error of Reg.=  61262.2
    Log(likelihood)  =   -543.630      Durbin-Watson    =   1.54648
    Schwarz Criterion =  -556.874      F ( 6,    37)    =   206.818
    Akaike Criterion  =  -550.630      Significance     =   .000000
```

(c5gap)

Since the time^2 variable is significant, it appears that Gap sales have indeed been increasing *at an increasing rate* over time. Our impressions are confirmed by the regression equation. Two of the seasonal dummy variables are statistically significant; this confirms our impression of the seasonality of the data. The SP500 variable was included to account for the general level of economic activity in the economy over time; it is also significant.

Overall, the regression appears to be a reasonable fit, as seen in the graph of actual and predicted values below.

The equation for Gap sales here takes seasonality into account in a very different manner than the one in Chapter 4 (which seasonally adjusted the data before running the model). The results, however, are quite similar.

In this model we have also added time-squared as a variable to take into account that sales seem to be increasing at an increasing rate over time. The Standard & Poor's 500 stock index adds some further explanatory power. The results do not seem much different from the simple regression results of Chapter 4, but the difference lies in the explanatory power of this model in the forecast horizon.

(c5gap)

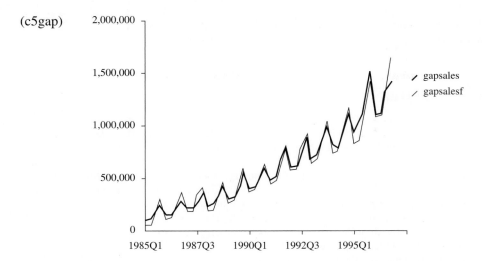

3. The SP500 variable was forecast for the four quarters of 1996 with a simple trend equation. The results are as follows:

	GAPSALES	GAPSALES Forecast
1996Q1	1,113,154	1,109,740
1996Q2	1,120,335	1,140,530
1996Q3	1,383,996	1,290,420
1996Q4	1,667,896	1,454,800

The RMSEs for the historic period and the 1996 forecast horizon are:

1985Q1–1995Q4 Root-mean-squared error = 56,178.1

1986Q1–1996Q4 Root-mean-squared error = 116,620

If we compare these results with the results presented at the end of Chapter 4, we find that the historic period forecast has much the same RMSE, but the forecast horizon RMSE is much lower with the multiple regression. This is due in part to the explanatory power of the nonlinear time-squared variable. For the present multiple-regression model, the RMSE is only 55 percent of the RMSE for the simple regression in the forecast horizon.

TABLE 5–13   Summary Table of RMSEs for Gap Sales

Chapter	Method	Period	RMSE
1	Naive—with 4-period lag	Historic before '96	107,150.0
		Holdout 96Q1–96Q4	227,029
2	Not applicable	Historic before '96	na
		Holdout 96Q1–96Q4	na
3	Winters' exponential smoothing	Historic before '96	37,935.5
		Holdout 96Q1–96Q4	84,460.7
	Holt's exponential smoothing	Historic before '96	31,272.5
	With seasonal readjustment	Holdout 96Q1–96Q4	33,341.3
4	Linear trend of deseasonalized	Historic before '96	56,110.6
	data with forecast	Holdout 96Q1–96Q4	211,550.0
5	Multiple regression	Historic before '96	56,178.1
		Holdout 96Q1–96Q4	116,620.0

USING SORITEC FOR MULTIPLE-REGRESSION FORECASTS

Getting the Data

The first thing we need to do is to get some data to work with in estimating a regression model. To do so, go to **FILE** on the main menu and select **OPEN DATA FILE,** then select a data file (typically a .SAL file) or a database file (a .SDB file) such as the ECONDATA file that came with your text.

For this example we will assume that you have opened the C5T1.SAL file and want to develop a forecast of retail sales (named RS in C5T1.SAL) as a function of the disposable personal income (named DPI in C5T1.SAL) and the mortgage interest rate (named MR in C5T1.SAL). All these variables are in C5T1.SAL on a quarterly basis, with retail sales not seasonally adjusted in millions of dollars. The mortgage rate is in percent per year, and disposable personal income is in constant 1992 dollars.

(c5t1)

Let us use data from the first quarter of 1986 through the fourth quarter of 1995 (40 observations) to forecast retail sales for the four quarters of 1996. The following shows how to set up the time period, including the forecast horizon, so that we can check the accuracy of our forecast and set up the variables with the names we desire.

If you have read C5T1.SAL into memory, clicking on **VIEW,** then on **SYMBOLS** will show what we have in the workspace, as follows:

```
SORITEC symbol table:
User variables

SYM NO NAME          ADDRESS TYPE     LENGTH
 141 RS          3455750 SERIES  44  1986Q1-1996Q4
 155 MR          3455668 SERIES  40  1986Q1-1995Q4
 169 DPI         3455586 SERIES  40  1986Q1-1995Q4
```

Estimating a Multiple-Regression Model

We hypothesize from economic theory that retail sales may be related to disposable personal income and the interest rate, so we want to regress RS on DPI and MR. To do this we first click the **Y** icon on the main menu to define the dependent variable. The **Single Variable Selection** dialog box appears. We highlight **RS,** click on **SELECT,** then click on **OK.** This is illustrated below.

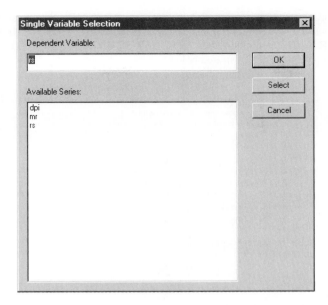

Next we need to select the independent variables. This is done by clicking the $\mathcal{X}$ icon on the main menu. The **Variables Selection** dialog box appears, as shown below. To select both DPI and MR, you highlight **DPI** and **MR** separately, then click on **SELECT,** then click on **OK.**

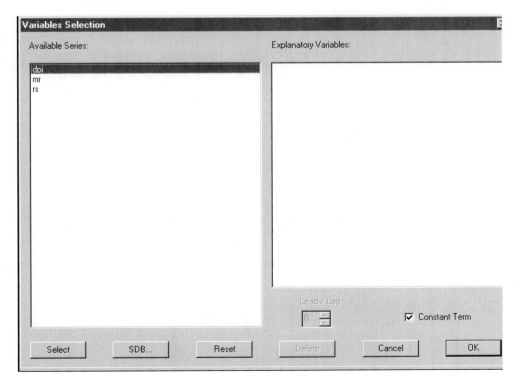

To estimate the regression model for RS = *f*(DPI, MR), first be sure the **use** period is 1986Q1–1995Q4 (on the command line type **USE 1986Q1 1995Q4** to be sure), then click on **LINEAR** on the main menu, then on **LEAST SQUARES,** then on **OLS** (for ordinary least squares regression), as illustrated below.

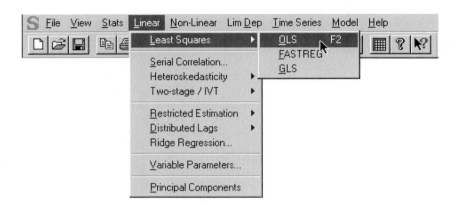

This will produce the following regression results:

```
REGRESS : dependent variable is RS

Using    1986Q1-1995Q4


     Variable          Coefficient       Std Err          T-stat          Signf

^CONST                 -.142327E+07      268992.          -5.29113          .000
DPI                     112.952          12.9653           8.71185          .000
MR                    -14150.5           5654.04          -2.50273          .017


                          Equation Summary
     No. of Observations =       40      R2=    .8381    (adj)=    .8294
     Sum of Sq. Resid. =    .369254E+11  Std. Error of Reg.=   31590.9
     Log(likelihood)    =  -469.623      Durbin-Watson      =    2.60588
     Schwarz Criterion  =  -475.157      F (  2,   37)      =   95.7747
     Akaike Criterion   =  -472.623      Significance       =    .000000
```

Rather than using the menus to define the dependent variable (RS), the independent variables (DPI and MR), and to select OLS regression, this same result can be obtained by typing the following command on the command line: **regress RS DPI MR.** Without any other modifiers SORITEC knows to do OLS regression and that the first variable named is the dependent variable. Some users find typing the regress command the preferable method, but both approaches yield the same result.

Once the variables are defined, you may also simply press the **(F2)** key and the OLS regression will be run, and then the results will be as seen above. Many users find it handy to specify the variables in a multiple regression first, using the Y and X keys, and then when the **(F2)** key is pressed the regression is run.

At this point you should evaluate the estimated regression equation using the criteria discussed in Chapters 4 and 5.

Developing Forecasts Based on Simple Regression Models

There is a "forecast" button, 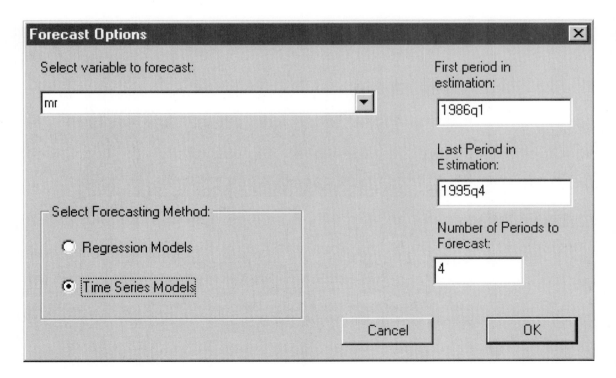, on the SORITEC toolbar that can be used to facilitate developing a multiple-regression forecast. (It can be used for other forecasting methods as well.) We will use this graphic interface to prepare a multiple-regression forecast of retail sales as a function of the mortgage rate and disposable personal income. In this section we assume that the variables RS, DPI, and MR are already in the workspace (see above discussion "Getting the Data") for the 1986Q1 through 1995Q4 period (note that C5T1.SAL also includes actual values of RS for 1996Q1 through 1996Q4, the forecast horizon). We will consider 1986Q1 to 1995Q4 as the historic period on which to base the forecast and 1996Q1 to 1996Q4 as a holdout period to allow us to evaluate the accuracy of our forecast "out of sample."

Forecasting the Independent Variables.   To use the mortgage rate and disposable personal income as a causal variables to forecast retail sales, we must first develop a forecast of both MR and DPI for the forecast horizon (1996Q1–1996Q4). Arbitrarily, we will use Holt's smoothing to forecast both variables (just as we did earlier in the chapter in the section titled "Forecasting with a Multiple-Regression Model."

Now click on the icon and the **Forecast Options** dialog box appears.

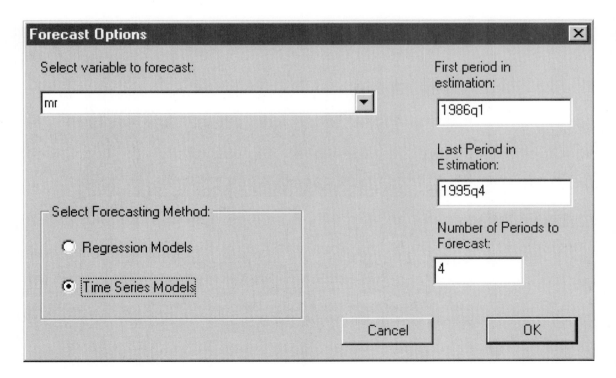

From the pull-down box (**Select Variable to Forecast**) select **MR.** Click on **Time Series Models** as the forecasting method, type in **1986Q1** as the **First Period in Estimation,**

1995Q4 as the **Last Period in Estimation,** and **6** as the **Number of Periods to Forecast.**
Then click on **OK** and the following dialog box appears.

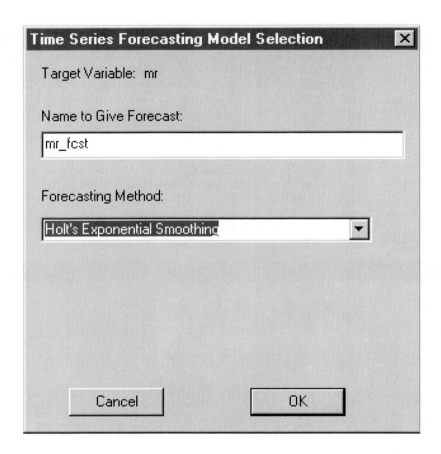

Select Holt's exponential smoothing as the forecasting model. Then click on **OK.**

You will be prompted with the **Smoothing Methods** dialog box to select or confirm the
independent variable for the Holt model. Make certain the **Optimal Solution** box is checked
and that the **Result Series Name** is correct (we used MR_FCST) and click on **OK.** This
Smoothing Methods dialog box will look like this:

```
┌──────────────────────────────────────────────────────────────────┐
│ Smoothing Methods                                            [X] │
├──────────────────────────────────────────────────────────────────┤
│                                                                    │
│  Smoothing Method: holt          ┌─ Parameter Values: ──────┐     │
│                                  │                          │     │
│                                  │  ┌──────────┐            │     │
│                                  │  │ 0.1      │  Alpha     │     │
│                                  │  └──────────┘            │     │
│  ☑ Optimal Solution              │                          │     │
│                                  │  ┌──────────┐            │     │
│  Forecast Horizon:               │  │ 0.1      │  Beta      │     │
│                                  │  └──────────┘            │     │
│  ┌────────────────────────────┐  │                          │     │
│  │ 4                          │  │  ┌──────────┐            │     │
│  └────────────────────────────┘  │  │ 0.1      │  Gamma     │     │
│                                  │  └──────────┘            │     │
│  Series to Forecast:             └──────────────────────────┘     │
│                                                                    │
│  ┌────────────────────────────┐     ┌──────┐                      │
│  │ mr                         │     │ 12   │  Season Length       │
│  └────────────────────────────┘     └──────┘                      │
│                                                                    │
│  Result Series Name:                                               │
│                                                                    │
│  ┌────────────────────────────┐   ┌──────────┐  ┌──────────┐      │
│  │ mr_fcst                    │   │  Cancel  │  │    OK    │      │
│  └────────────────────────────┘   └──────────┘  └──────────┘      │
│                                                                    │
└──────────────────────────────────────────────────────────────────┘
```

At this point the smoothing model will be calculated and the results will be printed. For our MR forecast the optimal value of alpha was 0.999 and the optimal beta was 0.100. This is not a particularly good fit for MR but it will provide us with the same results we obtained earlier in the chapter. The variable MR_FCST now contains forecasts of MR using the Holt model we just estimated. The original values of MR remain under the heading MR:

```
Holt's Two-Parameter Linear Exponential Smoothing

    Alpha= .999    Beta= .100

    Period        Actual        Forecast        Error        Pct Error
    1986Q1        10.5600
    1986Q2        10.2600        10.1233         .1367         1.3320%
    1986Q3        10.2400         9.8368         .4032         3.9375%
    1986Q4         9.6667         9.8567        -.1900         1.9654%
    1987Q1         9.1067         9.2650        -.1583         1.7388%
    1987Q2        10.3233         8.6892        1.6341        15.8290%
    1987Q3        10.5000        10.0667         .4333         4.1267%
    1987Q4        10.8500        10.2877         .5623         5.1823%
```

1988Q1	10.0667	10.6936	-.6269	6.2270%
1988Q2	10.3733	9.8491	.5242	5.0538%
1988Q3	10.5033	10.2067	.2966	2.8241%
1988Q4	10.3933	10.3664	.0269	.2585%
1989Q1	10.8033	10.2594	.5439	5.0348%
1989Q2	10.6733	10.7230	-.0497	.4656%
1989Q3	10.0000	10.5886	-.5886	5.8864%
1989Q4	9.8200	9.8573	-.0373	.3798%
1990Q1	10.1233	9.6730	.4503	4.4479%
1990Q2	10.3367	10.0207	.3160	3.0575%
1990Q3	10.1067	10.2656	-.1589	1.5727%
1990Q4	9.9500	10.0203	-.0703	.7065%
1991Q1	9.5033	9.8565	-.3532	3.7164%
1991Q2	9.5300	9.3750	.1550	1.6267%
1991Q3	9.2767	9.4166	-.1399	1.5081%
1991Q4	8.6900	9.1496	-.4596	5.2889%
1992Q1	8.7100	8.5175	.1925	2.2099%
1992Q2	8.6767	8.5560	.1206	1.3905%
1992Q3	8.0100	8.5348	-.5248	6.5514%
1992Q4	8.2033	7.8165	.3868	4.7153%
1993Q1	7.7233	8.0474	-.3241	4.1964%
1993Q2	7.4500	7.5359	-.0859	1.1529%
1993Q3	7.0767	7.2538	-.1771	2.5026%
1993Q4	7.0533	6.8629	.1904	2.6998%
1994Q1	7.3000	6.8582	.4418	6.0527%
1994Q2	8.4400	7.1485	1.2915	15.3016%
1994Q3	8.5867	8.4162	.1704	1.9849%
1994Q4	9.1000	8.5810	.5190	5.7035%
1995Q1	8.8133	9.1456	-.3323	3.7703%
1995Q2	7.9500	8.8267	-.8767	11.0281%
1995Q3	7.7033	7.8767	-.1734	2.2504%
1995Q4	7.3533	7.6121	-.2587	3.5185%
1996Q1		7.2364		
1996Q2		7.1192		
1996Q3		7.0020		
1996Q4		6.8848		

```
Mean Pct Error (MPE) or bias       =         .7267%
Mean Squared Error (MSE)           =        .239125
Mean Absolute Pct Error (MAPE)     =        4.0306%
```

In like manner the forecast of DPI will yield the following results. Note that our forecast values of DPI are called DPI_FCST and the actual values of DPI retain the name DPI.

```
Holt's Two Parameter Linear Exponential Smoothing

  Alpha= .734    Beta= .036
```

Period	Actual	Forecast	Error	Pct Error
1986Q1	16951.7000			
1986Q2	17064.7000	16970.7000	94.0000	.5508%
1986Q3	17107.3000	17061.1552	46.1448	.2697%
1986Q4	17032.3000	17117.7118	-85.4118	.5015%
1987Q1	17162.0000	17075.4811	86.5189	.5041%
1987Q2	16956.0000	17161.6929	-205.6929	1.2131%
1987Q3	17159.7000	17028.0583	131.6417	.7672%
1987Q4	17378.7000	17145.4278	233.2722	1.3423%
1988Q1	17622.7000	17343.5247	279.1753	1.5842%
1988Q2	17623.3000	17582.6674	40.6326	.2306%
1988Q3	17704.3000	17647.8418	56.4582	.3189%
1988Q4	17760.3000	17726.1179	34.1821	.1925%
1989Q1	17919.7000	17788.9495	130.7505	.7296%
1989Q2	17804.0000	17926.0902	-122.0902	.6857%
1989Q3	17833.7000	17874.4793	-40.7793	.2287%
1989Q4	17858.7000	17881.4580	-22.7580	.1274%
1990Q1	18034.7000	17901.0603	133.6397	.7410%
1990Q2	18062.7000	18038.9500	23.7500	.1315%
1990Q3	18031.3000	18096.8302	-65.5302	.3634%
1990Q4	17855.7000	18087.4694	-231.7694	1.2980%
1991Q1	17748.0000	17950.0117	-202.0117	1.1382%
1991Q2	17861.3000	17829.0622	32.2378	.1805%
1991Q3	17815.3000	17880.8525	-65.5525	.3680%
1991Q4	17811.0000	17859.1566	-48.1566	.2704%
1992Q1	18000.3000	17848.9556	151.3444	.8408%
1992Q2	18085.7000	17989.1375	96.5625	.5339%
1992Q3	18035.3000	18091.6677	-56.3677	.3125%
1992Q4	18330.0000	18080.4929	249.5071	1.3612%
1993Q1	17962.3000	18300.3458	-338.0458	1.8820%
1993Q2	18132.3000	18080.1438	52.1562	.2876%
1993Q3	18143.0000	18147.6431	-4.6431	.0256%
1993Q4	18305.7000	18173.3413	132.3587	.7230%
1994Q1	18081.7000	18303.0605	-221.3605	1.2242%
1994Q2	18366.3000	18167.3867	198.9133	1.0830%
1994Q3	18436.0000	18345.3509	90.6491	.4917%
1994Q4	18564.3000	18446.2628	118.0372	.6358%
1995Q1	18697.7000	18570.3848	127.3152	.6809%
1995Q2	18668.3000	18704.6725	-36.3725	.1948%
1995Q3	18818.7000	18717.8888	100.8112	.5357%
1995Q4	18971.3000	18834.4277	136.8723	.7215%
1996Q1		18981.0375		
1996Q2		19027.2120		
1996Q3		19073.3865		
1996Q4		19119.5610		

```
Mean Pct Error (MPE) or bias      =         .1437%
Mean Squared Error (MSE)          =       19799.3
Mean Absolute Pct Error (MAPE)    =         .6480%
```

Now we want to take the forecasted values of MR and DPI (which are called MR_FCST and DPI_FCST) and append the 1996Q1–1996Q4 values onto the original data sets. That will give us two series that contain the original values from 1986Q1 to 1995Q4 and the forecasted values from 1996Q1 to 1996Q4. The following commands accomplish this task easily:

```
USE 1996Q1 1996Q4
REVISE MR = MR_FCST
REVISE DPI = DPI_FCST
```

The series MR and DPI now contain the original values of these variables for 1986Q1 through 1995Q4 and the Holt model forecast values of these variables for 1996Q1 through 1996Q4 (the forecast horizon). Thus, MR and DPI are set up to be used as independent variables for a regression forecast of RS. The actual MR and DPI values will be used to develop the RS model, but the forecast values of MR and DPI will be used to make the forecast of RS.

Making the Forecast of the Dependent Variable. As you would expect, the process of forecasting the dependent variable (RS in this example) with a multiple-regression model is very much like the above description of using a Holt model to forecast the independent variables.

Click on the forecast icon and the **Forecast Options** dialog box appears. From the pull-down box (**Select Variable to Forecast**) select **RS.** Click on **Regression Models** as the forecasting method, type in **1986Q1** as the **First Period in Estimation, 1995Q4** as the **Last Period in Estimation,** and **4** as the **Number of Periods to Forecast.** Then click on **OK** and the **Regression Forecasting Models** dialog box will appear.

In this dialog box select **OLS** as the **Forecasting Model** and type in **RS_FCST** as the **Target Variable.** Then click on **OK.** RS_FCST is the name we will give to the forecast values of retail sales.

You will be prompted to select or confirm the independent variable for the regression model. Click on **OK** and a new dialog box appears, in which you select the independent variables. Highlight MR, then click on **SELECT.** Now highlight DPI, then click on **SELECT** and **OK** in that order. This will give you the regression model, some SORITEC commands, and the forecast values for the forecast horizon (1996Q1–1996Q4). The regression equation, the statistical results, and the forecasts for 1996Q1 through 1996Q4 are shown below.

$$\text{The equation is: RS} = -1{,}423{,}270 - 14{,}150.5\ (\text{MR}) + 112.952\ (\text{DPI})$$

The forecast values for 1996Q1 through 1996Q4 are:

	RS	RS_FCST
1996Q1	552928.	618273.
1996Q2	617069.	625147.
1996Q3	612813.	632021.
1996Q4	662486.	638895.

Checking the Fit and Accuracy of the Model Using RMSEs. The series RS_FCST that we now have contains the forecast values of retail sales for the entire 1986Q1 through 1996Q4 period (that is, including the historic period and the forecast horizon).

Now you can determine the RMSEs in the historic period and the forecast (holdout) period as follows:

```
USE 1986Q1 1995Q4
ACTFIT RB RS_FCST
USE 1996Q1 1996Q4
ACTFIT RS RS_FCST
```

For this example the RMSEs are:

```
Comparison of      Actual   = RS
Time Series        Predicted = RS_FCST



Using    1986Q1-1995Q4


Correlation Coefficient =   .915483          Regression Coefficient of
             (squared) =   .838109           Actual on Predicted =  1.00000
Root Mean Squared Error =  30383.2
    Mean Absolute Error =  24178.5           Theil Inequality
            Mean Error =   .582077E-09       Coefficient          =  .321422E-01


Fraction of error due to                 Alternate interpretation
               Bias =  .367024E-27                      Bias =  .367024E-27
    Different Variation =  .441230E-01      Difference of Regression
    Different Covariation =  .955877        Coefficient from one =  .881775E-27
                                            Residual Variance =  1.00000


Comparison of      Actual   = RS
Time Series        Predicted = RS_FCST



Using    1996Q1-1996Q4


Correlation Coefficient =   .931646          Regression Coefficient of
             (squared) =   .867965           Actual on Predicted =  4.71960
Root Mean Squared Error =  36265.6
    Mean Absolute Error =  29055.7           Theil Inequality
            Mean Error =  -17260.2           Coefficient          =  .292183E-01


Fraction of error due to                 Alternate interpretation
               Bias =  .226517                         Bias = .226517
    Different Variation =  .742382          Difference of Regression
    Different Covariation =  .311005E-01    Coefficient from one = .621316
                                            Residual Variance = .152166
```

26>

Suggested Readings

Aykac, Ahmed; and Antonio Borges. "Econometric Methods for Managerial Applications." In *The Handbook of Forecasting: A Managers Guide.* Eds. Spyros Makridakis and Steven C. Wheelwright. New York: John Wiley & Sons, 1982, pp. 185–203.

Bassin, William M. "How to Anticipate the Accuracy of a Regression Based Model." *Journal of Business Forecasting* 6, no. 4 (Winter 1987–88), pp. 26–28.

Brennan, Michael J.; and Thomas M. Carroll. *Preface to Quantitative Economics & Econometrics.* Cincinnati: South-Western Publishing, 1987. Especially Part III, "Econometrics."

Doran, Howard; and Jan Kmenta. "Multiple Minima in the Estimation of Models with Autoregressive Disturbances." *Review of Economics and Statistics* 24 (May 1992), pp. 354–57.

Jarrell, Stephen B. *Basic Business Statistics.* Boston: Allyn & Bacon, 1988. Especially Chap. 23, "Regression," and Chap. 24, "Evaluating and Forecasting: Two Variable Regression Models."

Johnson, Aaron C., Jr.; Marvin B. Johnson; and Reuben C. Buse. *Econometrics: Basic and Applied.* New York: Macmillan, 1987.

Judge, George G.; R. Carter Hill; William E. Griffiths; Helmut Lutkepohl; and Tsoung-Chao Lee. *Introduction to the Theory and Practice of Econometrics.* 2nd ed. New York: John Wiley & Sons, 1988.

Lewis-Beck, Michael S. *Applied Regression: An Introduction.* Beverly Hills, Calif.: Sage Publications, 1980.

Neter, John; William Wasserman; and Michael H. Kutner. *Applied Linear Statistical Models.* Homewood, Ill.: Richard D. Irwin, 1990.

Ostrom, Charles W., Jr. *Time Series Analysis: Regression Techniques.* Beverly Hills, Calif.: Sage Publications, 1978.

Wesolowsky, George O. *Multiple Regression and Analysis of Variance: An Introduction for Computer Users in Management and Economics.* New York: John Wiley & Sons, 1976.

Exercises

1. Explain why the adjusted R-squared should be used in evaluating multiple-regression models rather than the unadjusted value.

2. Review the three quick checks that should be used in evaluating a multiple-regression model. Apply these to the model for domestic car sales discussed in this chapter, using your own words to describe each step and the conclusions you reach.

3. Explain what dummy variables are and how they can be used to account for seasonality. Give an example of how you might use dummy variables to measure seasonality for a good or service of your choice. Explain the signs you would expect on each. Assume that you are working with quarterly data.

4. The following regression results relate to a study of fuel efficiency of cars as measured by miles per gallon of gas. (adjusted R-squared = 0.569; n = 120)

Variable*	Coefficient	Standard Error	t-Ratio
Intercept	6.51	1.28	
CID	0.031	0.012	
D	9.46	2.67	
M4	14.64	2.09	
M5	14.86	2.42	
US	4.64	2.48	

*CID = Cubic-inch displacement (engine size)

D = 1 for diesel cars and 0 otherwise

M4 = 1 for cars with a four-speed manual transmission and 0 otherwise

M5 = 1 for cars with a five-speed manual transmission and 0 otherwise

US = 1 for cars made in the United States and 0 otherwise

a. Calculate the *t*-ratios for each explanatory variable.

b. Use the three quick-check regression-evaluation procedures to evaluate this model.

5. Develop a multiple-regression model for auto sales as a function of population and household income from the following data for 10 metropolitan areas (c5p5):

Area	Auto Sales (AS)($000)	Household Income (INC)($000)	Population (POP)(000s)
1	$185,792	$23,409	133.17
2	85,643	19,215	110.86
3	97,101	20,374	68.04
4	100,249	16,107	99.59
5	527,817	23,432	289.52
6	403,916	19,426	339.98
7	78,283	18,742	89.53
8	188,756	18,553	155.78
9	329,531	21,953	248.95
10	91,944	16,358	102.13

a. Estimate values for b_0, b_1, and b_2 for the following model:

$$AS = b_0 + b_1(INC) + b_2(POP)$$

b. Are the signs you find for the coefficients consistent with your expectations? Explain.

c. Are the coefficients for the two explanatory variables significantly different from zero? Explain.

d. What percentage of the variation in AS is explained by this model?

e. What point estimate of AS would you make for a city where INC = $23,175 and POP = 128.07? What would the approximate 95 percent confidence interval be?

6. In Exercises 7 and 8 of Chapter 4 you worked with data on sales for a line of skiwear that is produced by HeathCo Industries. Barbara Lynch, product manager for the skiwear, has the responsibility of providing forecasts to top management of sales by quarter one year ahead. One of Ms. Lynch's colleagues, Dick Staples, suggested that unemployment and income in the regions in which the clothes are marketed might be causally connected to sales. If you worked the exercises in Chapter 4, you have developed three bivariate regression models of sales as a function of time (TIME), unemployment (NRUR), and income (INC). Data for these variables and for sales are as follows (c5p6):

Period	TIME	SALES	INC	NRUR
1988Q1	1	72,962	218	8.4
1988Q2	2	81,921	237	8.2
1988Q3	3	97,729	263	8.4
1988Q4	4	142,161	293	8.4
1989Q1	5	145,592	318	8.1
1989Q2	6	117,129	359	7.7
1989Q3	7	114,159	404	7.5
1989Q4	8	151,402	436	7.2
1990Q1	9	153,907	475	6.9
1990Q2	10	100,144	534	6.5
1990Q3	11	123,242	574	6.5
1990Q4	12	128,497	622	6.4
1991Q1	13	176,076	667	6.3
1991Q2	14	180,440	702	6.2
1991Q3	15	162,665	753	6.3
1991Q4	16	220,818	796	6.5
1992Q1	17	202,415	858	6.8
1992Q2	18	211,780	870	7.9
1992Q3	19	163,710	934	8.3
1992Q4	20	200,135	1,010	8.0
1993Q1	21	174,200	1,066	8.0
1993Q2	22	182,556	1,096	8.0
1993Q3	23	198,990	1,162	8.0
1993Q4	24	243,700	1,187	8.9
1994Q1	25	253,142	1,207	9.6
1994Q2	26	218,755	1,242	10.2
1994Q3	27	225,422	1,279	10.7
1994Q4	28	253,653	1,318	11.5
1995Q1	29	257,156	1,346	11.2
1995Q2	30	202,568	1,395	11.0
1995Q3	31	224,482	1,443	10.1
1995Q4	32	229,879	1,528	9.2
1996Q1	33	289,321	1,613	8.5
1996Q2	34	266,095	1,646	8.0
1996Q3	35	262,938	1,694	8.0
1996Q4	36	322,052	1,730	7.9
1997Q1	37	313,769	1,755	7.9
1997Q2	38	315,011	1,842	7.9
1997Q3	39	264,939	1,832	7.8
1997Q4	40	301,479	1,882	7.6

a. Now you can expand your analysis to see whether a multiple-regression model would work well. Estimate the following model:

$$SALES = b_0 + b_1(INC) + b_2(NRUR)$$

$$SALES = \_\_\_ + / - \_\_\_(INC) + / - \_\_\_(NRUR)$$

(Circle + or − as appropriate for each variable)

Do the signs on the coefficients make sense? Explain why.

b. Test to see whether the coefficients you have estimated are statistically different from zero, using a 95 percent confidence level and a one-tailed test.

c. What percentage of the variation in sales is explained by this model?

d. Use this model to make a sales forecast (SF1) for 1998Q1 through 1998Q4, given the previously forecast values for unemployment (NRURF) and income (INCF) as follows:

Period	NRURF	INCF	SF1
1998Q1	7.6	1,928	—
1998Q2	7.7	1,972	—
1998Q3	7.5	2,017	—
1998Q4	7.4	2,062	—

e. Actual sales for 1998 were: Q1 = 334,271; Q2 = 328,982; Q3 = 317,921; Q4 = 350,118. On the basis of this information, how well would you say the model worked? What is the root-mean-squared error (RMSE)?

f. Plot the actual data for 1998Q1 through 1998Q4 along with the values predicted for each quarter based on this model, for 1998Q1 through 1998Q4.

7. *a.* If you have not looked at a time-series graph of the sales data for HeathCo's line of skiwear (see data in Exercise 6), do so now. On this plot write a 1 next to the data point for each first quarter, a 2 next to each second quarter, and so forth for all four quarters. Does there appear to be a seasonal pattern in the sales data? Explain why you think the results are as you have found. (c5p6)

b. It does seem logical that skiwear would sell better from October through March than from April through September. To test this hypothesis, begin by adding two dummy variables to the data: dummy variable Q2 = 1 for each second quarter (April, May, June) and Q2 = 0 otherwise; dummy variable Q3 = 1 for each third quarter (July, August, September) and Q3 = 0 otherwise. Once the dummy variables have been entered into your data set, estimate the following trend model:

$$SALES = b_0 + b_1(TIME) + b_2Q2 + b_3Q3$$

$$SALES = \underline{\quad} + / - \underline{\quad} TIME$$

$$+/ - \underline{\quad} Q2 + / - \underline{\quad} Q3$$

(Circle + or − as appropriate for each variable)

Evaluate these results by answering the following:
· Do the signs make sense?
· Are the coefficients statistically different from zero at a 95 percent confidence level (one-tailed test)?
· What percentage of the variation in SALES is explained by this model?

c. Use this model to make a forecast of SALES (SF2) for the four quarters of 1998 and calculate the RMSE for the forecast period.

Period	SALES	SF2
1998Q1	334,271	—
1998Q2	328,982	—
1998Q3	317,921	—
1998Q4	350,118	—

d. Prepare a time-series plot of SALES (for 1988Q1 through 1997Q4) and SF2 (for 1988Q1 through 1988Q4) to illustrate how SALES and SF2 compare.

8. Consider now that you have been asked to prepare a forecast of wholesale furniture sales for the entire United States. You have been given the monthly time-series data in the accompanying table:

Data for Problem 8

	WFS	UR	PHS
1990M1	1,226.00	8.60000	843.000
1990M2	1,287.00	8.90000	866.000
1990M3	1,473.00	9.00000	931.000
1990M4	1,383.00	9.30000	917.000
1990M5	1,208.00	9.40000	1,025.00
1990M6	1,344.00	9.60000	902.000
1990M7	1,161.00	9.80000	1,166.00
1990M8	1,221.00	9.80000	1,046.00
1990M9	1,367.00	10.1000	1,144.00
1990M10	1,380.00	10.4000	1,173.00
1990M11	1,310.00	10.8000	1,372.00
1990M12	1,302.00	10.8000	1,303.00
1991M1	1,344.00	10.4000	1,586.00
1991M2	1,362.00	10.4000	1,699.00
1991M3	1,694.00	10.3000	1,606.00
			continued

(c5p8)

Data for Problem 8

	WFS	UR	PHS
1991M4	1,611.00	10.2000	1,472.00
1991M5	1,648.00	10.1000	1,776.00
1991M6	1,722.00	10.1000	1,733.00
1991M7	1,488.00	9.40000	1,785.00
1991M8	1,776.00	9.50000	1,910.00
1991M9	1,839.00	9.20000	1,710.00
1991M10	2,017.00	8.80000	1,715.00
1991M11	1,920.00	8.50000	1,785.00
1991M12	1,778.00	8.30000	1,688.00
1992M1	1,683.00	8.00000	1,897.00
1992M2	1,829.00	7.80000	2,260.00
1992M3	2,012.00	7.80000	1,663.00
1992M4	2,033.00	7.70000	1,851.00
1992M5	2,305.00	7.40000	1,774.00
1992M6	2,007.00	7.20000	1,843.00
1992M7	1,941.00	7.50000	1,732.00
1992M8	2,027.00	7.50000	1,586.00
1992M9	1,922.00	7.30000	1,698.00
1992M10	2,173.00	7.40000	1,590.00
1992M11	2,097.00	7.20000	1,689.00
1992M12	1,687.00	7.30000	1,612.00
1993M1	1,679.00	7.40000	1,711.00
1993M2	1,696.00	7.20000	1,632.00
1993M3	1,826.00	7.20000	1,800.00
1993M4	1,985.00	7.30000	1,821.00
1993M5	2,051.00	7.20000	1,680.00
1993M6	2,027.00	7.30000	1,676.00
1993M7	2,107.00	7.40000	1,684.00
1993M8	2,138.00	7.10000	1,743.00
1993M9	2,089.00	7.10000	1,676.00
1993M10	2,399.00	7.20000	1,834.00
1993M11	2,143.00	7.00000	1,698.00
1993M12	2,070.00	7.00000	1,942.00
1994M1	1,866.00	6.70000	1,938.00
1994M2	1,843.00	7.20000	1,869.00
1994M3	2,001.00	7.10000	1,873.00
1994M4	2,165.00	7.20000	1,947.00
1994M5	2,211.00	7.20000	1,847.00
1994M6	2,321.00	7.20000	1,845.00
1994M7	2,210.00	7.00000	1,789.00
1994M8	2,253.00	6.90000	1,804.00
1994M9	2,561.00	7.00000	1,685.00
1994M10	2,619.00	7.00000	1,683.00
1994M11	2,118.00	6.90000	1,630.00
1994M12	2,169.00	6.70000	1,837.00
1995M1	2,063.00	6.60000	1,804.00
1995M2	2,032.00	6.60000	1,809.00
1995M3	2,349.00	6.50000	1,723.00
1995M4	2,218.00	6.40000	1,635.00
1995M5	2,159.00	6.30000	1,599.00

continued

Data for Problem 8

	WFS	UR	PHS
1995M6	2,240.00	6.20000	1,583.00
1995M7	2,335.00	6.10000	1,594.00
1995M8	2,388.00	6.00000	1,583.00
1995M9	2,865.00	5.90000	1,679.00
1995M10	2,829.00	6.00000	1,538.00
1995M11	2,432.00	5.90000	1,661.00
1995M12	2,395.00	5.80000	1,399.00
1996M1	1,995.00	5.70000	1,382.00
1996M2	2,232.00	5.70000	1,519.00
1996M3	2,355.00	5.70000	1,529.00
1996M4	2,188.00	5.50000	1,584.00
1996M5	2,177.00	5.60000	1,393.00
1996M6	2,333.00	5.40000	1,465.00
1996M7	2,124.00	5.50000	1,477.00
1996M8	2,463.00	5.60000	1,461.00
1996M9	2,435.00	5.40000	1,467.00
1996M10	2,688.00	5.30000	1,533.00
1996M11	2,604.00	5.30000	1,558.00
1996M12	2,393.00	5.30000	1,524.00
1997M1	2,171.00	5.40000	1,678.00
1997M2	2,136.00	5.20000	1,465.00
1997M3	2,428.00	5.00000	1,409.00
1997M4	2,264.00	5.30000	1,343.00
1997M5	2,402.00	5.20000	1,308.00
1997M6	2,320.00	5.30000	1,406.00
1997M7	2,258.00	5.30000	1,420.00
1997M8	2,675.00	5.30000	1,329.00
1997M9	2,676.00	5.30000	1,264.00
1997M10	2,629.00	5.30000	1,428.00
1997M11	2,610.00	5.30000	1,361.00

(c5p8)

WFS is wholesale furniture sales in millions of dollars. It is not seasonally adjusted. PHS measures new private housing starts in thousands. UR is the unemployment rate as a percent. You believe that furniture sales are quite probably related to the general state of the economy and decide to test whether the unemployment rate affects furniture sales. You expect that as the unemployment rate rises (and the economy thus shows some sign of difficulty), furniture sales will decline.

a. Summarize the results of your bivariate regression by completing the following table:

Independent Variable	Intercept	Slope	t-Ratio	R^2
UR				

R-squared =
Durbin-Watson =

b. After discussing the results at a staff meeting, someone suggests that you fit a multiple-regression model of the following form:

$$\text{WFS} = b_0 + b_1(\text{UR}) + b_2(\text{M1}) + b_3(\text{M2}) + b_4(\text{M4}) + b_5(\text{M9}) + b_6(\text{M10})$$

where

M1 = A dummy variable for January
M2 = A dummy variable for February
M4 = A dummy variable for April
M9 = A dummy variable for September
M10 = A dummy variable for October

Summarize the results in the following table:

Independent Variable	Intercept	Slope	t-Ratio
UR			
M1			
M2			
M4			
M9			
M10			

Adjusted R-squared =
Durbin-Watson =

· Do the signs of the coefficients make sense?
· Are the coefficients statistically significant at a 95 percent confidence level (one-tailed test)?
· What percentage of the variation in WFS is explained by the model?

c. After a staff meeting where these results were presented, another analyst suggested that serial correlation can cause problems in such regression models. Interpret the Durbin-Watson statistic in part (*b*) and suggest what problems could result if serial correlation is a problem.

Add PHS lagged three months and time-squared (T^2) to the model and again examine the results for serial correlation. Summarize the results:

Independent Variable	Intercept	Slope	t-Ratio	R^2
UR				
M1				
M2				
M4				
M9				
M10				
T^2				
PHS(-3)				

Adjusted R-squared =
Durbin-Watson =

Have the additional two variables affected the existence of serial correlation?

d. A different way to handle serial correlation is to use the Cochrane-Orcutt procedure described in the chapter. Use the same independent variable you used in part (*c*) and apply the Cochrane-Orcutt procedure to the model. Summarize the results:

Independent Variable	Intercept	Slope	t-Ratio
UR			
M1			
M2			
M4			
M9			
M10			
T^2			
RHO			

Adjusted R-squared =
Durbin-Watson =

Has the Cochrane-Orcutt procedure affected the existence of serial correlation?

9. AmeriPlas, Inc., produces 20-ounce plastic drinking cups that are embossed with the names of prominent beers and soft drinks. In Chapter 4, Exercise 12, you may have developed a trend model for the company's sales from the following data:

Period	T	SALES	Period	T	SALES
1994M1	1	857	1996M1	25	1,604
1994M2	2	921	1996M2	26	1,643
1994M3	3	1,071	1996M3	27	1,795
1994M4	4	1,133	1996M4	28	1,868
1994M5	5	1,209	1996M5	29	1,920
1994M6	6	1,234	1996M6	30	1,953
1994M7	7	1,262	1996M7	31	1,980
1994M8	8	1,258	1996M8	32	1,989
1994M9	9	1,175	1996M9	33	1,897
1994M10	10	1,174	1996M10	34	1,910
1994M11	11	1,123	1996M11	35	1,854
1994M12	12	1,159	1996M12	36	1,957
1995M1	13	1,250	1997M1	37	1,955
1995M2	14	1,289	1997M2	38	2,008
1995M3	15	1,448	1997M3	39	2,171
1995M4	16	1,497	1997M4	40	2,202
1995M5	17	1,560	1997M5	41	2,288
1995M6	18	1,586	1997M6	42	2,314
1995M7	19	1,597	1997M7	43	2,343
1995M8	20	1,615	1997M8	44	2,339
1995M9	21	1,535	1997M9	45	2,239
1995M10	22	1,543	1997M10	46	2,267
1995M11	23	1,493	1997M11	47	2,206
1995M12	24	1,510	1997M12	48	2,226

(c5p9)

monthly sales forecast that incorporates monthly fluctuations. She has asked you to develop a trend model that includes dummy variables, with January as the base period (i.e., 11 dummy variables for February through December). Use M2 for the February dummy variable, which will equal 1 for each February and zero otherwise; M3 for the March dummy variable, which will equal 1 for each March and zero otherwise; and so forth to M12 for the December dummy variable, which will equal 1 for each December and zero otherwise. Summarize your results:

Variable	Coefficient	t-Ratio
Intercept		
T		
M2		
M3		
M4		
M5		
M6		
M7		
M8		
M9		
M10		
M11		
M12		

$$\text{Adjusted } R\text{-squared} =$$
$$\text{Durbin-Watson} =$$

a. Prepare a time-series plot of the sales data. Does there appear to be a regular pattern of movement in the data that may be seasonal? Ronnie Newton, the product manager for this product line, believes that her brief review of sales data for the four-year period indicates that sales are slower in the colder months of November through February than in other months. Do you agree?

b. Since production is closely related to orders for current shipment, Ronnie would like to have a

Do these results support Ronnie Newton's observations? Explain.

c. While sales of this new product have experienced considerable growth in the first four years, Ronnie believes that there has been some decrease in the rate of growth. To test this and to include such a possibility in the forecasting effort, she has asked that you add the square of the time index (T) to your model (call this new term $T2$). Summarize the new results:

Variable	Coefficient	t-Ratio
Intercept		
T		
T2		
M2		
M3		
M4		
M5		
M6		
M7		
M8		
M9		
M10		
M11		
M12		

Adjusted R-squared =
Durbin-Watson =

Is there any evidence of a slowing of sales growth? Compare the results of this model with those found in part (*b*).

d. Use the model in part (*c*) to forecast sales for 1993 and calculate the RMSE for the forecast period. Actual sales are as follows:

Month	Actual Sales	Forecast Sales	Squared Error
Jan	2,318		
Feb	2,367		
Mar	2,523		
Apr	2,577		
May	2,646		
Jun	2,674		
Jul	2,697		
Aug	2,702		
Sep	2,613		
Oct	2,626		
Nov	2,570		
Dec	2,590		

Sum of squared errors = _____
RMSE = _____

How does this model compare with the model developed in Exercise 12 of Chapter 4?

10. Norm Marks has recently been assigned the responsibility of forecasting the demand for P2CL, a coating produced by ChemCo that is used to line beer cans. He has decided to begin by trying to forecast beer production and has hired you as an outside consultant for this purpose.

a. Go to the *Survey of Current Business* and/or *Business Statistics* and gather data on monthly beer production in millions of barrels for a recent four-year period. Prepare a time-series plot of the data.

b. Develop a multiple-regression trend model with monthly dummy variables for February (M2) through December (M12) for beer production (i.e., use January as the base period). Summarize your findings:

Variable	Coefficient	t-Ratio
Intercept		
T		
M2		
M3		
M4		
M5		
M6		
M7		
M8		
M9		
M10		
M11		
M12		

Adjusted R-squared =
Durbin-Watson =

Write a paragraph in which you communicate your findings to Norm Marks.

c. Prepare a forecast for the year following the four years for which you collected data.

6　Time-Series Decomposition

Many business and economic time series contain underlying components that, when examined individually, can help the forecaster better understand data movements and therefore make better forecasts. As discussed in Chapter 2, these components include the long-term trend, seasonal fluctuations, cyclical movements, and irregular or random fluctuations. Time-series decomposition models can be used to identify such underlying components by breaking the series into its component parts and then reassembling the parts to construct a forecast.

The information provided by time-series decomposition is consistent with the way managers tend to look at data and often helps them to get a better handle on data movements by providing concrete measurements for factors that are otherwise not quantified.

These models are among the oldest of the forecasting techniques available and yet remain very popular today. Their popularity is due primarily to three factors. First, in many situations, time-series decomposition models provide excellent forecasts. Second, these models are relatively easy to understand and to explain to forecast users. This enhances the likelihood that the forecasts will be correctly interpreted and properly used. Third, the information provided by time-series decomposition is consistent with the way managers tend to look at data and often helps them to get a better handle on data movements by providing concrete measurements for factors that are otherwise not quantified.

There are a number of different methods for decomposing a time series. The one we will use is usually referred to as *classical time-series decomposition* and involves the ratio-to-moving-average technique. The classical time-series decomposition model uses the concepts of moving averages presented in Chapter 3 and trend projections discussed in Chapter 4. It also accounts for seasonality in a multiplicative way that is similar to what you have seen in Winters' exponential smoothing and to the way we used seasonal indices from the ADJUST command in Chapters 3 and 4.[1]

---

[1] Remember that you have also accounted for seasonality using dummy variables in regression models. That method uses additive factors rather than multiplicative ones to account for seasonal patterns.

(c6t1)   T<small>ABLE</small> **6–1**   **Private Housing Starts (PHS), 1961–1995 (000s)**

	PHS		*PHS*		*PHS*
1961Q1	183.1	1973Q1	255.8	1985Q1	215.3
1961Q2	284.6	1973Q2	366.9	1985Q2	317.9
1961Q3	284.2	1973Q3	306.0	1985Q3	295.0
1961Q4	222.4	1973Q4	203.3	1985Q4	244.1
1962Q1	187.5	1974Q1	177.8	1986Q1	234.1
1962Q2	305.1	1974Q2	297.8	1986Q2	369.4
1962Q3	272.3	1974Q3	243.9	1986Q3	325.4
1962Q4	226.4	1974Q4	168.4	1986Q4	250.6
1963Q1	178.2	1975Q1	142.3	1987Q1	241.4
1963Q2	324.3	1975Q2	260.9	1987Q2	346.5
1963Q3	288.9	1975Q3	268.0	1987Q3	321.3
1963Q4	221.0	1975Q4	221.0	1987Q4	237.1
1964Q1	202.6	1976Q1	219.0	1988Q1	219.7
1964Q2	294.0	1976Q2	339.6	1988Q2	323.7
1964Q3	261.7	1976Q3	333.6	1988Q3	293.4
1964Q4	212.1	1976Q4	270.1	1988Q4	244.6
1965Q1	181.5	1977Q1	268.7	1989Q1	212.7
1965Q2	296.7	1977Q2	440.1	1989Q2	302.1
1965Q3	266.2	1977Q3	410.3	1989Q3	272.1
1965Q4	219.4	1977Q4	331.8	1989Q4	216.5
1966Q1	180.2	1978Q1	257.5	1990Q1	217.0
1966Q2	258.8	1978Q2	449.1	1990Q2	271.3
1966Q3	197.9	1978Q3	403.9	1990Q3	233.0
1966Q4	141.7	1978Q4	322.9	1990Q4	173.6
1967Q1	147.1	1979Q1	226.6	1991Q1	146.7
1967Q2	254.7	1979Q2	386.9	1991Q2	254.1
1967Q3	244.2	1979Q3	342.9	1991Q3	239.8
1967Q4	197.8	1979Q4	237.7	1991Q4	199.8
1968Q1	179.9	1980Q1	150.9	1992Q1	218.5
1968Q2	266.2	1980Q2	203.3	1992Q2	296.4
1968Q3	249.0	1980Q3	272.6	1992Q3	276.4
1968Q4	204.2	1980Q4	225.3	1992Q4	238.8
1969Q1	171.1	1981Q1	166.5	1993Q1	213.2
1969Q2	259.0	1981Q2	229.9	1993Q2	323.7
1969Q3	214.5	1981Q3	184.8	1993Q3	309.3
1969Q4	165.9	1981Q4	124.1	1993Q4	279.4
1970Q1	136.7	1982Q1	113.6	1994Q1	252.6
1970Q2	231.6	1982Q2	178.2	1994Q2	354.2
1970Q3	228.8	1982Q3	186.7	1994Q3	325.7
1970Q4	215.8	1982Q4	184.1	1994Q4	265.9
1971Q1	204.8	1983Q1	202.9	1995Q1	214.2
1971Q2	348.5	1983Q2	322.3	1995Q2	296.7
1971Q3	321.5	1983Q3	307.5	1995Q3	308.2
1971Q4	276.2	1983Q4	234.8	1995Q4	257.2
1972Q1	263.9	1984Q1	236.5		
1972Q2	386.9	1984Q2	332.6		
1972Q3	370.9	1984Q3	280.3		
1972Q4	287.6	1984Q4	234.7		

FIGURE 6–1

Private Housing Starts in Thousands of Units by Quarter: 1961Q1– 1995Q4
(c6f1)

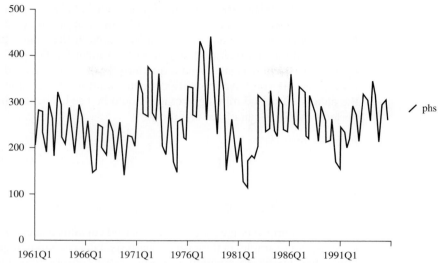

This plot of private housing starts shows the volatility in the data. There are repeated sharp upward and downward movements that appear regular and may be of a seasonal nature. There also appears to be some wavelike cyclical pattern and perhaps a slight positive trend.

The Basic Time-Series Decomposition Model

Look at the data on private housing starts (PHS) that are shown in Table 6–1 and Figure 6–1. While the series appears quite volatile, there is also some pattern to the movement in the data. The sharp increases and decreases in housing starts appear to follow one another in a reasonably regular manner, which may reflect a seasonal component. There also appears to be some long-term wavelike movement to the data as well as a slight positive trend. Patterns such as these are relatively common and can best be understood if they can each be isolated and examined individually. The classical time-series decomposition forecasting technique is a well-established procedure for accomplishing this end.

The model can be represented by a simple algebraic statement, as follows:

$$Y = T \times S \times C \times I$$

where Y is the variable that is to be forecast, T is the long-term (or secular) trend in the data, S is a seasonal adjustment factor, C is the cyclical adjustment factor, and I represents irregular or random variations in the series. Our objective will be to find a way to decompose this series into the individual components.

Deseasonalizing the Data and Finding Seasonal Indexes

The first step in working with this model is to remove the short-term fluctuations from the data so that the longer-term trend and cycle components can be more clearly identified. These short-term fluctuations include both seasonal patterns and irregular variations. They can be removed by calculating an appropriate moving average (MA) for the series. The moving average should contain the same number of periods as there are in the seasonality that you want to identify. Thus, if you have quarterly data and suspect seasonality on a quarterly basis, a four-period moving average is appropriate. If you have monthly data and want to identify the monthly pattern in the data, a 12-period moving average should be used. The moving average for time period t (MA_t) is calculated as follows:

For quarterly data:

$$MA_t = (Y_{t-2} + Y_{t-1} + Y_t + Y_{t+1})/4$$

For monthly data:

$$MA_t = (Y_{t-6} + Y_{t-5} + \cdots + Y_t + Y_{t+1} + \cdots + Y_{t+5})/12$$

The moving average for each time period contains one element from each of the seasons. For example, in the case of quarterly data, each moving average would contain a first-quarter observation, a second-quarter observation, a third-quarter observation, and a fourth-quarter observation (not necessarily in that order). The average of these four quarters should therefore not have any seasonality. Thus, the moving average represents a "typical" level of Y for the year that is centered on that moving average. When an even number of periods are used in calculating a moving average, however, it is really not centered in the year. The following simple example will make that clear and also help you verify your understanding of how the moving averages are calculated.

Let Y be the sales of a line of swimwear for which we have quarterly data (we will look at only six quarters of the data stream). MA_3 is the average of quarters 1 through 4. To be centered in the first year it should be halfway between the second and third quarters, but the convention is to place it at the third quarter ($t = 3$). Note that each of the three moving averages shown contains a first, second, third, and fourth quarter observation. Thus, seasonality in the data is removed. Irregular fluctuations are also largely removed, since such variations are random events that are likely to offset one another over time.

As was noted, when an even number of periods are used, the moving averages are not really centered in the middle of the year. To center the moving averages, a two-period moving average of the moving averages is calculated.[2] This is called a *centered moving average*. The centered moving average for time period t (CMA_t) is found as follows:

$$CMA_t = (MA_t + MA_{t+1})/2$$

For the swimwear data used in our example we have:

$$CMA_3 = (15.0 + 15.5)/2 = 15.25$$
$$CMA_4 = (15.5 + 16.0)/2 = 15.75$$

Thus, the moving average represents a "typical" level of Y for the year that is centered on that moving average.

---

[2]If the number of periods used is odd, the moving averages will automatically be centered, and no further adjustment is usually made.

	Time Index	Y	Moving Average	Centered Moving Average
Year 1:				
First quarter	1	10	MISSING	MISSING
Second quarter	2	18	MISSING	MISSING
Third quarter	3	20	15.0(MA$_3$)	15.25(CMA$_3$)
Fourth quarter	4	12	15.5(MA$_4$)	15.75(CMA$_4$)
Year 2:				
First quarter	5	12	16.0(MA$_5$)	MISSING
Second quarter	6	20	MISSING	MISSING

$$\text{MA}_3 = (10 + 18 + 20 + 12)/4 = 15.0$$

$$\text{MA}_4 = (18 + 20 + 12 + 12)/4 = 15.5$$

$$\text{MA}_5 = (20 + 12 + 12 + 20)/4 = 16.0$$

This second moving average further helps to smooth out irregular or random fluctuations in the data.

Note the "MISSINGS" that appear under the moving average and centered moving average columns in the data table. With just six data points, we could not calculate four-period moving averages for the first, second, or sixth time period. We then lose one more time period in calculating the centered moving average. Thus, the smoothing process has a cost in terms of the loss of some data points. If an *n*-period moving average is used, *n*/2 points will be lost at each end of the data series by the time the centered moving averages have been calculated. This cost is not without benefit, however, since the process will eventually provide clarification of the patterns in the data.

By comparing the actual value of the series in any time period (Y_t) with the deseasonalized value (CMA$_t$), you can get a measure of the degree of seasonality.

The centered moving averages represent the deseasonalized data (i.e., seasonal variations have been removed through an averaging process). By comparing the actual value of the series in any time period (Y_t) with the deseasonalized value (CMA$_t$), you can get a measure of the degree of seasonality. In classical time-series decomposition this is done by finding the ratio of the actual value to the deseasonalized value. The result is called a *seasonal factor* (SF$_t$). That is:

$$\text{SF}_t = Y_t/\text{CMA}_t$$

A seasonal factor greater than 1 indicates a period in which *Y* is greater than the yearly average, while the reverse is true if SF is less than 1. For our brief swimwear sales example, we can calculate seasonal factors for the third and fourth time periods as follows:

$$\text{SF}_3 = Y_3/\text{CMA}_3 = 20/15.25 = 1.31$$
$$\text{SF}_4 = Y_4/\text{CMA}_4 = 12/15.75 = 0.76$$

We see that the third period (third quarter of year 1) is a high-sales quarter while the fourth period is a low-sales quarter. This makes sense, since swimwear would be expected to sell well in July, August, and September, but not in October, November, and December.

When we look at all of the seasonal factors for an extended time period, we generally see reasonable consistency in the values for each season. We would not expect all first-quarter seasonal factors to be exactly the same, but they are likely to be similar. To establish a seasonal index (SI), we average the seasonal factors for each season. This will now be illustrated for the private housing starts data shown initially in Table 6–1 and Figure 6–1.

The data for private housing starts are reproduced in part in Table 6–2. Only the first and last two years of the entire 35-year period are shown, but that is sufficient to illustrate all of the necessary calculations. The moving average for private housing starts is denoted as PHSMA (private housing starts moving average) and is shown in the third column of Table 6–2. The elements included in two values of PHSMA are shown with brackets in the table and are calculated as follows:[3]

For 1961Q3: PHSMA = (183.1 + 284.6 + 284.2 + 222.4)/4 = 243.575

For 1995Q3: PHSMA = (214.2 + 296.7 + 308.2 + 257.2)/4 = 269.075

The centered moving average (PHSCMA) is shown in the next column. The calculations of PHSCMA for 1961Q3 and 1995Q2 are:

For 1961Q3: PHSCMA = (243.575 + 244.675)/2 = 244.125

For 1995Q2: PHSCMA = (271.250 + 269.075)/2 = 270.162

Notice that for PHSCMA there is a "MISSING" for each of the first two and last two quarters. This loss of four quarters of data over 35 years (140 quarters) is not too severe. The two lost quarters that are most critical are 1995Q3 and 1995Q4, since they are the closest to the period to be forecast (1996Q1 through 1996Q4).

Figure 6–2 shows a plot of the original private housing starts (PHS) data (dashed line) along with the deseasonalized data (solid line) represented by the centered moving averages (PHSCMA). Notice how much smoother the data appear once seasonal variations and random fluctuations have been removed.

The seasonal factors for each quarter are shown in the seventh column of Table 6–2. Recall that the seasonal factors measure the extent to which the observed value for each quarter is above or below the deseasonalized value (SF > 1 and SF < 1, respectively). For this example:

$$SF_t = PHS_t/PHSCMA_t$$

For the first two and the last two quarters, seasonal factors cannot be calculated, since there are no centered moving averages for those quarters. The calculations of the two

---

[3]In Table 6–2 you see that the SORITEC software positions the moving average at the last of the four quarters rather than at the third quarter. Since this is an intermediate step in time-series decomposition, doing so does not affect the results. The centered moving averages are positioned at the third quarter as described above.

TABLE 6–2   Time-Series Decomposition of Private Housing Starts (c6t2)

	PHS	PHSMA	PHSCMA	PHSCMAT	CF	SF	SI
1961Q1	183.1	MISSING	MISSING	240.099	MISSING	MISSING	0.788982
1961Q2	284.6	MISSING	MISSING	240.312	MISSING	MISSING	1.20983
1961Q3	284.2	MISSING	244.125	240.524	1.01497	1.16416	1.11339
1961Q4	222.4	243.575	247.238	240.737	1.02700	0.899540	0.887793
1962Q1	187.5	244.675	248.313	240.949	1.03056	0.755097*	0.788982
1962Q2	305.1	249.800	247.325	241.162	1.02556	1.23360	1.20983
1962Q3	272.3	246.825	246.663	241.374	1.02191	1.10394	1.11339
1962Q4	226.4	247.825	247.900	241.587	1.02613	0.913271	0.887793
⋮	⋮	⋮	⋮	⋮	⋮	⋮	⋮
1994Q1	252.6	291.250	300.925	268.155	1.12221	0.839412	0.788982
1994Q2	354.2	298.875	301.288	268.367	1.12267	1.17562	1.20983
1994Q3	325.7	302.975	294.800	268.580	1.09763	1.10482	1.11339
1994Q4	265.9	299.600	282.813	268.792	1.05216	0.940199	0.887793
1995Q1	214.2	290.000	273.438	269.005	1.01648	0.783360	0.788982
1995Q2	296.7	275.625	270.162	269.217	1.00351	1.09823*	1.20983
1995Q3	308.2	271.250	MISSING	269.430	MISSING	MISSING	1.11339
1995Q4	257.2	269.075	MISSING	269.642	MISSING	MISSING	0.887793

PHS = Private housing starts (in thousands)
PHSMA = Private housing starts moving average
PHSCMA = Private housing starts centered moving average
SF = Seasonal factor (PHS/PHSCMA)
PHSCMAT = Private housing starts centered moving-average trend (trend component)
CF = Cycle factor (PHSCMA/PHSCMAT)
SI = Seasonal indices (normalized mean of seasonal factors)

FIGURE 6–2

Private Housing Starts (PHS) with the Centered Moving Average of Private Housing Starts (PHSCMA) in Thousands of Units

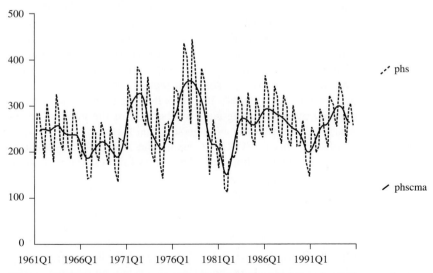

The centered moving-average series, shown by the solid line, is much smoother than the original series of private housing starts data (dashed line) because the seasonal pattern and the irregular or random fluctuations in the data are removed by the process of calculating the centered moving averages.

(c6t3)   **TABLE 6–3   Seasonal Factors for Private Housing Starts (Selected Years)**

Obs	Q1	Q2	Q3	Q4
1961	MISSING	MISSING	1.164	0.900
1962	0.755	1.234	1.104	0.913
1963	0.706	1.278	1.128	0.865
1964	0.816	1.206	1.091	0.892
⋮	⋮	⋮	⋮	⋮
1992	0.898	1.173	1.076	0.920
1993	0.798	1.171	1.080	0.947
1994	0.839	1.176	1.105	0.940
1995	0.783	1.098	MISSING	MISSING

This table is abbreviated to save space. All of the SFs are in the data files c6t3 (.sal or .txt).

seasonal factors marked with an asterisk in Table 6–2 are as follows:

$$\text{For 1962Q1: SF} = 187.5/248.313 = 0.755$$
$$\text{For 1995Q2: SF} = 296.7/270.162 = 1.098$$

It makes sense that a first quarter would have a low SF (less than 1), since January, February, and March are often not good months in which to start building. The reverse is true in the second quarter (April, May, and June).

In Table 6–2 there are three seasonal factors for third quarters: 1.164, 1.104, and 1.105. These are all above 1 and all indicate that third quarters are generally high for private housing starts. See Table 6–3 for additional seasonal factors for private housing starts. Since the seasonal factors for each period are bound to have some variability, we calculate a seasonal index (SI) for each period, which is a standardized average of all of that period's seasonal factors.

The determination of the seasonal indexes are calculated as follows. The seasonal factors for each of the four quarters are summed and divided by the number of observations to arrive at the average, or mean, seasonal factors for each quarter.[4] The sum of the average seasonal factors should equal the number of periods (4 for quarters, 12 for months). If it does not, the average seasonal factors should be normalized by multiplying each by the ratio of the number of periods (4 for quarterly data) to the sum of the average seasonal factors.

Doing this in SORITEC using the ADJUST command we find that seasonal indexes for private housing starts are as follows (rounded to three decimal places):

First quarter: 0.789

Second quarter: 1.210

Third quarter: 1.113

Fourth quarter: 0.888

These add to 4.000 as expected. As expected, the warmer spring and summer months of quarters 2 and 3 are the strongest seasons for housing starts.

---

[4]A medial average is sometimes used to reduce the effect of outliers. The medial average is the average that is calculated after the highest and lowest values are removed from the data.

The process of deseasonalizing the data has two useful results:

The deseasonalized data allow us to see better the underlying pattern in the data.

1. The deseasonalized data allow us to see better the underlying pattern in the data, as illustrated in Figure 6–2.
2. It provides us with measures of the extent of seasonality in the form of seasonal indexes.

As shown above, the private housing starts' seasonal index for the first quarter is 0.789. This means that the typical first-quarter figure is only 78.9 percent of the average quarterly value for the year. Thus, if the housing starts for a year totaled 400, we would expect 78.9 to occur in the first quarter. The 78.9 is found by dividing the yearly total (400) by 4, and then multiplying the result by the seasonal index $[(400/4) \times 0.789 = 78.9]$. Following this process for the other three quarters gives us 121.0 for the second quarter, 111.3 for the third quarter, and 88.8 for the fourth quarter.

Another useful application of seasonal indexes is in projecting what one quarter's observation may portend for the entire year. For example, assume that you were working for a manufacturer of major household appliances in April 1995 and heard that housing starts for the first quarter were 214.2. Since your sales depend heavily on new construction, you want to project this forward for the year. Let's see how you would do this, taking seasonality into account. Once the seasonal indexes are known you can deseasonalize data by dividing by the appropriate index. That is:

$$\text{Deseasonalized data} = \text{Raw data/Seasonal index}$$

For 1995Q1 we have:

$$\text{Deseasonalized data} = 214.2/0.789 = 271.483$$

Multiplying this deseasonalized value by 4 would give a projection for the year of 1,085.932.

Finding the Long-Term Trend

The long-term trend is estimated from the deseasonalized data for the variable to be forecast. Remember that the centered moving average (CMA) is the series that remains after the seasonality and irregular components have been smoothed out by using moving averages. Thus, to find the long-term trend, we estimate a simple linear equation as:[5]

$$\text{CMA} = f(\text{TIME})$$
$$= a + b(\text{TIME})$$

where $\text{TIME} = 1$ for the first period in the data set and increases by 1 each quarter thereafter. The values of a and b are normally estimated by using a computer

---

[5] A linear trend is most often used, but a nonlinear trend may also be used. Looking at a graph such as the one shown in Figure 6–2 is helpful in determining which form would be most appropriate for the trend line.

FIGURE 6–3

Private Housing Starts (PHS) with Centered Moving Average (PHSCMA) and Centered Moving-Average Trend (PHSCMAT) in Thousands of Units (c6f3)

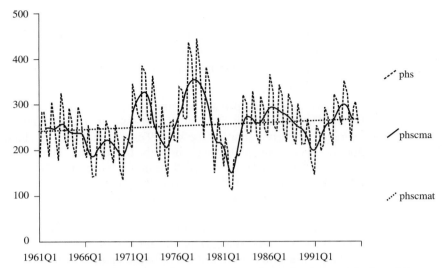

The long-term trend in private housing starts is shown by the straight dotted line (PHSCMAT). The dashed line is the raw data (PHS), while the wavelike solid line is the deseasonalized data (PHSCMA). The long-term trend is seen to be slightly positive. The equation for the trend line is: PHSCMAT = 239.89 + 0.213(TIME).

regression program, but they can also be found quickly on most hand-held business calculators.

Once the trend equation has been determined, it is used to generate an estimate of the trend value of the centered moving average for the historic and forecast periods. This new series is the centered moving-average trend (CMAT).

For our example involving private housing starts, the linear trend of the deseasonalized data (PHSCMA) has been found to be slightly positive. The centered moving-average trend for this example is denoted PHSCMAT, for "private housing starts centered moving-average trend." The equation is:

$$PHSCMAT = 239.89 + 0.213(TIME)$$

where TIME = 1 for 1961Q1. This line is shown in Figure 6–3, along with the graph of private housing starts (PHS) and the deseasonalized data (PHSCMA).

Measuring the Cyclical Component

The cyclical component of a time series is the extended wavelike movement about the long-term trend. It is measured by a cycle factor (CF), which is the ratio of the centered moving average (CMA) to the centered moving-average trend (CMAT). That is:

$$CF = CMA/CMAT$$

A cycle factor greater than 1 indicates that the deseasonalized value for that period is above the long-term trend of the data. If CF is less than 1, the reverse is true.

The cycle factor is the most difficult component of a time series to analyze and to project into the forecast period. If analyzed carefully, however, it may also be the component that has the most to offer in terms of understanding where the industry may be headed. Looking at the length and amplitude of previous cycles may enable us to anticipate the next turning point in the current cycle. This is a major advantage of the time-series decomposition technique. An individual familiar with an industry can often explain cyclic movements around the trend line in terms of variables or events that, in retrospect, can be seen to have had some import. By looking at those variables or events in the present, one can sometimes get some hint of the likely future direction of the cycle component.

> Looking at the length and amplitude of previous cycles may enable us to anticipate the next turning point in the current cycle.

Overview of Business Cycles

Business cycles are long-term wavelike fluctuations in the general level of economic activity. They are often described by a diagram such as the one shown in Figure 6–4. The period of time between the beginning trough (*A*) and the peak (*B*) is called the *expansion phase,* while the period from peak (*B*) to the ending trough (*C*) is termed the *recession,* or *contraction, phase.*

The vertical distance between *A* and *B'* provides a measure of the degree of the expansion. The start of the expansion beginning at point *A* is determined by three consecutive months of increase in economic activity. Thus, the preceding recession is only officially over three months after the economy has turned around. Similarly, the severity of a recession is measured by the vertical distance between *B''* and *C*, and the official beginning of the recession is dated as the first of three consecutive months of decline.

If business cycles were true cycles, they would have a constant amplitude. That is, the vertical distance from trough to peak and peak to trough would always be the same. In addition, a true cycle would also have a constant periodicity. That would mean that the length of time between successive peaks (or troughs) would always be

FIGURE 6–4

The General Business Cycle

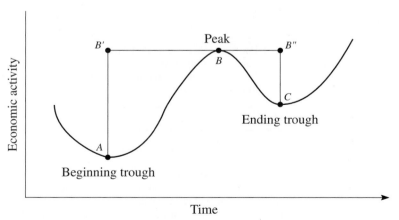

A business cycle goes through successive periods of expansion, contraction, expansion, contraction, and so on.

the same. However, with economic and business activity this degree of regularity is unlikely. As you will see when we look at the cyclical component for private housing starts and for domestic car sales, the vertical distances from trough to peak (or peak to trough) have some variability, as does the distance between successive peaks and successive troughs.

Business Cycle Indicators

There are a number of possible business cycle indicators but three are particularly noteworthy:

1. The index of leading economic indicators
2. The index of coincident economic indicators
3. The index of lagging economic indicators

The individual series that make up each index are:

Index of Leading Economic Indicators

Average weekly hours of production of nonsupervisory workers, manufacturing
Average weekly initial claims for unemployment insurance, state programs
Manufacturers' new orders in constant dollars, consumer goods and materials industries
Index of stock prices, 500 common stocks
Contracts and orders for plant and equipment in constant dollars
Index of new private housing units authorized by local building permits
Vendor performance, percent of companies receiving slower deliveries
Change in manufacturing and trade inventories on hand and on order in constant dollars
Change in sensitive materials price
Money supply, M2, in constant dollars
Change in business and consumer credit outstanding

Index of Coincident Economic Indicators

Employees on nonagricultural payrolls
Index of industrial production
Personal income less transfer payments in constant dollars
Manufacturing and trade sales in constant dollars

Index of Lagging Economic Indicators

Index of labor cost per unit of output, manufacturing
Ratio, manufacturing and trade inventories to sales in constant dollars
Average duration of unemployment in weeks
Ratio, consumer installment credit outstanding to personal income
Commercial and industrial loans outstanding in constant dollars
Average prime rate charged by banks

It is possible that one of these indexes, or one of the series that make up an index, may be useful in predicting the cycle factor in a time-series decomposition. This could be done in a regression analysis with the cycle factor (CF) as the dependent variable. These indexes, or their components, may also be quite useful as independent variables in other regression models, such as those discussed in Chapters 4 and 5.

Figure 6–5 shows what are considered the official business cycles for the United States economy in recent years. This graph focuses on real gross domestic product per capita as a broad measure of economic activity. The shaded vertical bars identify the officially designated periods of recession.

The Cycle Factor for Private Housing Starts

Let us return to our example involving private housing starts to examine how to calculate the cycle factor and how it might be projected into the forecast period. In Table 6–2 the cycle factors (CF) are shown in column 6. As indicated previously, each cycle factor is the ratio of the deseasonalized data (CMA) to the trend value (CMAT). For the private housing starts data, we have:

$$CF = PHSCMA/PHSCMAT$$

The actual calculations for 1962Q1 and 1995Q2 are:

$$1962Q1: CF = 248.313/240.949 = 1.03056$$
$$1995Q2: CF = 270.162/269.217 = 1.00351$$

You can see in Figure 6–3 that in 1962Q1 the centered moving average was above the trend line and that in 1995Q2 it was almost at the same level as the trend line.

The cycle factor is plotted in Figure 6–6. You can see that the cycle factor (CF) moves above and below the line at 1.00 in Figure 6–6 exactly as the centered moving average moves above and below the trend line in Figure 6–3. By isolating the cycle factor in Figure 6–6, we can better analyze its movements over time.

You see that the cyclical component for private housing starts does not have a constant amplitude or periodicity. The dates for peaks and troughs are shown in Figure 6–6, along with the values of the cycle factor at those points. Identification of these dates and values is often helpful in considering when the cycle factor may next turn around (i.e., when the next trough or peak may occur). For example, for the PHS cycle factor the decline from 1963Q3 through 1966Q4 covered 13 quarters, the 1972Q3 to 1975Q1 decline was 10 quarters long, the 1977Q3 through 1982Q1 decline was 18 quarters in duration, and the decline from 1986Q3 through 1991Q1 also lasted 18 quarters. The average of these four contractions was 14.75 quarters, with standard deviation of 3.9. The corresponding troughs had cycle factors of 0.759, 0.821, 0.583, and 0.763, for an average of about 0.73 (with a standard deviation of about 0.10). The most recent peak of the CF in Figure 6–6 was 1994Q2, and so a trough may be likely sometime near the beginning of 1998, perhaps with a cycle factor in the vicinity of 0.73. Thus the next trough is expected beyond our 1996 forecast horizon.

The determination of where the cycle factor will be in the forecast horizon is a difficult task. One approach would be to examine the past pattern visually,

Figure 6–5

Official Business Cycles in the United States

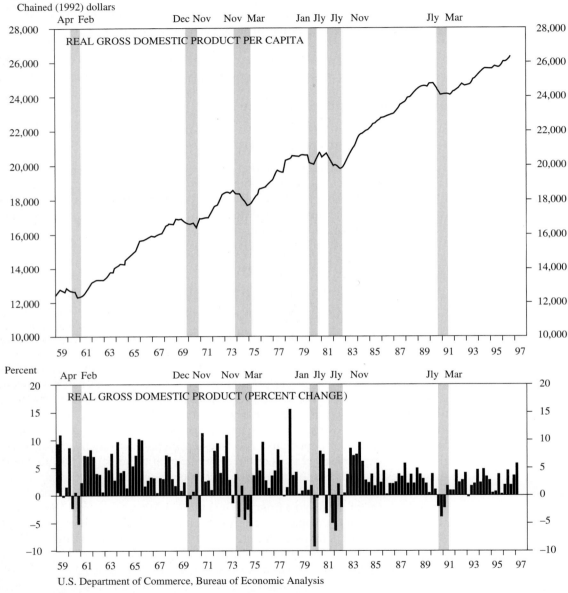

Percent changes shown are based on quarter-to-quarter changes and are expressed at seasonally adjusted annual rates; the levels are also expressed at a seasonally adjusted annual rate. Source: Survey of Current Business, July 1997.

FIGURE 6–6

Cycle Factor (CF) for Private Housing Starts (c6f6)

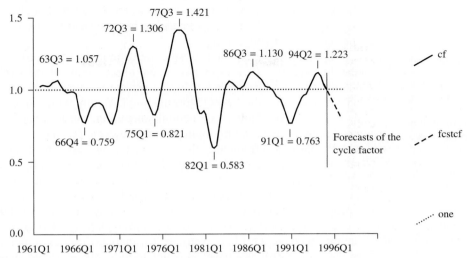

The cycle factor is the ratio of the centered moving average to the long-term trend in the data. As this plot shows, the cycle factor moves slowly around the base line (1.00) with little regularity. Dates and values of cycle factors at peaks and troughs are shown.

focusing on prior peaks and troughs, with particular attention to their amplitude and periodicity, and then making a subjective projection into the forecast horizon. Another approach would be to use another forecasting method to forecast values for CF. Holt's exponential smoothing may sometimes be a good candidate for this task, but one must remember that such a model will not pick up a turning point until after it has occurred. Thus, the forecaster would never predict that the current rise or fall in the cycle would end. If we have recently observed a turning point and have several quarters of data since the turning point, and *if* we believe another turning point is unlikely during the forecast horizon, then Holt's exponential smoothing may be useful. Holt's exponential smoothing forecast of the cycle factor for the private housing starts data based only on the period since the last turning point (1994Q2) is as follows:

Period	CF Forecast
1995Q3	0.97
1995Q4	0.94
1996Q1	0.91
1996Q2	0.88
1996Q3	0.85
1996Q4	0.82

We see that the Holt's exponential smoothing forecast projects continual downward movement in the cycle factor in a manner that is quite consistent with what we have observed from prior cycles. The Holt exponential smoothing forecast of the cycle factor (fcstcf) is shown by the dashed line in Figure 6–6. Note that we have to forecast

It is important
to recognize that
there is no way
to know exactly
where the cycle
factor will be
in the forecast
horizon, and there
is no a priori way
to determine the
best technique
for projecting the
cycle factor. A
thorough review of
the past behavior
of the cycle
factor, along
with alternative
forecasts, should
be evaluated for
consistency and
congruity before
selecting values
of the cycle factor
for the forecast
horizon.

the cycle factor for the last two quarters of 1995, even though we had original PHS data for all of 1995. This is because we lost the last two observations in developing the centered moving averages.

To use Holt's exponential smoothing model to forecast the cycle factor, you should have at least four or five actual observations of the cycle factor following the most recent turning point. In this private housing starts example, we have just enough data after the 1994Q2 turning point. You might try to use a regression model as well as trying Holt's exponential smoothing, but it is usually difficult to find a good regression model to use in forecasting cycle factors.

Perhaps most frequently the cycle factor forecast is made on a largely judgmental basis by looking carefully at the historic values, especially historic turning points and the rates of descent or rise in the historic series. You might look at the peak-to-peak, trough-to-trough, peak-to-trough, and trough-to-peak distances by dating each turning point, such as we show in Figure 6–6. Then, as we did above, you could calculate the average distance between troughs (or peaks) to get a feeling for when another such point is likely. You can also analyze the rates of increase and/or decrease in the cycle factor as a basis on which to judge the expected slope of the forecast of the cycle factor.

In our private housing starts example, Holt's forecast seems reasonable and is the one we shall use for the purpose of this example. It is important to recognize that there is no way to know exactly where the cycle factor will be in the forecast horizon, and there is no a priori way to determine the best technique for projecting the cycle factor. A thorough review of the past behavior of the cycle factor, along with alternative forecasts, should be evaluated for consistency and congruity before selecting values of the cycle factor for the forecast horizon.

The Time-Series Decomposition Forecast

You have seen that a time series of data can be decomposed into the product of four components:

$$Y = T \cdot S \cdot C \cdot I$$

where Y is the series to be forecast. The four components are:

T = The long-term trend based on the deseasonalized data. It is often called the *centered moving-average trend* (CMAT), since the deseasonalized data are centered moving averages (CMA) of the original Y values.

S = Seasonal indexes (SI). These are normalized averages of seasonal factors that are determined as the ratio of each period's actual value (Y) to the deseasonalized value (CMA) for that period.

C = The cycle component. The cycle factor (CF) is the ratio of CMA to CMAT and represents the gradual wavelike movements in the series around the trend line.

I = The irregular component. This is assumed equal to 1 unless the forecaster has reason to believe a shock may take place, in which case I could be different from 1 for all or part of the forecast period.

Previous sections of this chapter have illustrated how these components can be isolated and measured.

To prepare a forecast based on the time-series decomposition model, we simply reassemble the components. In general terms the forecast for Y (FY) is:

$$FY = (CMAT)(SI)(CF)(I)$$

For our private housing starts example we will denote the forecast value based on the model as PHSFTSD. Thus,

$$PHSFTSD = (PHSCMAT)(SI)(CF)(I)$$

where PHSCMAT is the private housing starts centered moving-average trend. The irregular factor (I) is assumed equal to 1, since we have no reason to expect it to be greater or less than 1 because of its random nature. These calculations are shown in Table 6–4 for 1961Q1–1962Q4 and 1994Q1–1996Q4. You will note that this method takes the trend (PHSCMAT) and makes two adjustments to it: the first adjusts it for seasonality (with SI), and the second adjusts it for cycle variations (with CF).

The actual and forecast values for private housing starts are shown for 1991Q1 through 1996Q4 in Figure 6–7. The actual values (PHS) are shown by the solid

(c6t4)   TABLE 6–4   **The Time-Series Decomposition Forecast**

	PHSCMAT	SI	CF	PHSFTSD
1961Q1	240.099	0.788982	MISSING	MISSING
1961Q2	240.312	1.20983	MISSING	MISSING
1961Q3	240.524	1.11339	1.01497	271.806
1961Q4	240.737	0.887793	1.02700	219.495
1962Q1	240.949	0.788982	1.03056	195.914
1962Q2	241.162	1.20983	1.02556	299.223
1962Q3	241.374	1.11339	1.02191	274.632
1962Q4	241.587	0.887793	1.02613	220.084
⋮	⋮	⋮	⋮	⋮
1994Q1	268.155	0.788982	1.12221	237.425
1994Q2	268.367	1.20983	1.12267	364.507
1994Q3	268.580	1.11339	1.09763	328.229
1994Q4	268.792	0.887793	1.05216	251.079
1995Q1	269.005	0.788982	1.01648	215.738
1995Q2	269.217	1.20983	1.00351	326.850
1995Q3	269.430	1.11339	0.970000e	290.981
1995Q4	269.642	0.887793	0.940000e	225.023
1996Q1	269.855	0.788982	0.910000e	193.749
1996Q2	270.067	1.20983	0.880000e	287.527
1996Q3	270.280	1.11339	0.850000e	255.788
1996Q4	270.493	0.887793	0.820000e	196.916

Notes:

1. The *e* beside cycle factors for 1995Q3–1996Q4 indicates that those are estimated values rather than actual ratios of PHSCMA to PHSCMAT.

2. Forecast values for private housing starts (PHSFTSD) are determined as follows:
PHSFTSD = (PHSCMAT)(SI)(CF)

3. The full set of data are in the files c6t4 (.sal or .txt).

FIGURE 6–7

Private Housing Starts (phs) and a Time-Series Decomposition Forecast (phsftsd) for 1991Q1 Through 1996Q4 (c6f7)

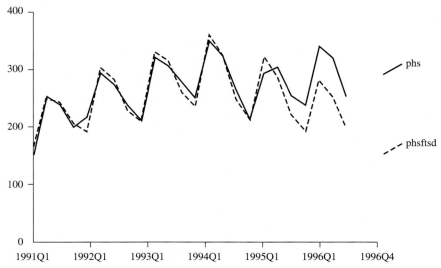

The actual values for private housing starts are shown by the solid line, and the time-series decomposition forecast values are shown by the dashed line.

FIGURE 6–8

Domestic Car Sales Time-Series Decomposition

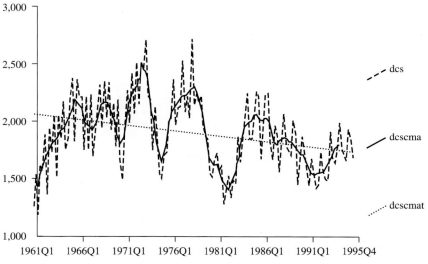

Actual domestic car sales (DCS) are shown by the dashed line, the centered moving averages (DCSCMA) are shown by the solid line, and the long-term trend values (DCSCMAT) are shown by the dotted line.

lines; forecast values based on the time-series decomposition model are shown by the dashed lines. The RMSE for this forecast, based on the four quarters of 1996, is 57.26.

Because time-series decomposition models do not involve a lot of mathematics or statistics, they are relatively easy to explain to the end user. This is a major advantage, because if the end user has an appreciation of how the forecast was developed, he or she may have more confidence in its use for decision making.

Forecasting Domestic Car Sales by Using Time-Series Decomposition

We have applied the classical time-series decomposition method, as described in this chapter, to the problem of forecasting domestic car sales. Figure 6–8 shows the original series (DCS) as the dashed line that fluctuates widely. The deseasonalized series, represented by the centered moving averages (DCSCMA) and the trend (DCSCMAT), are shown by solid and dotted lines, respectively. Note how the original series moves above and below the deseasonalized series in a fairly regular seasonal pattern. The seasonal indexes, based on the normalized mean of the seasonal factors for domestic car sales, are:

Quarter	Seasonal Index
1	0.966
2	1.105
3	0.950
4	0.980

The long-term trend (DCSCMAT), as shown in Figure 6–8, has a negative slope.

The cycle factor (CF) is shown in Figure 6–9. The values of CF from 1961Q3 through 1994Q2 were calculated as follows:

$$CF = DCSCMA/DCSCMAT$$

and are shown by the CF curve in Figure 6–9. For 1994Q3 through 1995Q4 they were determined through an analysis and projection of the behavior of the cycle pattern from 1961Q3 through 1994Q2. The dashed line labeled CFFH represents a forecast of the cycle factor based on Holt's exponential smoothing model.

The classical time-series decomposition forecast of domestic car sales (DCSFTSD) is found by multiplying the trend (DCSCMAT) by the seasonal indexes (SI) and the cycle factors (CF). That is:

$$DCSFTSD = DCSCMAT \times SI \times CF$$

The actual and forecast values for 1991Q1 through 1995Q4 are shown in Figure 6–10 by the solid and dashed lines, respectively.

We now have six different forecasts of domestic car sales for 1995Q1–1995Q4. The fit and accuracy of these six models are summarized in Table 6–5.

FIGURE 6–9

The Domestic Car Sales Cycle Factor (c6f9)

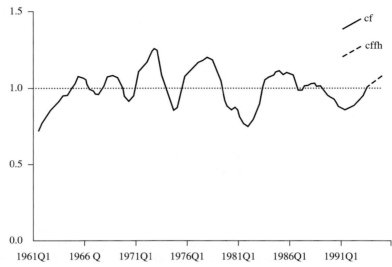

The cycle factor (CF) for domestic car sales is shown along with a forecast using Holt's exponential smoothing (CFFH).

FIGURE 6–10

The Time-Series Decomposition Forecast of Domestic Car Sales (c6f10)

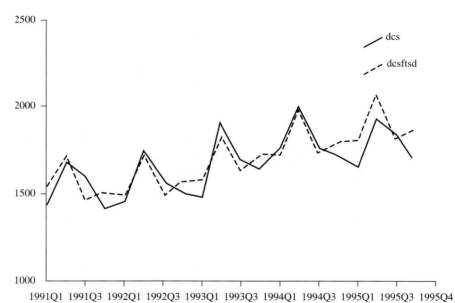

The actual values for domestic car sales (DCS) are shown by the solid lines, while the values forecast using the time-series decomposition method (DCSFTSD) are shown by the dashed lines.

TABLE 6–5   Summary Table of RMSEs for Domestic Car Sales

Chapter	Method	Period	RMSE
1	Naive–with 4-period lag	Historic before '95	207.3
		Holdout 95Q1–95Q4	74.9
2	Not applicable	Historic before '95	na
		Holdout 95Q1–95Q4	na
3	Winters' exponential smoothing	Historic before '95	177.1
		Holdout 95Q1–95Q4	55.8
	ADRES with	Historic before '95	169.5
	seasonal adjustment	Holdout 95Q1–95Q4	64.2
4	Simple regression model using seasonally adjusted DCS as a function of the University of Michigan Index of Consumer Satisfaction	Historic before '95	134.570
		Holdout 95Q1–95Q4	102.242
5	Multiple regression	Historic before '95	106.8
		Holdout 95Q1–95Q4	56.9
6	Time-series decomposition	Historic before '95	130.185
		Holdout 95Q1–95Q4	140.930

How to Evaluate and Improve a Forecasting Process

By Mark Walden
Sales Forecasting Manager, Partylite Gifts, Inc.

One of the fundamentals of making good forecasts is to understand exactly what comprises the historical data to be used in preparing forecasts. Do not accept the data at face value. In fact, this is one of the reasons why forecasts, and the resulting financial decisions based on those forecasts, can go awry. This may also be part of the reason a forecast department can lack credibility. The best statistical model in the world is only as good as the input data. To provide effective forecasts and market analyses, one has to fully understand the business. The best way to begin is to inquire into the systems that feed your source data. There is no single answer as to what constitutes the best data.

Source: *Journal of Business Forecasting* 15, no. 2 (Summer 1996), p. 23.

Forecasting Winter Daily Natural Gas Demand at Vermont Gas Systems

By Mike Flock,
Distribution Engineer, Vermont Gas Systems, Inc.

Vermont Gas Systems is a natural gas utility with approximately 26,000 residential, business and industrial customers in 13 towns and cities in northwestern Vermont. Vermont Gas Systems' Gas Control Department forecasts the gas demand and arranges the gas supply and transportation from suppliers in western Canada and storage facilities along the Trans-Canada Pipeline which delivers the gas to our pipeline. The quantities of gas must be specified to the suppliers at least 24 hours in advance. The Gas Control Department must request enough natural gas to meet the needs of the customers but must not over-request gas which will needlessly and expensively tax Trans-Canada Pipelines' facilities. Because Vermont Gas Systems has the storage capacity for only one hour use of gas as a buffer between supply and demand, an accurate forecast of daily natural gas demand is critical.

Source: *Journal of Business Forecasting* 13, no. 1 (Spring 1994), p. 23.

INTEGRATIVE CASE
The Gap

Part 6: Forecasting The Gap Sales Data with Time-Series Decomposition

The sales of Gap stores for the 44 quarters covering 1985 quarter 1 through 1995 quarter 4 are once again shown below.

(c6gap)

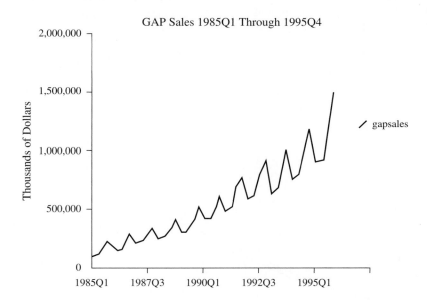

GAP Sales 1985Q1 Through 1995Q4

Case Questions

1. Describe what you see in the 1985–1995 Gap sales in the terms used in time-series decomposition: *trend, seasonality,* and *cycle.*

2. Using the Gap sales data for 1985Q1 through 1995Q4, calculate the 4-period centered moving average of Gap sales (call it GAPCMA). Then, using a time index that goes from 1 for 1985Q1 through 48 for 1996Q4, estimate the trend of GAPCMA (call this trend GAPCMAT and extend it through the entire 1985Q1–1996Q4 period). Plot Gap sales, GAPCMA, and GAPCMAT on the same graph for the period from 1985Q1 through 1995Q4.

3. Calculate the seasonal factors and seasonal indices (SI) based on the 1985–1995 data. Are they consistent with your expectations? Explain.

4. Calculate the cycle factors (CF) for this situation and plot CF along with a horizontal line at one. Your calculated cycle factors end at 1995Q2. Why do they not extend farther? Make a forecast of CF for 1995Q3 through 1996Q4, explaining why you forecast as you do.

5. Prepare a forecast of Gap sales for the four quarters of 1996 using the trend (GAPCMAT), cycle factors (CF), and the seasonal indices (SI) determined above. Plot the actual and forecast sales.

6. Use the historic period (1985Q1–1995Q4) and hold-out period (1996Q1–1996Q4) RMSEs to evaluate your results and to compare them with forecasts of Gap sales prepared using other methods.

Solutions to Case Questions

1. The Gap sales exhibit a substantial positive trend over the time frame being evaluated and a very clear seasonal pattern that repeats itself year to year. It appears that the seasonality may be more pronounced in the more recent years than it was in the early years. From this graph it is not clear that there are the long-term swings that are normally associated with a seasonal pattern. However, because of the long-term nature of cycles, it may be that these 11 years of data are insufficient to make an identification of a cyclical pattern.

2. The actual Gap sales are shown by the dotted line in the graph below. The centered moving average is the solid line, and the centered moving-average trend is the dashed line.

3. The seasonal factors (SF; SF = GAPSALES/GAPCMA) and the normalized seasonal indices (SI) are shown below.

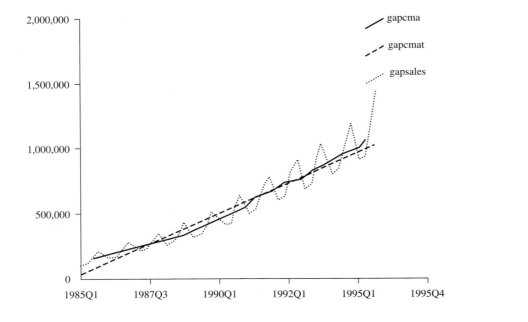

(c6gap)

	SF	SI		SF	SI		SF	SI
1985Q1	MISSING	0.8540	1988Q1	0.829765	0.8540	1991Q1	0.875554	0.8540
1985Q2	MISSING	0.8462	1988Q2	0.866608	0.8462	1991Q2	0.861170	0.8462
1985Q3	1.07741	1.0459	1988Q3	1.00359	1.0459	1991Q3	1.09346	1.0459
1985Q4	1.32510	1.2538	1988Q4	1.25394	1.2538	1991Q4	1.20689	1.2538
1986Q1	0.833460	0.8540	1989Q1	0.870753	0.8540	1992Q1	0.850008	0.8540
1986Q2	0.805002	0.8462	1989Q2	0.854437	0.8462	1992Q2	0.847917	0.8462
1986Q3	1.02936	1.0459	1989Q3	0.993622	1.0459	1992Q3	1.10748	1.0459
1986Q4	1.28986	1.2538	1989Q4	1.26880	1.2538	1992Q4	1.21808	1.2538
1987Q1	0.864566	0.8540	1990Q1	0.891111	0.8540	1993Q1	0.822485	0.8540
1987Q2	0.844446	0.8462	1990Q2	0.855332	0.8462	1993Q2	0.858264	0.8462
1987Q3	1.01606	1.0459	1990Q3	1.01467	1.0459	1993Q3	1.07314	1.0459
1987Q4	1.28933	1.2538	1990Q4	1.20097	1.2538	1993Q4	1.23149	1.2538

continued

	SF	SI		SF	SI		SF	SI
1994Q1	0.852103	0.8540	1995Q1	0.848873	0.8540	1996Q1	MISSING	0.8540
1994Q2	0.847695	0.8462	1995Q2	0.819529	0.8462	1996Q2	MISSING	0.8462
1994Q3	1.04824	1.0459	1995Q3	MISSING	1.0459	1996Q3	MISSING	1.0459
1994Q4	1.25119	1.2538	1995Q4	MISSING	1.2538	1996Q4	MISSING	1.2538

Notice that while the values for SF vary from year to year, the SI values repeat year after year. The seasonal factors for Gap sales in quarters one through four indicate strong sales during the fall back-to-school buying season, followed by even stronger sales in their fourth quarter due to the Christmas season.

4. The cycle factors are calculated as: CF = GAPCMA/GAPCMAT. The cycle factors are missing for 1985Q1, 1985Q2, 1995Q3, and 1995Q4 because the GAPCMA cannot be calculated for those quarters. The solid line in the graph of the cycle factors represents the actual values (CF), and the dashed line shows the forecast values (CFF). Because of the lack of peaks and troughs in the cycle, the six values for the forecast quarters have been set equal to the most recent actual value.

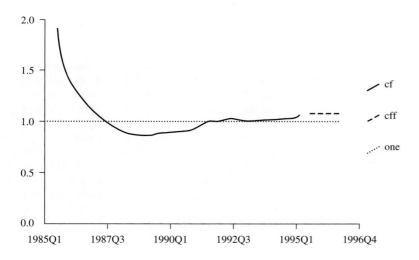

5. The forecast of Gap sales based on the time-series decomposition method is calculated as: GAPFTSD = GAPCMAT ∗ SI ∗ CF. A time-series plot of these results follows.

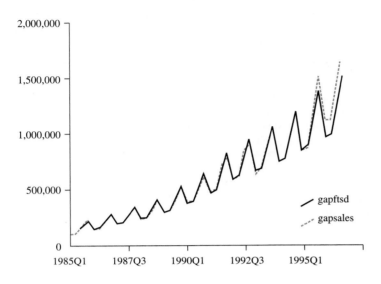

6. The actual (GAPSALES) and time-series decomposition forecast (GAPFTSD) of Gap sales are shown below for the four quarters of 1996.

	GAPSALES	GAPFTSD
1996Q1	1,113,154	968,619
1996Q2	1,120,335	980,720
1996Q3	1,383,996	1,238,100
1996Q4	1,667,896	1,515,290

The root-mean-squared errors for the historic period (1985Q1–1995Q4) and for the holdout forecast period (1996Q1–1996Q4) are:

Using 1985Q1–1995Q4:

Root-mean-squared error = 25,706.9

Using 1996Q1–1996Q4:

Root-mean-squared error = 145,488

It is not uncommon for time-series decomposition models to yield historic RMSEs that are relatively small. This is because these models simply decompose the data and then reassemble the parts. As long as the seasonal factors are not dramatically different, the historic fit of the model will be excellent. However, due to the difficulty of projecting the cycle factor into the forecast horizon, forecast RMSEs are often considerably higher than those in the historic period. This is a good reason to test models in a holdout forecast horizon so that you get a realistic measure of forecast accuracy.

Table 6–6 provides a summary of root-mean-squared errors for various methods used thus far to forecast GAP sales.

TABLE 6–6   Summary Table of RMSEs for Gap Sales

Chapter	Method	Period	RMSE
1	Naive–with 4-period lag	Historic before '96	107,150.0
		Holdout 96Q1–96Q4	227,029.0
2	Not applicable	Historic before '96	na
		Holdout 96Q1–96Q4	na
3	Winters' exponential smoothing	Historic before '96	37,935.5
		Holdout 96Q1–96Q4	84,460.7
	Holt's exponential smoothing	Historic before '96	31,272.5
	with seasonal readjustment	Holdout 96Q1–96Q4	33,341.3
4	Linear trend of deseasonalized	Historic before '96	56,110.6
	data with forecast reseasonalized	Holdout 96Q1–96Q4	211,550.0
5	Multiple regression	Historic before '96	56,178.1
		Holdout 96Q1–96Q4	116,620.0
6	Time-series decomposition	Historic before '96	25,706.9
		Holdout 96Q1–96Q4	145,448.0

USING SORITEC FOR TIME-SERIES DECOMPOSITION FORECASTS

Getting the Data

The first thing we need to do is to get data with which to work. To do so, go to **FILE** on the main menu and select **OPEN DATA FILE,** then select a data file (typically a .SAL file) or a database file (a .SDB file) such as the ECONDATA file that came with your text.

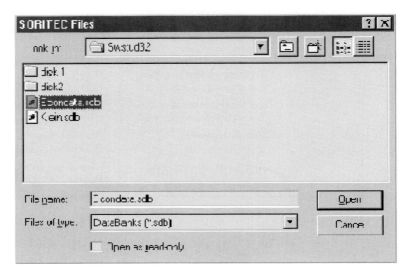

For this example we will assume that you have opened the ECONDATA file and want to develop a time-series decomposition forecast of new home sales (named HZNS in ECON-DATA). This variable is in ECONDATA on a monthly basis. We will call new home sales NHS and will use data from 1966Q1 through 1995Q4 (120 observations) to forecast new home sales for the four quarters of 1996. The following shows how to set up the time period, including the forecast horizon, so that we can check the accuracy of our forecast, and how to set up the initial variables with the names we desire.

```
1> access 'econdata'    {echoed from our use of the menu above
                          to open ECONDATA}
  *** File opened  ( 1): econdata.sdb
2> use 66q1 95q4  {sets up the time period for which we get
                    the new home sales data}
3> convert (sum) nhs = hzns   {brings new home sales into the
                                workspace with the name nhs}
4> use 66q1 96q4  {sets the period to 124 quarters to
                    include the historic period (66Q1–95Q4) and
                    the forecast "holdout" period (96Q1–96Q4)}
5> time t   {sets up a time index equal to 1 for
              1996Q1 through 124 for 1996Q4}
```

Pressing the (**F10**) key (or clicking on **VIEW** in the main menu, then on **SYMBOLS**) shows what is in the workspace, as follows:

```
>6 symbols (full)
SORITEC symbol table:
User variables
SYM NO NAME                  ADDRESS    TYPE       LENGTH
    197 HZNS                 2333606    SERIES        412  1963M1-1997M4
ONE FAMILY HOUSES SOLD:TOTAL U.S. (THOUS.U.)NSA
    211 NHS                  2333314    SERIES        138  1966Q1-1996Q4
    225 T                    2330842    SERIES        126  1966Q1-1996Q4
```

Finding the Seasonal, Trend, and Cyclical Components

The first thing we should do is to look at a graph of new home sales (NHS) to see what characteristics the data exhibit. Such a time-series plot for the historic period (1966Q1 through 1995Q4) is shown to the right. We see that there is some upward trend, considerable seasonality, and a cyclical component.

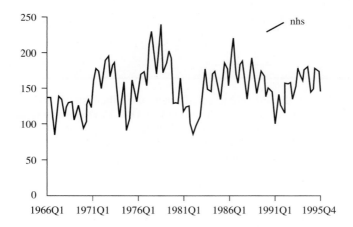

The Seasonal Factors and Seasonal Indices. The seasonal factors (SF) for each quarter are found by dividing new home sales by the centered moving average of new home sales (NHSCMA): that is, SF = NHS/NHSCMA. The seasonal indices are the arithmetic average of the seasonal factors (standardized to equal 1). While this can be done using commands, the efficient way is to use the ADJUST feature of SORITEC.

Click on **ADJUST** and the **Seasonal Adjustment** dialog box will appear.

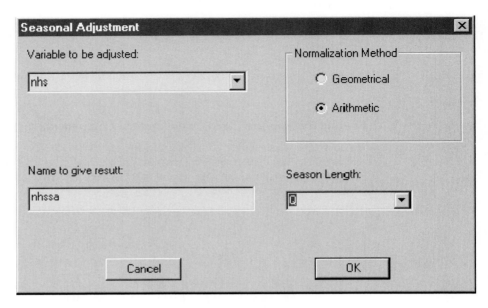

Select **NHS** as the variable to be adjusted, name the result NHSSA, click on **Arithmetic,** and select **Q** for quarterly data. Then click on **OK.** The following values will appear on your screen (and will be stored for 1966Q1–1995Q4 as ^FACTOR): 0.998376, 1.12537, 1.02680, and 0.849451. These are what we have called the seasonal indices (SI). To name these SI and project them into the next four quarters, type the following commands:

```
> SI = ^FACTOR
> USE  96Q1  96Q4
> REVISE  SI = SI(-4)
```

If you tried to extend SI for more than four quarters (such as through 1997Q4), you would get an error because when you look for a value for 1997Q1 there is nothing yet in 1996Q1. When using a longer forecast horizon you can get around this problem by issuing the following command prior to the REVISE command: ON DYNAMIC. This will have each quarter revised in sequence rather than all at once.

The Long-Term Trend.   The trend is based on the deseasonalized data as represented by the centered moving average of the original series. To find the centered moving average of NHS, we use the centered moving-average command (CMA) in SORITEC as follows:

```
> USE  66Q1  95Q4
> CMA  NHSCMA  NHS  4
```

where NHSCMA is a name we assign for the new series to be calculated from the base series (NHS) and 4 is the number of periods per year (quarters in our example).

NHSCMA only exists for 1966Q3 through 1995Q2, and that is the period we need to use to estimate the long-term trend. You may remember from the text that in calculating the centered moving averages we lose two periods at the beginning and at the end of our original time span (six periods at each end of a monthly series). To get the trend equation, first define a new variable, named NHSCMAT, to be the centered moving-average trend, then regress that as a function of T. Type the following three commands on the command line:

```
> NHSCMAT = NHSCMA
> USE  1966Q3  1995Q2    {alternatively you could type USEALL NHSCMA}
> REGRESS  NHSCMAT  T
```

This produces the following regression trend equation:

```
REGRESS : dependent variable is NHSCMA
 Using  1966Q3-1995Q2

 Variable     Coefficient      Std Err         T-stat        Signf
^CONST         137.701         5.00501        27.5127        .000
   T           .232065         .723806E-01     3.20617       .002
```

Now to use this equation to calculate the trend values for the entire historic and forecast period, type the following:

```
> USEALL   T
> FORECAST  ^FOREQ
```

You now have measures for the trend (NHSCMAT) component as well as the seasonal component (SI). The following graph shows NHS, NHSCMA, and NHSCMAT for the historic period:

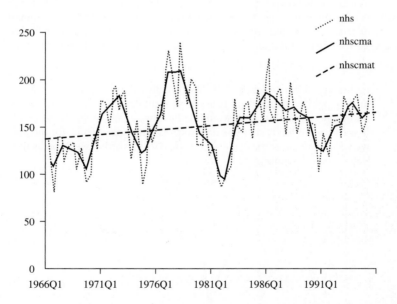

The Cycle Factor. The cycle factor (CF) measures how far the centered moving average (NHSCMA) is above or below the long-term trend (NHSCMAT), measured by the ratio of NHSCMA to NHSCMAT. This is calculated in SORITEC by the following:

```
> CF  = NHSCMA / NHSCMAT
```

(Note: values will not be calculated for the four time periods in which NHSCMA is missing.)

Next you will want to look at a plot of CF. In doing so it is helpful to have a horizontal line at one. To create a new series equal to one type:

```
> ONE = 1
```

Use the plot button and select both **CF** and **ONE** to get the following graph:

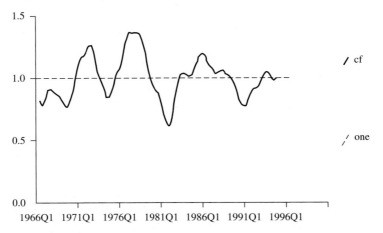

The task now is to project CF forward for the next six quarters, 1995Q3 through 1996Q4. This is done by examining the historic CFs, looking for the peaks and troughs, and evaluating the distances between them. Dating the peaks and troughs, such as in Figure 6–6, is also helpful. To see a list of the exact values of the cycle factor at each quarter, type:

```
> PRINT CF
```

In this case it is a judgment call about whether the downturn beginning in 1993Q4 is in fact a turning point in the cycle or just a short-term deviation from a longer-term rise. If it is a true turning point, the last peak would be the lowest peak in the history of the series since 1966. It seems more likely that this downturn is temporary. Thus, for the purpose of this example we will assume that the cycle will resume its upward movement, as illustrated by the dashed line in the following graph.

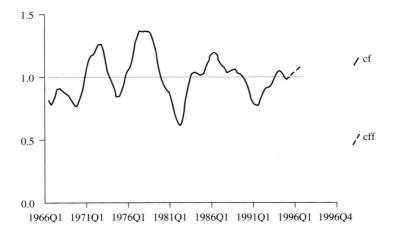

We now have all the components necessary to make the time-series decomposition forecast. But first we need to combine the historic cycle factor (CF) with the forecast of the cycle factor (CFF) into one single series. One way to do this is as follows:

```
> USE  95Q3  96Q4
> CFF = (Enter your six estimates of CFF each separated by a space.)
> REVISE CF = CFF
```

Making the Time-Series Decomposition Forecast.   We will name the time-series decomposition forecast of new home sales NHSFTSD. To calculate this value, we want to multiply the trend (NHSCMAT) by the seasonal indices (SI) and by the cycle factor (CF). Be sure to have the **USE** period set to the historical period plus the forecast horizon (1966Q1 through 1996Q4 in our example).

```
> USE  66Q1  96Q4
> NHSFTSD = NHSCMAT*SI*CF
```

To obtain a time-series plot of your forecast in comparison to the actual, including the 1996 holdout period, use the graph tool and select both NHS and NHSFTSD. You will get the following graph:

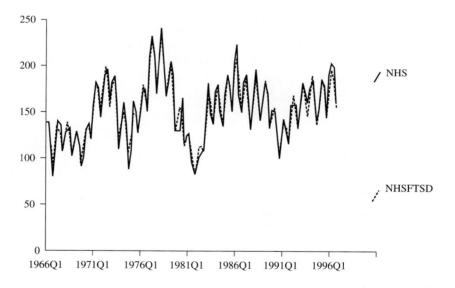

To better illustrate the comparison between NHS and NHSFTSD in recent years, these two series are graphed below for 1991Q1 through 1996Q4.

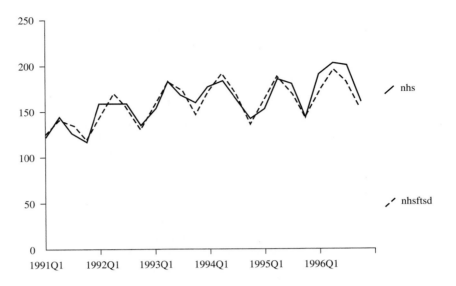

Checking the Fit and Accuracy of the Model Using RMSEs.   The series NHS contains the actual new home sales for 1966Q1 through 1996Q4, and NHSFTSD is the time-series decomposition forecast values of new home sales for the same period. Now you can determine the RMSEs in the historic period and the forecast (holdout) period as follows:

```
> USE 66Q1   95Q4
> ACTFIT  NHS   NHSFTSD
> USE  96Q1   96Q4
> ACTFIT  NHS    NHSFTSD
```

The results are:

Using 1966Q1–1995Q4: Root-mean-squared error = 8.16191 (historic period)

Using 1996Q1–1996Q4: Root-mean-squared error = 14.2458 (forecast, or holdout, period)

The RMSE for the holdout period is about 7.5 percent of the mean of the actual values in that period (1996Q1–1996Q4).

Suggested Readings

Austin, John S. "How to Use and Interpret Seasonal Factors." *Business Economics* 16, no. 4 (September 1981), pp. 40–42.

Espasa, Antoni; and Daniel Pena. "The Decomposition of Forecast in Seasonal ARIMA Models." *Journal of Forecasting* 14, no. 7 (December 1995), pp. 565–83.

Hurwood, David L.; Elliott S. Grossman; and Earl L. Bailey. *Sales Forecasting*. The Conference Board,

1978. Chapter 5, "Traditional Time-Series Analysis," contains five company examples as well as a discussion of decomposition methods.

Layton, Allan P. "Dating and Predicting Phase Changes in the U.S. Business Cycle." *International Journal of Forecasting* 12, no. 3 (September 1996), pp. 417–28.

Majani, Bernard E. "Decomposition Methods for Medium-Term Planning and Budgeting." In *The*

Handbook of Forecasting. Eds. Spyros Makridakis and Steven C. Wheelwright. New York: John Wiley & Sons, 1982, pp. 153–72.

Makridakis, Spyros; Steven C. Wheelwright; and Victor E. McGee. *Forecasting Methods and Applications.* 2nd ed. New York: John Wiley & Sons, 1983, pp. 130–78.

Sommers, Albert T. *The U.S. Economy Demystified.* Rev. ed. Lexington, Mass.: Lexington Books, 1988.

Veloce, William. "An Evaluation of the Leading Indicators for the Canadian Economy Using Time Series Analysis." *International Journal of Forecasting* 12, no. 3 (September 1996), pp. 403–16.

Zellner, Arnold, ed. *Seasonal Analysis of Economic Time Series.* U.S. Department of Commerce, Bureau of the Census, 1978.

Exercises

1. Using your own words, write a description of each of the four components of the classical time-series decomposition technique. Avoid using mathematical relationships and technical jargon as much as possible so that your explanations can be understood by almost anyone.

2. Define each of the components of the classical time-series decomposition method. Explain how the trend, seasonal, and cyclical components are determined.

3. Suppose that sales of a household appliance are reported to be 13,000 units during the first quarter of the year. The seasonal index for the first quarter is 1.24. Use this information to make a forecast of sales for the entire year. Actual sales for the year were 42,000 units. Calculate your percentage error for the year. What percentage error would result if you forecast sales for the year by simply multiplying the 13,000 units for the first quarter by 4?

4. In a time-series decomposition of sales (in millions of units), the following trend has been estimated:

$$CMAT = 4.7 + 0.37(T)$$

The seasonal indexes have been found to be:

Quarter	Seasonal Index
1	1.24
2	1.01
3	0.76
4	0.99

For the coming year the time index and cycle factors are:

Quarter	T	CF
1	21	1.01
2	22	1.04
3	23	1.06
4	24	1.04

a. From this information prepare a forecast for each quarter of the coming year.

b. Actual sales for the year you forecast in part (*a*) were 17.2, 13.2, 10.8, and 14.2 for quarters 1, 2, 3, and 4, respectively. Use these actual sales figures along with your forecasts to calculate the root-mean-squared error for the forecast period.

5. A tanning parlor located in a major shopping center near a large New England city has the following history of customers over the last four years (data are in hundreds of customers):

(c6p5)

Year	Quarter			
	Q1	Q2	Q3	Q4
1	3.5	2.9	2.0	3.2
2	4.1	3.4	2.9	3.6
3	5.2	4.5	3.1	4.5
4	6.1	5.0	4.4	6.0
Yearly totals	18.9	15.8	12.4	17.3

a. Construct a table in which you show the actual data (given in the table), the centered moving average, the centered moving-average trend, the seasonal factors, and the cycle factors for every quarter for which they can be calculated in years 1 through 4.

b. Determine the seasonal index for each quarter.

c. Do the best you can to project the cycle factor through year 5.

d. Make a forecast for each quarter of year 5.

e. The actual numbers of customers served per quarter in year 5 was 6.8, 5.1, 4.7, and 6.5 for quarters 1 through 4, respectively. Calculate the RMSE for year 5.

f. Prepare a time-series plot of the actual data, the centered moving averages, the long-term trend, and the values predicted by your model for years 1 through 5 (where data are available).

6. Barbara Lynch, the product manager for a line of skiwear produced by HeathCo Industries, has been working on developing sales forecasts for the skiwear that is sold under the Northern Slopes and Jacque Monri brands. She has had various regression-based forecasting models developed (see Exercises 7 and 8 in Chapter 4 and Exercises 6 and 7 in Chapter 5). Quarterly sales for the first quarter of 1988 through the fourth quarter of 1997 are as follows:

(c6p6)

	Sales			
Year	*Q1*	*Q2*	*Q3*	*Q4*
1988	72,962	81,921	97,729	142,161
1989	145,592	117,129	114,159	151,402
1990	153,907	100,144	123,242	128,497
1991	176,076	180,440	162,665	220,818
1992	202,415	211,780	163,710	200,135
1993	174,200	182,556	198,990	243,700
1994	253,142	218,755	225,422	253,653
1995	257,156	202,568	224,482	229,879
1996	289,321	266,095	262,938	322,052
1997	313,769	315,011	264,939	301,479

a. Prepare a time-series plot of the data and, on the basis of what you see in the plot, write a brief paragraph in which you explain what patterns you think are present in the sales series.

b. Smooth out seasonal influences and irregular movements by calculating the centered moving averages. Add the centered moving averages to the original data you plotted in part (a). Has the process of calculating centered moving averages been effective in smoothing out the seasonal and irregular fluctuations in the data? Explain.

c. Determine the degree of seasonality by calculating seasonal indexes for each quarter of the year. Do this by finding the normalized average of the seasonal factors for each quarter, where the seasonal factors are actual sales divided by the centered moving average for each period. If you worked Exercise 7 in Chapter 5, explain how these seasonal indexes compare with the seasonality identified by the regression model.

d. Determine the long-term trend in the sales data by regressing the centered moving average on time, where $T = 1$ for 1988Q1. That is, estimate the values for b_0 and b_1 for the following model:

$$\text{CMAT} = b_0 + b_1(T)$$

Plot this equation, called the *centered moving-average trend* (CMAT), along with the raw data and the CMA on the same plot developed in part (a).

e. Find the cycle factor (CF) for each quarter by dividing the CMA by the CMAT. Plot the cycle factors on a new graph and project (CF) forward through 1998Q4.

f. Develop a forecast for Ms. Lynch for the four quarters of 1998 by calculating the product of the trend, the seasonal index, and the cycle factor. Given that actual sales were 334,271, 328,982, 317,921, and 350,118 for quarters 1 through 4, respectively, calculate the RMSE for this model based only on the 1998 forecast period.

g. If you have done Exercises 7 and 8 in Chapter 4 and Exercises 6 and 7 in Chapter 5, write a comparison of your findings.

7. Mr. Carl Lipke is the marketing VP for a propane gas distributor. He would like to have a forecast of sales on a quarterly basis, and he has asked you to prepare a time-series decomposition model. The data for 1985Q1 through 1996Q4 follow:

(c6p7) **Propane Gas Sales in Millions of Pounds**

Year	Q1	Q2	Q3	Q4
1985	6.44	4.85	4.67	5.77
1986	6.22	4.25	4.14	5.34
1987	6.07	4.36	4.07	5.84
1988	6.06	4.24	4.20	5.43
1989	6.56	4.25	3.92	5.26
1990	6.65	4.42	4.09	5.51
1991	6.61	4.25	3.98	5.55
1992	6.24	4.34	4.00	5.36
1993	6.40	3.84	3.53	4.74
1994	5.37	3.57	3.32	5.09
1995	6.03	3.98	3.57	4.92
1996	6.16	3.79	3.39	4.51

a. To help Mr. Lipke see how propane gas sales have varied over the 12-year period, prepare a time-series plot of the raw data and the deseasonalized data (i.e., the centered moving averages).

b. Prepare seasonal indexes for quarters 1 through 4 based on the normalized averages of the seasonal factors (the seasonal factors equal actual values divided by the corresponding centered moving averages). Write a short paragraph in which you explain to Carl Lipke exactly what these indexes mean.

c. Estimate the long-term trend for the sales series by using a bivariate linear regression of the centered moving average as a function of time, where TIME = 1 for 1985Q1.

d. Develop cycle factors for the sales data, and plot them on a graph that extends from 85Q1 through 96Q4. Analyze the plot of the cycle factor and project it through the four quarters of 1997. Write a brief explanation of why you forecast the cycle factor as you did.

e. Plot the values of sales that would be estimated by this model along with the original data. Does the model appear to work well for this data series?

f. Prepare a forecast for 1997 quarters 1 through 4 from your time-series decomposition model. Write your forecast values in the accompanying table. Given the actual values shown in the table, calculate the root-mean-squared error (RMSE) for 1997.

Period	Sales Forecast	Actual	Squared Error
1997Q1		5.39	
1997Q2		3.56	
1997Q3		3.03	
1997Q4		4.03	

Sum of squared errors =
Mean-squared error =
Root-mean-squared error =

8. Kim Brite and Larry Short have developed a series of exclusive mobile-home parks in which each unit occupies a site at least 100 × 150 feet. Each site is well landscaped to provide privacy and a pleasant living environment. Kim and Larry are considering opening more such facilities, but to help manage their cash flow they need better forecasts of mobile-home shipments (MHS), since MHS appears to influence their vacancy rates and the rate at which they can fill newly opened parks. They have 16 years of data on mobile-home shipments, beginning with the first quarter of 1980 and ending with the last quarter of 1995, as shown:

(c6p8) **Mobile Home Shipments (MHS) (000s)**

Year	Q1	Q2	Q3	Q4
1980	56.6	49.1	58.5	57.5
1981	54.9	70.1	65.8	50.2
1982	53.3	67.9	63.1	55.3
1983	63.3	81.5	81.7	69.2
1984	67.8	82.7	79.0	66.2
1985	62.3	79.3	76.5	65.5
1986	58.1	66.8	63.4	56.1
1987	51.9	62.8	64.7	53.5
1988	47.0	60.5	59.2	51.6
1989	48.1	55.1	50.3	44.5
1990	43.3	51.7	50.5	42.6
1991	35.4	47.4	47.2	40.9
1992	43.0	52.8	57.0	57.6
1993	56.4	64.3	67.1	66.4
1994	69.1	78.7	78.7	77.5
1995	79.2	86.8	87.6	86.4

Assuming that Kim Brite and Larry Short have hired you as a forecasting consultant:

a. Provide a time-series plot of the actual MHS data along with the deseasonalized data. Write a brief memo in which you report the nature and extent of the seasonality in the data. Include seasonal indexes in your report.

b. Develop a long-term linear trend for the data, based on the centered moving averages. Let time equal 1 for 1980Q1 in your trend equation. On the basis of this trend, does the future look promising for Brite and Short?

c. One of the things Ms. Brite and Mr. Short are concerned about is the degree to which MHS is subject to cyclical fluctuations. Calculate cycle factors and plot them in a time-series graph, including projections of the cycle factor through 1996. In evaluating the cycle factor, see whether interest rates appear to have any effect on the cyclical pattern. The prime rate for 1980Q1 through 1995Q4 is provided in the following table, should you wish to use this measure of interest rates.

(c6p8) **Prime Interest Rate**

Year	Q1	Q2	Q3	Q4
1980	16.4	16.3	11.6	16.7
1981	19.2	18.9	20.3	17.0
1982	16.3	16.5	14.7	12.0
1983	10.9	10.5	10.8	11.0
1984	11.1	12.3	13.0	11.8
1985	10.5	10.2	9.5	9.5
1986	9.4	8.6	7.9	7.5
1987	7.5	8.0	8.4	8.9
1988	8.6	8.8	9.7	10.2
1989	11.0	11.4	10.7	10.5
1990	10.0	10.0	10.0	10.0
1991	9.2	8.7	8.4	7.6
1992	6.5	6.5	6.0	6.0
1993	6.0	6.0	6.0	6.0
1994	6.0	6.9	7.5	8.1
1995	8.8	9.0	8.8	8.7

d. Demonstrate for Ms. Brite and Mr. Short how well your time-series decomposition model follows the historical pattern in the data by plotting the actual values of MHS and those estimated by the model in a single time-series plot.

e. Prepare a forecast for 1996 and calculate the root-mean-squared error (RMSE), given the actual values of MHS for 1996 shown:

	MHS		
Period	*Forecast*	*Actual*	*Squared Error*
1996Q1		35.4	
1996Q2		47.3	
1996Q3		47.2	
1996Q4		40.9	

Sum of squared errors =
Mean-squared error =
Root-mean-squared error =

9. The Bechtal Tire Company (BTC) is a supplier of automotive tires for U.S. car companies. BTC has hired you to analyze their sales. Data from the first quarter of 1976 through the fourth quarter of 1997 are given in the following table (in thousands of units):

(c6p9) **BTC Sales of Tires**

Year	Q1	Q2	Q3	Q4
1976	2,029	2,347	1,926	2,162
1977	1,783	2,190	1,656	1,491
1978	1,974	2,276	1,987	2,425
1979	2,064	2,517	2,147	2,524
1980	2,451	2,718	2,229	2,190
1981	1,752	2,138	1,927	1,546
1982	1,506	1,709	1,734	2,002
1983	2,025	2,376	1,970	2,122
1984	2,128	2,538	2,081	2,223
1985	2,027	2,727	2,140	2,270
1986	2,155	2,231	1,971	1,875
1987	1,850	1,551	1,515	1,666
1988	1,733	1,576	1,618	1,282
1989	1,401	1,535	1,327	1,494
1990	1,456	1,876	1,646	1,813
1991	1,994	2,251	1,855	1,852
1992	2,042	2,273	2,218	1,672
1993	1,898	2,242	2,247	1,827
1994	1,669	1,973	1,878	1,561
1995	1,914	2,076	1,787	1,763
1996	1,707	2,019	1,898	1,454
1997	1,706	1,878	1,752	1,560

a. Write a report to Bechtal Tire Company in which you explain what a time-series decomposition analysis shows about their tire sales. Include in your discussion seasonal, cyclical, and trend components. Show the raw data, the deseasonalized data, and the long-term trend on one time-series plot. Also provide a plot of the cycle factor with a projection through 1998.

b. In the last section of your report, show a time-series graph with the actual data and the values that the time-series decomposition model would predict for each quarter from 1976Q3 through 1997Q4, along with a forecast for 1998. If actual sales for 1998 were Q1 = 1,445.1, Q2 = 1,683.8, Q3 = 1,586.6, and Q4 = 1,421.3, what RMSE would result from your 1998 forecast?

10. A national supplier of jet fuel is interested in forecasting their sales. These sales data are shown for the period from the first quarter of 1980 to the fourth quarter of 1995 (data in billions of gallons):

(c6p10) **Jet Fuel Sales (Billions of Gallons)**

Year	Q1	Q2	Q3	Q4
1980	23.86	23.97	29.23	24.32
1981	23.89	26.84	29.36	26.30
1982	27.09	29.42	32.43	29.17
1983	28.86	32.10	34.82	30.48
1984	30.87	33.75	35.11	30.00
1985	29.95	32.63	36.78	32.34
1986	33.63	36.97	39.71	34.96
1987	35.78	38.59	42.96	39.27
1988	40.77	45.31	51.45	45.13
1989	48.13	50.35	56.73	48.83
1990	49.02	50.73	53.74	46.38
1991	46.32	51.65	52.73	47.45
1992	49.01	53.99	55.63	50.04
1993	54.77	56.89	57.82	53.30
1994	54.69	60.88	63.59	59.46
1995	61.59	68.75	71.33	64.88

a. Convert these data to a time-series plot. What, if any, seasonal pattern do you see in the plot? Explain.

b. Deseasonalize the data by calculating the centered moving average, and plot the deseasonal-

ized data on the same graph used in part (*a*). Calculate the seasonal index for each quarter, and write a short explanation of why the results make sense.

c. Develop a trend for the data based on the centered moving averages, and plot that trend line on the graph developed in part (*a*). Compare the deseasonalized data (CMA) and the trend line. Does there appear to be a cyclical pattern to the data? Explain.

d. Calculate the cycle factors and plot them on a separate time-series graph. Project the cycle factor ahead one year.

e. For the historical period, plot the values estimated by the time-series decomposition model along with the original data.

f. Make a forecast of sales for the four quarters of 1996 and, given the following actual data for that year, calculate the root-mean-squared error:

	Jet Fuel Sales		
Period	*Forecast*	*Actual*	*Squared Error*
1		64.81	
2		75.52	
3		81.93	
4		72.89	

Sum of squared errors =
Mean-squared error =
Root-mean-squared error =

g. Develop two other forecasts of jet fuel sales with:
1. An exponential smoothing method; and
2. A regression model using just time and quarterly dummy variables.

Compare the RMSE for the three models you have developed and comment on what you like or dislike about each of the three models for this application.

11. The following table contains quarterly data on foreign car sales (FCS) in the United States for 1975Q1 through 1995Q4:

Foreign Car Sales (FCS)

Year	Q1	Q2	Q3	Q4
1975	407.6	431.5	441.6	306.2
1976	328.7	381.3	422.6	369.4
1977	456.3	624.3	557.5	436.7
1978	485.0	564.3	538.3	412.5
1979	555.0	682.7	581.3	509.7
1980	662.7	591.1	616.9	529.7
1981	641.2	632.7	576.6	475.0
1982	542.8	558.9	581.7	537.8
1983	588.1	626.5	590.9	580.1
1984	589.2	643.2	593.9	612.2
1985	586.1	699.4	734.4	753.8
1986	691.6	793.4	864.9	840.8
1987	653.9	754.8	883.6	797.7
1988	722.2	788.6	769.9	725.5
1989	629.3	738.6	732.0	598.8
1990	603.9	653.6	606.1	539.7
1991	461.3	548.0	548.4	480.4
1992	476.6	528.2	480.4	452.6
1993	407.2	498.5	474.3	403.7
1994	418.6	470.2	470.7	375.7
1995	371.1	425.5	397.3	313.5

a. Prepare a time-series plot of foreign car sales from 1975Q1 through 1995Q4.
b. On the basis of these data, calculate the centered moving average (FCSCMA) and the centered moving-average trend (FCSCMAT). Plot FCS, FCSCMA, and FCSCMAT on a single time-series plot.
c. Calculate a seasonal factor (SF = FCS/FCSCMA) for each quarter from 1975Q3 through 1995Q2. Calculate the seasonal indexes (SI) for this series. (c6p11)
d. Determine the cycle factors CF = FCSCMA/FCSCMAT for the period from 1975Q3 through 1995Q2 and plot them along with a horizontal line at 1.
e. Evaluate the cycle factor (CF) and project it forward from 1995Q3 through 1996Q4.
f. Prepare a time-series decomposition forecast of FCS (FCSFTSD = FCSCMAT × SI × CF).
g. Calculate the historic RMSE as a measure of fit; then calculate the RMSE for the 1996Q1– 1996Q4 forecast horizon as a measure of accuracy, given that the actual values of FCS for 1996

were:

1996Q1	301.1
1996Q2	336.7
1996Q3	341.8
1996Q4	293.5

h. Prepare a Winters exponential smoothing forecast of FCS using data from 1975Q1 through 1995Q4 as the basis for a forecast of 1996Q1– 1996Q4. Compare these results in terms of fit and accuracy with the results from the time-series decomposition forecast.

12. a. Use the following data on retail truck sales (TS) to prepare a time-series decomposition forecast of DTS for 1996Q1–1996Q4:

Truck Sales

Year	Q1	Q2	Q3	Q4
1975	478124	612719	613902	646312
1976	712170	821845	784493	725615
1977	848323	934438	817396	885389
1978	894359	1126400	946504	947141
1979	921967	838559	764035	711234
1980	634427	568758	532143	496188
1981	499968	559593	495349	417391
1982	597296	605965	516173	528238
1983	582202	722965	663528	740694
1984	852774	979159	828721	877681
1985	993431	1047300	982917	959867
1986	901757	1095580	1098730	932177
1987	935125	1145360	1071020	1022050
1988	1139130	1252900	1116670	1099110
1989	1080950	1222890	1195190	983803
1990	1085270	1172960	1081380	921370
1991	845992	1044490	1028720	922831
1992	957733	1240610	1171230	1143440
1993	1145370	1493980	1328300	1350470
1994	1430080	1636760	1456740	1502440
1995	1438960	1661130	1490620	1500120

(c6p12)

b. Evaluate your model in terms of fit and accuracy using RMSE.
c. Plot your forecast values of TS along with the actual values.
d. Compare the results from your time-series decomposition model with those obtained using a Winters exponential smoothing model in terms of both fit and accuracy.

7   ARIMA (BOX-JENKINS) TYPE FORECASTING MODELS

Introduction

A time series of data is a sequence of numerical observations naturally ordered in time. Some examples would be:

- Hourly temperatures at the entrance to Grand Central Station
- Daily closing price of IBM stock
- Weekly automobile production by the Pontiac Division of General Motors
- Data from an individual firm: sales, profits, inventory, back orders
- An electrocardiogram

When a forecaster examines time-series data, two questions are of paramount importance:

1. Do the data exhibit a discernible pattern?
2. Can this pattern be exploited to make meaningful forecasts?

We have already examined some time-series data by using regression analysis to relate sequences of data to explanatory variables. Sales (as the dependent variable), for instance, might be forecast by using the explanatory (or independent) variables of product price, personal income of potential purchasers, and advertising expenditures by the firm. Such a model is a structural or causal forecasting model that requires the forecaster to know in advance at least some of the determinants of sales. But in many real-world situations, we do not know the determinants of the variable to be forecast, or data on these causal variables are not readily available. It is in just these situations that the ARIMA technique has a decided advantage over standard regression models. ARIMA is also used as a benchmark for other forecasting models; we could use an ARIMA model, for example, as a criterion for our best structural regression model. The acronym ARIMA stands for "Auto-Regressive Integrated Moving Average." Exponential smoothing, which we examined in Chapter 3, is actually just a special case of an ARIMA model.

The Box-Jenkins methodology of using ARIMA models is a technically sophisticated way of forecasting a variable by looking *only* at the past pattern of the time series.

The Box-Jenkins methodology of using ARIMA models is a technically sophisticated way of forecasting a variable by looking *only* at the past pattern of the time series. Box-Jenkins thus ignores information that might be contained in a structural regression model; instead, it uses the most recent observation as a starting value and proceeds to analyze recent forecasting errors to select the most appropriate adjustment for future time periods. Since the adjustment usually compensates for only part of the forecast error, the Box-Jenkins process is best suited to longer-range rather than shorter-range forecasting (although it is used for short-, medium-, and long-range forecasts in actual practice).

The Box-Jenkins methodology of using ARIMA models has some advantages over other time-series methods such as exponential smoothing, time-series decomposition, and simple trend analysis. Box-Jenkins methodology determines a great deal of information from the time series (more so than any other time-series method), and it does so while using a minimum number of parameters. The Box-Jenkins method allows for greater flexibility in the choice of the "correct" model (this, we will see, is called "identification" in Box-Jenkins terminology). Instead of a priori choosing a simple time trend or a specific exponential smoothing method, for example, as the correct model, Box-Jenkins methodology includes a process that allows us to examine a large variety of models in our search for the correct one. This "open-ended" characteristic alone accounts for its appeal to many forecasters.

The Philosophy of Box-Jenkins

Pretend for a moment that a certain time series is generated by a "black box":

$$\text{Black box} \rightarrow \text{Observed time series}$$

In standard regression analysis we attempt to find the causal variables that explain the observed time series; what we take as a given is that the black box process is actually approximated by a linear regression technique:

$$\begin{array}{c}\text{Explanatory}\\\text{variables}\end{array} \rightarrow \begin{array}{c}\text{Black box}\\\text{(approximated}\\\text{by linear}\\\text{regression)}\end{array} \rightarrow \begin{array}{c}\text{Observed}\\\text{time series}\end{array}$$

In the Box-Jenkins methodology, on the other hand, we do not start with any explanatory variables, but rather with the observed time series itself; what we attempt to discern is the "correct" black box that could have produced such a series from some white noise:

$$\text{White noise} \rightarrow \text{Black box} \rightarrow \text{Observed time series}$$

The term *white noise* deserves some explanation. Since we are to use no explanatory variables in the ARIMA process, we assume instead that the series we are observing started as white noise and was transformed by the black box process into the series we are trying to forecast.

White noise is essentially a purely random series of numbers.

White noise is essentially a purely random series of numbers. Some examples of white noise may serve to make its meaning clearer:

1. The winning numbers in the Illinois lottery's "Pick Four" game (where the four winning digits are drawn daily from four separate urns, each with 10 marked balls inside). Would knowledge of the numbers drawn for the past year help you pick a winner? (No, but there are those who actually believe some numbers are "better" than others.)
2. The last digit in the daily closing Dow Jones Industrial Average (or the last digit in the day-to-day change in the average). Would knowing the digit for the last two weeks help you to pick today's final digit?

White noise, then, has two characteristics:

1. There is no relationship between consecutively observed values.
2. Previous values do not help in predicting future values.

White noise is important in explaining the difference between the standard regression process and the Box-Jenkins methodology. The steps required in each method are shown in Table 7–1. In standard regression analysis we move from the explanatory variables (which we choose as a result of some knowledge of the real

---

TABLE 7–1   Comparison of Standard Regression Analysis and Box-Jenkins Methodology

For standard regression analysis:

1. Specify the causal variables.
2. Use a linear (or other) regression model.
3. Estimate the constant and slope coefficients.
4. Examine the summary statistics and try other model specifications.
5. Choose the most desirable model specification (perhaps on the basis of RMSE).

Start here:

Explanatory variables	$\rightarrow$	Black box	$\rightarrow$	Observed time series

For Box-Jenkins methodology:

1. Start with the observed time series.
2. Pass the observed time series through a black box.
3. Examine the time series that results from passage through the black box.
4. If the black box is correctly specified, only white noise should remain.
5. If the remaining series is not white noise, try another black box.

Start here:

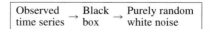

Observed time series	$\rightarrow$	Black box	$\rightarrow$	Purely random white noise

world) to applying the linear regression technique in order to estimate the constant and slope coefficients of the model. We then use the regression equation to actually make up forecasts about future values of the time series. If our regression model does not have good summary statistics (e.g., t-statistics, R^2), we may change some or all of the explanatory variables and try again until we are satisfied with the summary statistics (including the root-mean-squared error).

In Box-Jenkins methodology, however, we start instead with the observed time series itself (with no explanatory variables) and examine its characteristics in order to get an idea of what black box we might use to transform the series into white noise. We begin by trying the most likely of many black boxes, and if we get white noise, we assume that this is the "correct" model to use in generating forecasts of the series. If we try a particular black box and do not wind up with white noise, we try other likely black boxes until we finally wind up with white noise. The test to see whether we have succeeded in winding up with only white noise serves the same purpose as the set of summary statistics we generate with standard regression models.

When choosing the "correct" black box, there are really only three basic types of models for us to examine; there are, however, many variations within each of these three types. The three types of models are: (1) moving-average (MA) models, (2) autoregressive (AR) models, and (3) mixed autoregressive–moving-average models (called ARMA models). We will examine each of these three models in turn in the following sections.

Moving-Average Models

A moving-average (MA) model is simply one that predicts Y_t as a function of the past forecast errors in predicting Y_t. Consider e_t to be a white noise series; a moving-average model would then take the following form:

$$Y_t = e_t + W_1 e_{t-1} + W_2 e_{t-2} + \cdots + W_q e_{t-q}$$

where:

$$e_t = \text{The value at time } t \text{ of the white noise series}$$
$$Y_t = \text{The generated moving-average time series}$$
$$W_{1,2,\cdots,q} = \text{The coefficients (or "weights")}$$
$$e_{t-1,t-2,\cdots,t-q} = \text{Previous values of the white noise series}$$

The name *moving-average* is actually not very descriptive of this type of model; we would do better to call it a *weighted-average model,* since it is similar to exponential smoothing. An example of a moving-average model is constructed in Table 7–2. Table 7–2 is an abbreviated listing of the entire 200-observation data set. The complete data set is included on the CD accompanying this book.

In the first column of Table 7–2 we show a white noise series generated by randomly selecting numbers between 0 and 1. The moving-average series was constructed from the white noise series by using the following equation:

$$Y_t = e_t + W_1 e_{t-1}$$

(c7t2) **TABLE 7–2 Box-Jenkins Example Data Series**

	White Noise	MA1	AR1	AR2	ARIMA111
1	0.256454	0.399867	0.240000	0.160000	0.160000
2	0.230240	0.409758	0.350240	0.040000	0.569758
3	0.675186	0.836354	0.850306	0.735186	1.40611
4	0.0475159	0.520146	0.472669	0.570146	1.92626
5	0.716827	0.750089	0.953162	1.26297	2.67635
6	0.854614	1.35639	1.33120	1.85272	4.03274
7	0.557983	1.15621	1.22358	2.10748	5.18895
8	0.0390320	0.429620	0.650822	1.88481	5.61857
9	0.184616	0.211938	0.510027	1.92548	5.83051
10	0.0167999	0.146031	0.271814	1.74160	5.97654
11	0.596069	0.607829	0.731976	2.20029	6.58437
12	0.235672	0.652921	0.601660	2.12419	7.23729
13	0.0724487	0.237419	0.373279	1.99944	7.47471
14	0.858917	0.909631	1.04556	2.68336	8.38434
15	0.830856	1.43210	1.35363	3.10910	9.81644
16	0.215927	0.797527	0.892744	2.92897	10.6140
17	0.223007	0.374156	0.669379	2.89511	10.9881
18	0.254166	0.410271	0.588855	2.86653	11.3984
19	0.764038	0.941954	1.05847	3.34963	12.3403
20	0.286438	0.821265	0.815671	3.20449	13.1616
191	0.323975	0.782538	0.820131	4.36400	150.720
192	0.162109	0.388892	0.572175	4.12794	151.109
193	0.702011	0.815488	0.988099	4.46437	151.924
194	0.854660	1.34607	1.34871	4.80531	153.270
195	0.480850	1.07911	1.15520	4.73744	154.349
196	0.843475	1.18007	1.42108	5.12074	155.530
197	0.408600	0.999033	1.11914	4.94061	156.529
198	0.581711	0.867731	1.14128	5.06429	157.396
199	0.975937	1.38313	1.54658	5.50906	158.779
200	0.683960	1.36712	1.45725	5.55316	160.147

where:

Y_t = The series generated, which appears in column 2
e_t = The white noise series appearing in column 1
W_1 = A constant (equal here to 0.7)
e_{t-1} = The white noise value lagged one period

This series [called an MA(1) series because it contains one lag of the white noise term] was constructed with known characteristics. Imagine how we might decide that a time series of unknown origin that we want to forecast could be similar to this known series. How could we go about examining this time series to determine whether it is an MA(1) series like that in column 2 of Table 7–2? We can get an insight into the answer by examining two characteristics of the time series we have

First, we examine the autocorrelation (or "serial correlation") among successive values of the time series; this will be the first of two key tools in determining which model (or black box) is the appropriate representation of any given time series.

purposely constructed to be an MA(1) series in Table 7–2. These characteristics are the autocorrelations and the partial autocorrelations.

First, we examine the autocorrelation (or "serial correlation") among successive values of the time series; this will be the first of two key tools in determining which model (or black box) is the appropriate representation of any given time series. As described in Chapter 2, autocorrelation is the concept that the association between values of the same variable at different time periods is nonrandom—that is, that if autocorrelation does exist in a time series, there is correlation or mutual dependence between the values of the time series at different time periods.

As a simple example of autocorrelation, consider the data in Table 7–3. The first column could represent sales of an item during successive periods; the second column is the first column lagged one period; the third column is the first column lagged two periods. We can now calculate the simple correlation coefficient between the numbers in the first column and the numbers in the second column, treating each column as if it were a separate variable. Remember that the correlation coefficient will always vary between +1 and −1. If it is +1, it indicates that there is a perfect positive correlation between the two columns—that is, as one increases, so does the other. If the correlation coefficient is −1, it indicates a perfect negative correlation—that is, as one goes up, the other goes down. The closer the number is to +1, the more positively correlated the columns; the closer the number is to −1, the more negatively correlated the columns.

Here the correlation between the first and second columns is +0.867; the correlation between the first and third columns is +0.898. These values indicate the extent to which the original series values are correlated with themselves, lagged one and two periods (called *auto*correlation since the second and third columns of our table are not variables separate from column 1, but are actually the same variable at different periods).

Apparently, autocorrelation exists in this variable for both one and two lags, and the autocorrelation coefficients are approximately equal. These autocorrelations

(c7t3)

TABLE 7–3   A Simple Example of Autocorrelation

Original Variable	One Time Lag	Two Time Lags
121	—	—
123	121	—
134	123	121
133	134	123
151	133	134
141	151	133
176	141	151
187	176	141
183	187	176
214	183	187

Correlation between original variable and one time lag = +0.867.
Correlation between original variable and two time lags = +0.898.

provide us with the first important tool for identifying the correct model; if the original data in Table 7–3 had been completely random white noise (ours were not), the correlation among lagged values (one, two, or more lags) would have been approximately equal to zero, given a large enough data set. We will find that the pattern of the autocorrelations will help us identify a series that behaves as a moving-average model.

The partial autocorrelation coefficient is the second tool we will use to help identify the relationship between the current values and past values of the original time series. Partial autocorrelation coefficients measure the degree of association between Y_t and Y_{t-k} *when all the other time lags on Y are held constant.* The calculation of the partial autocorrelation terms is beyond the scope of this text, but they are calculated by SORITEC and most other statistical packages that deal with time-series analysis. It is possible, however, to indicate how these coefficients are calculated without presenting the rather lengthy derivation.

The partial autocorrelation coefficient is defined in terms of the last autoregressive (AR) term of an AR-type model with m lags. Partial autocorrelations are calculated when we are unsure of the correct order of the autoregressive process to fit the time series. Consider the AR(m) model (which will be explained in more detail in the section "Autoregressive Models") represented in the following equations:

$$Y_t = A_1 Y_{t-1} + e_t$$
$$Y_t = A_1 Y_{t-1} + A_2 Y_{t-2} + e_t$$
$$\vdots$$
$$Y_t = A_1 Y_{t-1} + A_2 Y_{t-2} + \cdots + A_m Y_{t-m} + e_t$$

By solving this system of equations for the $A_1, A_2, \ldots, A_{t-m}$ terms (which are the partial autocorrelation coefficients), we could determine their actual values.

It is most common to view both the autocorrelation coefficients and the partial autocorrelation coefficients in graphic form by constructing a correlogram of the autocorrelation coefficients and a partial correlogram for the partial autocorrelation coefficients; both graphics look very much like the residuals output in the SORITEC program.

Consider the typical MA(1) correlogram and partial correlogram in Figure 7–1. Two distinctive patterns in the autocorrelation and partial autocorrelation functions are characteristic of an MA(1) model. The *a* frame of Figure 7–1 displays the first of these patterns. Note the gradual falling to zero of the partial autocorrelation function and the single spike in the autocorrelation function. In general, if the autocorrelation function abruptly stops at some point, we know the model is of the MA type; the number of spikes (commonly referred to as q) before the abrupt stop tells us the "order" of the MA model. In frame *a* there is only one spike, and so we know the model is likely to be of the MA(1) variety.

Frame *b* represents a variation of this distinctive pattern; here the single spike (now negative) still appears in the autocorrelation function, but the partial autocorrelation function shows alternating positive and negative values, gradually falling to zero. This also would indicate to us an MA(1)-type model.

The partial autocorrelation coefficient is the second tool we will use to help identify the relationship between the current values and past values of the original time series.

FIGURE 7–1

Examples of Theoretical Autocorrelation and Partial Autocorrelation Plots for MA(1) and MA(2) Models

Autocorrelation Function   Partial Autocorrelation Function

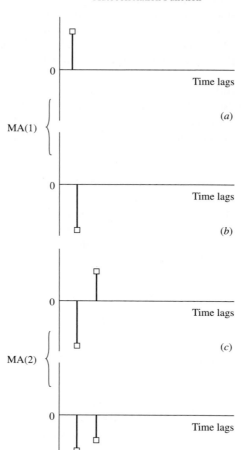

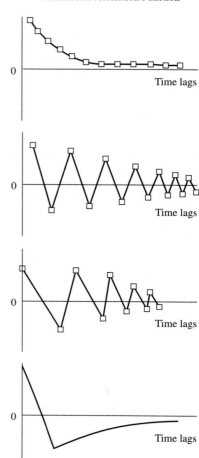

In any given data there may be more than one significant moving-average term; if there were two significant moving-average terms, for instance, we could find either of the patterns in frames *c* and *d*. Both of these situations are characteristic of an MA(2) model; both frames show two distinct spikes in the autocorrelation function while the partial autocorrelation function gradually slides to zero, either monotonically decreasing or alternating between positive and negative values.

We are now ready to examine the autocorrelation and partial autocorrelation functions for the MA(1) series in column 2 of Table 7–2. The correlograms for each are shown for the first 24 lags in Table 7–4. If we had not previously known that this was an MA(1) series, we should have been able to deduce this from the characteristic patterns shown in Table 7–4: note that the autocorrelation function has only one spike that appears to be significantly different from zero. Also note that the partial autocorrelation function alternates from positive to negative *and* decreases in

(c7t2) **TABLE 7–4 Autocorrelation and Partial Autocorrelation Plots for the MA(1) Series in Table 7–2**

Lag	Auto-covariance	Auto-correlation	Partial Auto-correlation	Std. Err. of Partial Auto-correlation
0	.129851	1.00000	1.00000	0.000000
1	.542185E-01	.417545	.421515	.708881E-01
2	-.135794E-01	-.104577	-.337905	.710669E-01
3	-.343114E-04	-.264238E-03	.272432	.712470E-01
4	.636634E-02	.490282E-01	-.168474	.714286E-01
5	-.524059E-03	-.403586E-02	.109371	.716115E-01
6	-.525653E-02	-.404814E-01	-.120424	.717958E-01
7	-.557553E-02	-.429381E-01	.485062E-01	.719816E-01
8	.401314E-02	.309058E-01	.281939E-01	.721688E-01
9	.444087E-02	.341999E-01	-.256219E-01	.723575E-01
10	-.985669E-02	-.759080E-01	-.839896E-01	.725476E-01
11	-.418902E-02	-.322603E-01	.930016E-01	.727393E-01
12	.575895E-02	.443506E-01	-.573834E-01	.729325E-01
13	.247514E-03	.190615E-02	.291750E-01	.731272E-01
14	-.239745E-02	-.184632E-01	-.177614E-01	.733236E-01
15	.319008E-02	.245673E-01	.556947E-01	.735215E-01
16	.797794E-02	.614394E-01	.242707E-01	.737210E-01
17	.470914E-02	.362659E-01	-.491480E-02	.739221E-01
18	-.508594E-02	-.391676E-01	-.534288E-01	.741249E-01
19	-.572213E-02	-.440670E-01	.213730E-01	.743294E-01
20	-.302769E-02	-.233167E-01	-.731403E-01	.745356E-01
21	-.744002E-02	-.572968E-01	-.222845E-01	.747435E-01
22	.262650E-03	.202271E-02	.876585E-01	.749532E-01
23	.174190E-02	.134146E-01	-.102610	.751646E-01
24	-.272315E-02	-.209715E-01	.750637E-01	.753778E-01.

Note that your results may vary slightly from those printed here.

absolute value as it approaches zero. This pattern is similar to that shown in frame *b* of Figure 7–1 and identifies the time series for us as one of the MA(1) variety. This knowledge of what the autocorrelation and partial autocorrelation functions look like in an MA(1) model will allow us later to use Box-Jenkins methodology to model and forecast any similar time series accurately.

Autoregressive Models

The second of the three classes of models we need to examine is the autoregressive (AR) model. The equation for the autoregressive model is similar to the moving-average model, except that the dependent variable Y_t depends on its own previous values rather than the white noise series or residuals. The autoregressive model is produced from a white noise series by using an equation of the form:

$$Y_t = A_1 Y_{t-1} + A_2 Y_{t-2} + \cdots + A_p Y_{t-p} + e_t$$

(c7t2)   ___TABLE 7–4   The MA(1) Series (*concluded*)___

```
        Plot of Autocorrelation (+) and Partial Autocorrelation (*)

Lag  -1.0                              0.0                            1.0
     |--------------------------------+-----------------------------|
  1  |                                |   [*************+           |
  2  |                     ********+**]     |                       |
  3  |                                |   +*********               |
  4  |                          *****] +  |                         |
  5  |                                |   +***  |                   |
  6  |                                |***+]    |                   |
  7  |                                |  +[**   |                   |
  8  |                                |   [+    |                   |
  9  |                                |  *]+    |                   |
 10  |                                | *+*]    |                   |
 11  |                                |  +[***  |                   |
 12  |                                |  **]+   |                   |
 13  |                                |   +*    |                   |
 14  |                                |   +]    |                   |
 15  |                                |   [+*   |                   |
 16  |                                |   [*+   |                   |
 17  |                                |   [+    |                   |
 18  |                                |  *+]    |                   |
 19  |                                |  +[*    |                   |
 20  |                                |  *+]    |                   |
 21  |                                |  +*]    |                   |
 22  |                                |   +***  |                   |
 23  |                                | ***+    |                   |
 24  |                                |  +[**   |                   |
     |--------------------------------+-----------------------------|
```

where:

$$Y_t = \text{The moving-average time series generated}$$
$$A_1, A_2, \cdots, A_p = \text{Coefficients}$$
$$Y_{t-1}, Y_{t-2}, \cdots, Y_{t-p} = \text{Lagged values of the time series (hence the name \textit{autos})}$$
$$e_t = \text{White noise series}$$

If the model has only the Y_{t-1} term on the right-hand side, it is referred to as an AR(1) model; if it has Y_{t-1} and Y_{t-2} terms, it is an AR(2); and so on. Column 3 of Table 7–2 is an AR(1) series produced by the following equation:

$$Y_t = A_1 Y_{t-1} + e_t$$

where

$$Y_t = \text{The series generated, which appears in column 2}$$
$$e_t = \text{The white noise series appearing in column 1}$$
$$A_1 = \text{A constant (equal here to 0.5)}$$
$$Y_{t-1} = \text{The series lagged one period}$$

(Note: The first number in the column [i.e., 0.24] is chosen arbitrarily.)

Once again, as with the MA(1) model presented in the previous section, the AR(1) series in column 3 is constructed from the white noise series with known characteristics [that is, it is an AR(1) series because we constructed it to be one]. Again, ask the question: How might we decide that another time series, of unknown origin, that we were given to forecast could be similar to this AR(1) series? In other words, how would we go about examining a series to determine whether it is an AR(1)-type series?

We will answer the question by again examining the characteristics of the known series [the AR(1) series in column 3 of Table 7–2]. Once again we first examine the autocorrelation function of the series and then examine the partial autocorrelation function of the series. We are looking for distinctive patterns in each of these functions that will indicate that any time series under examination is an AR(1)-type series.

The typical correlograms and partial correlograms for an AR(1) series are shown in frames *a* and *b* of Figure 7–2. Either of two patterns is distinctive for an AR(1)

FIGURE 7–2

Examples of Theoretical Autocorrelation and Partial Autocorrelation Plots of AR(1) and AR(2) Models

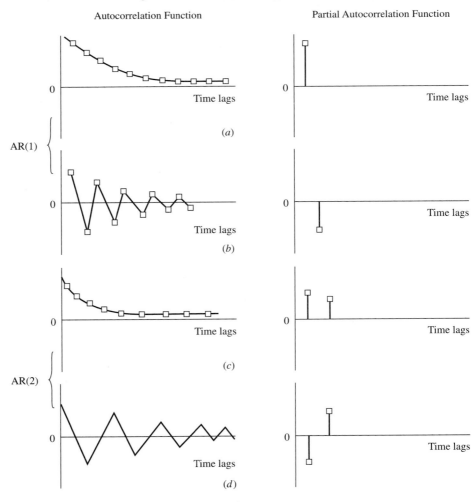

(c7t2)   **TABLE 7–5**   **Autocorrelation and Partial Autocorrelation Plots for the AR(1) Series in Table 7–2**

Lag	Auto-covariance	Auto-correlation	Partial Auto-correlation	Std. Err. of Partial Auto-correlation
0	.113009	1.00000	1.00000	0.000000
1	.536882E-01	.475078	.483297	.708881E-01
2	.167068E-01	.147836	-.932125E-01	.710669E-01
3	.135955E-01	.120304	.117125	.712470E-01
4	.744831E-02	.659089E-01	-.300365E-01	.714286E-01
5	.719179E-03	.636391E-02	-.168899E-01	.716115E-01
6	-.186763E-02	-.165264E-01	-.217102E-01	.717958E-01
7	-.238697E-02	-.211219E-01	-.674433E-02	.719816E-01
8	.197890E-02	.175109E-01	.521990E-01	.721688E-01
9	.459300E-02	.406428E-01	.232898E-01	.723575E-01
10	-.634984E-02	-.561887E-01	-.107391	.725476E-01
11	-.963362E-03	-.852464E-02	.893408E-01	.727393E-01
12	.381008E-02	.337148E-01	-.269253E-02	.729325E-01
13	-.289091E-03	-.255812E-02	-.105092E-01	.731272E-01
14	-.472363E-03	-.417987E-02	.109537E-01	.733236E-01
15	.382253E-02	.338250E-01	.309884E-01	.735215E-01
16	.682703E-02	.604113E-01	.373457E-01	.737210E-01
17	.412714E-02	.365204E-01	-.142391E-01	.739221E-01
18	-.254154E-02	-.224897E-01	-.468830E-01	.741249E-01
19	-.513539E-02	-.454423E-01	-.162182E-01	.743294E-01
20	-.820002E-02	-.725607E-01	.212161E-01	.745356E-01
21	-.663416E-02	-.587046E-01	-.817149E-01	.747435E-01
22	.204159E-03	.180657E-02	.122802	.749532E-01
23	.699044E-03	.618573E-02	-.614686E-01	.751646E-01
24	-.178466E-02	-.157922E-01	-.403011E-03	.753778E-01

model. In frame *a* the autocorrelation function falls monotonically to zero while the partial autocorrelation function shows a single spike; note that this is the exact opposite of the pattern exhibited by an MA(1) time series. In general, if the partial autocorrelation function abruptly stops at some point, the model is of the AR type; the number of spikes (*p*) before the abrupt stop is equal to the "order" of the AR model. In frame *a* there is just one spike in the partial autocorrelation function, and so the model is of the AR(1) type.

Frame *b* represents the second of two characteristic patterns for an AR(1) model; here the single spike (now negative) still appears in the partial autocorrelation function, but the autocorrelation function tends to zero by alternating between positive and negative values.

As in MA-type models, there may be more than one significant autoregressive term; if this is the case, patterns like those shown in frames *c* and *d* of Figure 7–2 could result. Patterns like those in either frame *c* or *d* would indicate an AR(2)-type model because of the two significant spikes in the partial autocorrelation function.

(c7t2)   **TABLE 7–5   The AR(1) Series (*concluded*)**

```
         Plot of Autocorrelation (+) and Partial Autocorrelation (*)

Lag   -1.0                          0.0                           1.0
      |--------------------------------+----------------------------|
   1  |                              |     [**************+          |
   2  |                              | ***]      +                   |
   3  |                              |    [***+|                      |
   4  |                              |  *] +  |                       |
   5  |                              |  *+    |                       |
   6  |                              |  +]    |                       |
   7  |                              |  +[    |                       |
   8  |                              |   [+*  |                       |
   9  |                              |   [+   |                       |
  10  |                              | *+*]   |                       |
  11  |                              |  +***  |                       |
  12  |                              |  ]+    |                       |
  13  |                              |  +     |                       |
  14  |                              |  +     |                       |
  15  |                              |  [+    |                       |
  16  |                              |  [*+   |                       |
  17  |                              |  [+    |                       |
  18  |                              | *+]    |                       |
  19  |                              |  +]    |                       |
  20  |                              |  +*    |                       |
  21  |                              | *+*]   |                       |
  22  |                              |  +****|                        |
  23  |                              |  **+   |                       |
  24  |                              |  +[    |                       |
      |--------------------------------+----------------------------|
```

Note again that the autocorrelation function in both cases falls to zero, either mono-tonically (as in frame *c*) or alternating between positive and negative values (as in frame *d*).

We should now be able to evaluate the autocorrelation and partial autocorrelation functions for the AR(1) series in column 3 of Table 7–2. Recall that we know that this particular time series was produced from a white noise series by using the equation

$$Y_t = A_1 Y_{t-1} + e_t$$

The correlograms for each are shown for the first 24 lags in Table 7–5. If we had not known that this was an AR(1) series, we should have been able to deduce this from the characteristic patterns in Table 7–5: note that the partial autocorrelation function has only one significant spike (i.e., it has only one spike that appears significantly different from zero, and so the order is $p = 1$). Also note that the auto-correlation function decreases in value, approaching zero. This pattern is similar to that shown in frame *a* of Figure 7–2, and this fact identifies the time series as one of the AR(1) variety.

Mixed Autoregressive and Moving-Average Models

The third and final of the three classes of models that we need examine is really a combination of an AR and an MA model. This third class of general models is called *ARMA*, which stands for *autoregressive–moving-average model.* This model could be produced from a white noise series by introducing the elements we have already seen in both moving-average and autoregressive models:

$$Y_t = A_1 Y_{t-1} + A_2 Y_{t-2} + \cdots$$
$$+ A_p Y_{t-p} + e_t + W_1 e_{t-1}$$
$$+ W_2 e_{t-2} + \cdots + W_q e_{t-q}$$

This equation defines a mixed autoregressive–moving-average model of order *p, q* and is usually written as ARMA(*p, q*). To identify an ARMA model, we again look for characteristic patterns in the autocorrelation and partial autocorrelation functions.

Figure 7–3 shows the characteristic patterns for an ARMA(1, 1) model; note that *any* of the four frames in Figure 7–3 could be patterns that would identify an ARMA(1, 1) model. In Figure 7–3, in each of the frames, both the autocorrelations and partial autocorrelations gradually fall to zero *rather than abruptly stop.* This observation (both functions falling off gradually) is characteristic of any ARMA(*p, q*) model.

To identify the order of the AR and MA terms, we need to count the number of AR and MA terms significantly different from zero. In frame *b*, for instance, there is one spike in the AR process and one spike in the MA process; this would imply an ARMA(1, 1) model. The other patterns exhibited in Figure 7–3 are less easily identified as ARMA(1, 1) processes.

In fact, the particular identification process we have outlined requires some experience to apply in the real world. We have, however, outlined the basic steps to be followed in applying the identification process; skill in actual application requires the consideration of many examples and learning from past mistakes. We have already seen that according to Box-Jenkins methodology, if we are able to identify the type and order of model we are faced with when we are given a time series, then the repetitive pattern in that original time series offers us the method for forecasting it. When we are given a time series in the real world, however, we are not told the type of model that will fit it, and the first task is to figure out which of the infinite variations of the three models (autoregressive, moving-average, or mixed) is the "correct" model for our data.

Many real-world processes, once they have been adjusted for seasonality, can be adequately modeled with the low-order models.

Fortunately, for low-order processes like the ones we have examined so far, the correct specification of the *p* and *q* values is rather simple to make. Many real-world processes, once they have been adjusted for seasonality, can be adequately modeled with the low-order models [e.g., MA(1), MA(2), AR(1), AR(2), ARMA(1, 1)]. If low-order models are not adequate (how to determine whether a model is adequate will be explained in the section "The Box-Jenkins Identification Process"), the selection of the proper *p* and *q* becomes more difficult. As a rule of thumb, however, spikes in the autocorrelation function indicate moving-average terms, and spikes in the partial autocorrelation function indicate autoregressive terms.

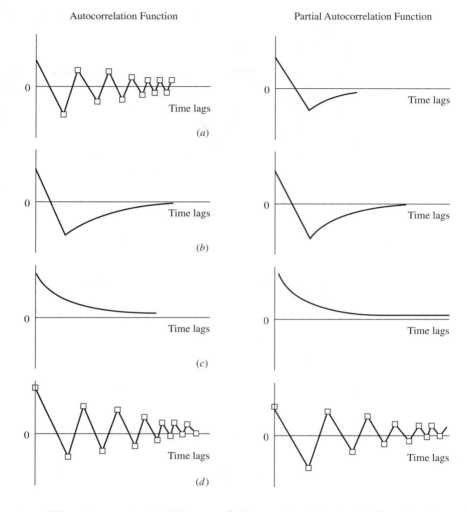

FIGURE 7–3

Examples of Theoretical Autocorrelation and Partial Autocorrelation Plots of ARMA (1, 1) Models

Autocorrelation Function

Partial Autocorrelation Function

When the correct model is not of a low order, you may be forced to determine an adequate p and q by trial and error; it will be possible, you will see, to check your guesses after the parameters of each model have been determined.

Stationarity

A *stationary* time series is one in which two consecutive values in the series depend *only* on the time interval between them and not on time itself.

In general we have been approaching our data as if they were stationary. A *stationary* time series is one in which two consecutive values in the series depend *only* on the time interval between them and *not* on time itself. For all practical purposes this would be consistent with a series whose mean value did *not* change over time. Real-world time series are most often nonstationary; that is, the mean value of the time series changes over time, usually because there is some trend in the series so that the mean value is either rising or falling over time. Nonstationarity can result in other ways (it could be that the variability of the time series changes over time; perhaps the variability becomes exaggerated through time), but the most common cause is simply some trend in the series.

If the series we examine are nonstationary, the autocorrelations are usually significantly different from zero at first and then gradually fall off to zero, or they show a spurious pattern as the lags are increased. Because autocorrelations dominate the pattern of a nonstationary series, it is necessary for us to modify a nonstationary series to make it stationary *before* we try to identify as the "correct" model one of the three models we have so far examined.

There is no single way to remove nonstationarity, but two methods help achieve stationarity most often in actual practice. First, if the nonstationarity is caused by a trend in the series, then differencing the time series may effectively remove the trend. Differencing refers to subtracting the previous observation from each observation in the data set:

$$Y'_t = Y_t - Y_{t-1}$$

where

Y'_t = The first difference of observation at time t
Y_t = Time-series observation at time t
Y_{t-1} = Time-series observation at time period $t - 1$

In some cases the first difference will not remove the trend and it may be necessary to try a higher order of differencing. For example, second-order differences can be found as follows:

$$Y''_t = Y'_t - Y'_{t-1}$$

where:

Y''_t = The second difference
Y'_t = The first difference of observation at time t
Y'_{t-1} = The first difference of observation at time $t - 1$

The second method for removing nonstationarity is used when there is a change in the variability of the series (i.e., when there is a trend in the variance). This method involves taking logs of the original time series, which usually transfers the trend in variance to a trend in the mean; this trend can then be handled by differencing. Other, more sophisticated methods of removing nonstationarity are sometimes used but will not be covered here.

Consider the series in column 6 of Table 7–2. Glancing at the numbers down the column, we can easily see that this series has some trend; the numbers are monotonically increasing throughout the time period. Table 7–6 shows the autocorrelation function for this series. This autocorrelation function is entirely characteristic of series with a trend; that is, it shows dominant autocorrelations for the 24 lags shown, and these autocorrelations only gradually become smaller. Table 7–7 shows the correlograms for the same series *after* first differences have been taken. Apparently, this series contains a trend and could probably easily be modeled with a simple time trend or a low-order ARMA model. Table 7–7 (which shows the data after taking first

(c7t2)

TABLE 7–6 Autocorrelation and Partial Autocorrelation Plots for the ARIMA(1, 1, 1) Series in Table 7–2

Lag	Auto-covariance	Auto-correlation	Partial Auto-correlation	Std. Err. of Partial Auto-correlation
0	2214.66	1.00000	1.00000	0.0000
1	2182.23	.985357	.999971	.708881E-01
2	2149.83	.970729	-.406591	.710669E-01
3	2117.71	.956226	.346934	.712470E-01
4	2085.52	.941691	-.259058	.714286E-01
5	2053.40	.927188	.178227	.716115E-01
6	2021.67	.912861	-.983310E-01	.717958E-01
7	1990.23	.898662	.131931	.719816E-01
8	1958.90	.884517	-.374041E-01	.721688E-01
9	1927.38	.870285	-.182291E-01	.723575E-01
10	1895.47	.855875	.349478E-01	.725476E-01
11	1863.51	.841446	.944669E-01	.727393E-01
12	1831.51	.826997	-.829834E-01	.729325E-01
13	1799.20	.812407	.667361E-01	.731272E-01
14	1767.13	.797924	-.194268E-01	.733236E-01
15	1735.45	.783620	.287790E-01	.735215E-01
16	1703.63	.769253	-.446979E-01	.737210E-01
17	1671.44	.754718	-.134605E-01	.739221E-01
18	1639.00	.740071	.149961E-01	.741249E-01
19	1606.83	.725544	.647935E-01	.743294E-01
20	1574.86	.711108	-.114008E-01	.745356E-01
21	1542.69	.696582	.839457E-01	.747435E-01
22	1510.38	.681992	.331218E-01	.749532E-01
23	1477.98	.667364	-.754106E-01	.751646E-01
24	1445.54	.652713	.116459	.753778E-01

differences) could perhaps be best modeled as an ARMA(3, 1), since there appear to be one dominant autocorrelation spike and three dominant partial autocorrelation spikes.

When differencing is used to make a time series stationary, it is common to refer to the resulting model as an ARIMA(p, d, q)-type model. The "I" that has been added to the name of the model refers to the integrated or differencing term in the model; the d inside the parentheses refers to the degree of differencing. An ARIMA(p, d, q) model is then properly referred to as an *autoregressive integrated moving-average model.* For example, a model with one autoregressive term, one degree of differencing, and no moving-average term would be written as an ARIMA(1, 1, 0) model. An ARIMA model is thus classified as an "ARIMA(p, d, q)" model, where:

- p is the number of autoregressive terms,
- d is the number of differences, and
- q is the number of moving-average terms.

(c7t2)   <u>TABLE **7–6**</u>   **The ARIMA(1, 1, 1) Series (*concluded*)**

```
              Plot of Autocorrelation (+) and Partial Autocorrelation (*)

  Lag    -1.0                              0.0                              1.0
         |-----------------------------------+-----------------------------------|
   1  |                                 |      [*******************************+
   2  |                   *************]      |                                +|
   3  |                                 |      [**********                     +|
   4  |                      ********]   |                                   +  |
   5  |                                 |      [******                       +  |
   6  |                                 |   ***]     |                        +  |
   7  |                                 |      [****|                         +  |
   8  |                                 |     *]    |                          +  |
   9  |                                 |     *]    |                          +  |
  10  |                                 |      [*   |                           + |
  11  |                                 |      [*** |                           + |
  12  |                                 |   ***]    |                            + |
  13  |                                 |      [**  |                            + |
  14  |                                 |     *]    |                            + |
  15  |                                 |      [*   |                           +  |
  16  |                                 |     *]    |                           +  |
  17  |                                 |      [    |                          +   |
  18  |                                 |      [    |                          +   |
  19  |                                 |      [**  |                         +    |
  20  |                                 |      [    |                         +    |
  21  |                                 |      [*** |                        +     |
  22  |                                 |      [*   |                        +     |
  23  |                                 |   **]     |                       +      |
  24  |                                 |      [****|                       +      |
         |-----------------------------------+-----------------------------------|
```

The Box-Jenkins Identification Process

We are finally in a position to set down the Box-Jenkins methodology in a patterned format. The approach is an iterative one, in which we may loop through the process many times before reaching a model with which we are comfortable. The four steps of the Box-Jenkins process are outlined in Figure 7–4.

As a first step the raw series is examined to *identify* one of the many available models that we will tentatively select as the best representation of this series.

As a first step the raw series is examined to *identify* one of the many available models that we will tentatively select as the best representation of this series. If the raw series is not stationary, it will initially be necessary to modify the original series (perhaps using first differences) to produce a stationary series to model.

The first step in the process is usually accomplished by using an *identify* function, which is a part of every standard Box-Jenkins software package; the identify function simply calculates and displays the autocorrelation and partial autocorrelation functions for the time series in question. Table 7–4 shows these functions for the series in column 2 of Table 7–2 [which you will recall is the MA(1) data we

(c7t2)   TABLE 7–7   **Autocorrelation and Partial Autocorrelation Plots for the ARIMA(1, 1, 1) Series in Table 7–2 after First Differences Have Been Taken**

Lag	Auto-covariance	Auto-correlation	Partial Auto-correlation	Std. Err. of Partial Auto-correlation
0	.129689	1.00000	1.00000	.000000
1	.536975E-01	.414048	.417943	.710669E-01
2	-.135740E-01	-.104666	-.336466	.712470E-01
3	-.601690E-03	-.463948E-02	.270032	.714286E-01
4	.629757E-02	.485590E-01	-.168044	.716115E-01
5	.606777E-03	.467871E-02	.109990	.717958E-01
6	-.454693E-02	-.350602E-01	-.120175	.719816E-01
7	-.633505E-02	-.488479E-01	.480541E-01	.721688E-01
8	.285517E-02	.220155E-01	.281776E-01	.723575E-01
9	.314189E-02	.242263E-01	-.257070E-01	.725476E-01
10	-.102968E-01	-.793959E-01	-.839645E-01	.727393E-01
11	-.451227E-02	-.347929E-01	.931994E-01	.729325E-01
12	.463891E-02	.357695E-01	-.570985E-01	.731272E-01
13	.462511E-03	.356630E-02	.291821E-01	.733236E-01
14	-.113269E-02	-.873391E-02	-.178227E-01	.735215E-01
15	.319588E-02	.246426E-01	.557735E-01	.737210E-01
16	.714261E-02	.550748E-01	.244277E-01	.739221E-01
17	.392444E-02	.302603E-01	-.458567E-02	.741249E-01
18	-.484056E-02	-.373243E-01	-.539046E-01	.743294E-01
19	-.572166E-02	-.441182E-01	.221210E-01	.745356E-01
20	-.390965E-02	-.301463E-02	-.726716E-01	.747435E-01
21	-.852480E-02	-.657325E-01	-.217545E-01	.749532E-01
22	.407578E-04	.314273E-03	.876084E-01	.751646E-01
23	.202870E-02	.156428E-01	-.102989	.753778E-01
24	-.322497E-02	-.248669E-01	.759765E-01	.755929E-01

produced from white noise]. By examining these correlograms we can observe the distinctive pattern (like that in frame *b* of Figure 7–1), which we earlier identified as representing an MA(1) type model. It is this pattern produced by the identify function that leads us to the tentative choice of an MA(1) model. The general rules to be followed in this identification stage of the process can be summed up as follows:

1. If the autocorrelation function abruptly stops at some point—say, after *q* spikes—then the appropriate model is an MA(*q*) type.
2. If the partial autocorrelation function abruptly stops at some point—say, after *p* spikes—then the appropriate model is an AR(*p*) type.
3. If neither function falls off abruptly, but both decline toward zero in some fashion, the appropriate model is an ARMA(*p, q*).

The second step in the process begins after the tentative model has been identified; the actual *estimation* of the parameters of the model is similar to fitting a

(c7t2)   **TABLE 7–7**   **The ARIMA(1, 1, 1) Series after First Differences (*concluded*)**

```
         Plot of Autocorrelation (+) and Partial Autocorrelation (*)

Lag   -1.0                              0.0                              1.0
      |-------------------------------+-------------------------------|
   1 |                               |    [***********+               |
   2 |                       ********+**]      |                      |
   3 |                               |  +*********                    |
   4 |                           *****]  +    |                       |
   5 |                               |    +****|                      |
   6 |                               |***+]    |                      |
   7 |                               |  + [**  |                      |
   8 |                               |   [+    |                      |
   9 |                               |  *]+    |                      |
  10 |                               | +**]    |                      |
  11 |                               |  +[***  |                      |
  12 |                               | **]+    |                      |
  13 |                               |  +*     |                      |
  14 |                               |  *+     |                      |
  15 |                               |   [+*   |                      |
  16 |                               |   [*+   |                      |
  17 |                               |   [+    |                      |
  18 |                               |  *+]    |                      |
  19 |                               |  +[*    |                      |
  20 |                               |  *+]    |                      |
  21 |                               |  +*]    |                      |
  22 |                               |   +***  |                      |
  23 |                               | ***]+   |                      |
  24 |                               |  +[**   |                      |
      |-------------------------------+-------------------------------|
```

The second step in the process begins after the tentative model has been identified; the actual *estimation* of the parameters of the model is similar to fitting a standard regression to a set of data.

standard regression to a set of data. If an MA(1) model had been tentatively identified as the "correct" model, we would fit the equation

$$Y_t = e_t + W_1 e_{t-1}$$

The Box-Jenkins software package would estimate the value for W_1, using a mean-squared error minimization routine in order to select the optimal value.

Consider again the series in column 2 of Table 7–2; we "identified" these data as being distinctive of an MA(1)-type model when we examined the autocorrelation and partial autocorrelation functions in Table 7–4. If we now specify an MA(1)-type model [this could also be written as an ARIMA(0, 0, 1) model] in the software package, the output will be as shown in Table 7–8.

Table 7–8 reports the estimated ARIMA equation to be:

$$Y_t = 0.790035 - 0.821751 e_{t-1}$$
$$(-20.5580)$$

FIGURE 7–4

*The Box-Jenkins
Methodology*

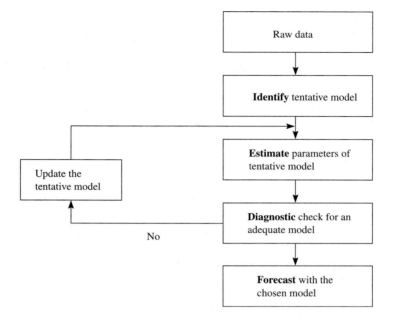

The third step in
the Box-Jenkins
process is to
diagnose in order
to determine
whether the
"correct" model
has been chosen.

The third step in the Box-Jenkins process is to *diagnose* in order to determine whether the "correct" model has been chosen. In order to do this, again for the example in column 3 of Table 7–2, we will examine the autocorrelation function of the residuals produced by the estimation program; this is also presented in Table 7–8. Recall that we originally produced the "raw data" series from white noise by specifying a function we knew would behave as an MA(1) model. That is, we passed an MA(1) box over the white noise and turned it into an MA(1) data set. If we now reverse the process and pass an MA(1) box over the contrived data set, we should wind up with white noise. A look at the autocorrelation function will tell us whether we have been left with just white noise, or whether we will have some unaccounted-for pattern in the series.

The autocorrelation function of the residual series in Table 7–8 shows virtually no significant spikes. Apparently the MA(1)-type model we estimated was an accurate representation of the data. It is most importantly the autocorrelation function that tells the forecaster when the tentative model is actually the correct one. If you are left with only white noise in the residual series, the model chosen is likely the correct one.

A second test for the correctness of the model (but again, not a definitive test) is the Box-Pierce chi-square statistic (sometimes referred to as a *Q*-statistic). Most Box-Jenkins packages will compute this statistic as a matter of routine. The chi-square statistic is calculated as:

$$Q = (n - d) \sum_{i}^{k} p_i^2(e)$$

TABLE 7–8 Parameter Estimates, Statistics, and Residual Autocorrelation Plot for the MA(1) Model Estimate

```
Multivariate ARMA Estimation

Using    1-200
Terms in Moving Average Process: 1
Parameters to Be Estimated: 2
Initial parameter values and their associated subscripts
(  1)  .000000     (  0)  .00000
Non-linear Gaussian Estimation Procedure
200 Observations, 2 Parameters
Convergence achieved at 5 iterations.
Relative change in sum of squares less than   .100000E-02
Variance of residuals =      .885354E-01, 199 degrees of freedom
Parameter Estimates

          Dependent Variable Is MA1
     Coefficient       Estimated       Standard        t-
     Description       Coefficient     Error           Statistic
      ^CONST            .790035        .381249E-01      20.7223
      _MA-TERM(-1)     -.821750        .321525E-01     -25.5579
ARMA Structure Information for the Error Term
Coefficients in the Infinite Autoregression
    1.00000     -.821750      .675273     -.554905      .455993     -.374712
                 .307920     -.253033      .207930     -.170866      .140409
                -.115381      .948146E-01 -.779139E-01  .640275E-01 -.526131E-01
                 .432348E-01 -.355282E-01  .291953E-01 -.239912E-01  .197148E-01
                -.162006E-01  .133128E-01 -.109398E-01  .898980E-02 -.738737E-02
                 .607057E-02 -.498849E-02  .409929E-02 -.336859E-02  .276814E-02
                -.227472E-02  .186925E-02 -.153605E-02  .126225E-02 -.103726E-02
                 .852364E-03 -.700430E-03  .575578E-03 -.472981E-03  .388672E-03
                -.319391E-03  .262460E-03 -.215676E-03  .177232E-03 -.145640E-03
                 .119680E-03 -.983469E-04  .808166E-04 -.664110E-04  .545732E-04
                -.448455E-04  .368518E-04 -.302830E-04  .248850E-04 -.204493E-04
                 .168042E-04 -.138088E-04  .113474E-04 -.932472E-05  .766259E-05
                -.629673E-05  .517434E-05 -.425201E-05  .349409E-05 -.287127E-05
                 .235946E-05 -.193889E-05  .159328E-05 -.130928E-05  .107590E-05
Total Multiplier =    .548923
Autocorrelations of Residuals
    Lags                                       N SUM (R(k)**2)
    1- 5   -.125    .000   -.053    .100   -.060   6.39730
    6-10    .040   -.079    .037    .039   -.081   9.86777
   11-15   -.014    .049   -.026    .019   -.018  10.6629
   16-20    .059   -.011    .014   -.075    .068  13.4591
   21-25   -.119    .057    .003   -.035    .024  17.2937
   26-30    .036   -.088   -.018    .030    .040  19.6830
Sum of Squares of Residuals =   17.6185
Variance of Residuals      =    .885354E-01
Durbin-Watson Statistic    =   2.12227
R-Squared =      .3216
```

(c7t2)

(c7t2)   TABLE 7–8   **The MA(1) Model Estimate (*continued*)**

Lag	Auto- covariance	Auto- correlation	Auto- correlation	Std. Err. of Partial Auto- correlation
0	.880229E-01	1.00000	1.00000	0.00000
1	-.110997E-01	-.126101	-.126283	.708881E-01
2	-.339655E-04	-.385871E-03	-.170743E-01	.710669E-01
3	-.466000E-02	-.529407E-01	-.576611E-01	.712470E-01
4	.871212E-02	.989755E-01	.905876E-01	.714286E-01
5	-.530580E-02	-.602775E-01	-.462290E-01	.716115E-01
6	.354395E-02	.402616E-01	.329214E-01	.717958E-01
7	-.693126E-02	-.787438E-01	-.723692E-01	.719816E-01
8	.326715E-02	.371170E-01	.139905E-01	.721688E-01
9	.341815E-02	.388324E-01	.567583E-01	.723575E-01
10	-.721697E-02	-.819896E-01	-.863849E-01	.725476E-01
11	-.130147E-02	-.147856E-01	-.193269E-01	.727393E-01
12	.425566E-02	.483471E-01	.416908E-01	.729325E-01
13	-.238868E-02	-.271371E-01	-.343662E-01	.731272E-01
14	.160119E-02	.181906E-01	.287537E-01	.733236E-01
15	-.162057E-02	-.184108E-01	-.173574E-01	.735215E-01
16	.512217E-02	.581912E-01	.641845E-01	.737210E-01
17	-.101682E-02	-.115518E-01	.142808E-02	.739221E-01
18	.111462E-02	.126628E-01	.732673E-02	.741249E-01
19	-.667138E-02	-.757914E-01	-.700590E-01	.743294E-01
20	.587885E-02	.667876E-01	.480507E-01	.745356E-01
21	-.105397E-01	-.119738	-.131093	.747435E-01
22	.494171E-02	.561412E-01	.490885E-01	.749532E-01
23	.184343E-03	.209426E-02	.253370E-01	.751646E-01
24	-.320801E-02	-.364451E-01	-.622562E-01	.753778E-01

with $k - p - q$ degrees of freedom, where:

Q = Box-Pierce test statistic (or Q-statistic)
n = Length of the time series
k = First k correlations being checked
p = Number of AR terms
q = Number of MA terms
$p_i(e)$ = Sample autocorrelation function of the ith residual
d = Degree of differencing used

The Box-Pierce statistic tests whether the residual autocorrelations as a set are significantly different from zero. If the residual autocorrelations are significantly different from zero, the model should be reformulated.

The Box-Pierce statistic calculated for the Table 7–8 model is 19.7 for the first 30 autocorrelations (which result in 29 degrees of freedom). A check with the chi-square table (see the appendix to this chapter) shows the critical value to be *about* 39 at the 0.10 significance level. Since the calculated value is less than the table

(c7t2)   <u>TABLE 7–8</u>   **The MA(1) Model Estimate (*concluded*)**

```
          Plot of Autocorrelation (+) and Partial Autocorrelation (*)

Lag   -1.0                          0.0                           1.0
     |-------------------------------+-----------------------------|
  1 |                              |+***]   |                      |
  2 |                              |  *+    |                      |
  3 |                              |  +*]   |                      |
  4 |                              |   [**+ |                      |
  5 |                              |  +*]   |                      |
  6 |                              |   [+   |                      |
  7 |                              | +**]   |                      |
  8 |                              |   [+   |                      |
  9 |                              |   [+*  |                      |
 10 |                              | +**]   |                      |
 11 |                              |  *+    |                      |
 12 |                              |   [*+  |                      |
 13 |                              |   +]   |                      |
 14 |                              |   [+   |                      |
 15 |                              |   +]   |                      |
 16 |                              |   [*+  |                      |
 17 |                              |   +    |                      |
 18 |                              |   +    |                      |
 19 |                              |  +*]   |                      |
 20 |                              |   [*+  |                      |
 21 |                              |+***]   |                      |
 22 |                              |   [*+  |                      |
 23 |                              |   +*   |                      |
 24 |                              |  *+]   |                      |
     |-------------------------------+-----------------------------|
```

value, the model is considered appropriate, that is, we believe the residuals to be uncorrelated. If this is the correct model, the residuals should be normally distributed and independent of one another (i.e., the residuals should resemble white noise).

If either the check of the residual series autocorrelations or the Box-Pierce statistic test had shown the model to be inappropriate, the tentative model would have been updated by trying another variation of the possible models. In Box-Jenkins methodology it is possible for two or more models to be very similar in their fit of the data; Occam's razor would suggest that the simpler of the similar models be chosen for actual forecasting. It is important to realize that the selection of an ARIMA model is an art and not a science.

The final step in the Box-Jenkins process is to actually *forecast* using the chosen model.

The final step in the Box-Jenkins process is to actually *forecast* using the chosen model. SORITEC performs this function by substituting into the chosen model in much the same manner as a standard regression forecast would be made. It should be remembered that as forecasts are made more than one period into the future, the size of the forecast error is likely to become larger.

When new observations of the time series become available, the model should be reestimated and checked again by the Box-Jenkins process; it is quite likely that the parameters of the model will have to be recalculated, or perhaps a different model altogether will be chosen as the best representation of the series. Consistent errors observed in estimation as more data become available are an indication that the entire model may require a change.

ARIMA: A Set of Numerical Examples

Example 1

Return to the first column of Table 7–2; this is the column containing white noise from which we constructed the other time series in the table. When we run an *identify* test on the white noise (that is, observe the autocorrelation and partial autocorrelation functions), we should be able to see that this column actually contains white noise. Table 7–9 contains these correlograms; in each case there is no distinctive pattern of spikes or significant but descending values as we observed with earlier time series.

(c7t2) **TABLE 7–9   Autocorrelation and Partial Autocorrelation Plots for the White Noise Series in Table 7–2 (Example 1)**

Lag	Auto-covariance	Auto-correlation	Partial Auto-correlation	Std. Err. of Partial Auto-correlation
0	.850123E-01	1.00000	1.00000	0.000000
1	.193794E-02	.227960E-01	.228712E-01	.708881E-01
2	-.116087E-01	-.136553	-.138489	.710669E-01
3	.403701E-02	.474874E-01	.545402E-01	.712470E-01
4	.266408E-02	.313375E-01	.976230E-02	.714286E-01
5	-.469832E-03	-.552663E-02	.662718E-02	.716115E-01
6	-.126252E-02	-.148510E-01	-.110233E-01	.717958E-01
7	-.356677E-02	-.419559E-01	-.462644E-01	.719816E-01
8	.994636E-03	.116999E-01	.941529E-02	.721688E-01
9	.643146E-02	.756532E-01	.699240E-01	.723575E-01
10	-.964245E-02	-.113424	-.117610	.725476E-01
11	-.263787E-03	-.310293E-02	.249500E-01	.727393E-01
12	.395163E-02	.464831E-01	.801757E-02	.729325E-01
13	-.997266E-03	-.117308E-01	-.632679E-02	.731272E-01
14	-.948544E-03	-.111577E-01	.300165E-04	.733236E-01
15	.710060E-03	.835244E-02	.967439E-02	.735215E-01
16	.351717E-02	.413725E-01	.442418E-01	.737210E-01
17	.199813E-02	.235040E-01	.234144E-01	.739221E-01
18	-.195123E-02	-.229523E-01	-.222668E-01	.741249E-01
19	-.454374E-02	-.534481E-01	-.440123E-01	.743294E-01
20	.379596E-02	.446519E-01	.339773E-01	.745356E-01
21	-.869090E-02	-.102231	-.135402	.747435E-01
22	.333491E-02	.392285E-01	.840719E-01	.749532E-01
23	.153990E-02	.181138E-01	-.157393E-01	.751646E-01
24	-.438818E-02	-.516181E-01	-.349634E-01	.753778E-01

(c7t2)   **TABLE 7–9   The White Noise Series (*Example 1 concluded*)**

```
            Plot of Autocorrelation (+) and Partial Autocorrelation (*)

Lag   -1.0                              0.0                              1.0
      |-------------------------------+-------------------------------|
   1 |                              |    [+  |                              |
   2 |                              |+***]   |                              |
   3 |                              |    [*+  |                              |
   4 |                              |    [+  |                              |
   5 |                              |    +   |                              |
   6 |                              |    +   |                              |
   7 |                              |    +]  |                              |
   8 |                              |    +   |                              |
   9 |                              |    [*+  |                              |
  10 |                              |+***]   |                              |
  11 |                              |    +*  |                              |
  12 |                              |    [+  |                              |
  13 |                              |    +   |                              |
  14 |                              |    +   |                              |
  15 |                              |    +   |                              |
  16 |                              |    [+  |                              |
  17 |                              |    [+  |                              |
  18 |                              |    +]  |                              |
  19 |                              |    +*] |                              |
  20 |                              |    [+  |                              |
  21 |                              |*+**]   |                              |
  22 |                              |    [+**  |                              |
  23 |                              |    +]+  |                              |
  24 |                              |    +*] |                              |
      |-------------------------------+-------------------------------|
```

In this case the appropriate model would be an ARIMA(0, 0, 0); in other words, the best forecast would just be the mean value of the original time series (which is about 0.47).

Example 2

The series in column 3 of Table 7–2 was constructed to be an AR(1) or ARIMA(1, 0, 0) model. When we examined the autocorrelation and partial autocorrelation functions in Table 7–5, one of the characteristic patterns for an ARIMA(1, 0, 0) model appeared; in addition, no trend is apparent in the series and so it is likely that no differencing is required. We should then be able to specify an ARIMA(1, 0, 0) model and correctly model the time series.

Table 7–10 presents the results from estimating an AR(1) or ARIMA(1, 0, 0) model. The value of the AR(1) term is 0.466440; it has a significant *t*-statistic ($t = 7.43$). Two tests will determine whether this model is an appropriate model: first, the examination of the autocorrelation coefficients of the residual series and, second, the Box-Pierce statistic.

TABLE 7–10 Parameter Estimates, Statistics, and Residual Autocorrelation Plot for the AR(1) Model Estimate (Example 2)

```
Multivariate ARMA Estimation
Using     1-200
Terms in Autoregressive Process: 1
Parameters to be Estimated: 2
Initial parameter values and associated subscripts
(  1)  .000000     (  0)  .000000
Non-linear Gaussian Estimation Procedure
200 Observations, 2 Parameters
Convergence achieved at 6 iterations.
Relative change in sum of squares less than   .100000E-02
Variance of residuals =      .953710E-01, 199 degrees of freedom
Parameter Estimates

        Dependent Variable is AR1
    Coefficient          Estimated       Standard        t-
    Description          Coefficient     Error           Statistic
      ^CONST             .908109         .407406E-01     22.2900
    /_AR-TERM{-1}        .466439         .627551E-01     7.43269
ARMA Structure Information for the Error Term
Coefficients in the Infinite Moving Average
    1.00000        .466439       .217566       .101481     .473348E-01 .220788E-01
                   .102984E-01   .480358E-02   .224058E-02 .104509E-02 .487473E-03
                   .227376E-03   .106057E-03   .494693E-04 .230744E-04 .107628E-04
                   .502020E-05   .234162E-05   .109222E-05
Total Multiplier =    1.87420
Autocorrelations of Residuals
  Lags                                           N SUM(R(k)**2)

   1- 5   -.012    -.071    .015     .031     .018      1.34715
   6-10    .015    -.045    .017     .036    -.078      3.33575
  11-15    .004     .004    .000     .026     .010      3.50004
  16-20    .038     .001    .009    -.041     .038      4.41931
  21-25   -.108     .040    .037    -.051     .033      8.08038
  26-30    .026    -.076   -.026     .043     .035     10.1145
Sum of Squares of Residuals =   18.9788
Variance of Residuals       =   .953710E-01
Durbin-Watson Statistic     =   1.96607
R-Squared =      .1603
        Autocorrelation Structure of ^RES

                                       Partial     Std. Err. of
                  Auto-       Auto-       Auto-     Partial Auto-
    Lag           covariance  correlation correlation correlation
    ------------------------------------------------------------
     0            .944611E-01  1.00000     1.00000     0.00000
     1           -.144643E-02 -.153124E-01 -.157132E-01 .708881E-01
     2           -.716003E-02 -.757987E-01 -.800120E-01 .710669E-01
     3            .108920E-02  .115307E-01  .146586E-01 .712470E-01
     4            .252224E-02  .267014E-01  .187856E-01 .714286E-01
     5            .135270E-02  .143202E-01  .199344E-01 .716115E-01
```

(c7t2)

(c7t2)   **TABLE 7–10   The AR(1) Model Estimate (*Example 2 concluded*)**

6	.113233E-02	.119873E-01	.168382E-01	.717958E-01
7	-.454428E-02	-.481074E-01	-.534925E-01	.719816E-01
8	.131684E-02	.139406E-01	.170051E-01	.721688E-01
9	.312583E-02	.330912E-01	.260898E-01	.723575E-01
10	-.776652E-02	-.822193E-01	-.861871E-01	.725476E-01
11	.486318E-04	.514835E-03	.145811E-01	.727393E-01
12	-.130466E-04	-.138116E-03	-.229651E-01	.729325E-01
13	-.445950E-03	-.472099E-02	-.921884E-03	.731272E-01
14	.214992E-02	.227599E-01	.303892E-01	.733236E-01
15	.568561E-03	.601900E-02	.923682E-02	.735215E-01
16	.316367E-02	.334918E-01	.457208E-01	.737210E-01
17	-.409677E-03	-.433699E-02	-.137160E-01	.739221E-01
18	.376907E-03	.399007E-02	.956910E-02	.741249E-01
19	-.428110E-02	-.453213E-01	-.503056E-01	.743294E-01
20	.314836E-02	.333297E-01	.320929E-01	.745356E-01
21	-.106919E-01	-.113188	-.147042	.747435E-01
22	.333268E-02	.352810E-01	.672326E-01	.749532E-01
23	.298338E-02	.315832E-01	.124883E-01	.751646E-01
24	-.540941E-02	-.572660E-01	-.475083E-01	.753778E-01

```
           Plot of Autocorrelation (+) and Partial Autocorrelation (*)
   Lag   -1.0                            0.0                             1.0
          |-------------------------------+-------------------------------|
     1 |                               |  *+    |                          |
     2 |                               | *+*]   |                          |
     3 |                               |   +    |                          |
     4 |                               |  [+    |                          |
     5 |                               |  +*    |                          |
     6 |                               |  +*    |                          |
     7 |                               |  +*]   |                          |
     8 |                               |  +*    |                          |
     9 |                               |  [+    |                          |
    10 |                               | +**]   |                          |
    11 |                               |   +    |                          |
    12 |                               |  *+    |                          |
    13 |                               |   +    |                          |
    14 |                               |  [+    |                          |
    15 |                               |   +    |                          |
    16 |                               |  [+    |                          |
    17 |                               |   +    |                          |
    18 |                               |   +    |                          |
    19 |                               |  *+]   |                          |
    20 |                               |  [+    |                          |
    21 |                             *+***]     |                          |
    22 |                               |  [+*   |                          |
    23 |                               |  [+    |                          |
    24 |                               |  +*]   |                          |
          |-------------------------------+-------------------------------|
```

The autocorrelation function for the residual series shows no distinctive pattern; it appears to be white noise. This would imply that we have chosen the correct model because when the original time series is modified by the model only white noise remains.

The Box-Pierce statistic offers further evidence that the correct model has been chosen. The calculated Box-Pierce Q is 10.1 for 30 autocorrelations (which give us 29 degrees of freedom). Checking the chi-square table shows the critical value to be *about* 39.087 at the 0.10 significance level. (See the appendix to this chapter for the chi-square table.) Since the calculated Box-Pierce is less than the table value, the model is termed appropriate.

Example 3

The AR(2) series in column 4 of Table 7–2 may be examined in like manner. Assume that we did not know the appropriate model for these data and examine the identification data presented in Table 7–11. The autocorrelation function gradually

(c7t2) **TABLE 7–11   Autocorrelation and Partial Autocorrelation Plots for the AR(2) Series in Table 7–2 (Example 3)**

Lag	Auto-covariance	Auto-correlation	Partial Auto-correlation	Std. Err. of Partial Auto-correlation
0	1.09633	1.00000	1.00000	0.000000
1	.999882	.912024	.955159	.708881E-01
2	.916565	.836027	.171619	.710669E-01
3	.858717	.783263	.142185	.712470E-01
4	.791719	.722152	.160459E-02	.714286E-01
5	.736237	.671545	-.466672E-04	.716115E-01
6	.696107	.634940	.155049E-01	.717958E-01
7	.661047	.602961	.213206E-01	.719816E-01
8	.626623	.571563	.717921E-01	.721688E-01
9	.593740	.541569	.408047E-01	.723575E-01
10	.545864	.497900	-.717030E-01	.725476E-01
11	.517522	.472048	.112197	.727393E-01
12	.486195	.443473	.162459E-01	.729325E-01
13	.445457	.406316	.276080E-02	.731272E-01
14	.420306	.383374	.241426E-01	.733236E-01
15	.406738	.370998	.201528E-01	.735215E-01
16	.388108	.354005	.222025E-01	.737210E-01
17	.363196	.331282	-.247695E-01	.739221E-01
18	.334025	.304674	-.143719E-01	.741249E-01
19	.314717	.287063	.117792E-01	.743294E-01
20	.301049	.274597	.732573E-01	.745356E-01
21	.274703	.250565	-.492899E-01	.747435E-01
22	.257091	.234501	.147721	.749532E-01
23	.239169	.218154	-.373975E-01	.751646E-01
24	.220766	.201368	-.866331E-02	.753778E-01

(c7t2)   T ABLE **7–11**   **The AR(2) Series of Example 3 (*concluded*)**

```
             Plot of Autocorrelation (+) and Partial Autocorrelation (*)

     Lag   -1.0                              0.0                            1.0
           |-------------------------------+-----------------------------|
       1   |                               |   [***************************+**|
       2   |                               |   [*****                       + |
       3   |                               |   [*****                     +   |
       4   |                               |   [    |                   +     |
       5   |                               |   [    |                +        |
       6   |                               |   [    |               +         |
       7   |                               |   [*   |              +          |
       8   |                               |   [**  |           +             |
       9   |                               |   [*   |          +              |
      10   |                               | **]    |        +                |
      11   |                               |   [****|       +                 |
      12   |                               |   [*   |      +                  |
      13   |                               |   [    |     +                   |
      14   |                               |   [*   |   +                     |
      15   |                               |   [*   |   +                     |
      16   |                               |   [*   |  +                      |
      17   |                               |  *]    |  +                      |
      18   |                               |   [    |    +                    |
      19   |                               |   [    |   +                     |
      20   |                               |   [**  |   +                     |
      21   |                               | **]    | +                       |
      22   |                               |   [*****  +                      |
      23   |                               |  *]    | +                       |
      24   |                               |   [    |+                        |
           |-------------------------------+-----------------------------|
```

falls over almost the entire 24 lags presented; the partial autocorrelation function shows two clear spikes (and possibly a third). The pattern looks like that in frame *c* of Figure 7–2; this identifies the tentative model as an AR(2) or ARIMA(2, 0, 0). No differencing *appears* to be needed, because there does not appear to be any trend.

When the AR(2) model is run, however, the coefficients fail to damp to zero, indicating a possible problem. In many cases like this, the use of a differencing term eliminates the problem. Table 7–12 presents the results of applying an ARIMA(2, 1, 0) model to this series. The first AR term is -0.188469 and the second AR term is -0.129900.

The autocorrelation function for the residuals shows only white noise with no significant values in any of the 24 lags. The Box-Pierce statistic is 11.7173 for the 30 autocorrelations (which give us 28 degrees of freedom). The table value from the chi-square table is about 37.916; this would indicate that the ARIMA(2, 1, 0) model chosen is an accurate representation of the series.

TABLE 7–12   **Parameter Estimates, Statistics, and Residual Autocorrelation Plot for the ARIMA(2, 1, 0) Model Estimate (Example 3)**

```
Multivariate ARMA Estimation

Using    1-200
Terms in Autoregressive Process: 2
Differencing on Dependent Variable, Order: 1
Parameters to Be Estimated: 3
Initial parameter values and their associated subscripts
(  1)  .000000    (  2)  .000000        (  0)  .000000
Non-linear Gaussian Estimation Procedure
199 Observations, 3 Parameters
Convergence achieved at 5 iterations.
Relative change in sum of squares less than   .100000E-02
Variance of residuals =      .927328E-01, 197 degrees of freedom
Parameter Estimates

        Dependent Variable is AR2
    Coefficient      Estimated    Standard          t-
    Description      Coefficient    Error        Statistic
     ^CONST          .268810E-01  .164015E-01      1.63894
    /_AR-TERM{-1}    -.188469     .706786E-01     -2.66656
    /_AR-TERM{-2}    -.129901     .709492E-01     -1.83090
ARMA Structure Information for the Error Term
Coefficients in the Infinite Moving Average
   1.00000      -.188469     -.943802E-01  .422700E-01  .429347E-02 -.630009E-02
                 .629648E-03   .699717E-03 -.213667E-03 -.506242E-04  .372966E-04
                -.453122E-06  -.475945E-05
Total Multiplier =   .758513
Autocorrelations of Residuals
   Lags                                           N SUM (R(k)**2)
   1- 5   .003    .012    .027    .018   -.007      .247688
   6-10  -.013   -.032    .006    .084   -.093     3.61306
  11-15   .026    .040   -.001    .009    .014     4.12757
  16-20   .049    .017    .001   -.061    .068     6.32600
  21-25  -.098    .058    .023   -.027    .040     9.47733
  26-30   .032   -.082   -.011    .036    .045    11.7173
Sum of Squares of Residuals =   18.2684
Variance of Residuals      =   .927328E-01
Durbin-Watson Statistic    =   1.99580
R-Squared =      .9162

        Autocorrelation Structure of  ^RES
```

| | | Partial | Std. Err. of |
| | Auto- | Auto- | Auto- | Partial Auto- |
Lag	covariance	correlation	correlation	correlation
0	.918008E-01	1.00000	1.00000	0.000000
1	.272688E-03	.297043E-02	.297535E-02	.710669E-01
2	.107893E-02	.117529E-01	.118687E-01	.712470E-01
3	.245383E-02	.267300E-01	.270319E-01	.714286E-01
4	.169188E-02	.184300E-01	.188040E-01	.716115E-01

TABLE 7–12   The ARIMA(2, 1, 0) Model Estimate (*Example 3 concluded*)

5	-.615314E-03	-.670271E-02	-.715272E-02	.717958E-01
6	-.121510E-02	-.132363E-01	-.145825E-01	.719816E-01
7	-.288920E-02	-.314725E-01	-.354724E-01	.721688E-01
8	.524661E-03	.571521E-02	.351659E-02	.723575E-01
9	.769842E-02	.838601E-01	.894732E-01	.725476E-01
10	-.855073E-02	-.931444E-01	-.966638E-01	.727393E-01
11	.242066E-02	.263686E-01	.270088E-01	.729325E-01
12	.369886E-02	.402922E-01	.382770E-01	.731272E-01
13	-.433975E-04	-.472736E-03	-.310817E-02	.733236E-01
14	.831659E-03	.905938E-02	.950488E-02	.735215E-01
15	.127447E-02	.138830E-01	.164820E-01	.737210E-01
16	.452093E-02	.492471E-01	.531756E-01	.739221E-01
17	.160561E-02	.174901E-01	.210298E-01	.741249E-01
18	.115850E-03	.126198E-02	-.262077E-02	.743294E-01
19	-.561305E-02	-.611437E-01	-.552369E-01	.745356E-01
20	.621467E-02	.676973E-01	.687956E-01	.747435E-01
21	-.896622E-02	-.976703E-01	-.109285	.749532E-01
22	.533524E-02	.581176E-01	.826205E-01	.751646E-01
23	.210720E-02	.229540E-01	.326211E-01	.753778E-01
24	-.251879E-02	-.274376E-01	-.300397E-01	.755929E-01

Plot of Autocorrelation (+) and Partial Autocorrelation (*)

```
Lag  -1.0                             0.0                            1.0
     |-------------------------------+-------------------------------|
  1 |                              |    +    |                       |
  2 |                              |    +    |                       |
  3 |                              |   [+    |                       |
  4 |                              |   [+    |                       |
  5 |                              |    +    |                       |
  6 |                              |    +    |                       |
  7 |                              |    +]   |                       |
  8 |                              |    +    |                       |
  9 |                              |   [**+  |                       |
 10 |                              | +**]    |                       |
 11 |                              |   [+    |                       |
 12 |                              |   [+    |                       |
 13 |                              |    +    |                       |
 14 |                              |    +    |                       |
 15 |                              |    +*   |                       |
 16 |                              |   [*+   |                       |
 17 |                              |   [+    |                       |
 18 |                              |    +    |                       |
 19 |                              |  +*]    |                       |
 20 |                              |   [*+   |                       |
 21 |                              | +**]    |                       |
 22 |                              |   [*+*  |                       |
 23 |                              |   [+    |                       |
 24 |                              |    +]   |                       |
     |-------------------------------+-------------------------------|
```

(c7t13)

TABLE 7–13 Example 4 Data Series

ARIMA

....

1	.	0.160000	68	. 44.7896	135	. 97.2641
2	.	0.544113	69	. 45.2098	136	. 98.4736
3	.	1.35744	70	. 46.0228	137	. 99.5781
4	.	1.81007	71	. 46.5587	138	. 100.248
5	.	2.55541	72	. 47.2307	139	. 101.396
6	.	3.84012	73	. 47.9890	140	. 102.778
7	.	4.91087	74	. 49.2088	141	. 103.951
8	.	5.28469	75	. 50.5534	142	. 105.195
9	.	5.49273	76	. 51.9717	143	. 106.493
10	.	5.62030	77	. 52.5793	144	. 107.602
11	.	6.22645	78	. 52.7499	145	. 108.921
12	.	6.81976	79	. 53.1405	146	. 109.953
13	.	7.03361	80	. 53.3826	147	. 110.384
14	.	7.93600	81	. 54.3375	148	. 111.074
15	.	9.28220	82	. 55.8604	149	. 112.112
16	.	9.99665	83	. 57.3969	150	. 113.163
17	.	10.3492	84	. 58.2719	151	. 113.903
18	.	10.7372	85	. 59.1758	152	. 114.280
19	.	11.6537	86	. 60.4877	153	. 115.156
20	.	12.3986	87	. 61.6198	154	. 116.267
21	.	12.7508	88	. 62.2831	155	. 116.826
22	.	13.0273	89	. 62.6991	156	. 117.822
23	.	13.7149	90	. 63.5748	157	. 118.461
24	.	14.6099	91	. 64.3452	158	. 118.806
25	.	15.1324	92	. 65.0968	159	. 119.679
26	.	15.6525	93	. 65.4967	160	. 120.198
27	.	16.3994	94	. 66.4900	161	. 120.534
28	.	17.3193	95	. 67.6714	162	. 121.418
29	.	18.1561	96	. 68.1611	163	. 121.895
30	.	19.0496	97	. 68.2980	164	. 122.030
31	.	19.8106	98	. 68.9562	165	. 122.893
32	.	20.7518	99	. 70.3170	166	. 123.409
33	.	21.2347	100	. 71.5608	167	. 123.898
34	.	21.5877	101	. 72.3279	168	. 124.924
35	.	22.7092	102	. 73.2702	169	. 125.618
36	.	23.8470	103	. 74.0750	170	. 125.903
37	.	24.4950	104	. 74.7422	171	. 126.771
38	.	24.7342	105	. 75.1037	172	. 128.169
39	.	25.0825	106	. 76.1463	173	. 129.070
40	.	25.6879	107	. 76.9680	174	. 130.199
41	.	26.9086	108	. 77.2119	175	. 131.363
42	.	27.6985	109	. 78.1276	176	. 132.159
43	.	27.9592	110	. 78.8356	177	. 132.600
44	.	29.0047	111	. 79.2148	178	. 132.974
45	.	30.5438	112	. 79.4252	179	. 133.496
46	.	31.8912	113	. 80.0609	180	. 134.223
47	.	32.7602	114	. 81.1088	181	. 134.735
48	.	33.0873	115	. 81.5818	182	. 135.831
49	.	33.2974	116	. 82.5728	183	. 136.911
50	.	33.7224	117	. 83.4074	184	. 137.315
51	.	34.4206	118	. 84.0063	185	. 137.517
52	.	35.0356	119	. 84.8875	186	. 137.859
53	.	35.6169	120	. 86.0977	187	. 138.897

TABLE 7–13   Example 4 Data Series (*concluded*)

54	. 35.9999	121	. 87.1734	188	. 139.979
55	. 36.4831	122	. 88.2206	189	. 140.426
56	. 36.8279	123	. 88.9342	190	. 141.150
57	. 37.0943	124	. 89.6704	191	. 141.867
58	. 37.6164	125	. 90.6897	192	. 142.224
59	. 38.7882	126	. 91.4675	193	. 143.023
60	. 39.9187	127	. 91.7072	194	. 144.299
61	. 40.9344	128	. 92.1157	195	. 145.293
62	. 41.5441	129	. 92.9512	196	. 146.425
63	. 42.5229	130	. 93.4450	197	. 147.339
64	. 43.1073	131	. 94.4363	198	. 148.166
65	. 43.4389	132	. 95.6413	199	. 149.491
66	. 44.2401	133	. 96.2160	200	. 150.761
67	. 44.6401	134	. 96.6762		

TABLE 7–14   Autocorrelation and Partial Autocorrelation Plots for the Series in Table 7–13 (Example 4)

Lag	Auto- covariance	Auto- correlation	Partial Auto- correlation	Std. Err. of Partial Auto- correlation
0	1961.94	1.00000	1.00000	0.000000
1	1933.21	.985353	.999970	.708881E-01
2	1904.49	.970718	-.382559	.710669E-01
3	1876.04	.956217	.318632	.712470E-01
4	1847.52	.941679	-.221419	.714286E-01
5	1819.07	.927175	.135345	.716115E-01
6	1790.97	.912853	-.599595E-01	.717958E-01
7	1763.10	.898652	.942096E-01	.719816E-01
8	1735.34	.884501	-.144946E-02	.721688E-01
9	1707.42	.870270	-.368652E-01	.723575E-01
10	1679.14	.855857	.327451E-01	.725476E-01
11	1650.84	.841429	.100367	.727393E-01
12	1622.49	.826982	-.768804E-01	.729325E-01
13	1593.86	.812389	.540393E-01	.731272E-01
14	1565.45	.797905	-.689468E-02	.733236E-01
15	1537.40	.783609	.184541E-01	.735215E-01
16	1509.21	.769244	-.319634E-01	.737210E-01
17	1480.70	.754712	-.239833E-01	.739221E-01
18	1451.96	.740063	.172910E-01	.741249E-01
19	1423.46	.725534	.587811E-01	.743294E-01
20	1395.14	.711100	.176763E-01	.745356E-01
21	1366.64	.696572	.606047E-01	.747435E-01
22	1338.01	.681980	.636266E-01	.749532E-01
23	1309.32	.667357	-.931125E-01	.751646E-01
24	1280.58	.652712	.114263	.753778E-01

TABLE 7–14   The Series in Table 7–13 of Example 4 (*concluded*)

```
            Plot of Autocorrelation (+) and Partial Autocorrelation (*)

Lag   -1.0                              0.0                              1.0
      |------------------------------+------------------------------|
  1 |                                |  [******************************+
  2 |                    ************]      |                          +|
  3 |                                |  [*********             +|
  4 |                      *******]          |                   +  |
  5 |                                |   [****|                  +  |
  6 |                                |  **]   |                +  |
  7 |                                |  [***  |                +  |
  8 |                                |  [     |              +    |
  9 |                                |  *]    |              +    |
 10 |                                |  [*    |            +      |
 11 |                                |  [***  |            +      |
 12 |                                |  **]   |          +        |
 13 |                                |  [**   |          +        |
 14 |                                |  [     |          +        |
 15 |                                |  [*    |        +          |
 16 |                                |  *]    |        +          |
 17 |                                |  *]    |      +            |
 18 |                                |  [*    |      +            |
 19 |                                |  [**   |    +              |
 20 |                                |  [     |    +              |
 21 |                                |  [**   |  +                |
 22 |                                |  [**   |  +                |
 23 |                                | ***]   |  +                |
 24 |                                |  [****| |  +                |
      |------------------------------+------------------------------|
```

Example 4

Consider finally the time-series data in Table 7–13 and assume we are given no clues to its origin. Applying the Box-Jenkins methodology, we would first use an identification function to examine the autocorrelation and partial autocorrelation functions; these are presented in Table 7–14.

The autocorrelation function in Table 7–14 is entirely characteristic of a series with a trend; that is, it shows dominant autocorrelations for the 24 lags shown. Look at the actual numbers in the original series in Table 7–13 and observe how they gradually creep upward in value. These data apparently have a trend and are therefore nonstationary. Before the Box-Jenkins process can be continued, the series must be transformed to a stationary series. The most common method of achieving stationarity is to take first differences of the original series; taking these first differences and again applying the identification program to the resulting series gives the autocorrelation and partial autocorrelation functions in Table 7–15.

TABLE 7–15   Autocorrelation and Partial Autocorrelation Plots for the Series in Table 7–13 *after* **First Differences Have Been Taken (Example 4)**

Lag	Auto-covariance	Auto-correlation	Partial Auto-correlation	Std. Err. of Partial Auto-correlation
0	.118227	1.00000	1.00000	0.00000
1	.461761E-01	.390573	.394001	.710669E-01
2	-.125682E-01	-.106306	-.308087	.712470E-01
3	-.245247E-03	-.207438E-02	.232433	.714286E-01
4	.568930E-02	.481220E-01	-.124907	.716115E-01
5	.541642E-03	.458138E-02	.714366E-01	.717958E-01
6	-.397041E-02	-.335830E-01	-.822910E-01	.719816E-01
7	-.577292E-02	-.488292E-01	.120861E-01	.721688E-01
8	.247539E-02	.209376E-01	.467390E-01	.723575E-01
9	.314265E-02	.265816E-01	-.236570E-01	.725476E-01
10	-.960279E-02	-.812236E-01	-.899128E-01	.727393E-01
11	-.393530E-02	-.332861E-01	.871041E-01	.729325E-01
12	.424912E-02	.359405E-01	-.445029E-01	.731272E-01
13	.379891E-03	.321324E-02	.166361E-01	.733236E-01
14	-.100805E-02	-.852640E-02	-.754020E-02	.735215E-01
15	.275200E-02	.232774E-01	.429641E-01	.737210E-01
16	.634891E-02	.537011E-01	.347483E-01	.739221E-01
17	.349449E-02	.295575E-01	-.673490E.02	.741249E-01
18	-.423258E-02	-.358006E-01	-.479760E-01	.743294E-01
19	-.533467E-02	-.451224E-01	.876099E-02	.745356E-01
20	-.307605E-02	-.260182E-01	-.492860E-01	.747435E-01
21	-.808971E-02	-.684254E-01	-.525704E-01	.749532E-01
22	.316778E-03	.267941E-01	.105405	.751646E-01
23	.186638E-02	.157865E-01	-.101101	.753778E-01
24	-.317800E-02	-.268806E-01	.589193E-01	.755929E-01

The pattern exhibited here (after differencing) is similar to frame *d* of Figure 7–3; perhaps the model is a mixed model, with both AR and MA terms in addition to the differencing required to make the series stationary. Table 7–16 displays the results of estimating an ARIMA(3, 1, 2), that is, a model with three AR terms, one degree of differencing, and two MA terms.

The results in the residual series autocorrelation function indicate that only white noise remains after applying the model. The Box-Pierce statistic is 15.5414 for the 30 autocorrelations. The value from the chi-square table is about 34.382 for 25 degrees of freedom. We would then accept the ARIMA(3, 1, 1) model specification as a "correct" forecasting model for this series. Note the low *t*-statistics on the autoregressive and moving-average terms of the model; the standard errors and *t*-statistics in any of these ARIMA models are calculated from the last iteration of the nonlinear estimation process, and thus the *t*-statistics are limited in their meaning. The *t*-statistics

TABLE 7–15   The Series in Table 7–13 *after* First Differences from Example 4 (*concluded*)

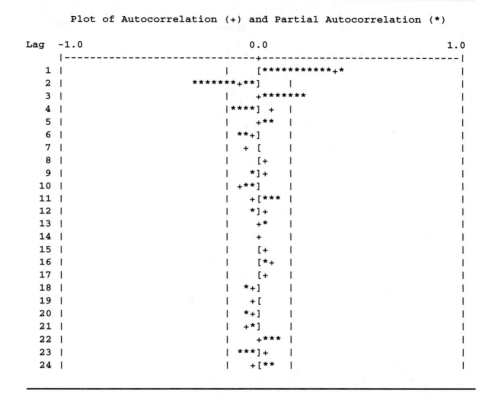

```
           Plot of Autocorrelation (+) and Partial Autocorrelation (*)

Lag   -1.0                           0.0                              1.0
      |-----------------------------+-----------------------------|
    1 |                             |    [***********+*            |
    2 |                   *******+**]     |                        |
    3 |                             |    +*******                  |
    4 |                          |****] +  |                       |
    5 |                          |    +**  |                       |
    6 |                          | **+]    |                       |
    7 |                          |  + [    |                       |
    8 |                          |    [+   |                       |
    9 |                          |   *]+   |                       |
   10 |                          | +**]    |                       |
   11 |                          |   +[*** |                       |
   12 |                          |   *]+   |                       |
   13 |                          |   +*    |                       |
   14 |                          |   +     |                       |
   15 |                          |   [+    |                       |
   16 |                          |   [*+   |                       |
   17 |                          |   [+    |                       |
   18 |                          | *+]     |                       |
   19 |                          |  +[     |                       |
   20 |                          | *+]     |                       |
   21 |                          | +*]     |                       |
   22 |                          |   +***  |                       |
   23 |                          | ***]+   |                       |
   24 |                          |   +[**  |                       |
```

indicate only the significance of the least-squares parameter estimates for the *last* iteration; the R^2 is calculated in the same manner and also has limited usefulness. Despite very low *t*-statistics and a low R^2, the predictive power of the model could be considerable.

Forecasting Seasonal Time Series

Seasonality can cause some problems in the Box-Jenkins process, since a model fitted to such a series would likely have a very high order.

In many actual business situations the time series to be forecast are quite seasonal. Recall that seasonality refers to a consistent shape in the series that recurs with some periodic regularity (sales of lawn mowers during summer months, for instance, are always higher than in winter months). This seasonality can cause some problems in the ARIMA process, since a model fitted to such a series would likely have a very high order. If monthly data were used and the seasonality occurred in every 12th

TABLE 7–16 Parameter Estimates, Statistics, and Residual Autocorrelation Plot for the ARIMA(3, 1, 2) Model Estimate (Example 4)

```
Multivariate ARMA Estimation

Using      1-200
Terms in Autoregressive Process: 3
Terms in Moving Average Process: 2
Differencing on Dependent Variable, Order: 1
Parameters to be Estimated: 6
Initial parameter values and associated subscripts
(  1)  .000000     (  2)  .000000     (  3)  .000000     (  1)  .000000
(  2)  .000000     (  0)  .000000
Non-linear Gaussian Estimation Procedure
199 Observations,  6 Parameters
Convergence acheived at 7 iterations.
Relative change in sum of squares less than  .100000E-02
Variance of residuals =       .866577E-01,  194 degrees of freedom
Parameter Estimates
```

	Dependent Variable is ARIMA		
Coefficient Description	Estimated Coefficient	Standard Error	t-Statistic
^CONST	.752411	.331103E-01	22.7244
/_AR-TERM{-1}	.232708	1.40629	.165476
/_AR-TERM{-2}	-.142550	.159945	-.891242
/_AR-TERM{-3}	.683236E-01	.151137	.452063
_MA-TERM{-1}	-.443462	1.40571	-.315472
_MA-TERM{-2}	.140670	1.00342	.140190

```
ARMA Structure Information for the Error Term
Coefficients in the Infinite Autoregression
   1.00000      -.676170      .583076      -.422012      .269168      -.178730
                 .117124     -.770820E-01  .506588E-01 -.333084E-01  .218972E-01
                -.143961E-01  .946438E-02 -.622219E-02  .409066E-02 -.268933E-02
                 .176805E-02 -.116237E-02  .764178E-03 -.502395E-03  .330290E-03
                -.217143E-03  .142757E-03 -.938526E-04  .617016E-04 -.405646E-04
                 .266684E-04 -.175327E-04  .115265E-04 -.757789E-05  .498194E-05
                -.327529E-05  .215328E-05 -.141563E-05
Total Multiplier =   .645935
Coeffecients in the Infinite Moving Average
   1.00000       .676170     -.125870      -.573554E-01  .507941E-01  .113963E-01
                -.850741E-02 -.133856E-03  .196022E-02 -.106017E-03 -.313246E-03
                 .761471E-04  .551298E-04 -.194277E-04 -.717710E-05  .486592E-05
Total Multiplier = 1.54814
Autocorrelations of Residuals
  Lags                                            N SUM(R(k)**2)
   1- 5   -.047    .033   -.011    .030    .008      .875700
   6-10   -.032   -.031   -.045    .075   -.114     5.40366
  11-15   -.003    .022    .022   -.017    .015     5.69636
  16-20    .013    .029   -.009   -.086    .048     7.86385
  21-25   -.126    .065   -.017   -.024    .008    12.0560
  26-30    .045   -.111    .013    .008    .054    15.5414
Sum of Squares of Residuals =  16.8116
Variance of Residuals        =  .866577E-01
Durbin-Watson Statistic      =  2.01981
```

(c7t13)   **TABLE 7–16   (Example 4) (*continued*)**

Autocorrelation Structure of   ^RES

Lag	Auto-covariance	Auto-correlation	Partial Auto-correlation	Std. Err. Of Partial Auto-correlation
0	.844208E-01	1.00000	1.00000	0.00000
1	-.399953E-02	-.473761E-01	-.480623E-01	.710669E-01
2	.273672E-02	.324176E-01	.311339E-01	.712470E-01
3	-.961489E-03	-.113892E-01	-.881900E-02	.714286E-01
4	.256366E-02	.303677E-01	.293382E-01	.716115E-01
5	.684139E-03	.810391E-02	.101868E-01	.717958E-01
6	-.269149E-02	-.318819E-01	-.336615E-01	.719816E-01
7	-.256611E-02	-.303966E-01	-.345031E-01	.721688E-01
8	-.375123E-02	-.444349E-01	-.475162E-01	.723575E-01
9	.636401E-02	.753843E-01	.781168E-01	.725476E-01
10	-.967560E-02	-.114611	-.110785	.727393E-01
11	-.287798E-03	-.340908E-02	-.175686E-01	.729325E-01
12	.178409E-02	.211333E-01	.319170E-01	.731272E-01
13	.184751E-02	.218845E-01	.172144E-01	.733236E-01
14	-.145374E-02	-.172202E-01	-.164513E-01	.735215E-01
15	.122418E-02	.145010E-01	.193863E-01	.737210E-01
16	.103992E-02	.123183E-01	.110268E-01	.739221E-01
17	.243883E-02	.288890E-01	.321699E-01	.741249E-01
18	-.799791E-03	-.947385E-02	-.208245E-01	.743294E-01
19	-.730359E-02	-.865141E-01	-.854725E-01	.745356E-01
20	.402484E-02	.476759E-01	.402816E-01	.747435E-01
21	-.107028E-01	-.126779	-.135842	.749532E-01
22	.542510E-02	.642626E-01	.666937E-01	.751646E-01
23	-.146002E-02	-.172945E-01	.100758E-01	.753778E-01
24	-.212207E-02	-.251368E-01	-.453549E-01	.755929E-01

month, the order of the model might be 12 or more. There is a process for estimating "seasonal MA" and "seasonal AR" terms for the ARIMA process, but the details of estimating such terms are quite complicated. There is, however, an easier approach to using ARIMA with seasonal data, which uses a method already covered in Chapter 6.

This easier approach to handling seasonal data is to first deseasonalize the series, then estimate using ARIMA, and finally transform the forecasts by "reseasonalizing" them:

1. Deseasonalize the original time series as explained in Chapter 6.
2. Apply ARIMA and make the forecasts as you normally would.
3. Seasonalize the forecasts to reintroduce the seasonality into the model.

(c7t13)   **TABLE 7–16**   **(Example 4)** *(concluded)*

```
            Plot of Autocorrelation (+) and Partial Autocorrelation (*)

   Lag   -1.0                            0.0                               1.0
          |-----------------------------------+-----------------------------------|
      1 |                                  |  +*]  |                             |
      2 |                                  |  [+   |                             |
      3 |                                  |   +   |                             |
      4 |                                  |  [+   |                             |
      5 |                                  |   +   |                             |
      6 |                                  |  +]   |                             |
      7 |                                  |  +]   |                             |
      8 |                                  |  *+]  |                             |
      9 |                                  |  [*+  |                             |
     10 |                                  |+***]  |                             |
     11 |                                  |  *+   |                             |
     12 |                                  |  [+   |                             |
     13 |                                  |  [+   |                             |
     14 |                                  |  +]   |                             |
     15 |                                  |  +*   |                             |
     16 |                                  |  +    |                             |
     17 |                                  |  [+   |                             |
     18 |                                  |  *+   |                             |
     19 |                                  |+**]   |                             |
     20 |                                  |  [*+  |                             |
     21 |                                  |+***]  |                             |
     22 |                                  |  [*+  |                             |
     23 |                                  |  +[   |                             |
     24 |                                  |  +]   |                             |
```

Domestic Car Sales

Recall once again that the domestic car sales figures we have examined in past chapters show some trend and appear to exhibit a high degree of seasonality. For ARIMA purposes, we will have to difference the series in the manner that was discussed in the section "Stationarity." The mean of the series also shifts significantly from period to period because of a strong seasonal variation. We will first seasonally adjust the series in order to remove most of the seasonality. This method is described in the section "Forecasting Seasonal Time Series."

We begin by seasonally adjusting the domestic cars sales (DCS) series. Since the data are quarterly, we obtain a seasonal factor for each quarter (see Chapter 6 for a complete description of these seasonal factors and their calculation):

Quarter	Seasonal Factor
Quarter 1	0.967907
Quarter 2	1.10423
Quarter 3	1.01002
Quarter 4	0.926355

The domestic car sales data are seen again to be very seasonal. Quarters one and four appear to be "off" quarters for car sales, while quarter two is about 10 percent above average in sales.

Examining the autocorrelation and partial autocorrelation structure (Table 7–17A) note the clear pattern of the autocorrelation plot. This pattern is very much like the one in Table 7–6 and this suggests that the series is nonstationary. Using a single degree of differencing on this series eliminates the pattern of nonstationarity. See Table 7–17B and examine the plot; the nonstationarity characteristic is now absent and the data appear to be stationary.

(c7t17)   TABLE 7–17A   **Autocorrelation and Partial Autocorrelation Plots for the Seasonally Adjusted Domestic Car Sales Series. Note that the Series Appears to Be Nonstationary.**

Lag	Auto-covariance	Auto-correlation	Partial Auto-correlation	Std. Err. of Partial Auto-correlation
0	44637.4	1.00000	1.00000	0.00000
1	29661.6	.664501	.669843	.130189
2	26109.2	.584918	.240949	.131306
3	24077.3	.539398	.155484	.132453
4	22150.9	-.496242	.874145E-01	.133631
5	18895.4	.423310	-.301416E-01	.134840
6	12797.4	.286698	-.226116	.136083
7	5710.08	-.127921	-.291552	.137361
8	3083.14	-.690708E-01	-.726820E-01	.138675
9	-482.568	-.108109E-01	-.980263E-01	.140028
10	-4171.91	-.934623E-01	-.127175	.141421
11	-4541.32	-.101738	.146882	.142857
12	-11057.2	-.247712	-.224942	.144338

Plot of Autocorrelation (+) and Partial Autocorrelation (*)

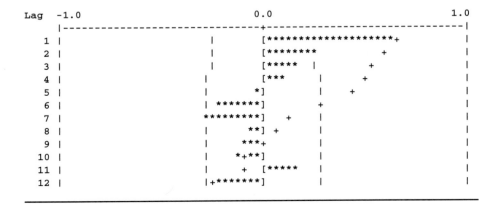

(c7t17)   TABLE **7–17B**   **Autocorrelation and Partial Autocorrelation Plots for the Seasonally Adjusted Domestic Car Sales Series after First-Degree Differencing. Note that the Series Now Appears to Be Stationary.**

Lag	Auto-covariance	Auto-correlation	Partial Auto-correlation	Std. Err. of Partial Auto-correlation
0	29729.8	1.00000	1.00000	0.00000
1	-9929.47	-.333991	-.362689	.131306
2	-1945.72	-.654469E-01	-.232821	.132453
3	-976.843	-.328574E-01	-.142011	.133631
4	1469.66	.494338E-01	-.184051E-01	.134840
5	4137.58	.139173	.163840	.136083
6	376.809	.126745E-01	.197648	.137361
7	-3490.28	-.117400	-.580661E-01	.138675
8	588.182	.197843E-01	-.501695E-01	.140028
9	428.570	.144155E-01	-.465960E-01	.141421
10	-3206.74	-.107863	-.293230	.142857
11	5553.25	.186791	.101647	.144338
12	-8332.67	-.280281	-.234067	.145865

```
       Plot of Autocorrelation (+) and Partial Autocorrelation (*)

Lag  -1.0                            0.0                              1.0
      |-----------------------------+-------------------------------|
  1 |                    *+**********]             |                  |
  2 |                    |*****+*]                 |                  |
  3 |                    |  ****+]                  |                  |
  4 |                    |     *] +                 |                  |
  5 |                    |    [***+*                |                  |
  6 |                    |     +******              |                  |
  7 |                    |   + **]                  |                  |
  8 |                    |    **]+                  |                  |
  9 |                    |     *+                   |                  |
 10 |              ******+**]                       |                  |
 11 |                    |       [***   +           |                  |
 12 |              + *******]                       |                  |
```

Since the series now appear stationary, we may attempt to identify a model that we could use in forecasting. While no one pattern we examined in Figures 7–1, 7–2, and 7–3 fits this situation very well, frame *b* of Figure 7–3 comes the closest to representing our current data. This suggests an ARMA(1, 1)-type model.

Table 7–18 is the estimation for an ARMA(1, 1) model *with first-degree ordinary differencing*. The residual plot for the first 12 lags of the residuals is also shown in Table 7–18. Note that we now appear to have only white noise in the residuals, and so the choice of ARMA(1, 1) with ordinary differencing is probably an accurate one.

TABLE 7–18   Parameter Estimates, Statistics, and Residual Autocorrelation Plot
for the ARIMA(1, 1, 1) Model Estimate with First-Degree Ordinary Differencing
(of the Seasonally Adjusted Domestic Car Sales Series)

```
Multivariate ARMA Estimation

Using  1980Q1-1994Q4
Terms in Autoregressive Process: 1
Terms in Moving Average Process: 1
Differencing on Dependent Variable, Order:  1
Parameters to be Estimated: 3
Initial parameter values and associated subscripts
 ( 1)  .000000     ( 1)  .000000     ( 0)  .000000
Non-linear Gaussian Estimation Procedure
59 Observations, 3 Parameters
Convergence achieved at 4 iterations.
Relative change in sum of squares less than  .100000E-02
Variance of residuals =     24268.1    , 57 degrees of freedom
Parameter Estimates

          Dependent Variable is ADJDCS
      Coefficient     Estimated    Standard        t-
      Description     Coefficient    Error       Statistic
       ^CONST          5.44639      10.0630       .541229
      /_AR-TERM{-1}   -.906555E-01   .245501     -.369268
       _MA-TERM{-1}    .458845       .209034      2.19507
ARMA Structure Information for the Error Term
Coefficients in the Infinite Autoregression
   1.00000      .549501      .252136      .115691      .530843E-01   .243575E-01
                .111763E-01  .512819E-02  .235305E-02  .107968E-02   .495408E-03
                .227315E-03  .104303E-03  .478587E-04  .219597E-04   .100761E-04
                .462337E-05  .212141E-05
Total Multiplier =   2.01542
Coefficients in the Infinite Moving Average
   1.00000     -.549501      .498152E-01 -.451603E-02  .409403E-03 -.371146E-04
                .336464E-05
Total Multiplier =   .496174
Autocorrelations of Residuals
   Lags                                        N SUM(R(k)**2)
   1- 5    .099   -.044   -.008    .112    .216    4.20824
   6-10    .033   -.133   -.061   -.053   -.076    6.04261
  11-15    .041   -.220    .015   -.232   -.187   14.2388
  16-20    .115   -.010    .020   -.076   -.109   16.0992
  21-25    .108    .116    .009   -.105   -.212   20.8952
  26-30    .003    .068   -.163    .071   -.036   23.0979
Sum of Squares of Residuals =  .138328E+07
Variance of Residuals      =  24268.1
Durbin-Watson Statistic    =  1.79162
R-Squared =    .4807
```

(c7t17)

(c7t17)   TABLE 7–18   **The ARIMA(1, 1, 1) Model Estimate (*concluded*)**

Lag	Auto-covariance	Auto-correlation	Partial Auto-correlation	Std. Err. of Partial Auto-correlation
0	23347.1	1.00000	1.00000	0.00000
1	2275.05	.97446E-01	.103525	.131306
2	-1049.51	-.449523E-01	-.556702E-01	.132453
3	-253.843	-.108722E-01	-.865778E-01	.133631
4	2530.34	.108379	.121631	.134840
5	5003.72	.214319	.242394	.136083
6	691.469	.296169E-01	-.270984E-01	.137361
7	-3188.64	-.136575	-.158962	.138675
8	-1480.14	-.633971E-01	-.372576E-01	.140028
9	-1285.83	-.550746E-01	-.107068	.141421
10	-1812.17	-.776187E-01	-.173538	.142857
11	891.422	.381812E-01	.104350	.144338
12	-5229.30	-.223980	-.188094	.145865

```
    Plot of Autocorrelation (+) and Partial Autocorrelation (*)

Lag  -1.0                            0.0                          1.0
     |-----------------------------+-----------------------------|
  1  |                             |      [**+    |                |
  2  |                             |     *+]       |               |
  3  |                       |     +      |                        |
  4  |                       |     [**+*  |                        |
  5  |                       |     [******+* |                     |
  6  |                       |      *]+    |                        |
  7  |                       | *+***]      |                        |
  8  |                       |    +*]      |                        |
  9  |                       |   *+*]      |                        |
 10  |                       | ****+*]     |                        |
 11  |                       |      [+**   |                        |
 12  |                       | +******]    |                        |
```

The Box-Pierce statistic for the first 30 lags is 23.0979 and confirms the accuracy of the model.

Calculating the RMSE for the ARMA(1, 1) model *with first-degree ordinary differencing* gives 68.79. We can compare this with our previous results using other forecasting techniques.

Summary Table of RMSEs for DCS

Chapter	Method	Period	RMSE
1	Naive—with 4 period lag	Historic before '95	207.3
		Holdout 95Q1–95Q4	74.9
2	Not applicable	Historic before '95	na
		Holdout 95Q1–95Q4	na
3	Winters' exponential smoothing	Historic before '95	177.1
		Holdout 95Q1–95Q4	55.8
	ADRES with seasonal adjustment	Historic before '95	169.5
		Holdout 95Q1–95Q4	64.2
4	Simple regression model using seasonally adjusted DCS as a function of the University of Michigan Index of Consumer Sentiment	Historic before '95	134.570
		Holdout 95Q1–95Q4	102.242
5	Multiple regression	Historic before '95	106.8
		Holdout 95Q1–95Q4	56.9
6	Time-series decomposition	Historic before '95	130.185
		Holdout 95Q1–95Q4	140.930
7	ARMA(1,1) model with first-degree ordinary differencing on seasonally adjusted DCS	Historic before '95	*
		Holdout 95Q1–95Q4	68.79

*Unavailable with this technique

Comments from the Field

An Overview of INTELSAT Forecasting[1]
INTELSAT

At the International Telecommunications Satellite Organization (INTELSAT), forecasting techniques have been employed to assist in developing estimates of future demand for international satellite telecommunications. This is accomplished by using as a base the demand projections provided by each of the approximately 200 worldwide telecommunications entities located within 130 countries and territories. Every year, a new 15-year projection, which is needed for long-range financial and new spacecraft planning, is developed.

The provision of international telephone satellite trunk circuits represents a fundamental portion of INTELSAT business. It is practically impossible for INTELSAT to attempt to assemble accurate worldwide point-to-point forecasts, because of the number of technical and economic details required on each system user. In order to develop such forecasts, an annual global traffic meeting (GTM) is held, attended by each of the system users. During this week-long meeting, users can discuss and negotiate with each of their worldwide correspondents their estimates of future mutual traffic demand. These discussions are based on the network planning and preliminary traffic projections each system user develops prior to the GTM. The GTM delegates submit their mutually agreed forecasts as they are completed, and these are entered into a database (Oracle) for subsequent analysis and processing.

In developing their forecast of satellite circuits, established system users will typically make use of quantitative forecasting methods, because there exists a historical base of measured or known traffic. In the new and emerging countries, such as the members of the Commonwealth of Independent States (formerly USSR), where there are either few data or none available, the less experienced system users tend to accept the suggestions of their larger, more established correspondent countries. In some instances, user forecast estimates will not be determined from an analysis of computed demand, but decided by the funds projected to be available to purchase the necessary telecommunications equipment.

An additional significant service category that INTELSAT offers to telecommunications entities is leases for satellite capacity. These users' inputs describe the technical operating qualities needed for each lease along with information on anticipated start date, duration, and renewal potential. These requests from all users are aggregated and sorted by geographic region. The aggregated near-term user data can provide, on a systemwide basis, fairly accurate estimates of the potential growth trends to be expected. The 15-year, long-term demand for leases is developed using nonlinear regression analysis, historical trend analysis, and the three- to five-year near-term growth rate projections. Studies indicate that historically, these projected trends closely correlate to the realized system usages.

Recently, work was begun to look into methodologies to supplement the forecasts as provided by the system users. Two approaches that are currently being investigated are econometric demand models and stochastic time-series models. The development of an econometric model is recognized as a considerable endeavor, and one method that is being considered is to define the model in terms of geographic groups of countries so as to limit the complexity of the demand function.

As a specific example of INTELSAT's forecasting, consider the occasional-use television channel-hours provided to TV broadcasters needing satellites to relay news coverage around the world. Data on such occasional-use television satellite use date back to 1983. A Box-Jenkins, second-order autoregressive-integrated moving-average model [ARIMA (2, 1, 1)] was applied to the quarterly data of usage statistics from 1983 through the fourth-quarter of 1992. The parameters of the model were estimated by excluding the 1992 data (holdout period), and an "ex-post" forecast was developed and compared with the 1992 period. Having accepted the model performance, an "ex-ante" forecast, for a future time period, was generated.

For the future, work will continue on evaluation and development of forecasting models appropriate to each of INTELSAT's many telecommunications services.

---

[1]This overview of forecasting at INTELSAT was provided by Martin J. Kelinsky, forecasting manager, INTELSAT, Washington, D.C.

INTEGRATIVE CASE
Forecasting Sales of The Gap

Case Questions

1. From your previous experience plotting the Gap sales over time, what ARIMA techniques should you keep in mind when approaching this data?

2. Prepare a plot of the autocorrelation and partial autocorrelation coefficients of the Gap sales data. Does this correlogram suggest an ARIMA approach that could be used for forecasting Gap sales?

3. Apply a model suggested by the correlogram plot and calculate the RMSE for your forecast of the four quarters of 1996. Recall that the actual 1996 sales (in thousands) were: Quarter 1—1,113,154; Quarter 2—1,120,335; Quarter 3—1,382,996; Quarter 4—1,667,896.

Solutions to Case Questions

1. The seasonal pattern and trend should now be familiar. These data will not be stationary and some adjustment will have to be made to obtain stationarity. The strong seasonal pattern could require some adjustment. It is also the case that the pattern of the data is quite regular and some ARIMA technique should do an excellent job of fitting a model.

(c7t19)

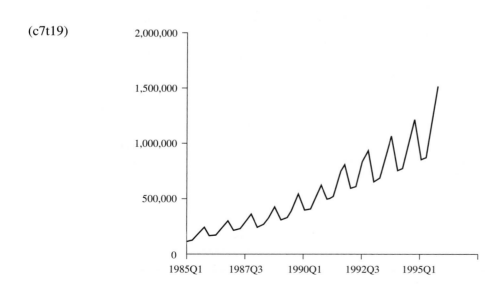

2. The correlogram for the unadjusted Gap sales shows the possibility of nonstationarity (see Table 7–19). Since we already know that the data are seasonal, the nonstationarity and the seasonality might be accounted for by using seasonal differencing. Applying two degrees of seasonal differencing to the data produces a correlogram that is much more easily interpreted (see Table 7–20).

3. While a number of models may perform quite well, ARIMA(2, 0, 0) model *with two degrees of seasonal differencing* seems to provide a good fit. The model estimation indicates that the Box-Pierce statistic is 10.7970 for the 30 autocorrelations, which confirms the accuracy of the model.

The correlogram of the residuals to the model shows only white noise (see Table 7–20).

The actual and predicted values for 1996Q1 through 1996Q4 are shown below. The RMSE for these four quarters is: RMSE = 96,975.1. This is about a 7.3 percent error based on the average quarterly sales for the year (1,321,095.25). See Table 7–21 for parameter estimates and forecasted values.

(c7t19) **TABLE 7–19   Autocorrelation and Partial Autocorrelation Plots for Gap Sales (For the Historic Period of 1985Q1 Through 1995Q4)**

Lag	Auto-covariance	Auto-correlation	Partial Auto-correlation	Std. Err. of Partial Auto-correlation
0	.109001E+12	1.00000	1.00000	0.00000
1	.845640E+11	.775806	.889461	.152499
2	.681288E+11	.625026	.107430E-01	.154303
3	.716136E+11	.656997	.706029	.156147
4	.797347E+11	.731502	.949389	.158114
5	.609908E+11	.559541	-.598983	.160128
6	.468076E+11	.429422	.218828	.162221
7	.487297E+11	.447055	-.296877E-01	.164399
8	.550319E+11	.504873	.793343E-01	.166667
9	.388595E+11	.356505	.156733	.169031
10	.257134E+11	.235900	-.823453E-01	.171499
11	.263205E+11	.241470	.902321E-01	.174078
12	.312458E+11	.286655	.305214	.176777

```
       Plot of Autocorrelation (+) and Partial Autocorrelation (*)

Lag   -1.0                          0.0                           1.0
     |-------------------------------+-----------------------------|
  1  |                               |    [*********************+***    |
  2  |                               |    [        |        +          |
  3  |                               |    [****************+**          |
  4  |                               |    [********************+******* |
  5  |           *****************]   |        +                        |
  6  |                               |    [*******  |   +              |
  7  |                               |    *]        |  +               |
  8  |                               |    [***      |    +             |
  9  |                               |    [*****    +   |              |
 10  |                               |  ***]       +   |              |
 11  |                               |    [***    +  |                |
 12  |                               |    [********+*|                |
```

(c7t19) TABLE 7–20 **Autocorrelation and Partial Autocorrelation Plots for Gap Sales after Two Degrees of Seasonal Differencing Have Been Applied (Which Allows the Model to Be More Easily Identified). This Examination Covers Only the Historic Period 1985Q1 Through 1995Q4.**

Lag	Auto-covariance	Auto-correlation	Partial Auto-correlation	Std. Err. of Partial Auto-correlation
0	.211802E+10	1.00000	1.00000	0.00000
1	.108179E+10	.510754	.613612	.169031
2	.194360E+09	.917652E-01	-.346585	.171499
3	-.287574E+09	-.135775	-.118042	.174078
4	-.465808E+09	-.219926	-.101815	.176777
5	-.359238E+09	-.169611	.168907	.179605
6	-.145019E+09	-.684690E-01	-.496876E-01	.182574
7	.896622E+08	.423331E-01	.344514E-02	.185695
8	-.105950E+09	-.500232E-01	-.171607	.188982
9	-.130168E+09	-.614576E-01	.381428E-01	.192450
10	-.294517E+08	-.139053E-01	-.130007	.196116
11	-.310190E+09	-.146453	-.347512	.200000
12	-.614111E+09	-.289946	-.496578	.204124

```
Plot of Autocorrelation (+) and Partial Autocorrelation (*)

Lag  -1.0                            0.0                              1.0
  |------------------------------+------------------------------|
 1 |                        |         [***************+****        |
 2 |              **********]    +          |                      |
 3 |                    |   +***]           |                      |
 4 |                    |  +   ***]         |                      |
 5 |                    |     +  [*****      |                      |
 6 |                    |       +*]         |                      |
 7 |                    |       [+          |                      |
 8 |                    |    ***+*]         |                      |
 9 |                    |     + [*          |                      |
10 |                    |     ****+         |                      |
11 |              |  ******+****]           |                      |
12 |              *******+********]          |                      |
```

	GAPSALES	ARIMA Forecast
1996Q1	1,113,154	1,075,320
1996Q2	1,120,335	1,025,480
1996Q3	1,383,996	1,334,130
1996Q4	1,667,896	1,825,350

(c7t19) TABLE **7–21** **Parameter Estimates, Statistics, and Residual Autocorrelation Plot for Gap Sales ARIMA(2,0) Model Estimate *with* Two Orders of Common Seasonal Differencing**

```
Multivariate ARMA Estimation

Using 1985Q1-1995Q4
Terms in Autoregressive Process: 2
Common Seasonal Differencing---Season Length: 4
Common Seasonal Differencing---Season, order:  2
Parameters to Be Estimated: 3
Initial parameter values and associated subscripts
( 1)  .000000      ( 2)  .000000      ( 0)  .000000
Non-linear Gaussian Estimation Procedure
36 Observations, 3 Parameters
Convergence achieved at 4 iterations.
Relative change in sum of squares less than   .100000E-03
Variance of residuals =       .122734E+10,  34 degrees of freedom
Parameter Estimates

          Dependent Variable is GAPSALES
        Coefficient        Estimated      Standard        t-
        Description        Coefficient      Error       Statistic
         ^CONST             15027.1        11665.8       1.28814
        /_AR-TERM{-1}       0.957545       0.182777      5.23888
        /_MA-TERM{-2}      -0.427542       0.190452     -2.24382
ARMA Structure Information for the Error Term
Coefficients in the Infinite Moving Average
    1.00000        .957545        .489350       .591834E-01 -.152547      -.171
                  -.988781E-01  -.214105E-01   .217731E-01   .300026E-01  .194
                   .576806E-02  -.277966E-02  -.512774E-02  -.372162E-02 -.137
                   .278078E-03   .852557E-03   .697472E-03   .303356E-03 -.772
                  -.137091E-03  -.127970E-03  -.639245E-04  -.649802E-05  .211
                   .229903E-04   .129896E-04   .260876E-05  -.305559E-05 -.404
                  -.256326E-05
Total Multiplier =   2.12767
Autocorrelation of Residuals
  Lags                                          N SUM(R(k)**2)
   1- 5    -.048    .026    .080   -.203    .036      1.85992
   6-10    -.046    .046   -.029   -.088   -.060      2.45129
  11-15    -.003   -.124   -.221   -.018   -.169      5.80611
  16-20     .052    .321   -.028    .023    .007      9.66818
  21-25    -.087    .071    .017    .007    .113     10.5975
  26-30    -.049    .031    .017   -.037   -.021     10.7940
Sum of Squares of Residuals =   .417296E+11
Variance of Residuals       =   .122734E+10
Durbin-Watson Statistic     =   1.86369
R-Squared =      .9810
```

(c7t19) TABLE 7–21   The ARIMA(2,0) Model Estimate (*concluded*)

```
              Autocorrelation Structure of ^RES

                                                Partial      Std. Err. of
                          Auto-        Auto-      Auto-       Partial Auto-
          Lag           covariance   correlation correlation correlation
          ----------------------------------------------------------------
           0            .115850E+10    1.00000     1.00000      0.00000
           1           -.544221E+08  -.469762E-01 -.521474E-01  .169031
           2            .318641E+08   .275045E-01  .232446E-01  .171499
           3            .950107E+08   .820116E-01  .107417      .174078
           4           -.232893E+09  -.201028     -.214544      .176777
           5            .430757E+08   .371822E-01 -.184142E-01  .179605
           6           -.514482E+08  -.444091E-01 -.432301E-01  .182574
           7            .544949E+08   .470390E-01  .111760      .185695
           8           -.330629E+08  -.285393E-01 -.869309E-01  .188982
           9           -.991963E+08  -.856245E-01 -.153333      .192450
          10           -.688316E+08  -.594142E-01 -.946960E-01  .196116
          11           -.215258E+07  -.185807E-02  .386386E-01  .200000
          12           -.142977E+09  -.123415     -.282525      .204124
```

```
        Plot of Autocorrelation (+) and Partial Autocorrelation (*)

    Lag  -1.0                        0.0                          1.0
         |---------------------------+----------------------------|
      1  |                          |    +*]                |              |
      2  |                          |    [+                 |              |
      3  |                          |    [**+               |              |
      4  |                          | *+*****]              |              |
      5  |                          |   *]+                 |              |
      6  |                          |   +]                  |              |
      7  |                          |    [*+**              |              |
      8  |                          | **+]                  |              |
      9  |                          | **+**]                |              |
     10  |                        |    *+*]                 |              |
     11  |                        |    +*                   |              |
     12  |                        | *****+***]              |              |
```

	GAPSALES		*GAPSALES*		*GAPSALES*		*GAPSALES*
1985Q1	105715	1988Q1	241348	1991Q1	490300	1994Q1	751670
1985Q2	120136	1988Q2	264328	1991Q2	523056	1994Q2	773131
1985Q3	181669	1988Q3	322752	1991Q3	702052	1994Q3	988346
1985Q4	239813	1988Q4	423669	1991Q4	803485	1994Q4	0.120979E+07
1986Q1	159980	1989Q1	309925	1992Q1	588864	1995Q1	848688
1986Q2	164760	1989Q2	325939	1992Q2	614114	1995Q2	868514
1986Q3	224800	1989Q3	405601	1992Q3	827222	1995Q4	0.152212E+07
1986Q4	298469	1989Q4	545131	1992Q4	930209	1996Q1	0.107532E+07
1987Q1	211060	1990Q1	402368	1993Q1	643580	1996Q2	0.102548E+07
1987Q2	217753	1990Q2	404996	1993Q2	693192	1996Q3	0.133413E+07
1987Q3	273616	1990Q3	501690	1993Q3	898677	1995Q3	0.115593E+07
1987Q4	359592	1990Q4	624726	1993Q4	0.106023E+07	1996Q4	0.182535E+07

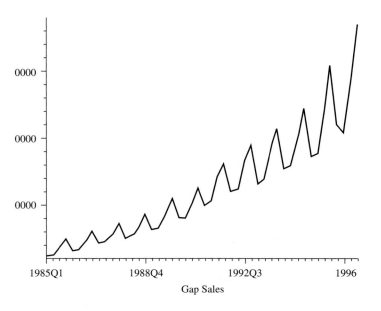

Gap Sales

Summary Table of RMSEs for GAP Sales

Chapter	Method	Period	RMSE
1	Naive—with 4-period lag	Historic before '95	107,150
		Holdout 96Q1–96Q4	227,027
2		Historic before '95	na
		Holdout 96Q1–96Q4	na
3	Winters' exponential smoothing	Historic before '95	37,935.5
		Holdout 96Q1–96Q4	84,460.7
	Holt's exponential smoothing with seasonal readjustment	Historic before '95	31,272.5
		Holdout 96Q1–96Q4	33,341.3
4	Linear trend of deseasonalized data with forecast	Historic before '95	56,110.6
		Holdout 96Q1–96Q4	211,550.0
5	Multiple regression	Historic before '95	56,178.1
		Holdout 96Q1–96Q4	116,620.0
6	Time-series decomposition	Historic before '95	25,706.9
		Holdout 96Q1–96Q4	145,488.0
7	ARMA(2,0) with two degrees of seasonal differencing	Historic before '95	*
		Holdout 96Q1–96Q4	96,975.1

*Unavailable with this technique

USING SORITEC FOR ARIMA ANALYSIS

There are two new commands needed in order to handle ARIMA-type forecasting; these are the **EXAMINE AUTOCORRELATIONS** and **ARIMA** commands. **EXAMINE AUTO-CORRELATIONS** is used to calculate and display tables of autocorrelations and partial autocorrelations of any time series. **EXAMINE AUTOCORRELATIONS** will always be the first command used when attempting to specify an ARIMA model; **EXAMINE AUTO-CORRELATIONS** provides the data you need in order to perform the identification of the tentative model.

Begin by turning on the plot flag (so that you will automatically produce the plots of the correlograms) and loading 🖝 the data for the MA(1) model in the chapter (loading the data in Table 7–2 will read in all five of the series included in Table 7–2). To turn on the plot flag type:

ON PLOT

Use the **SYMBOLS** command (from the **View** menu) to inspect the names of the various series in this SAL (SORITEC Alternate Load) file. First, select the variable to be examined (**MA1**) by using the **Y-Variable** selection button 𝓨.

Determining the Appropriate Model in ARIMA

The series called MA1 is the series you are currently interested in; it contains 200 observations. You may inspect the first 24 autocorrelations and partial autocorrelations with the **EXAMINE AUTOCORRELATIONS** command in the **Time Series** menu (this produces the data and plot in Table 7–4):

(c7t2)

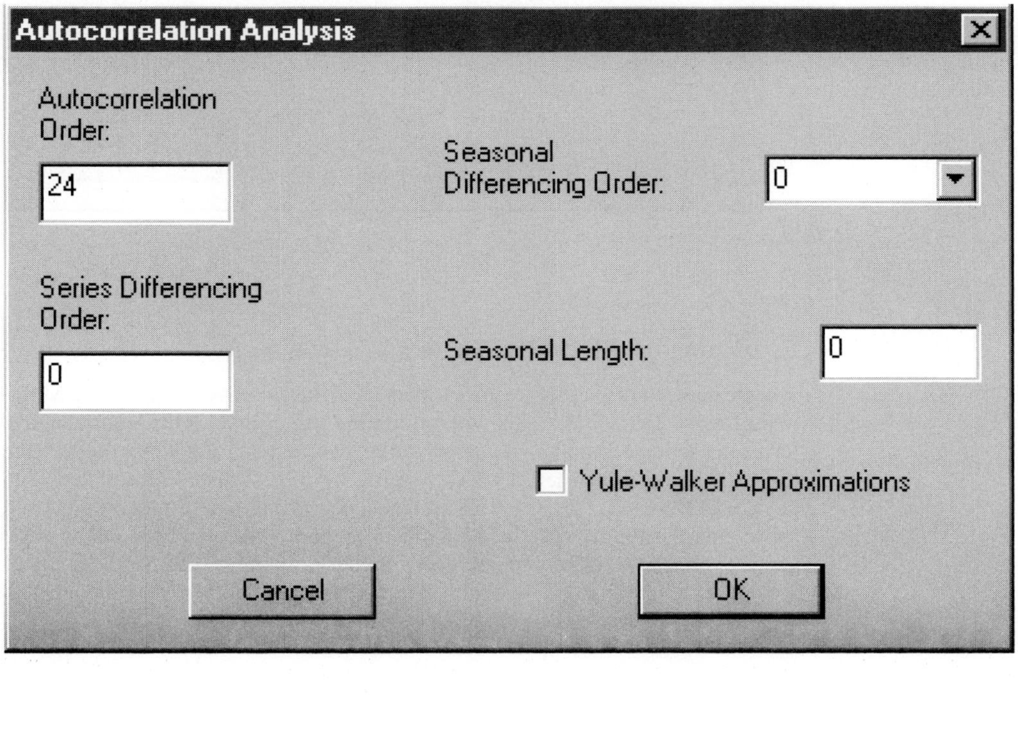

To inspect the correlograms and table for the series labeled AR1, select the variable to be examined (AR1) by using the **Y-Variable** selection button **Y** and again use the **EXAMINE AUTOCORRELATIONS** selection from the **Time Series** menu. This will produce the plot in Table 7–5.

To produce the results in Table 7–6 for an ARIMA(1,1,1) model, select the variable to be examined (ARIMA111) by using the **Y-Variable** selection button **Y** and again use the **EXAMINE AUTOCORRELATIONS** selection from the **Time Series** menu.

Note that "ARIMA111" is the name of the series and not a SORITEC command. Also recall that the ARIMA111 data is nonstationary; in order to remove the nonstationarity it was necessary to take first differences of the series (this produced Table 7–7). The first differences can be easily specified with the **EXAMINE AUTOCORRELATIONS** dialog box in the following manner:

(c7t2)

Note the change in the series differencing order box

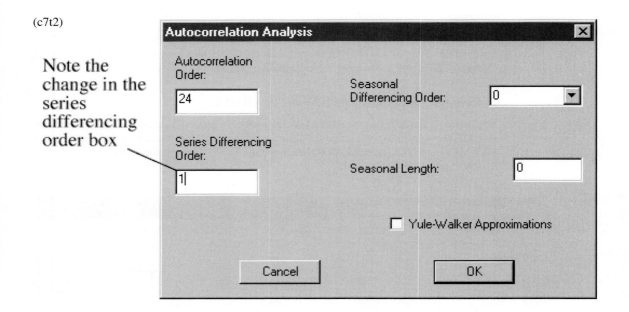

Estimating the Model Parameters in ARIMA

You are now ready to estimate the parameters of the tentative model for the MA1 series (which will produce Table 7–8). This will require the use of the **ARIMA** command. **ARIMA** performs the actual estimation of a large variety of dynamic time-series models; the modifiers of the **ARIMA** command select which type of model is estimated. Recall that you must first use the **EXAMINE AUTOCORRELATIONS** command to help suggest what type of ARIMA model you wish to fit with the **ARIMA** command. Since you have already done this above, you are ready to proceed with the actual model estimation. The **ARIMA** command includes a modifier to allow you to compute forecasts for any number of periods into the future (but we will set the forecast horizon to zero for now).

To estimate an MA(1)-type model on the MA1 series use the **ARIMA** dialog box in the **Time Series** menu:

(c7t2)

Set the MA Order box to 1.

Be certain that the Forecast Horizon box is set to zero.

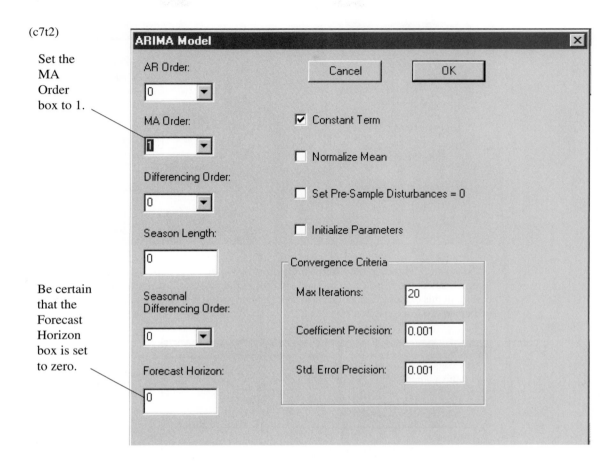

Forecasting with ARIMA Using the "Forecast Button"[1]

If you wish to compute the model **and** forecast for one period into the future with the estimated model, this is accomplished by using the "forecast tool" or button ⚏.

Run the estimation of the model and the one-period forecast by filling in the **ARIMA** dialog box as follows:

---

[1] You should always use the forecast button when you are attempting to make a forecast using an ARIMA model. Do not use the ARIMA selection from the **Time Series** menu to prepare actual forecasts.

(c7t2)

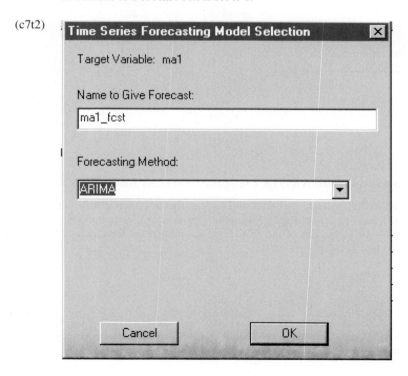

Note carefully that in the **Forecast Options** dialog box you must indicate the variable to forecast, select the forecasting method, and fill in the first and last periods in the estimation period. In this example we will forecast out just one period into the future and so the **Number of Periods to Forecast** box is set to 1.

(c7t2)

In the **Model Selection** dialog box you must select the method you will use to forecast the data series. In this example ARIMA is chosen from the options.

(c7t2)

The **ARIMA Model** dialog box appears and you must select the type of model to estimate. Since we have already determined that the appropriate model is an MA(1)-type model, we select one moving average term. The **Forecast Horizon** box is automatically filled in; do not change the value in this box. When you exit this menu the model will again be estimated and the value(s) of the forecast will be computed and placed under a different variable name (here that name is MA1_fcst).

A plot of the MA1 variable and the model's forecast may be plotted using the plot button and selecting the appropriate variable name to plot.

(c7t2)

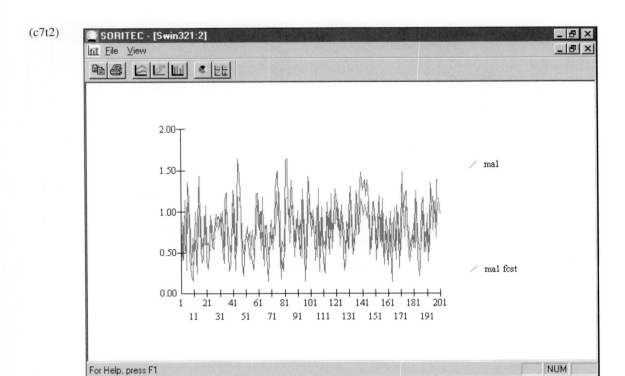

Diagnosing the Appropriateness of the Model

The third step in the Box-Jenkins process is to diagnose the appropriateness of the tentative model. When you used the "forecast button" above, SORITEC calculated the residuals produced by the estimation procedure and stored them as a variable called ^RES. Note carefully that the carat is a part of this variable's name.

To diagnose the appropriateness of the tentative model, you must inspect the correlograms of those residuals. To do this you again use the **EXAMINE AUTOCORRELATIONS** command. If the plot flag is on (**ON PLOT**), you will see the table and the correlogram (which are part of Table 7–8).

Before producing Table 7–9, it may be useful to use the **FRESH** command to clear your memory. Reload ☞ the Table 7–2 data before continuing.

Reproducing Table 7–9 (the "Whitenoise" Series)

To produce Table 7–9, which inspects the series called whitenoise, you should select the whitenoise series as the "Y" variable 🇾 and again use the **EXAMINE AUTOCORRELATIONS** command:

(c7t2)

Estimating the AR(1) Model

To estimate the AR(1) model as shown in Table 7–10, select the AR1 data series as the "Y" variable $\mathcal{Y}$ and choose ARIMA from the **Time Series** menu:

(c7t2)

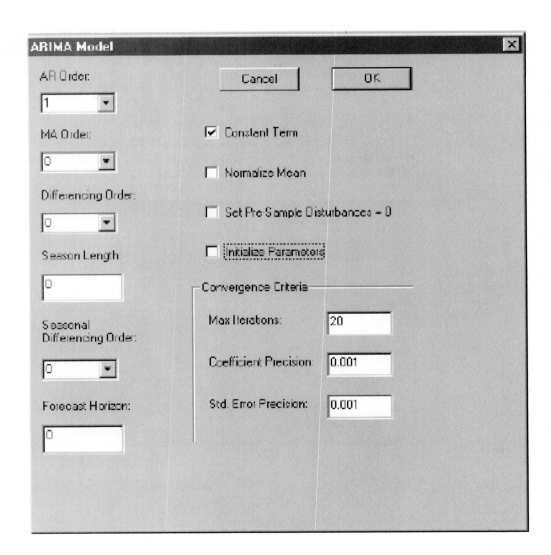

To diagnose the appropriateness of the AR(1) model of Table 7–10, first select ^RES $\mathcal{Y}$ as the variable to be examined and then use the **EXAMINE AUTOCORRELATIONS** command:

(c7t2)

Autocorrelation Analysis ⊠

Autocorrelation
Order:

24

Seasonal
Differencing Order: 0 ▼

Series Differencing
Order:

0

Seasonal Length: 0

☐ Yule-Walker Approximations

Cancel   OK

Note that as you estimate each new model, the residuals for that model are always stored under the ^RES name, thus overwriting any residuals previously calculated for other models. So, if you wish to inspect the residuals for a particular model, you must first run that model (i.e., use the **ARIMA** command) and then inspect the residuals before estimating another model.

Reproducing Some Other Tables from the Text

To inspect the series called AR2, as shown in Table 7–11, begin by selecting 🅨 the AR2 variable and using the **EXAMINE AUTOCORRELATIONS** command:

(c7t2)

Autocorrelation Analysis ⊠

Autocorrelation
Order:

24

Seasonal
Differencing Order: 0 ▼

Series Differencing
Order:

0

Seasonal Length: 0

☐ Yule-Walker Approximations

Cancel   OK

The AR(2) model estimation in Table 7–12 is obtained by using the **ARIMA** command with the AR(2) model specified with one degree of differencing:

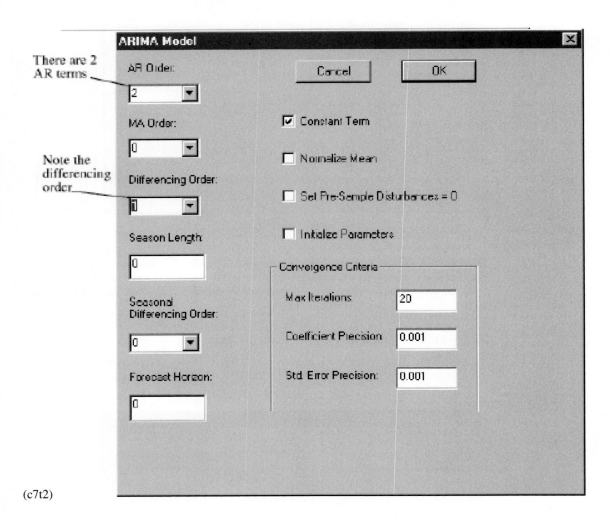

There are 2 AR terms

Note the differencing order

(c7t2)

Again the autocorrelation structure of the residuals is given by changing the **use** period to allow for the differencing:

```
USE 2 200
```

Then select **Y** the ^RES variable and use the **EXAMINE AUTOCORRELATIONS** command:

(c7t2)

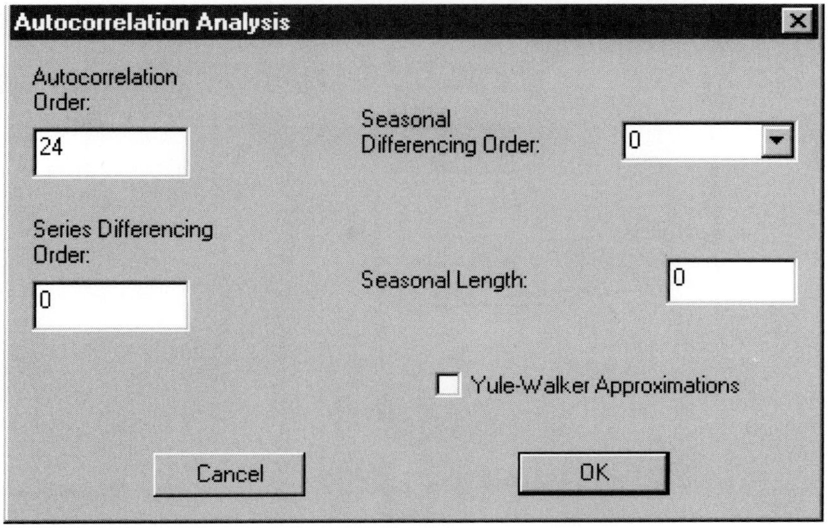

Autocorrelation Analysis ☒

Autocorrelation
Order:

24

Seasonal
Differencing Order: 0 ▼

Series Differencing
Order:

0

Seasonal Length: 0

☐ Yule-Walker Approximations

Cancel   OK

The data in Table 7–13 must be read 🖼 into SORITEC before analysis. It would be best to use the **FRESH** command before continuing (be sure to turn the plot flag on):

ON PLOT

to examine the characteristics of the **SYMBOLS** command from the **View** menu.

You may wish to visually examine the series by printing the variable named ARIMA:

PRINT ARIMA

To inspect the series, as shown in Table 7–14, first select 📈 ARIMA as the variable to be examined and then use the **EXAMINE AUTOCORRELATIONS** command:

(c7t13)

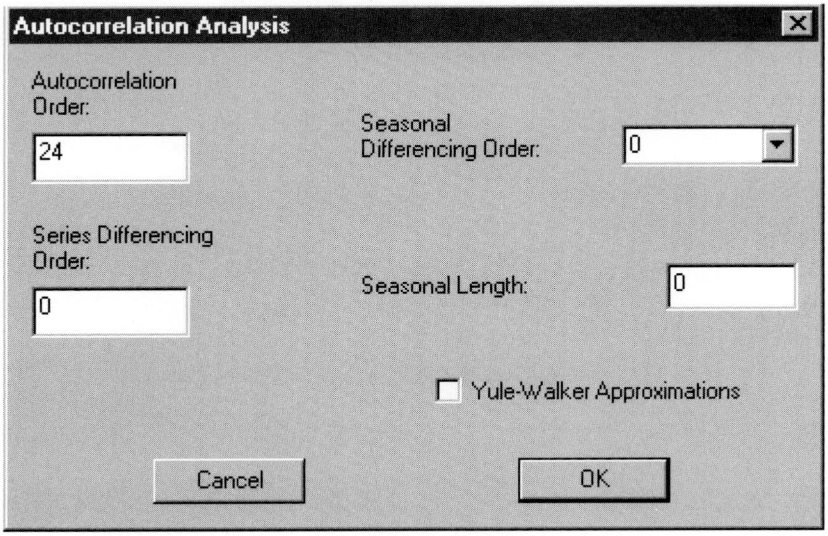

Autocorrelation Analysis ☒

Autocorrelation
Order:

24

Seasonal
Differencing Order: 0 ▼

Series Differencing
Order:

0

Seasonal Length: 0

☐ Yule-Walker Approximations

Cancel   OK

To inspect the series *after* taking first differences as in Table 7–15:

(c7t13)

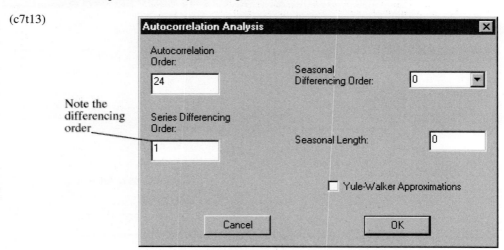

The ARIMA(3,1,2) model of Table 7–16, which was suggested as the tentative model, is estimated by using the **ARIMA** command with numerous modifiers, as noted below. Be patient; this estimation procedure is quite complex and it will take a few moments for SORITEC to complete.

(c7t13)

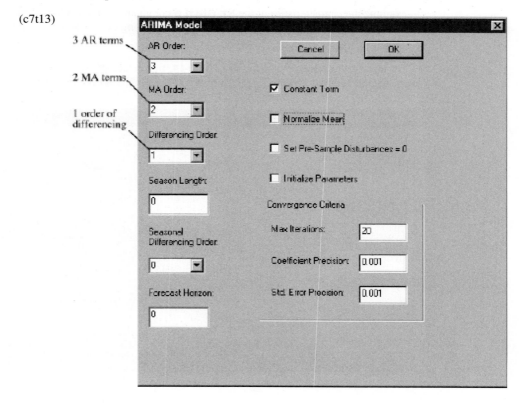

Since you have used first differences in the estimation procedure, you will have one less observation in the series; you adjust for this before you inspect the residuals with:

(c7t13)

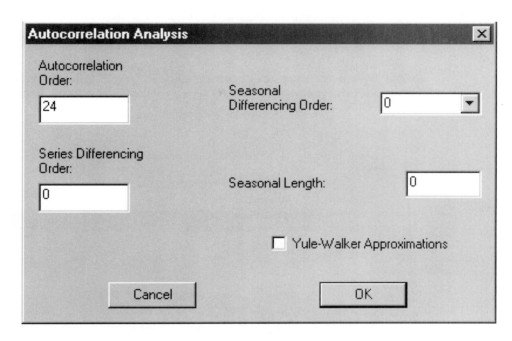

Now you may inspect the residuals with the familiar:

(c7t13)

Using ARIMA Analysis on the Domestic Car Sales Data

To estimate an ARIMA model for the domestic car sales data, you must first load 📂 the data. It would be best to quit SORITEC and start a new session before continuing (be sure to turn the plot flag to **on**):

```
ON PLOT
```

We will first adjust the domestic car sales data for seasonality, using the **ADJUST** command. The created variable, which is the seasonally adjusted domestic car sales, will be called ADJDCS:

```
ADJUST ADJDCS DCS
```

In the inspection of the seasonally adjusted domestic car sales series (Table 7–17A) you will use:

(c7t17)

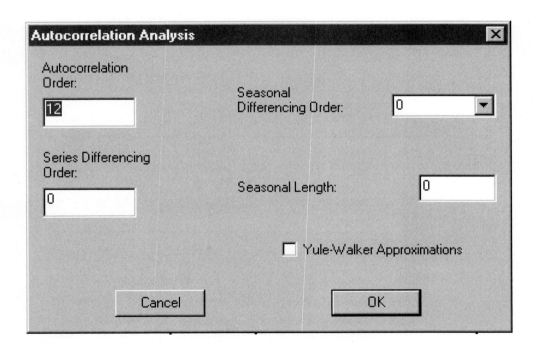

Since Table 7–17A clearly shows nonstationarity, you will again examine the correlogram, this time *with* ordinary first-degree differencing. This produces the plot in Table 7–17B:

(c7t17)

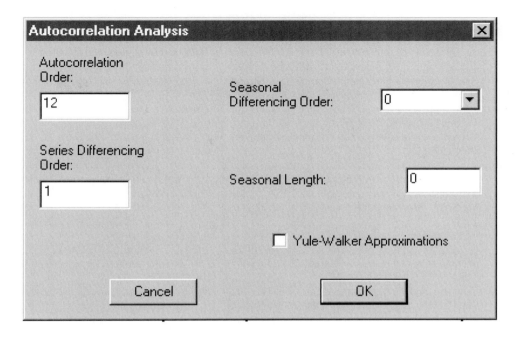

The estimation of the ARIMA(1,1,1) model *with* ordinary differencing, as seen in Table 7–18, is given by:

(c7t17)

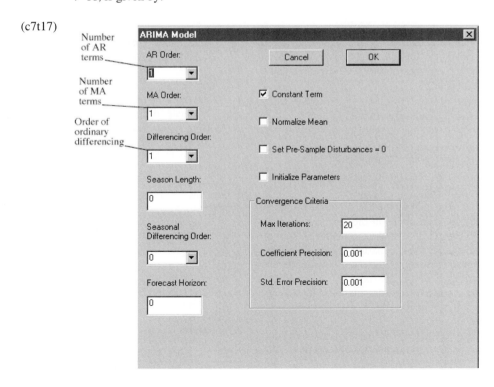

Suggested Readings

Armstrong, Scott J.; and Edward J. Lusk. "Research on the Accuracy of Alternative Extrapolation Models: Analysis of a Forecasting Competition Through Open Peer Review." *Journal of Forecasting* 2 (1983), pp. 259–62.

Box, G.; and G. Jenkins. *Time Series Analysis: Forecasting and Control.* Rev. ed. San Francisco: Holden-Day, 1976.

Brandon, Charles H.; Jeffrey E. Jarrett; and Saleha Khumawala. "Revising Forecasts of Accounting Earnings: A Comparison with the Box-Jenkins Method." *Management Science* 29 (1983), pp. 256–63.

Brown, Lawrence D.; and Michael S. Rozeff. "The Superiority of Analyst Forecasts as Measures of Expectations: Evidence from Earnings." *Journal of Finance* 33 (1978), pp. 1–16.

Chatfield, C.; and D. L. Prothero. "Box-Jenkins Seasonal Forecasting Problems in a Case Study." *Journal of the Royal Statistical Society* Series A 136 (1973), pp. 295–352.

Hill, Gareth; and Robert Fildes. "The Accuracy of Extrapolation Methods: An Automatic Box-Jenkins Package (SIFT)." *Journal of Forecasting* 3 (1984), pp. 319–23.

Libert, G. "The M-Competition with a Fully Automatic Box-Jenkins Procedure." *Journal of Forecasting* 3 (1984), pp. 325–28.

Lusk, Edward J.; and Joao S. Neves. "A Comparative ARIMA Analysis of the 111 Series of the Makridakis Competition." *Journal of Forecasting* 3 (1984), pp. 329–32.

Nelson, Charles R. *Applied Time Series Analysis for Managerial Forecasting.* San Francisco: Holden-Day, 1973.

Pankratz, Alan. *Forecasting with Univariate Box-Jenkins Models.* New York: John Wiley & Sons, 1983.

Pindyck, Robert S.; and Daniel L. Rubinfeld. *Econometric Models and Economic Forecasts.* 3rd ed. New York: McGraw-Hill, 1991.

Exercises

1. A student collects data on the use of the university library on an hourly basis for eight consecutive Mondays. What type of seasonality would you expect to find in these data?

2. When would you use differencing and when would you employ seasonal differencing?

3. Evaluate the following statement: "If an ARIMA model is properly constructed, it has residual autocorrelations that are all equal to zero."

4. Of what use is the chi-square test as applied to residual autocorrelations?

5. *a.* Calculate and display the first 50 autocorrelations for the four data series in the accompanying table, labeled A, B, C, and D; consider each of the four data series to be a quarterly time series. How many of the autocorrelations fall outside the two-standard-deviation range (positive or negative)?

   b. Is there a pattern to those autocorrelation coefficients falling outside the two-standard-deviation range?

   c. Calculate and display the first 50 partial autocorrelations for the 100 time-series observations. How

many of the partial autocorrelation coefficients fall outside the two-standard-deviation range?

   d. Is there a pattern to those partial autocorrelation coefficients falling outside the two-standard-deviation range?

   e. Estimate the appropriate model as determined from your inspections carried out in parts *a* through *d* and forecast for four quarters into the future. Calculate the RMSE for each model.

EXERCISE 5   Four Data Series

A	B	C	D	A	B	C	D
1.62	0.38	0.68	1.11	0.41	1.11	4.22	40.27
1.55	1.02	0.71	2.27	0.40	0.80	3.97	40.68
1.59	0.70	1.22	3.71	1.13	0.41	4.29	41.19
1.55	1.16	1.29	4.52	1.06	0.93	4.22	41.58
1.10	1.11	1.53	5.04	0.31	0.66	4.34	42.23
0.82	0.93	1.52	6.10	0.67	1.29	4.85	43.33
1.06	1.32	1.53	7.61	0.68	1.11	4.39	44.27
0.69	0.78	2.08	8.89	0.72	1.16	4.74	44.89
0.74	0.50	2.57	9.73	0.58	1.52	5.09	45.41

EXERCISE 5 Four Data Series (*concluded*)

A	B	C	D	A	B	C	D
0.73	0.72	3.15	10.85	0.74	1.28	4.83	45.69
0.44	0.69	3.71	11.99	1.14	0.76	5.21	46.39
0.98	0.41	3.76	12.87	1.42	0.74	4.74	46.96
0.62	1.16	3.73	13.44	0.94	0.53	4.90	47.34
0.44	1.35	3.49	14.26	0.59	0.44	5.06	47.61
0.66	0.98	3.94	14.91	0.32	0.92	5.29	48.21
0.83	1.21	4.01	15.37	0.68	0.57	4.90	48.77
1.25	0.69	3.97	15.90	1.40	0.33	4.90	49.17
0.89	0.35	4.35	17.10	1.52	0.99	4.80	49.85
1.02	0.70	3.84	18.39	1.20	1.24	4.88	50.55
0.72	0.74	3.60	18.98	1.33	0.77	4.46	51.55
0.79	0.52	3.43	19.50	0.69	0.48	5.09	52.20
0.77	0.26	3.43	20.21	0.30	1.16	4.56	53.06
1.18	0.21	3.69	20.85	0.49	0.62	4.37	54.46
1.26	1.06	3.85	21.69	0.43	0.83	4.20	55.70
0.81	1.27	4.20	22.69	0.95	0.62	4.65	56.51
1.05	1.63	4.05	23.56	1.50	1.11	4.37	57.41
0.63	0.98	4.33	24.65	1.58	0.73	4.67	58.81
0.71	0.98	4.76	25.92	0.92	0.61	5.00	60.10
1.02	1.13	4.79	26.87	0.40	0.90	5.03	61.00
0.79	1.30	4.69	28.07	0.47	1.01	4.78	61.69
1.22	1.61	4.65	29.63	1.03	1.01	5.21	62.63
1.01	1.31	4.49	30.41	1.33	0.61	5.31	63.12
0.43	1.20	4.91	31.42	1.11	1.13	5.14	63.28
0.27	1.26	5.01	32.66	0.60	1.05	5.18	63.52
0.41	1.32	4.59	33.49	0.30	0.89	4.92	64.08
0.94	0.85	4.62	34.23	0.93	1.21	5.24	64.45
1.42	1.13	4.83	35.00	0.92	1.48	4.80	64.62
1.22	1.24	4.86	36.27	0.85	1.62	5.37	64.78
1.31	1.08	4.53	37.07	0.52	1.15	5.19	65.52
0.67	0.85	4.44	37.25	0.07	1.43	4.71	66.18
0.22	1.32	4.74	38.10	0.41	1.33	4.62	67.16
0.50	1.53	4.54	39.51	1.21	1.26	4.42	68.63
0.64	1.75	4.13	40.20	0.96	1.16	5.00	69.67
0.72	1.16	4.74	44.89	1.42	1.39	4.74	74.74
0.58	1.52	5.09	45.41	1.29	1.51	4.31	75.15
0.74	1.28	4.83	45.69	0.87	1.11	4.74	75.81
1.14	0.76	5.21	46.39	0.86	1.42	4.64	76.86
1.42	0.74	4.74	46.96	0.76	1.38	4.39	77.83
0.94	0.53	4.90	47.34	0.36	1.68	4.15	78.95
0.59	0.44	5.06	47.61	0.17	1.49	4.35	80.27

6. *a.* Calculate and display the first 50 autocorrelations for the four data series in the table for this exercise, labeled A, B, C,and D; consider each of the four data series to be a quarterly time series. How many of the autocorrelations fall outside the two-standard-deviation range (positive or negative)?

b. Is there a pattern to those autocorrelation coefficients falling outside the two-standard-deviation range?

c. Calculate and display the first 50 partial autocorrelations for the 100 time-series observations. How many of the partial autocorrelation coefficients fall outside the two-standard-deviation range?

d. Is there a pattern to those partial autocorrelation coefficients falling outside the two-standard-deviation range?

e. Which frame in Figures 7–1, 7–2, and 7–3 does this pattern of autocorrelation and partial autocorrelation coefficients most closely resemble?

f. Estimate the appropriate model as determined from your inspections carried out in parts *a* through *e* and forecast for four quarters into the future. Calculate the RMSE for each model.

EXERCISE 6 Four Data Series

A	B	C	D	A	B	C	D
0.77	0.37	0.20	0.93	1.07	0.97	4.68	43.00
0.31	0.32	0.93	1.24	1.00	1.11	4.64	44.01
0.88	0.95	1.62	2.12	0.90	1.05	4.56	65.15
1.48	1.40	1.66	3.60	1.11	1.30	4.57	46.02
0.99	1.04	2.41	4.59	0.71	0.81	4.46	46.73
1.16	1.44	2.63	5.75	0.38	0.68	4.46	47.12
1.26	1.33	2.75	7.01	0.61	0.76	4.71	47.73
0.86	1.10	2.64	7.87	0.99	1.07	4.69	48.72
0.48	0.73	2.66	8.35	0.99	1.04	4.61	49.71
0.39	0.63	2.75	8.74	0.74	0.86	4.87	76.58
0.55	0.68	2.97	9.29	0.28	0.46	4.11	50.73
0.76	0.85	2.84	10.05	0.27	0.49	3.95	50.99
0.56	0.63	3.55	10.62	0.42	0.49	3.72	51.42
1.12	1.29	3.55	11.74	0.30	0.38	3.49	51.72
1.18	1.14	3.30	12.91	0.19	0.29	3.33	51.91
0.45	0.68	3.16	13.37	0.21	0.28	4.01	52.12
0.21	0.48	3.13	13.58	1.08	1.13	3.91	53.21
0.36	0.50	3.71	13.93	1.12	0.99	4.09	54.33
1.06	1.13	3.77	15.00	0.85	1.05	3.94	55.18
1.17	1.12	3.50	16.17	0.68	0.82	4.50	55.86
0.50	0.67	3.86	16.67	1.13	1.33	4.30	56.99
0.74	0.99	3.72	17.41	1.00	1.03	4.03	57.99
0.78	0.82	3.54	18.19	0.38	0.64	4.61	58.37
0.39	0.57	3.92	18.58	1.02	1.25	4.11	59.39
0.82	0.99	4.31	19.39	0.73	0.71	4.11	60.12
1.35	1.35	4.28	20.74	0.36	0.66	4.20	60.48
1.08	1.16	4.70	21.82	0.71	0.83	3.81	61.19
1.18	1.42	4.56	23.00	0.40	0.47	3.56	61.59
1.00	1.12	4.71	24.00	0.09	0.29	3.57	61.69

EXERCISE 6 **Four Data Series** (*concluded*)

A	B	C	D	A	B	C	D
0.87	1.14	5.19	24.87	0.35	0.46	4.05	62.04
1.38	1.55	5.26	26.25	1.06	1.07	4.12	63.09
1.37	1.46	5.24	27.62	1.16	1.10	4.19	64.25
1.01	1.26	5.63	28.62	0.90	1.02	4.97	44.91
1.28	1.54	5.77	29.90	1.15	1.33	4.23	66.30
1.42	1.55	5.43	31.32	0.76	0.86	4.18	67.06
0.82	1.04	5.36	32.13	0.45	0.74	4.59	67.51
0.59	0.93	5.15	32.72	1.03	1.18	5.02	68.54
0.60	0.78	5.05	33.32	1.54	1.56	5.40	70.08
0.59	0.75	5.56	33.91	1.65	1.75	5.44	71.73
1.25	1.37	5.22	35.16	1.33	1.53	4.91	73.07
1.02	1.01	5.65	36.18	0.48	0.79	5.33	73.55
1.11	1.39	5.85	37.29	0.82	1.20	5.62	74.37
1.47	1.55	5.53	38.76	1.48	1.51	5.11	75.84
0.90	1.08	5.23	39.66	0.74	0.91	4.18	50.45
0.40	0.73	5.14	40.06	0.25	0.60	4.81	76.83
0.50	0.73	4.68	40.56	0.50	0.68	5.25	77.33
0.29	0.40	4.47	40.86	1.18	1.25	5.45	78.51
0.19	0.37	4.07	41.05	1.45	1.44	5.37	79.95
0.12	0.19	4.50	41.17	1.08	1.23	5.35	81.03
0.76	0.85	4.51	41.93	0.86	1.11	5.02	81.89

7. *a.* An autoregressive model is given by:

$$Y_t = 20.58 + 0.046Y_{t-1} + 0.019Y_{t-2}$$

where Y_t = sales of a product. Explain the meaning of the terms in this autoregressive model.

b. Write the expressions for the following models:

AR(3)   MA(4)

AR(4)   ARMA(1, 2)

MA(3)   ARIMA(2, 1, 2)

APPENDIX
Critical Values of Chi-Square

This table contains the values of χ^2 that correspond to a specific right-tail area and specific numbers of degrees of freedom (df).

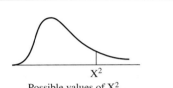

Possible values of X^2

Degrees of Freedom (df)	Right-Tail Area			
	0.10	0.05	0.02	0.01
1	2.706	3.841	5.412	6.635
2	4.605	5.991	7.824	9.210
3	6.251	7.815	9.837	11.345
4	7.779	9.488	11.668	13.277
5	9.236	11.070	13.388	15.086
6	10.645	12.592	15.033	16.812
7	12.017	14.067	16.622	18.475
8	13.362	15.507	18.168	20.090
9	14.684	16.919	19.679	21.666
10	15.987	18.307	21.161	23.209
11	17.275	19.675	22.618	24.725
12	18.549	21.026	24.054	26.217
13	19.812	22.362	25.472	27.688
14	21.064	23.685	26.873	29.141
15	22.307	24.996	28.259	30.578
16	23.542	26.296	29.633	32.000
17	24.769	27.587	30.995	33.409
18	25.989	28.869	32.346	34.805
19	27.204	30.144	33.687	36.191
20	28.412	31.410	35.020	37.566
21	29.615	32.671	36.343	38.932
22	30.813	33.924	37.659	40.289
23	32.007	35.172	38.968	41.638
24	33.196	36.415	40.270	42.980
25	34.382	37.652	41.566	44.314
26	35.563	38.885	42.856	45.642
27	36.741	40.113	44.140	46.963
28	37.916	41.337	45.419	48.278
29	39.087	42.557	46.693	49.588
30	40.256	43.773	47.962	50.892

Source: From Owen P. Hall, Jr., and Harvey M. Adelman, *Computerized Business Statistics* (Homewood, Ill.: Richard D. Irwin, 1987), p. 95.

8 COMBINING FORECAST RESULTS

Introduction

The use of combinations of forecasts has been the subject of a great deal of research in forecasting. An indication of the importance of this concept is the fact that the prestigious *International Journal of Forecasting* had a special section, composed of seven articles, entitled "Combining Forecasts" in the year-end issue of the volume for 1989. These articles are listed in the "Suggested Readings" section at the end of this chapter. In December 1992 an article in the same journal provided strong evidence on the importance of combining forecasts to improve accuracy. It was found that 83 percent of expert forecasters believe that combining forecasts will produce more accurate forecasts than could be obtained from the individual methods![1]

The idea of combining business forecasting models was originally proposed by Bates and Granger.[2] Since the publication of their article, this strategy has received immense support in almost every empirical test of combined forecasts versus individual uncombined forecasts.

Throughout this book we have emphasized the use of the root-mean-squared error (RMSE) as a measure of the effectiveness of a particular forecasting model (*forecast optimality*). The emphasis is very different in this chapter; instead of choosing

---

[1]Fred Collopy and J. Scott Armstrong, "Expert Opinions about Extrapolation and the Mystery of the Overlooked Discontinuities," *International Journal of Forecasting* 8, no. 4 (December 1992), pp. 575–82.

[2]Some of the material in this chapter is taken from the original Bates and Granger article; we recommend that readers consult the original article and other articles listed in the bibliography for more detail. J. M. Bates and C. W. J. Granger, "The Combination of Forecasts," *Operational Research Quarterly* 20, no. 4 (1969), pp. 451–68.

We have also drawn from and highly recommend J. Scott Armstrong's book, which is a virtual encyclopedia of forecasting methods. J. Scott Armstrong, *Long-Range Forecasting from Crystal Ball to Computer,* 2nd ed. (New York: John Wiley & Sons, 1985). For a nice overview of the state of the art in combining forecasts, see Robert T. Clemen, "Combining Forecasts: A Review and Annotated Bibliography," *International Journal of Forecasting* 5, no. 4 (1989), pp. 559–83.

the best model from among two or more alternatives, we are going to combine the forecasts from these different models to obtain *forecast improvement.* It may actually be unwise to simply determine which of a number of forecasting methods yields the most accurate predictions. A more reasoned approach, according to the empirical evidence, is to combine the forecasts already made in order to obtain a combined forecast that is more accurate than any of the separate predictions.

Any time a particular forecast is ignored because it is not the "best" forecast produced, it is likely that valuable independent information contained in the discarded forecast has been lost. The information lost may be of two types:

1. Some variables included in the discarded forecast may not be included in the "best" forecast.
2. The discarded forecast may make use of a type of relationship ignored by the "best" forecast.

In the first of these cases it is quite possible for several forecasts to be based on different information; thus, ignoring any one of these forecasts would necessarily exclude the explanatory power unique to the information included in the discarded model. In the second situation, it is often the case that different assumptions are made in different models about the form of the relationship between the variables. Each of the different forms of relationship tested, however, may have some explanatory value. Choosing only the "best" of the relationships could exclude functional information.

Bias

To be useful, forecasts we wish to combine must be unbiased. That is, each of the forecasts cannot consistently overestimate or underestimate the actual value. Note that if we combined an unbiased forecast with one that consistently overestimated the true value, we would always wind up with a biased estimate. Combining forecasts is not a method for eliminating bias in a forecast.

Bias can arise from a number of sources, but perhaps the most common source is the forecaster's preconceived notions. Predictions of forecasters not only reflect what they believe to be the truth, but also what they would *like* the truth to be. This statement is best demonstrated by the results obtained by Hayes in a survey of voters two weeks before the Roosevelt-Hoover election. Hayes found that of the people who intended to vote for Hoover, 84 percent thought that he would win the election. Of the people who intended to vote for Roosevelt, however, only 6 percent thought that Hoover would win. Apparently those who intended to vote for a particular candidate are biased in the sense that they also believe that their favorite will actually win the election.[3]

---

[3]S. P. Hayes, Jr., "The Predictive Ability of Voters," *Journal of Social Psychology* 7 (1936), pp. 183–91.

A forecaster should spend some time examining multiple forecasting models in the hope of combining some or all of these models into a combined forecast that is superior to any of the individual forecasts.

Professional forecasters may suffer from the same bias as voters—they may look for forecasting models that confirm their own preconceived ideas. To eliminate bias a forecaster will have to examine models that may contradict his or her current beliefs. What this means is that you must do something that runs counter to your intuition in order to examine models you may feel are incorrect; you must examine forecasting models that you may believe to be inferior to your "favorite" model. This prescription is more difficult to implement than it sounds. Much of a forecaster's time is spent in confirming existing beliefs of how the world works. However, we are suggesting that a forecaster should spend some time examining multiple forecasting models in the hope of combining some or all of these models into a combined forecast that is superior to any of the individual forecasts.

An Example

Consider a situation in which two separate forecasts are made of the same event. It is not atypical for a forecaster to attempt in this situation to choose the "best" of the two forecasting models on the basis of some error-minimization criterion such as RMSE. The model not chosen is discarded as being second-best and, therefore, unusable.

If, however, the two forecasting models use different methods, or if the two models use different information, discarding one of the models may cause the loss of some valuable information. To prevent this loss of useful information requires some method for combining the two forecasts into a single "better" forecast.

To illustrate, we will use a classic example taken from an appendix to the original Bates and Granger article. In Table 8–1 we show output indexes for the gas, electricity, and water sectors of the economy, drawn from the 1966 edition of *National Income and Expenditure*. The actual index data in column 2 are in 1958 dollars. Our task is to estimate a forecasting model for these data that has a low RMSE.

We will use two separate forecasting techniques that have already been introduced in the text:

1. A linear time-series regression model (see Chapter 4)
2. An exponential or logarithmic model (see Chapter 5)

The regression model for forecasting with a simple linear trend in Chapter 4 was:

$$Y = b_0 + b_1(\text{TIME})$$

where Y is the series we wish to forecast. The linear-trend forecast in column 3 of Table 8–1 is calculated by using the year in column 1 as the independent variable and the actual data in column 2 as the dependent variable. The equation—estimated with simple linear regression—for making the first forecast (the one for 1950) used only the data for 1948 and 1949:

$$Y = -7,734 + 4(\text{YEAR})$$

TABLE 8–1 Forecast of Output Indexes for Gas, Electricity, and Water

1	2	3	4	5	6	7	8	9	10
Year	Actual Index Data	Linear Forecast	Squared Deviations	Exponential Forecast	Squared Deviations	Combined Forecast (0.16 Weight)*	Squared Deviations	Combined Forecast (0.5 Weight)†	Squared Deviations
1948	58								
1949	62								
1950	67	66.000	1.0	66.276	0.5	66.23	0.59	66.14	0.74
1951	72	71.333	0.4	71.881	0.0	71.79	0.04	71.61	0.15
1952	74	76.500	6.3	77.385	11.5	77.24	10.52	76.94	8.66
1953	77	79.200	4.8	80.289	10.8	80.11	9.70	79.74	7.53
1954	84	81.933	4.3	83.215	0.6	83.01	0.98	82.57	2.03
1955	88	87.000	1.0	88.632	0.4	88.37	0.14	87.82	0.03
1956	92	91.607	0.2	93.656	2.7	93.33	1.76	92.63	0.40
1957	96	95.972	0.0	98.476	6.1	98.08	4.31	97.22	1.50
1958	100	100.200	0.0	103.187	10.2	102.71	7.34	101.69	2.87
1959	103	104.345	1.8	107.843	23.4	107.28	18.34	106.09	9.57
1960	110	108.106	3.6	112.108	4.4	111.47	2.15	110.11	0.01
1961	116	112.846	9.9	117.444	2.1	116.71	0.50	115.15	0.73
1962	125	117.967	49.5	123.241	3.1	122.40	6.77	120.60	19.32
1963	133	124.152	78.3	130.228	7.7	129.02	14.02	127.19	33.76
1964	137	130.850	37.8	137.864	0.7	136.74	0.07	134.36	6.99
1965	145	136.978	64.4	145.034	0.0	143.74	1.58	141.01	15.95
Sum of squares =			263.3		84.4		78.82		110.25
RMSE =			4.06		2.30		2.22		2.63

*The 0.16 weight refers to the weight on the linear model. The weight on the exponential model must then be 0.84, since the two weights must sum to 1.
†The 0.5 weight refers to the weight on the linear model. The weight on the exponential model must then be 0.5, since the weights must sum to 1. Note also that the RMSE for the column 9 combined model is not as low (and, therefore, not as good) as the RMSE for the column 7 combined model.

SOURCE: J. M. Bates and C. W. J. Granger, "The Combination of Forecasts," *Operational Research Quarterly* 20, no. 4 (1969), pp. 451–68.

Substituting the year 1950 gives the linear forecast for 1950, which appears in column 3:

$$Y = -7{,}734 + 4(1950) = 66$$

The simple linear-trend estimating equation is then estimated again, this time using the data for the first three years (1948–50); this equation is used to forecast for the year 1951, and that value (which is 71.3) is placed in column 3 of Table 8–1. This procedure is repeated for each year, so that the forecast for year t is always made by extrapolating the regression line formed by the least-squares regression of the actual figures for 1948 through the year $t - 1$. The results obtained and displayed in the table would be similar to the results an actual forecaster might record as he or she makes annual forecasts by always using new data as they become available.

For each forecast in column 3, we also calculate the squared deviation from the actual figure as an intermediate step in calculating the RMSE (see Chapter 1 for an explanation of root-mean-squared error). The RMSE for the simple linear-trend approach to forecasting the index is given at the bottom of column 4.

The second model used to forecast the index is the exponential model (it is sometimes called the *logarithmic* or *constant-rate-of-growth* model). The assumption in this model is that the value we are forecasting does not produce a straight-line plot when graphed over time. Instead the data may plot as a curve on arithmetic paper but as a straight line on semilogarithmic paper (graph paper with one arithmetic axis and one logarithmic axis). The equation to estimate is:

$$Y = b_0 m^x$$

where:

Y = The actual value of the index
b_0 = Value of the trend when $x = 0$
m = The constant rate of growth (which could be negative)
x = The time value (in the present case, 1948 = 1, 1949 = 2, etc.)

The equation can be estimated with a standard regression package by using the equation:

$$\ln Y = \ln b_0 + x \ln m$$

To obtain the equation for the first exponential estimate in Table 8–1, the natural logs of the actual index data for the years 1948 and 1949 were taken and regressed on time (with 1948 = 1 and 1949 = 2). This produced the estimate:

$$\ln Y = \ln 3.994 + (\text{Year}) \ln 0.067$$

Taking the antilogs of the log values gives the following equation:

$$Y = (54.258)(1.069)^{\text{Year}}$$

Note that the antilog of 3.994 = 54.258 and the antilog of 0.067 = 1.069. The first forecast (the one for 1950) is calculated by making the substitution for year into this equation (recall that the year 1950 = 3):

$$Y = (54.258)(1.069)^3 = 66.276$$

This first exponential forecast is the first number (66.276) in column 5 of Table 8–1. The forecast for the following year (71.9) requires the fitting of another equation of the same form, utilizing the actual index data from all three previous years. Each subsequent forecast then requires the equation to be estimated once again.

For each forecast in column 5 we again calculate the squared deviation from the actual figure as an intermediate step in calculating the RMSE. The results in column 6 are again what could be expected if a forecaster were to use the exponential method over time and keep careful track of the errors made each year as the current year's actual data became available. The RMSE for the exponential model over the 16-year period from 1950 to 1965 is given at the bottom of column 6.

The RMSE for the exponential forecasting model is clearly smaller (and therefore better) than the corresponding figure for the simple linear-trend forecasting model. If we were to choose the "best" model, the exponential model would be the clear choice.

However, since the two forecasts assume different forms of the relationship between the variables, there may be a combination of the two forecasts that will yield considerable improvements from either single model. A combined forecast is a weighted average of the different forecasts, with the weights reflecting in some sense the confidence the researcher has in each of the models. Some forecasters have suggested that the weights should be selected before the forecasts are generated in order to reduce the possibility of bias introduced by the researcher. The use of a mechanical rule to make the selection of weights would also satisfy this objection and will be discussed in what follows.

In our particular situation it appears that we should have more confidence in the exponential model because it has the lower RMSE. This would suggest that in combining the two forecasts we should weight the exponential model more heavily than the simple linear-trend model. In column 7 of Table 8–1 we have arbitrarily weighted the simple linear-trend model by 0.16 and the exponential model by 0.84 (the two weights must sum to 1). The first forecast in column 7 is then calculated as follows:

$$(0.16)(\text{Linear forecast}) + (0.84)(\text{Exponential forecast}) = \text{Combined forecast}$$
$$(0.16)(66.000) + (0.84)(66.276) = 66.23$$

This procedure is repeated for each of the years from 1950 to 1965. Column 8 contains the squared deviations of the combined forecast from the actual index data, and the RMSE for the combined forecast (2.22) is at the bottom of the column.

Note that the RMSE for the combined forecast is better (i.e., lower) than for either individual forecasting model. The combining of forecasts is a practical tool for increasing forecast accuracy and has the attraction of being both automatic and conceptually quite simple; apparently even the less accurate simple linear-trend model contained important information that made it possible to obtain a better forecast. Following this approach, it should be clear that most forecast methods contain some information that is independent of the information contained in other forecast methods. If this is the case, combination forecasts will, quite likely, outperform individual forecasts.

Two important observations need to be made about the results in Table 8–1:

1. Considerable improvements in forecast accuracy can be achieved by combining forecast models with an optimal weight. In this case the optimal weight turned out to be 0.16 for the simple linear trend model (and therefore, 0.84 for the exponential model).

2. While the forecaster cannot assume that combining forecasts will always yield better results, it can be shown that the combined forecasts will have an error variance not greater than the smallest error variance of the individual forecasts.[4]

What Kinds of Forecasts Can Be Combined?

The example of combining forecasts we used in the previous section is one of the simpler combinations a researcher could try. In actual practice it would be more common to find a forecaster using very different types of models in order to construct a combination forecast.

Recall that the premise in constructing combined forecasts is:

1. That the different forecasting models *extract different predictive factors* from essentially the same data, or

2. That the different models offer different predictions because they *use different variables.*

We should expect that combinations of forecasts that use very different models are likely to be effective in reducing forecast error.

> We should expect that combinations of forecasts that use very different models are likely to be effective in reducing forecast error.

Consider Figure 8–1, which conceptually presents a 10-year forecast of air travel in the United States. The judgmental method represents a mail survey of experts outside the airline industry. The extrapolation method could be a form of exponential smoothing. The segmentation method surveys airline travelers in different segments of the market and then combines the results to obtain a total picture of the industry. The econometric method refers to a causal regression model. All four methods could be employed and predictions weighted by the values w_1 to w_4 in order to calculate the combined forecast. Such a diverse combined forecast would benefit from both the use of the different techniques *and* from the use of different sources of data. If each of the methods employed was also constructed and estimated by a different forecaster, another source of possible bias may also have been minimized; this provides a safeguard by making it difficult to cheat.

---

[4]David A. Bessler and Jon A. Brandt, "Composite Forecasting: An Application with U.S. Hog Prices," *American Journal of Agricultural Economics* 63 (1981), pp. 135–40.

FIGURE 8–1

Combined Forecasts from Different Methods

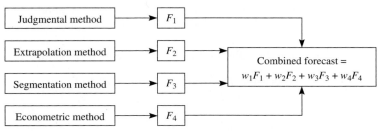

Note: The *w*'s, the relative weights on various forecasts, should sum to 1.0.

Considerations in Choosing the Weights for Combined Forecasts

Combined forecasts are used in place of individual forecasts in order to reduce forecast error, and the results of the combined method are quite often impressive. Armstrong has reported results from reanalyzing eight separate studies that provided sufficient information to test the combined forecasting method against individual forecast models.[5] In each case Armstrong used equal weights for the individual forecasts, following his belief that weight should be chosen *ex ante*. The combinations of two forecasts reduced error (measured as mean absolute percentage error) by a significant 6.6 percent. In no single case did the accuracy ever suffer; when more than two forecasts were combined, further improvements were noted (in one case observed by Armstrong, the forecast error was reduced by 17.9 percent).

Even though the use of equal weights for each of the individual forecasts offers the advantage of simplicity and also precludes the forecaster's own bias in the selection of weighting factors, there may be a good reason for weighting one individual forecast more than another, as we have done in the previous example. Equal weights do not take into account the relative accuracy of the individual forecasting models that are combined. Bates and Granger were the first to indicate that by weighting the more accurate of the methods more heavily, the overall forecast could be improved.[6] You have seen in Table 8–1 that the combination using equal weights is not as effective, on the basis of RMSE, as a combination that assigns a smaller weight to the individual forecast having the larger RMSE.

In general, a combined forecast will have a smaller error, as measured by RMSE, *unless individual forecasting models are almost equally good and their forecast errors are highly correlated.*

Consider Table 8–2, which presents data on the gross national product (GNP) of the communications industry for the years 1968 to 1985 (i.e., the total value of all goods and services produced by the communications industry, valued at market prices). The actual GNP figures appear in column 2; in columns 3 and 5, respectively,

[5] See Armstrong, *Long-Range Forecasting,* p. 292.
[6] See Bates and Granger, p. 452.

TABLE 8–2   GNP: Communications, 1982 Dollars (Billions)

1 Year	2 Actual Data	3 Linear Forecast	4 Squared Deviations	5 Exponential Forecast	6 Squared Deviations	7 Combined Forecast (0.9 Weight)	8 Squared Deviations	9 Combined Forecast (0.8 Weight)	10 Squared Deviations	11 Combined Forecast (0.7 Weight)	12 Squared Deviations	13 Combined Forecast (0.5 Weight)	14 Squared Deviations	15 Combined Forecast (0.3 Weight)	16 Squared Deviations
1968	33.9														
1969	37.4														
1970	40.9	40.9	0.0	41.3	0.1	40.94	0.00	40.97	0.01	41.01	0.01	41.08	0.03	41.15	0.06
1971	43	44.4	2.0	45.0	4.0	44.46	2.13	44.52	2.30	44.58	2.49	44.70	2.87	44.81	3.29
1972	47	46.5	0.3	47.2	0.1	46.57	0.18	46.65	0.13	46.72	0.08	46.87	0.02	47.01	0.00
1973	50.5	50.0	0.3	51.0	0.2	50.08	0.18	50.18	0.10	50.28	0.05	50.48	0.00	50.68	0.03
1974	53	53.5	0.3	54.8	3.4	53.64	0.41	53.77	0.60	53.91	0.82	54.17	1.38	54.44	2.07
1975	55.2	56.5	1.6	58.1	8.6	56.64	2.07	56.81	2.58	56.97	3.14	57.31	4.44	57.64	5.95
1976	58.1	59.0	0.9	61.0	8.5	59.23	1.29	59.43	1.78	59.63	2.34	60.03	3.72	60.43	5.41
1977	61.9	61.7	0.0	64.0	4.5	61.95	0.00	62.18	0.08	62.41	0.26	62.87	0.95	63.34	2.06
1978	67.7	64.8	8.3	67.5	0.0	65.09	6.81	65.36	5.47	65.63	4.28	66.17	2.33	66.72	0.97
1979	72.5	68.9	12.9	72.1	0.1	69.23	10.69	69.55	8.70	69.87	6.91	70.51	3.94	71.16	1.81
1980	78.4	73.3	26.2	77.1	1.7	73.66	22.46	74.04	18.99	74.42	15.81	75.19	10.32	75.95	6.00
1981	82.8	78.2	21.5	82.7	0.0	78.62	17.47	79.07	13.88	79.53	10.70	80.44	5.57	81.35	2.11
1982	85.6	83.0	6.9	88.4	7.6	83.51	4.38	84.05	2.41	84.59	1.03	85.66	0.00	86.74	1.30
1983	92.1	87.3	23.2	93.6	2.2	87.91	17.54	88.54	12.67	89.17	8.59	90.43	2.80	91.68	0.17
1984	92.7	92.2	0.3	99.5	45.6	92.89	0.04	93.62	0.85	94.35	2.73	95.81	9.67	97.27	20.87
1985	93.2	96.1	8.3	104.4	124.4	96.90	13.71	97.73	20.52	98.56	28.71	100.21	49.19	101.87	75.15
Sum of squares =			112.8		211.1		99.4		91.1		87.94		97.24		127.25
RMSE =		2.66		3.63		2.49		2.39		2.34		2.47		2.82	

Note that the weights listed in parentheses are those assigned to the linear forecasting model. The exponential model must then have a weight of 1 minus the weight listed in parentheses.
Source: CITIBASE, Citicorp Database Services.

379

are the linear and exponential forecasts calculated in the manner of the previous example. The squared deviations of these forecasts from the actual data are given in columns 4 and 6. By calculating the RMSE for each of the forecasting models, it is clear that the linear model is a superior forecasting tool (RMSE of 2.66 for the linear model versus 3.63 for the exponential model).

Of interest here is the correlation of the forecast errors (squared) between the two models. To do this we calculate the correlation coefficient between columns 4 and 6 of Table 8–2, which yields −0.62; from this low correlation coefficient it is apparent that these two forecasting models are not highly correlated. This result indicates that possible improvements would result from some combination of the two models.

The simplest combination of the two models is obtained by weighting each equally; this is done in column 13 of Table 8–2. The RMSE for this combined model is 2.47, which is lower (and therefore better) than for either the linear or the exponential model.

If, however, the forecast model with the lower RMSE is more heavily weighted, the combined forecast should improve even further. In column 9 of Table 8–2, a weight of 0.8 is applied to the linear model and a weight of 0.2 to the exponential model. This results in an RMSE of 2.39, which is the best yet. Further experimentation shows that a weighting of 0.7 for the linear model (and 0.3 for the exponential model) yields even better results (an RMSE of 2.34).

If, however, you ignore the rule of thumb that the more accurate forecast should receive the larger weight, the accuracy of the combined forecast may deteriorate. Notice that in the final two columns of the table we use a weighting of 0.3 for the linear model (and 0.7 for the exponential model), which results in an RMSE that is larger than that for the linear model alone.

In Table 8–3 the data for GNP in the retail trade industry for the same years are presented. Again we calculate a linear forecast and an exponential forecast by using the same methods we have employed, so that the data represent what a forecaster would have collected during 16 years of forecasting these numbers one year at a time and using only the data available in the given year.

In this case both forecasts have very similar errors, as shown by their RMSEs (11.23 for the linear model and 11.53 for the exponential model). In addition, the correlation between the squared deviations of the linear model and the squared deviations of the exponential model (located in columns 4 and 6) is high—the coefficient is 0.81. We should expect little, if any, improvement by using a combined forecast in this situation.

It is the diversity of information included in the individual models that allows the combined forecast model to assemble the pieces to form a more powerful forecasting model than any one of the parts.

Using an equal-weighting scheme for the two models yields a combined forecast with an RMSE of 11.28, which is better than the exponential model but worse than the linear model. By using heavier weights for the "better" forecasting model (in this case the linear model), we are able to improve the forecast only slightly. Weights of 0.9 or 0.8 for the linear model (and correspondingly 0.1 or 0.2, respectively, for the exponential model) result in an RMSE of 11.22 for the combined model. This result emphasizes that it is the diversity of information included in the individual models that allows the combined forecast model to assemble the pieces to form a more powerful forecasting model than any one of the parts.

TABLE 8–3   GNP: Retail Trade, 1982 Dollars (Billions)

1	2	3	4	5	6	7	8	9	10	11	12	13	14	15	16
Year	Actual Data	Linear Forecast	Squared Deviations	Exponential Forecast	Squared Deviations	Combined Forecast (0.9 Weight)	Squared Deviations	Combined Forecast (0.8 Weight)	Squared Deviations	Combined Forecast (0.7 Weight)	Squared Deviations	Combined Forecast (0.5 Weight)	Squared Deviations	Combined Forecast (0.3 Weight)	Squared Deviations
1968	211.6														
1969	212.7														
1970	215.6	213.8	3.2	213.8	3.2	213.80	3.24	213.80	3.24	213.80	3.23	213.80	3.23	213.80	3.23
1971	224.5	217.3	51.8	217.3	51.5	217.30	51.80	217.31	51.77	217.31	51.73	217.31	51.66	217.32	51.58
1972	239.8	226.5	176.9	226.6	173.9	226.51	176.59	226.52	176.29	226.53	176.00	226.56	175.40	226.58	174.81
1973	255.6	241.3	204.5	241.7	193.9	241.34	203.41	241.38	202.34	241.41	201.27	241.49	199.14	241.56	197.02
1974	245.2	257.7	155.1	258.6	180.1	257.75	157.50	257.85	159.94	257.94	162.40	258.14	167.37	258.33	172.41
1975	247.5	259.4	141.6	260.7	274.0	259.53	144.70	259.66	147.82	259.79	150.98	260.05	157.39	160.30	163.93
1976	262.8	261.0	3.3	262.5	0.1	261.13	2.80	261.27	2.33	261.42	1.90	261.72	1.17	262.01	0.62
1977	275.1	268.3	45.9	270.2	24.3	268.51	43.43	268.69	41.04	268.88	38.71	269.25	34.25	269.62	30.06
1978	288.1	277.7	108.3	280.0	65.7	277.92	103.57	278.15	98.94	278.38	94.42	278.84	85.70	279.30	77.40
1979	294.4	288.5	34.7	291.4	9.2	288.79	31.45	289.08	28.32	289.37	25.35	289.94	19.90	290.51	15.12
1980	286.9	298.0	122.6	301.5	213.5	298.33	130.53	298.68	138.75	299.03	147.21	299.74	164.88	300.45	183.56
1981	288.9	302.3	179.4	306.3	303.9	302.70	190.34	303.10	201.66	303.50	213.30	304.31	237.56	305.12	263.13
1982	287.5	305.8	335.9	310.3	518.6	306.27	352.43	306.72	369.31	307.16	386.59	308.05	422.33	308.94	459.65
1983	307	307.9	0.8	312.6	31.5	308.39	1.93	308.86	3.46	309.33	5.42	310.27	10.67	311.21	17.69
1984	328.6	314.2	207.0	319.4	85.0	314.73	192.40	315.25	178.34	315.76	164.81	316.80	139.35	317.83	116.03
1985	339.8	324.1	246.5	329.8	99.2	324.67	228.81	325.25	211.77	325.82	195.39	326.97	164.60	328.12	136.46
Sum of squares =			2,017.6		2,127.7		2,015.0		2,015.3		2,018.70		2,034.63		2,062.72
RMSE =			11.23		11.53		11.22		11.22		11.23		11.28		11.35

Note that the weights listed in parentheses refer to the weighting on the linear forecasting model. The exponential model must then have a weight of 1 minus the weight listed in parentheses.

SOURCE: CITIBASE, Citicorp Database Services.

Three Techniques for Selecting Weights When Combining Forecasts

Is there any way to choose the weights to use in combining the individual forecasts other than by trying all possible combinations? Yes; several researchers have suggested techniques for choosing weights that take advantage of the facts we have just demonstrated. We will present three of these techniques here.

First, Bates and Granger have suggested a method that assumes the individual forecasts are consistent over time and that minimizes the variance of the forecast errors over the time period covered. The weight assigned to the first forecast model, k, is calculated in the following manner (note that the second forecast model would receive a weight of $1 - k$):

$$k = \frac{(\sigma_2)^2 - \rho\sigma_1\sigma_2}{(\sigma_1)^2 - (\sigma_2)^2 - 2\rho\sigma_1\sigma_2}$$

where:

k = The weight assigned to the first forecast model
$(\sigma_1)^2$ = The variance of errors for the first model
$(\sigma_2)^2$ = The variance of errors for the second model
ρ = The coefficient of correlation between the errors in the first set of forecasts and those in the second set

A second, and quite different, approach to selecting the best weighting scheme involves allowing the weights to adapt or change from period to period. The power of this method rests on the assumption that forecasting models may not have a constant performance over time. An adaptive set of weights may be calculated in the following manner:

$$\alpha_{1,T+1} = \sum_{t=T-\nu}^{T} \frac{e_{2t}^2}{e_{1t}^2 + e_{2t}^2}$$

where:

$\alpha_{1,T+1}$ = The weight assigned to forecast model 1 in period $T + 1$
e_{it} = The error made by forecast model i in period t
ν = The choice variable, which represents the number of periods included in the adaptive weighting procedure
T = The total number of periods for which there is a history of forecast errors

What is not clear is the superiority of these two methods for choosing weights in a combined model. Bessler and Brandt[7] examined the two weighting methods and

---

[7] See Bessler and Brandt, p. 139.

concluded:

1. Forecasts from individual models are not likely to be the most accurate forecasts.
2. Even with no record of prior forecast performance, it may make some sense to combine forecasts using a simple averaging method (i.e., equal weights).
3. If prior forecasting records are available, the user should weight forecasts on the basis of past performance (with the most accurate forecast receiving the highest weight).

At least one other technique is used to combine forecasts in order to improve accuracy. This technique involves the use of a regression analysis in determining the weights. Charles Nelson[8] suggests that if we are trying to weight a portfolio of forecasts in order to minimize the forecast error, an optimal linear composite forecast would be:

$$F* = b_1 F(1) + b_2 F(2)$$

where:

$$F* = \text{Optimal combined forecast}$$
$$F(1) = \text{First individual forecast}$$
$$F(2) = \text{Second individual forecast}$$
$$b_1 = \text{Weight allocated to the first forecast}$$
$$b_2 = \text{Weight allocated to the second forecast}$$

The actual values of b_1 and b_2 would be calculated by running a regression with the past actual values as the dependent variable and the forecasted values for each individual model as the independent variables. Note that this is not exactly the type of regression we have run before in the text; this regression has no intercept term, and so the equation must be calculated in a manner different from that we have used earlier.

Using this method, if the two (or more) individual forecasts are free of systematic bias, the values of b_1 and b_2 will sum to roughly 1. The t-ratios for the regression essentially answer the question: Does individual forecast 1 add any explanatory power to what is already present in forecast 2? and similarly for forecast 2. If the b_1 value passed the t-test at some reasonable confidence level, we would be assured that the first individual model, $F(1)$, did add explanatory power when combined with the second model, $F(2)$, using the weights calculated by the regression.

To apply this method and to determine the best values for b_1 and b_2, a two-step regression process is used. First, you perform a standard multiple regression of the actual values (dependent variable) on the values predicted from the individual forecasting methods (independent variables in this regression). We can express this as:

$$A = a + b_1 F(1) + b_2 F(2)$$

---

[8]Charles R. Nelson, "A Benchmark for the Accuracy of Econometric Forecasts of GNP," *Business Economics* 19, no. 3 (April 1984), pp. 52–58.

The value of the intercept (a) should be zero if there is no bias in the combined forecast. A standard t-test can be used to test whether the intercept is significantly different from zero.[9] Note that a two-tailed test would be appropriate here.

Assuming that you conclude that $a = 0$, you then redo the regression, forcing the regression through the origin. Most regression programs provide an option that allows this to be done quite easily. The result of regressing the actual values on the two forecast series, without an intercept, yields the desired result to determine the best weights to be used in combining the forecasts. We have:

$$F* = b_1 F(1) + b_2 F(2)$$

Using these values of b_1 and b_2, along with the $F(1)$ and $F(2)$ forecast series, the optimal combined forecast, $F*$, is easily determined.

As was indicated, the values of b_1 and b_2 should sum roughly to 1. On occasion one of these weights may be negative, in which case interpretation is tenuous. Some forecasters use such a model even if b_1 or b_2 is negative, as long as the RMSE for $F*$ is lower than for $F(1)$ or $F(2)$ alone. However, we advise using this method only when both weights are positive. It should be noted that this method can be extended to include more than two forecast series in the combination process. Remember, however, that each method should have unique information content.

An Application of the Regression Method for Combining Forecasts

To illustrate the widely used regression method of combining forecasts we will apply it to the problem of forecasting private housing starts (PHS) using data from 1991M1 through 1996M12. Regressing PHS as a function of the mortgage rate (MR) yields:

$$PHS = 143.43 - 6.61(MR)$$
$$(RMSE = 17.4)$$

Forecasts based on this model will be referred to as RFCST. A Winters exponential smoothing model ($\alpha = 0.405$, $\beta = 0.863$, $\gamma = 0.018$) for PHS results in an RMSE of 7.9. We will refer to the Winters forecast as WFCST.

Regressing PHS on RFCST and WFCST, and using standard method including an intercept term, yields the following results (using 1992M2 to 1996M12):

$$PHS = -22.5 + 0.398(RFCST) + 0.831(WFCST)$$
$$(-1.2) \quad (1.9) \quad\quad\quad (17.9)$$

The values in parentheses are t-ratios. On the basis of these t-ratios, the intercept (-22.5) is not significantly different from zero, but the slope terms are significantly positive. Since the intercept is essentially zero, we conclude that there is no bias in combining these two methods.

---

[9]This is one of the few cases for which we are interested in testing to see whether the intercept is different from zero. Normally, we do this test only for the slope terms.

Repeating the regression without an intercept yields the following (again using 1992M2 to 1996M12):

$$PHS = 0.171(RFCST) + 0.812(WFCST)$$
$$(3.7) \qquad (18.8)$$
$$(RMSE = 6.4)$$

We see that the combined RMSE of 6.4 is less than the root-mean-squared error of either the regression model (RMSE = 17.4) or the Winters model (RMSE = 7.9). Notice also that the coefficients sum nearly to 1 (0.171 + 0.812 ≈ 1).

Note that the two methods combined in this example contain quite different information. The regression model includes only the effect of mortgage rates on private housing starts, while the Winters model takes into account trend and seasonal components of the time series (but not the effect of the mortgage rate). Incidentally, the correlation coefficient between the squared errors for the two individual models is −0.14 in this case (quite small, as we would expect).

The values for PHS, RFCST, WFCST, and CFCST (the combined forecast) are shown in Table 8–4. Figure 8–2 shows the combined forecast (CFCST) and the actual PHS data for the historic period, as well as CFCST. The period is missing early observations for CFCST because of the loss of initial data in developing the Winters forecast. The forecast values for 1992M2–1996M12 certainly appear reasonable.

FIGURE 8–2

Private Housing Starts (PHS) and the Combined Forecast (CFCST) (c8t4)

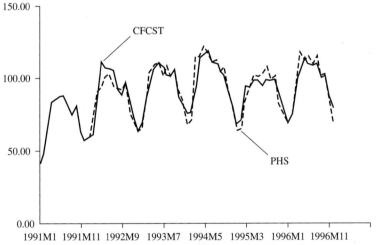

This plot shows actual private housing starts (PHS) and the forecast based on a combination of a regression forecast (RFCST) with a Winters' exponential smoothing forecast (WFCST). The combined forecast is:

$$CFCST = 0.171(RFCST) + 0.812(WFCST)$$

(c8t4)

TABLE 8–4   Private Housing Starts (PHS) and Three Forecasts of PHS

	PHS	RFCST	WFCST	CFCST
1991M1	39.2	79.6891	MISSING	MISSING
1991M2	46.1	81.4745	MISSING	MISSING
1991M3	61.4	80.6149	MISSING	MISSING
1991M4	82.8	80.6149	MISSING	MISSING
1991M5	84.5	80.8133	MISSING	MISSING
1991M6	86.8	79.8213	MISSING	MISSING
1991M7	87.4	80.0858	MISSING	MISSING
1991M8	78.7	82.3342	MISSING	MISSING
1991M9	73.7	83.8552	MISSING	MISSING
1991M10	80.9	84.8471	MISSING	MISSING
1991M11	62.6	85.8390	MISSING	MISSING
1991M12	56.3	87.2277	MISSING	MISSING
1992M1	58.4	87.6906	MISSING	MISSING
1992M2	69.2	85.5084	56.7895	60.6729
1992M3	90.9	84.3181	83.8210	82.4067
1992M4	93.5	84.9132	118.978	111.039
1992M5	100.2	86.1036	112.815	106.241
1992M6	102.7	87.1616	112.521	106.183
1992M7	93.2	89.6745	111.119	105.474
1992M8	91.8	90.6664	95.0476	92.6003
1992M9	91.4	91.0632	89.1842	87.9097
1992M10	96.1	89.9390	100.445	96.8564
1992M11	74.8	88.4842	77.5463	78.0253
1992M12	67.9	89.1455	69.7888	71.8426
1993M1	62.8	90.6003	58.5257	62.9505
1993M2	65.5	92.6503	66.1144	69.4586
1993M3	84.9	93.8406	84.0754	84.2376
1993M4	104.4	94.1051	97.4895	95.1686
1993M5	109.2	94.0390	110.922	106.058
1993M6	110.1	94.3696	116.491	110.634
1993M7	100.4	95.7583	111.138	106.527
1993M8	108.3	96.4196	105.016	101.671
1993M9	100.6	97.7422	104.040	101.105
1993M10	105.5	98.2712	110.178	106.176
1993M11	90.6	96.0890	85.2234	85.5527
1993M12	83.3	96.0229	79.9676	81.2762
1994M1	67.2	96.6841	72.3169	75.1802
1994M2	70.8	96.1551	73.8298	76.3178
1994M3	114.6	92.6503	93.3597	91.5690
1994M4	114.3	88.4181	121.093	113.353
1994M5	122.3	86.5665	125.144	116.325
1994M6	117.6	87.8890	128.034	118.896
1994M7	110.4	86.5003	117.717	110.287
1994M8	110.1	87.1616	120.628	112.762
1994M9	105.2	86.3019	109.882	103.894
1994M10	101.3	84.3842	115.056	107.766
1994M11	87.8	82.7971	90.6736	87.7083
1994M12	76.8	82.5987	80.8396	79.6939

TABLE 8–4   *concluded*

	PHS	RFCST	WFCST	CFCST
1995M1	63.6	82.9294	66.2136	67.8809
1995M2	65.3	85.0455	69.4208	70.8446
1995M3	85.3	87.4923	98.2635	94.6687
1995M4	93.9	88.4181	96.4836	93.3822
1995M5	102.3	90.7987	102.383	98.5758
1995M6	100.5	93.3777	101.954	98.6676
1995M7	102.0	93.1132	97.1130	94.6939
1995M8	108.5	91.4600	102.390	98.6943
1995M9	97.7	92.9148	101.293	98.0522
1995M10	101.5	93.9729	101.540	98.4332
1995M11	82.0	94.6342	88.2243	87.7399
1995M12	73.7	95.8245	76.4776	78.4101
1996M1	68.9	96.9487	63.2264	67.8482
1996M2	74.2	96.6180	68.9531	72.4392
1996M3	96.9	93.0471	98.7029	95.9728
1996M4	117.9	90.9971	107.880	103.071
1996M5	111.6	90.0713	121.719	114.143
1996M6	115.0	88.4181	116.305	109.468
1996M7	109.1	88.8810	114.527	108.104
1996M8	115.6	90.5342	116.496	109.984
1996M9	99.3	89.0132	106.799	101.855
1996M10	101.0	91.0632	107.369	102.667
1996M11	82.6	93.0471	87.5610	86.9309
1996M12	68.8	93.1793	77.6912	78.9438

RFCST = Regression forecast of PHS
WFCST = Winters' exponential smoothing forecast of PHS
CFCST = A combination forecast of PHS, where CFCST =
0.171(RFCST) + 0.812(WFCST)

Forecasting Domestic Car Sales with a Combined Forecast

We will now apply the forecasting concepts of this chapter to the problem of forecasting domestic car sales. We will combine two of the forecasting models we have presented in previous chapters (using a holdout period). The models chosen for combination are a multiple-regression model (Chapter 5) and a Winters' exponential smoothing model (Chapter 3). These two models were chosen because they differ in both the variables included and in the type of relationship hypothesized.

The multiple-regression model contains information from disposable personal income and the prime interest rate. The regression model appeared in the upper section of Table 5–10.

$$DCS = 1793.92 + 0.004637(DPI) - 12.1914(PR)$$

The root-mean-squared error for this forecasting model is 233.47 in the historic period and 115.53 in the 1995Q1–1995Q4 forecast horizon.

```
REGRESS : dependent variable is DCS

Using    1981Q2-1994Q4
```

Variable	Coefficient	Std Err	T-stat	Signf
^CONST	-21.2530	924.613	-.229858E-01	.982
DCSFR	.279164	.538849	.518074	.607
DCSFW	.744144	.971241E-01	7.66179	.000

```
                       Equation Summary
     No. of Observations =      55     R2=   .5490   (adj)=   .5316
     Sum of Sq. Resid. =   .148824E+07  Std. Error of Reg.=  169.174
     Log(likelihood)   =  -358.700     Durbin-Watson    =   1.80431
     Schwarz Criterion =  -364.711     F ( 2,    52)    =   31.6476
     Akaike Criterion  =  -361.700     Significance     =    .000000
```

```
REGRESS : dependent variable is DCS

Using    1981Q2-1994Q4
```

Variable	Coefficient	Std Err	T-stat	Signf
DCSFR	.266978	.956301E-01	2.79178	.007
DCSFW	.744209	.961633E-01	7.73902	.000

```
                       Equation Summary
     No. of Observations =      55     R2=   .9914   (adj)=   .9910
     Sum of Sq. Resid. =   .148826E+07  Std. Error of Reg.=  167.572
     Log(likelihood)   =  -358.701     Durbin-Watson    =   1.80422
     Schwarz Criterion =  -362.708     F ( 2,    53)    =   3040.60
     Akaike Criterion  =  -360.701     Significance     =    .000000
```

The Winters' exponential smoothing model takes both trend and seasonality into account. The parameters of the optimal Winters model are $\alpha = 0.397$, $\beta = 0.658$, and $\gamma = 0.037$. The root-mean-squared error for the Winters forecasting model for DCS is 177.08 in the historic period and 55.75 in the 1995Q1–1995Q4 forecast horizon.

If we were to simply choose the optimum forecasting model from only these two, we would choose the smoothing model. The RMSE for the smoothing model of about 56 is less than the RMSE of the regression model (115). Recall, however, that the objective in combining forecasts is not to choose the optimum forecasting model (forecast optimality) but to improve the forecast (forecast improvement).

Let us see what happens when we combine these forecasts using the regression method of selecting the best set of weights. For notational simplicity we will let DCSFR—Domestic Car Sales Forecast Regression—refer to the multiple-regression forecast and DCSFW—Domestic Car Sales Forecast Winters—refer to the Winters forecast. DCSCF—Domestic Car Sales Combined Forecast—will be used to represent the combined forecast.

We begin by regressing the actual values of domestic car sales (DCS) on DCSFR and DCSFW, using standard regression techniques to determine whether the intercept is essentially equal to zero. The results are:

$$DCS = -21.2530 + 0.279164(DCSFR) - 0.744144(DCSFW)$$
$$(0.02) \qquad (0.52) \qquad\qquad (7.66)$$

where the *t*-ratios are in parentheses. Given a *t*-ratio of 0.02 for the intercept, we would conclude that it is not statistically different from zero at any meaningful significance level.

Next we do the same regression, except that this time we force it through the origin by eliminating the constant term (i.e., the intercept). The new regression results are:

$$DCS = 0.266978(DCSFR) + 0.744209(DCSFW)$$
$$(2.79) \qquad\qquad (7.74)$$

where the *t*-ratios are in parentheses. These results are interesting. First, they show that the coefficients do sum approximately to 1 ($0.266978 + 0.744209 = 1.01$). Second, we see that by far the greatest weight is assigned to the smoothing model, which has an RMSE about three-quarters the size of the RMSE for the regression model. Third, we see that after accounting for the contribution of the regression model, the amount of explanatory power added by the Winters model is substantial (note the large *t*-ratio for DCSFW). This is not surprising, since the correlation coefficient between the squared error terms resulting from DCSFR and DCSFW is quite low. These results suggest that the amount of improvement from combining these models may be significant.

Using this set of weights to determine the combined forecast (DCSCF), we have:

$$DCSCF = 0.266978(DCSFR) + 0.744209(DCSFW)$$

The resulting root-mean-squared error of 164.49 does not show improvement over the 106.8 RMSE based on the multiple-regression model alone. The forecast values based on DCSCF are plotted for the historic period as well as for the 1995Q1–1995Q4 forecast horizon, along with actual DCS for 1980Q1 through 1994Q4, in Figure 8–3. The data are shown in tabular form in Table 8–5.

Table 8–6 contains a summary of RMSEs for various models we have used to forecast domestic car sales throughout the text. We see that, on the basis of known information, the combined forecast has one of the lowest RMSEs during the historic period. However, during the forecast horizon (for which we assumed we did not

FIGURE 8–3

Domestic Car
Sales (DCS)
and Combined
Forecast (DCSCF)

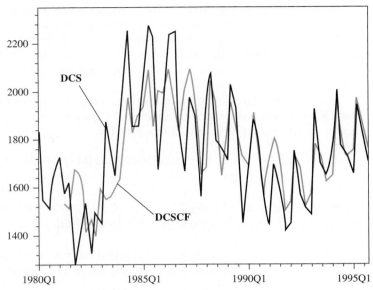

This graphic shows actual DCS and a combined forecast (DCSCF)
that is based on a combination of a multiple-regression forecast
(DCSFR) and a Winters' exponential smoothing forecast (DCSFW)
The combined forecast is:

$$DCS = 0.266978(DCSFR) + 0.744209(DCSFW)$$

(c8t5)

TABLE 8–5   Domestic Car Sales (DCS) and Three
Forecasts of DCS

	DCS	*DCSFR*	*DCSFW*	*DCSCF*
1980Q1	1849.90	1663.40	MISSING	MISSING
1980Q2	1550.80	1662.96	MISSING	MISSING
1980Q3	1515.30	1720.96	MISSING	MISSING
1980Q4	1665.40	1659.43	MISSING	MISSING
I981Q1	1733.00	1629.52	MISSING	MISSING
1981Q2	1576.00	1632.27	1475.58	1532.46
1981Q3	1618.50	1616.52	1459.68	1516.24
1981Q4	1281.30	1656.52	1652.98	1671.25
1982Q1	1401.40	1665.11	1610.06	1641.71
1982Q2	1535.30	1662.89	1313.29	1420.25
1982Q3	1327.90	1684.12	1365.40	1464.95
1982Q4	1493.60	1718.02	1262.26	1397.66
1983Q1	1456.90	1731.27	1522.41	1594.95
1983Q2	1875.80	1736.38	1452.78	1544.56
1983Q3	1646.20	1733.66	1479.29	1563.53
1983Q4	1814.10	1732.43	1574.67	1634.16
1984Q1	1994.60	1733.12	1742.61	1759.33
1984Q2	2251.80	1719.27	2033.52	1971.94
1984Q3	1854.30	1711.97	1844.20	1829.02
1984Q4	1851.00	1726.50	1920.93	1890.18

TABLE 8–5 *concluded*

	DCS	DCSFR	DCSFW	DCSCF
1985Q1	2042.20	1741.88	1977.63	1936.66
1985Q2	2272.60	1747.28	2186.22	2093.39
1985Q3	2217.70	1755.23	1860.82	1853.46
1985Q4	1672.20	1755.77	2053.12	1996.71
1986Q1	1898.70	1758.39	2043.95	1990.62
1986Q2	2242.20	1768.10	2171.86	2088.52
1986Q3	2246.90	1777.46	1942.27	1920.28
1986Q4	1827.20	1781.46	1816.63	1827.91
1987Q1	1669.30	1782.06	2067.77	2014.95
1987Q2	1972.80	1774.44	2177.14	2094.22
1987Q3	1878.20	1771.12	1930.08	1909.44
1987Q4	1560.60	1766.40	1583.90	1650.51
1988Q1	1914.00	1770.93	1627.68	1684.35
1988Q2	2076.00	1768.59	2081.90	2021.71
1988Q3	1787.10	1757.68	1974.35	1938.63
1988Q4	1762.30	1752.11	1585.18	1647.48
1989Q1	1707.40	1743.17	1838.90	1833.79
1989Q2	2018.60	1738.01	2000.88	1952.88
1989Q3	1898.50	1746.64	1832.32	1829.85
1989Q4	1453.60	1748.72	1684.34	1720.32
1990Q1	1706.20	1755.17	1642.94	1691.32
1990Q2	1878.20	1755.76	1929.02	1904.36
1990Q3	1752.10	1755.62	1757.50	1776.68
1990Q4	1560.40	1754.81	1475.17	1566.37
1991Q1	1445.10	1764.13	1678.04	1719.93
1991Q2	1683.90	1771.11	1783.60	1800.43
1991Q3	1586.60	1774.10	1616.61	1677.00
1991Q4	1421.30	1783.90	1376.36	1500.96
1992Q1	1455.40	1798.14	1423.24	1539.82
1992Q2	1746.10	1798.54	1675.51	1727.65
1992Q3	1571.70	1804.32	1605.58	1677.23
1992Q4	1503.40	1805.78	1394.92	1520.88
1993Q1	1483.50	1804.06	1465.04	1572.58
1993Q2	1917.90	1804.85	1733.75	1772.76
1993Q3	1690.30	1804.90	1665.87	1722.26
1993Q4	1642.30	1805.66	1529.97	1621.34
1994Q1	1762.30	1804.36	1570.40	1651.06
1994Q2	2001.50	1795.00	2017.16	1980.90
1994Q3	1766.60	1787.96	1797.75	1815.67
1994Q4	1724.80	1780.85	1671.02	1719.37
1995Q1	1658.20	1776.89	1720.60	1755.16
1995Q2	1938.40	1772.97	2008.62	1968.40
1995Q3	1845.30	1769.06	1789.17	1804.00
1995Q4	1686.90	1765.15	1708.30	1742.73

DCSFR = Multiple-regression forecast of DCS

DCSFW = Winters' exponential smoothing forecast of DCS

DCSCF = A combination forecast of DCS, where
DCSCF = 0.266978(DCSFR) + 0.744209(DCSFW)

TABLE 8–6   **Summary Table of RMSEs for DCS**

Chapter	Method	Period	RMSE
1	Naive—with 4-period lag	Historic before '95	207.3
		Holdout 95Q1–95Q4	74.9
2	Not applicable	Historic before '95	na
		Holdout 95Q1–95Q4	na
3	Winters' exponential smoothing	Historic before '95	177.1
		Holdout 95Q1–95Q4	55.8
	ADRES with seasonal adjustment	Historic before '95	169.5
		Holdout 95Q1–95Q4	64.2
4	Simple regression model using seasonally adjusted DCS as a function of the University of Michigan Index of Consumer Sentiment	Historic before '95	134.570
		Holdout 95Q1–95Q4	102.242
5	Multiple regression	Historic before '95	106.8
		Holdout 95Q1–95Q4	56.9
6	Time-series decomposition	Historic before '95	130.185
		Holdout 95Q1–95Q4	140.930
7	ARMA(1,1) model with first-degree ordinary differencing on seasonally adjusted DCS	Historic before '95	*
		Holdout 95Q1–95Q4	68.79
8	Combined Winters' and multiple-regression forecast (note: regression model includes only DPI and MR as explanatory variables)	Historic before '95	164.496
		Holdout 95Q1–95Q4	61.4922

*Unavailable with this technique

know the actual values of DCS), some models, most notably multiple regression, outperformed the combined forecast. Isn't hindsight wonderful!

Comments from the Field

Combining Forecasts Can Improve Results

Delfield

This statement was made by Deborah Allison-Koerber, a product-line manager at the Delfield Company, a leading manufacturer of food-service equipment. Delfield uses a production-planning system consisting of a master production schedule and a corresponding material requirements planning (MRP) system. The MRP system is driven in large part by sales forecasts. For some time, management had been relying on a heavily judgmental sales forecast that started with a three-month moving average, incorporated judgmental factors from an informal "jury of executive opinion," and was finally adjusted by "add factors" provided by the person who was responsible for the MRP system.

According to Ms. Allison-Koerber, the results from this approach to forecasting were unsatisfactory from an operational perspective, and so she started to test some more quantitative forecasting methods. She focused her initial attention on a particular three-door reach-in freezer that represented a large cost when held in inventory, and so accurate forecasts of sales were important. A review of the sales history for this product showed some trend and some seasonality. Thus, Ms. Allison-Koerber believed that a multiple-regression model and a Winters' exponential smoothing model would be good candidates.

For a multiple-regression model she "reviewed a large set of potential causal variables but settled on GNP and the prime interest rate as the most important." In addition, "dummy variables were used to account for seasonality and a temporary demand surge" that reflected the rollout of new menu items by a large fast-food chain that purchases Delfield food-service equipment. Ms. Allison-Koerber commented,

> A regression model based on this information is comprehensive enough to forecast sales of these freezers and yet simple enough to be easily communicated to others in the organization. In addition, the model is desirable because it necessitates having to develop forecasts for only two independent variables.

For the first six months of actual use, this model resulted in an RMSE of 20.185, which compared with an RMSE of 42.821 based on the traditional subjective method.

Ms. Allison-Koerber found a Winters exponential smoothing forecast to also outperform the subjective forecast by producing an RMSE of 29.081 for the first six months of use. Because the regression model and the Winters model contain different information, they were combined. The resulting RMSE was 17.198, lower than the regression model (20.185) or the Winters model (29.081) and much better than the subjective approach (42.821).

However, as Ms. Allison-Koerber commented, it was felt that "the personnel who make the subjective forecasts have good insights about the industry and these insights should be utilized when possible." Thus, she used a regression technique to combine the quantitative and subjective forecasts. Even though the RMSE for the subjective forecast was much higher, the results demonstrated that the subjective method contained information not found in the other models. The results are summarized in the following table:

Model	RMSE
A. Regression	20.185
B. Winters'	29.081
C. Subjective	42.821
D. A and B combined	17.198
E. C and A combined	17.944
F. C and B combined	16.724
G. C and D combined	16.168

These results confirmed for Delfield that the use of quantitative forecasting methods and the combination of subjective and quantitative forecasts can improve results.

INTEGRATIVE CASE
The Gap Part 8

Forecasting The Gap Sales Data with a Combination Model

The sales of Gap stores for the 44 quarters covering 1985 quarter 1 through 1995 quarter 4 are again shown in the graph below. Recall that the Gap sales data are quite seasonal and are increasing over time.

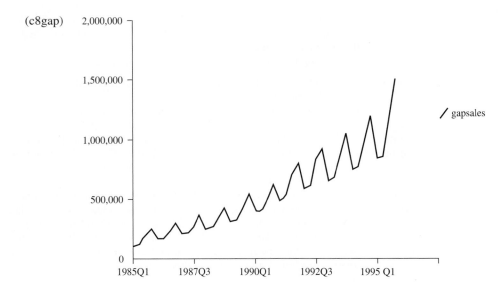

Case Questions

1. Assume you would like to use a Winters model and combine the forecast results with the multiple-regression model presented previously (see Chapter 5). Use the regression technique to decide on the weighting to attach to each forecast.

2. Combine the two methods (i.e., the Winters and the multiple-regression model) with the calculated weighting scheme and make a combined forecast.

3. Calculate the root-mean-squared errors for both the historic period and for the 1996Q1 through 1996Q4 forecast horizon.

Solutions to Case Questions

1. To see if both models may reasonably be used in a combined forecast, run the regression that uses Gap sales as the dependent variable and the two forecasts (one from the Winters model and the other from the multiple-regression model) as the explanatory variables. The regression (shown below) indicates that there is little significance attached to the constant term (because of its *t*-statistic of -1.34), and so we may reasonably attempt to combine the models.

```
REGRESS : dependent variable is GAPSALES

Using   1986Q2-1995Q4


      Variable          Coefficient      Std Err        T-stat        Signf

^CONST                    -17832.3       12755.7       -1.39799         .171
GAPSALES_RFCST            .150525         .113992       1.32049         .195
GAPSALES_WFCST           .889250         .115491       7.69976         .000


                          Equation Summary
      No. of Observations =       39      R2=    .9880   (adj)=    .9874
      Sum of Sq. Resid.  =   .470185E+11  Std. Error of Reg.=  36139.6
      Log(likelihood)   =  -463.088      Durbin-Watson    =   1.31127
      Schwarz Criterion =  -468.584      F ( 2,   36)     =   1486.83
      Akaike Criterion  =  -466.088      Significance     =    .000000
```

2. The two models are combined by running the same regression through the origin (shown below). Here the dependent variable is again Gap sales (here called "cfcst," so that this variable becomes the combined forecast when we use the forecast command). Note that the weight on the Winters forecast is larger than the weight on the multiple-regression forecast; this seems appropriate because the Winters forecast alone has a lower RMSE than does the multiple-regression forecast when considered separately.

Note the very close association of the forecast with the original data:

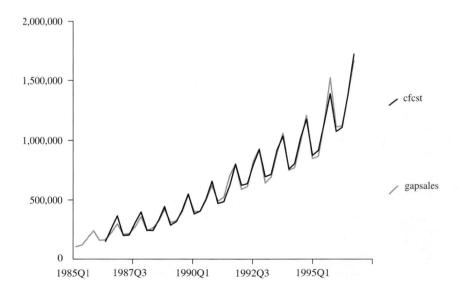

```
REGRESS : dependent variable is GAPSALES

Using   1986Q2-1995Q4

     Variable          Coefficient      Std Err        T-stat        Signf

GAPSALES_RFCST           .136756         .115021       1.18897         .242
GAPSALES_WFCST           .879360         .116751       7.53193         .000

                        Equation Summary
    No. of Observations =        39     R2=   .9972   (adj)=   .9971
    Sum of Sq. Resid.  = .495710E+11    Std. Error of Reg.= 36602.7
    Log(likelihood)    = -464.119       Durbin-Watson    = 1.24546
    Schwarz Criterion  = -467.783       F ( 2,   37)     = 6695.28
    Akaike Criterion   = -466.119       Significance     = .000000
```

3. The combined forecast gives the following results in the forecast horizon:

	GAPSALES	Combined Forecast
1996Q1	1,113,154	1,040,120
1996Q2	1,120,335	1,070,170
1996Q3	1,383,996	1,380,010
1996Q4	1,667,896	1,744,940

The RMSEs for the (shortened) historic period and the 1996 forecast horizon are:

1986Q2–1995Q4   Root-mean-squared error = 35,657
(shortened period due to missing data)

1996Q1–1996Q4   Root-mean-squared error = 58,724

If we compare these results with the results presented at the end of Chapters 3 and 5 (see Table 8–7), we find that both the historic period RMSE and the forecast

TABLE 8–7   **Summary Table of RMSEs for Gap Sales**

Chapter	Method	Period	RMSE
1	Naive—with 4-period lag	Historic before '95	107,150
		Holdout 96Q1–96Q4	227,027
2		Historic before '95	na
		Holdout 96Q1–96Q4	na
3	Winters' exponential smoothing	Historic before '95	37,935.5
		Holdout 96Q1–96Q4	84,460.7
	Holt's exponential smoothing with seasonal readjustment	Historic before '95	31,272.5
		Holdout 96Q1–96Q4	33,341.3
4	Linear trend of deseasonalized data with forecast	Historic before '95	56,110.6
		Holdout 96Q1–96Q4	211,550.0
5	Multiple regression	Historic before '95	56,178.1
		Holdout 96Q1–96Q4	116,620
6	Time-series decomposition	Historic before '95	25,706.9
		Holdout 96Q1–96Q4	145,488.0
7	ARMA(2,0) model with two-degrees of seasonal differencing	Historic before '95	*
		Holdout 96Q1–96Q4	96,975.1
8	Combined Winters' and the multiple regression from Chapter 5	Historic before '95	35,652
		Holdout 96Q1–96Q4	58,734

*Unavailable with this technique

horizon RMSE are lower with the combination forecast than with either individual method. Each forecasting method must be adding some unique explanatory power to the combined regression.

(c8gap)

	GAPSALES	CFCST
1985Q1	105715.	MISSING
1985Q2	120136.	MISSING
1985Q3	181669.	MISSING
1985Q4	239813.	MISSING
1986Q1	159980.	MISSING
1986Q2	164760.	155856.
1986Q3	224800.	263171.
1986Q4	298469.	364018.
1987Q1	211060.	202742.
1987Q2	217753.	204766.
1987Q3	273616.	298301.
1987Q4	359592.	395183.
1988Q1	241348.	256726.
1988Q2	264328.	251268.
1988Q3	322752.	327135.
1988Q4	423669.	438045.
1989Q1	309925.	291253.
1989Q2	325939.	321820.
1989Q3	405601.	405970.
1989Q4	545131.	538137.

continued

	GAPSALES	CFCST
1990Q1	402368.	384306.
1990Q2	404996.	409179.
1990Q3	501690.	507545.
1990Q4	624726.	667581.
1991Q1	490300.	475326.
1991Q2	523056.	484821.
1991Q3	702052.	616015.
1991Q4	803485.	811545.
1992Q1	588864.	633736.
1992Q2	614114.	647868.
1992Q3	827222.	814828.
1992Q4	930209.	932907.
1993Q1	643580.	696248.
1993Q2	693192.	716383.
1993Q3	898677.	936756.
1993Q4	.106023E+07	.104056E+07
1994Q1	751670.	747034.
1994Q2	773131.	804955.
1994Q3	988346.	.103276E+07
1994Q4	.120979E+07	.119317E+07
1995Q1	848688.	860345.
1995Q2	868514.	895457.
1995Q3	.115593E+07	.114091E+07
1995Q4	.152212E+07	.139421E+07
1996Q1	.111315E+07	.104003E+07
1996Q2	.112034E+07	.107006E+07
1996Q3	.138300E+07	.137985E+07
1996Q4	.166790E+07	.174480E+07

USING SORITEC TO COMBINE FORECASTS

The SORITEC software that accompanies this text is ideally suited for developing optimal combinations of forecasts. If you have already developed the individual forecasts, the combined forecast can be developed with a few short commands. In this section, however, we will start from scratch by entering six years of quarterly sales data, developing two alternative forecasts, using the regression technique to combine them, and plotting graphs with each individual forecast as well as the combined forecast along with actual sales.

Begin by entering the SORITEC software and opening the **Data Tool** from the **View** menu, or by clicking on the ▦ button on the toolbar. To enter data:

1. Enter the date and time of the first observation in the first column, second row (the column labeled Date). Our first date will be 1992Q1.
2. If you desire, SORITEC will complete the date series in the Date column:
    a. With the mouse, select the date you just entered in column 1, row 2.
    b. Hold down the left mouse button, and drag down to highlight the cells to hold the dates.
    c. Click on the **Fill** button and SORITEC will fill the selected cells with sequential dates and times.
3. Enter the name of the variable (i.e., Sales) in the first row, second column (labeled Series 1).
4. Beneath the variable name "Sales" begin entering the data values in row 2, column 2.
5. When the data are completely entered, click on the **Update** button to enter the data into the workspace.

The data values you should enter in order are:

12 14 18 19 19 20 22 23 25 26 27 28 28 31 32 33 36 39 40 43 47 48 49 49

The Data Tool should now look like the following figure:

	Type/Date	Series1	Series2	Series3
1		sales		
2	1992q1	12		
3	1992Q2	14		
4	1992Q3	18		
5	1992Q4	19		
6	1993Q1	19		
7	1993Q2	20		
8	1993Q3	22		
9	1993Q4	23		
10	1994Q1	25		
11	1994Q2	26		
12	1994Q3	27		
13	1994Q4	28		
14	1995Q1	28		
15	1995Q2	31		
16	1995Q3	32		
17	1995Q4	33		
18	1996Q1	36		
19	1996Q2	39		
20	1996Q3	40		
21	1996Q4	43		
22	1997Q1	47		
23	1997Q2	48		
24	1997Q3	49		

Update	Cancel	Display...	Calc	Fill

To see what the sales series looks like, use the **Plot** button to create the following plot:

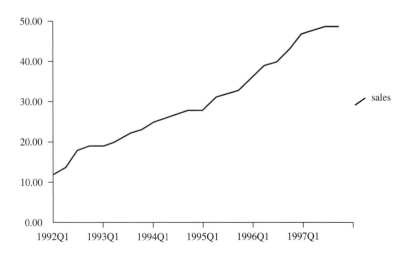

We will begin with a trend-forecasting model, and so you should first extend the **use** period to include 1998Q1–1998Q4 as a forecast horizon and then create a time index variable (T) that runs from 1992Q1 (T = 1) through 1998Q4 (T = 28) by entering the following two commands:

```
USE 1992Q1 1998Q4
TIME T
```

Now, to develop the regression trend model and forecast you may use the forecasting tool: 🔭. Select the variable to be forecast (Sales) in the dialog box and set the estimation period to 1992Q1–1997Q4; request 4 periods to forecast:

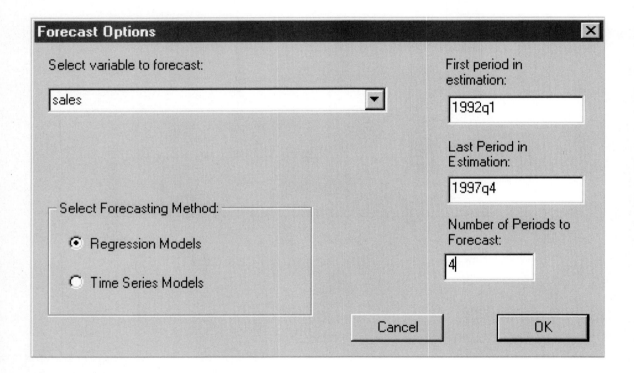

The time index (T) should be selected as the only explanatory variable. Make certain that the **Target Variable** name is set to **SFT** so that the time-series forecast has a different name than the original Sales time series.

Your regression equation should be:

$$SFT = 10.4746 + 1.5887(T)$$

Next, you should develop a Holt's exponential smoothing forecast of sales and call the forecast SFH. Once again, you may use the forecast tool 🔭 for this purpose. Make certain that the **results series name is SFH.** For this model, α will be 0.999 and β will be 0.001.

Before combining the two forecasts (SFT and SFH), check the root-mean-squared error of each by using the **ACTFIT** command from the **Stats** menu. Recall that the first variable selected must be the "actual" variable (in this case Sales) and the second variable selected must be the "fitted" variable (in this case either SFT or SFH). The RMSE for SFT will be 1.66816, and for SFH it will be 1.17548.

Now, to develop a combined forecast, you will want to regress Sales on SFT and SFH. To do so you'll need to use the 1992Q2–1997Q4 period (since 1992Q1 will be missing for SFH). Enter the following command and then run the regression from the **Linear** menu (with SALES as the dependent variable and SFT and SFH as the explanatory variables):

```
USE 1992Q2 1997Q4
```

The results of the regression are as follows:

```
REGRESS : dependent variable is SALES

Using   1992Q2-1997Q4


    Variable          Coefficient      Std Err        T-stat        Signf

^CONST               .282521E-01      .766610       .368533E-01      .971
SFT                  .237264          .145811       1.62720          .119
SFH                  .764498          .144355       5.29595          .000


                        Equation Summary
    No. of Observations =      23       R2=    .9894   (adj)=    .9883
    Sum of Sq. Resid.  =   27.7984      Std. Error of Reg.=  1.17895
    Log(likelihood)    =  -34.8147      Durbin-Watson    =   1.61855
    Schwarz Criterion  =  -39.5179      F ( 2,   20)     =   932.000
    Akaike Criterion   =  -37.8147      Significance     =    .000000
```

In this regression you want to check to see whether the constant term is essentially zero. Your results show a constant term of about 0.028 with a *t*-ratio of about 0.037 and a two-tailed significance of 0.971. Thus, you can conclude that the constant term is essentially equal to zero.

Next, to get the appropriate weights for SFT and SFH, you will want to again regress Sales on SFT and SFH, but this time you'll force the regression through the origin. Again, use the **Linear** menu and select the regression as before (with SALES as the dependent variable and SFT and SFH as the explanatory variables), but this time deselect the "constant term" selection in the dialog box. This will cause the regression to be forced through the origin (and there will be no constant term reported). The resulting regression is reported as:

```
REGRESS : dependent variable is SALES

Using   1992Q2-1997Q4


    Variable          Coefficient      Std Err        T-stat        Signf

SFT                  .238092          .140601       1.69339          .105
SFH                  .764484          .140881       5.42647          .000
```

```
                           Equation Summary
No. of Observations =       23      R2=   .9989   (adj)=    .9988
Sum of Sq. Resid. =    27.8003      Std. Error of Reg.=   1.15058
Log(likelihood)   =   -34.8154      Durbin-Watson    =    1.61857
Schwarz Criterion =   -37.9509      F ( 2,   21)     =    9397.10
Akaike Criterion  =   -36.8154      Significance     =    .000000
```

Notice that the coefficients sum approximately to 1 and that the Holt's forecast (which had the lower RMSE) is given the greater weight (i.e., the larger regression coefficient).

To actually forecast values for the combined forecast, use the Forecast Tool. To calculate the RMSE for the historical period (1992Q1 through 1997Q4) use the **ACTFIT** command from the **Stats** menu. This RMSE is 1.09941, which represents an improvement over either of the individual forecasts. You may wish to use the **PLOT** command to compare the actual Sales values with each of the forecasts.

Suggested Readings

Armstrong, J. Scott. "Combining Forecasts: The End of the Beginning or the Beginning of the End?" *International Journal of Forecasting* 5, no. 4 (1989), pp. 585–88.

———. *Long-Range Forecasting from Crystal Ball to Computer.* 2nd ed. New York: John Wiley & Sons, 1985.

Bates, J. M.; and C. W. J. Granger. "The Combination of Forecasts." *Operational Research Quarterly* 20, no. 4 (1969), pp. 451–68.

Bessler, David A.; and Jon A. Brandt. "Composite Forecasting: An Application with U.S. Hog Prices." *American Journal of Agricultural Economics* 63 (1981), pp. 135–40.

Clemen, Robert T. "Combining Forecasts: A Review and Annotated Bibliography." *International Journal of Forecasting* 5, no. 4 (1989), pp. 559–83.

———. "Linear Constraints and the Efficiency of Combined Forecasts." *Journal of Forecasting* 5 (1986), pp. 31–38.

Collopy, Fred; and J. Scott Armstrong. "Expert Opinions about Extrapolation and the Mystery of the Overlooked Discontinuities." *International Journal of Forecasting* 8, no. 4 (December 1992), pp. 575–82.

Diebold, Francis X. "Forecast Combination and Encompassing: Reconciling Two Divergent Literatures." *International Journal of Forecasting* 5, no. 4 (1989), pp. 589–92.

Flores, Benito E.; David L. Olson; and Christopher Wolfe. "Judgmental Adjustment of Forecasts: A Comparison of Methods." *International Journal of Forecasting* 7, no. 4 (1992), pp. 421–33.

Fullerton, Thomas M., Jr. "A Composite Approach to Forecasting State Government Revenues: Case Study of the Idaho Sales Tax." *International Journal of Forecasting* 5, no. 3 (1989), pp. 373–80.

Hayes, Samuel P., Jr. "The Predictive Ability of Voters." *Journal of Social Psychology* 7 (1936), pp. 183–91.

Hogarth, Robin M. "On Combining Diagnostic 'Forecasts': Thoughts and Some Evidence." *International Journal of Forecasting* 5, no. 4 (1989), pp. 593–97.

Lobo, Gerald I. "Analysis and Comparison of Financial Analysts' Time Series, and Combined Forecasts of Annual Earnings." *Journal of Business Research* 24 (1992), pp. 269–80.

Mahmoud, Essam. "Combining Forecasts: Some Managerial Issues." *International Journal of Forecasting* 5, no. 4 (1989), pp. 599–600.

Makridakis, Spyros. "Why Combining Works." *International Journal of Forecasting* 5 (1989), pp. 601–603.

Moriarity, Mark M.; and Arthur I. Adams. "Management Judgment Forecasts, Composite Forecasting Models, and Conditional Efficiency." *Journal of Marketing Research* 21 (1984), pp. 239–50.

Nelson, Charles R. "A Benchmark for the Accuracy of Econometric Forecasts of GNP." *Business Economics* 19, no. 3 (April 1984), pp. 52–58.

Wilson, J. Holton; and Deborah Allison-Koerber. "Combining Subjective and Objective Forecasts Improve Results." *Journal of Business Forecasting* 11, no. 3 (1992), pp. 3–8.

Winkler, Robert L. "Combining Forecasts: A Philosophical Basis and Some Current Issues." *International Journal of Forecasting* 5, no. 4 (1989), pp. 605–609.

Exercises

1. Explain why a combined model might be better than any of the original contributing models. Could there be cases in which a combined model would show no gain in forecast accuracy over the original models? Give an example where this situation might be likely to occur.

2. Outline the different methods for combining forecast models explained in the chapter. Can more than two forecasting models be combined into a single model? Does each of the original forecasts have to be the result of the application of a quantitative technique?

3. *Air Carrier Traffic Statistics Monthly* is a handbook of airline data published by the U.S. Department of Transportation. In this book you will find revenue passenger-miles (RPM) traveled on major airlines on international flights. Airlines regularly try to predict accurately the RPM for future periods; this gives the airline a picture of what equipment needs might be and is helpful in keeping costs at a minimum.

   The revenue passenger-miles for international flights on major international airlines is shown in the accompanying table for the period January 1979 to February 1984. Also shown is personal income during the same period, in billions of dollars.

Date	RPM	Personal Income
Jan-79	4,114,904	1,834.3
Feb-79	3,283,488	1,851.4
Mar-79	4,038,611	1,872.1
Apr-79	4,312,697	1,880.7
May-79	4,638,300	1,891.6
Jun-79	6,661,979	1,905.1
Jul-79	6,221,612	1,933.2
Aug-79	6,489,078	1,946.5
Sep-79	5,258,750	1,960.1
Oct-79	4,720,077	1,979.2
Nov-79	4,037,529	2,000.0
Dec-79	4,240,862	2,022.5

continued

Date	RPM	Personal Income
Jan-80	4,222,446	2,077.2
Feb-80	3,540,027	2,086.4
Mar-80	4,148,262	2,101.0
Apr-80	4,106,723	2,102.1
May-80	4,602,599	2,114.1
Jun-80	5,169,789	2,127.1
Jul-80	5,911,035	2,161.2
Aug-80	6,236,392	2,179.4
Sep-80	4,700,133	2,205.7
Oct-80	4,274,816	2,235.3
Nov-80	3,611,307	2,260.4
Dec-80	3,794,631	2,281.5
Jan-81	3,513,072	2,300.7
Feb-81	2,856,083	2,318.2
Mar-81	3,281,964	2,340.4
Apr-81	3,694,417	2,353.8
May-81	4,240,501	2,367.4
Jun-81	4,524,445	2,384.3
Jul-81	5,156,871	2,419.2
Aug-81	5,465,791	2,443.4
Sep-81	4,320,529	2,462.6
Oct-81	4,036,149	2,473.5
Nov-81	3,272,074	2,487.6
Dec-81	3,514,227	2,492.1
Jan-82	3,558,273	2,499.1
Feb-82	2,834,658	2,513.8
Mar-82	3,318,250	2,518.6
Apr-82	3,660,038	2,535.5
May-82	4,014,541	2,556.2
Jun-82	4,487,598	2,566.3
Jul-82	5,088,561	2,588.3
Aug-82	5,292,201	2,592.0
Sep-82	4,320,181	2,597.2
Oct-82	4,069,619	2,611.5
Nov-82	3,125,650	2,621.3
Dec-82	3,381,049	2,636.8
Jan-83	3,513,758	2,652.6
Feb-83	2,876,672	2,650.5
Mar-83	3,536,871	2,670.1
Apr-83	3,744,696	2,689.0
May-83	4,404,939	2,719.3

continued

Date	RPM	Personal Income
Jun-83	5,201,363	2,732.6
Jul-83	5,915,462	2,747.6
Aug-83	6,022,431	2,756.4
Sep-83	5,000,685	2,781.6
Oct-83	4,659,152	2,812.8
Nov-83	3,592,160	2,833.1
Dec-83	3,818,737	2,857.2
Jan-84	3,828,367	2,897.4
Feb-84	3,221,633	2,923.5

Quarter	Loan Volume	Assets	Members	Prime Rate
Jan-77	$2,583,718	$4,036,809	3,522	6.25%
Apr-77	2,801,104	4,164,720	3,589	6.75%
Jul-77	2,998,237	4,362,676	3,632	7.13%
Oct-77	3,032,719	4,482,993	3,676	7.75%
Jan-78	3,094,578	4,611,301	3,668	8.00%
Apr-78	3,372,678	4,696,723	3,689	8.63%
Jul-78	3,499,348	4,844,957	3,705	9.41%
Oct-78	3,553,706	4,893,452	3,722	11.55%
Jan-79	3,651,868	5,089,835	3,732	11.75%
Apr-79	3,832,437	5,185,361	3,770	11.65%
Jul-79	4,013,310	5,381,136	3,845	12.90%
Oct-79	3,950,097	5,413,716	3,881	15.30%
Jan-80	3,925,097	5,574,156	3,923	18.31%
Apr-80	3,717,475	5,838,994	3,941	12.63%
Jul-80	3,712,296	6,150,349	3,955	12.23%
Oct-80	3,677,937	6,133,033	3,943	20.35%
Jan-81	3,724,771	6,119,032	3,960	18.05%
Apr-81	3,787,763	6,221,092	3,971	20.03%
Jul-81	3,981,623	6,228,997	3,993	20.08%
Oct-81	3,848,656	6,412,229	4,011	15.75%
Jan-82	3,619,831	6,795,825	4,040	16.50%
Apr-82	3,623,585	7,538,214	4,103	16.50%
Jul-82	3,632,124	8,496,079	4,133	13.50%
Oct-82	3,481,999	9,979,388	4,173	11.50%
Jan-83	3,378,499	11,475,342	4,218	10.50%
Apr-83	3,433,468	12,116,883	4,266	10.50%
Jul-83	3,615,426	12,686,543	4,305	11.00%
Oct-83	3,865,780	13,457,558	4,657	11.00%
Jan-84	3,955,265	14,118,299	4,741	11.21%
Apr-84	4,394,137	14,448,570	4,826	12.60%
Jul-84	4,803,632	14,687,215	4,943	12.97%
Oct-84	4,952,742	14,885,789	4,945	11.06%
Jan-85	5,249,756	16,106,298	5,007	10.50%
Apr-85	5,943,392	17,079,365	5,112	9.78%
Jul-85	6,387,001	17,846,796	5,164	9.50%
Oct-85	6,435,753	19,435,550	5,210	9.50%
Jan-86	6,482,777	19,714,146	5,255	9.10%
Apr-86	6,683,801	21,185,825	5,289	8.50%
Jul-86	7,094,214	22,716,730	5,391	7.50%
Oct-86	7,329,765	23,790,539	5,461	7.50%

a. Build a multiple-regression model for the data to predict RPM for the next month. Check the data for any trend, and be careful to account for any seasonality. You should easily be able to obtain a forecast model with an R^2 of about 0.70 that exhibits little serial correlation.

b. Use the same data to compute a time-series decomposition model and again forecast for one month in the future.

c. Judging from the root-mean-squared error, which of the models in parts (a) and (b) proved to be the best forecasting model? Now combine the two models, using a weighting scheme like that shown in Table 8–1; choose various weights until you believe you have come close to the optimum weighting scheme. Does this combined model perform better (according to RMSE) than either of the two original models? Why do you believe the combined model behaves in this way?

d. Try one other forecasting method of your choice on these data and combine the results with the multiple-regression model. Do you obtain a better forecast (according to RMSE) than either of your two original models?

4. Estimating the volume of loans that will be made at a credit union is crucial to effective cash management in those institutions. In the table that follows are quarterly data for a real credit union located in a midwestern city. Credit unions are financial institutions similar to banks, but credit unions are not-for-profit firms whose members are the actual owners (remember their slogan, "It's where you belong"). The members may be both depositors in and borrowers from the credit union.

a. Estimate a multiple-regression model to estimate loan demand and calculate its root-mean-squared error.

b. Estimate a time-series decomposition model to estimate loan demand with the same data and calculate its root-mean-squared error.

c. Combine the models in parts (*a*) and (*b*) and determine whether the combined model performs better than either or both of the original models. Try to explain why you obtained the results you did.

5. HeathCo Industries, a producer of a line of skiwear, has been the subject of problems in several earlier chapters of the text. The data for its sales and two potential causal variables, income (INC) and the northern-region unemployment rate (NRUR), are repeated in the following table:

Obs	TIME	SALES	INC	NRUR
1988Q1	1	72,962	218	8.4
1988Q2	2	81,821	237	8.2
1988Q3	3	97,729	263	8.4
1988Q4	4	142,161	296	8.4
1989Q1	5	145,592	318	8.1
1989Q2	6	117,129	359	7.7
1989Q3	7	114,159	404	7.5
1989Q4	8	151,402	436	7.2
1990Q1	9	153,907	475	6.9
1990Q2	10	100,144	435	6.5
1990Q3	11	123,242	574	6.5
1990Q4	12	128,497	622	6.4
1991Q1	13	176,076	667	6.3
1991Q2	14	180,440	702	6.2
1991Q3	15	162,665	753	6.3
1991Q4	16	220,818	796	6.5
1992Q1	17	202,415	858	6.8
1992Q2	18	211,780	870	7.9
1992Q3	19	163,710	934	8.3
1992Q4	20	200,135	1,010	8.0
1993Q1	21	174,200	1,066	8.0
1993Q2	22	182,556	1,096	8.0
1993Q3	23	198,990	1,162	8.0
1993Q4	24	243,700	1,187	8.9
1994Q1	25	253,142	1,207	9.6
1994Q2	26	218,755	1,242	10.2
1994Q3	27	225,422	1,279	10.7
1994Q4	28	253,653	1,318	11.5
1995Q1	29	257,156	1,346	11.2
1995Q2	30	202,568	1,395	11.0

Continued

Obs	TIME	SALES	INC	NRUR
1995Q3	31	224,482	1,443	10.1
1995Q4	32	229,879	1,528	9.2
1996Q1	33	289,321	1,613	8.5
1996Q2	34	266,095	1,646	8.0
1996Q3	35	262,938	1,694	8.0
1996Q4	36	322,052	1,730	7.9
1997Q1	37	313,769	1,755	7.9
1997Q2	38	315,011	1,842	7.9
1997Q3	39	264,939	1,832	7.8
1997Q4	40	301,479	1,882	7.6

a. Develop a multiple-regression model of SALES as a function of both INC and NRUR:

$$\text{SALES} = a + b_1(\text{INC}) + b_2(\text{NRUR})$$

Use this model to forecast sales for 1998Q1–1998Q4 (call your regression forecast series SFR), given that INC and NRUR for 1998 have been forecast to be:

Quarter	INC	NRUR
1998Q1	1,928	7.6
1998Q2	1,972	7.7
1998Q3	2,017	7.5
1998Q4	2,062	7.4

b. Calculate the RMSE for your regression model for both the historic period (1988Q1–1997Q4) and the forecast horizon (1998Q1–1998Q4).

Period	RMSE
Historic	_____
Forecast	_____

c. Now prepare a forecast through the historic period and the forecast horizon (1998Q1–1998Q4) using Winters' exponential smoothing. Call this forecast series SFW, and fill in the RMSEs for SFW:

Period	RMSE
Historic	_____
Forecast	_____

d. Solely on the basis of the historic data, which model appears to be the best? Why?

e. Now prepare a combined forecast (SCF) using the regression technique described in this chapter. In the standard regression:

$$\text{SALES} = a + b_1(\text{SFR}) + b_2(\text{SFW})$$

Is the intercept essentially zero? Why? If it is, do the following regression as a basis for developing SCF:

$$\text{SALES} = b_1(\text{SFR}) + b_2(\text{SFW})$$

Given the historic RMSEs found in parts (*b*) and (*c*), do the values for b_1 and b_2 seem plausible? Explain.

f. Calculate the RMSEs for SCF:

Period	RMSE
Historic	_____
Forecast	_____

Did combining models reduce the RMSE in the historic period? What about the actual forecast?

6. Annual U.S. billings for the Leo Burnett advertising agency (LBB) for the period from 1950 through 1990 are shown in the following table (data are from various issues of *Advertising Age*):

Year	LBB*	Year	LBB*	Year	LBB*
1950	22.0	1964	160.1	1978	604.0
1951	28.0	1965	184.7	1979	639.8
1952	37.6	1966	212.2	1980	734.6
1953	46.4	1967	250.0	1981	838.4
1954	55.0	1968	255.6	1982	919.8
1955	69.2	1969	288.2	1983	914.1
1956	79.0	1970	283.6	1984	1,132.9
1957	78.7	1971	296.8	1985	1,269.9
1958	98.7	1972	313.6	1986	1,361.6
1959	110.5	1973	330.9	1987	1,550.0
1960	116.7	1974	366.1	1988	1,765.0
1961	136.1	1975	400.0	1989	1,945.3
1962	151.9	1976	508.0	1990	2,035.2
1963	139.3	1977	575.0	1991	MISSING

*Data are in billions of dollars.

a. Prepare an exponential trend forecast of LBB through 1995, calling this forecast LBBFET. The development of such a trend was discussed in this chapter in the section "An Example." Start by entering the LBB data; then establish a time index (T) equal to 1 for 1950 through 46 for 1995. The model you want is:

$$\text{LBB} = b_0 m^T$$

Thus, start by regressing the natural log of LBB on T, to obtain

$$\ln \text{LBB} = \ln b_0 + T(\ln m)$$

Forecast $\ln$ LBB throughout the 1950–1995 period; then convert back to LBBFET as follows:

$$\text{LBBFET} = e^{\ln \text{LBB}}$$

or

$$\text{LBBFET} = \exp(\ln \text{LBB})$$

(Note: The regression must be done using the 1950–1990 time frame; then forecast [fit] the model for 1950–1995.)

b. Calculate the root-mean-squared error for this forecast model during the historic period.

c. Plot actual LBB for 1950–1990 along with the predicted or forecast values (LBBFET) for 1950–

1995. On the basis of this plot, does the forecast seem reasonable? Why or why not?

d. Now use Holt's exponential smoothing to make a forecast of this series through 1995. Call this forecast the LBBFH. What is the historic RMSE for your Holt's forecast?

e. Plot LBB and LBBFH using the 1950–1995 period. On the basis of this plot, does the forecast seem reasonable? Why or why not?

f. Now use the regression method described in this chapter to prepare a combined forecast (called LBBCF). For the regression model

$$LBB = a + b_1(LBBFET) + b_2(LBBFH)$$

is the intercept essentially zero? How can you tell? For the regression model

$$LBB = b_1(LBBFET) + b_2(LBBFH)$$

do the values of b_1 and b_2 seem logical? Explain.

g. Complete the following table:

Model	RMSE
LBBFET	_____
LBBFH	_____
LBBCF	_____

On the basis of this information, which of these models would you expect to provide the best forecast for the 1991–1995 forecast horizon? Explain.

h. Calculate the correlation coefficient between the squared forecast errors from LBBFET and LBBFH. Is the value consistent with your other findings? Explain.

9   FORECAST IMPLEMENTATION

In this chapter we discuss the forecasting process and provide a framework that will help you get the most out of any forecasting effort. While every forecasting problem has unique features, there is enough commonality in forecasting that guidelines can be helpful in several ways. First, the guidelines we provide will help you come to grips with some of the nuts-and-bolts issues related to data problems. Second, these guidelines will help you in making certain that the effort that goes into forecasting has the desired result in terms of the decision process. Finally, the guidelines discussed in this chapter will help you make logical choices regarding the technique(s) you should use for any particular situation.

The Forecast Process

The forecast process begins with a need to make one or more decisions that depend, at least in part, on the future value(s) of some variable(s) or on the future occurrence of some event. Subjective forecasting methods, such as the Delphi method, are usually the most useful in forecasting future events such as the nature of the home computer market 20 years from now. The quantitative techniques you have studied in this text are widely used in providing forecasts of variables such as sales, occupancy rates, income, inventory needs, and personnel requirements. Regardless of the specific scenario, the forecast is needed to help in making the best possible decision.

Communication and cooperation are critical if forecasting is to have the desired positive effect on decisions.

    We have divided the entire forecasting process into the nine steps first introduced in Chapter 2 and shown again in Figure 9–1. These begin and end with communication and cooperation between the managers who use the forecasts and the technicians who prepare them. This communication and cooperation are critical if forecasting is to have the desired positive effect on decisions. Most of the students who study this text will probably be managers and will be better able to communicate with their

FIGURE 9–1

*A Nine-Step
Forecasting
Process*

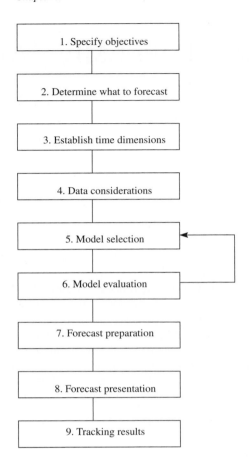

professional forecasters because they have developed an understanding of the methods that can be used.

Step 1. Make Objectives Clear

The objectives related to the decisions for which a forecast is important should be stated clearly. Management should articulate the role that the forecast will have in the decision process. If the decision will be the same regardless of the forecast, then any effort devoted to preparing the forecast is wasted. This may sound too obvious to deserve mention. However, it is not uncommon for a manager to request a forecast only to ignore it in the end. One reason that this happens is that the manager does not understand or have faith in the forecast. This issue will be addressed more fully in steps 7, 8, and 9, but a grounding of faith and understanding should begin here in step 1. If the manager who needs the information from a forecast and the technician who prepares the forecast take the opportunity to discuss the objectives and how the forecast will be used, there is increased likelihood that the ultimate forecast will be one that the manager understands and has faith in using.

Step 2. Determine What to Forecast

Once your overall objectives are clear, you must decide exactly what to forecast. For example, it is not sufficient to say that you want a sales forecast. Do you want a forecast of sales revenue or unit sales? Do you want an annual forecast or a quarterly, monthly, or weekly forecast? It is generally better to base sales forecasts on units rather than dollars so that price changes do not cloud actual variations in unit sales. The unit sales forecast can then be converted to a dollar figure easily enough. If the effect of price on sales is important, you may want to use a regression-based technique that incorporates causality. Good communication between forecast user and forecast preparer is important in making certain that the appropriate variables are being forecast.

Step 3. Establish Time Dimensions

There are two types of time dimensions to consider. First, one must establish the length of the forecast horizon. For annual forecasts this might be from one to five years or more, although forecasts beyond a few years are likely to be influenced by unforeseen events that are not incorporated into the model used. Quarterly forecasts are probably best used for one or two years (four to eight quarters), as are monthly forecasts (perhaps as long as 12 to 18 months). The objectives dictate the time interval (year, quarter, etc.) that is appropriate in preparing the forecast. For inventory control, short time periods are often necessary, whereas an annual forecast may be sufficient for the preparation of an estimated profit-and-loss statement for the coming year.

Second, the manager and the forecaster must agree on the urgency of the forecast. Is it needed tomorrow? Is there ample time to explore alternative methods? Proper planning is appropriate here. If their forecasting process is integrated into ongoing operations, then the forecasting personnel can plan an appropriate schedule, which will contribute to better forecasts.

Step 4. Database Considerations

The data necessary in preparing a forecast may come from within or may be external. Let us first consider internal data. Some people may believe that internal data are readily available and easy to incorporate into the forecasting process. It is surprising how often this turns out to be far from correct. Data may be available in a technical sense yet not readily available to the person who needs them to prepare the forecast. Or the data may be available but not expressed in the right unit of measurement (e.g., in sales dollars rather than units sold).

Data are often aggregated across both variables and time, but it is best to have disaggregated data. For example, data may be kept for refrigerator sales in total but not by type of refrigerator, type of customer, or region. In addition, what data are maintained may be kept in quarterly or monthly form for only a few years and annually thereafter. Such aggregation of data limits what can be forecast and may limit the appropriate pool of forecasting techniques. Communication and cooperation among the personnel involved in database maintenance, forecast preparation, and forecast use can help alleviate many unnecessary problems in this regard.

External data are available from a wide variety of sources, many of which have been discussed in Chapter 1. Data from national, state, and local government agencies are generally available at low cost. The more local the level of government unit, the more likely it is that the data will not be available as quickly as one might like or in the desired detail. Other sources of secondary data include industry or trade associations and private companies, such as some of the major banks. Often secondary data are available on computer disk, a CD, or on the Internet.[1] The ECONDATA database file (ECONDATA.SDB) that accompanies this text has provided you with the opportunity to use such a database.

Step 5. Model Selection

There are many methods to select from when you set out to make any forecast. There are subjective or judgmental methods, some of which were reviewed in Chapter 1, and a growing set of quantitative methods is available. The most widely used of these quantitative methods have been discussed in the previous chapters. Now, how can you decide which methods are most appropriate for a particular situation? Some of the things that should be included in making the selection are:

1. The type and quantity of data available
2. The pattern that the data have exhibited in the past
3. The urgency of the forecast
4. The length of the forecast horizon
5. The technical background of the people preparing and using the forecast

This issue of selecting the appropriate methods to use is of sufficient importance that we will come back to it in the next section. There we provide specific guidelines for each of the methods discussed in the text.

Step 6. Model Evaluation

Once the methods that we want to use have been selected we need to do some initial evaluation of how well they work. For the subjective or judgmental methods, this step is less appropriate than for the quantitative methods that have been stressed in this text. For those subjective methods the comparable sixth step would be to organize the process to be used (e.g., setting up procedures for gathering information from a sales force or Delphi panel).

For quantitative methods we should apply the techniques to historical series and evaluate how well they work in a retrospective sense. We have referred to this as an evaluation of the "fit" of the model. If they do not work well in the historical context

[1] At this time one of the best economic databases on the Internet is found at: http://bus.business.uab.edu/data/data.htm

there is little reason to believe that they will perform any better in the unknown domain of the future.

If we have sufficient historical data, a good approach to model testing is to use a "holdout" period for evaluation. For example, suppose we have quarterly data on sales for 10 years. We might use only the earliest nine years (36 data points) and make a forecast for the 10th year. If the model performs well when the forecast values are compared with the known values for the four quarters of year 10, we have reason to believe that the technique may also work well when the forecast period is indeed unknown. Out-of-sample evaluations such as this provide a measure of forecast "accuracy."

Once you are satisfied with a model based on historic and holdout period evaluations, you should respecify the model using all the available data (historic and holdout) and then use it for your actual forecast.

Suppose a technique turns out not to perform well when tested. The purpose of testing is, at least in part, to help us avoid applying a method that does not work well in our unique situation. Therefore, we should go back to step 5 and select another method that is appropriate to the problem at hand. It is not always possible to tell ahead of time how well a particular method will actually perform in a specific forecasting environment. We can apply reasoned judgment to our initial selection, but ultimately "the proof is in the pudding." We must apply the method to see whether it performs adequately for the purpose at hand.

Step 7. Forecast Preparation

At this point some method or set of methods has been selected for use in developing the forecast, and from testing you have reasonable expectations that the methods will perform well. We recommend using more than one forecasting method when possible, and it is desirable for these to be of different types (e.g., a regression model and Holt's exponential smoothing rather than two different regression models). The methods chosen should be used to prepare a range of forecasts. You might, for example, prepare a worst-case forecast, a best-case forecast, and a most likely forecast. The latter may be based on a combination of forecasts developed by following the procedures suggested in Chapter 8.

Step 8. Forecast Presentation

For a forecast to be used as intended, it must be presented to management clearly, in a way that provides an understanding of how the numbers were obtained and that elicits confidence in the forecast. It does not matter how much work is put into developing the forecast. It does not matter how confident the preparer is in the results. It does not matter how sophisticated the methodology may be. What matters is whether or not the manager understands and has confidence in the forecast. All too often, quantitative analyses are put on a shelf and do not play the role in decision making that they should, because the results are not effectively presented to management. Mark J. Lawless, who has been involved with forecasting within a number of corporations, including Chrysler, NCR, Ponderosa, and Hanson Industries Housewares

Group, has commented that:

> In communicating the forecast results to management, the forecaster must be capable of communicating the findings in language which the functional managers can understand and which is compatible with the corporate culture.[2]

The forecast should be communicated to management both in written form and in an oral presentation. The written document should be at a level that is appropriate to the reader. In most cases the managers who read the forecast document will have little interest in technical matters. They need just enough information to give them a general understanding of the method used. They do not need the amount of background and detail to be able to prepare the forecast themselves.

Tables should be kept relatively short. Rarely would it be desirable to include an entire history of the data used and historical forecasts. The most recent observations and forecasts are usually sufficient. The long series should, however, be shown graphically and should include both actual and forecast values. In such graphic displays colors and/or patterns can be used effectively to distinguish actual and forecast values.

The oral presentation should follow the same form and be made at about the same level as the written document. Generous use should be made of flip charts, slides, overheads, or projections of computer displays to heighten interest and involvement in the presentation. This oral presentation provides an excellent opportunity for discussion and clarification, which help the manager gain a more complete understanding of the forecast and confidence in its usefulness.

Step 9. Tracking Results

Neither the preparer nor the user is done with the forecast after the presentation and incorporation of results into the relevant decisions. The *process* continues. Deviations from the forecast and the actual events should be discussed in an open, objective, and positive manner. The objectives of such discussions should be to understand why errors occurred, to determine whether the magnitude of the errors was sufficient to have made a difference in the decisions that were based on the forecast, and to reevaluate the entire process with the intent of improving performance in the next round of forecasts. Input from both managers and technicians is important for the continual refinement of the forecasting process.

It is important to stress once more the critical role that communication and cooperation between managers and technicians play in building and maintaining a successful forecasting process. This is true whether forecasts are prepared "in house" or by outside suppliers. Without a commitment to communication and cooperation it is not likely that any organization can get a maximum return from the forecasting effort.

---

[2]Mark J. Lawless, "Effective Sales Forecasting: A Management Tool," *Journal of Business Forecasting* 9, no. 1 (Spring 1990), p. 10.

Choosing the Right Forecasting Techniques

In the Spring 1991 issue of the *Journal of Business Forecasting,* Charles W. Chase, Jr. (director of forecasting at Johnson & Johnson Consumer Products, Inc., at the time of this publication), commented that:

"The key task of a practicing forecaster is to determine at the outset the best match possible between the situation and the methods...."

> The key task of a practicing forecaster is to determine at the outset the best match possible between the situation and the methods before doing anything else.[3]

Now that you have an understanding of a variety of forecasting techniques, you need a general framework that will help you determine when to use each method. There are few hard-and-fast rules in this regard, but there are guidelines to assist in making the determination. If you understand how to use the methods discussed in this text, you have a good start toward determining when each method is likely to be useful. For example, if you are preparing a quarterly forecast of sales for a product that exhibits considerable seasonality, you would want to use one of the methods that are designed to handle such seasonal fluctuations.

In this section we evaluate the forecasting methods presented earlier in the text relative to the underlying conditions for which they are most likely to be useful.[4] There are many characteristics of a forecasting situation that might be considered in selecting an appropriate method. We will focus attention on three major areas: data, time, and personnel. For data we consider the type and quantity of data that are available as well as any pattern that may exist in the data (e.g., trend, cycle, and/or seasonality). The time dimension focuses on the forecast horizon. Within personnel we consider the necessary technical background of both the preparer and the user of the forecast. We begin with the methods discussed in Chapter 1 and progress sequentially through the text, ending with the ARIMA technique. Table 9–1 provides a quick reference summary of the discussion that follows.

Sales Force Composite (SFC)

In using the sales force composite method, little or no historical data are necessary. The data required are the current estimates of salespeople regarding expected sales for the forecast horizon. Historical data may be considered by the sales force, but not necessarily. Thus, this method may not reflect patterns in the data unless they are obvious to the sales force (e.g., Christmas season sales of jewelry). The method may, however, provide early warning signals of pending change (positive or negative) because of the closeness of the sales force to the customer. SFC is probably best used for short- to medium-term forecasts.[5] The preparation time is relatively short once a

---

[3]Charles W. Chase, Jr., "Forecasting Consumer Products," *Journal of Business Forecasting* 10, no. 1 (Spring 1991), p. 3.

[4]Some of the guidelines used are adapted from David M. Georgoff and Robert G. Murdick, "Manager's Guide to Forecasting," *Harvard Business Review* (January–February 1986), pp. 110–20.

[5]Short-term, medium-term, and long-term forecasts will be mentioned throughout this section. Short-term forecasts include up to three months, medium-term forecasts cover four months to about two years, and long-term forecasts are for periods longer than two years.

TABLE 9–1   A Guide to Selecting an Appropriate Forecasting Method

Forecasting Method	Data Pattern	Quantity of Historical Data (Number of Observations)	Forecast Horizon	Quantitative Background
Subjective Methods				
Sales force composite	Any	Little	Short to medium	Little
Customer surveys	Not applicable	None	Medium to long	Knowledge of survey methods
Jury of executive opinion	Any	Little	Any	Little
Delphi	Any	Little	Long	Little
Naive				
	Stationary[a]	1 or 2	Very short	None
Moving Averages				
	Stationary[a]	Number equal to the periods in the moving average	Very short	Very little
Exponential Smoothing				
Simple	Stationary[a,b]	5 to 10	Short	Little
Adaptive response	Stationary[a,b]	10 to 15	Short	Moderate
Holt's	Linear trend[b]	10 to 15	Short to medium	Little
Winters'	Trend and seasonality	At least 4 or 5 per season	Short to medium	Moderate
Regression-Based				
Trend	Linear and nonlinear trend with or without seasonality	Minimum of 10 with 4 or 5 per season if seasonality is included	Short to medium	Little
Causal	Can handle nearly all data patterns	Minimum of 10 per independent variable	Short, medium, and long	Moderate
Time-Series Decomposition				
	Can handle trend, seasonal, and cyclical patterns	Enough to see 2 peaks and troughs in the cycle	Short, medium, and long	Little
ARIMA				
	Stationary or transformed to stationary	Minimum of 50	Short, medium, and long	High

[a]Or data that have been transformed to a stationary series

[b]May be used for seasonal data if the data are first deseasonalized

system for gathering data from the sales force is in place. This method requires little quantitative sophistication on the part of the preparer or the user, which contributes to its ease of use and to ready acceptance of results.

Customer Surveys (CS)

Forecasts that are based on surveys of buyers' intentions require no historical data, and thus the past plays no explicit role in forecasting the future. Customer surveys are most appropriate for medium- to long-term forecasting. For example, a natural gas utility has used this method to help in long-term planning by gathering survey data on customers' plans for future energy use, including long-term capital expansion plans. The time necessary to develop, conduct, and analyze a survey research project can be relatively extensive. Rarely can such a project be completed in less than two to three months. If the same survey is used year after year, however, this time can be shortened considerably. CS is not a method to consider if there is a sense of urgency in getting the forecast. Those involved in preparing such a forecast need considerable technical expertise in the area of survey research. Users, on the other hand, need not have a sophisticated technical background, as long as they know enough about survey research to interpret the results appropriately.

Jury of Executive Opinion (JEO)

The executives included do not need a formal data set. They need only the body of experience that they have developed to make judgments concerning the most likely value of the forecast variable during the period of interest. Historical data patterns may or may not be reflected in the opinions expressed, although regular patterns such as seasonality are very likely to receive attention, albeit implicit attention. JEO may be used for any forecast horizon and is generally a relatively quick procedure. This method does not require much quantitative sophistication on the part of either preparers or users, but it does require a substantial base of expertise on the part of the participants.

Delphi Method

The Delphi method does not require a historical data series, other than what is in the knowledge base of the panel members, and therefore does not necessarily reflect patterns that may have existed in the past. It is most often applicable for long-range forecasting but can be applied to medium-term projects as well. In these respects it is much like JEO. However, the time to develop the Delphi forecast can be considerable unless the responses of panel members stabilize quickly. Computers can be effectively used to speed the flow of information and thus shorten the time considerably. The Delphi method requires only modest technical sophistication on the part of the preparer, and no particular technical sophistication is necessary for the end user, other than to understand the process through which the forecast was developed.

Naive

The basic naive model requires only one historical value as a basis for the forecast. An extended naive model that takes the most recent trend into account requires just two past values. This method is best suited to situations in which the data are stationary or in which any trend is relatively stable. Seasonality can sometimes be accounted for in a reasonably stationary series using a seasonal time lag, such as was demonstrated for domestic car sales and Gap sales in Chapter 1. The naive approach is suited only for very short-term forecasts. Preparation time is minimal, and no technical sophistication is necessary on the part of either the preparer or the user.

Moving Averages

Moving averages are most appropriate when the data are stationary and do not exhibit seasonality. Relatively few historic data are necessary. The number of past observations must be at least equal to the number of periods in the moving average. For example, if a four-period moving average is used, one needs at least four historic data points. Moving averages are normally used to forecast just one period ahead and require very little quantitative sophistication.

Simple Exponential Smoothing (SES)

Historical data are necessary to establish the best weighting factor in simple exponential smoothing, but thereafter only the most recent observed and forecasted values are required. Five to ten past values are sufficient to determine the weighting factor. The data series should be stationary (i.e., have no trend and no seasonality) when SES is used. This method is appropriate for short-term forecasting and requires little technical sophistication. While the arithmetic work can be done by hand, a computer can be helpful in determining the best weighting factor. Once the weighting factor is known, forecasts can be developed very quickly.

Adaptive-Response Exponential Smoothing (ADRES)

The adaptive-response exponential smoothing model may be used when the data are stationary and exhibit no seasonality. Ten to fifteen historic observations should be available when ADRES is used, and forecasts should be for only a short forecast horizon, typically one or two periods ahead. This method requires a bit more quantitative sophistication by the preparer than does SES, but users need little quantitative background.

Holt's Exponential Smoothing (HES)

As in SES, Holt's exponential smoothing model requires historical data to determine weighting values, but only the very recent past is required to apply the model. It is desirable to have at least 10 to 15 historical observations in determining the two weights. HES can be used effectively with data series that exhibit a positive or negative trend, and thus this method has a much wider scope of application than SES. However, it should not be used when the data contain a seasonal pattern unless the data have been deseasonalized. HES is appropriate for short- and medium-term forecasts and, like SES, can be implemented rapidly once the weights have been selected. Some technical expertise is required of the preparer, but users with little sophistication can understand HES well enough to use it properly. A computer is desirable, but not necessary, for model development.

Winters' Exponential Smoothing (WES)

Sufficient historical data to determine the weights are necessary in using Winters' exponential smoothing model. A minimum of four or five observations per season should be used (i.e., for quarterly data, 16 or 20 observations should be used). Since this method incorporates both trend and seasonal components, it is applicable to a wide spectrum of data patterns. Like HES this method is most appropriate for short- to medium-term forecasts. Once the weights have been determined, the process of making a forecast moves quickly. The preparer needs some technical expertise, but the nature of the method can be understood by users with little technical sophistication. Use of a computer is recommended for the process of selecting the best values for the weights in the WES model. Even if weights are restricted to one decimal place, the number of combinations that might be evaluated becomes too cumbersome to do by hand.

Regression-Based Trend Models

The data requirement for using a regression-based trend depends to a considerable extent on the consistency in the trend and whether or not the trend is linear. We look for enough data that the *t*-statistic for the slope term (i.e., the trend) is significant (a *t*-value of 2 or more in absolute value is a handy rule of thumb). For a simple linear trend, 10 observations may be quite sufficient. A simple trend model can be effective when the series being forecast has no pattern other than the trend. Such a model is appropriate for short- to medium-term forecasts and can be developed and implemented relatively quickly. The preparer needs to have a basic understanding of regression analysis but does not need a sophisticated background for simple linear trends. More complex nonlinear trends require deeper understanding. Using a computer simplifies preparation of the forecast. The method is sufficiently straightforward that the user needs little technical sophistication.

Regression-Based Trend Models with Seasonality

To include seasonality in a regression-based trend model, it is desirable to have at least four or five observations per season. Thus, for quarterly data a minimum of 16 observations would be appropriate. For monthly data 48 or more observations should be used. Regular seasonal patterns in the series are often modeled quite well by using dummy variables. As with simple trend models, linear or nonlinear forms can be used; the models are best for short- to medium-term forecasts, and the time necessary for preparation is short. Except when nonlinear models are used, little mathematical sophistication is necessary on the part of either the preparer or the user of the forecast. A computer regression program is a virtual necessity, however.

Comments from the Field

James G. Steen,
Forecasting Analyst
Sensormatic Electronics Corporation

Team Work: Key to Successful Forecasting

Sensormatic Electronics is a manufacturer of electronic article surveillance equipment. The most challenging part of our forecasting effort is getting the market management and product development groups together to come up with a consensus forecast. This is important because they are in frequent contact with salespeople, customers, and account managers, and thus have access to information vital for forecasting. But, due to their hectic schedule, the information is often not communicated in a timely manner to be used effectively in preparing forecasts. Because of the lead time of certain products, ample time is needed to plan and manufacture products. We often don't hear of a large order or potential order until the end of our fiscal quarter. At that point, there is little or no time left to react.

Once every quarter we have a meeting in which we discuss, review, and update our forecasts. Such meetings are very helpful but not quite adequate to do the job. Many things change during the period between one meeting and the next. But the information about the changes is not passed on to those responsible for preparing the forecasts. We are currently working on improving the flow of information from our sales force to those involved in forecasting at our head office.

The "team" approach is the only way we can be successful since no one person has all the necessary information to prepare forecasts. By working together, we can all benefit and keep our customers satisfied.

Adapted from: *Journal of Business Forecasting* 11, no. 2 (Summer 1992), p. 22. Reprinted by permission.

Regression Models with Causality

The quantity of data required for the development of a causal regression model depends on the number of independent variables in the model and on how much contribution each of those variables makes in explaining variation in the dependent variable. One rule of thumb is that you should expect to have a minimum of 10 observations per independent variable. Thus, for a model with three independent variables you should have at least 30 observations. You can see that developing and maintaining a database for multiple-regression models can be a significant undertaking. The effort may be worthwhile, however, since multiple-regression models are often effective in dealing with complex data patterns and may even help identify turning points. Seasonality can be handled by using dummy variables. Causal regression models can be useful for short-, medium-, or long-term forecasts. Because the causal variables must usually be forecast as well, regression models may take more effort to develop. It can take a long time to develop a good causal regression model. Once the model is developed, preparation of a forecast can be done reasonably quickly. In using causal regression models, you should reestimate equations at least once a year so that structural changes are identified in a timely manner. The technician who prepares regression forecasts needs to have a solid background in regression analysis. Managers, on the other hand, can use such forecasts effectively as long as they have a basic understanding of regression methods.

Comments from the Field

Debra M. Schramm
Manager, Sales Forecasting
Parke-Davis

How to Sell Forecasts to Management

One of the universal problems forecasters have is "selling" their forecast to others, especially Marketing Management. Management is reluctant, at best, to use numbers from a group or individual who is viewed as only able to analyze numbers. They question why our crystal ball should be any better than theirs. Our company was no exception. Five years ago the forecast area was viewed as a department that did something with the sales numbers. No one seemed to know what our role was in the organization or how we meshed with the big picture. Although our forecasts were used to feed manufacturing and distribution, they were not considered in the management review process, which took place each month, to determine the division's sales numbers. It became our goal to change our image or the lack of it.

Today the forecasting department and its forecasts are an integral part of the management process. Our system-forecasts are used as the basis for the monthly review, the annual, and longer term plans. We continue to support Marketing with reliable information, anticipating their future needs, and experimenting with external data in order to improve the forecasts. There is no point lower than to work at something, then find you are the only one who believes in what you do. If we as forecasters are to raise our image in business we must be able to prove ourselves and prove the integrity of the data we supply. The process can be long and frustrating, but it is attainable with determination, patience, and perseverance. Once achieved it is immensely rewarding.

Adapted from: *Journal of Business Forecasting* 10, no. 4 (Winter 1991–92), p. 22. Reprinted by permission.

Time-Series Decomposition (TSD)

The quantity of data needed for time-series decomposition should be enough for you to see at least two peaks and two troughs in the cycle factor, if the cycle factor is important. If the cycle factor does not appear important (i.e., has not been far above or below 1.0 during the historic period), then the quantity of data needed should be determined by what is necessary to adequately identify the seasonal pattern. A rule of thumb would be at least four or five observations per season (e.g., for quarterly data you should have at least 16 to 20 observations). TSD is quite good at picking up patterns in the data. The challenge is for the analyst to successfully project the patterns through the forecast horizon. This is generally fairly easy for the trend and seasonal pattern but is more difficult for the cyclical pattern. TSD is especially appropriate for short-term and medium-term forecasting. If the cycle pattern is not important or if it can be projected with confidence, the method can also be used effectively for long-term forecasts. This method may be one of the best in terms of being able to identify and incorporate turning points. Doing so is dependent on the analyst's ability to correctly interpret when the cycle factor may turn up or down. The preparation time for a TSD forecast is relatively short, and this method does not require much sophistication on the part of the preparer or the user. In fact, most managers find the concepts inherent in the TSD model quite consistent with how they see the world.

ARIMA

A long data series (at least 50 data points—more if data are seasonal) is necessary to make use of the ARIMA models. These models can handle variability in the data as long as the series is stationary or can be transformed to a stationary series. This method can be applied to short-, medium-, or long-term forecast horizons. Because of the complexity of model identification, forecast preparation can take an extended period of time. This complexity also means that the preparer needs a highly sophisticated technical background. Users of ARIMA forecasts must also be quite sophisticated, because even achieving a basic understanding of the method is not easy. It is rare to find a manager who has a good feel for how an ARIMA forecast is developed and rarer still to find a manager capable of explaining the forecast derivation to others who must use the results. This may be part of the reason that ARIMA models have had relatively low ratings in terms of importance, accuracy, and use by business managers.

Artificial Intelligence and Forecasting

As you discovered earlier in this chapter, a manager must make a number of potentially difficult decisions during the forecast process. For example, to select an appropriate forecasting method, a manager must first consider the many characteristics of the forecasting situation and then choose a specific forecasting technique from a large number of available judgmental and quantitative techniques. Fortunately, recent improvements in microcomputer hardware and software technology have aided managers in making more effective and efficient forecasting decisions. One computer technology application that shows significant promise for improving forecasting decision making involves the use of artificial intelligence.

Artificial intelligence (AI) is concerned with making machines perform in ways that we would normally associate with human intelligence. AI includes (1) natural language processing, the focus of which is on computer programs that are able to speak, read, and understand spoken language; (2) robotics, which is concerned with providing machines with human abilities such as vision, a sense of touch, and intelligent movement; and (3) reasoning abilities that can solve problems, such as expert systems and neural networks. Expert systems and neural networks have the potential to make significant contributions to business forecasting.

Expert systems are intelligent computer programs that use expert knowledge and reasoning to solve problems. In developing an expert system one begins by interviewing recognized experts to capture their knowledge about a problem area and the problem-solving logic they apply when making related decisions. Then a computer program is developed that replicates the experts' problem-solving process. There are commercially available expert system "shells," which provide a structure in which the knowledge base can be operationalized.

An example of the use of an expert system would be in the selection of an appropriate forecast method. The software would lead a manager through some simple questions concerning such things as data availability, data patterns, and other issues like those shown in Table 9–1. The program could combine the manager's responses to these questions with the knowledge base that has been supplied from forecast experts to determine an appropriate forecast method to be used in the manager's current situation.

Neural networks are computer programs that take inputs similar to those used in the forecasting methods discussed in this text and process them to provide an output that is the forecast. In a limited way neural networks are similar to the methods you have already learned. Exponential smoothing models have inputs (past data and weights) that combine to yield an output (the forecast). Regression analysis takes inputs (past data and a statistical model), which are combined to produce an output in the form of a forecast. What is different about neural networks is that they incorporate artificial intelligence in the process that connects inputs to outputs.[6]

In a neural network there are input and output pairs that are used to "train" the network. There can be multiple inputs (causal factors) and multiple outputs (forecasts of different variables) in a neural network. Between the inputs and outputs there is a layer (or multiple layers) of processing that mimics the working of the human mind attempting to reason out the logical connections between inputs and outputs. Then, given a new set of inputs, the neural network can produce a new output (forecast) based on what it has learned from the pairs of actual inputs and outputs that were provided. The analyst can control some aspects of the process, such as the learning rate and the desired precision of the output (forecast). As with expert systems there are commercially available neural network "shells" that simplify the development of a neural network forecast system.

---

[6]For a more complete description of neural networks and an example of their potential application in a forecasting environment, see Chin Kuo and Arthur Reitsch, "Neural Networks vs. Conventional Methods of Forecasting," *Journal of Business Forecasting* 14, no. 4 (Winter 1995–96), pp. 17–22.

Comments from the Field

Mark J. Lawless
Senior Vice President of the Business Group,
National Fire Protection Association

Forecasts Must Be Relevant and Effective

The environment of business is continuing to change at an increasing rate, and the demands on management to create value are increasing with it. The role of forecasters is changing as well, and the value created by the forecaster is very much a consideration in the role which forecasting plays in the management decision process.

If management must create value for the shareholder, the forecaster must create value for the shareholder as well. Hence, rather than pining for earlier times when things were better for forecasters, we need to adapt to the changing environment as well. We need to be continuously asking: "How can we create value? How can we enhance value? How can we assist others in creating value?" If forecasters will ask themselves these simple questions, and act upon their answers, the ability of forecast functions to be effective and credible will take care of itself. Looking to the needs of the management decisions, using whatever information that is available (imperfect though it may be), and developing the forecasts and recommendations in the context of these management needs are important parts of the forecast function.

To be successful in the future, there are two important ground rules for all forecasters—be relevant and be effective.

Adapted from: "Ten Prescriptions for Forecasting Success," *Journal of Business Forecasting* 16, no. 1 (Spring 1997), pp. 3–5.

Summary

The forecasting process begins with the need to make decisions that are dependent on the future values of one or more variables. Once the need to forecast is recognized, the steps to follow can be summarized as follows:

1. Make the objectives clear
2. Determine what to forecast
3. Establish time dimensions
4. Database considerations
5. Model selection
6. Model evaluation
7. Forecast preparation
8. Forecast presentation
9. Tracking results

Throughout the process, open communication between managers who use the forecasts and the technicians who prepare them is essential.

You have been introduced to the most widely used forecasting methods and need to know when each is appropriate. The section entitled "Choosing the Right Forecasting Techniques" provides a guide to help you in determining when to use each technique and when each should not be used. Table 9–1 also provides a handy summary of that discussion.

As you have seen, there is potential for the application of artificial intelligence technology to the forecast process. For example, expert-system decision-support tools would allow managers to make better forecasting decisions in forecasting method selection. Artificial intelligence concepts are also applied to forecasting through the use of neural networks. These are computer programs that take inputs and process them to provide an output that is the forecast. In a limited way neural networks are similar to other forecast methods but they differ in that they incorporate artificial intelligence in the process that connects inputs to outputs. As with expert systems, there are commercially available neural network "shells" that simplify the development of a neural network forecast system.

Suggested Readings

Armstrong, J. Scott. "Research Needs in Forecasting." *International Journal of Forecasting* 4, no. 3 (1988), pp. 449–65.

Chase, Charles W., Jr. "Business Forecasting: A Process Not an Application." *Journal of Business Forecasting* 11, no. 3 (Fall 1992), pp. 12–13.

Cummings, Steve. "Built-In Expert Systems Streamline Business Forecasts." *PC Week* 5, no. 19 (1988), pp. 95–99.

Keating, Barry; and J. Holton Wilson. "Forecasting Practices and Teachings." *Journal of Business Forecasting* 7, no. 4 (Winter 1987–88), pp. 10–13, 16.

Larréché, Jean-Claude; and Reza Moinpour. "Managerial Judgement in Marketing: The Concept of Expertise." *Journal of Marketing Research* 20, no. 2 (May 1983), pp. 110–21.

Lawless, Mark J. "Effective Sales Forecasting: A Management Tool." *Journal of Business Forecasting* 9, no. 1 (Spring 1990), pp. 2–11.

———. "Ten Prescriptions for Forecasting Success." *Journal of Business Forecasting* 11, no. 4 (Spring 1997), pp. 3–5.

LeLee, Gary S. "The Key to Understanding the Forecasting Process." *Journal of Business Forecasting* 11, no. 4 (Winter 1992–93), pp. 12–16.

Mentzer, John T.; and Kenneth B. Kahn. "State of Sales Forecasting Systems in Corporate America." *Journal of Business Forecasting* 11, no. 4 (Spring 1997), pp. 6–13.

O'Clock, George D.; and Priscilla M. O'Clock. "Political Realities of Forecasting." *Journal of Business Forecasting* 8, no. 1 (Spring 1989), pp. 2–6.

Reyes, Luis. "The Forecasting Function: Critical Yet Misunderstood." *Journal of Business Forecasting* 14, no. 4 (Winter 1995–96), pp. 8–9.

Szmania, Joe; and John Surgent. "An Application of an Expert System Approach to Business Forecasting." *Journal of Business Forecasting* 8, no. 1 (Spring 1989), pp. 10–12.

Weitz, Rob R. "NOSTRADAMUS—A Knowledge-Based Forecast Advisor." *International Journal of Forecasting* 2, no. 1 (1986), pp. 273–83.

Wilson, J. Holton; and Hugh G. Daubek. "Marketing Managers Evaluate Forecasting Models." *Journal of Business Forecasting* 8, no. 1, (Spring 1989), pp. 19–22.

Exercises

1. You have read the statement that the forecast process begins with a need to make one or more decisions that depend on the future value of some variable. Think about this as it relates to the daily weather forecast you hear, and write a list of five decisions that might depend on such a forecast.

2. Why do you think communication between the person preparing a forecast and the forecast user is important? Give several specific places in the nine-step forecast process where you think such communication is especially important and explain why.

3. The availability and form of data to be used in preparing a forecast are often seen as especially critical areas. Summarize, in your own words, the database considerations in the forecasting process (step 4).

4. Suppose that you have been asked to recommend a forecasting technique that would be appropriate to prepare a forecast, given the following situational characteristics:

   a. You have 10 years of quarterly data.
   b. There is an upward trend to the data.
   c. There is a significant increase in sales prior to Christmas each year.
   d. A one-year forecast is needed.
   e. You, as the preparer of the forecast, have good technical skills, but the manager who needs the forecast is very nontechnical.
   f. You need to have the forecast done and the presentation ready in just a few days.

   What method(s) would you consider using and why?

5. Write an outline of what you would like to see in a forecast presentation from the perspective of a manager who needs to use the forecast.

6. Explain in your own words how artificial intelligence can be used in a forecasting environment.

10 COMPUTATIONALLY INTENSIVE STATISTICS: THE BOOTSTRAP

Computationally Intensive Statistical Techniques

Up to this point in the text, we have used what statisticians would call *classical* statistical techniques. Many of these techniques and their related measures of accuracy have been known and widely used for a very long time (for example, regression analysis dates back to about the 1870s). During the period when most of these methods developed, computation was performed by hand or by crude calculator at best. The expense of complicated and repetitious calculations was quite large. Since statistical analysis had to be done by hand, the classical methods tend to use calculations simplified by formulas that assumed the data conformed to unverifiable assumptions.

Classical statistical techniques rely for their power on these unverifiable assumptions about the data being examined.

Classical statistical techniques (such as the Pearson coefficient described in Chapter 2) rely for their power on these unverifiable assumptions about the data being examined. The most important assumption made by classical statistics is that of the normal, or Gaussian, distribution (named after the mathematician Karl Friedrich Gauss, 1777–1855). We presented this normal distribution in some detail in Chapter 2 because its assumption underlies many of the techniques we have presented. When the normal distribution is assumed, we are saying that random deviations, or errors, in the observed sample values of some quantity are scattered symmetrically about the real or true value of the quantity. Most often we further assume that the larger the deviations or errors between the sample value and the true value are, the less is the likelihood that the true value will be observed in a sample.

We would not have discussed such assumptions and applied their results in later chapters if long experience had not shown that the Gaussian theory works quite well even when the assumptions we make are only approximated in the real-world data. For almost 200 years statisticians have made remarkably reliable forecasts with a minimum of computation by making these assumptions about the data.

Whenever our data do not match the assumptions we make in applying a statistical technique, however, the results we obtain are far less reliable. Experience suggests that the classical validation techniques are overly optimistic because our data quite often do not fit the classical assumptions.[1] The technique we present in this chapter does not rely on the classical Gaussian distribution of the data. The technique's accuracy, then, is not affected by how closely our assumptions about the data are matched.

There is a second characteristic of the *computationally intensive,* or resampling, statistical techniques (as they are called) we will study in this chapter that sets them apart from the classical techniques. The classical statistical techniques (such as Pearson's correlation coefficient) are calculations that are greatly simplified by the assumptions we make about the data. Most of the classical techniques require only modest computation by the researcher. In part, this is the reason why these techniques are called classical; because, in older practice, the techniques used had to economize on the researcher's time to some extent. If they did not, the techniques were unmanageable. The computationally intensive techniques, on the other hand, typically require massive calculation. While it is instructive to perform some of these calculations by hand, we have provided a tool for you to use that makes full use of the power of modern microcomputers.

The New York Times had this to say about the resampling technique presented in this chapter (i.e., the bootstrap):

> A new technique that involves powerful computer calculations is greatly enhancing the statistical analysis of problems in virtually all fields of science. The method, which is now surging into practical use after a decade of refinement, allows statisticians to determine more accurately the reliability of data analysis in subjects ranging from politics to medicine to particle physics . . .
>
> "There's no question but that it's very, very important," said Frederick Mosteller, a statistician at Harvard University . . . Jerome H. Friedman, a Stanford statistician who has used the new method, called it "the most important new idea in statistics in the last 20 years, and probably the last 50." He added, "Eventually, it will take over the field, I think." (Nov. 8, 1988, C1, C6)

The generalized procedure of any computationally intensive statistic (or resampling technique, including bootstrapping) consists of four steps[2]:

Step 1. Construct a simulated "population" so that composition is similar to the population whose behavior we wish to describe and investigate.

Step 2. Specify the procedure that produces artificial data sets that simulate the real-life sample in which we are interested. That is, specify the procedural rules by which the artificial samples are drawn from the simulated population. These rules must correspond to the behavior of the real population in which you are interested.

---

[1] See Richard D. Cramer, Jeffrey D. Bunce, David E. Patterson, and Ildiko E. Frank, "Crossvalidation, Bootstrapping, and Partial Least Squares Compared with Multiple Regression in Conventional QSAR Studies," *Quantitative Structure-Activity Relationships* 7, no. 1 (1988), p. 19.

[2] These steps are taken from the *Chance* article by Julian Simon and Peter Bruce.

Step 3. If several simple events must be combined into a composite event, and if the composite event was not described in the procedure in step 2, this becomes the third step.

Step 4. Calculate from the tabulation of outcomes of the resampling trials.

The Bootstrap

The bootstrap method (invented by Bradley Efron) is a simple method of creating "pseudo-data" from the data in an original sample.

The particular computationally intensive method used in this chapter is called the *bootstrap.* It is not the only technique in this category, but it is the one most often used.[3] The bootstrap method (invented by Bradley Efron) is a simple method of creating "pseudo-data" from the data in an original sample. These pseudo-data sets, or artificial data sets, are constructed to mimic the process originally used to select the real sample. We can then estimate the statistical accuracy of our classical measures by comparing them with the results provided by analyzing the artificial data sets.

To illustrate how the bootstrap method is applied, consider the data presented in Chapter 2 in the section titled "Using SORITEC for Exploratory Data Analysis and Basic Statistics." We entered the following two series as data and suggested that the corresponding *X* and *Y* values were related:

X	Y	X	Y	X	Y
3	7	4	14	6	24
1	3	2	4	4	12
1	2	6	25	3	7
3	8	5	20	3	9
2	4	7	30	2	5

We suppose that the *X* and *Y* values are proportional to each other; that is, we believe that as the observed value of *X* rises, the correspondent value of *Y* is greater. It is quite likely, however, that the true relationship is not a perfectly proportional one. We desire to know how close the relationship between the two variables is to proportionality. We do not, however, have every value for *X* and *Y* that exists; we have only the 15 values we were able to measure. What we would really like to know is whether the sample of 15 values we have observed allows us to view an accurate picture of the true relationship between all the *X* and *Y* values.

Since we have collected only a sample of all the existing *X* and *Y* values, the classical statistical measure of the proportionality between *X* and *Y* would be the sample Pearson correlation coefficient. Remember that the correlation coefficient

---

[3] Another technique that is similar to the bootstrap is the "jackknife." See Bradley Efron and Gail Gong, "A Leisurely Look at the Bootstrap, the Jackknife, and Cross-Validation," *American Statistician* 37, no. 1 (February 1983), pp. 36–48.

measures the degree to which the plotted pairs of the sample data cluster along a straight line. Some of the possibilities were shown in Figure 2–7. The value of 0.0 for the correlation coefficient (as in frame F of Figure 2–7) indicated that the points of the sample were scattered at random, while a value of either $+1$ (as in frame A) or -1 (as in frame B) indicated that the points in the sample tended to cluster along a straight line (of positive slope if $r = +1$ and of negative slope if $r = -1$).

Some values in the real world we expect to be perfectly proportional; for example, inches are perfectly proportional to centimeters. The correlation coefficient for various lengths measured in both centimeters and inches would be $+1$. A given distance measured in centimeters is directly proportional to the same distance measured in inches.

Other variables in the real world are related, but not directly proportional to one another. The miles per gallon an automobile achieves is roughly (inversely) proportional to the gross weight of the car. The proportionality is not exact, because other factors such as engine displacement (i.e., size) and aerodynamic characteristics also affect mileage.

For the sample we have chosen to repeat from Chapter 2, the correlation coefficient is 0.975. This indicates that there appears to be a strong positive linear association between the variables Y and X. Recall that the correlation coefficient measures only apparent *linear* associations. If two variables were associated in nonlinear fashion, the plotted points would not tend to cluster along a straight line. In such cases the calculated correlation coefficient might well be close to zero.

Since we have examined only a sample of the XY combinations (with 15 observations in the sample), what certainty do we have that the true relationship between X and Y is $r = 0.975$? The population from which our sample of 15 observations was drawn might very well have a correlation coefficient larger or smaller than 0.975. Since a sample with only 15 observations is quite small, the calculated value of 0.975 could be quite inaccurate.

If we had access to *all* the X and Y pairs available instead of only our sample of 15, we would be able to calculate the correlation coefficient for the population. We would then have an exact measure of the association between X and Y, because every existing combination of the two variables had been measured and examined.

But is there a method for us to check the statistical accuracy of a calculated correlation coefficient if we have access to only a small portion of the XY population? By statistical accuracy, we mean the probability that our calculated correlation coefficient is the one that would apply to the entire population of XY pairs. The bootstrap is one procedure that will allow such a measure.[4]

We could get a better (but still not perfect) idea of what the real coefficient value is if we were to obtain a few more samples of XY pairs. Suppose that we were able to obtain 10 more samples of 15 observations on X and Y. We could calculate a new correlation coefficient for each sample. If all the coefficients were quite close to our original number of 0.975, we would feel more confident that our original estimate was in the ballpark.

---

[4]The example we use here is modeled after Persi Diaconis and Bradley Efron, "Computer-Intensive Methods in Statistics," *Scientific American,* May 1983, pp. 116–30.

If, on the other hand, the coefficients for the 10 new samples ranged from -1 to $+1$ and were spread out evenly along the spectrum, we would be much less confident that our original estimate of 0.975 was representative of the true relationship between all X and Y combinations in the population.

The most common situation analysts face in the real world is that only limited data are available. You may be able to obtain only a single sample of 15 observations to represent a much larger population of XY combinations.

This is the precise situation in which the bootstrap is useful for determining the statistical accuracy of the correlation coefficient from a single sample. The essence of the bootstrap technique is to imitate the process of selecting our original sample of 15 observations. In fact, we will imitate the process not once, but many times over. This gives us many "artificial samples" of 15 observations each, from which we may find the probability that the values of their correlation coefficients fall within various intervals.

Steps in the Bootstrapping Process

The process of selecting the artificial samples is called *bootstrapping* and consists of a number of steps outlined in Figure 10–1. While the bootstrapping process appears, at first glance, to be rather complicated, it is actually quite simple. First, we make many copies of each of our 15 data points.

Pretend that the XY coordinates of a single data point—say, the first observation of (3, 7)—are written on a note card. This note card is then duplicated many times over (say, 10^9 times), and the resulting large stack of cards is placed in a hopper.

We continue this process, producing 10^9 duplicates of every one of our original 15 data points. All the note cards are placed in turn in the hopper. The hopper is then turned a sufficient number of times to ensure that the cards are truly randomly mixed. This produces a simulated universe (step 1 of any resampling process).

In order to create the first artificial sample, we draw one card from the hopper, list its represented point as the first observation in the artificial sample, and replace the card in the hopper. Note that all 15×10^9 cards are available in the hopper again and ready for us to draw the second data point. We continue the process (with replacement) until we have created a single artificial sample with 15 data points.

We repeat the process, creating more artificial samples. Each time we create an artificial sample, we calculate the correlation coefficient between X and Y for the sample. This production of the artificial data sets is step 2 of any resampling process.

Figure 10–1 outlines a rather novel way of actually carrying out the process, but it would be quite onerous in practice. The method actually used to select bootstrap samples involves selecting random numbers with a computer and matching the numbers drawn to points in the original sample (assuming that the rows of the sample are all numbered consecutively). This type of calculation is called a *computer-intensive* statistical technique, because the generation of large numbers of artificial samples requires a high degree of computing power.

We will now have a large number of correlation coefficients, each one calculated from an artificial sample that in turn was generated from the 15 data points in the

FIGURE 10–1

The Bootstrapping Process Creates Many Artificial Samples

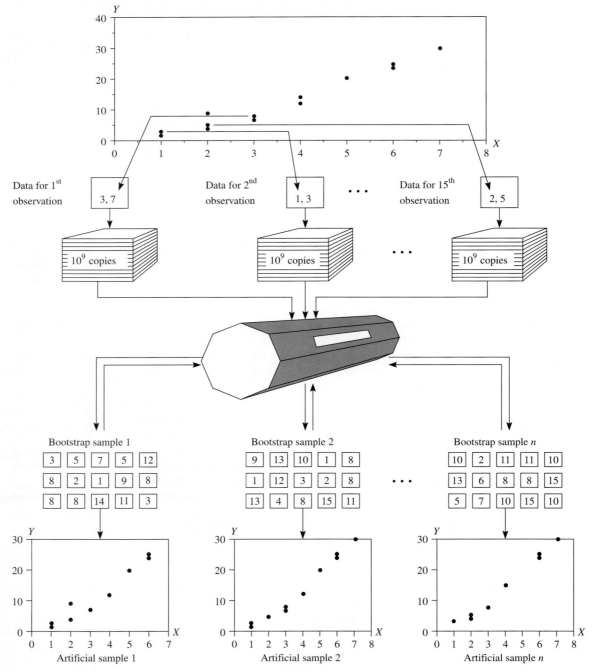

original sample. This large number of correlation coefficients (one for each artificial sample) can be viewed as if they were the product of real samples drawn from the real population. The calculation of the correlation coefficients for each artificial data set is the third step in the procedure.

It is the distribution of these correlation coefficients that gives us a measure of the statistical accuracy of the single correlation coefficient we calculated from the original real sample. This is the fourth and final step in the procedure. For demonstration purposes, we actually created 100 artificial samples using the method we just described (three of these 100 artificial data sets are shown in Table 10–1). Of the 100 correlation coefficients we computed (one for each artificial sample), 68 percent fell between 0.945 and 1.00. This interval (0.055) can be thought of as the bootstrap measure of accuracy for the value of the correlation coefficient of the original sample (which was 0.975). Half this interval (0.055/2 = 0.0275) may be thought of as the average amount by which the observed correlation coefficient will vary from the true correlation coefficient.

Thus, for our original sample of 15 observations, the true correlation coefficient might be 1.00 or 0.945, but we can be almost certain that it is not zero. It appears that the original estimate of 0.975 was quite accurate.

> It is the distribution of these correlation coefficients that gives us a measure of the statistical accuracy of the single correlation coefficient we calculated from the original real sample.

(C10T1.SAC)

TABLE 10–1   Bootstrapped Samples (Artificial Data Sets)*

1st Bootstrapped Artificial Sample		2nd Bootstrapped Artificial Sample		. . .	100th Bootstrapped Artificial Sample	
X	Y	X	Y		X	Y
1	2	5	20		7	30
2	4	3	7		1	3
2	4	7	30		6	24
2	4	3	7		6	24
4	12	6	25		3	7
6	25	3	7		3	7
1	3	4	12		4	14
3	7	1	2		6	25
6	25	3	7		3	7
1	3	4	12		4	14
3	7	1	2		6	25
5	20	1	3		6	25
6	25	6	25		2	5
6	25	3	7		2	4
6	25	3	8		2	4
2	9	6	25		7	30
6	24	2	5		2	5
1	2	6	24		7	30
$r = 0.983$		$r = 1.00$			$r = 0.994$	

68 percent of the r's fell between 0.945 and 1.00.
*The SORITEC Alternate Command File (SAC file) that produced this table is contained on the CD accompanying this text. You may modify and rerun this file to compute your own bootstrap procedures (C10T1.SAC).

How dependable is this bootstrap measure of accuracy? Diaconis and Efron[5] have shown in their theoretical work that the accuracy of the measure is "dependable in a wide variety of situations." Theoretical investigations indicate that for the correlation coefficient and a wide variety of other statistics, the interval associated with the bootstrap method and the corresponding interval for the statistic calculated from the larger population (and not just the smaller sample) have the same width. Diaconis and Efron cite intervals with 68 percent of the observations because in a normal (bell-shaped) distribution, 68 percent of the sample statistics lie within one standard error of the mean.

The bootstrap technique can at times provide a less-than-accurate picture of the real data. Since we are essentially trying to construct a picture of a complete data set from only a small fragment or sample of the data set, we may be misled from time to time. The bootstrap, then, does not guarantee accuracy in our estimates, but it will give a better picture of the original data set than classical statistical techniques most of the time. The one best reason for using the bootstrap technique remains that it involves absolutely no simplifying assumptions about the underlying probability distribution.

Extensions of the Bootstrap Technique

The bootstrap technique may be applied to statistics other than the correlation coefficient. Perhaps the most useful suggested application of the bootstrap technique for forecasters is to test the variability of the summary statistics (especially R^2 and the standard error of the regression) in traditional least-squares regression analysis. The problem we wish to address is quite similar to that of examining the variability of the correlation coefficient.

In Chapter 4 we presented simple regression as an estimation technique that can be used to model a great deal of real-world data. The full statistical term for that regression analysis, you will recall, is *linear least-squares regression analysis.* As the name implies, regression analysis is carried out by making our available data conform as closely as possible to the linear model. In Chapter 4 we converted the simplest case, in which the model is a straight line. In Chapter 5, we presented the more complicated cases in which a plane (when there are two independent variables) and the higher-dimensional analogues of the plane (when there are more than two independent variables) were all linear as well. There arises some difficulty when the real-world data do not conform to our assumptions of linearity in using regression (or when the data do not conform to our other common data assumptions such as independence of the independent variables).

Consider again the four dissimilar data sets we presented in Chapter 4. They are presented here once again for convenience in Table 10–2. Each of the four data sets contains 11 observations, and all four data sets surprisingly yield the same regression

---

[5] Ibid., p. 120.

(c10t2)

TABLE 10–2   Four Dissimilar Data Sets with Similar Regression Results

Set A		Set B		Set C		Set D	
X	Y	X	Y	X	Y	X	Y
10	8.04	10	9.14	10	7.46	8	6.58
8	6.95	8	8.14	8	6.77	8	5.76
13	7.58	13	8.74	13	12.74	8	7.71
9	8.81	9	8.77	9	7.11	8	8.84
11	8.33	11	9.26	11	7.81	8	8.47
14	9.96	14	8.10	14	8.84	8	7.04
6	7.24	6	6.13	6	6.08	8	5.25
4	4.26	4	3.10	4	5.39	19	12.50
12	10.84	12	9.13	12	8.15	8	5.56
7	4.82	7	7.26	7	6.42	8	7.91
5	5.68	5	4.74	5	5.73	8	6.89

SOURCE: F. J. Anscombe, "Graphs in Statistical Analysis," *American Statistician* 27 (February 1973), pp. 17–21; as reported in Edward R. Tufte, *The Visual Display of Quantitative Information* (Cheshire, Conn.: Graphics Press, 1983), p. 13.

line (and identical R^2's and standard errors):

$$Y = 3 + 0.5X$$

$$R^2 = 0.67 \qquad \text{s.e.} = 1.24$$

In all cases, the mean value of Y is 7.5 and the mean value of X is 9.0. The data sets differed quite dramatically, however, when we examined their scatterplots (these are reproduced in Figure 10–2). Only the plot in the upper left-hand corner of Figure 10–2 appeared to meet our expectations of near linearity. We suggested in Chapter 4 the use of scatterplots to identify dramatic deviations from our assumptions. However, the difficulty of identifying these deviations is compounded in multiple regression. There is simply no easy way to visualize hyperplanes (hyperplanes are the n-dimensional analogues of planes in three-space). Without such a visualization tool, we need a method for measuring the variability of our estimated regressions, since the original data may very well not match the assumptions we have taken as given.

If bootstrapping is applied to regression data, we can generate artificial data sets, and the least-squares regression technique can be applied to each artificial data set in order to fit a new line (or plane or hyperplane). By examining the fluctuation in these lines (or planes or hyperplanes), the bootstrap method will indicate the variability of the least-squares estimator for these data points.

Let's consider the four data sets in Table 10–2 and apply the bootstrap technique to each one in order to estimate which linear least-squares regressions have the highest variability (and therefore reflect the highest probability that our original

FIGURE 10–2

Scatterplots of Four XY Data Sets That Have Very Similar Statistical Properties but Are Visually Quite Different
(c10t2)

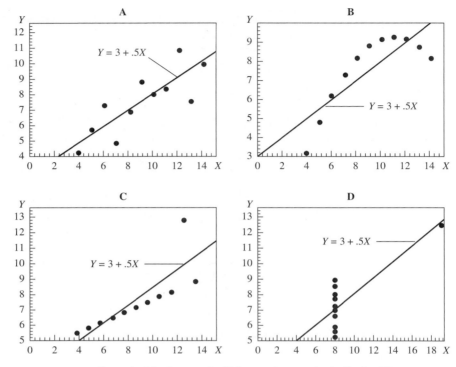

For each of the data sets the OLS regression equation is: $Y = 3 + .5X$.

assumptions about the data were incorrect). It is the highly variable regressions that alert us to the possibility that the model we have used may not fit the data.

We generate our bootstrap samples in the manner we used previously. In Figure 10–3 we have drawn a schematic diagram of the process we are using. To generate one bootstrap sample, we draw a random sample of 11 rows from the original data set. The artificial sample is drawn with replacement. Thus, the artificial sample may very likely contain duplicate rows from the original data set. This process is repeated many times over, with each process resulting in a bootstrapped artificial sample.

We actually created 10 bootstrapped artificial data sets for each data set represented in Table 10–2. The first two of these artificial data sets for the "set A" sample appear in Table 10–3. A linear least-squares regression was run on each of the 10 artificial data sets, and the R^2 and standard error of the regression statistics were accumulated.

It is the fluctuation in these summary statistics that indicates whether the original estimates of R^2 and standard error are accurate.

The regression results for the first two artificial data sets drawn from set A of Table 10–2 are displayed in Table 10–3. It is the fluctuation in these summary statistics that indicates whether the original estimates of R^2 and standard error are accurate. This method is capable of warning an investigator when "something else is going on." That is, the bootstrap technique may warn of inappropriate applications of a model.

FIGURE 10–3

Artificial Data Sets Are Selected by Choosing Entire Rows at Random

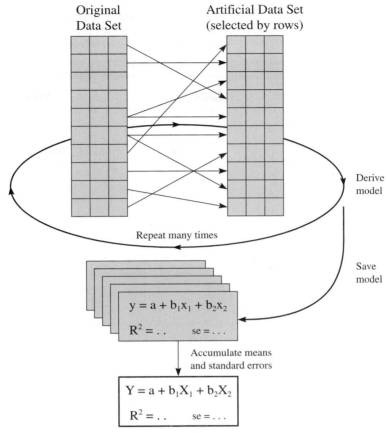

Regressions run on the artificial data sets are used to accumulate means and standard errors. This figure is modeled after a similar diagram in Richard D. Cramer, Jeffrey D. Bunce, David E. Patterson, and Ildiko E. Frank, "Crossvalidation, Bootstrapping, and Partial Least Squares Compared with Multiple Regression in Conventional QSAR Studies," Quantitative Structure-Activity Relationships *7, no. 1 (1988), p. 21.*

In Table 10–4 we present a measure of the variability of the R^2 and standard error of the regression for the bootstrapped data sets. Remember that data set A is the closest to approximating a straight line, while data sets B, C, and D are all quite deviant. Since all of the four original data sets have identical R^2's and standard errors, the conventional regression analysis would tell us little about the reliability of each regression compared with the other regressions.

Bootstrapping has, however, clearly differentiated the four data sets. The bootstrapped data set A has a relatively low standard deviation of the R^2. We could interpret this as telling us that our calculated R^2 for the original data set is probably quite accurate.

TABLE 10–3   Two Bootstrapped Data Sets Drawn from Set A of Table 10–2

First Artificial Data Set

	Y_1	X_1		Y_1	X_1
1	6.95	8.00	7	8.04	10.00
2	8.81	9.00	8	8.04	10.00
3	8.33	11.00	9	7.24	6.00
4	8.81	9.00	10	9.96	14.00
5	10.84	12.00	11	9.96	14.00
6	9.96	14.00			

$$Y_1 = 4.68744 + 0.387848(X_1)$$
$$R^2 = 0.6878 \quad \text{s.e.} = 0.731600$$

Second Artificial Data Set

	Y_1	X_1		Y_1	X_1
1	9.96	14.00	7	4.26	4.00
2	4.82	7.00	8	8.04	10.00
3	4.26	4.00	9	9.76	14.00
4	6.95	8.00	10	8.04	10.00
5	7.24	6.00	11	10.84	12.00
6	4.82	7.00			

$$Y_1 = 1.80353 + 0.618241(X_1)$$
$$R^2 = 0.8364 \quad \text{s.e.} = 1.03184$$

(C10T4A.SAC)
(C10T4B.SAC)
(C10T4C.SAC)
(C10T4D.SAC)

TABLE 10–4   Summary Data for 10 Bootstrapped Regressions on Each of the Four Original Data Sets*

	Data Set A	Data Set B	Data Set C	Data Set D
Average R^2	0.703	0.647	0.843	0.607
Standard deviation of R^2	0.105	0.259	0.182	0.422
Average s.e. of regression	1.032	0.921	0.639	1.097
Standard deviation of s.e.	0.201	0.305	0.681	0.259

*The SAC files that created this table are contained on the CD accompanying the book. The files may be executed (i.e., run) as is or modified to fit other situations (C10T4A.SAC, C10T4B.SAC, C10T4C.SAC, C10T4D.SAC).

The standard deviations of the R^2 values we calculated for data sets B, C, and D are much larger (more than 4 times as large in the case of data set D). We could interpret this as "failing" the test for variability in the R^2. The question we should ask is: What does it mean to "fail" this type of test? In general, despite identical conventional regression statistics, greater variability in bootstrapped results means that for data sets B, C, and D the estimated equations are "not as good" as the equation estimated for data set A.

The data in Table 10–4 concerning the variability of the standard error of the bootstrapped regressions produce a similar picture. For data set A the standard deviation of the standard errors of the 10 bootstrapped equations was 0.201. Once again this was the lowest standard deviation of the four. For data set C the standard deviation of the standard errors was more than 3 times as large (i.e., 0.681). This result is interpreted in the same manner as the variability of the R^2. Because data sets B, C, and D have substantially larger variability in the bootstrapped standard errors, the regression equations we originally estimated for these data sets are suspect; the originally calculated standard errors of the regressions may be significantly understated. According to Bradley Efron,[6] while the bootstrap is not the only method for estimating the variability of standard errors in complex situations, all other computationally intensive methods rely on a very similar procedure and would likely produce similar results.

Bootstrapping Time-Series Data

Bootstrapping in actual practice is, however, most often used with multiple-regression models and often with time-series data.

The four examples we presented in the previous section all involved cross-sectional data and simple regression. Bootstrapping in actual practice is, however, most often used with multiple-regression models and often with time-series data.

For our example we will use the data presented below.

(c10t5)

	Sales	Income	Price	Competitor's Price
1990Q4	20	2,620	5.00	5.00
1991Q1	16	2,733	5.20	4.80
1991Q2	16	2,898	5.32	4.80
1991Q3	14	3,056	5.48	4.50
1991Q4	16	3,271	5.60	4.44
1992Q1	19	3,479	5.80	4.55
1992Q2	17	3,736	6.03	4.60
1992Q3	18	3,868	6.01	4.85
1992Q4	21	4,016	5.92	5.10
1993Q1	26	4,152	5.90	5.40
1993Q2	30	4,336	5.85	5.00
1993Q3	26	4,477	5.80	4.95
1993Q4	27	4,619	5.85	5.00
1994Q1	29	4,764	5.80	5.00

[6]See Bradley Efron, "Computer-Intensive Methods in Statistical Regression," *SIAM Review* 30, no. 3 (September 1988), p. 433.

We will assume that sales are affected by or caused by the price we choose (PRICE), our competitor's price (C_PRICE), and the income of potential purchasers (INCOME). If we run a regression with sales as the dependent variable and the independent variables of price, competitor's price, and income, we obtain the regression results shown in Table 10–5.

Performing the "three quick checks" on this model (as suggested in Chapter 4) requires us to examine the signs of the coefficients, the t-statistics, and the coefficient of multiple determination (or adjusted R^2).

For our current model, the signs appear to be what we would expect from economic theory. The income coefficient (0.00857807) is positive, suggesting that as incomes rise more of our good is purchased, all other things remaining unchanged. The price coefficient (-9.05741) is negative, as we also would expect, indicating that as we raise our price our sales will fall, all other things remaining the same. The coefficient on the competitor's price (5.09168) is positive, indicating that as our competitor raises price, our sales increase, all other variables remaining unchanged. Thus, we seem to pass the first of the three quick checks.

The t-statistics for price and income are well above 2 and are significant at well above the 95 percent confidence level. The t-statistic on our competitor's price is just below what is needed for the 95 percent confidence level; it is significant at the 92.3 percent confidence level (note the "Signf," or significance, column in Table 10–5).

The last of the three quick checks involves examining the adjusted R^2 value (0.8669), which suggests that 86.69 percent of the variation in sales is explained by the variations in price, income, and competitor's price.

Note also that the Durbin-Watson statistic of 1.81371 indicates that you can be confident that there is no serial correlation.

(C10T5.SAC)

TABLE 10–5   Regression with Actual Data*

```
REGRESS: dependent variable is SALES
Using   1  -  14

   Variable      Coefficient     Std Err        t-stat      Signf
   ---------------------------------------------------------------
   ^CONST        15.9393         20.7687        0.767465    0.461
   INCOME        0.857807E-02    0.154568E-02   5.54971     0.000
   PRICE         -9.05741        3.11926        -2.90371    0.016
   C_PRICE       5.09168         2.58162        1.97229     0.077

   ---------------------Equation Summary----------------------
   No. of Observations   =   14      R2 = 0.8976 (adj) = 0.8669
   Sum of Sq. Resid. = 39.4199      Std. Error of Reg. = 1.98545
   Log(likelihood) = -27.1116       Durbin-Watson = 1.81371
   Schwarz Criterion = -32.3898     F (3,10) = 29.2161
   Akaike Criterion = -31.1116      Significance = 0.000029
```

*The SAC file that created this table is contained on the CD accompanying this book. The file may be executed (i.e., run) as is or modified to fit other situations (C10T5.SAC).

The regression output in Table 10–5 is the best estimate we can obtain through regression analysis. But is this estimate reliable? The summary statistics we have already introduced have given us some confidence in the results. Recall, however, that the technique of regression analysis as a way of estimating a model has assumed that the data conform closely to a predetermined model.

To be exact, we have assumed in running this linear least-squares regression model that sales is a linear function of price, income, and competitor's price. We have derived our estimates for the variable coefficients from the classical assumption that the independent variables are normally and independently distributed. The experience of recent researchers indicates that the classical measures of the accuracy of multiple-regression results (such as adjusted R^2 and the standard error of the regression) are far too optimistic.[7] It is bootstrapping that provides an acceptable alternative to making the classical assumptions about the data. Recall that bootstrapping makes no assumptions about the data; it replaces the assumptions with massive calculations for assessing the "correctness" of a relationship found within a particular sample.

We proceed to assess our original regression (the one in Table 10–5) by creating numerous artificial data sets using the technique presented in Figure 10–3. We numbered each row in the original data set with the numbers from 2 to 14. We then drew 14 random numbers (with replacement) from a range from 1 to 14. We selected rows from the actual data set.

The first artificial data set we created appears in Table 10–6. Note that the first row in the data set is actually the 14th row (i.e., the 1994Q1 observation) from the actual data set. This row was chosen because the first random number generated was the number 14. The second random number generated was 10 (and so now 10 was chosen from the actual data set to be the second row of the artificial data set). Note carefully that rows 10, 11, and 14 of the artificial data set are identical. That is because the number 7 was chosen three times as one of our 14 picks.

Next we ran the same form of regression on this artificial data set as the one we ran on our actual data set. This regression is reported at the bottom of Table 10–6.

The resulting regression is not identical to our original regression, but it is similar. The adjusted R^2 is quite close to the original adjusted R^2, and the standard error of the regression is only modestly different.

What we are looking for are wide deviations in either of these statistics. A wide deviation would make us suspect that the original linear least-squares model might have been an incorrect way to characterize the relationship and therefore our coefficient estimates may be quite misleading.

In actual practice, bootstrapping would be carried out by performing the process of creating an artificial sample and running a regression on the artificial sample many times over. How many artificial samples would be taken? Again, somewhere between 10 and 100 samples are suggested by statisticians. The summary statistics for those samples would be averaged and the standard deviation of this average calculated. It is this standard deviation that is of interest.

---

[7]See Cramer, Bunce, Patterson, and Frank, p. 19.

(C10T6.SAC)   TABLE 10–6   **First Artificial Data Set and Regression***

	SIMS	SIMI	SIMP	SIMCP
1	29.0000	4,764.00	5.80000	5.00000
2	26.0000	4,152.00	5.90000	5.40000
3	21.0000	4,016.00	5.92000	5.10000
4	20.0000	2,620.00	5.00000	5.00000
5	30.0000	4,336.00	5.85000	5.00000
6	26.0000	4,152.00	5.90000	5.40000
7	21.0000	4,016.00	5.92000	5.10000
8	27.0000	4,619.00	5.85000	5.00000
9	19.0000	3,479.00	5.80000	4.55000
10	17.0000	3,736.00	6.03000	4.60000
11	17.0000	3,736.00	6.03000	4.60000
12	29.0000	4,764.00	5.80000	5.00000
13	16.0000	3,271.00	5.60000	4.44000
14	17.0000	3,736.00	6.03000	4.60000

SIMS is simulated sales, SIMI is simulated income, SIMP is
simulated price, and SIMCP is simulated competitor's price.

```
REGRESS: dependent variable is SIMS
Using  1  -  14

    Variable     Coefficient        Std Err          t-stat         Signf
    -------------------------------------------------------------------
    ^CONST        26.1637          17.1434          1.52617         0.158
    SIMI          0.816356E-02     0.122797E-02     6.64803         0.000
    SIMP          -9.94924         2.51939          -3.94906        0.003
    SIMCP         4.45759          1.94582          2.29086         0.045

    --------------------Equation Summary------------------
    No. of Observations  =  14      R2 = 0.9059 (adj) = 0.8777
    Sum of Sq. Resid.  = 32.1366    Std. Error of Reg. = 1.79267
    Log(likelihood) =    -25.6817   Durbin-Watson = 1.96436
    Schwarz Criterion = -30.9598    F (3,10) = 32.0883
    Akaike Criterion =  -29.6817    Significance = 0.000019
```

*The SAC file that created this table is contained on the CD accompanying this book. The file may be executed
(i.e., run) as is or modified to fit other situations'(C10T6.SAC).

Statisticians
have found that
if this standard
deviation is not
"greatly" in excess
of 0.05 (and
ours is not), the
actual regression-
adjusted R^2 is a
true representation
of the goodness
of fit of the
regression.

The standard deviation of the adjusted R^2 for the 10 regressions is reported in Table 10–7 and was only 0.045. Statisticians have found that if this standard deviation is not "greatly" in excess of 0.05 (and ours is not), the actual regression-adjusted R^2 is a true representation of the goodness of fit of the regression. Another way of interpreting our low standard deviation would be to say that it implies that "nothing else is going on." If this number had been much larger, say, equal to 0.5, then we should be very suspecting of our original regression; further examination would be indicated.

TABLE 10–7   Summary for 10 Regressions on the 10 Artificial Data Sets

Regression	R^2	Standard Error of Regression
1	0.8777	1.79267
2	0.8665	2.29708
3	0.9140	1.64544
4	0.9885	0.524396
5	0.9698	1.02025
6	0.9361	1.33311
7	0.8724	1.89077
8	0.9074	1.26409
9	0.8553	2.14069
10	0.8952	1.72330
Total	9.0829	15.631796

R^2 avg. $= 9.0829/10 = 0.90829$
s.e. avg. $= 15.631796/10 = 1.5631796$
Standard deviation of $R^2 = 0.045$
Standard deviation of s.e. $= 0.535$

Now examine the standard errors of the regression for the 10 regressions reported in Table 10–7. The average of the standard errors (1.563) is actually smaller than that reported in Table 10–5 for the actual regression (1.985). However, the standard deviation of the standard errors of the 10 regressions in Table 10–7 is quite large (0.535). This is not at all unusual; it indicates that the standard error of the true regression might be a bit larger than calculated.

Freedman and Peters report that the variability in bootstrapped standard errors is appreciably larger than that in nominal standard errors.[8] Once again, the reason is that our original data do not exactly match the standard regression assumptions. According to Freedman and Peters, the bootstrapped standard errors in Table 10–7 are much better estimates than conventional standard errors, even though they still may be biased downward. Bootstrapped standard errors may in some cases show that the nominal standard error is too small by a factor of 2 or 3.

> Bootstrapped standard errors may in some cases show that the nominal standard error is too small by a factor of 2 or 3.

For our particular regression, it appears that the originally calculated adjusted R^2 is quite accurate and that the standard error of the regression, while perhaps mildly understated, is also quite accurate. The bootstrap procedure, then, is not commonly used as another forecasting tool, but rather as a means of further evaluating regression models we have estimated from actual data. If our actual data deviate from the standard assumptions of classical statistics, standard regression analysis will provide a poorer fit than if our actual data fit the standard assumptions. Bootstrapping gives us another tool to measure whether our regressions are accurate.

---

[8]See Freedman and Peters (1984), p. 101.

Conclusion

How many bootstrap data sets should be created in testing the variability of R^2 and the standard error of the regression? The number of bootstrapped data sets does not need to be very large. Some statisticians indicate that little is lost by using only 10 samples rather than 100. Others point out that there is essentially no difference in the results between using 40 and 100 as the number of bootstrapped samples. It is a safe bet that in critical or important situations, more bootstrapped samples are better than fewer but that the total number may be kept quite small.

The bootstrap is not the only computer-intensive method for handling statistical analysis. Other methods, such as the jackknife and cross-validation, actually predate the bootstrap, but all of them are quite similar in that they involve the creation of artificial data sets manufactured from an original data set. All the methods also rely on measuring and comparing the variability of some statistic calculated from the artificial data sets. Only the methods used to create the artificial data sets differ among the computer-intensive methods.

The SORITEC Sampler software provided with this book is capable of performing the sampling procedure required in the bootstrapping technique. Exercise 3 below will allow you to actually try bootstrapping.

USING SORITEC FOR BOOTSTRAPPING

Bootstrapping is, of course, best accomplished with the aid of a computer to handle the repetitive sampling involved in the construction of the artificial data sets. The SORITEC statistical package offers an easy method to handle this computationally intensive technique.

The SORITEC software has the ability to execute small programs written by a user. These small programs are files that contain a standard set of commands drawn from the SORITEC Analysis Language. We will use one of these small programs to examine the data presented in the section titled "Bootstrapping Time-Series Data." These time-series data included information on four variables:

Sales

Income

Price

Competitor's Price

The data are reproduced here for convenience:

(c10using)

	Sales	*Income*	*Price*	*Competitor's Price*
1990Q4	20	2,620	5.00	5.00
1991Q1	16	2,733	5.20	4.80
1991Q2	16	2,898	5.32	4.80
1991Q3	14	3,056	5.48	4.50
1991Q4	16	3,271	5.60	4.44
1992Q1	19	3,479	5.80	4.55
1992Q2	17	3,736	6.03	4.60
1992Q3	18	3,868	6.01	4.85
1992Q4	21	4,016	5.92	5.10
1993Q1	26	4,152	5.90	5.40
1993Q2	30	4,336	5.85	5.00
1993Q3	26	4,477	5.80	4.95
1993Q4	27	4,619	5.85	5.00
1994Q1	29	4,764	5.80	5.00

We used bootstrapping earlier in the chapter to examine a regression using these data, which assumed that our sales were affected by the income of potential purchasers (income), the price we chose to charge (price), and the price our competitor chose to charge (comp. price). The reliability of the time-series regression was examined using the standard diagnostic statistics (e.g., R^2, standard error of the regression). We used bootstrapping to examine the reliability of the estimated regression without the confining classical assumptions.

To use bootstrapping, however, requires the "manufacture" of numerous artificial data sets. This is where we will use the SORITEC programming language to help the analysis. The short program below is an easy way to prepare any number of artificial data sets. In SORITEC parlance this file is called a "**SAC**" file or **S**oritec **A**lternate **C**ommand file. Each artificial data set is prepared in precisely the manner described earlier (sampling with replacement).

The commands in this file will look a bit strange, since we have not used the SORITEC programming language previously. There is actually no reason for you to learn the entire programming language. In fact, you need not learn any of the language; you may simply modify the SAC files presented here (which are included on the enclosed CD) with the SORITEC Procedures Editor ▦ and insert your own data for different situations. The Procedures Editor is opened either by selecting "Proc Editor" from the **File** menu or by pressing the special button assigned to this task ▦.

The file below performs four steps:

1. creates a matrix of the original data set;
2. draws a row number at random (i.e., a number between 1 and 14);
3. repeats step two 14 times (because we need 14 observations);
4. prints out the simulated data set.

```
! First, Read the values of the four original variables into the program !

USE 1990q4 1994q1

SERIES SALES 20 16 16 14 16 19 17 18 21 26 30 26 27 29

SERIES INCOME 2620 2733 2898 3056 3271 3479 3736 3868 4016 4152 4336
4477 4619 4764

SERIES PRICE 5 5.2 5.32 5.48 5.6 5.8 6.03 6.01 5.92 5.9 5.85 5.8 5.85 5.8

SERIES C_PRICE 5 4.8 4.8 4.5 4.44 4.55 4.6 4.85 5.1 5.4 5 4.95 5 5

! Next, create a matrix of the original data set !

MATRIX A
MMAKE A SALES INCOME PRICE C_PRICE


! Draw a random number between 1 and 14 to select a row of the original data set !
! Do this 14 times to create an artificial data set with 14 rows!

RANDOM DRAW
DRAW=14*DRAW
DRAW=CEILING(DRAW)
PRINT DRAW

B=ROW(A,DRAW)
PRINT B

!Take the artificial data in matrix format and return it to SORITEC
variable format and print it !


UNMAKE B SIMS SIMI SIMP SIMCP
PRINT SIMS SIMI SIMP SIMCP
```

This SAC file appears on the CD accompanying this text as "**C10T5A.SAC**".

Note that comments are included between exclamation marks; these are not executable statements. If you wished to bootstrap different data, you could use the same file by replacing the "SERIES" statements with statements containing your own data. The number of observations you have would need to match the number in the **DRAW** command (so that your artificial data set would contain the same number of observations as the original data set).

The file is executed by choosing the **EXECUTE**... command from the **File** menu or by opening the file into the Procedures Editor ▦ and selecting the "Execute" button.

Each time this file is executed, a new (and different) artificial data set is created. Each new data set could be subjected to the examination we performed earlier in the chapter. This exact file was the one used to create the artificial data sets we used earlier in the chapter.

Using SORITEC for Bootstrapping Time-Series Data

In the chapter section titled "Bootstrapping Time-Series Data" we demonstrated how the bootstrapping technique could help determine the reliability of a time-series regression result. The technique we employed was to use the original sample as the basis for creating numerous artificial samples, and we then used the artificial sample to run the same regression we had run with the original sample; the process was repeated many times and the standard deviation of the R^2 for the regressions was examined.

A single SAC file can contain both commands for creating the artificial sample and for running the regression. A new result is created each time the file is executed.

```
USE 1990q4 1994q1

SERIES SALES 20 16 16 14 19 17 18 21 26 30 26 27 29

SERIES INCOME 2620 2733 2898 3056 3271 3479 3736 3868 4016 4152 4336 4477
4619 4764

SERIES PRICE 5 5.2 5.32 5.48 5.6 5.8 6.03 6.01 5.92 5.9 5.85 5.8 5.85 5.8

SERIES C_PRICE 5 4.8 4.8 4.5 4.44 4.55 4.6 4.85 5.1 5.4 4.95 5 5

! CREATE A MATRIX OF THE ORIGINAL DATASET !
MATRIX A

MMAKE A SALES INCOME PRICE C_PRICE

! DRAW A RANDOM NUMBER FROM 1 TO  FOURTEEN !
RANDOM DRAW
DRAW=14*DRAW

DRAW=CEILING(DRAW)
PRINT DRAW

B=ROW(A,DRAW)
PRINT B

UNMAKE B SIMS SIMI SIMP SIMCP
PRINT SIMS SIMI SIMP SIMCP

! RUN THE REGRESSION SIMILAR TO THE ONE IN TABLE 10.5 IN THE TEXT !
! NOTE THAT THE REGRESSION WILL BE DIFFERENT EACH TIME THIS SAC !
! FILE IS EXECUTED !

REGRESS SIMS SIMI SIMP SIMCP
```

This SAC file appears on the CD accompanying this text as "**C10T5.SAC**".

Running this file produces an artificial sample and runs a regression of the type shown in Table 10–6. Each time the file is executed it will produce a different regression because the particular artificial sample will be unique.

By modifying the file to read in your own data you can easily examine any sample.

Using SORITEC to Complete Exercise 3

Exercise 3 in the exercises below contains a much larger data set than the one used above. In exercise 3 you are asked to complete a bootstrapping procedure by hand; this is highly recommended for first-time users of the technique. The exercise will fix in your mind the exact steps in the bootstrapping procedure. Performing the technique by hand many times over, however, can be very onerous. This is a situation in which the power of the small executable SORITEC command files becomes apparent. Consider the following SORITEC Alternate Command file (also called a SAC File).

```
! Read in the original 15 observation sample drawn from the larger population !

USE 1 15

SERIES MPG 10 24 23.2 21.1 16 17.5 28 19 15 11 28 24.3 13 34.1 13

SERIES CYL 8 4 4 4 8 8 4 6 8 8 4 4 8 4 8

SERIES DISP 307 116 156 134 400 305 90 232 318 400 97 151 350 86 351

SERIES HP 200 75 105 95 230 145 75 100 150 150 75 90 165 65 158

SERIES WEIGHT 4376 2158 2745 2515 4278 3880 2125 2901 3777 4997 2155 3003 4274
1975 4363

! Create a matrix of this original data set !

MATRIX A
MMAKE A MPG CYL DISP HP WEIGHT

! Draw a random number between 1 and 15 to select a row of the data set !

RANDOM DRAW
DRAW=15*DRAW
DRAW=CEILING(DRAW)
PRINT DRAW

B=ROW(A,DRAW)
PRINT B

!Take the simulated data in matrix format and return it to SORITEC variable !
!format and print it !

UNMAKE B SIMMPG SIMCYL SIMDISP SIMHP SIMWEIGHT
PRINT SIMMPG SIMCYL SIMDISP SIMHP SIMWEIGHT

! Run the regression called for in  problem 3 !

REGRESS SIMMPG SIMCYL SIMDISP SIMHP SIMWEIGHT
```

This SAC file appears on the CD accompanying this text as "**C10P3.SAC**".

In this file the original sample of 15 observations is read into the program, an artificial data set is created through bootstrapping, the artificial data set is printed, and finally the regression is run on the artificial data set. Each time this executable file is run, a different artificial data set is created and a new regression is run. The process can be replicated many times over in just a few seconds.

After completing exercise 3 by hand you will appreciate the power of the small SAC file listed above. While the two files above use relatively small samples as their starting point, much larger original samples are often used in actual practice.

Suggested Readings

Adler, Yu P.; I. V. Gadolina; and M. N. Lyandres. "Bootstrap Simulation for the Construction of Confidence Intervals from Curtailed Samples." *Industrial Laboratories* 53, no. 10. New York: Plenum Publishing Corporation, 1988, pp. 994–98.

Bickel, Peter J.; and David A. Freedman. "Some Asymptotic Theory for the Bootstrap." *Annals of Statistics* 9, no. 6 (1981), pp. 1196–217.

Cramer, Richard D.; Jeffrey D. Bunce; David E. Patterson; and Ildiko E. Frank. "Crossvalidation, Bootstrapping, and Partial Least Squares Compared with Multiple Regression in Conventional QSAR Studies." *Quantitative Structure-Activity Relationship* 7, no. 1 (1988), pp. 18–25.

Diaconis, Persi; and Bradley Efron. "Computer-Intensive Methods in Statistics." *Scientific American* 248 (May 1983), pp. 116–30.

Efron, Bradley. "Bootstrap Methods: Another Look at the Jackknife." *Annals of Statistics* 7, no. 1 (1979), pp. 1–26.

———. "Computer-Intensive Methods in Statistical Regression." *SIAM Review* 30, no. 3 (September 1988), pp. 421–49.

Efron, Bradley; and Gail Gong. "A Leisurely Look at the Bootstrap, the Jackknife, and Cross-Validation." *The American Statistician* 37, no. 1 (February 1983), pp. 36–48.

Efron, B.; and Tibshirani, R. J. *An Introduction to the Bootstrap.* New York: Chapman & Hall, 1993.

Freedman, D. A. "Bootstrapping Regression Models." *Annals of Statistics* 9, no. 6 (1981), pp. 1218–28.

Freedman, David A.; and Stephen C. Peters. "Bootstrapping an Econometric Model: Some Empirical Results." *Journal of Business and Economic Statistics* 2, no. 2 (April 1984), pp. 150–58.

———. "Bootstrapping a Regression Equation: Some Empirical Results." *Journal of the American Statistical Association* 79, no. 385 (March 1984), pp. 97–106.

Good, P. *Permutation Tests: A Practical Guide to Resampling Methods for Testing Hypotheses.* New York: Springer-Verlag, 1994.

Hall, Peter. "Theoretical Comparison of Bootstrap Confidence Intervals." *Annals of Statistics* 16, no. 3 (1988), pp. 927–53.

Marais, M. Laurentius. "An Application of the Bootstrap Method to the Analysis of Squared, Standardized Market Model Prediction Errors." *Journal of Accounting Research* 22, Supplement 1984, pp. 34–54.

Simon, J. L. "What Some Puzzling Problems Teach About the Theory of Simulation and the Use of Resampling." *American Statistician* 48, no. 4 (November 1994), pp. 1–4.

Simon, J. L.; and Peter C. Bruce. "Resampling: A Tool for Everyday Statistical Work." *Chance* 4, no. 1 (1991), pp. 22–32.

Vinod, H. D.; and Baldev Raj. "Economic Issues in the Bell Divestiture: A Bootstrap Application." *Applied Statistics* 37, no. 2 (1988), pp. 251–61.

Exercises

1. Assume you had estimated a multiple-regression equation you wanted to use to forecast sales. At the time you estimated the equation, only three years of monthly data were available. What steps would you

follow if you wished to test the validity of the model with the bootstrap technique?

2. Explain under what conditions a bootstrap approach might yield significantly different results from a conventional approach.

3. In this problem we ask you to perform a bootstrap operation by hand. With the complete SORITEC package it is possible to perform this entire operation with just a few commands. The SORITEC Sampler software that is included with this book is capable of performing the sampling procedure required in the bootstrap technique.

Consider the data set abbreviated in the accompanying table, which includes actual data from the United States Department of Transportation covering 392 automobiles sold from 1971 to 1983. The complete data set is located on the CD accompanying this book. Information is given for each of these types of automobiles, covering miles per gallon (mpg), number of cylinders, cubic-inch displacement of the engine, engine horsepower (hp), and gross vehicle weight.

The data set represents a complete population. The correlation coefficient relating miles per gallon to gross vehicle weight is -0.83224. The correlation coefficient for the relationship between miles per gallon and cubic inch displacement is -0.805127.

a. Suppose now that you did not have available the entire population, but only 15 observations. Simulate this situation by randomly selecting 15 of the 392 observations. Calculate the correlation coefficients for both miles per gallon and cubic-inch displacement. Explain why your calculations differ from the population parameters.

Now bootstrap the sample you have selected by preparing 10 artificial samples. Calculate the correlation coefficient for each sample and then calculate the standard deviations of the 10 samples taken as a group.

If you truly had only the one sample of 15 observations and the bootstrap results, would you have been misled by the results?

b. Run the regression of the following form on all 392 data points:

$$\text{Mileage} = f(\text{weight, displacement})$$

Now use the first sample of 15 data points selected in part (*a*) and run the same regression. Why is it different?

Automobile Data
U.S. Department of Transportation: 1971–1983

Obs	mpg	Cylinders	Displacement in Cubic Inches	hp	Weight
1	18.000	8	307	130	3,504
2	15.000	8	350	165	3,693
3	18.000	8	318	150	3,436
4	16.000	8	304	150	3,433
5	17.000	8	302	140	3,449
6	15.000	8	429	198	4,341
7	14.000	8	454	220	4,354
8	14.000	8	440	215	4,312
9	14.000	8	455	225	4,425
10	15.000	8	390	190	3,850
11	15.000	8	383	170	3,563
12	14.000	8	340	160	3,609
13	15.000	8	400	150	3,761
14	14.000	8	455	225	3,086
15	24.000	4	113	95	2,372
16	22.000	6	198	95	2,833
17	18.000	6	199	97	2,774
18	21.000	6	200	85	2,587
19	27.000	4	97	88	2,130
20	26.000	4	97	46	1,835
21	25.000	4	110	87	2,672
22	24.000	4	107	90	2,430
23	25.000	4	104	95	2,375
24	26.000	4	121	113	2,234
25	21.000	6	199	90	2,648
⋮	⋮	⋮	⋮	⋮	⋮
382	38.000	6	262	85	3,015
383	26.000	4	156	92	2,585
384	22.000	6	232	112	2,835
385	32.000	4	144	96	2,665
386	36.000	4	135	84	2,370
387	27.000	4	151	90	2,950
388	27.000	4	140	86	2,790
389	44.000	4	97	52	2,130
390	32.000	4	135	84	2,295
391	28.000	4	120	79	2,625
392	31.000	4	119	82	2,720

(c10p3)
(C10P3.SAC)

Run the same regression on each of the 10 bootstrapped samples. Record the R^2 and standard error of the regression for each equation. Calculate the standard deviation of the R^2 and the standard deviation of the 10 standard-error calculations. What do these values tell you about the accuracy of the regression on the sample data?

Perform the same operation with the second sample selected in part (*a*).

4. Some businesses incur special problems with accounts collection. The number of days since billing for a sample of 20 accounts receivable of a particular business is shown below.

Establish a 90 percent confidence interval for the average number of "days since billing" for all the physicians' accounts, using the "bootstrap" procedure.

If we could, we would take additional samples from the universe of accounts receivable. That is deemed to be too time-consuming and too expensive in this particular situation. Instead, let the sample serve as a proxy universe.

You can imagine replicating each of the sample observations millions of times to create our "bootstrap" universe. Even this is time-consuming, so we achieve the same effect by putting each observation back in after we sample it—sampling with replacement. Draw samples of size 20, because this is the sample size whose behavior we wish to observe.

Account no.	Days since billing
1	17
2	57
3	10
4	35
5	26
6	3
7	21
8	11
9	7
10	72
11	5
12	86
13	6
14	20
15	105
16	40
17	14
18	42
19	12
20	32

(C10P4.SAC)

5. A poll has been taken by a national service showing that 54 percent of 150 prospective customers for your type of product prefer your particular brand. What degree of confidence would you place in such a poll?

Use the bootstrap procedure.

If we could, we would run additional polls by selecting additional samples from the universe of voters, but that is too time-consuming and too expensive. Instead, we let our 54 percent "for our brand" and 46 percent "for another brand" sample serve as a proxy universe. We can imagine replicating each of the sample observations millions of times to create our "bootstrap" universe. Even this is time-consuming, so we achieve the same effect by putting each observation back in after we sample it—sampling with replacement. Draw samples of size 150 because this is the sample size whose behavior we wish to observe.

6. In Exercise 5 of Chapter 5 you were asked to develop a multiple-regression model for auto sales as a function of population and household income. The data covered 10 metropolitan areas and hence were cross-sectional data.

Use these data to bootstrap 10 artificial samples. The bootstrap procedure may be used on cross-sectional as well as time-series data. Calculate the standard deviation of the R^2 for those samples. Does the original model developed in Chapter 5 seem reliable?

7. In Exercise 6 of Chapter 5 you developed a model for the sales of skiwear. These data were time-series data. Use the original data to create 10 artificial samples and examine the regressions of those artificial samples. Calculate the standard deviation of the R^2 for these artificial samples. Does your original model estimate (the one developed in Chapter 5) appear reliable?

USER'S GUIDE TO BEA INFORMATION[1]

The Bureau of Economic Analysis (BEA) provides basic information on such key issues as economic growth, regional development, and the nation's role in the world economy. This guide lists the most recent and most frequently requested BEA products and helps users locate and obtain that information.

The guide contains program descriptions and entries for specific products. The first section, entitled "General," describes the products that cut across the range of BEA's work. The following sections describe the products related to BEA's national, regional, and international economics programs.

General

BEA's current national, regional, and international estimates usually appear first in news releases. The information in news releases is available to the general public in a variety of forms: on recorded telephone messages, online through the Economic Bulletin Board (EBB), by fax through STAT-USA/FAX, on the Internet through STAT-USA Internet, and in printed BEA reports. This section describes these products, as well as the SURVEY OF CURRENT BUSINESS—BEA's monthly journal of record. General information products produced by BEA, including BEA's home page on the Internet, are discussed first. This is followed by descriptions of electronic products and services available through the Department of Commerce's STAT-USA, which also disseminates BEA's economic data.

For more information on BEA's programs and products, write to the Public Information Office, BE-53, Bureau of Economic Analysis, U.S. Department of Commerce, Washington, DC 20230, or call (202) 606-9900; for telecommunications

---

[1] Source: http://www.bea.doc.gov/bea/aboutbea/uguide.txt. Updates maybe found at this URL. We have not included here a listing of phone numbers for BEA contacts on various topics nor the current year's release dates for information. Both of these are available from the Internet. You may also want to explore http://www.bea.doc.gov for other related information.

device for the deaf (TDD), call (202) 606-5335. For information about STAT-USA's services, call (202) 482-1986.

What's New?

New products include: SURVEY OF CURRENT BUSINESS on CD-ROM (see entry 1.2); summary BEA data now available on BEA's Internet site (see entry 1.5); change in SURVEY cover dates (see SURVEY OF CURRENT BUSINESS—Cover Dates); transfer of business cycle indicators to The Conference Board (see entry 6.0); State Personal Income, 1929–93 (see entry 8.2); BEA Regional Projections to 2045: Volume 1, States (see entry 9.3); Foreign Direct Investment in the United States: 1992 Benchmark Survey, Final Results (see entry 12.2).

How to Use This Guide

Entries in this guide are arranged by program area. Each program area includes descriptions and schedules of current estimates, a list of products available, and telephone numbers for users who have questions or need assistance. Near the end of this guide is a subject list of BEA products. Each BEA product is available from one of three sales agents, abbreviated as follows: BEA—Bureau of Economic Analysis; GPO—U.S. Government Printing Office, Superintendent of Documents; NTIS—National Technical Information Service.

Each product's listing identifies the sales agent and includes a stock or accession number to be used when ordering. An order form from each sales agent, including specific ordering information, is provided at the end of this guide. Each sales agent accepts credit cards. BEA data are also available electronically from STAT-USA (see entries 1.6–1.9).

BEA Products

1.1. SURVEY OF CURRENT BUSINESS (publication).

A monthly journal containing estimates and analyses of U.S. economic activity. Most of BEA's work is presented in the SURVEY, either in full or in summary form. Includes the "Business Situation"—a review of current economic developments—and regular and special articles pertaining to the national, regional, and international economic accounts and related topics. Among the special articles that appeared in the past year were "Mid-Decade Strategic Review of BEA's Economic Accounts: Maintaining and Improving Their Performance," "Improved Estimates of the National Income and Product Accounts for 1959–95: Results of the Comprehensive Revision," "An Ownership-Based Disaggregation of the U.S. Current Account, 1982–93," and "Regional and State Projections of Economic Activity and Population to the Year 2005." Current estimates of the national income and product accounts (see program description 2.0) appear every month. The SURVEY is available from the U.S. Government Printing Office (GPO): List ID SCUB, price $49.00 per year (domestic second-class mail), $61.25 (foreign second-class mail), or $90.00 (domestic first-class mail); single-copy price, $11.00 (domestic) and $13.75 (foreign). Foreign airmail delivery rates are available upon request from GPO.

SURVEY OF CURRENT BUSINESS—Cover Dates

Beginning in 1996, the cover date designation for the SURVEY was changed to match the month of publication. As a result, the issues in which regular quarterly and annual articles appear will have a different monthly designation than those in which the article had previously appeared. For example, in 1996 (and henceforth), the article on the annual revision of the international transactions accounts will appear in the July issue; in previous years, this article had appeared in the June issue.

1.2. SURVEY OF CURRENT BUSINESS (CD-ROM).
All of the issues of 1994 and selected articles from 1987–93 with the look and feel of the printed version. A Windows version of Acrobat Exchange LE software is included on the CD-ROM, enabling searches across the entire set of files for 1987–94. In addition, a "Copy Table to Clipboard" plug-in allows Windows users to easily extract statistical material from the SURVEY into spreadsheet format. The SURVEY files on CD-ROM are in portable document format (PDF), a graphically oriented format that preserves document fidelity across all major computer platforms and printers. Available from BEA: Accession No. 53-95-30-001, price $35.00. To order, contact BEA's Public Information Office at (202) 606-9900.

NOTE: The availability of a CD-ROM containing all the issues of the SURVEY for 1995 and selected articles for 1987–94 will be announced in the SURVEY.

1.3. Recorded Telephone Messages.
Brief (3–5 minutes) recorded telephone messages summarizing key estimates immediately after their release. The messages are available 24 hours a day for several days following release. The usual time of release (eastern standard or eastern daylight time) and the telephone numbers to call are as follows:

Gross domestic product (8:30 A.M.) . . . . (202) 606-5306
Personal income and outlays (8:30 A.M.) . . . . -5303
U.S. international transactions (10:00 A.M.) . . . . -5362

1.4. BEA Reports (EBB, STAT-USA/FAX, Internet, news release).
Four sets of reports that present the information contained in the BEA news releases for the following areas: gross domestic product; personal income and outlays; regional reports; and international reports. The reports contain summary estimates. All reports are available on-line through the EBB (see entry 1.6), by fax through STAT-USA/FAX (see entry 1.7), and on the Internet through STAT-USA Internet (see entry 1.9). The printed reports are mailed the day after the estimates are released. Annual subscriptions to the printed reports may be ordered for individual sets or for all four sets. Order information for the four printed sets is given below.

For information on individual sets, see the following corresponding entries: gross domestic product, entry 2.1; personal income and outlays, entry 2.2; regional reports, entry 7.1; and international reports, entry 10.1. All four sets (usually a total of 37 printed reports) are available from BEA: Accession No. 53-91-11-019, price $74.00 per year.

1.5. BEA's Home Page on the Internet.

Summary data—including the latest figures on GDP, personal income, and balance of payments—are available free of charge on BEA's Internet site. The "User's Guide to BEA Information," a telephone contact list, the news release schedule, and other information are also available. Go to http://www.bea.doc.gov. For more-detailed economic data and BEA's news releases, subscribe to STAT-USA at http://www.stat-usa.gov (see entry 1.9).

Available through STAT-USA

BEA's economic statistics are also made available in the following electronic formats through the Commerce Department's STAT-USA.

1.6. Economic Bulletin Board.

Online computer access to news releases and other information. BEA news releases are available on the Economic Bulletin Board (EBB) shortly after their release. Selected national, regional, and international estimates and articles from the SURVEY OF CURRENT BUSINESS are also available. (Other items in this guide that are available through the EBB are marked "EBB" after the title.) The EBB may be accessed by personal computer equipped with a modem and communications software; the information available on it—which includes information from several other federal agencies—may either be viewed on the user's screen or downloaded. Instant hookup is available. For more information, including subscription rates, call STAT-USA at 1-800-782-8872.

1.7. STAT-USA/FAX.

Facsimile-based service that provides access to BEA news releases and other BEA information on the EBB, usually within 1 hour of the time of the release. The STAT-USA/FAX is available by dialing (202) 482-0005 from a facsimile machine's handset. Subscriptions start at $29.95, and instant access is available. This service is available 24 hours a day, 7 days a week. For more information, call STAT-USA at (202) 482-1986.

1.8. The National Trade Data Bank (CD-ROM).

BEA places a significant amount of its statistics in the National Trade Data Bank (NTDB). These statistics include international transactions, foreign direct investment, balance of payments, annual and quarterly national income and product accounts, and others. The NTDB contains over 150 information programs from over 30 government agencies, including export and import statistics, foreign marketing reports, "how-to" guides for exporters, and names of companies overseas that want to do business with U.S. exporters. The NTDB is produced monthly and may be ordered from STAT-USA by calling (202) 482-1986; an individual monthly issue (two discs) costs $59.00, and an annual subscription (12 monthly issues) is $575.00. The NTDB is also available for public use at over 1,100 Federal Depository Libraries throughout the nation.

1.9. STAT-USA Internet (Internet).

BEA's economic information is available on the Internet by subscription through STAT-USA. Users can obtain BEA news releases shortly after their release, SURVEY OF CURRENT BUSINESS issues and articles, and detailed files from BEA's national, regional, and international economic accounts, as well as a variety of information from other federal agencies. Subscriptions start at $50.00; to find out more, go to http://www.stat-usa.gov.

National Economics

BEA's national economics program encompasses the national income and product accounts, government transactions on a national income and product accounting basis, the input-output accounts, and estimates of expenditures on pollution abatement and control.

National Income and Product Accounts

2.0

The national income and product accounts (NIPAs) show the value and composition of the nation's output and the distribution of incomes generated in its production. The accounts include estimates of gross domestic product (GDP)—the market value of the nation's output of goods and services—in current and real terms, GDP price measures, the goods and services that make up GDP in current and real terms, national income, personal income, and corporate profits. In addition, BEA produces specialized measures such as estimates of auto and truck output, GDP of corporate business, housing output, and business inventories and sales. Estimates of gross product originating by industry are prepared annually in current and real terms. Measures of the inventory and fixed capital stocks consistent with the NIPA output measures are also provided. Further, the accounts provide a consistent framework within which estimates of analytical interest—such as the role of research and development in the U.S. economy or the interaction of the economy and the environment—can be developed.

The estimates of GDP are prepared each quarter in the following sequence: Advance estimates are released near the end of the first month after the end of the quarter; as more detailed and comprehensive data become available, preliminary and final estimates are released near the end of the second and third months, respectively. Monthly estimates of personal income and outlays are released near the end of the month following the reference month; estimates for the two to four most recent months are revised at that time. Ordinarily, annual NIPA revisions are carried out each summer and cover the months and quarters of the most recent calendar year and the preceding two years. (For example, the July 1994 revision covered 1991, 1992, and 1993.) These revisions are timed to incorporate newly available major annual source data. Comprehensive (benchmark) revisions are carried out at about five-year intervals; a comprehensive revision was released in January 1996. Current quarterly NIPA estimates appear in a set of 54 "selected" tables each month in the SURVEY OF CURRENT BUSINESS. The full set of NIPA tables (138 tables) usually is published at the time of annual revisions and comprehensive revisions. Annual estimates of the fixed capital stock are reported shortly thereafter.

In addition to the current and historical estimates described in the entries that follow, additional component detail (for example, purchases of private structures by type and change in business inventories by industry) is available. For further information about this detail or about the listed printouts and diskettes, write to National Income and Wealth Division, BE-54, Bureau of Economic Analysis, U.S. Department of Commerce, Washington, DC 20230, or call (202) 606-9700. For specific questions, the following telephone numbers may be used:

GDP . . . . (202) 606-5304
Personal income and outlays . . . . -5301
Corporate profits . . . . -9738
Personal consumption expenditures . . . . -5302
Gross private domestic investment . . . . -9711
GDP by industry . . . . -5307

A recorded telephone message summarizing the latest GDP estimates is available by calling (202) 606-5306 (see entry 1.3). A recorded message summarizing the latest personal income and outlays estimates is available at (202) 606-5303.

Current Estimates

2.1. BEA Reports: Gross Domestic Product
(EBB, STAT-USA/FAX, Internet, news release).
Monthly reports with summary NIPA estimates that feature GDP and corporate profits. Reports are available on-line through the EBB (see entry 1.6), by fax through STAT-USA/FAX (see entry 1.7), and on the Internet (see entry 1.9). Printed reports are mailed the day after estimates are released. (This set of reports is included in the four sets of BEA Reports; see entry 1.4.) The gross domestic product printed reports are available from BEA on a subscription basis: Accession No. 53-91-11-015, price $24.00 per year.

2.2. BEA Reports: Personal Income and Outlays
(EBB, STAT-USA/FAX, Internet, news release).
Monthly reports with summary NIPA estimates that feature personal income and outlays. Reports are available on-line through the EBB (see entry 1.6), by fax through

STAT-USA/FAX (see entry 1.7), and on the Internet (see entry 1.9). Printed reports are mailed the day after estimates are released. (This set of reports is included in the four sets of BEA Reports; see entry 1.4.) The personal income and outlays printed reports are available from BEA on a subscription basis: Accession No. 53-91-11-014, price $24.00 per year.

2.3. Monthly Advance National Income and Product Accounts Tables (EBB, Internet, diskette, or printout).

NIPA estimates as they appear in the current issue of the SURVEY OF CURRENT BUSINESS. Updated monthly. Available on-line through the EBB (see entry 1.6) and on the Internet (see entry 1.9). Diskettes are available the day of release of GDP, and printouts are available one day after the release from BEA on a subscription basis: Diskette (3 1/2″ HD). Accession No. 54-85-41-401, price $200.00 per year. Printout-Accession No. 54-83-21-201, price $100.00 per year.

2.4. Key Source Data and Assumptions (EBB, Internet, printed table).

Available source data and assumptions for missing source data that are used to prepare the advance estimates of GDP for each quarter. Available on-line through the EBB (see entry 1.6) and on the Internet (see entry 1.9). Annual subscriptions for the printed table are available from BEA: Accession No. 54-84-21-209, price $25.00 per year.

Historical Estimates

2.5. National Income and Product Accounts (diskette).

The full set of NIPA tables, most with estimates from 1959 to the present. Diskettes (3 1/2″ HD). Available from BEA: Accession No. 54-89-40-401, price $40.00 (two diskettes).

2.6. National Income and Product Accounts of the United States (forthcoming).

Two volumes will present the full set of NIPA tables for 1929–92. Includes statistical conventions and the definitions and classifications underlying the NIPAs. Volume 1: 1929–58 and Volume 2: 1959–92 will be available from GPO.

NIPA Methodology

Summary tables listing the principal source data and estimating methods used to prepare the NIPA estimates are included in the articles in the SURVEY OF CURRENT BUSINESS that describe annual revisions to the NIPAs. These tables were last published in the July 1994 issue of the SURVEY. The availability of updated tables will be announced in a future issue. A number of papers that provide detailed descriptions of NIPA concepts and methodologies have been published (see next entry).

Methodology Papers (publications).

A series of papers that document the conceptual framework of the NIPAs and the methodology used to prepare the estimates. To date, six papers are available.

NOTE: The methodologies described in these papers are subject to periodic improvements that are typically introduced as part of the annual and comprehensive revisions of the NIPAs. These improvements—which consist of definitional changes, new source data, and new estimating methods—are described in the SURVEY articles that cover these revisions. For example, the major improvements introduced in the most recent comprehensive revision are described in articles in the July 1995, September 1995, October 1995, and January/February 1996 issues. For more information, write or call the National Income and Wealth Division.

2.7. An Introduction to National Economic Accounting (NIPA Methodology Paper No. 1).

An introduction to the concepts of the U.S. NIPAs that places these accounts within the larger framework of national economic accounting. Shows the step-by-step derivation of a general national economic accounting system from the conventional accounting statements used by business and government and inferred for other transactors. Also shows how the income and product accounts, the capital finance accounts, and the input-output accounts—the major branches of national economic accounting in the United States today—are derived from this general system. Also appeared in the March 1985 SURVEY OF CURRENT BUSINESS. Available from NTIS: Accession No. PB 85-247567, price $12.50.

2.8. Corporate Profits: Profits Before Tax, Profits Tax Liability, and Dividends (NIPA Methodology Paper No. 2).

A description of the concepts, sources, and methods of the corporate profits components of the NIPAs. (1985) Available from NTIS: Accession No. PB 85-245397, price $27.00.

2.9. Foreign Transactions (NIPA Methodology Paper No. 3).

A description of the preparation of estimates in the NIPAs of net exports (both current- and constant-dollar), transfer payments to foreigners, capital grants received by the United States, interest paid by the government to foreigners, and net foreign investment. Also describes the relationship between foreign transactions estimates in the NIPAs and those in the balance of payments accounts. (1987) Available from NTIS: Accession No. PB 88-100649, price $27.00.

2.10. GNP: An Overview of Source Data and Estimating Methods (NIPA Methodology Paper No. 4).

Basic information about GNP, including the conceptual basis for the account that presents GNP, definitions of each of the components on the income and product sides of that account, and a summary, presented in tabular form, of the source data and methods used in preparing estimates of current- and constant-dollar GNP. Also provides an annotated bibliography, with a directory, of the more than 50 items over the last decade that provided methodological information about GNP. Appeared in the July 1987 SURVEY OF CURRENT BUSINESS. Available from NTIS: Accession No. PB 88-134838, price $24.50. The summary tables of source data and methods were last updated in the July 1994 issue of the SURVEY (tables 7 and 8, pages 28–45); the availability of updated tables will be announced in a future issue.

2.11. Government Transactions (NIPA Methodology Paper No. 5).

Presents the conceptual basis and framework of government transactions in the NIPAs, describes the presentation of the estimates, and details the sources and methods used to prepare estimates of federal transactions and of state and local transactions. (1988) Available from NTIS: Accession No. PB 90-118480, price $31.50.

NOTE: Major changes in methodology have occurred since the publication of this methodology paper. These changes include the recognition of government investment, treatment of federal retirement programs, enterprise definition changes, treatment of Commodity Credit Corporation loans, and deposit insurance changes. See "The Comprehensive Revision of the U.S. National Income and Product Accounts: A Review of Revisions and Major Statistical Changes," SURVEY 71 (December 1991) and "Preview of the Comprehensive Revision of the National Income and Product Accounts: Recognition of Government Investment and Incorporation of a New Methodology for Calculating Depreciation," SURVEY 75 (September 1995).

2.12. Personal Consumption Expenditures (NIPA Methodology Paper No. 6).

Presents the conceptual basis and framework for personal consumption expenditures (PCE) in the NIPAs, describes the presentation of these estimates, and details the sources and methods used to prepare annual, quarterly, and monthly estimates of PCE. Includes a bibliography, definitions, and convenient tabular summaries of estimating procedures. (1990) Available from NTIS: Accession No. PB 90-254244, price $27.00.

GDP by Industry Estimates

Gross product originating (GPO) by industry is the contribution of each industry—including government—to GDP. GPO, also known as GDP by industry or value added, equals an industry's gross output less intermediate goods and services purchased from other industries or imported. Annual estimates are expressed in both current dollars (1947–93) and in real terms (1977–93). These estimates, published in the April 1995 (1991–93) and November 1993 (1947–90) issues of the SURVEY OF CURRENT BUSINESS, are provided at approximately the two-digit standard industrial classification (SIC) level. Industry classifications are based on the 1987 SIC for 1988–93, on the 1972 SIC for 1947–86, and on both the 1972 and 1987 SICs for 1987. For further information, write to the Industry Economics Division, BE-51, Bureau of Economic Analysis, U.S. Department of Commerce, Washington, DC 20230, or call (202) 606-5307.

2.13. Gross Product by Industry.

Current-dollar estimates are provided for 1947–93. Constant-dollar estimates, which are calculated with benchmark years and fixed 1987 weights, are provided for

1977–93. Includes the components of gross domestic income that define current-dollar GPO for each industry. Includes estimates of gross output and intermediate inputs for double-deflated industries.

> Diskette (3 1/2″ HD)—Accession No. 51-91-40-406, price $20.00.
> Printout—Accession No. 51-91-20-206, price $20.00.

2.14. Gross Output by Detailed Industry.

Annual estimates (1977–93) of gross output in current and constant dollars (fixed 1987 weights) for double-deflated industries that were used to prepare the estimates of GPO. Industry detail generally exceeds that available in the Gross Product by Industry data products (see entry 2.13). Gross output for manufacturing industries on these files is at the two-digit GPO level of industry detail; see entry numbers 2.15 and 2.16 for more detailed data for manufacturing.

> Diskette (3 1/2″ HD)—Accession No. 51-91-40-410, price $20.00.
> Printout—Accession No. 51-91-20-210, price $20.00.

2.15. Manufacturing Establishment Shipments.

Annual estimates (1977–93) in current and constant dollars (fixed 1987 weights) of manufacturing establishment shipments by four-digit SIC. These estimates were used to prepare the estimates of gross output that underlie the GPO estimates for manufacturing industries.

> Diskette (3 1/2″ HD)—Accession No. 51-91-40-407, price $20.00.
> Printout—Accession No. 51-91-20-207, price $35.00.

2.16. Manufacturing Product Shipments.

Annual estimates (1977–92) in current and constant dollars (fixed 1987 weights) of manufacturing product shipments by five-digit Census Bureau product class defined on a wherever-made basis. Estimates for 1993 are not available. Estimates are based on the 1972 Census Bureau product-class system for 1977–86, on the 1987 system for 1988–92, and on both the 1972 and 1987 systems for 1987.

> Diskette (3 1/2″ HD)—Accession No. 51-91-40-408, price $20.00.
> Printout—Accession No. 51-91-20-208, price $35.00.

Other Information Related to the NIPAs

2.17. The Underground Economy: An Introduction (reprint).

A discussion of the coverage, measurement methods, and implications of the underground economy. Part of the discussion features the relation between the NIPAs and the underground economy: illegal activities in the context of the NIPAs, three sets of NIPA estimates sometimes misunderstood as being measures of the underground economy, and the effect on NIPA estimates of possible misreporting in source data due to the underground economy. Articles appeared in the May, June, and July 1984 issues of the SURVEY OF CURRENT BUSINESS. Available upon request from BEA's Public Information Office.

2.18. Alternative Measures of Change in Real Output and Prices (reprint).

Four articles that appeared in the SURVEY OF CURRENT BUSINESS describing the two alternatively weighted measures of real output and of prices that BEA prepares to supplement its featured fixed-weighted measures. These alternative measures are especially useful for studies of long-term economic growth, for comparisons of business cycles, and for gauging the effect of changes in the economy's relative price structure on the measurement of real gross domestic product. (1993) Available upon request from BEA's Public Information Office. (For recent information about BEA's improved chain-type measures of real output and prices, see "Improved Estimates of the National Income and Product Accounts: Results of the Comprehensive Revision," SURVEY 76 (January/February 1996): 1–31.)

2.19. Evaluation of the GNP Estimates (reprint).

An evaluation of the GNP estimates, covering the reliability of estimates, sources of error and types of statistical improvement, status of source data, documentation of methodology, release schedules, and security before release. This article appeared in the August 1987 SURVEY OF CURRENT BUSINESS. Available upon request from BEA's Public Information Office. (For a more recent study, see Allan H. Young, "Reliability of the Quarterly Estimates of GDP," SURVEY 73 (October 1993): 29–43.)

2.20. The Use of National Income and Product Accounts for Public Policy: Our Successes and Failures (BEA Staff Paper No. 43).

An evaluation using two indirect approaches. The first reviews the "accuracy" of the estimates, using the size of revisions to GNP estimates as an indicator. The second reviews users' recommendations drawn from publications issued over the last 30 years. (1985) Available from NTIS: Accession No. PB 86-191541, price $17.50.

2.21. The United Nations System of National Accounts: An Introduction (reprint).

Describes the United Nations System of National Accounts (SNA), which is followed by most other countries, and contrasts it with the U.S. economic accounts. The article also presents estimates prepared by BEA to approximate some of the major SNA aggregates and describes the revision of the SNA that is under way. This article appeared in the June 1990 SURVEY OF CURRENT BUSINESS. Available upon request from BEA's Public Information Office. (For a more recent description, see New International Guidelines in Economic Accounting, SURVEY 73 (February 1993): 43–44.)

2.22. Economic-Environmental Accounts (reprint).

Two articles that describe a BEA framework for integrated economic and environmental satellite accounts and that present prototype estimates of mineral stocks, and changes in those stocks, for the past several decades. The new set of accounts, which supplements the existing system of national economic accounts, provides a statistical picture of the interaction of the economy and the environment. These articles appeared in the April 1994 SURVEY OF CURRENT BUSINESS. Available upon request from BEA's Public Information Office.

2.23. A Satellite Account for Research and Development (diskette).

The Satellite Account for Research and Development is designed to facilitate analysis of the role of research and development (R&D) in the U.S. economy. In the R&D satellite account, R&D expenditures are treated as a form of investment, and the resulting investment flows are used to estimate stocks of R&D fixed intangible capital. For most series, summary tables include data for 1953–92. (For a description of the R&D accounts, see "A Satellite Account for Research and Development," SURVEY 74 [November 1994]: 37–71.) The complete set of data in the R&D satellite account is available on diskette (3 1/2" HD) from BEA's Public Information Office: Accession No. 53-94-40-001, price $20.00.

Wealth and Related Estimates

These estimates are being updated to reflect the results of the recently released comprehensive revision of the NIPAs. The data products that follow will become available when the updating of the estimates is completed; their availability will be announced in the SURVEY OF CURRENT BUSINESS.

2.24. Fixed Reproducible Tangible Wealth in the United States, 1925–92 (publication).

Annual estimates of net stocks, depreciation, and average ages of net stock for fixed nonresidential and private capital and residential capital, for government-owned fixed capital, and for durable goods owned by consumers.

2.25. Wealth (diskette).

Annual estimates of net stocks and depreciation for fixed nonresidential private and residential capital, for government-owned fixed capital, and for durable goods owned by consumers.

2.26. Detailed Investment by Industry (diskette).

Annual estimates of investment purchased by industry for each detailed NIPA type of equipment and structure.

2.27. Detailed Wealth by Industry (diskette).

Annual estimates of net stocks, depreciation, and discards for fixed nonresidential capital by industry for each detailed NIPA type of equipment and structure.

Government Transactions

3.0

BEA's estimates of government receipts, expenditures, and surplus or deficit are on a national income and product accounting basis. The estimates are prepared separately for federal and for state and local governments on the same schedule as that described for the NIPAs (see program description 2.0). Reconciliations of the federal sector on a NIPA basis and the budget prepared by the Office of Management and Budget are the basis for an article in the SURVEY OF CURRENT BUSINESS, shortly after the release of the budget, about federal fiscal programs for the next fiscal year, and for detailed tables in the NIPA annual revision issue. These reconciliations, and more specialized work such as described in the papers that follow, facilitate analysis of the effects of government fiscal policies on the economy. An article on the fiscal position of state and local governments is usually published in the February or March SURVEY. For further information, write to the Government Division, BE-57, Bureau of Economic Analysis, U.S. Department of Commerce, Washington, DC 20230, or call (202) 606-5590. For specific questions, the following telephone numbers may be used:

Federal . . . . (202) 606-5591

National defense . . . . -5592

Nondefense . . . . -5593

State and local . . . . -5594

3.1. Government Transactions (NIPA Methodology Paper No. 5).

Presents the conceptual basis and framework of government transactions in the national income and product accounts, describes the presentation of the estimates, and details the sources and methods used to prepare estimates of federal transactions and of state and local transactions. (1988) Available from NTIS: Accession No. PB 90-118480, price $31.50.

NOTE: Major changes in methodology have occurred since the publication of this methodology paper. These changes include the recognition of government investment, treatment of federal retirement programs, enterprise definition changes, treatment of Commodity Credit Corporation loans, and deposit insurance changes. See "The Comprehensive Revision of the U.S. National Income and Product Accounts: A Review of Revisions and Major Statistical Changes," SURVEY 71 (December 1991) and "Preview of the Comprehensive Revision of the National Income and Product Accounts: Recognition of Government Investment and Incorporation of a New Methodology for Calculating Depreciation," SURVEY 75 (September 1995).

3.2. National Income and Product Accounts Translation of the Federal Budget (printed tables).

Package of tables that provide a more detailed translation than appears in the Budget of the United States Government, Analytical Perspectives. (See item 3.1 to obtain information on the differences between the budget and NIPA concepts that lead to the translation.) The translation package will include the annual article on the federal budget after it is published this summer in the SURVEY OF CURRENT BUSINESS. Available from BEA: Accession No. 57-91-20-101, price $12.00.

Input-Output Accounts

4.0

Input-output (I-O) accounts for the United States show how industries interact—providing input to, and taking output from, each other—to produce GDP. Benchmark tables, based largely on the economic censuses, are prepared every five years; the latest benchmark tables are for 1987. Annual tables are prepared using basically the same procedures as used for the benchmark tables, but with less comprehensive and less reliable source data. The preparation of annual tables was suspended after the 1987 annual table; the preparation of annual tables will resume after publication of the 1992 benchmark table. For benchmark years, associated benchmark tables showing capital flows from producing to using industries are also prepared. Diskettes are available at the summary level (95 industries) and detailed level (480 industries), listed below. For further information, write to the Industry Economics Division, BE-51, Bureau of Economic Analysis, U.S. Department of Commerce, Washington, DC 20230, or call (202) 606-5585.

4.1. Benchmark Input-Output Accounts of the United States, 1987 (publication).

This volume contains the use and make tables and total output multipliers for BEA's 1987 benchmark I-O study at the summary and detailed I-O industry levels. Includes discussion of concepts and of analytical and statistical uses of estimates, description of sources and methods, and overview of industry and commodity classification. Provides benchmark I-O commodity composition of NIPA final demand, personal consumption expenditures, and producers' durable equipment expenditures. (1994) Available from GPO: Stock No. 003-010-00251-4, price $29.00.

4.2. 1987 Benchmark I-O Tables (diskettes).

Estimates from the 1987 benchmark I-O accounts at the summary and the detailed levels. Each product includes information on the mathematical derivation of the coefficients tables. Available from BEA: 1987 Benchmark Detailed Transactions. Contains the make table, use table, direct requirements coefficients table, and estimates by commodity of transportation costs and of wholesale and retail trade margins. Accession No. 51-94-40-001, price $40.00.

1987 Benchmark Detailed, Industry-by-Commodity Total Requirements. Accession No. 51-94-40-002, price $40.00.

1987 Benchmark Detailed, Commodity-by-Commodity Total Requirements. Accession No. 51-94-40-003, price $40.00.

1987 Benchmark Summary, All. Contains the make table, use table, direct requirements coefficients table, estimates by commodity of transportation costs and of wholesale and retail trade margins, and industry-by-commodity and commodity-by-commodity total requirements coefficients. Accession No. 51-94-40-004, price $20.00.

1987 Benchmark Commodity Composition of NIPA Final Demand at the Detailed Level. Accession No. 51-94-40-005, price $20.00.

1987 Benchmark PCE and PDE By NIPA Category. Contains the detailed I-O commodity composition of NIPA personal consumption expenditures and producers' durable equipment expenditures. Accession No. 51-94-40-006, price $20.00.

4.3. 1982 Benchmark 85-Industry Input-Output Tables (diskette).
Five tables: (1) Use table, (2) make table, (3) commodity-by-industry direct requirements table, (4) commodity-by-commodity total requirements table, and (5) industry-by-commodity total requirements table. Diskette (3 1/2″ HD)—Available from BEA: Accession No. 51-91-40-008, price $20.00.

Environmental Estimates

5.0
BEA maintains a set of annual current- and constant-dollar estimates of capital expenditures and operating costs for pollution abatement and control. These estimates, which are prepared within the framework of the national income and product accounts, are classified by sector (consumers, business, and government) and by type of pollution abatement and control (PAC) activity (air PAC, water PAC, and solid waste management). The most recent SURVEY OF CURRENT BUSINESS article reporting the total expenditures (including capital and operating spending) appeared in May 1995. For further information, write to the Environmental Economics Division, BE-62, Bureau of Economic Analysis, U.S. Department of Commerce, Washington, DC 20230, or call (202) 606-5350.

5.1. BEA Reports: Pollution Abatement and Control Expenditures (EBB, Internet, news release).
News release on annual pollution abatement and control expenditures. Available online through the EBB (see entry 1.6) and on the Internet (see entry 1.9). Printed report available by calling or writing the Environmental Economics Division.

5.2. Stocks and Underlying Data for Air and Water Pollution Abatement Plant and Equipment (printout).
Estimates of the gross and net capital stocks at historical, constant, and current cost; estimates of capital expenditures in constant and current dollars; price indexes by media (air and water) and for selected industry groups (manufacturing, electric utilities, and other nonmanufacturing); and estimates of lifetimes by media for pollution abatement plant and equipment. Available from BEA: Accession No. 62-82-20-001, price $35.00.

Business Cycle Indicators

6.0
Effective in late 1995, responsibility for the preparation and dissemination of the composite indexes of leading, coincident, and lagging indicators was transferred to The Conference Board. The Conference Board is now producing these indexes and is maintaining and publishing a set of data similar to that previously available in the "Business Cycle Indicators" section of the SURVEY OF CURRENT BUSINESS. For more information, call The Conference Board at (212) 339-0345. In addition, many of the business cycle indicator series are available on the Economic Bulletin Board (see entry 1.6).

Regional Economics

BEA's regional economics program provides estimates, analyses, and projections by region, state, metropolitan area, and county.

7.1. BEA Reports: Regional Reports (EBB, STAT-USA/FAX, Internet, news release).
Reports (usually six a year) with summary estimates of state personal income (quarterly and annual) and of county and metropolitan area personal income (annual). Reports are available on-line through the EBB (see entry 1.6). (The EBB carries, in addition to the news release, estimates of personal income by state and by county, and earnings and wages by industry and by state; see entry 8.4.) The news releases are also available through STAT-USA/FAX (see entry 1.7) and on the Internet (see entry 1.9). The printed reports are mailed the day after the estimates are released. (This set of reports is included in the four sets of BEA Reports; see entry 1.4.) These printed regional reports are available from BEA on a subscription basis: Accession No. 53-91-11-017, price $12.00 per year.

Regional Estimates

8.0
Current quarterly state personal income estimates are released in January, April, July, and October. The annual estimates of state and local area personal income for a given year are subject to successive improvement. Preliminary annual state estimates, based on the current quarterly series, are released four months after the close of the reference year. Revised annual estimates based on more reliable source data are released in August. These estimates are subsequently revised to incorporate newly available information used to prepare the current local area estimates. The revised state estimates, together with the current local area estimates, are released the following April. The annual estimates emerging from this process are subject to further revision for several succeeding years (the state estimates in April and August

and the local estimates in April) as additional data become available. These routine revisions are completed three years after the preliminary state estimates were prepared and two years after the local area estimates were prepared. The state and local area estimates are normally revised again only to incorporate a comprehensive revision of the national income and product accounts, which takes place approximately every five years, or to make important improvements to the estimates through the use of additional or more current state and local area data. Estimates of personal income and employment by state, metropolitan area, and county are available through the Regional Economic Information System (REIS). The system includes an information retrieval service that provides a variety of analytical tabulations for counties and combinations of counties. All of the tabulations are available in several media. BEA also makes its regional estimates available through the BEA User Group, members of which include state agencies, universities, and Census Bureau Primary State Data Centers. BEA provides its estimates of income and employment for all states and counties to these organizations with the understanding that they will make the estimates readily available.

For further information, write to the Regional Economic Measurement Division, BE-55, Bureau of Economic Analysis, U.S. Department of Commerce, Washington, DC 20230, or call (202) 606-5360.

8.1. Regional Economic Information System (REIS) CD-ROM, 1969–94 (CD-ROM).

Estimates of annual personal income by major source, per capita personal income, earnings by two-digit SIC industry, full- and part-time employment by one-digit SIC industry, regional economic profiles, transfer payments by major program, and farm income and expenses for states, metropolitan areas, and counties. The CD-ROM contains over 450 megabytes of data and documentation. All the estimates are stored as ASCII files that can be accessed in either sequential or random mode. The CD-ROM includes a REIS program (both DOS- and Windows-based) that allows the user to display, print, or copy one or more of the standard tables from the historical personal income series.

In addition, the CD-ROM includes BEA estimates of quarterly personal income by state (1969:I–1995:IV); Census Bureau data on intercounty flows for 1960, 1970, 1980, and 1990; BEA's latest gross state product estimates for 1977–92; its projections to 2045 of income and employment for states and metropolitan areas; and total commuters' income flows, 1969–94. Updated annually. (June 1996) Available from BEA: Accession No. 55-94-30-599, price $35.00.

8.2. State Personal Income, 1929–93 (publication).

Presents detailed annual estimates for states and regions of personal income for 1929–93, including estimates of per capita personal income, personal income by major source, and earnings by industry. Also presents annual estimates for states and regions of disposable personal income and per capita disposable personal income for 1969–93. Provides information about the sources and methods used to prepare the estimates for 1987–93 and samples all of the detailed tables of personal income and employment that are available for regions, states, counties, and metropolitan areas. (1995) Available from GPO: Stock No. 003-010-00257-3, price $27.00.

8.3. Local Area Personal Income, 1969–92 (publication).

Presents the estimates of personal income and per capita personal income for 1969–92 for the United States, regions, states, counties, and metropolitan areas. Also presents the Census Bureau's estimates of population that were used in the derivation of per capita personal income. Provides information about the source and methods used to prepare the estimates for 1987–92 and samples of all the detailed tables of personal income and employment that are available for regions, states, counties, and metropolitan areas. (1994) Available from GPO: Stock No. 003-010-00249-2, price $41.00.

Special-Order Regional Products

8.4. Regional Income and Employment.

The products listed in section 8.4 must be special-ordered from BEA for the specific area(s) needed. Items 8.4.1 through 8.4.12 are for the United States, regions, and states. Items 8.4.13 through 8.4.24 are for the United States, states, metropolitan areas, and counties. All items are available on several media and can be purchased for a single area (a county, a metropolitan area, a state), for groups of areas (several counties, several metropolitan areas, all counties in a state, several states), or for all counties or all states in the United States. Some items are available on-line through the EBB (see entry 1.6). Before placing an order, write to the Regional Economic Measurement Division, REIS, BE-55, Bureau of Economic Analysis, Washington, DC 20230, or call (202) 606-5360 for accession numbers, prices, and availability. Call the same number to place charge orders using MasterCard or VISA.

Products for Regions and States

The items in section 8.4 must be special-ordered. Refer to the text at the beginning of section 8.4 for instructions.

8.4.1. Quarterly Personal Income, 1969–95 (EBB, Internet, printout).

Total personal income by quarter for the United States, regions, and states. (1996)

8.4.2. Quarterly Personal Income by Major Source and Earnings by Industry, 1969–95 (EBB, Internet, computer tape, printout, diskette).

Major sources of personal income and earnings by one-digit SIC industry by quarter for the United States, regions, and states. (1996)

8.4.3. Quarterly Wages and Salaries by Major Source and Major Industry, 1969–95 (EBB, Internet, computer tape, printout, diskette).

Wage and salary distributions by one-digit SIC industry by quarter for the United States, regions, and states. (1996)

8.4.4. Personal Income, Per Capita Personal Income, and Total Population, 1929–95 (EBB, Internet, computer tape, printout, diskette).

Total and per capita personal income and population annually for the United States, regions, and states. (1996)

8.4.5. Personal Income by Major Source and Earnings by Industry, 1929–94 (EBB, Internet, computer tape, printout, diskette).

Major sources of personal income and earnings by two-digit SIC industry annually for 1958–94 and by one-digit SIC industry annually for 1929–57 for the United States, regions, and states. (1995)

8.4.6. Wage and Salary Disbursements by Industry, 1929–94 (EBB, Internet, computer tape, printout, diskette).

Wages and salaries by two-digit SIC industry annually for 1958–94 and by one-digit SIC industry annually for 1929–57 for the United States, regions, and states. (1995)

8.4.7. Full-Time and Part-Time Employment by Industry, 1969–94 (computer tape, printout, diskette).

Total employment by place of work by two-digit SIC industry annually for the United States, regions, and states. (1995)

8.4.8. Full-Time and Part-Time Wage and Salary Employment by Industry, 1969–94 (computer tape, printout, diskette).

Wage and salary employment by place of work by two-digit SIC industry annually for the United States, regions, and states. (1995)

8.4.9. Transfer Payments, 1948–94 (computer tape, printout, diskette).

Transfer payments by type annually for the United States, regions, and states. (1995)

8.4.10. Farm Income and Expenses, 1969–94 (computer tape, printout, diskette).

Major categories of farm income and expenses and gross and net farm income aggregates annually for the United States, regions, and states. (1995)

8.4.11. Personal Tax and Nontax Payments, 1948–94 (computer tape, printout, diskette).

Personal tax and nontax payments by level of government and by type of payment (includes total and per capita disposable personal income and population) annually for the United States, regions, and states. (1995)

8.4.12. Disposable Personal Income, Per Capita Disposable Personal Income, and Total Population, 1948–95 (EBB, Internet, printout, diskette).

Total and per capita disposable personal income and population annually for the United States, regions, and states. (1996)

Products for States, Metropolitan Areas, and Counties

8.4.13. Personal Income, Per Capita Personal Income, and Total Population, 1969–94 (EBB, Internet, computer tape, printout, diskette).

Total and per capita personal income and population annually for the United States, states, metropolitan areas, and counties. (June 1996)

8.4.14. Per Capita Personal Income Ranking, 1994 (printout).

Ranking in the United States and in regions (highest and lowest 250 counties). (June 1996) Available from BEA: Printout—Accession No. 55-94-20-541, price $20.00. Rankings among all counties. Printout—Accession No. 55-94-20-542, price $20.00. Rankings among counties with total personal incomes greater than $50 million. The items in section 8.4 must be special-ordered. Refer to the text at the beginning of section 8.4 for instructions.

8.4.15. Personal Income by Major Source and Earnings by Major Industry, 1969–94 (computer tape, printout, diskette).

Major sources of personal income and earnings by one-digit SIC industry annually for the United States, states, metropolitan areas, and counties. (June 1996)

8.4.16. Personal Income by Major Source and Earnings by Industry, 1969–94 (computer tape, printout).

Major sources of personal income and earnings by two-digit SIC industry annually for the United States, states, metropolitan areas, and counties. (June 1996)

8.4.17. Full-Time and Part-Time Employment by Major Industry, 1969–94 (computer tape, printout, diskette.)

Total employment one-digit SIC industry annually for the United States, states, metropolitan areas, and counties. (June 1996)

8.4.18. Regional Economic Profile, 1969–94 (computer tape, printout, diskette).

Summary of income and employment by place of work and residence annually for the United States, states, metropolitan areas, and counties. (June 1996)

8.4.19. Total Wages and Salaries, Total Wage and Salary Employment, and Average Wage Per Job, 1969–94 (computer tape, printout, diskette).

Annually for the United States, states, metropolitan areas, and counties. (1995)

8.4.20. Transfer Payments, 1969–94 (computer tape, printout, diskette).

Transfer payments by type annually for the United States, states, metropolitan areas, and counties. (1995)

8.4.21. Farm Income and Expenses, 1969–94 (computer tape, printout, diskette).

Major categories of farm income and expenses and gross and net farm aggregates annually for the United States, states, and counties. (June 1996)

8.4.22. BEARFACTS, 1993–94 or 1984–94 (printout, diskette).
One-page computer-generated narrative. Describes an area's personal income using current estimates, growth rates, and a breakdown of the sources of personal income for that area for states, metropolitan areas, and counties. (June 1996)

**8.4.23. Journey-to-Work, 1960, 1970, 1980, 1990
(computer tape, printout, diskette).**
Data on commuting flows to and from counties from decennial census by place of work or by place of residence. (1990)

**8.4.24. Total Commuters' Income Flows, 1969–94
(computer tape, printout, diskette).**
Total gross commuters' income flows (inflows and outflows) annually for all counties. (June 1996)

Regional Analyses and Projections

9.0
BEA prepares analyses to identify and measure factors that determine area differences in levels and growth rates of total and per capita personal income and of industrially detailed earnings, employment, and gross state product. Annual estimates of gross state product—the market value of the goods and services produced by the labor and property located in a state—are prepared by component and industry eight years after the release of national GDP by industry. Special tabulations from the Regional Input-Output Modeling System (RIMS II) of regional economic multipliers for any combination of counties are prepared on a reimbursable basis for use in analyzing the economic effects of events, such as the conversion of military bases and the expansion of airports. Long-term and midterm projections of personal income and gross state product, employment, and earnings by industry for states, as well as long-term projections of employment and earnings for metropolitan areas and BEA economic areas are prepared for use by planners and marketing analysts. The segmentation of the nation into 172 BEA economic areas facilitates regional economic analysis for businesses that want to assess potential plant locations and sales territories and for public-sector and university groups that want to conduct small-area, geographically exhaustive regional economic studies. For further information, write to the Regional Economic Analysis Division, BE-61, Bureau of Economic Analysis, U.S. Department of Commerce, Washington, DC 20230, or call (202) 606-3700. For specific questions, the following telephone numbers may be used:

Gross state product by industry . . . . (202) 606-5340
Regional input-output multipliers . . . . -5343
Long-term regional projections . . . . -5341
Midterm regional projections . . . . -5342
BEA economic areas . . . . -9219

9.1. Revised Gross State Product, Annual Estimates, 1977–92 (EBB, Internet, diskette, CD-ROM).

These estimates are the state equivalent of GDP and provide the most comprehensive measure of state production now available. Gross state product (GSP) is measured in current dollars as the sum of four components for each industry: compensation of employees; proprietors' income; indirect business tax and nontax liability; and other, mainly capital-related, charges. A statement of sources and methods for the estimates was published in the December 1993 SURVEY OF CURRENT BUSINESS. The estimates are for the 50 states, eight BEA regions, and the United States and for 61 industries. Estimates are in current and constant (1987) dollars. Available on-line through the EBB (see entry 1.6), on CD-ROM (see entry 8.1), and on the Internet (see entry 1.9).

Diskette (3 1/2" HD) available from BEA: Accession No. 61-95-40-421 for GSP with DOS, price $20.00 (one diskette) or 61-95-40-423 for GSP with Windows, price $40.00 (two diskettes).

9.2. Regional Multipliers: A User Handbook for the Regional Input-Output Modeling System (RIMS II), second edition (publication).

Presents tables of regional input-output multipliers by industry, for output, earnings, and employment, for all states and the District of Columbia. Multipliers are shown on a direct-effect and a final-demand basis. Explains how to obtain multipliers for over 500 industries for any geographic area composed of one or more U.S. counties or county equivalents. Includes case studies. (1992) Available from NTIS: Accession No. PB 92-204-262, price $27.00.

9.3. BEA Regional Projections to 2045 (publication, EBB, Internet, diskette, CD-ROM).

Estimates for 1978, 1983, and 1993 and projections for 2000, 2005, 2010, 2015, 2025, and 2045 for total personal income, population, per capita personal income, and gross state product, employment and earnings by industry for the United States, BEA regions, and states. These estimates and projections, as well as estimates and projections of employment and earnings for metropolitan areas and BEA economic areas, were available on-line through the EBB (see entry 1.6) on the Internet (see entry 1.9), and on CD-ROM (see entry 8.1) as of June 1996 and in other media as follows:

Volume 1. States.

Publication—Available from GPO: Stock No. 003-010-00256-5, price $13.00. Diskette (3 1/2" HD)—Available from BEA: Accession No. 61-95-40-201, price $40.00 (two diskettes).

Metropolitan Statistical Areas.

Diskette (3 1/2" HD)—Available from BEA: Accession No. 61-96-40-202, price $40.00 (two diskettes).

BEA Economic Areas.
Diskette (3 1/2″ HD)—Available from BEA: Accession No. 61-96-40-203, price $40.00 (two diskettes).

9.4. BEA Economic Areas, 1995
(EBB, Internet, diskette, CD-ROM).

This segmentation of the nation on an economic basis has 172 economic areas, and it replaces the 183-area segmentation that BEA first drafted in 1977 and then revised slightly in 1983. Each economic area consists of one or more centers of economic activity and the surrounding counties that are economically related to the centers. Economic data assembled by economic area can be used to analyze local area economic activity, local interindustry economic relationships, and interarea population movements. The codes, names, and numbers of the counties in each economic area are available on-line through the EBB (see entry 1.6), on the Internet (see entry 1.9), and on CD-ROM (see entry 8.1). Diskette (3 1/2″ HD)—Available from BEA: Accession No. 61-95-40-101, price $20.00.

A 26″ × 40″ map of the economic areas is also available from BEA: Accession No. 61-95-10-500, price $15.00.

International Economics

BEA's international economics program encompasses the international transactions accounts (balance of payments), including related estimates of the U.S. international investment position, and the direct investment estimates. The international transactions accounts, which measure U.S. transactions with foreign countries, include merchandise trade, trade in services, the current-account balance, and capital transactions. The direct investment estimates cover estimates of U.S. direct investment abroad and foreign direct investment in the United States, income and other flows associated with these investments, and other aspects of the operations of multinational enterprises.

10.1. BEA Reports: International Reports
(EBB, STAT-USA/FAX, Internet, news release).

Reports (usually seven a year) with summary estimates of international transactions (quarterly); international investment position (annual); and related topics. Reports are available on-line through the EBB (see entry 1.6), by fax through STAT-USA/FAX (see entry 1.7), and on the Internet (see entry 1.9). Printed reports are mailed the day after estimates are released. (This set of reports is included in the four sets of BEA Reports; see entry 1.4.) The printed international reports are available from BEA on a subscription basis: Accession No. 53-91-11-018, price $14.00 per year.

U.S. International Transactions

11.0

The international transactions accounts provide a detailed and comprehensive view of economic transactions between the United States and foreign countries. The accounts include estimates of merchandise exports and imports; travel, transportation, and other services; foreign aid; and private and official capital flows, including direct investment. (Information about direct investment and international services is provided in program description 12.0.) Current estimates are reported in the January, April, July, and October issues of the SURVEY OF CURRENT BUSINESS. (Prior to 1996, the current estimates appeared in the March, June, September, and December issues; see SURVEY OF CURRENT BUSINESS—Cover Dates.) Estimates include detail for the current and capital accounts, classified by type of transaction and by area. Each July, estimates for the last four years are revised. Estimates of the international investment position of the United States appear in July. For further information, write to the Balance of Payments Division, BE-58, Bureau of Economic Analysis, U.S. Department of Commerce, Washington, DC 20230, or call (202) 606-9545. For specific questions, the following telephone numbers may be used:

Current-account estimates . . . . (202) 606-9573
Merchandise trade . . . . -3384
Capital-account transactions . . . . -9579
Government transactions . . . . -9574

A recorded telephone message summarizing key estimates of U.S. international transactions is available at (202) 606-5362 (see entry 1.3).

NOTE: Monthly estimates of U.S. international trade in goods and services are released jointly by the Bureau of the Census and BEA. For information on goods, contact the Bureau of the Census at (301) 457-2311; for information on services, contact BEA at (202) 606-9545. For information about the availability of the news releases, contact the Bureau of the Census at (301) 457-4100.

11.1. U.S. Merchandise Trade Data (printout, diskette).

Seasonally adjusted and unadjusted exports and imports for the end-use categories used by BEA to derive trade totals on a Census Bureau basis. Series begin in 1978. Updated monthly or quarterly. Available from BEA on a subscription basis: U.S. Merchandise Trade Data, Monthly. Printout—Accession No. 58-86-21-201, price $100.00 per year. Diskette (5 1/4″)—Accession No. 58-86-41-401, price $200.00 per year. U.S. Merchandise Trade Data, Quarterly. Also includes, on a balance of payments basis, exports of agricultural products, nonagricultural products, and nonmonetary gold and imports of petroleum and products, nonpetroleum products, and nonmonetary gold. Printout—Accession No. 58-86-21-202, price $40.00 per year. Diskette (5 1/4″)—Accession No. 58-86-41-402, price $80.00 per year.

11.2. U.S. Merchandise Trade: Exports and Imports by End-Use Category, Monthly (printout).

Monthly end-use detail (not seasonally adjusted) on a Census Bureau basis for exports and imports for 70 countries and areas. Series begin in 1978. Available by subscription from BEA: U.S. Merchandise Exports, Monthly. Accession No. 58-86-20-001, price $880.00 per year. U.S. Merchandise Imports, Monthly. Accession No. 58-86-20-002, price $880.00 per year.

11.3. U.S. Merchandise Trade: Exports and Imports by End-Use Category, Quarterly (printout).

Quarterly end-use detail (not seasonally adjusted) on a Census Bureau basis for exports and imports for 70 countries and areas. Series begin in 1978. Available by subscription from BEA: U.S. Merchandise Exports, Quarterly. Accession No. 58-86-20-003, price $275.00 per year. U.S. Merchandise Imports, Quarterly. Accession No. 58-86-20-004, price $275.00 per year.

11.4. U.S. Merchandise Trade: Exports and Imports by End-Use Category, Annually (printout).

Annual end-use detail on a Census Bureau basis for exports and imports for 70 countries and areas. Series begin in 1978. Available by subscription from BEA: U.S. Merchandise Exports, Annually. Accession No. 58-86-20-005, price $110.00. U.S. Merchandise Imports, Annually. Accession No. 58-86-20-006, price $110.00.

11.5. An Analysis of the Use of Time-Series Models to Improve Estimates of International Transactions (BEA Working Paper No. 7).

An investigation to see whether the use of time-series models could improve the accuracy and decrease the bias of the initial estimates of international transactions data in both the national income and product accounts and the international transactions accounts. Currently, these estimates require a considerable degree of judgment in lieu of complete source data. (1993) Available upon request from BEA's Public Information Office.

11.6. The Balance of Payments of the United States: Concepts, Data Sources, and Estimating Procedures (publication).

Describes in detail the methodology used in constructing the U.S. balance of payments (U.S. international transactions) estimates and the international investment position of the United States. Explains underlying principles and describes the presentation of the estimates. Includes a comprehensive list of data sources. (1990) Available from NTIS: Accession No. PB 90-268715, price $39.00

NOTE: The methodologies described in this paper are subject to periodic improvements that are typically introduced as part of the annual revisions of the international transactions accounts. These improvements are described in the SURVEY articles that cover the annual revisions, most recently in "U.S. International Transactions, Revised Estimates for 1983–94," SURVEY 75 (June 1995): 69–75.

11.7. Current and Historical Data for U.S. International Transactions (diskettes).

In March, September, and December, a current-period diskette with data for the most recent one to two years will be available three working days after the U.S. international transactions news release. In June, a current-period diskette with data for the most recent three years will be available five to six working days after the news release. In late June, a historical data diskette will be available; this diskette will include data that begin with the earliest period available for individual tables and that end with the fourth quarter of the previous year. (1995) For order information, call (202) 606-9545. Available as follows: Subscription—Accession No. 58-94-41-001, price $80.00 per year. Current-period diskette—Accession No. 58-94-41-001, price $20.00. Historical diskette—Accession No. 58-94-40-002, price $20.00.

11.8. U.S. International Sales and Purchases of Private Services (diskette).

The diskette contains data on cross-border transactions for 1986–94 and on sales by majority-owned affiliates for 1989–93. The estimates cover transactions by type of service, by area, and by industry. Available from BEA: Accession No. 58-93-40-501, price $20.00.

Direct Investment and International Services

12.0

BEA conducts quarterly, annual, and benchmark surveys of U.S. direct investment abroad and of foreign direct investment in the United States. The information collected relates to the direct investment position and flows of capital, income, royalties and license fees, and other service charges between parent companies and affiliates; the financial structure and operations of U.S. parent companies and their foreign affiliates; the financial structure and operations of U.S. affiliates of foreign companies; and U.S. business enterprises acquired or established by foreign direct investors. Survey information on the quarterly and annual surveys usually appears in the SURVEY OF CURRENT BUSINESS on the following schedule.

Foreign Direct Investment in the United States

The position and balance of payments flows, in July, with additional detail in September. (Prior to 1996, these estimates were published in June and August, respectively. In 1993, the additional detail was published in July.)

Operations of U.S. affiliates of foreign companies, in June (or subsequent months). (Prior to 1996, these estimates were published in May or subsequent months.)

U.S. business enterprises acquired or established by foreign direct investors, in June. (Prior to 1996, these estimates were published in May.)

U.S. Direct Investment Abroad

The position and balance of payments flows, in July, with additional detail in September. (Prior to 1996, these estimates were published in June and August, respectively. In 1993, the additional detail was published in July.)

Operations of U.S. parent companies and their foreign affiliates, in July (or subsequent months). (Prior to 1996, these estimates were published in June or subsequent months.)

BEA's data on direct investment are collected and published at the enterprise (company) level. In 1992, highly detailed establishment- (plant) level data on foreign direct investment in the United States, which complement BEA's enterprise data, became available for the first time as a result of a joint project between BEA and the Bureau of the Census. A volume containing data for 1987 on the number, employment, payroll, and shipments or sales of foreign-owned U.S. establishments was published in June 1992 (see entry 12.4), and an article analyzing the data appeared in the October 1992 SURVEY OF CURRENT BUSINESS. Expanded information for 1988–91 for manufacturing establishments, including most of the items covered by the Census Bureau's annual survey of manufactures, was subsequently published. Articles in the January 1994 and March 1996 issues of the SURVEY analyzed the results.

The information BEA provides on U.S. international sales and purchases of services covers cross-border (balance of payments) services transactions, sales of services abroad by nonbank majority-owned foreign affiliates of U.S. companies, and sales of services in the United States by nonbank majority-owned U.S. affiliates of foreign companies. The information on cross-border services transactions is derived from a variety of sources, including BEA surveys, surveys by other government agencies, and nongovernment sources. The information on sales of services by affiliates is obtained from BEA's benchmark and annual direct investment surveys. From 1990 to 1995, the data on international services were published in a detailed and unified format in the September issue of the SURVEY. As of 1996, these data appear in the October issue of the SURVEY.

For further information on direct investment and international services, write to the International Investment Division, BE-50, Bureau of Economic Analysis, U.S. Department of Commerce, Washington, DC 20230, or call (202) 606-9800. For specific questions, the following telephone numbers may be used:

Foreign direct investment in the United States . . . . . . (202) 606-9804

Operations of U.S. affiliates of foreign companies . . . . -9893

Establishment-level data on foreign direct investment in the
United States . . . . -9898

U.S. direct investment abroad . . . . -9867

Operations of U.S. parent companies and their foreign affiliates-9867

International services . . . . -9804

Foreign Direct Investment in the United States

12.1. Foreign Direct Investment in the United States: Operations of U.S. Affiliates of Foreign Companies (publication, diskette).

The most detailed results of BEA's annual survey of foreign direct investment in the United States (only summary information appears in articles in the SURVEY OF CURRENT BUSINESS). Contains information on the financial structure and operations of nonbank U.S. affiliates of foreign direct investors. Data are classified by industry of U.S. affiliate, by country and industry of ultimate beneficial owner, and, for selected data, by industry of sales and by state. Estimates from annual surveys are first released on a preliminary basis; revised estimates are released one year later. Available as follows:

Foreign Direct Investment in the United States: Operations of U.S. Affiliates of Foreign Companies, Preliminary 1993 Estimates. (1995) Publication—Available from GPO: Stock No. 003-010-00255-7, price $6.50. Diskette (3 1/2″ HD)—Available from BEA: Accession No. 50-95-40-402, price $20.00.

Foreign Direct Investment in the United States: Operations of U.S. Affiliates of Foreign Companies, Revised 1991 Estimates. (1994) Publication—Available from BEA: Accession No. 50-94-10-101, price $6.00. Diskette (3 1/2″ HD)—Available from BEA: Accession No. 50-94-40-401, price $20.00.

Foreign Direct Investment in the United States: Operations of U.S. Affiliates of Foreign Companies, Revised 1990 Estimates. (1993) Publication—Available from NTIS: Accession No. PB 93-216224, price $19.50. Diskette (3 1/2″ HD)—Available from BEA: Accession No. 50-93-40-401, price $20.00.

NOTE: For 1992, a benchmark survey was conducted instead of an annual survey (see entry 12.2).

12.2. Foreign Direct Investment in the United States, Benchmark Survey Results (publication, diskette).

The results of BEA's benchmark survey of foreign direct investment in the United States. Benchmark surveys are BEA's most comprehensive surveys, both in terms of companies covered and information gathered. Contains information on the financial structure and operations of the U.S. affiliates of foreign direct investors. Data are classified by industry of U.S. affiliate, by country and industry of foreign parent or ultimate beneficial owner, and, for selected data, by industry of sales and by state. Results from benchmark surveys are first released on a preliminary basis; final results are released one year later.

Foreign Direct Investment in the United States, 1992 Benchmark Survey, Final Results. (1995) Publication—Available from GPO: Stock No. 003-010-00259-0, price $20.00. Diskette (3 1/2″ HD)—Available from BEA: Accession No. 50-95-40-401, price $20.00.

Foreign Direct Investment in the United States, 1987 Benchmark Survey, Final Results. (1990) Publication—Available from NTIS: Accession No. PB 91-108316, price $48.00. Diskette (3 1/2″ HD)—Available from BEA: Accession No. 50-90-40-401, price $20.00.

12.3. Foreign Direct Investment in the United States: Establishment Data for Manufacturing (publication, diskette).

Presents detailed annual data for 1988–91 on the manufacturing establishments of U.S. affiliates of foreign companies. The data were obtained by linking BEA enterprise, or company, data on foreign direct investment in the United States with Census Bureau establishment, or plant, data for all U.S. companies. Data for the foreign-owned manufacturing establishments were extracted from the Census Bureau's annual survey of manufactures (ASM) and cover most of the ASM items, including value added, shipments, employment, total employee compensation, employee benefits, hourly wage rates of production workers, cost of materials and energy used, inventories by stage of fabrication, and expenditures for new plants and equipment. The data are presented by detailed manufacturing industry (they are classified into the 459 Standard Industrial Classification four-digit industries), by country of the ultimate beneficial owner of the establishment, and by state. Available as follows:

Foreign Direct Investment in the United States: Establishment Data for Manufacturing, 1991. (1994) Publication—Available from GPO: Stock No. 003-010-00250-6, price $14.00. Diskette (3 1/2″ HD)—Available from BEA: Accession No. 50-94-40-791, price $20.00.

Foreign Direct Investment in the United States: Establishment Data for Manufacturing, 1990. (1993) Publication—Available from BEA: Accession No. 50-93-10-790, price $14.00. Diskette (3 1/2″ HD)—Available from BEA: Accession No. 50-93-40-790, price $20.00.

Foreign Direct Investment in the United States: Establishment Data for Manufacturing, 1989. (1993) Publication—Available from BEA: Accession No. 50-93-10-789, price $13.00. Diskette (3 1/2″ HD)—Available from BEA: Accession No. 50-93-40-789, price $20.00.

Foreign Direct Investment in the United States: Establishment Data for Manufacturing, 1988. (1994) Publication—Available from BEA: Accession No. 50-94-10-788, price $13.00. Diskette (3 1/2″ HD)—Available from BEA: Accession No. 50-94-40-788, price $20.00.

12.4. Foreign Direct Investment in the United States: Establishment Data for 1987 (publication, diskette).

Presents detailed results from linking BEA's data for foreign-owned U.S. business enterprises to the Census Bureau's data for the establishments (or plants) of those enterprises. Detailed estimates of the number, employment, payroll, and shipments or sales of foreign-owned U.S. establishments and, for comparative purposes, of all U.S. establishments are presented. Data are classified by detailed industry (four-digit SIC), by country of the ultimate beneficial owner of the investment, and by state. (1992) Available as follows: Publication—Available from BEA: Accession No. 50-92-10-777, price $36.00. Diskette (3 1/2″ HD)—Available from BEA: Accession No. 50-92-40-777, price $20.00.

12.5. Foreign Direct Investment in the United States: Balance of Payments and Direct Investment Position Estimates, 1980–86 (publication).

Contains estimates of the foreign direct investment position in the United States and balance of payments transactions between foreign parent groups and their U.S. affiliates for 1980–86. Includes estimates by country of foreign parent and industry of U.S. affiliate. Note that the data in this publication do not incorporate methodological changes made in June 1992 to the data for 1982 forward. (1990) Available from BEA: Accession No. 50-90-10-109, price $5.00.

12.6. Foreign Direct Investment in the United States: Direct Investment Position and Related Capital and Income Flows (printed tables, diskette).

Annual estimates of the foreign direct investment position in the United States and selected capital and income flows between U.S. affiliates and their foreign parent companies. In June 1992, a number of methodological changes were made to the data on capital and income flows for 1982 forward. To the extent they could be carried to the detailed country and industry level presented, these changes have been incorporated in this item. Available from BEA: 1987–94: Printed tables—Accession No. 50-96-20-606, price $10.00 for each year. Diskettes (3 1/2″ HD)—Accession No. 50-95-40-606, price $20.00. 1980–86: Diskettes (3 1/2″ HD)—Accession No. 50-91-40-605, price $20.00.

12.7. U.S. Business Enterprises Acquired or Established by Foreign Direct Investors, Supplementary Tables (printed tables, diskette).

The results of BEA's survey of new foreign direct investments in the United States. Summary tables appeared in the May 1995 SURVEY OF CURRENT BUSINESS article. This set of supplementary tables contains additional detail for 1992–94 on the number of investments and investors, investment outlays, and selected operating data on the U.S. business enterprises acquired or established. (1995) Comparable tables for 1980–86 are also available. Available from BEA: Printed tables:

    1992–94—Accession No. 50-95-20-105, price $10.00.
    1987–91—Accession No. 50-95-20-106, price $18.00.
    1980–86—Accession No. 50-89-20-106, price $18.00.

Diskettes (3 1/2″ HD):

    1992–94—Accession No. 50-95-40-405, price $20.00.
    1980–91—Accession No. 50-96-40-405, price $20.00.

12.8. A Guide to BEA Statistics on Foreign Direct Investment in the United States (reprint).

Explains the types of data on foreign direct investment in the United States that are collected and published by BEA and clarifies the differences between those data sets. This article appeared in the February 1990 SURVEY OF CURRENT BUSINESS. (1990) Available upon request from the International Investment Division.

12.9. U.S. Direct Investment Abroad: Operations of U.S. Parent Companies and Their Foreign Affiliates (publication, diskette).

The most detailed results of BEA's annual survey of the worldwide operations of U.S. multinational companies (only summary information appears in the SURVEY OF CURRENT BUSINESS). Contains information on the financial structure and operations of both U.S. parent companies and their foreign affiliates. Data are classified by country and industry of foreign affiliate and by industry of U.S. parent. Estimates from annual surveys are first released on a preliminary basis; revised estimates are released one year later. Available as follows:

U.S. Direct Investment Abroad: Operations of U.S. Parent Companies and their Foreign Affiliates, Preliminary 1993 Estimates. (1995) Publication—Available from GPO: Stock No. 003-010-00254-9, price $6.50. Diskette (3 1/2″ HD)—Available from BEA: Accession No. 50-95-40-404, price $20.00.

U.S. Direct Investment Abroad: Operations of U.S. Parent Companies and Their Foreign Affiliates, Revised 1992 Estimates. (1995) Publication—Available from GPO: Stock No. 003-010-00253-1, price $6.50. Diskette (3 1/2″ HD)—Available from BEA: Accession No. 50-95-40-403, price $20.00.

U.S. Direct Investment Abroad: Operations of U.S. Parent Companies and Their Foreign Affiliates, Revised 1991 Estimates. (1994) Publication—Available from NTIS: Accession No. PB 94-196425, price $19.50. Diskette (3 1/2″ HD)—Available from BEA: Accession No. 50-94-40-403, price $20.00.

12.10. U.S. Direct Investment Abroad: 1989 Benchmark Survey, Final Results (publication, diskette).

Final results of BEA's 1989 benchmark survey of U.S. direct investment abroad. Benchmark surveys are BEA's most comprehensive surveys, both in terms of companies covered and information gathered. Presents a detailed account of U.S. direct investment abroad in 1989, including data on balance sheets; income statements; employment; employee compensation; U.S. merchandise trade; sales of goods and services; research and development expenditures; property, plant, and equipment; and taxes. Data are classified by country and industry of affiliate and industry of U.S. parent. (1992) Available as follows: Publication—Available from NTIS: Accession No. PB 93-127702, price $57.00. Diskette—Available from BEA: Accession No. 50-92-40-403, price $20.00.

12.11. U.S. Direct Investment Abroad: Balance of Payments and Direct Investment Position Estimates, 1982–88 (publication).

Contains estimates of the U.S. direct investment position abroad and balance of payments transactions between U.S. parent companies and their foreign affiliates for 1982–88. The data are presented by country and industry of affiliate. (1995) Available from GPO: Stock No. 003-010-00258-1, price $6.50.

12.12. U.S. Direct Investment Abroad: Direct Investment Position and Related Capital and Income Flows (printed tables, diskette).

(These data, together with additional data, are also available on diskette (see entry 11.8).) Annual estimates of the U.S. direct investment position abroad and selected capital and income flows between U.S. parent companies and their foreign affiliates. Available from BEA: 1989–94: Printed tables—Accession No. 50-96-20-577, price $10.00 for each year. 1982–94: Diskette (3 1/2″ HD)—Accession No. 50-95-40-577, price $20.00.

12.13. A Guide to BEA Statistics on U.S. Multinational Companies (reprint). Explains the types of data on U.S. multinational companies that are collected and published by BEA and clarifies the differences between those data sets. This article appeared in the March 1995 SURVEY OF CURRENT BUSINESS. (1995) Available upon request from the International Investment Division.

International Services

12.14. U.S. International Sales and Purchases of Services (reprint). Presents information on services in a detailed and unified format. Includes data on cross-border transactions in services (for 1991–94) and on sales of services by majority-owned foreign affiliates of U.S. companies and by majority-owned U.S. affiliates of foreign companies (for 1992–93). (These data, together with additional data, are also available on diskette (see entry 11.8).) This article appeared in the September 1995 SURVEY OF CURRENT BUSINESS; data are updated annually. (1995) (Beginning with 1996, the article will appear in the October issue of the SURVEY.) Available upon request from the International Investment Division.

Subject Guide to BEA Products

Balance of Payments

Balance of Payments of the United States 11.6
International Reports: BEA Reports 10.1
U.S. International Transactions 11.5, 11.7
U.S. International Transactions: Recorded Telephone Message 1.3

Environment

Economic-Environmental Accounts 2.22
Pollution Abatement and Control Expenditures: BEA Reports 5.1
Stocks and Underlying Data for Pollution Abatement Plant and Equipment 5.2

Government

Federal Budget 3.2
Government Transactions 3.1

Gross Domestic Product

Gross Domestic Product: BEA Reports 1.3
Gross Domestic Product: Recorded Telephone Message 1.3
Key Source Data and Assumptions 2.4
(Also see "National Income and Product Accounts.")

Gross State Product

Revised Gross State Product, Annual Estimates, 1977–92 9.1

Input-Output

National
Benchmark Input-Output Accounts of the United States, 1987 4.1, 4.2
1982 Benchmark 85—Industry Input-Output Tables 4.3
Regional
Regional Multipliers: Input-Output Modeling System (RIMS II) 9.2

Investment

Detailed Investment by Industry 2.26
Research and Development Satellite Account Data 2.23

Foreign Direct Investment in the United States (FDIUS)

FDIUS: Balance of Payments and Direct Investment Position, 1980–86 12.5
FDIUS: Benchmark Survey Results 12.2
FDIUS: Direct Investment Position and Related Capital and Income Flows 12.6
FDIUS: Establishment Data 12.3, 12.4
FDIUS: Operations of U.S. Affiliates of Foreign Companies 12.1
Guide to BEA Statistics on FDIUS 12.8
U.S. Business Enterprises Acquired or Established by Foreign Direct Investors 12.7

U.S. Direct Investment Abroad (USDIA)

Guide to BEA Statistics on U.S. Multinational Companies 12.13
USDIA: Direct Investment Position, Capital and Income Flows 12.12
USDIA: Operations of U.S. Parent Companies and Their Foreign Affiliates 12.9
USDIA: 1989 Benchmark Survey Results 12.10
U.S. International Sales and Purchases of Services 12.13

National Income and Product Accounts

Alternative Measures of Change in Real Output and Prices 2.18
Corporate Profits 2.8
Foreign Transactions 2.9
Government Transactions 2.11

Gross Domestic Product: BEA Reports 2.1
Gross National Product 2.10, 2.19
Gross Product by Industry 2.13, 2.14
National Income and Product Accounts 2.3, 2.5, 2.6, 2.7, 2.20
Personal Consumption Expenditures 2.12
Personal Income and Outlays: BEA Reports 2.2
Underground Economy: An Introduction 2.17
United Nations System of National Accounts: An Introduction 2.21

Personal Income

National
Personal Income and Outlays: BEA Reports 2.2
Personal Income and Outlays: Recorded Telephone Message 1.3
Regional
BEARFACTS (personal income on regional basis, in narrative form) 8.4.22
Farm Income and Expenses 8.4.10, 8.4.21
Local Area Personal Income, 1969–92 8.3
Personal Income by Major Source, Earnings by Industry 8.2, 8.4.2, 8.4.5, 8.4.15, 8.4.16
Personal Income, Per Capita, and Total Population 8.3, 8.4.4, 8.4.12, 8.4.13, 8.4.14
Regional Economic Profile 8.4.18
Regional Economic Information System CD-ROM 1969–94 8.1
Regional Reports: BEA Reports 7.1
State Personal Income, 1929–93 8.2
Transfer Payments 8.4.9, 8.4.20
Wages and Salaries 8.4.3, 8.4.6, 8.4.19

Projections, Regional

BEA Regional Projections to 2045 9.3

Trade

U.S. Merchandise Trade Data 11.1, 11.2, 11.3, 11.4

Wealth

Fixed Reproducible Tangible Wealth in the United States 2.24
Detailed Investment by Industry 2.26
Detailed Wealth by Industry 2.27
Wealth 2.25

NOTE: This is a guide to finding products by general subject area, not a complete listing of BEA products.